Excavations 1998

Excavations 1998:
Summary accounts of archaeological excavations in Ireland

Edited by Isabel Bennett

Index 1969–1997
compiled by Eoin Bairéad

First published in 2000
Wordwell Ltd
PO Box 69, Bray, Co. Wicklow
Copyright © The contributors

ISBN 1-869857-35-6

British Library Cataloguing-in-Publication Data.
A catalogue record for this book is available from the British Library.

Typeset in Ireland by Wordwell Ltd.
Origination by Impress Ltd

Cover design: Rachel Dunne

Copy editor: Aisling Flood
Index editor: Emer Condit

Printed by Brookfield Printing Company.

INTRODUCTION

There was a great, positive reaction to the 1997 edition of *Excavations*, and all of us involved in its preparation and publication were very happy to see that. We hope the readership will continue to be pleased with the new format.

Continuing the trend of increasing excavation work in Ireland, again the number of licences issued has grown, with an increase of over 100 on those issued during 1997. The vast majority of those sites (*c.* 700) are reported on in this volume, with the remainder being listed. Every one of the 32 counties is represented this year, even if it's only by one site, as is the case in County Carlow. As is to be expected, Dublin is again the county where most work took place, much of it in urban areas (118 sites altogether). Louth this year takes second place (58 sites), with Tipperary and Kildare joint third (50 sites each).

The huge increase in archaeological excavations taking place in Ireland, which grows every year, has meant a great increase in the workload of the staff of the Excavation Licensing Section of *Dúchas*, their colleagues elsewhere in the National Monuments Section, and also in the National Museum. This increase does not seem to have been adequately recognised by the Department of Finance, who hold the purse-strings regarding the employment of more professional staff in those areas. Perhaps it is time that we archaeologists work together to lobby the Department to improve that situation, as it can only be to our benefit in the long run.

As it is still a relatively new condition that archaeologists who are issued with excavation licences must supply a summary of their work for publication in the relevant issue of this bulletin, some people may have omitted to send their reports in time for inclusion in this volume. Can I use this medium, therefore, to ask people who may have carried out excavations during 1999, and in future years, to send their summaries to me as soon as possible after the work has been completed, but certainly no later than 1 March of the following year. Otherwise it cannot be guaranteed that their summary will be included in the relevant bulletin. The reports should be sent to: Isabel Bennett, Glen Fahan, Ventry, Tralee, Co. Kerry.

ACKNOWLEDGEMENTS

The editor and the publisher wishes to thanks David Sweetman, Chief Archaeologist, and Edward Bourke, of the Excavation Licensing Section, Dúchas, for facilitating the production of this bulletin and providing the relevant information for licences issued in the Republic of Ireland. Ciara O'Donnell, formerly of the Excavation Licensing Section, is also to be thanked. North of the border, Declan Hurl of the DoE Environment Service was my first port of call, as usual, for sites investigated there, and he is to be thanked for all the information provided.

The editor and publisher would particularly like to thank Eoin Bairéad for compiling the three indexes of excavations 1969–97 given at the end of this volume.

The Heritage Council provided a grant, some years ago, to acquire equipment that is used for this work, for which they are to be thanked.

As usual, for their patience, I must thank Seán, Áedán and Eoin Ó hUallacháin.

Index of sites

103.	Churchland Quarters, Carndonagh	Donegal	Early ecclesiastical	Heather A. King and Richard Crumlish
104.	Crockahenny (Inishowen)	Donegal	No archaeological significance	Eoin Halpin
105.	Doe Castle	Donegal	Tower-house	Heather A. King
106.	Site 9, Drumhinny Lower	Donegal	Prehistoric	Sylvia Desmond
107.	Site 11, Drumhinny Lower	Donegal	Prehistoric	Sylvia Desmond
108.	Glenfinn to Glenmore (R252) Road Improvement Scheme	Donegal	Burnt mound, pit	Eoin Halpin
109.	Fishery Cottage, Magheracar	Donegal	Midden	Stephen Gilmore
110.	Fortstewart, Ramelton	Donegal	No archaeological significance	Audrey Gahan
111.	Jordan's Castle, Ardglass	Down	Tower-house	M. Gardiner
112.	Newark Castle, Ardglass	Down	Tower-house	Tom McNeill
113.	Old Bridge Court, Ballyvalley, Banbridge	Down	Ringfort	Alan Reilly
114.	IDB Development Site, Belfast Road, Downpatrick	Down	Multi-period	Ciara MacManus
115.	Cathedral Hill, Downpatrick	Down	Multi-phase landscape	Eoin Halpin
116.	Castle Mill Gardens, Newtownards	Down	Post-medieval garden	Steve Lawrence
117.	Airport–Balbriggan Northern Motorway Bypass	Dublin	No archaeological significance	Hilary Opie
118.	The Royal Dublin Society, Simmonscourt Road, Ballsbridge	Dublin	Urban post-medieval	Malachy Conway
119.	Ballycullen	Dublin	Testing	Colin D. Gracie
120.	Ballyfermot Upper	Dublin	Graveyard	Edmond O'Donovan
121.	Southern Cross Route Motorway, Balrothery/Firhouse/Scholarstown/ Ballycullen/Newtown/ Edmonstown/Tibradden/ Marley Grange/Taylor's Grange	Dublin	Monitoring	Colin D. Gracie
122.	Southern Cross Route Motorway Balrothery/Ballycullen/ Edmondstown/Kilmashogue/ Taylorsgrange/Kellystown	Dublin	Monitoring	Martin Reid
123.	'The Bungalow', Ards, Cabinteely	Dublin	Cemetery (site of)	Kenneth Hanley
124.	Mount Offaly, Cabinteely	Dublin	Early medieval enclosed cemetery	Malachy Conway
125.	Carrickmines–Bray Gas Pipeline, Carrickmines Great/Laughanstown/ Tiknick/Rathmichael/ Shankill/Ballyman	Dublin	Wedge tomb, *fulachta fiadh*	John Ó Néill
126.	Carrickmines and Jamestown	Dublin	Pits, *fulachta fiadh* and Pale Ditch	Niall Brady
127.	Science and Technology Park, Cherrywood	Dublin	Multi-period	John Ó Néill
128.	Cherrywood and Laughanstown	Dublin	Prehistoric/post-medieval	Edmond O'Donovan
129.	Kilcarberry Distribution Park, Nangor, Clondalkin	Dublin	Monitoring	Dermot Nelis
130.	1–7 St Agnes Road (rear of), Crumlin	Dublin	Medieval ditches and fields	Alan Hayden
131.	Castle Street, Dalkey	Dublin	Urban medieval	Rob Lynch
132.	Castle Street/Ulverton Road, Dalkey	Dublin	Urban medieval	Margaret Gowen
133.	21/22 St Patrick's Road, Dalkey	Dublin	Adjacent to site of castle	Avril Purcell
134.	Meánscoil Iognaid Rís CBS, Drimnagh Castle, Drimnagh	Dublin	Vicinity of medieval castle	James Eogan
135.	St Patrick's College, Drumcondra	Dublin	Environs of 17th-century house	Martin E. Byrne
136.	Augustine Street/ 16/17 John Street West, Dublin	Dublin	Urban medieval	Una Cosgrove
137.	Baggot Lane, Dublin	Dublin	No archaeological significance	Malachy Conway
138.	Croppies Acre, Benburb Street, Dublin	Dublin	Possible graveyard	Rónán Swan
139.	15A Bishop Street, Dublin	Dublin	Urban medieval	Helen Kehoe
140.	6–7 Bow Lane West, Dublin	Dublin	Urban medieval	Una Cosgrove

141.	St Patrick's Hospital, Bow Lane/ Stephen's Lane, Dublin	Dublin	No archaeological significance	Alan Hayden
142.	Iveagh Hostel, Bride Road, Dublin	Dublin	Urban medieval	James Eogan
143.	Bride Street, Dublin	Dublin	Urban medieval	Una Cosgrove
144.	Bridgefoot Street/Island Street/ Bonham Street/Marshal Lane, Dublin	Dublin	Urban	Daire O'Rourke
145.	89–93 Capel Street/ 16, 17, 21 and 22 Green Street/ 195–196 North King Street, Dublin	Dublin	Urban	Claire Walsh
146.	98–102 Capel Street, Dublin	Dublin	Urban post-medieval	Claire Walsh
147.	17–35 Carman's Hall (odd nos only)/1–7 Ash Street/ 33–34 Garden Lane, Dublin	Dublin	Medieval, post-medieval	Claire Walsh
		Dublin	Urban medieval	Helen Kehoe
148.	27–31 Church Street, Dublin			
149.	102–108 Church Street/ 6–7 Catherine Lane, Dublin	Dublin	No archaeological significance	Alan Hayden
150.	Sisters of the Holy Faith, The Coombe, Dublin	Dublin	Urban medieval	Malachy Conway
151.	57–58 The Coombe, Dublin	Dublin	Urban	Audrey Gahan
152.	3–4 Crane Lane/ 16–19 Crampton Court, Dublin	Dublin	Urban	Helen Kehoe
153.	Belvedere College, Denmark Street Great North, Dublin	Dublin	Urban	Avril Purcell
154.	18 Earl Street, Dublin	Dublin	Urban	Dermot G. Moore
155.	35 Essex Street East, Dublin	Dublin	Urban medieval	Helen Kehoe
156.	The Project Arts Centre, 37 Essex Street East, Dublin	Dublin	Urban medieval	Helen Kehoe
157.	8–10 Exchange Street Upper/ 1 Essex Gate, Dublin	Dublin	Urban medieval	Georgina Scally
158.	7A Fownes Street, Dublin	Dublin	17th-century reclamation	Linzi Simpson
159.	10 Fownes Street Upper, Dublin	Dublin	Urban	James Eogan
160.	88 Francis Street, Dublin	Dublin	Suburban medieval	Alan Hayden
161.	23–27a Gardiner Street Middle, Dublin	Dublin	Urban	Alan Hayden
162.	41–43 George's Street Great North (rear of), Dublin	Dublin	Urban medieval	Helen Kehoe
163.	1–5 Green Street, Dublin	Dublin	Urban medieval	Helen Kehoe
164.	6–10 Hanbury Lane/ rear 38 Thomas Street, Dublin	Dublin	Urban post-medieval	Claire Walsh
165.	14 Hanbury Lane (site adjoining), Dublin	Dublin	Urban	Rónán Swan
166.	Hill Street/Parnell Street, Dublin	Dublin	Urban medieval	Helen Kehoe
167.	15–17 Island Street/ 33 Watling Street, Dublin	Dublin	Urban	Claire Walsh
168.	Former churchyard, John Dillon Street, Dublin	Dublin	Medieval friary	Claire Walsh
169.	6–11 Kevin Street Lower, Dublin	Dublin	Urban medieval and post-medieval	Cia McConway
170.	1–3 King Street North/ 62–63 Bolton Street, Dublin	Dublin	Urban	Claire Walsh
171.	4–6 King Street North, Dublin	Dublin	No archaeological significance	Mary McMahon
172.	189–194 King Street North, Dublin	Dublin	Graveyard	Daire O'Rourke
173.	King Street North/Church Street/Stirrup Lane, Dublin	Dublin	Urban	Conor McHale
174.	Abbey Mall, 13–15 Liffey Street, Dublin	Dublin	Urban medieval	Helen Kehoe
175.	4–7 Lurgan Street, Dublin	Dublin	No archaeological significance	Mary McMahon

176.	Marshal Lane (rear of 138–141 Thomas Street), Dublin	Dublin	Urban	Rosanne Meenan
177.	51–52 Mary Street, Dublin	Dublin	No archaeological significance	Martin E. Byrne
178.	22 Mary Street Little, Dublin	Dublin	Urban	Martin Reid
179.	61–63 Meath Street, Dublin	Dublin	No archaeological significance	Mary McMahon
180.	The Houses of the *Oireachtas*, Merrion Square, Dublin	Dublin	Urban medieval	Tim Coughlan
181.	Richmond Hospital, Morning Star Avenue, Dublin	Dublin	No archaeological significance	Alan Hayden
182.	Parkgate Street, Dublin	Dublin	Urban	Eoin Halpin
183.	19 Parliament Street, Dublin	Dublin	Urban medieval	Helen Kehoe
184.	1–4a Red Cow Lane/ 62–63, 67–76 King Street North/ 71–72 Brunswick Street North, Dublin	Dublin	Urban, post-medieval	Claire Walsh
185.	New Physiotherapy Building, St James's Hospital, Dublin	Dublin	Unknown	Rosanne Meenan
186.	St Mary's Church, Saint Mary's Street/ Wolfe Tone Street, Dublin	Dublin	Urban medieval	Tim Coughlan
187.	St Stephen's Green, Dublin	Dublin	Urban medieval	Helen Kehoe
188.	Ship Street (Phase V), Dublin	Dublin	Urban medieval	Helen Kehoe
189.	13–15 Spitalfields, Dublin	Dublin	Urban medieval	Helen Kehoe
190.	Temple Bar West, Dublin	Dublin	North-east corner of Viking town	Linzi Simpson
191.	St Catherine's Church, Thomas Street, Dublin	Dublin	Urban medieval	Tim Coughlan
192.	Townsend Street/Luke Street, Dublin	Dublin	17th-century river revetment	Claire Walsh
193.	109 Townsend Street, Dublin	Dublin	Post-medieval	Claire Walsh
194.	Berkley Library Building Extension, Trinity College, Dublin	Dublin	Urban medieval	Helen Kehoe
195.	Library Square, Trinity College, Dublin	Dublin	Site of All Hallows Priory and early college	Linzi Simpson
196.	Science of Materials Building, Trinity College, Dublin	Dublin	Urban medieval	Helen Kehoe
197.	15/16 Werburgh Street, Dublin	Dublin	Urban	Daire O'Rourke
198.	22–31 Wolfe Tone Street, extending to Jervis Lane, Dublin	Dublin	Urban	Claire Walsh
199.	St Michael's Holy Faith Convent, Wellmount Road, Finglas	Dublin	Zone of archaeological potential	Eoghan Moore
200.	Holy Faith Convent, Glasnevin	Dublin	Medieval	Richard N. O'Brien
201.	Corr Castle, Howth Road, Howth	Dublin	Tower-house	Rónán Swan
202.	28–31 Conyngham Road, Islandbridge	Dublin	No archaeological significance	Georgina Scally
203.	Ballyogan Road, Jamestown	Dublin	Pale ditch	Laurence Dunne
204.	Ballyogan, Jamestown	Dublin	Pale ditch	Martin Reid
205.	Kellystown and Ticknock	Dublin	No archaeological significance	Niall Brady
206.	Bow Bridge House, Bow Lane West, Kilmainham	Dublin	Urban post-medieval	Ruairí Ó Baoill
207.	7 Rowserstown Lane (site adjoining), Kilmainham	Dublin	Post-medieval	Georgina Scally
208.	Kingston	Dublin	No archaeological significance	Martin Reid
209.	Lambay Island	Dublin	Neolithic axe production site with associated activity	Gabriel Cooney
210.	10 Main Street, Lucan	Dublin	Medieval borough	Martin E. Byrne
211.	Main Street/The Square, Lucan	Dublin	Zone of archaeological potential	Jim Higgins
212.	'The Orchard', Old Leixlip Road, Lucan	Dublin	No archaeological significance	Eoghan Moore
213.	Post Office Road, Lusk	Dublin	Possible Early Christian/medieval	Deirdre Murphy
214.	Quarryvale, Palmerstown Upper	Dublin	Area of burning	Orla Scully, C. Kelleher

256.	High Island	Galway	Early Christian monastery	Georgina Scally
257.	Church Street, Loughrea	Galway	Urban	Dave Pollock
258.	Moanmore, Loughrea	Galway	No archaeological significance	Martin Fitzpatrick
259.	Mainistir Chiaráin, Oghil (Inis Mór)	Galway	Early Christian/medieval monastery	Sinéad Ní Ghabhláin
260.	Oranmore Sewerage Scheme	Galway	Various	Jim Higgins
261.	Oranmore	Galway	No archaeological significance	Billy Quinn
262.	Portumna Castle, Portumna	Galway	Post-medieval castle	Donald Murphy
263.	Portumna Sewerage Scheme, Portumna	Galway	Post-medieval brick kiln	Donald Murphy
264.	Raheen	Galway	No archaeological significance	Martin Fitzpatrick
265.	Rinville West	Galway	Environs of possible souterrain	Margaret Gowen
266.	*An Raingiléis*, Ballywiheen	Kerry	Early Christian monastic site	Margaret McCarthy
267.	Bray Head (Valencia Island)	Kerry	Early medieval farmhouses	Alan Hayden
268.	Caherlehillan	Kerry	Early ecclesiastical enclosure	John Sheehan
269.	Tailor's Row, Castlegregory	Kerry	Castle site	Laurence Dunne
270.	'The Canon's Garden', Green Street, Dingle	Kerry	Town wall	Isabel Bennett
271.	Garvey's Supermarket, Holyground, Dingle	Kerry	Monitoring	Isabel Bennett
272.	John Street, Dingle	Kerry	Monitoring	Isabel Bennett
273.	Main Street, Dingle	Kerry	Town wall site	Laurence Dunne
274.	Main Street, Dingle	Kerry	Urban	Isabel Bennett
275.	Garranbane	Kerry	Children's burial-ground/ringfort	Laurence Dunne
276.	Skellig Michael (Monks' Garden), Great Skellig	Kerry	Monastic site	Edward Bourke
277.	Killarney Sewerage Scheme	Kerry	Urban	Billy Quinn
278.	Castleconway, Killorglin	Kerry	Tower-house	Laurence Dunne
279.	Killoughane Church, Killoughane	Kerry	Medieval church site	Isabel Bennett
280.	Kilmaniheen West	Kerry	Possible hillfort?	Michael Connolly
281.	Listowel Castle, Listowel	Kerry	Castle	Florence M. Hurley
282.	Lissyvigeen	Kerry	Stone circle	William O'Brien
283.	Meanus	Kerry	Cropmark enclosure	John Tierney
284.	Scrahane 1	Kerry	Enclosure and smelting site	Mary O'Donnell
285.	Ballyvelly, Tralee	Kerry	Flat cemetery and crematoria	Laurence Dunne
286.	Cloghers, Tralee	Kerry	Neolithic house	Jacinta Kiely
287.	Clounalour House, Tralee	Kerry	Monitoring	Margaret McCarthy
288.	Dromthacker, Tralee	Kerry	Ringfort	Rose M. Cleary
289.	Lower Abbey Street, Tralee	Kerry	Dominican priory	Laurence Dunne
290.	Monavally, Tralee	Kerry	Pit burials	Frank Coyne
291.	Cloch an Oigair (Carrigeendaniel), Mount Hawk, Tralee	Kerry	No archaeological significance	Isabel Bennett
292.	Mounthawk 2, Tralee	Kerry	Cultivation furrows	Laurence Dunne
293.	St John's Lane, Athy	Kildare	Urban medieval	Martin E. Byrne
294.	Church Road, Ballymore Eustace	Kildare	Urban medieval	Clare Mullins
295.	Ballyshannon Demesne	Kildare	Medieval/post-medieval	Martin E. Byrne
296.	Barreen	Kildare	Vicinity of church	Rosanne Meenan
297.	Bawnogue/Tipperkevin/ Walshestown	Kildare	No archaeological significance	Dominic Delany
298.	Boherhole	Kildare	Earthwork	Thaddeus C. Breen
299.	Athy Road, Castledermot	Kildare	Urban medieval	Clare Mullins
300.	Castlefarm	Kildare	Prehistoric complex	Clare Mullins
301.	Castlereban South	Kildare	Proximity to various sites	Clare Mullins
302.	New Medical Complex, Main Street, Celbridge	Kildare	Urban	Rónán Swan
303.	Clane	Kildare	No archaeological significance	Niall Brady
304.	Clane	Kildare	Urban medieval	Martin Reid
305.	Jones' Pub, Main Street, Clane	Kildare	No archaeological significance	Eoin Halpin
306.	Corbally/Brownstown/ Silliot Hill	Kildare	Neolithic structures and prehistoric activity	Avril Purcell
307.	Corbally	Kildare	Peripheral activity associated with	Avril Purcell

			Neolithic settlement	
308.	The Curragh	Kildare	Prehistoric and later	Breandán Ó Ríordáin
309.	The Curragh	Kildare	Enclosure/ringfort	Martin Reid
310.	Dowdenstown Great	Kildare	Adjacent to enclosure site	Martin E. Byrne
311.	Grange Castle, Grange	Kildare	Late medieval/ post-medieval tower-house	Dave Pollock
312.	Harristown	Kildare	Medieval borough	Martin E. Byrne
313.	Main Street, Johnstown	Kildare	Urban medieval	Breandán Ó Ríordáin
314.	Kildare	Kildare	Urban	Niall Brady
315.	Kildare	Kildare	Urban medieval	Breandán Ó Ríordáin
316.	Kildare	Kildare	Urban medieval	Hilary Opie
317.	Market Square, Kildare	Kildare	Urban medieval	Richard N. O'Brien
318.	St Brigid's Square, Kildare	Kildare	Environs of early monastic and urban medieval centre	Martin E. Byrne
319.	Kilhill, Kill	Kildare	Environs of archaeological complex	Clare Mullins
320.	Kill	Kildare	Urban	Breandán Ó Ríordáin
321.	Main Street, Leixlip	Kildare	Urban medieval	Clare Mullins
322.	18 Main Street, Leixlip	Kildare	Urban medieval	Martin E. Byrne
323.	Mayfield	Kildare	*Fulacht fiadh*	Breandán Ó Ríordáin
324.	Main Street/Mill Street, Maynooth	Kildare	Urban	Colin D. Gracie
325.	Monasterevin	Kildare	No archaeological significance	Carmel Duffy
326.	Moone Abbey, Moone	Kildare	Early Christian monastery	Miriam Clyne
327.	Naas	Kildare	Urban	Breandán Ó Ríordáin
328.	Abbey Street/Canal Street, Naas	Kildare	Urban medieval	Martin E. Byrne
329.	Friary Road, Naas	Kildare	Urban medieval	Clare Mullins
330.	Main Street, Naas	Kildare	Post-medieval	Jim Higgins
331.	South Main Street, Naas	Kildare	Urban medieval	Clare Mullins
332.	Old Kilcullen	Kildare	Environs of ecclesiastical remains	Martin E. Byrne
333.	Ballysax Road, Old Kilcullen	Kildare	Environs of Dún Áillinne archaeological complex	Clare Mullins
334.	Glebe North, Old Kilcullen	Kildare	Early monastic and medieval centre	Clare Mullins
335.	Oldtown/Aghards	Kildare	No archaeological significance	Rónán Swan
336.	Punchestown Little	Kildare	No archaeological significance	Christiaan Corlett
337.	Rathmore West	Kildare	Burials	Clare Mullins
338.	Rathmore West	Kildare	Medieval	Emmet Byrnes
339.	Tully East	Kildare	Medieval	Breandán Ó Ríordáin
340.	Green Street/Mill Street, Callan	Kilkenny	Graveyard	Sheila Lane
341.	Callan Co-op, West Street, Callan	Kilkenny	Urban medieval and post-medieval	Jo Moran
342.	Dungarvan	Kilkenny	No archaeological significance	Cathy Sheehan
343.	St Mary's Church, Gowran	Kilkenny	Medieval church	Dave Pollock
344.	Main Street, Graiguenamanagh	Kilkenny	Urban medieval	Clare Mullins
345.	'Abbey House', Jerpoint Abbey	Kilkenny	Environs of deserted settlement and abbey	Martin E. Byrne
346.	Abbey Street, Kilkenny	Kilkenny	Urban	Sylvia Desmond
347.	Evan's Lane, Kilkenny	Kilkenny	Urban medieval	Paul Stevens
348.	14 High Street, Kilkenny	Kilkenny	Urban	Jacinta Kiely
349.	5–7 James's Street, Kilkenny	Kilkenny	Urban medieval	Paul Stevens
350.	10 John Street, Kilkenny	Kilkenny	Urban	Sheila Lane
351.	Bridge House, John Street, Kilkenny	Kilkenny	Urban medieval	Edmond O'Donovan
352.	10–13 Kieran Street, Kilkenny	Kilkenny	Urban medieval	Hilary Opie
353.	Maudlin Street, Kilkenny	Kilkenny	Urban medieval	Paul Stevens
354.	New Building Lane, Kilkenny	Kilkenny	Urban medieval	Sheila Lane
355.	New Street Lower, Kilkenny	Kilkenny	Urban	Jacinta Kiely
356.	26–29 Patrick Street, Kilkenny	Kilkenny	Urban medieval	Judith Carroll
357.	33 Patrick Street, Kilkenny	Kilkenny	Urban medieval	Judith Carroll
358.	Patrick Street/Pudding Lane/ Pennyfeather Lane, Kilkenny	Kilkenny	Urban medieval	Judith Carroll
359.	St Francis' Abbey, Smithwick's Brewery, Kilkenny	Kilkenny	Medieval	Margaret Gowen
360.	8 William Street, Kilkenny	Kilkenny	Urban medieval	Martin Reid
361.	21 William Street, Kilkenny	Kilkenny	Urban	James Eogan

415.	Ballinalee	Longford	Post-medieval	Jim Higgins
416.	Ballinalee or Saint Johnstown	Longford	Stone structure	Judith Carroll
417.	Kilsallagh, Edgeworthstown	Longford	Proximity to ringfort	Deirdre Murphy
418.	Forgney	Longford	Vicinity of ringfort	Dermot Nelis
419.	Carlingford	Louth	Urban	Dermot G. Moore
420.	Kilcurry, Carrickedmond	Louth	No archaeological significance	Deirdre Murphy
421.	Carstown	Louth	*Fulacht fiadh*	Donald Murphy
422.	Castlelumnny	Louth	Vicinity of castle site	Donald Murphy
423.	Charlestown	Louth	Vicinity of medieval church	Donald Murphy
424.	Clonmore	Louth	Vicinity of Early Christian monastery	Deirdre Murphy
425.	Bachelors Lane, Drogheda	Louth	Urban medieval	Donald Murphy
426.	2 Bessexwell Lane, Drogheda	Louth	Urban medieval	Rosanne Meenan
427.	3–4 Bessexwell Lane, Drogheda	Louth	Urban medieval	Rosanne Meenan
428.	Blind Quay/Merchant's Row, Drogheda	Louth	Urban post-medieval	Rosanne Meenan
429.	Chord Road/North Strand, Drogheda	Louth	Unknown	Rosanne Meenan
430.	Sienna Convent, Chord Road, Drogheda	Louth	Urban medieval	Deirdre Murphy
431.	Fair Green, Drogheda	Louth	Medieval town	Donald Murphy
432.	Haymarket/John Street, Drogheda	Louth	Urban medieval	Edmond O'Donovan
433.	30 Magdalene Street, Drogheda	Louth	Urban post-medieval	Donald Murphy
434.	Mill Lane, Drogheda	Louth	Vicinity of medieval town	Deirdre Murphy
435.	9/10 Mill Lane, Drogheda	Louth	Vicinity of medieval town	Deirdre Murphy
436.	Donaghy's Mill, Mill Lane, Drogheda	Louth	18th-century mill	Deirdre Murphy
437.	Millmount, Drogheda	Louth	Urban post-medieval	Donald Murphy
438.	Shop Street/Bessexwell Lane, Drogheda	Louth	Urban medieval	Deirdre Murphy
439.	12/13 Shop Street/Dyer Street, Drogheda	Louth	Urban medieval	Donald Murphy
400.	Wellington Quay, Drogheda	Louth	No archaeological significance	Deirdre Murphy
441.	78/79 West Street, Drogheda	Louth	Urban medieval, post-medieval	Deirdre Murphy
442.	Gleeson's Lounge, West Street, Drogheda	Louth	Urban medieval	Deirdre Murphy
443.	Dromiskin	Louth	Vicinity of Early Christian monastic site	Donald Murphy
444.	49 Anne Street, Dundalk	Louth	Medieval town	Donald Murphy
445.	Castletown Cross, Castleblayney Road, Dundalk	Louth	No archaeological significance	Finola O'Carroll
446.	Castletown, Dundalk	Louth	Urban	Rob Lynch
447.	Castletown, Dundalk	Louth	*Fulacht fiadh*	Rob Lynch
448.	Chapel Street, Dundalk	Louth	Urban medieval	Rosanne Meenan
449.	AIB Bank, 96 Clanbrassil Street, Dundalk	Louth	Urban	Rónán Swan
450.	Crowe Street/Demesne, Dundalk	Louth	Medieval town	Donald Murphy
451.	69 Dublin Street, Dundalk	Louth	Urban	Rosanne Meenan
452.	2A Earl Street, Dundalk	Louth	Urban medieval	Rosanne Meenan
453.	19 Jocelyn Street, Dundalk	Louth	Urban medieval	Cóilín Ó Drisceoil
454.	Laurels Road, Dundalk	Louth	Urban medieval/post-medieval	Finola O'Carroll
455.	Market Square, Dundalk	Louth	Urban medieval	Deirdre Murphy
456.	Mill Road, Castletown, Dundalk	Louth	No archaeological significance	Finola O'Carroll
457.	Mill Road, Castletown, Dundalk	Louth	18th-century mill race	Linzi Simpson
458.	66–67 Park Street, Dundalk	Louth	Urban medieval	Deirdre Murphy
459.	66–67 Park Street, Dundalk	Louth	Medieval town	Deirdre Murphy
460.	Credit Union, Ramparts Road,	Louth	Medieval town	Deirdre Murphy

	Dundalk			
461.	Dundealgan Athletic Club, Seatown, Dundalk	Louth	Urban medieval	Deirdre Murphy
462.	Dunleer	Louth	Vicinity of ecclesiastical enclosure	Rosanne Meenan
463.	Farrandreg	Louth	Souterrain	Deirdre Murphy
464.	Knocklore	Louth	Circular enclosure (site of), cemetery (site of)	Colin D. Gracie
465.	Knocknagoran	Louth	Earthwork site	Finola O'Carroll
466.	Priorstate, Louth	Louth	Medieval borough	Donald Murphy
467.	Richard Taaffes Holding, Louth	Louth	Urban medieval	Deirdre Murphy
468.	Mullagharlin and Haggardstown	Louth	Enclosure	Dermot G. Moore
469.	Mullagharlin and Haggardstown	Louth	Possible ringfort	Audrey Gahan
470.	Phillipstown	Louth	Vicinity of holy well	Rosanne Meehan
471.	Tattyboys/Knocklore/ Cookstown/Rahanna/Harristown/ Glebe	Louth	Group of *fulacht fiadh*-type features	Thaddeus C. Breen
472.	Credit Union, Big Street, Termonfeckin	Louth	Vicinity of Early Christian monastery site	Donald Murphy
473.	Strand Road, Termonfeckin	Louth	Vicinity of Early Christian monastic site	Donald Murphy
474.	Aghtaboy	Mayo	Rath	Leo Morahan
475.	Ahena	Mayo	Cemetery	Deirdre Murphy
476.	Balla	Mayo	No archaeological significance	Gerry Walsh
477.	High Street, Ballinrobe	Mayo	No archaeological significance	Gerry Walsh
478.	Ballyhaunis Sewerage Scheme	Mayo	Urban	Martin E. Byrne
479.	Carrowbeg	Mayo	Rath	Leo Morahan
480.	Knockacroghery, Castlebar	Mayo	Urban	Gerry Walsh
481.	Castlegar	Mayo	Burnt spread	Gerry Walsh
482.	Clare	Mayo	*Fulacht fiadh*	Suzanne Zajac
483.	Clare	Mayo	No archaeological significance	Suzanne Zajac
484.	Coolroe	Mayo	*Fulachta fiadh*	Richard Gillespie
485.	Corimla South	Mayo	Enclosure	Suzanne Zajac
486.	Doogort (Achill Island)	Mayo	No archaeological significance	Richard Gillespie
487.	Farranoo/Garrankeel/ Belleek/Kilmore–Moy	Mayo	*Fulachta fiadh*	Paula King
488.	Frenchgrove	Mayo	Crannog	Conor McDermott
489.	Garrankeel	Mayo	19th-century tree ring	Donald Murphy
490.	Tulrahan Graveyard, Kildarra	Mayo	No archaeological significance	Gerry Walsh
491.	Lecarrow	Mayo	No archaeological significance	Gerry Walsh
492.	Rushbrook East	Mayo	Mound	Paula King
493.	Shrule	Mayo	Adjacent to church	Gerry Walsh
494.	The Deserted Village, Slievemore (*Tuar* and *Tuar Riabhach*), Achill Island	Mayo	Multi-phase landscape	Theresa McDonald
495.	Strade Abbey, Strade	Mayo	Medieval priory	Donald Murphy
496.	Terryduff	Mayo	No archaeological significance	Gerry Walsh
497.	Westport–Belclare, R335 Road Realignment Scheme	Mayo	No archaeological significance	Martin E. Byrne
498.	Abbeyland South and Blackcastle Demesne	Meath	Medieval/post-medieval	Niall Brady
499.	Abbeyland South and Blackcastle Demesne	Meath	Corn-drying kiln	Niall Brady
500.	Athlumney	Meath	Vicinity of castle and graveyard	Rosanne Meenan
501.	Bettystown	Meath	No archaeological significance	Finola O'Carroll
502.	Bettystown (Betaghstown Townland)	Meath	Iron Age cemetery	Rosanne Meenan
503.	Bettystown	Meath	Prehistoric/multi-period site	James Eogan
504.	Moynagh Lough, Brittas	Meath	Late Mesolithic settlement site	John Bradley
505.	Corstown	Meath	Environs of archaeological complex	Martin E. Byrne
506.	Main Street, Drumconrath	Meath	Medieval borough	Deirdre Murphy
507.	Main Street, Duleek	Meath	Medieval borough	Donald Murphy

508.	Dunshaughlin	Meath	Urban	Thaddeus C. Breen
509.	Irishtown, Gormanstown	Meath	Early Christian	Edmond O'Donovan
510.	Knockcommon	Meath	Medieval church site	Deirdre Murphy
511.	Knowth	Meath	Multi-period	George Eogan
512.	Loughsallagh	Meath	Unknown	Rosanne Meenan
513.	Monknewtown	Meath	No archaeological significance	Rónán Swan
514.	Navan Sewerage Scheme	Meath	Monitoring	Clare Mullins
515.	Navan Inner Relief Road	Meath	Urban	Fiona Reilly
516.	The Lyric Cinema, Brew's Hill, Navan	Meath	Urban	Rosanne Meenan
517.	40–42 Canon Row, Navan	Meath	Urban	James Eogan
518.	28 Trimgate Street, Navan	Meath	Urban medieval	Rosanne Meenan
519.	The Knockans, Teltown, Oristown	Meath	Linear earthwork	John Waddell and Madeline O'Brien
520.	Prioryland	Meath	Site of enclosure	Rosanne Meenan
521.	Curragha Road, Ratoath	Meath	Zone of archaeological potential	Rosanne Meenan
522.	Main Street, Ratoath	Meath	Urban medieval	Rosanne Meenan
523.	Rossan	Meath	No archaeological significance	Dermot Nelis
524.	Roughgrange	Meath	Vicinity of archaeological complex	Donald Murphy
525.	Roughgrange	Meath	Vicinity of archaeological complex	Donald Murphy
526.	Simonstown	Meath	Prehistoric burial/ritual site	Cóilín Ó Drisceoil
527.	Abbey Lane, Trim	Meath	Urban medieval	Matthew Seaver
528.	Bridge Street, Trim	Meath	Urban medieval	Martin E. Byrne
529.	Haggard Street, Trim	Meath	Urban medieval	Rosanne Meenan
530.	Newtown, Trim	Meath	Medieval borough	Deirdre Murphy
531.	Peterstown, Trim	Meath	Possible Early Christian cemetery	Deirdre Murphy
532.	Trim Castle, Trim	Meath	Medieval castle	Alan Hayden
533.	Castleblaney Water Scheme	Monaghan	No archaeological significance	Martin E. Byrne
534.	Cara Street, Clones	Monaghan	Zone of archaeological potential	Eoghan Moore
535.	Corkeeran	Monaghan	Vicinity of ringfort	Deirdre Murphy
536.	Cornapaste	Monaghan	Near the Black Pig's Dyke/ Worm Ditch linear earthwork	Eoghan Moore
537.	Drumlane I	Monaghan	Environs of ringfort	Martin E. Byrne
538.	Drumlane II	Monaghan	Environs of ringfort	Martin E. Byrne
539.	Dunmadigan	Monaghan	No archaeological significance	Martin E. Byrne
540.	Ulster Bank, The Diamond, Monaghan	Monaghan	Possible castle site	Rónán Swan
541.	Temporary Bank, Glasslough Street Carpark, Glasslough Street, Monaghan	Monaghan	No archaeological significance	Rónán Swan
542.	Ballicknahee	Offaly	Cemetery	Donald Murphy
543.	Ballyburley	Offaly	Adjacent to church and graveyard	Clare Mullins
544.	Banagher	Offaly	Urban	Jacinta Kiely
545.	Kylebeg, Banagher	Offaly	17th-century and later military fortification	Jim Higgins
546.	Main Street, Banagher	Offaly	Urban	Martin Fitzpatrick
547.	Clonmacnoise	Offaly	Early medieval wooden bridge	Aidan O'Sullivan, Niall Brady and Donal Boland
548.	New Graveyard, Clonmacnoise	Offaly	Early Christian settlement	Heather A. King
549.	Deerpark	Offaly	Close to archaeological complex	Clare Mullins
550.	Derryvilla	Offaly	Medieval	Clare Mullins
551.	Frankfort	Offaly	Shrunken settlement	Brian Hodkinson
552.	Frankfort	Offaly	Shrunken settlement	Brian Hodkinson
553.	Lemanaghan	Offaly	Trackway	Conor McDermott
554.	Tumbeagh Bog, Tumbeagh	Offaly	Bog body	Nóra Bermingham
555.	Aughamore Village, Ballykilcline	Roscommon	19th-century tenant village	Charles E. Orser, Jr
556.	Ballyphesan	Roscommon	No archaeological significance	Martin Fitzpatrick
557.	Demesne	Roscommon	Possible tree ring?	Anne Connolly
558.	Drumsillagh	Roscommon	No archaeological significance	Gerry Walsh
559.	Glebe	Roscommon	Adjacent to castle	Leo Morahan
560.	Grallagh	Roscommon	Archaeological complex	Leo Morahan

561.	Kiltullagh Hill, Kiltullagh	Roscommon	Inhumations	M.E. Robinson and D.G. Coombs
562.	Rockingham–Cortober Road Project	Roscommon	Monitoring	Deirdre Murphy
563.	Vesnoy	Roscommon	No archaeological significance	Gerry Walsh
564.	Aghanagh	Sligo	No archaeological significance	Anne Marie Lennon
565.	Ballincar	Sligo	No archaeological significance	Richard Crumlish
566.	Carrowhubbuck South	Sligo	Adjacent to possible passage tombs	Suzanne Zajac
567.	Carrowmore	Sligo	Megalithic tombs	Göran Burenhult
568.	Caltragh, Cumeen	Sligo	Enclosure	Eoin Halpin
569.	Curlew Mountains Project	Sligo	*Fulachta fiadh*	Sylvia Desmond
570.	Grange	Sligo	Adjacent to castle	Gerry Walsh
571.	Grange East	Sligo	Pit	Eoin Halpin
572.	Grange West	Sligo	No archaeological significance	Martin A. Timoney
573.	Killaspugbrone	Sligo	Shell midden	Fiona Rooney
574.	Shroove (Lough Gara)	Sligo	Stone platform	Christina Fredengren
575.	Sligo and Environs Water Supply Scheme	Sligo	Urban	Martin A. Timoney
576.	Sligo Environs Water Scheme	Sligo	*Fulacht fiadh*	Anne Marie Lennon
577.	Abbey Street, Sligo	Sligo	Urban medieval/post-medieval	Ruairí Ó Baoill
578.	Abbey Street Lower, Sligo	Sligo	Urban	Audrey Gahan
579.	Abbey Street Lower, Sligo	Sligo	Urban post-medieval	Ruairí Ó Baoill
580.	8–9 Lower Abbey Street, Sligo	Sligo	Medieval limekiln and post-medieval burials	Alan Hayden
581.	14 Stephen Street, Sligo	Sligo	Urban	Eoin Halpin
582.	Water Lane, Sligo	Sligo	Urban post-medieval	Ruairí Ó Baoill
583.	Ballina	Tipperary	Urban	Celie O Rahilly
584.	Ballintotty	Tipperary	Medieval hall-house	Paul Logue
585.	Ballintotty	Tipperary	*Fulacht fiadh*	Richard N. O'Brien
586.	Ballybrado House	Tipperary	Mesolithic artefacts	Nyree Finlay and Peter Woodman
587.	Ballymackeogh–Mulkear Certified Drainage Scheme	Tipperary	Riverine sites	Tracy Collins
588.	Benedin	Tipperary	Bronze Age	Cia McConway
589.	Benedin	Tipperary	Possible Bronze Age	Cia McConway
590.	Abbey Street Lower, Cahir	Tipperary	Urban	Anne Marie Lennon
591.	Cahir Abbey Lower, Cahir	Tipperary	Urban	Mary Henry
592.	Carrick-on-Suir	Tipperary	Urban	Florence M. Hurley
593.	Carrigatogher/Tullahedy	Tipperary	Post-medieval	Cia McConway
594.	St Patricksrock/Ladyswell/ Moor/St Dominicks Abbey/ Cashel/and vicinity of a Cistercian Abbey, Loughnafina/Green/Wailer's Lot/Hore Abbey and country townlands, Cashel	Tipperary	Medieval and post-medieval town	Mary Henry
595.	Agar's Lane, Cashel	Tipperary	Urban	Richard N. O'Brien
596.	County Hospital, Cashel	Tipperary	Urban medieval	Rose M. Cleary
597.	Friar Street, Cashel	Tipperary	Urban medieval, post-medieval	Edmond O'Donovan
598.	Old Road, Cashel	Tipperary	Enclosure	Jo Moran
599.	Hughes Mill, Little Island,	Tipperary	No archaeological significance	Paul Stevens
600.	Coolbaun	Tipperary	Possible early fields	Dave Pollock
601.	Donohill Lands, Donohill	Tipperary	Linear feature	Mary Henry
602.	Main Street, Golden	Tipperary	Urban medieval and post-medieval	Jo Moran
603.	*Rian Bó Phádraig*, Kildanoge	Tipperary	Linear earthwork	Mary G. O'Donnell
604.	Kiltinan Castle, Kiltinan	Tipperary	Medieval and post-medieval castle	Dave Pollock
605.	Knockalton Lower	Tipperary	Prehistoric ditches	Richard N. O'Brien
606.	Knockalton Upper (Site A)	Tipperary	Unknown	Richard N. O'Brien
607.	Knockalton Upper (Site B)	Tipperary	Prehistoric structure?	Richard N. O'Brien
608.	Knockaunkennedy	Tipperary	*Fulacht fiadh*	Richard N. O'Brien
609.	Lahesseragh (Site A)	Tipperary	Prehistoric settlement	Richard N. O'Brien
610.	Lahesseragh (Site C)	Tipperary	Prehistoric house	Richard N. O'Brien
611.	Lahesseragh (Site D)	Tipperary	*Fulacht fiadh*	Richard N. O'Brien

612.	Lisheen Mine Complex, Barnalisheen/Cooleeney/ Derryfadda/Killoran	Tipperary	Archaeological complex	Paul Stevens
613.	Killoran 10	Tipperary	Bronze Age flat cremation cemetery	Paul Stevens
614.	Killoran 16	Tipperary	Iron Age house and Early Christian pit	Cara Murray
615.	Killoran 31	Tipperary	Early Christian settlement	Paul Stevens
616.	Listunny	Tipperary	Bronze Age house site	Richard N. O'Brien
617.	Loughnafina	Tipperary	Enclosure	Mary Henry
618.	Nenagh Bypass Road Scheme	Tipperary	Various	Richard N. O'Brien
619.	54 Pearse Street, Nenagh	Tipperary	Urban	Anne Connolly
620.	Cuckoo Hill, Nicholastown	Tipperary	Adjacent to enclosure	Mary Henry
621.	Roscrea Sewerage Scheme, Roscrea	Tipperary	No archaeological significance	John Ó Néill
622.	King John's Tower, Roscrea Castle, Roscrea	Tipperary	Medieval castle, curtain tower	Alan Hayden
623.	Riverrun House, Cornamult, Terryglass	Tipperary	Ditch features of unknown age	Kenneth Hanley
624.	Riverrun House, Cornamult, Terryglass	Tipperary	Ringitch	Paul Stevens
625.	The Munster Hotel, Cathedral Street, Thurles	Tipperary	Urban medieval	Paul Stevens
626.	Bohercrow Road, Murgasty, Tipperary	Tipperary	Burial-ground/kiln/hut site	Tony Cummins
627.	Tullahedy	Tipperary	Neolithic landscape	Cia McConway
628.	Tullahedy	Tipperary	Prehistoric/early medieval *fulachta fiadh*	Richard N. O'Brien
629.	Copney	Tyrone	Stone circle complex	Norman Crothers
630.	Lisdivin	Tyrone	Megalith	Declan P. Hurl
631.	Tremoge	Tyrone	Stone circle complex	Norman Crothers
632.	Ballyduff	Waterford	No archaeological significance	Florence M. Hurley
633.	Lisnakill, Butlerstown	Waterford	Adjacent to church	Orla Scully
634.	Church Street/Emmet Street, Dungarvan	Waterford	Late medieval/post-medieval urban	Dave Pollock
635.	Dungarvan Castle, Dungarvan	Waterford	Medieval and post-medieval castle	Dave Pollock
636.	44 Main Street, Dungarvan	Waterford	Late medieval/post-medieval urban	Dave Pollock
637.	Kilmovee	Waterford	Kilns, medieval?	Dave Pollock
638.	9 Arundel Square, Waterford	Waterford	Urban medieval	Joanna Wren
639.	Deanery Garden, Waterford	Waterford	Medieval undercroft	Orla Scully
640.	92 The Quay, Waterford	Waterford	No archaeological significance	Cathy Sheehan
641.	Waterside Motors Ltd, Waterside, Waterford	Waterford	City wall	Andrew Gittins
642.	Bastion Street, Athlone	Westmeath	Urban post-medieval	Paul Stevens
643.	Northgate Street, Athlone	Westmeath	Urban medieval	Martin E. Byrne
644.	Retreat Park, Athlone	Westmeath	Enclosure	Dominic Delany
645.	Seán Costello Street West (Irishtown Upper), Athlone	Westmeath	17th-century suburb	Martin E. Byrne
646.	Water Street, Castlepollard	Westmeath	Adjacent to church and graveyard	Martin E. Byrne
647.	Fore	Westmeath	No archaeological significance	Anne Connolly
648.	Kerinstown and Balrowan	Westmeath	Vicinity of castle site	Rosanne Meenan
649.	Austin Friars Street/ McCurtain Street, Mullingar	Westmeath	Urban post-medieval	Deirdre Murphy
650.	Austin Friars Street/ McCurtain Street, Mullingar	Westmeath	Urban medieval	Deirdre Murphy
651.	Barrack Street/Friar's Mill Road, Mullingar	Westmeath	Site of post-medieval friary?	Alan Hayden
652.	Blackhall Street, Mullingar	Westmeath	Urban medieval	Clare Mullins
653.	Church Avenue/Pearse Street, Mullingar	Westmeath	Post-medieval	Jim Higgins
654.	Dominic Street, Mullingar	Westmeath	Organic deposit	Thaddeus C. Breen
655.	28 Dominick Street, Mullingar	Westmeath	Urban medieval	Rosanne Meenan
656.	Friars Hill Road, Mullingar	Westmeath	Urban	Jim Higgins

657.	Lynnbury Terrace, Mullingar	Westmeath	Urban medieval	Donald Murphy
658.	McCurtain Street, Mullingar	Westmeath	Urban medieval	Deirdre Murphy
659.	11–13 Oliver Plunkett Street, Mullingar	Westmeath	Urban medieval	Rosanne Meenan
660.	Adamstown	Wexford	Adjacent to ecclesiastical site	Cathy Sheehan
661.	Ballyanne	Wexford	Medieval settlement	Jo Moran
662.	Courtown	Wexford	No archaeological significance	Edmond O'Donovan
663.	Murphy-Flood's Hotel, Irish Street, Enniscorthy	Wexford	Urban medieval	Sarah McCutcheon
664.	Parnell (Lemington) Road, Enniscorthy	Wexford	No archaeological significance	Isabel Bennett
665.	Ferns/Ferns Demesne/ Ferns Upper/Ferns Lower	Wexford	Medieval and post-medieval town and vicinity of abbey	Mary Henry
666.	Main Street, Ferns	Wexford	Adjacent to castle	Florence M. Hurley
667.	Fethard-on-Sea	Wexford	No archaeological significance	Helen Kehoe
668.	Town Centre, Gorey	Wexford	Urban post-medieval	Rob Lynch
669.	Haggardstown	Wexford	Zone of archaeological potential	Dermot Nelis
670.	Killurin	Wexford	Possible enclosure site	Isabel Bennett
671.	Killurin	Wexford	Medieval graveyard	Joanna Wren
672.	Ball Alley Lane, New Ross	Wexford	Medieval	Orla Scully
673.	Bishopsland, New Ross	Wexford	No archaeological significance	Orla Scully
674.	Priory Street, New Ross	Wexford	Urban medieval	Clare Mullins
675.	Mayglass, Pollwitch	Wexford	18th-century earthen farmhouse	Cathy Sheehan
676.	Salville	Wexford	Adjacent to motte and boulder burial	Isabel Bennett
677.	Main Street, Taghmon	Wexford	Vicinity of Early Christian and medieval sites	Clare Mullins
678.	13 The Faythe, Wexford	Wexford	No archaeological significance	Cathy Sheehan
679.	George's Street Upper, Wexford	Wexford	No archaeological significance	Cathy Sheehan
680.	King Street Upper, Wexford	Wexford	Viking Age (?)/urban medieval	Martin E. Byrne
681.	Rowe Street, Wexford	Wexford	Urban medieval	Joanna Wren
682.	Wexford Main Drainage	Wexford	Urban	Cathy Sheehan
683.	Arklow Bypass	Wicklow	Various	Breandán Ó Riordáin
684.	South Quay, Arklow	Wicklow	Urban medieval	Donald Murphy
685.	Ballinabarney	Wicklow	Monastic site	Rob Lynch
686.	Ballynattin	Wicklow	Prehistoric enclosure	Eamonn Cotter
687.	Presentation College, Newcourt, Bray	Wicklow	Unknown	Rosanne Meenan
688.	Carrickmines–Bray Gas Pipeline, Fassaroe/Kilbride/Kilcroney/ Wingfield/Hollybrook/ Ballywaltrin	Wicklow	Wedge tomb, *fulachta fiadh*	John Ó Néill
689.	Market Square, Dunlavin	Wicklow	Urban medieval	Clare Mullins
690.	Market Square, Dunlavin	Wicklow	Urban medieval	Martin E. Byrne
691.	Redford Park, Rathdown, Greystones	Wicklow	Medieval	Una Cosgrave
692.	Lott Lane, Kilcoole	Wicklow	Late medieval ironworking	Emmet Byrnes
693.	Kilquade	Wicklow	Adjacent to church	Christiaan Corlett
694.	Rath East	Wicklow	Adjacent to hillfort	Una Cosgrove
695.	1 Milton Villas, Church Hill, Wicklow	Wicklow	No archaeological significance	Eoin Halpin
696.	Church Hill Street, Wicklow	Wicklow	Urban	Dermot Nelis
697.	2 Church Street, Wicklow	Wicklow	Urban	James Eogan
698.	Church Street/Wentworth Place, Wicklow	Wicklow	Urban	Una Cosgrave
699.	Church Street/Wentworth Place, Wicklow	Wicklow	Urban	Dermot Nelis

ADDENDA

Reports of the following sites were received in press.

Ad1.	Orchard Lane/The Ninth Lock Road, Clondalkin	Dublin	Post-medieval	Edmond O'Donovan
Ad2.	43/44 Clarendon Street, Dublin	Dublin	Pre-Georgian wall containing fireplace; Georgian cellars	Noel Dunne
Ad3	Dundrum Castle House, Dundrum	Dublin	Medieval	E. Eoin Sullivan
Ad4.	Patrickswell Lane, Finglas	Dublin	Probable 17-century rampart	Noel Dunne
Ad5.	Punchestown Little	Kildare	No archaeological significance	Noel Dunne
Ad6.	Tholsel Street, Carlingford	Louth	Urban medieval/post-medieval	Kieran Campbell
Ad7.	Irishtown, New Ross	Wexford	Urban medieval	E. Eoin Sullivan
Ad8.	Ashton, Blessington	Wicklow	18th/19th/20th-century tillage features	Noel Dunne

The following is a list of sites for which excavation licences were issued during 1998 but for which summaries were not received in time for publication. It should also be noted that there may have been some other sites investigated during 1998, but for which licences were issued during 1997, which may have escaped being included in this bulletin.

CLARE

700. Ballymaley–Ennis Drainage Scheme
Monitoring
98E0400
Michael Tierney.

701. Cappalea North
?
98E0399
Tom Condit, Dúchas, 51 St Stephen's Green, Dublin 2.

702. Fanore Beg
?
98E0056
Christine Grant, 11 Balliny North, Craggagh PO, Co. Clare.

703. Cloondoon Castle, Rockvale
Castle
98E0067, 98E0079
Christine Grant, 11 Balliny North, Craggagh PO, Co. Clare.

CORK

704. Reenadisert
?
98E0446
John Tierney, Eachtra Archaeological Projects, Curragh, Ardmore, Co. Waterford.

DONEGAL

705. Donegal Bypass
Monitoring
97E0162
Paula King, 5 St Jarlath's Place, Bishop Street, Tuam.

DUBLIN

706. Killegar Road, Kiltiernan, Ballybetagh

?
98E0314
Sarah Cross.

707. Blackhall Place, Dublin
Urban
98E0562
Tim Coughlan, Margaret Gowen & Co., 2 Killiney View, Albert Road Lower, Glenageary, Co. Dublin.

708. Cork Hill, Dublin
Urban
98E0576
Helen Keogh, Margaret Gowen & Co., 2 Killiney View, Albert Road Lower, Glenageary, Co. Dublin.

709. Laughanstown
?
98E0261
Christine Grant, 11 Balliny North, Craggagh PO, Co. Clare.

710. Kiltalown, Tallaght
On bypass route
98E0118
Tadgh O'Keefe, Department of Archaeology, University College, Dublin.

GALWAY

711. Kinalehin Monastery, Friary
Monastery
98E0312
Tadgh O'Keefe, Department of Archaeology, University College, Dublin.

712. Victoria Place, Galway
Urban
98E0087
Christine Grant, 11 Balliny North, Craggagh PO, Co. Clare.

KILDARE

713. 3, 13 and 14 Emily Row, Athy
Urban
98E0211
Christine Grant, 11 Balliny North, Craggagh PO, Co. Clare.

714. 'Race of the Black Pig', The Curragh
Linear earthwork?
98E0059
Tadgh O'Keefe, Department of Archaeology, University College, Dublin.

KILKENNY

715. Kilkenny Sewerage Scheme, Stage 4
Urban
97E0481
Patrick Neary, 12 Willow Close, Ardmore, Kilkenny.

716. Thomastown
Urban
98E0353

John Tierney, Eachtra Archaeological Projects, Curragh, Ardmore, Co. Waterford.

LOUTH

717. Loughboy, Drogheda
Urban?
98E0285
Sarah Cross.

718. Dunleer–Dundalk Motorway
Monitoring
97E0475
Patricia Lynch, 10 Ashford Place, Dublin 7.

MAYO

719. Knock–Claremorris Bypass Route
Monitoring
98E0304
Joanna Nolan.

720. Knock–Claremorris Bypass
Monitoring
98E0551
Joanna Nolan.

MEATH

721. St Columba's, Canon Street, Kells
Urban
98E0307
Cara Murray, 10 Martello Ave., Dun Laoghaire, Co. Dublin.

722. Farrell Street, Kells
Urban
98E0222
Christine Grant, 11 Balliny North, Craggagh PO, Co. Clare.

723. Moyglare Church, Moyglare
Church
98E0207
Frank Ryan.

ROSCOMMON

724. Moydow
?
98E0519
John Tierney, Eachtra Archaeological Projects, Curragh, Ardmore, Co. Waterford.

725. Tully Lough, Tully
?
98E0364
Fionnbarr Moore, Dúchas, 51 St Stephen's Green, Dublin 2.

SLIGO

726. Drumcliff South and Drumcliff Glebe

?
98E0514
Cara Murray, 10 Martello Ave., Dun Laoghaire, Co. Dublin.
TIPPERARY

727. New Museum, Clonmel
Urban
98E0249
John Tierney, Eachtra Archaeological Projects, Curragh, Ardmore, Co. Waterford.

728. River House, New Quay, Clonmel
Urban
98E0099
John Tierney, Eachtra Archaeological Projects, Curragh, Ardmore, Co. Waterford.

729. 13 Sarsfield Street, Clonmel
Medieval/post-urban medieval
97E0464
Mary Henry, 1 Jervis Place, Clonmel, Co. Tipperary.

730. Spitalfield
?
98E0181
John Tierney, Eachtra Archaeological Projects, Curragh, Ardmore, Co. Waterford.

WATERFORD

731. Kilmacthomas Road Scheme, Ahanaglogh
Monitoring
98E0575
John Tierney, Eachtra Archaeological Projects, Curragh, Ardmore, Co. Waterford.

732. Dysert
?
98E0226
John Tierney, Eachtra Archaeological Projects, Curragh, Ardmore, Co. Waterford.

733. Scrahan
?
98E0564
John Tierney, Eachtra Archaeological Projects, Curragh, Ardmore, Co. Waterford.

APPENDICES

I. Irish Archaeological Wetland Unit (IAWU) Fieldwork 1998—Counties Offaly and Mayo.
Conor McDermott, Nóra Bermingham, Ellen O'Carroll and Jane Whitaker, Irish Archaeological Wetland Unit, Department of Archaeology, University College Dublin, Dublin 4.

II. A Fieldwalking Survey of the Knocknarea Mountain area, Co. Sligo (E998)
Stefan Bergh, Department of Archaeology, University of Stockholm, Sweden.

III. Correction to report on Templerainy, Co. Wicklow, published in *Excavations 1997*.
Breandán Ó Ríordáin, Burage More, Blessington, Co. Wicklow, for Valerie J. Keeley Ltd.

1. CASTLE WALLS, ANTRIM

Fortification

J14728690

During conservation work on the east castle wall the opportunity was taken to examine the fortification.

The trench, 2m x 2m, exposed cobbles on a metalled surface overlying a shallow ditch running north–south, flanking the wall and containing medieval glazed pottery. The examination of the bastion uncovered a series of ten gun-loops within its walls. A further trench, 2m x 1m, was opened at the rear of the bastion to determine whether there was a return, but neither this nor any other archaeologically interesting feature was found.

Paul Logue, Archaeological Excavations Unit, Built Heritage, EHS, 5–33 Hill Street, Belfast.

2. KILLYBEGS ROAD, ANTRIM

Rath and motte

J13768853

SMR 50:4

This was the location of an Early Christian ecclesiastical site and a rath converted into a motte, removed during previous development. An investigation took place ahead of factory expansion.

A roughly circular feature, 21m in diameter, was noted, but, following heavy rainfall, attempts to find it again failed. It was assumed to be the insubstantial remnant of an enclosing ditch. Several large timbers and some strands of hazel, all running approximately east–west, were also found. These turned out to be natural timbers along the bottom of a stream bed, subsequently removed.

J.C. McSparron, Northern Archaeological Consultancy Ltd, Unit 6, Farset Enterprise Centre, Springfield Road, Belfast.

3. BALLYUTOAG

No archaeological significance

J275790

Investigation took place ahead of quarry expansion through a possible booley-house complex. Nothing of archaeological relevance was uncovered.

J.C. McSparron, Northern Archaeological Consultancy Ltd, Unit 6, Farset Enterprise Centre, Springfield Road, Belfast.

4. BRITISH AND SEACASH

Multi-period

J143806

SMR 55:111, 55:135, 55:150, 55:238–9

An investigation was undertaken on suspected cropmarks within this archaeologically rich area ahead of commercial development.

Several suspected sites were shown to be modern drains or the result of waterlogging. Two, however, revealed archaeological features. One was a mound 45.2m in diameter and 1.2m high, containing three phases of occupation: the first phase was represented by post- and stake-holes, the second by a hearth and charcoal-rich soils containing souterrain ware, and the third by stone wall footings and more souterrain ware.

The second site consisted of a gully, 0.57m wide and 0.18m deep, from which several flints were recovered, and a pit, 1.3m x 0.8m and 0.3m deep, containing large stones and charcoal-rich soil.

Norman Crothers, Archaeological Development Services Ltd, Unit 48, Westlink Enterprise Centre, 30–50 Distillery Street, Belfast BT12 5BJ.

5. BUSHFOOT STRAND, PORTBALLINTRAE

Burial site

C93464263

SMR 3:113

The police contacted EHS to request an analysis of human remains found protruding from sand dunes outside Portballintrae on the north coast. A brief investigation revealed them to be from a skeleton several centuries old, and it was arranged to excavate them.

The find consisted of a coffined burial oriented east-north-east/west-south-west, with pieces of wood and corroded iron nails still *in situ*. The upper part of the skeleton had been removed by tidal action, although the bones of the legs, feet and right hand were discernible as those of a robust man of average height and in his late twenties or early thirties when he died. The results of radiocarbon analysis are awaited.

Declan P. Hurl, Built Heritage, EHS, 5–33 Hill Street, Belfast.

6. CASTLE UPTON, TEMPLEPATRICK

Bronze Age settlement

J225859

SMR 50:137

Excavation, ahead of the construction of a hotel and golf-course, continued on a site adjacent to Castle Upton where cropmark sites were identified, and monitoring revealed further archaeological survival (see also A. Gahan, *Excavations 1997*, 3.)

Four trenches were excavated. The first, 50m x 30m, exposed an area of charcoal staining, 7.5m in diameter, containing a central hearth; flint scrapers and flakes and Bronze Age pottery were recovered. Within the second trench, 20m x 30m, was a subcircular pit, 1.83m x 1.52m, containing Bronze Age pottery and burnt bone. The third trench, a machine-stripped area *c.* 28m in diameter, contained a stone-filled slot 5m long, 0.3m wide and 0.2m deep. Within the last trench, 30m x 19m, were a gully, 0.4m wide and 0.14m deep, and another pit, 0.64m in diameter and 0.16m deep.

Ciara McManus, Archaeological Development Services Ltd, Unit 48, Westlink Enterprise Centre, 30–50 Distillery Street, Belfast BT12 5BJ.

7. LINENHALL STREET, ARMAGH

Urban

H87684502

SMR 12:103

Armagh Museum informed EHS of the demolition of a public house in the centre of Armagh. The construction of new premises had been granted planning permission, although EHS had not been notified. With the permission of the new owner a brief, small-scale excavation was undertaken.

Several areas were cleared of rubble. The first trench, 5m x 4m, revealed five subcircular pits, ranging from 0.85m in diameter and 0.7m deep to 1.95m in diameter and 1.2m deep. They were found to contain sherds of everted-rim ware and green-glazed pottery, parts of amber beads, iron nails and pieces of bone and antler, within clearly stratified fills.

Two further, adjacent trenches, 1.5m x 2.5m and 2m x 3m, in the south of the site, revealed perpendicular stone walls, belonging to two post-medieval building phases, which cut through a gully, 1m wide and 0.7m deep, containing a sherd of red-glazed pottery and a piece of amber.

Declan P. Hurl, Built Heritage, EHS, 5–33 Hill Street, Belfast.

8. MARKET STREET, ARMAGH
Urban
H87564524
SMR 12:103

The building of a new theatre in Armagh city centre to the north of Market Square necessitated the presence of an archaeologist. Three trenches were sunk using heavy machinery.

Two were dug on the mound in the south-east corner, and one running east–west in the carpark to the north-east. The two trenches on the mound produced no features other than relatively modern pottery and house remains.

At the western end of the 6m-long carpark trench a large, square, organic-filled cesspit was uncovered. About 0.25m from the top of the organic material was a small, complete, glazed, early 18th-century pot, enabling close dating of the pit. Near this pit a house known as 'the Cottage' is shown on the 1st and 2nd edition OS maps. This pit may relate to this house.

At the eastern end of the third test-trench a filled-in ditch was uncovered. It was flat-bottomed and V-shaped, with its base at a depth of *c.* 2m below ground level, and *c.* 2.5–3m wide. It appeared to run in a north–south direction and was filled with grey, sticky clay with a large animal bone content. This ditch was uncovered to the north later in the excavation.

Part of the work involved the removal of several metres of land at the west of the site, part of the Archbishop's garden. The scarping of this area and topsoil-stripping in the northern part of the site uncovered a series of large pits and several ditches. These pits were up to 3m in both depth and diameter. They appeared to be rubbish pits as there was no sign of structural evidence or any sort of a pattern. They did contain large amounts of animal bone and antler. Several of the pits also contained late 18th-century pottery and glass. However, several pits contained material that gave an earlier date, including parts of an antler comb, souterrain ware pottery and part of a lignite bracelet.

At least three ditches were uncovered. The carpark ditch was traceable in the northern part of the carpark. It had been destroyed by the construction of the St Patrick's Trian carpark to the north. The ditch curved slightly to the west but appeared to run concentrically around the hilltop. It may be related to those found in the excavations on the site of St Patrick's Trian. There was no obvious dating evidence present, but again the ditch was full of animal bones. It also cut through some large pits, without dating evidence.

On removal of the mound in the area to the west of the two original test-trenches, a V-shaped ditch was discovered running east–west up the hill. It appeared to cut through a cobbled surface, had dark grey fills and was cut into subsoil. Part of the upper fill was composed of large limestone boulders. These occurred on the northern side of the ditch, suggesting that they had come in from this side.

Material found in the fills included souterrain ware, everted-rim ware, a piece of copper strip, one piece of Neolithic pot, part of a quernstone and a human skull. The skull, which had been deliberately placed, was found lying near the base of the ditch facing east, right way up. There was no lower jaw present. It was examined by Dr E. Murphy and was of a male aged between twenty-five and thirty-five who appeared to have been at least partially decapitated with a long, sharp object.

The third ditch was uncovered to the north-west of Ditch 2. It appeared to run north from a rounded terminal and was U-shaped, very steep-sided, relatively narrow and filled with an organic, almost peaty material. It contained animal bones but no artefacts. This ditch too was cut through the cobbled surface. It was not possible to trace it for any distance to the north.

Stephen Gilmore, Northern Archaeological Consultancy Ltd, Unit 6, Farset Enterprise Centre, Springfield Road, Belfast.

9. DRUMILLY DEMESNE, LOUGHGALL
Souterrain
H90435128

An underground passage was discovered during the construction of a new golf-course in Drumilly Demesne near Loughgall in County Armagh. Mechanical topsoil-stripping disturbed a roofing lintel of an air vent attached to the roof of the passage. This revealed a void that was found to be a drystone-lined and stone-roofed passage.

A geophysical survey was carried out by Martina McCarthy of Geoarch, within an area of *c.* 50m diameter of the displaced lintel. Within the same grid a 4m x 4m trench, centred on the displaced lintel, was excavated. After the geophysical results were processed it was decided to partially machine-excavate two trenches at either end of the passage.

Trench 1 revealed that the disturbed lintel had been displaced from a roughly square-sectioned, chimney-shaped air vent, built using around four layers of subrectangular stones (*c.* 0.4m max. dimensions) laid alternately longitudinally and traversely. These seem to have been stacked on a gap left between the lintels of the passage proper. This created a square-sectioned chimney the aperture of which had sides measuring *c.* 0.3–0.4m. This was encased in the stiff, orange clay.

A box-trench 1m by 2.4m within Trench 1 was excavated down a further 0.5m to the surface of the roofing lintels and the tops of the side-walls of the passage. This showed that the top of the air vent was *c.* 0.43m above any of the other lintels roofing the passage. The floor of the passage lay 1.54m below the top of the air vent. This implied a passage height at this point of 1.24m.

The excavated passage had been lined by drystone walling. The upper courses of the side-walls were partly corbelled, allowing the passage to be roofed by lintels, *c.* 0.5–0.6m wide. No finds were uncovered in any of the trenches.

The geophysical survey showed that the passage ran in a roughly south-west/north-east direction across the grid. However, the information became confused at both terminal points of the grid. In order to ascertain whether these anomalies represented structures or whether the passage terminated within the grid, two trenches were excavated in the area where the geophysics indicated that the ends of the passage were heading. Trench 2 was initially machine-excavated to a depth of *c.* 0.7m, without encountering the roof of the passage or a construction cut.

A narrow box-section was excavated to a deeper level. An area of this, *c.* 2.8m by 0.6m, was hand-excavated. This revealed that the passage continued in much the same form, orientation and dimensions indicated in Trench 1. At the roof level the passage was *c.* 0.5m wide, narrowing to *c.* 0.4m halfway down the side-walls. This may imply a slightly battered wall.

The displaced lintel and direct visual access to the passage allowed a camera to be hand-lowered into the passage. It could be seen that the passage came to a terminus *c.* 6m further west. Further observation showed that this appeared to be a T-junction.

Another trench, 2m wide and 10m long, was mechanically excavated in the area where the geophysics indicated that the passage reached the western side of the grid. A box-trench 0.6m wide, centred on this was excavated by a digger with a narrow bucket. One small lintel was lifted. The passage was again *c.* 1.3m deep, was similar in width to Trenches 1 and 2 and continued basically unchanged to the edge of the grid.

Flash photography revealed that the passage took a massive deliberate reduction in height (from *c.* 1.3m to *c.* 0.5m). It also seemed to reduce in width. This finely constructed restriction was carefully framed by a large, rectangular lintel.

The subterranean structure examined at Drumilly was a typical east Ulster souterrain. The main passage seems to have been relatively straight in plan (orientated roughly south-west/north-east) and over 40m long, making it one of the longest straight stretches of souterrain passage ever found in Ireland. There seems to have been a T-junction at the eastern end of the main passage and a dramatic, finely constructed, narrowing creep at the most westerly point visible. This narrowing may indicate that a chamber and possibly the end of the structure lie only a few metres beyond the eastern end of the grid. The chimney-type air vent is also a rare feature.
Alan Reilly, Northern Archaeological Consultancy Ltd, Unit 6, Farset Enterprise Centre, Springfield Road, Belfast.

10. NAVAN FORT
Multi-period
H84704523
SMR 12:15
The decision was taken to permit a trench to be cut through the external bank and ditch on the north-west side of the monument in an attempt to determine its age and dimensions.

The trench was stepped as the ditch was found to be 4.7m deep, mostly filled with natural timbers and peat. At its base was a thin layer of grey silt containing the remains of a wooden bowl and two charred oak beams, one of which was dendro-dated to 95BC, similar to the central post in the 40m structure in the main mound.
Jim Mallory, Department of Archaeology, Queen's University, Belfast.

11. HAUGHEY'S FORT, TRAY
Bronze Age settlement
SMR 12:13
H83504530
The research and training programme of excavations at Haughey's Fort continued this year. The investigation focused on the terminal of the inner ditch, both to complete previous work in the area (*Excavations 1997*, 3) and to ground-truth the results of a remote-sensing project.

An area of 271m² was investigated, mainly around the double series of post-holes previously uncovered. A pit, 1.7m in diameter and 1.3m deep, was found to contain Late Bronze Age pottery. A horizon of charcoal-rich soil was also uncovered; it too contained Late Bronze Age pottery, as well as struck flint and burnt bone.
Jim Mallory, Department of Archaeology, Queen's University, Belfast.

CARLOW

12. MILL LANE, CARLOW
Urban
S715771
98E0058
The development site at Mill Brook, Mill Lane, Carlow, was tested on 7 February 1998. It lies in the low-lying flood-plain immediately west of Carlow Castle and beside the River Barrow. Two test-trenches were excavated by mechanical digger.

Warehouse buildings had recently been demolished and removed from the site, and discarded stoneware bottles stamped 'Corcoran & Co. Carlow, Estd. 1827' were noted in profusion. Deposits consisted of river silts and gravels with no early structural remains. One surprising find was an intact human tibia, and this led to a recommendation that further groundworks be archaeologically monitored.
Martin Reid, 37 Errigal Road, Drimnagh, Dublin 12.

CAVAN

13. FAIR GREEN, CAVAN
Urban medieval
242020 304560
98E0496
Archaeological testing was carried out on a proposed apartment block in Fair Green, Cavan, for Cavan Urban District Council in October 1998. Two excavated trenches on the site failed to reveal any evidence of archaeological stratigraphy, with natural boulder clay being exposed quite close to the surface. It is possible that the construction of the pre-existing house on this site destroyed any stratigraphy that

may have been present. No further work was recommended.

Deirdre Murphy, Archaeological Consultancy Services Ltd, 15 Trinity Street, Drogheda, Co. Louth.

14. CORGREAGH/CORPORATION LANDS

No archaeological significance

O183322

97E0461 ext.

A final stage of monitoring at the site of the N3 Belturbet to Aghalane Road Realignment Scheme was undertaken in January 1998. Areas within farmland were topsoil-stripped immediately east and south-east of the proposed Staghall junction, to permit the construction of link roads for the new junction. The topsoil was cleared to an average depth of 0.3m, revealing undisturbed subsoil. No deposits, features or finds of archaeological significance were revealed during these works, and there are no further archaeological requirements for the development.

Malachy Conway, Margaret Gowen & Co. Ltd, 2 Killiney View, Albert Road Lower, Glenageary, Co. Dublin.

15. DERRYGARRA UPPER

Fulacht fiadh

240986 309765

98E0164

The site at Derrygarra Upper was uncovered during monitoring of road-stripping for the Cavan Bypass. Excavation has revealed a large burnt mound up to 0.4m high and up to 12m north–south by 6m east–west. It may reach 0.6m beyond the field boundary to the east of the site.

Small fragments of burnt stone, which took on a reddish-brown colour, and blackened earth, which contained a large percentage of charcoal, made up 80% of the mound. Several features were revealed under this mound in the natural soil, including a V-shaped gully that ran east–west along the northern limit of the site, possibly acting as a drainage channel for water.

No artefacts were recovered from the mound, which is characteristic of such monuments, and a radiocarbon date of 3656±46 years BP (cal. BC 2134–1972) was obtained for charcoal from the mound. The former presence nearby of a standing stone at Tullybuck (SMR 15:72) and the unclassified megalithic tomb at Drummany (SMR 15:40) attest to occupation of the area both before and during the Bronze Age.

A thin layer of peaty soil overlies the burnt mound, which in turn is overlain by a field bank constructed from redeposited natural soil against which was thrown clay and small stones, perhaps from field clearance. This field boundary may have been of considerable antiquity. East of the field boundary site inspection revealed further burnt material seen in the section of the stream. This may represent a further site and has been preserved intact.

Deirdre Murphy, Archaeological Consultancy Services Ltd, 15 Trinity Street, Drogheda, Co. Louth.

16. DRUMBO (SITE 1)

Fulacht fiadh/burnt spread

243242 309765

98E0164

Site 1 at Drumbo was discovered during stripping of

topsoil for the Cavan Bypass and consisted of a small spread of burnt stone and blackened earth to a maximum of 2.2m north-west/south-east by 0.3m north-east/south-west. This layer lay under 0.2m of light brown clay, which constituted the topsoil. The remainder of the mound appeared to have been truncated by recent machine activity, as was evident by piles of churned blackened earth and burnt stone. Even considering this, the mound does not appear to have been very large; no trough or underlying features were found. The site lies close to a stream.

A radiocarbon date of 2702±49 years BP (cal. BC 906–814) was obtained from charcoal from the mound.

Deirdre Murphy, Archaeological Consultancy Services Ltd, 15 Trinity Street, Drogheda, Co. Louth.

17. DRUMBO (SITE 2)

Fulacht fiadh/burnt spread

243042 307909

98E0164

Site 2 in Drumbo townland was uncovered during monitoring of road-stripping for the Cavan Bypass. The roughly oval area of burnt sandstone in a charcoal-rich soil measured 6.6m north–south and 11.6m east–west and had been levelled by ploughing. The mound had been partially truncated by field drains. The deposit was up to 0.17m deep.

A subrectangular trough dug into the natural soil was uncovered below the mound. It had three wooden planks lining the base. A circular area of burning on the natural soil was interpreted as a probable pyre. No artefacts were recovered. A dendrochronological date of 959±9 BC (QUB) was obtained for the timber in the trough.

Deirdre Murphy, Archaeological Consultancy Services Ltd, 15 Trinity Street, Drogheda, Co. Louth.

Wooden trough lining at Drumbo 2 *fulacht fiadh.*

18. DRUMCALPIN

Fulacht fiadh

242596 308271

98E0164

A *fulacht fiadh* was uncovered during road-stripping at Drumcalpin, Co. Cavan, in the course of road construction on the Cavan Bypass. It was badly disturbed by modern drainage ditches, field boundaries and pipe-trenches.

A deposit of heat-cracked sandstone in a friable,

Trough with post-holes at Drumcalpin *fulacht fiadh*.

black, sandy clay extended for 11m north–south and 11.4m east–west. Below this a separate deposit of heat-cracked sandstone in a friable, brown, sandy clay, 0.2m deep, with frequent inclusions of wood charcoal, was removed. This came down onto the boulder clay.

A rectangular trough had been dug through the natural soil and had four post-holes, one at each corner, two of which still contained butt-trimmed posts. Impressions of planks that must have lined the trough were visible on the sides, which were lined with a sticky, grey clay. The trough was filled with heat-cracked stone and friable, brown clay and was between 0.33m and 0.19m deep. It measured 1.4m north–south by 2.05m east–west. There was no nearby watercourse.

No artefacts were recovered; two samples sent for radiocarbon dating produced dates of 2865±65 years BP (cal. BC 1154–932) and 2921±40 years BP.
Deirdre Murphy, Archaeological Consultancy Services Ltd, 15 Trinity Street, Drogheda, Co. Louth.

19. DRUMMANY
Fulacht fiadh
240696 310632
98E0164
Archaeological monitoring of the Cavan Bypass in Drummany, Co. Cavan, revealed an area of heat-cracked stones that was subsequently excavated.

A cutting measuring 10.4m north–south by 6m east–west was opened. Topsoil overlay a layer of large, angular, shattered sandstone in a brown, sandy clay with inclusions of charcoal, which was up to 0.15m deep, 3.3m north–south and 0.02m east–west. It overlay a layer of smaller, angular, fire-cracked sandstone in a loose, black, charcoal-rich soil, was up to 0.3m deep and extended for 8.1m north–south and 5.8m east–west. A subrectangular trough with rounded corners measuring 1.8m north–south and 1.7m east–west was excavated and was filled with burnt stone. This feature was cut into the compact, grey-green natural.

Part of the site was truncated by a field boundary. No artefacts or bone were recovered. The site lies close to a small lake, an unclassified megalithic tomb, possibly a wedge tomb, a standing stone at Tullybuck and other *fulachta fiadh* excavated along the road's path.
Deirdre Murphy, Archaeological Consultancy Services Ltd, 15 Trinity Street, Drogheda, Co. Louth.

20. DRUMMANY
Multi-period site
240716 310513
98E0303
This site in Drummany townland, Butlersbridge, Co. Cavan, lay across an area of bogland periodically flooded by the Annalee River. It lay along the route of the Cavan Bypass, which has been under construction since 1997. The site was uncovered by Deirdre Murphy during monitoring of ground disturbance works for the bypass. The zone stretches from the laneway (accessed beside Butlersbridge post office) to the north of the site and from the Annalee River to the south. A *fulacht fiadh* was excavated at the northern limit of this area by D. Murphy (No. 19 above).

The present site lay in an area associated with a number of known archaeological monuments from various periods. To the east of the site lay a 16th-century cornmill, and earlier settlement is marked by the presence of a number of Late Neolithic/Early Bronze Age sites such as the wedge tomb that lies in a field to the north-west of the site and a standing stone that lies south of the site.

Some struck flint was recovered during the excavation, which appeared to indicate human activity in the area in the Later Mesolithic. The earliest find was a broken butt-trimmed flake, but no apparently prehistoric features were identified during the course of the excavation.

The next use of the site appears to be during the Early Christian period, but this date is as yet unconfirmed. A number of dumps of clay had been placed on top of fen peats in the south-east of the site and linked by a short stone causeway to an area of dry land to the north-west.

The naturally fallen wood component of the peat also included larger trunks, some of which were quite substantial. There was no indication that any of these timbers had been modified. An absence of identifiable silting episodes in the peat, other than that associated with the south-western side of the stone causeway, appears to suggest that during the period of peat formation water movement on the site was in this direction only. At that stage the hydrology of the area may have been independent of the river, and it was only when the river had silted up that flooding regularly occurred in the area around the site.

The area to the east of the clay 'platform' had been monitored during previous surface-stripping, but no archaeological deposits were found. A series of circular pits was excavated at both ends of the stone causeway. The deposits around the pits contained a metallic residue, which may be a by-product of (iron?) ore reduction or roasting. The residue may indicate that bog iron ore was being processed on the site, but it may be the result of mineralisation, as it was also present in non-archaeological contexts. Two fragments of iron were recovered from one feature, along with a lead pellet, but these may be intrusive as the feature was at the upper level of the site. The butt-trimmed flake and piece of flint debitage were also recovered from features at this level. The time-span of this activity is not known owing to the absence of a radiocarbon date.

At least 0.4m of peat had formed over the stone causeway when a deposit of boulders was thrown into the pool to the south-west of the causeway. This may be associated with the initial use of the 16th-century cornmill to the east of the site, as the mill-race was positioned to the south of the clay platform. The dump of boulders consolidated the edges of an existing pool as part of the outworks of the mill. The consolidation process may have been ongoing throughout the period of use of the mill and also later, as 19th- and 20th-century objects were present within this deposit. These included farmhouse pottery, cart fragments, 19th-century clay pipe fragments, a blue glass bottle and some amorphous iron objects. A number of sherds of blackware were also identified among the deposits within the millpond.

No evidence of archaeological activity in the peats to the east of the site was revealed, either from the previous surface-stripping or from examination of the drainage channels and dry-land margins. The main focus of the attempts to cross the wetlands on the site was in the area where the two dry headlands were closest.

The cornmill is reputed to have gone out of use during the mid-19th century, and a series of landfill dumps in areas around the mill-race and lake/pond edge was identified as dating to this period. A modern pathway and field drain were also identified on the site. A double post-row structure was identified above the earlier stone causeway. It may have been the pegged element from a now destroyed structure of early modern date.

John Ó Néill, for Margaret Gowen & Co. Ltd, 2 Killiney View, Albert Road Lower, Glenageary, Co. Dublin.

21. CATHLEEN'S FALL–ENNISKILLEN–GORTAWEE 110KM V-LINE
98E0592

Testing was undertaken at different locations along the proposed Gortawee 110km V-Line.

An archaeological assessment detailed the remains in the vicinity of the proposed 110km V-Line, and as a consequence it was recommended that angle-masts (AM) or intermediate pole-sets (IMP) close to archaeological sites be repositioned where possible so that the necessary groundworks would not to pose a threat to the monuments. Three areas were identified as requiring archaeological testing. In addition, all groundworks associated with the line were monitored.

Gortoorlan
Adjacent to linear feature and possible ringfort
2224 3187
SMR 10:16

AM4 stands within 10m of a large linear feature. A single trench was cut between the proposed angle-mast location and the feature. There was no indication of any archaeological layers or deposits within the exposed section, and it appears that this feature is the result of the diversion of a nearby stream.

AM391 stands within 30m of the linear feature. A single trench 6m long, 1.4m wide and 0.8m deep was cut to the west of AM391. There were no indications of any archaeological layers or deposits, nor was any archaeological material recovered from this trench.

Kilsallagh
Charcoal spread
2242 3710

AM360 stands on an upland slope overlooking an area of low-lying, marshy ground. This area was identified as being suitable terrain for *fulachta fiadh* and/or toghers.

A single trench to the south of the AM360 was positioned in an east–west direction. There was no indication of archaeological deposits within this trench.

IMP361 is to be positioned adjacent to a field boundary. The stratigraphy revealed topsoil, overlying a natural deposit of grey marl. No artefacts or archaeological deposits were identified within this cutting.

IMP362 stands within and towards the northern end of the zone of archaeological potential. Removal of the topsoil revealed a deposit of charcoal that was up to 0.1m thick, overlying a lens of natural clay mixed with charcoal. The full extent of this burnt area was revealed and measured 2.5m north–south x 2m, with an ovoid shape. No artefactual material was recovered from these deposits. Environmental analysis of these two layers was unable to determine whether this charcoal spread was a 'consequence of anthropogenic activity or the result of natural fires'. Immediately after this trench was opened the area was inundated with water, and further investigation at this site would not be possible.

Snugborough
Adjacent to ringfort
22634 31940
SMR 10:21

IMP9 and IMP386 stand within 30m of a ringfort, perched at the edge of a cliff overlooking a gully with steeply sloping sides. The power-line will span this gully, so it was not practical to reposition these pole-sets, which stand on a steep slope to the south-east of the ringfort.

IMP9 stood 28m from the ringfort. A trench was cut adjacent to the location of this pole-set. There was no indication of artefactual material or archaeological deposits within this cutting.

IMP386 stands 20m from the ringfort. A trench was cut 3m to the west of this pole-set. No archaeological deposits or artefacts were identified.

Rónán Swan, Arch-Tech Ltd, 32 Fitzwilliam Place, Dublin 2.

22. LISDRUMSKEA
No archaeological significance
27284 30556
SMR 23:36
98E0294

Archaeological monitoring was carried out at Lisdrumskea, Shercock, Co. Cavan, during the construction of a pitch-and-putt course. The site was in the vicinity of a large, bivallate ringfort. Topsoil was followed by natural boulder clay at 0.2m.

Donald Murphy, Archaeological Consultancy Services Ltd, 15 Trinity Street, Drogheda, Co. Louth.

23. MULLAGH
Proximity to ringfort
26836 28660
98E0530

Archaeological assessment of a site at Mullagh, Co.

Cavan, took place in advance of a proposed residential development. The site lay in close proximity to an enclosure site with traces of a fosse. Five trenches were dug across the site, and no archaeological features or objects were recovered.
Deirdre Murphy, Archaeological Consultancy Services Ltd, 15 Trinity Street, Drogheda, Co. Louth.

CLARE

24. BALLYCASEY MORE
Archaeological complex
R424634
SMR 51:176
98E0517

Test-trenching and a control survey were conducted in September and November 1998 in advance of sale of the land for development. The site is an extensive complex of rectilinear, linear and mound earthworks, covering an area of 540m x 232m. A comprehensive programme of excavation of twelve test-trenches was undertaken to identify the nature and morphology of all earthwork features.

This produced evidence of at least one burnt mound, as well as a substantial concentration of post-medieval activity. The burnt mound was situated in a later, undated, square enclosure close to an area of fen and was just outside the development area. The remaining earthworks were revealed to be of post-medieval origin, including field banks, field systems, a roadway and possible house—possibly a seasonal booleying camp—dating to the 18th century. Kenneth Hanley (*Excavations 1996*, 9, 95E133) excavated a similar complex close to this site at Latoon South. The site was substantially ploughed in recent times, with recent quarrying activity noted in two areas, undertaken some time after the 1950s.

Further archaeological wetland survey, archaeological monitoring of dry-land areas and preservation or full excavation of the burnt mound was recommended.
Paul Stevens, for Margaret Gown & Co. Ltd, 2 Killiney View, Albert Road Lower, Glenageary, Co. Dublin.

25. BALLYMALLEY
No archaeological significance
98E0277

The route of the drainage scheme runs from the townland of Ballymalley to the Corrovorrin housing estate, Ennis, Co. Clare. The project began in June 1998 and was initially monitored by Michael Tierney of Eachtra Archaeological Projects. In September 1998 the licence was transferred to this author. The remaining sections to be monitored included Work Area Nos 1 and 2 (on/near the Ennis–Gort road), the Ennis–Ruan road and the River Fergus.

Most of the work in Work Area No. 1 involved the insertion of pipes through part of the existing Ennis–Ruan road. Based on some early historical and mapping evidence this road would have been in use in the late medieval/post-medieval period; however, the monitoring evidence revealed nothing of archaeological significance. This also applied to the section of pipeline cut through the Ennis–Gort road. The small area stripped from 'Hogan's Field',

Ballymalley, also failed to reveal anything of archaeological significance owing to the area having been lowered by the landowner in recent years.

The area flanking the bank of the River Fergus, in Work Area No. 2, did produce some depositional activity. However, this appeared to have been caused by soil creep or by landfill, introduced in recent years. Nothing of archaeological interest was revealed.

Only about half of the outfall area could be developed owing to severe flooding problems. Monitoring revealed *c.* 0.3–0.4m of black silt overlying the bedrock and boulder clay. This silt did not reveal any archaeological activity. However, being associated with the marshy banks of the River Fergus, it does still have archaeological potential. Above this silt deposit was *c.* 1–2m of recently introduced landfill. It is intended to complete this section of pipeline in the spring of 1999.
Kenneth Hanley, 44 Eaton Heights, Cobh, Co. Cork.

26. BALLYMULCASHEL
Possible enclosure
SMR 43:84
98E0480

A site assessment consisting of two test-trenches was carried out in the area of the enclosure noted on a GSI map but not visible at ground level. No finds or features of archaeological significance were noted.
Sheila Lane, 1 Charlemont Heights, Coach Hill, Rochestown, Co. Cork.

27. AREA 7, BALLYNACRAGGA
No archaeological significance
1381 1692
98E0333

In the summer of 1998 an archaeological investigation was carried out in the townland of Latoon South, Co. Clare, as part of the proposed N18/19 (Ballycasey–Dromoland) Bypass Road Improvement Scheme. This followed an Environmental Impact Survey carried out by Celie O Rahilly and subsequent site assessments by Christine Grant, undertaken in 1998. It was established that this area, Area 7, contained erratic boulders and traces of linear arrangements of earth and stone, possibly early field systems.

Two 10m x 1m trenches, both orientated north–south, were excavated to limestone bedrock. Trench 1 was positioned to traverse an earth-and-stone bank. Trench 2 lay further to the west, in a clearing on higher ground.

Trench 1 was excavated to a depth of 0.3m. Before testing, much of the surrounding bush and scrub was cut back to reveal the earth-and-stone bank, which survived to a height of 0.7m above ground level and when excavated was shown to be a drystone wall. Despite clearance the wall was still overgrown and much disturbed by root action. The sod and topsoil layer of mid-brown silt, with more grass cover to the north than to the south, ran over and was banked up against the boundary wall. It had a maximum depth of 0.15m. The wall itself consisted of a number of large, limestone slabs set on edge, supported on a foundation of smaller packing-stones. In one instance an upright slab had been placed in a natural socket in the bedrock. There was no evidence of any toolmarks on the larger stones.

A stone alignment consisting of five stones running east–west across the trench to the north of the wall was investigated by opening two $1m^2$ extensions on both sides of the feature. The alignment proved to be natural. A brown silt layer with occasional small stones and a maximum thickness of 0.3m was found around the wall and appeared to be natural. An orange/brown, gravelly silt was found to the north of the wall and directly overlay the bedrock. It had a depth of 0.13m and was featureless. Trench 2 was excavated to a maximum depth of 0.35m. Sod and topsoil with a depth of 0.1m overlay a featureless brown silt, with frequent small stones. This overlay limestone bedrock.

Pre-development testing of Area 7 produced no archaeological finds. The wall in Trench 1 was the only notable feature but lacked any associated datable evidence. All of the layers excavated were sterile.

Billy Quinn, Archaeological Services Unit Ltd, Purcell House, Oranmore, Co. Galway.

28. AREA 11, BALLYNACRAGGA
No archaeological significance
98E0334
One week's pre-development testing commenced on 17 July 1998 as part of the N18/N19 (Ballycasey–Dromoland) Road Improvement Scheme.

No archaeological features or deposits were encountered. Natural soils of silty clay and silty sand were excavated and were found to be sterile and featureless.

Anne Connolly, Archaeological Services Unit Ltd, Purcell House, Oranmore, Co. Galway, for Valerie J. Keeley Ltd.

29. AREA 13, BALLYNACRAGGA
98E0335
One week's pre-development testing commenced on 24 July 1998 as part of the N18/N19 (Ballycasey–Dromoland) Road Improvement Scheme.

A possible stone alignment had been identified in an archaeological assessment report compiled by Celie O Rahilly. It consists of three earthfast boulders oriented north-west/south-east. A geophysical survey identified a possible ditch feature to the north of the stone alignment in an area within the road corridor.

No archaeological features or deposits were encountered during testing. Natural soils were excavated and found to be sterile and featureless.

Excavation of the trenches adjacent to the possible alignment revealed, for the most part, undisturbed natural layers. The recovery of two beads and some charcoal flecks from the subsoil suggests some activity in the vicinity of the stones rather than activity related to their original erection.

One of the stones of the possible alignment was seen to be deeply lodged in natural sand layers, in contrast to the depth of the other stone, revealed in an adjacent trench. This second stone was not earthfast in that it was found to be overlying a shallow, brown clay that had a depth of 0.1m.

Anne Connolly, Archaeological Services Unit Ltd, Purcell House, Oranmore, Co. Galway, for Valerie J. Keeley Ltd.

30. SITE 17, BALLYNACRAGGA
No archaeological significance
1381 1681
98E0336
An area to the west of Ballnacragga ringfort, SMR 51:15, was investigated in advance of construction of the Ballycasey–Dromoland Bypass. A geophysical survey identified possible ditches. Though under grass at the time of investigation, the field had been ploughed several times. Evidence of furrows was found in the subsoil. Nothing of archaeological significance was found.

Fiona Reilly, Wood Road, Cratloekeel, Co. Clare, for Valerie J. Keeley Ltd.

31. FORMER CREAMERY, BUNRATTY
Medieval borough
R450608
SMR 61:11 and 62:1
98E0434
The extension to the existing creamery building, installation of underground services and preparation of the carpark were monitored in accordance with a planning condition. The site lay to the west of the castle, just south of the Old Bunratty Road. Before the construction of the new road and buildings to the south of the castle this piece of ground abutted the castle, and it is possible that it was used as a fairground/market in the medieval period.

The work was monitored in stages. Initially two landscape cuttings were opened as it was proposed to reduce the level in certain areas close to the main building. Then the foundations for the extension at the rear of the main building (on the north side) were opened, followed by the drainage trenches. No finds, features or deposits of archaeological significance were noted in any of the cuttings.

Celie O Rahilly, Limerick Corporation, City Hall, Limerick.

32. SITE 18, CARRIGORAN
Field system
1385 1677
SMR 51:01802
98E0337
Three areas, identified by a geophysical survey as of possible interest, were excavated in this area before construction of the Ballycasey–Dromoland Bypass. The site is described as a field system in the SMR.

Area 1 did not produce any features. Among the finds were a musket ball and a possible copper-alloy stick-pin. Area 2 did not produce any archaeological features. Area 3 revealed a low drystone wall.

Further investigation was recommended.

Fiona Reilly, Wood Road, Cratloekeel, Co. Clare, for Valerie J. Keeley Ltd.

33. SITE 20, CARRIGORAN
Field system
1389 1671
SMR 51:171
98E0426
The site, investigated as part of the Ballycasey–Dromoland Bypass, is described in the SMR as a possible field system. A linear stone feature faced on one side was found running roughly north–south.

Clare

Among the finds were several samples of bone, part of an iron knife and a copper-alloy object.

Further investigation was recommended.

Fiona Reilly, Wood Road, Cratloekeel, Co. Clare, for Valerie J. Keeley Ltd.

34. SITE EX1, CARRIGORAN
Concentration of stone
1389 1671
98E0338

The areas investigated on this site were identified by a geophysical survey carried out in connection with the Ballycasey–Dromoland Bypass. Nothing of archaeological significance was found in the first area.

The second area revealed a concentration of stone as suggested by the geophysical survey.

Further investigations were recommended.

Fiona Reilly, Wood Road, Cratloekeel, Co. Clare, for Valerie J. Keeley Ltd.

35. CARROWNAKILLY
Close to possible crannog
98E0459

A small island in Lough Derg, marked on the early OS maps, is no longer visible owing to the rise in the lake level caused by the Shannon Scheme. Five test-trenches on a development site on the adjacent shore revealed no features of archaeological interest.

Brian Hodkinson, Annaholty, Birdhill, Co. Tipperary.

36. DROMOLAND CASTLE, DROMOLAND
Medieval castle (site of)
SMR 42:63
98E0561

It was proposed to construct a 24-bedroom extension to Dromoland Castle Hotel, Newmarket-on-Fergus, Co. Clare, on an area of raised ground on the south-eastern side of the driveway, opposite the new main entrance. This area consists of a low hillock, ranging from 6.75m OD to 9.74m OD, and is covered in part by trees and shrubbery.

The castle at Dromoland is believed to have originated from a late 15th- or early 16th-century tower-house, for which there are few documentary references. It is mentioned in the will of Murrough O'Brien, in 1551, when he left the castle and lands of 'Drumolune' to his third son, Donough MacMurrough O'Brien.

Four main trenches were dug by mechanical digger. These showed the hillock to be a natural feature, not imported soil as had been previously assumed. Soil cover on the hillock consisted mainly of *c.* 0.2–0.4m of sod and topsoil over natural, sandy boulder clay. The area at the foot of the hillock produced some depositional and structural activity in the form of pits and deposits associated with landscaping and drainage. Based on the associated finds, this activity appears to have taken place during the 18th/19th century. The outer kerbed paving area of a 19th-century tennis court was also identified, along with other, more modern deposits, many of which were associated with water mains and cabling.

No features of archaeological significance were identified in any of the excavated test-trenches.

Kenneth Hanley, 44 Eaton Heights, Cobh, Co. Cork.

37. DRUMCLIFF
Fulachta fiadh
R331790
SMR 33:146
98E0455

Monitoring of the digging for an ESB pole was carried out in order to comply with a planning condition. The pole stood within an area where a number of *fulachta fiadh* had been noted. It was close to the western bank of the River Fergus and liable to flooding. The ground was densely covered with scrub, with a high incident of rock outcrop.

The approach was made from the northern side. Some removal of the growth and outcrop was necessary to allow access. A cutting measuring *c.* 1m² was made. Nothing of archaeological interest was noted.

Celie O Rahilly, Limerick Corporation, City Hall, Limerick.

38. 49 ABBEY STREET, ENNIS (REAR OF)
Urban
98E0028

Pre-development testing was carried out at the rear of No. 49 Abbey Street, Ennis, from 2 to 12 February 1998, in advance of a proposed housing development at the site. The site was directly adjacent to Ennis Friary in an archaeologically sensitive area within Ennis town.

Four trial-trenches were excavated manually. Three of these revealed a homogeneous stratigraphy comprising mainly garden soil coming down onto natural, undisturbed clay and bedrock. The fourth trench excavated revealed an unprecedented depth of mortar and debris, indicating its use as a dump in recent times. Nothing of archaeological significance was revealed.

Anne Connolly, Archaeological Services Unit Ltd, Purcell House, Oranmore, Co. Galway.

39. BINDON LANE, ENNIS
No archaeological significance
R888360
98E0366

Monitoring was carried out of the excavation of foundations for an apartment building. Two warehouses (19th/20th century in date) that were demolished in advance of construction had occupied the development area.

There were no archaeological features or artefacts revealed during foundation excavations. The stratigraphy consisted of a layer of modern overburden, 0.5–0.7m deep, which overlay a layer of limestone rubble, with inclusions of plastic, brick and modern delph, 1.2m deep. Beneath this was a sterile, blue, boulder clay subsoil, 1.9m below present ground level.

Tony Cummins for Archaeological Services Unit, University College Cork.

40. 7 CHAPEL LANE, ENNIS
Urban
98E0258
13378 17741

Testing was carried out on the site of a demolished building in advance of construction. All finds were

post-medieval in date. The exterior back-yard of the demolished building may once have been cobbled, as cobbles were found in Con-text 1. Nothing of archaeological significance was discovered.
Fiona Reilly, Wood Road, Cratloekeel, Co. Clare.

41. CLONROAD BEG, ENNIS
Unknown
R339770
98E0305

The site is not within the zone of archaeological potential for Ennis, nor are there any known sites on it. A condition of planning was monitoring, but given the size of the area and the fact that it would be developed in stages it was recommended that testing be carried out in advance of any construction or site works.

The site lay just south of the town centre. To the north are houses fronting Station Road; to the west, houses fronting Clare Road; to the south, houses fronting Ardlee Road; and to the east, a factory (previously the State Inebriate Reformatory) and houses fronting Ard na Gréine.

One boundary divided the site east–west. Phase 1 lay to the south on north-facing, sloping ground. The northern part, Phase 2, was bisected by one north–south field boundary and consisted of fairly level grazing land, except on the east side. Here a ridge of rock outcrop ran north–south parallel to the factory wall but separated from it by a quarry pit and pond.

No finds, features or deposits of archaeological significance were noted in any of the eight cuttings. The only finds noted were late 18th/19th-century pottery and clay pipes.
Celie O Rahilly, Limerick Corporation, City Hall, Limerick.

42. ENNIS FRIARY, ENNIS
Medieval friary
98E0195

Dúchas, in advance of proposed conservation and development works, commissioned an excavation that extended over *c.* 70m^2 within the area of the former east range and cloister walk. Some medieval wall remnants were uncovered, but the principal focus of interest was around ninety early modern graves, all of which were unmarked. The remains were all skeletal: no clothing or coffins survived intact. Indeed, the earliest individuals appear to have been wrapped in shrouds or winding cloths rather than buried in coffins. The graves were generally shallow, and the cemetery was very congested.

The friary precinct was used as a cemetery from perhaps the mid- or late 1600s until its formal closure in the 1890s. The Church of Ireland congregation, who worshipped here from the 1600s until the 1870s, principally used it, but other denominations are also likely to be represented, especially amongst the earlier burials. A full palaeopathologist's study of fifty individuals has been compiled for publication (in prep., *Journal of Post-Medieval Archaeology*).
Jerry O'Sullivan for Glasgow University Archaeological Research Division (GUARD), 5 Bellevue Road, Edinburgh EH7 4DA, Scotland.

43. 15–16 MARKET STREET, ENNIS
Historic town
13378 17741
SMR 33:82
98E0320

Two test-trenches were excavated at the rear of this site, which is earmarked for a private retail development. In both trenches large-scale post-medieval intrusions were noted. In one trench was a large hole, backfilled with loose stone, interpreted as a drain. In the other trench was a rectangular, brick-lined pit that cut an earlier pit with a grey clay/silt fill from which two sherds of brownware and a fragment of green bottle glass were recovered. No features of medieval or earlier date were noted.
Brian Hodkinson, Annaholty, Birdhill, Co. Tipperary.

44. MILL ROAD, ENNIS
Urban
98E0068

Commissioned by the owner, this project involved the construction of 36 apartments at Mill Road, Ennis, Co. Clare. Initial site investigation by Anne Connolly (*Excavations 1997*, 7; 97E0424) had revealed a poorly preserved wall foundation.

Pre-development testing in the form of five trial-trenches took place. Nothing of archaeological significance was uncovered. It was found that the site had been disturbed since the initial investigations had been carried out.
Fiona Rooney, Archaeological Consultancy, Ballydavid South, Athenry, Co. Galway.

45. OLD FRIARY LANE, ENNIS
Historic town
SMR 33:82
13378 17741
98E0055

A test-trench *c.* 8m long by 1m wide on this private development revealed no features of archaeological interest. A single clay/silt layer varying from 0.35 to 0.55m deep overlay the subsoil and was sealed by brick and stone rubble. Two brownware sherds and a clay pipe stem date the layer to the post-medieval period.
Brian Hodkinson, Annaholty, Birdhill, Co. Tipperary.

46. 61/63 PARNELL STREET, ENNIS
No archaeological significance
98E0439

Pre-development testing in the form of four trial-trenches took place at this site. No evidence of features/deposits of archaeological significance was found. The layers present consisted of made-up ground or natural.
Fiona Rooney, Archaeological Consultancy, Ballydavid South, Athenry, Co. Galway.

47. POUND LANE, ENNIS
No archaeological significance
98E0130

The site on Pound Lane, which links Cornmarket Street and Considine Terrace, lies outside the area zoned by the Ennis Urban Archaeological Survey. An existing store, built around 20 years ago, was to be demolished and replaced by a series of office units in a small, two-storey structure. The development was

Clare

designed to retain (and build up from) the existing floor level.

Monitoring of foundation works took place on 10 April 1998, as part of the planning conditions. Four foundation trenches were excavated by machine to *c.* 1.3m below the existing ground surface. These trenches revealed nothing of archaeological significance.
Kenneth Hanley, 44 Eaton Heights, Cobh, Co. Cork.

48. FALLS HOTEL, ENNISTYMON
Tower-house
11279 18851
SMR 15:101
98E0270
Five test-trenches were excavated in the area of a proposed extension at the Falls Hotel, Ennistymon, to comply with a planning condition. The extension is to the north-west of the oldest section of the hotel. The MacNamara family built a Georgian house on the site of Ennistymon Castle, which was the seat of a branch of the O'Brien family. Recent survey work has revealed that much of the medieval tower-house was incorporated into the 18th-century house, which forms the front section of the hotel (Croinin and Breen, The hidden towers, *The Other Clare* **16** (1992), 5–10.).

Trench 1 was 6m north–south by 1.5m east–west. A stone drain was recorded in the trench; it overlay the natural. Trench 2 was 7.2m east–west by 2.1m. Six shallow layers of modern material overlay a dump of modern household rubbish that overlay a former yard surface; the yard overlay the natural. Trench 3 was 6m east–west by 1.5m; four modern layers overlay the natural. Trench 4 was 4.5m north–south by 1m and 1.2m deep; four layers of sandy silt overlay the natural. Trench 5 was 5m east–west by 1.5m; a layer of sand overlay the natural.

No medieval occupation layers or ancillary features associated with the tower-house, or any archaeological stratigraphy, features or artefacts, were recovered from any of the trenches.
Jacinta Kiely, Eachtra Archaeological Projects, Clover Hill, Mallow, Co. Cork.

49. ROYAL PARADE, KILLALOE
Historic town
R704728
SMR 45:33 (part of)
98E0009
This site was tested in advance of development both for archaeological reasons and for the purpose of identifying ground conditions for foundations. It lay within the zone of archaeological potential of Killaloe, opposite St Flannan's Cathedral, on the west side of Royal Parade, between a derelict site to the north and a newly restored building to the south. The garden of the bank, in which St Flannan's Well and a sheela-na-gig are situated, lay immediately behind the site.

The new development was recessed 4m from the existing frontage, resulting in an area 9.1m long and 7m wide. Two short, longitudinal cuttings were made; a third was opened against the adjoining building to the south to test how far its foundations extended. Nothing of archaeological interest was identified.
Celie O Rahilly, Limerick Corporation, City Hall, Limerick.

50. AREA 1, LATOON SOUTH
No archaeological significance
1378 1715
98E0330
In the summer of 1998 an archaeological investigation was carried out in the townland of Latoon South, Co. Clare, as part of the proposed N18/19 Ballycasey–Dromoland Bypass Road Improvements Scheme. This followed an Environmental Impact Survey carried out by Celie O Rahilly and subsequent site assessments by Christine Grant, undertaken in 1998. It was established that there were a number of earthworks in the townland. This investigation was conducted at Environmental Impact Survey Area 1.

Following Ms O Rahilly's and Ms Grant's recommendations, a non-intrusive geophysical and topographic survey was commissioned. The results of this survey highlighted a number of anomalies of sufficient archaeological interest to warrant further inspection. These anomalies were interpreted as a possible stony bank feature, a number of potential burnt spreads and a possible ring-ditch. In consultation with Valerie J. Keeley Ltd and *Dúchas* The Heritage Service it was decided to concentrate excavation on resolving the anomalies and assessing their archaeological worth.

Trench 1, to the south-east of the area, was excavated to a depth of 0.55m and measured 5m x 1m. It was sited to investigate an anomaly detected during the geophysical survey, which indicated the presence of either ferrous litter or fired materials. It was orientated in a general east–west direction and, before topsoil removal, showed no above-ground traces of earthworks.

The top layer consisted of sod and topsoil to a maximum depth of 0.22m. Finds recovered from this layer consisted of modern pottery/crockery. The underlying layer was compacted, brown silt with a maximum depth of 0.45m. Trench 1 was excavated to a deposit of boulder infill. The landowner confirmed that the area was the site of a boulder dump during land clearance work in 1988.

Trench 2, positioned to traverse a possible stony bank, was excavated to a depth of 0.6m. It measured 5m x 1m, was orientated north-west/south-east and lay to the west of Trench 1. The layers encountered were similar to those in Trench 1: sod and topsoil *c.* 0.2m thick above a mid-brown, silty material with occasional small stones. This overlay natural limestone bedrock. There were no finds.

Trench 3, excavated to a depth of 0.2m, was the northernmost trench, sited on a slope and orientated north-east/south-west. It cut across an area that, according to the geophysical report, had a high susceptibility to soil-filled structures such as pits or ditches. As in the previous trenches, soil cover was quite thin and bedrock was exposed directly under the sod. No finds or features were uncovered.
Billy Quinn, Archaeological Services Unit Ltd, Purcell House, Oranmore, Co. Galway.

51. AREA 2, LATOON SOUTH
No archaeological significance
1379 1709
98E0331
In the summer of 1998 an archaeological investigation was carried out in the townland of Latoon

South, Co. Clare, as part of the proposed N18/19 Ballycasey–Dromoland Bypass Road Improvements Scheme. This followed an Environmental Impact Survey carried out by Celie O Rahilly and subsequent site assessments by Christine Grant, undertaken in 1998. It was established that there were a number of earthworks and a disused quarry in the vicinity of Area 2.

Following Ms O Rahilly's and Ms Grant's recommendations, a non-intrusive geophysical and topographic survey was commissioned. The intrusive investigation concentrated on resolving the anomalies highlighted during the geophysical survey.

Two trenches, both measuring 5m east–west x 1m, were excavated to natural bedrock. Trench A was excavated to a depth of 0.35m and was positioned to investigate a horseshoe-shaped, soil-filled feature. Three contexts were encountered: the topsoil layer with a maximum depth of 0.05m, above a mid-brown, silty layer with a moderate amount of small stones, which overlay limestone bedrock. All of the layers were sterile.

Trench B was excavated to a maximum depth of 0.4m. To the west of Trench A, it was positioned to investigate a geophysical anomaly. The shallow sod and topsoil layer covered natural, brown, silty gravel with a depth of 0.35m. This directly overlay limestone bedrock. No archaeological features or deposits were found.

Billy Quinn, Archaeological Services Unit Ltd, Purcell House, Oranmore, Co. Galway.

52. AREA 3, LATOON SOUTH
No archaeological significance
1380 1708
98E0332
In the summer of 1998 an archaeological investigation was carried out in the townland of Latoon South, Co. Clare, as part of the proposed N18/19 Ballycasey–Dromoland Bypass Road Improvements Scheme. This followed an Environmental Impact Survey carried out by Celie O Rahilly and subsequent site assessments by Christine Grant, undertaken in 1998. It was established that Area 3 contained a standing stone consisting of an irregular lump of rough limestone. A geophysical survey of the immediate vicinity revealed a potential soil-filled feature, subcircular in plan with three radiating 'spokes'. The intrusive investigation sought to resolve this anomaly. No testing took place around the standing stone.

A trench was excavated to a depth of 0.95m. It lay *c.* 20m south-east of the standing stone and measured 10m x 1m. During the investigation a 1m² extension was dug 3m from the eastern end of the trench on the northern side. It was orientated in a general east–west direction. The purpose of the trench was to investigate a possible ditch feature detected during the geophysical survey of the area. The topsoil layer, of a mid-brown, loosely compacted silt with a maximum depth of 80mm, overlay a mid-grey, sandy layer. Below this and confined to the eastern end of the trench was a mid-orange/brown silt with occasional small stones. It was mildly compacted with a maximum depth of 0.25m. Underlying this was a layer quite similar to the last in colour and compaction but with a higher

clay content. This ran the full length of the trench and had an average thickness of 0.25m. Below was a grey, sandy clay, quite compacted and very uneven, which was again confined to the eastern end of the trench and was associated with a number of large limestone boulders. The extension was opened to further investigate this layer, which proved to be natural material. An undisturbed, pink, sandy layer lay under this, *c.* 0.5m below ground level.

This testing produced no archaeological features or deposits. All the layers excavated were sterile and featureless.

Billy Quinn, Archaeological Services Unit Ltd, Purcell House, Oranmore, Co. Galway.

53. CLARE 153, ROUGHAN HILL, PARKNABINNIA
Court tomb
98E0230
As part of a continuing programme of survey and excavation on Roughan Hill on the south-east edge of the Burren, excavation was begun on court tomb Cl. 153 and the survey of ancient field walls and farmsteads was expanded.

Survey and excavation on Roughan Hill in 1994 and 1995 identified a final Neolithic/Early Bronze Age landscape consisting of field systems, wedge tombs and at least one Beaker-period farmstead (*Excavations 1995*, 5, 95E0C '). In 1998 two additional farmsteads were discovered that appear to be contemporary with that excavated, which brings the total to four farmsteads. All four are embedded in the same field system of 'mound walls' and all appear to be contemporary.

Most of the prehistoric activity on Roughan Hill appears to date to the Beaker period, but there are also indications of activity in the Neolithic. The excavation of the court tomb was initiated in order to answer questions about the Neolithic activity on the hill and the transition to the intensive occupation during the Beaker period (see Jones and Walsh, *JRSAI* **126** (1996), 86–107, for site location and plan).

Two trenches were opened in 1998. Trench A was opened to investigate the form of the forecourt and the nature and depth of the deposit. This trench extended east away from the tomb entrance and encompassed the southern half of the forecourt. Excavation revealed a number of interesting features. The forecourt was found to be very narrow, no wider than the gallery, which is unusual but not unique (similar forecourts occur on the two nearest court tombs, Ballyganner North and Leamaneh North, and also farther south, in County Tipperary at Shanballyedmund). The stones that formed the forecourt had no sockets but were placed directly on the old ground surface and propped up with smaller stones. The forecourt was loosely filled with cobble-sized stones. Interestingly, the forecourt is built within a drop in the bedrock. It is not yet clear whether the tomb builders were making use of a natural depression or the drop was formed by stone quarrying before tomb construction.

Trench B was opened to explore the nature of the 'revetment' stones on the south side of the cairn. This trench extended south from Trench A and crossed the line of revetment stones. Before excavation began it was thought that these stones may be a later alteration of the tomb. Trench B revealed the revetment stones to be sitting directly on the old ground surface. Additionally the cairn between the edge of the forecourt and the inner row of revetment stones showed a distinctive patterning. This consisted of layers of stones laid with their long axes parallel to each other and perpendicular to the stones in the next layer. It now appears that the forecourt, cairn, and revetment stones were all built at the same time.

Finds consisted of human and animal bone, a leaf-shaped arrowhead, a few pieces of debitage, a small, flat grinding stone and potsherds. The potsherds are awaiting analysis, but preliminary inspection shows that they are quite thin-walled.
Carleton Jones and Alix Gilmer, Burren Archaeology Research, No. 5 River Lane House, Parnell Street, Ennis, Co. Clare.

54. SIXMILEBRIDGE
Town
R472659
SMR 52:16 (Part of)
98E0306
The proposed private housing development lay to the north-west of the village in a heavily overgrown rectangular field that sloped gently from west to east. The extant hedge defining the western limit is the townland boundary. Only the eastern end of the field was within the zone of archaeological potential.

A continuous cutting was made east–west with a north–south dog-leg, 5m long and 45.5m from the eastern end. No finds, features or deposits of archaeological significance were identified.
Celie O Rahilly, Limerick Corporation, City Hall, Limerick.

CORK

---

55. ADRIGOLE
Post-medieval ironworks
08078 05043
SMR 116:00501, 116:00502
98E0328
This site, on the south side of the Beara Peninsula, lies at the foot of Adrigole Mountain, which rises steeply to the north-west, and overlooks a plateau that slopes gently southwards towards the Adrigole River, close to where it flows into Adrigole Harbour.

The site is to be developed as a tourist amenity, and test-trenching and monitoring were required as the site is the location of a 17th/18th-century iron foundry (Power *et al.* 1992, 384).

A rectangular, one-storey, stone-built structure measuring 5.55m x 3.17m internally, with walls *c.* 0.65m thick, and *c.* 1.75m high survives on the site. It is depicted on the 1st edition 6-inch OS map as 'Old Furnace'. However, the present ruin is more likely to be a 19th/20th-century farm shed rather than a remnant of the 17th/18th-century ironworks, although it is probably built on their foundations.

A number of test-trenches were excavated in the area, but only those closest to the ruined structure contained archaeological remains. In a north–south trench, excavated immediately to the west of the ruin, a 2.55m-wide mortared stone wall foundation was uncovered directly under the thin sod. The wall was aligned west-north-west/east-south-east and was in line with the south wall of the ruined structure. The north face of the wall had been reddened by intense heat, and the area for *c.* 2.5m to the north was a mass of burnt stone rubble with some vitrified stone and iron slag.

On the east side of the ruin another trench, running north–south, was excavated. Near its north end was the base of a broad channel running east–west with a 0.05–0.1m-thick layer of black silt at its base. Over the remainder of the trench a *c.* 0.2m-deep layer of iron slag and vitrified stone lay underneath the sod. Beneath this layer, at the southern end of the trench, was a 0.3m-deep layer of bright red burnt stone. A thin (0.04m) layer of white clay lay underneath the stone, with a layer of sand under the clay.

Further remains of the silted channel were uncovered in a trench *c.* 13m west of the ruin.

Other trenches excavated further away from the ruin revealed no archaeological remains, nor did monitoring of development works on the western half of the development area.

The massive foundations and burnt stone uncovered to the west of the existing ruin suggest a furnace or foundry to the west of, and possibly running underneath, the ruin. The silted channel in the trenches to the east and west suggests a water channel running east–west, to the immediate north of the foundry, providing the power to drive the bellows wheel. The large quantities of slag and vitrified stone uncovered in the trench to the east of the ruin suggest a slag heap to the east of the foundry. The evidence, as a whole, suggests a site layout remarkably similar to that of a charcoal blast furnace shown in the *Dictionary of industrial archaeology* (Jones 1996, 29).

Local information indicates that a more extensive complex of buildings survived on the site into recent times, but these were demolished within living memory.

References
Power, D. *et al.* 1992 *Archaeological inventory of County Cork,* vol. 1. Dublin. Wordwell.
Jones, W. 1996 *Dictionary of industrial archaeology.* Gloucestershire. Sutton Publishing Ltd.

Eamonn Cotter, Ballynanelagh, Rathcormac, Co. Cork.

56. DUNASEAD CASTLE, BALTIMORE
Fortified house
10468 02649
SMR 150:03602
98E0186
Test-trenching at Baltimore was carried out on foot of an application for permission to renovate the castle for use as a residence.

Dunasead Castle is a 17th-century fortified house on the west end of a ridge of sandstone rock overlooking Baltimore town and harbour. It is a simple rectangular structure measuring 18.5m north–south x 5.82m internally and standing two storeys high, with an attic above within its high gables. The ground floor is dimly lit with slit windows in the north, east and south walls, while the first floor has two- and three-light ogee windows in the east and west walls. Several sections of the walls were repaired with concrete in the early part of this century. The house stands in the south-west corner of a small bawn measuring *c.* 28m north–south x *c.* 14m, enclosed by a dilapidated stone wall, much of which is rebuilt. Apart from the bawn wall the only defensive elements on the structure are the wall walk on the west wall and the bartizan clasping the south-west corner at eaves level, with shot holes facing east and south-west. There appears originally to have been a second bartizan on the north-east corner.

Documentary evidence suggests that the house was built in the late 1620s/early 1630s, possibly by Sir Walter Coppinger, following his acquisition of the site in 1629.

Trenches were excavated across the interior of the building and across the bawn. Within the building, removal of a surface layer of *c.* 0.3m of rubble revealed areas of hard-packed mortar and small shale fragments *c.* 0.1–0.15m thick in sections of two of the trenches. These may be the remains of an original floor surface, now extensively disturbed. Underneath this was a sub-floor layer of shale hard-core, which was archaeologically sterile and was obviously introduced to level up the rock surface before laying the floor. The hard-core lay on bedrock and boulder clay.

Three trenches were excavated in the bawn area. Two extended approximately east–west across the bawn from the castle wall to the east bawn wall, and the third ran north–south along the base of the east wall of the castle.

The main features of these trenches were the foundations of a garderobe tower at the south end of the east wall of the building, a stone-lined well (diameter 0.7m) *c.* 7m to the north, adjacent to the castle wall, and several paved and cobbled areas.

The garderobe tower was originally accessed via a first-floor doorway at the south end of the east wall of the castle. The only evidence of the garderobe that survives above ground are three long stones protruding from the wall face at each side of the doorway, which presumably were 'through stones', keying the garderobe tower into the castle wall.

Excavation indicated that the lower levels of the well existed before the construction of the house, although the stone lining of the well was raised by *c.* 1m after the house was built. The well was accessed from the north via three steps leading down from a paved surface that probably originally extended north to the ground-floor doorway.

A section of a stone-lined drain was uncovered in the bawn, as were the foundations of a wall running east–west across it, possibly remnants of an outbuilding. An area of fine cobblestones immediately east of the castle pre-dated it, while areas of larger cobblestones further north were contemporary with it.

Numerous sherds of late medieval pottery were found distributed over all the excavated areas of the site, with more dense concentrations at the east end of the most northerly trench and in the fill of the well. Included were two fragments of ceramic ridge tile, similar in appearance to fragments of North Devon ridge tiles found in excavations in Cork City (M.F. Hurley, *Excavations at the North Gate* (1997), 90).

A number of metal objects were also recovered, particularly in the area immediately to the north of the well, where a number of fragments had become solidly encrusted on the stone. The concentration of metal in this area suggests the possibility of a metal railing around the well. Unfortunately none of the pieces was readily identifiable as all were heavily corroded.
Eamonn Cotter, Ballynanelagh, Rathcormac, Co. Cork.

57. CASEMENT ROAD, BANDON
Town wall
W487545
98E0503
Archaeological testing was undertaken adjacent to the outer face of the town wall in Bandon in advance of a new housing development. Three test-trenches were placed within the area of the proposed site to assess the archaeological implications of the development. The excavation of the trenches revealed no trace of archaeological deposits within the proposed development site.
Margaret McCarthy, Archaeological Services Unit, University College Cork.

58. BAWNAGLOGH
Vicinity of burnt mound
22266 16613
98E0420
Test-trenches were opened in the vicinity of SMR 36:7, which had been uncovered and provisionally identified as a *fulacht fiadh* during the construction of the existing Bord Gáis pipeline through the townland. As a 100m-long domestic pipe was to intersect in the immediate vicinity, test-trenches were opened beforehand to relocate the site.

Although no evidence of a *fulacht fiadh* was recovered, the presence of heat-shattered stone in the topsoil of a trench to the south of the pipeline suggested that a burnt deposit had been disturbed by ploughing or lay further to the south of the proposed pipe-trench.

As a piece of iron slag was also recovered in the topsoil, it is possible that the site either is a burnt mound or comprises features associated with metalworking. The local subsoil, which is sandy and porous, would possibly be too free-draining for a trough to have been sited in the immediate area, again suggesting that the identification of the site as a *fulacht fiadh* is unlikely.

No archaeological deposits were disturbed during the construction of the pipe-trench.
John Ó Néill, for Margaret Gowen & Co. Ltd, 2 Killiney View, Albert Road Lower, Glenageary, Co. Dublin.

59. MYROSS WOOD, BRADE
Graveyard and church
SMR 142:01801 and 142:01802
98E0052
Margaret McCarthy, Archaeological Services Unit, University College Cork.
The report on this site was mistakenly included in *Excavations 1997*, 9. The editor regrets any confusion.

60. BRIDGETOWN ABBEY, BRIDGETOWN

Medieval priory

SMR 34:02702

98E0377

The Augustinian Priory complex at Bridgetown consists of a cloister, with church on the north side, refectory on the south and ruinous chapter range on the east side. At the west end of the church is an inserted two-storey tower. On the west side of the cloister, where the present excavations took place, the ground level is *c.* 4m higher than that within the cloister, and no structures survive above ground. The excavations are part of an ongoing programme of conservation and recording being carried out on the priory by Cork County Council, the owners of the site.

Ground level on the west side of the priory is *c.* 4m higher than that within it, and, because of water percolation through the west walls of the church tower and refectory, it was felt that conservation work would be necessary on these walls. These test excavations were carried out in advance of conservation.

On the west side of the refectory the foundations of two walls running west from the refectory wall were uncovered. These were constructed on a layer of stone rubble and are parts of two separate buildings. They appear to have been built after Bridgetown had ceased to function as a priory, possibly by the farmer to whom the buildings were granted in the period after the Dissolution. The most southerly of the two is well rendered internally and probably had a domestic function. A layer of slate and stone rubble found at the south end of the cutting represents the destruction of this building, while the cobblestones found at the base of the cutting are remains of its floor. As the foundation of the building is at the same level as the first floor of the refectory, it may have been used in conjunction with the refectory as domestic quarters long after the other priory buildings had fallen into disrepair. This protracted use could explain why the refectory remains the best preserved of the priory buildings.

Structures uncovered in the cutting to the west of the church were clearly built after the rebuilding of the church tower. They therefore belong to a late phase in the history of the priory and may be contemporary with the structures to the west of the refectory. They include a small, rectangular chamber measuring 2.6m x 2.4m, within which was a chimney *c.* 1m high. While the north wall of the chamber has shallow foundations, the foundations of the south and west walls go much deeper and were not uncovered. These may have been the walls of the original church, which was subsequently shortened. The lintel of the chimney is part of the jamb of a late medieval doorway with chamfered edge and rounded chamfer-stop. The lintel is unusually low so that the actual fireplace is a pit sunk below ground level.

It was evident that there are other buildings to the west of this extending under the baulk.

An isolated deposit of iron slag was found in this cutting. The location of the furnace that produced it is unknown, but it is unlikely to have been the chimney already noted as the intense heat required for the smelting process would have left a more obvious impression on the stonework and soil around it.

Because these were test excavations not all the exposed features were fully investigated. It is clear, however, that most of the features uncovered belong to a late phase in the history of the priory and, in all likelihood, to a period after its abandonment as a monastic site, i.e. late 16th/early 17th century. Possible exceptions to this are the west and south walls of the chamber to the west of the church, which may be part of the original church. However, only further excavations will determine whether this is the case.

Eamonn Cotter, Ballynanelagh, Rathcormac, Co. Cork.

61. BARRYSCOURT CASTLE, CARRIGTWOHILL

Late medieval castle

1822 0725

96E0238

A further season of excavations ahead of consolidation at Barryscourt (see *Excavations 1996*, 10–11, and *Excavations 1997*, 9, for previous reports), funded by the National Monuments Service, saw a large part of the bawn opened and a number of outstanding problems solved.

It is unlikely that any buildings on site pre-date the large tower-house (probably of 16th-, perhaps of 15th-century construction). A contemporary building has now been identified, probably a kitchen. The building is largely robbed but had mortared stone walls and a battered foot to the gable dropping down into a moat surrounding the site. There is no indication that the moat pre-dates the tower-house.

The kitchen was extended and then damaged, probably in 1581, but was rebuilt shortly thereafter with an enclosing mortared bawn wall and a range of buildings to the west. The new range included a hall, which appears to have been largely timbered on an insubstantial unmortared stone footing.

Garden beds and planting holes (several for trees?) have been identified in the bawn, within 10m of the hall. The arrangement clearly respects the new range and in part post-dates the kitchen. The pattern of beds is not symmetrical but provides indications of the position of the hall entrance.

At an early stage this corner of the bawn was enclosed from the rest of the yard (taking in an area much larger than the garden). At some stage (perhaps in the early 17th century) the far end of the enclosure was raised as a large platform, revetted with substantial mortared walls, perhaps as a garden feature, perhaps as an artillery platform.

Dave Pollock, 33 Woodlawn, Cashel, Co. Tipperary.

62. ADELAIDE STREET/KYLE STREET/ LIBERTY STREET/NORTH MAIN STREET/ PAUL STREET/SOUTH MAIN STREET, CORK

Urban medieval/post-medieval

W670720

96E0157

Excavation for the Cork Main Drainage Scheme took place within the archaeological zone of the medieval city from February until October 1998.

The medieval city walls were observed in three streets. Two portions were evident at the western end of Adelaide Street, one at the eastern end of Kyle Street and one at North Main Street. At North Main Street (the North Gate) a second wall, 4m thick and battered, was built against its south face. These walls

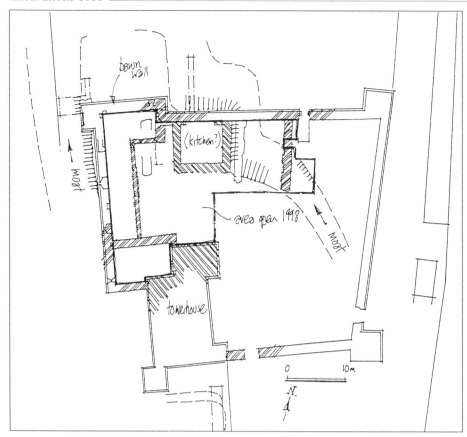

General plan of Barrystown Castle.

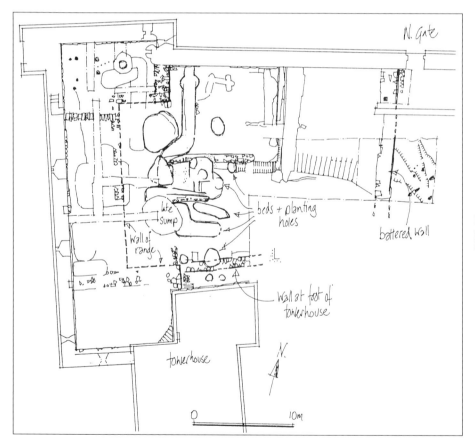

Plan of garden beds and planting holes in the bawn, Barrystown Castle.

Cork

were associated with horizontal timber beams and braces dating to the medieval period. Street metalling extended south from the city wall.

A 17th-century wooden barrel used as a cistern was recorded on Adelaide Street. It was stave built and bound by wooden hoops.

Medieval paving made of flat green sandstone and limestone was exposed for a length of 3.92m on Kyle Street. This was suggestive of the presence of a house. Six fragments of moulded Dundry stone, dating to the 13th/14th centuries, were found on Kyle Street. These originally came from at least one arch, possibly a church window.

Two substantial structural walls on Liberty Street are probably medieval; one was 12m long and 1m wide, while the second had a footing. Lanes and houses were excavated on Liberty Street; these are depicted on John Rocque's map of 1773. They were associated with North Devon Sgraffito wares, as well as a Cromwellian penny token from Clonmel. Excavations on Paul Street exposed walls of the original 18th-century buildings fronting the street.

A length of 3.26m of medieval street surface, laid on a foundation of small stones, was exposed on South Main Street. It ran in a north–south direction and was composed of flat red sandstone and limestone. Also on South Main Street two medieval timber structures were exposed. One of these is probably part of a fence or house. It consists of a row of wattling and a parallel row of upright timber planks associated with organic packing. The second structure consists of horizontal timbers associated with a row of posts. This may be the base of a boardwalk that is contiguous with an existing alleyway. An 18th/19th-century culvert built of red sandstone, running north–south, was recorded for the full length of trenching on South Main Street; 1.45m of its width was evident, while its height was recorded for 2.3m.

Catryn Power, Cork Corporation, City Hall, Cork.

63. BACHELORS QUAY/GRATTAN STREET, CORK
Urban
16702 07201
98E0283

A site assessment consisting of three archaeological test-trenches was carried out on 20 June 1998. All three trenches were opened to a depth of 2.5m and were found to contain loose rubble fill, 18th–20th century in date. No finds or features of archaeological significance were noted.

Sheila Lane, 1 Charlemont Heights, Coach Hill, Rochestown, Cork.

64. BARRACK STREET/COBH STREET, CORK
Urban
98E0507

A site assessment consisting of one test-trench was carried out on 2 November 1998. The trench was opened to a depth of 1.1m and was found to contain loose rubble fill. At 1.1m a layer containing earth, bone fragment, shell and organic material was noted. This was deemed an archaeological layer and was not investigated. The developer was advised to design foundations for the proposed building that would not interfere with this layer. No development has taken place on the site to date.

Sheila Lane, 1 Charlemont Heights, Coach Hill, Rochestown, Cork.

65. BLACKPOOL, CORK
Industrial
W1675007300
97E0457

Phase III of this road project involved the construction of a culvert from the Glen Road to Brewery Corner. The route of the culvert passes through sites dating to the 18th/19th centuries, such as Green's Distillery, a tannery at Corkeran's Quay, a mill at Assumption Road, Hewitt's Watercourse Distillery (now an industrial estate), Dunn's Tannery and Water's Mill. Before construction a complete architectural and industrial archaeological survey of

View from courthouse roof from south, showing excavation of medieval and post-medieval structures on Liberty Street.

sites on the route of the bypass was carried out.

Construction work uncovered the remains of the 18th-century corn- and flour-mill at Assumption Road and a row of 19th-century houses demolished in this century at Farrancleary Place. Following demolition of buildings associated with the distillery, the foundations of a steam mill and the structure of a chimney were recorded.

A group of five wooden tanning pits of plank-and-post construction was uncovered and excavated. The pits measured *c.* 1m², and the surviving depth was 0.4m–0.6m. The pits were filled with clay, stones, grit, red brick and red earthenware. At the base of one pit was a layer of oily debris containing animal hairs, scraps of leather and some scraps of metal. A Georgian halfpenny coin, dating from between 1769 and 1805, was found in the silty clay in which the pits were set.

A layer of residue from the tanning process was recorded at the site of Dunn's Tannery. This contained compacted oak chips and bark and possibly minerals that were used in the tanning process.

The sill-beam and other timbers of a sluice-gate were found *in situ* at the outlet of a culverted channel on the north side of the Back Watercourse below Hewitt's Watercourse Distillery. Tenoned upright and horizontal timbers were fixed into, or laid on top of, the beam. A row of holes bored into the horizontal timbers may indicate the presence of a grating. This site is probably of late 18th-/early 19th-century date.

Catryn Power, Cork Corporation, City Hall, Cork.

66. CARROLL'S QUAY/PINE STREET, CORK
Urban
16750 07208
98E0379

Five 19th-century warehouses on the site were surveyed and photographed in advance of their demolition. A site assessment consisting of two test-trenches was carried out on 16 November 1998. Both trenches were opened to a depth of 2m. Both were found to contain loose rubble fill. No finds or features of archaeological significance were noted.

Sheila Lane, 1 Charlemont Heights, Coach Hill, Rochestown, Cork.

Cork

67. 7 COACH STREET, CORK
Urban
SMR 74:34
98E0529

A test-trench was excavated in the rear of No. 7 Coach Street, Cork, to comply with a planning condition. The building is situated to the west of the walled medieval city of Cork, built on two islands in the River Lee. By the 14th century the city had expanded to include suburbs on the banks of the river. These suburbs declined in the 15th century, and the city did not expand again until after the Restoration in 1660. There is no evidence of building in the area of Coach Street until the 18th century. (J. Bradley *et al.*, *Urban archaeological survey of Cork* (1985)).

A trench, 2m east–west by 1.5m, was excavated by hand in the rear of the building, to a depth of 1.65m (1.283m OD). The surface of a layer of grey/black estuarine silt was recorded at this depth. Layers of rubble, red brick and an earlier concrete floor were recorded under the modern floor level. Three additional layers of sand, gravel and brick underlay the floor. They included a mix of modern, post-medieval and late medieval pottery, oyster shells, animal bone and clay pipe fragments. The estuarine silt was recorded in the base of the trench. A soil auger was used to ascertain the depth of the silt. It went down 1m, but that does not represent the full depth. The silt included oyster shells, a fragment of a 17th-century drinking glass and some late medieval and post-medieval sherds of pottery.

Monitoring of foundation and drainage trenches has yet to be undertaken.
Jacinta Kiely, Eachtra Archaeological Projects, Clover Hill, Mallow, Co. Cork.

68. GRATTAN STREET, CORK
City wall
16727 07202
98E0105

This test-trench excavation was carried out in advance of an apartment development at Grattan Street in order to confirm the location and extent of the city wall in this area. The northern end of the development area was excavated in 1996 by Maurice Hurley, and part of the west extent of the city wall, dating to the 17th century, was uncovered (*Excavations 1996*, 11).

A test-trench, 1.5m wide and 9m long, was opened at the south end of the wall exposed in the 1996 excavation and was extended to the south end of the development area. The wall was revealed at a depth of 0.5–0.6m below the present ground level and continued in a straight line to the south. The overburden consisted of brick, sand and slate, associated with 18th- and 19th-century houses known to have been present in this area. Excavation halted once the truncated surface of the wall was revealed (the wall was found to survive to a height of 1.2–1.3m, including foundations, in the 1996 excavation). The masonry was composed of roughly hewn limestone, ranging in size from 0.1m x 0.1m to 0.4m x 0.4m, with occasional sandstone and slate inclusions, and was bonded with lime mortar. A later wall, with brick inclusions, had been built along the truncated level of the city wall and dates to the 18th/19th century. This later wall was also

uncovered in the 1996 excavation to the north.
Tony Cummins for Archaeological Services Unit, University College Cork.

69. CORK SCHOOLS PROJECT, GRATTAN STREET, CORK
Urban
SMR 74:34
98E0543

Monitoring of all groundworks was undertaken in compliance with the archaeological planning condition. The development site lies within the walled medieval city of Cork, to the immediate west of Cross Court Lane, which runs at right angles to North Main Street. The street pattern of medieval Cork was linear. It was based on the north–south axis of North and South Main Streets. Lanes ran at right angles to give access to individual properties and to ·the town wall (J. Bradley *et al.*, *Urban archaeological survey of Cork* (1985)).

The ground disturbance work was divided into two phases. The first consisted of the excavation of nine piles by a small piling rig. In general the piles were 9–10m deep. A stone obstruction was encountered by the rig at a depth of *c.* 4m in the south-east corner and across the central line of the site. This meant that three additional pile holes had to be excavated. All of the soil that came to the surface with the auger was examined, and a number of artefacts were recovered. Four soil horizons were recorded. C1, the upper horizon, was a grey, sandy silt with frequent inclusions of slate, brick, glass and sherds of modern pottery. C2 was a black silt with occasional inclusions of oyster shells; the bones of mature cattle, young pig and sheep were recorded. C3 was a brown silt with frequent inclusions of wood. C4 was a grey clay.

The second phase consisted of removing 0.4m of C1 from the entire area of the site. The ground-beams, pile caps and drains were laid within this depth. The surface of the brick foundations of the school building that had been demolished before the commencement of works was uncovered when C1 was partially removed.
Jacinta Kiely, Eachtra Archaeological Projects, Clover Hill, Mallow, Co. Cork.

70. 21 MAIN STREET NORTH, CORK
Urban medieval
16708 07203
98E0241

Two test-trenches, 1m x 1m, were excavated in advance of a redevelopment to ascertain whether archaeological deposits were present. The stratigraphy in the west of the site, next to the street, consisted of 0.38m of modern overburden that overlay a 0.26m-deep, light brown, sandy layer containing inclusions of slates, ash, brick and mortar. Beneath this was a black layer of decayed organic material, 0.3m deep, with frequent inclusions of animal bone and oyster shells. The only artefact recovered from this layer was a clay pipe stem. A brown, silty clay deposit was found to a depth of 0.16m beneath the black, humic layer. This was medieval in date, as indicated by the ceramic finds, and overlay an extremely compact oxidised surface, 1.1m below modern ground surface. The excavation halted at this depth.

The stratigraphy at the east end of the property consisted of 0.7m of modern overburden that overlay a stony layer in a grey, silty clay matrix. This contained moderate amounts of butchered animal bones and oyster shells and was 0.3m deep. What appeared to be a paved surface was uncovered beneath the stony layer, at a depth of 1m below modern ground level. This consisted of two flat limestone slabs surrounded by a firmly packed surface of smaller, purple slates and sandstones. This surface continued under the baulks in all directions and was left *in situ*. A single sherd of medieval pottery was uncovered in the interface between the overlying stony layer and the paved surface.

Tony Cummins for Archaeological Services Unit, University College Cork.

71. BEAMISH AND CRAWFORD, MAIN STREET SOUTH, CORK

Urban post-medieval/medieval (?)

W672716

97E0344

Pre-development rescue excavation was carried out, in compliance with planning conditions, between 13 and 16 September 1997. The site lies near the southern boundary of the medieval walled city of Cork. An area of *c.* 5.5m x 4.5m was excavated to a depth of *c.* 1m. The remains of two stone walls were uncovered between *c.* 0.75m and 0.9m below modern ground level. Both walls had been disturbed by previous industrial development on the site. The only finds uncovered consisted of fragments of pottery (chinaware, red-glazed earthenware and willow ware) and animal bones. The features were recorded, and development plans were modified to ensure that further disturbance would be avoided.

Gina Johnson for Archaeological Services Unit, University College Cork.

Editor's note: This excavation, though carried out during 1997, was not received in time for inclusion in the bulletin for that year.

72. BEAMISH and CRAWFORD BREWERY, MAIN STREET SOUTH, CORK

Urban

16715 07214

98E0043

The site lies on the south island of Cork within the Beamish and Crawford brewery. The excavation consisted of two test-trenches, 1m wide and 17m long, excavated in advance of development works in the south-west area of the brewery grounds. The area was found to have been extensively disturbed by drainage works carried out in the 1970s, and there were no traces of archaeological remains at a depth of 0.5–0.6m below present ground level.

Tony Cummins for Archaeological Services Unit, University College Cork.

73. BOSTON SCIENTIFIC CORK LTD, MODEL FARM ROAD, CORK

No archaeological significance

98E0136

Planning conditions for the development of a large healthcare manufacturing plant by Boston Scientific at the IDA Cork Business and Technology Park, Model Farm Road, Cork, required archaeological monitoring of the site before construction. The site is part of the former Model Farm lands, and at the north-eastern corner of the development are some listed buildings known as the Munster Institute. The restoration and use of these buildings for research and training purposes is proposed as part of the development. The site covers an area of 30 acres and lies on relatively level terrain with some gradients to the north-west.

Topsoil was removed by mechanical excavator to the interface with the subsoil, and the ground was subsequently raised by infill material taken from high ground at the north-western end of the site. It was expected that subsidence features such as sinkholes would be encountered given the karstic nature of the geology of this region. A possible subsidence feature was observed on the surface, during the initial inspection by the site investigators, at a distance of 30m west of the site. Previous agricultural activity is likely to have obscured surface evidence of subsidence at the site itself, and it was only when the topsoil was removed that two buried karst phenomena became apparent.

On the exposed surface and before excavation these features resembled backfilled post-holes or substantial rubbish pits. On excavation, however, it was clear that they had not been artificially cut but were natural subsidence features commonly found in karst areas. Discarded domestic debris including broken floor tiles, modern earthenware and waste from a blacksmith's forge was found in one of the subsidence features.

Fill materials were encountered at the southern end of the site and consisted of construction debris from the demolition of poultry houses associated with the original Model Farm. Apart from the recovery of a number of sherds of post-medieval pottery, the area proved devoid of archaeological features and finds.

Margaret McCarthy, Archaeological Services Unit, University College Cork.

74. LINDVILLE HOUSE, OLD BLACKROCK ROAD, CORK

No archaeological significance

17020 07132

98E0015

Monitoring was carried out of a housing estate development within the grounds of a disused hospital dating to the 19th century. There have been no archaeological features or artefacts uncovered to date, and monitoring of the foundation excavations is ongoing.

Tony Cummins for Archaeological Services Unit, University College Cork.

75. PETER STREET/COACH STREET, CORK

Urban

16725 17192

98E0224

An 18th-century house on the site was considered structurally unsound, and permission was granted to demolish it. A photographic and descriptive record was made of the house in advance of its demolition. A site assessment, consisting of two test-trenches, was carried out on 24 May 1998. Both trenches were opened to a depth of 2.5m. Both were found to contain loose rubble fill. No finds or features of archaeological significance were noted.

Sheila Lane, 1 Charlemont Heights, Coach Hill, Rochestown, Cork.

76. 44–46 SHANDON STREET, CORK
Urban medieval
16714 7230
SMR 74:03102
98E0151

A site assessment, consisting of two test-trenches, was carried out on 21 March 1998. Two houses were demolished on the site in advance of the development. The trenches ran east–west across the site and were found to contain rubble fill dating to the 19th and 20th centuries. No finds or features of archaeological significance were noted.

Sheila Lane, 1 Charlemont Heights, Coach Hill, Rochestown, Cork.

77. SHARMAN CRAWFORD STREET/ WANDESFORD QUAY, CORK
Urban
16609 07110
SMR 74:37
98E0205

A site assessment consisting of two test-trenches was carried out on 9 May 1998. The trenches ran north–south across the site. They were opened to a depth of 3m and were found to contain loose rubble fill dating to the 19th and 20th centuries. No finds or features of archaeological significance were noted.

Sheila Lane, 1 Charlemont Heights, Coach Hill, Rochestown, Cork.

78. TRISKEL ARTS CENTRE, TOBIN STREET CORK
Urban post-medieval
W672717
97E0295

Two pre-development test-pits were excavated, in compliance with planning conditions, on 18 August 1997. The site lies on the south island of the medieval walled city of Cork. The development area was excavated to a depth 1.7m (maximum depth of developmental intrusion). The only feature present was a cobbled surface, probably from 18th-century stables. The finds consisted of modern pottery, a hone stone and a small quantity of animal bones and oyster shells.

Gina Johnson for Archaeological Services Unit, University College Cork.

Editor's note: This excavation, though carried out during 1997, was not received in time for inclusion in the bulletin for that year.

79. KILCOE CASTLE, KILCOE
Tower-house
10192 03282
SMR 140:32
98E0133

Kilcoe Castle is a 16th-century tower-house situated on a small rocky island off the shore of Roaringwater Bay in West Cork, the island being now linked by a bridge to the mainland. It consists of a main tower four storeys high, with a conjoined six-storey flanking tower on its north-east corner. Entrance is via ground- and first-floor doorways at the west end of the south wall of the main tower. The tower-house is in private ownership and is currently being restored as a residence. Test-trenching was carried out in advance of development.

Initial excavations on the site concentrated on a possible shell midden that was disturbed at the exterior north-east corner of the tower-house. The midden comprised a mound of black, humic material containing a dense concentration of shellfish (oysters, periwinkles and limpets) and bone (mainly cattle, with some sheep and pig). It covered an area *c.* 2m east–west x 2.8m to a maximum depth of 0.8m. Local information suggests that the material was dumped here from within the tower-house, and the discovery of two sherds of late 18th/early 19th-century pottery underneath the midden supports this assertion.

Excavations on the south side of the castle revealed part of a cobblestone yard from which steps lead up to the ground-floor door. To the east of the door a mortared stone base with steps at its east end appears to be the base of a flight of steps that originally led up to the first floor doorway, directly above that on the ground floor.

Some 3.5m south of the castle parts of the foundations of a clay-bonded wall running east–west were uncovered. Between it and the stone steps more of the cobblestone yard was revealed.

A trench excavated some 15m south-east of the castle revealed the foundations of a rectangular structure from which the north-west corner was missing. A break in the wall face on its north side suggests that there may formerly have been a wall running north from it. The remains indicate a structure measuring *c.* 1.3m north–south x *c.* 2m internally, suggesting that it may have been a rectangular corner tower on the bawn wall.

At the north end of a trench excavated within the ground floor of the main tower, flagstones were uncovered that were built into the castle walls. These are almost certainly the remains of an original paved floor. In the remainder of the trench only a loose fill of large stones was found, filling a deep gully in the bedrock.

The ground floor of the flanking tower is likely to have been the castle dungeon. It measures 2.15m x 2.25m and is covered by a vaulted roof *c.* 4m above floor level. The only point of access to the chamber is through a narrow shaft in the roof from the chamber above, and the only light is through a small rectangular opening high on the south wall.

Deposits *c.* 1m deep, consisting of humic, silty soil interspersed with thin layers of mortar, were excavated. Some hair and woven fabric were recovered from the lower levels of these deposits.

Eamonn Cotter, Ballynanelagh, Rathcormac, Co. Cork.

80. CHARLES FORT, FORTHILL, KINSALE
Star-shaped fort
W652495
SMR 125:7
98E0536

An excavation, funded by The National Monuments and Historic Properties Service, was undertaken at

Charles Fort, Kinsale, Co. Cork, in an area that will form the base of a large model of the fort. Archaeological supervision during service trenching in 1979 recorded the remains of a substantial wall close to the original citadel, as well as the possible outer edge of a ditch cut into the bedrock. As there was a possibility that this ditch extended as far as the area chosen for the display, an excavation was undertaken over a three-week period in December 1998.

A trench measuring 5m x 5m was opened in an area directly opposite the main entrance to the fort. The sod and topsoil were quite shallow and rarely exceeded 80mm. In places, particularly at the north-eastern corner of the trench, the bedrock became exposed at a very high level, resulting in a difference in height of almost 1m between the northern and southern ends of the trench.

The excavation uncovered traces of stone huts associated with the latest phase of military use of the site, as well as a series of recent post- and stake-holes interpreted as possible tent structures. Apart from the recovery of a small quantity of human remains representing a juvenile individual, nothing of archaeological significance was recovered.
Margaret McCarthy, Archaeological Services Unit, University College Cork.

81. GUARDWELL, KINSALE
Urban
16373 05043
SMR 112:03404
98E0007

The site lies in the centre of the medieval town of Kinsale and is overlooked to the north by St Multose Church. There was planning permission to demolish a large warehouse, in use as a bakery, that occupied the site. A photographic and descriptive survey of the building was carried out in advance of its demolition.

Following demolition, a site assessment consisting of two test-trenches was carried out on 3 January 1998. The trenches ran east–west along the site from the street front to the rear. Both were found to contain 19th/20th-century loose rubble fill to a depth of 0.5m. Below this was a layer of tightly packed soil (0.15m thick) containing tiny fragments of bone, brick, wood and stone. This lay on top of natural, yellow clay. No finds or features of archaeological significance were noted.
Sheila Lane, 1 Charlemont Heights, Coach Hill, Rochestown, Cork.

82. JAMES'S FORT, OLD-FORT, KINSALE
Star-shaped fort
16463 04963
SMR 112:36
98E0279

James's Fort, Kinsale, Co. Cork, is the site of a 17th-century, star-shaped fort with a central inner fortification. Part of this inner building was excavated over eight weeks from June to August 1998 at the request of *Dúchas* The Heritage Service.

The excavation was undertaken in advance of restoration/heightening of the outer revetment wall and restoration of the gateway to the inner fortification. There were four areas of excavation: Area 1, the south bastion; Area 2, the entrance; Area 3, the moat; and Area 4, the north bastion.

Area 1: the south bastion
The excavated areas included the entire inner area of the bastion and the area of the moat immediately to the south of the bastion. The excavation revealed that the inner work was made up of a rampart of sterile material, enclosed on three sides by the outer facing wall of the bastion and on the fourth by a modern stone wall. The rampart sloped up steeply from the northern edge of the cutting to the crest. A square stone setting was built on top of the crest of the bastion, and this may have been the base for a flagpole. A low stone wall extended across the edge of the crest. A 0.5m-thick layer of charcoal-enriched silt was uncovered on top of the bastion and covering the flagpole base. It contained post-medieval pottery, clay pipes, lead musket shot and animal bones. It did not extend to the north side of the dividing wall, but there was evidence of burning on the rampart slope, which had been covered by a layer of building collapse. This contained post-medieval pottery, clay pipes, iron nails, lead musket shot, glass and slate roof tiles.

All of the features in the area were covered by a 0.2–0.4m-thick layer of dark brown silt containing large amounts of fragmented roof slate, small fragments of mortar and small stones, which produced finds of animal bones, post-medieval pottery, lead musket balls and a 17th-century token.

The southern section of the bastion wall had collapsed outward into the moat. This collapse was removed, and the excavation was then halted.

Area 2: the entrance
An area *c.* 9m x 8m was opened in front of the entrance to the fort and included the area immediately inside the entrance. This trench linked with the cutting in the south bastion. The topsoil was removed from the moat outside the west wall, but the moat fills were left *in situ*.

The features uncovered included a causeway running across the moat to the bastion gateway and a flagstone surface bounded by a low, stepped stone wall to the west of the moat. The function of the flagstone surface was unclear. The presence of the boundary feature makes it unlikely that the surface was used to provide a level approach to the entrance.

Area 3: the moat
Three areas of the moat were investigated. A section of moat was cleared on either side of the entrance causeway and along the length of the west wall between the entrance and the south bastion. Only topsoil was removed from this area, which linked with the clearance of the moat around the south bastion wall, where the topsoil was also removed, and the rubble from the collapsed section of the outer facing wall of the bastion was removed from the moat.

The main area of excavation was along the outside of the wall between the south and east bastions, where three small trenches, Cuttings 1A, 2 and 3, were opened across the moat.

Excavation of the trenches revealed that the moat cut was 3.6m wide and 1.2–1.4m deep. The cut was wider and deeper close to the south-west bastion. In Cuttings 1A and 2 the moat cut was steep sided with a fairly flat base, apart from a small gully, 0.36m wide and 0.1–0.2m deep, which had been cut into the base in these areas. In Cutting 3, however, the cut sloped gently down to a rounded base and there was no evidence of a gully. There was a slight berm, 0.2m wide, on the inner edge of the moat between the moat and the walls of the fort.

The basic fill of the moat in all three trenches was a 0.16–0.2m-thick layer of building collapse under a mortar-rich layer, 0.24–0.6m thick. The finds from these layers were post-medieval pottery, clay pipes, lead musket shot, bottle glass and animal bone. A 0.1–0.18m-thick layer of mid-brown silt with frequent inclusions of slate fragments and small mortar fragments covered the mortar layer. Finds from this included post-medieval pottery and clay pipes.

The stratigraphy in Cutting 1A was a little more complex, with a series of thin lenses of silt and charcoal deposits under the building collapse layer. These may have related to the burning represented within the bastion by the charcoal-enriched silt on top of the south bastion, although the lenses F18 and F31 also contained frequent pieces of coal, something not found in the silt.

Area 4: the north bastion
Excavation here was limited to the removal of topsoil over the north and east walls to expose the level of the partially collapsed wall underneath. A roughly flagged surface was uncovered under the topsoil in the interior of the bastion.
Mary O'Donnell, Archaeological Services Unit, University College Cork.

83. LOTAMORE
Adjacent to ringfort
W713736
98M0022
In accordance with planning permission from Cork County Council archaeological monitoring of topsoil removal and the excavation of foundation trenches for a housing development by Cork Corporation was carried out over a period of two weeks in September–October 1998. No archaeological features or finds were uncovered during sod-stripping and excavation of house trenches.
Maurice F. Hurley, Cork Corporation, City Hall, Cork.

84. FAIR STREET, MALLOW
Urban
15589 09849
SMR 33:93
98E0281
A site assessment consisting of one test-trench was carried out on 22 June 1998 off Fair Street, Mallow. One east–west trench was opened to the depth of 1m. It was found to contain 20th-century loose rubble fill. No finds or features of archaeological significance were noted.
Sheila Lane, 1 Charlemont Heights, Coach Hill, Rochestown, Cork.

85. MISHELLS
Possible burial-ground
W486578
98E0516
An application to Cork County Council to construct a dwelling-house in the vicinity of a possible burial-ground at Mishells, Bandon, Co. Cork, led to archaeological conditions being imposed on the development. Three test-trenches were placed within the area of the proposed site to determine whether archaeological features or finds were present. The excavation of the trenches revealed no traces of archaeological deposits on the proposed house site, and there was no archaeological reason to prohibit the development.
Margaret McCarthy, Archaeological Services Unit, University College Cork.

86. MIDLETON
Sewerage scheme
W885737
98E0065
Cork County Council and Midleton Urban Development Council propose to commence a major sewerage scheme in Midleton town in 1999. The scheme includes the construction of a new sewerage treatment plant, three submersible pumping stations and a storm tank, as well as laying new sewerage pipelines. The new treatment plant will be built south-west of Midleton adjacent to the Cork–Midleton dual carriageway. The routes of the pipelines are confined mostly to the southern and western areas of the town, and a relatively small section will extend into the archaeological constraint zone as defined by the Urban Archaeological Survey of County Cork. A storm tank and one of the submersible pumping stations will also be built within the designated area.

Site investigation works commenced in April 1998. Archaeological monitoring of trial holes along the proposed routes of the pipeline revealed no features or finds of significance. Construction work on the sewerage treatment plant and the various pumping houses is scheduled to commence in 1999. An archaeologist will be present to monitor the excavation of foundations and associated service trenches.
Margaret McCarthy, Archaeological Services Unit, University College Cork.

87. TOWNLANDS, ROSS CARBERY
No archaeological significance
W287366
98E0234
Pre-development archaeological testing was undertaken in September 1998 in accordance with planning conditions for the construction of eight new houses around a central yard/carpark at the eastern end of Ross Carbery town close to the harbour. Topsoil removal and excavation of foundation trenches were subsequently monitored in early November.

The site was an undeveloped area of parkland with occasional trees, associated with the former Ross College (Academy) adjacent to St Fachtna's Cathedral. The area is close to the site of the ancient ecclesiastical foundation and to the possible line of the town wall. The Cork Archaeological Survey has suggested the likely location of the town wall, but the evidence of the existence of a later medieval wall remains equivocal.

No archaeological evidence of human occupation from any period was recorded in the course of the site testing and monitoring. A large deposit of

building rubble, including stone, mortar, brick and slate, occurred over part of the site, and appears to have resulted from the dumping of the debris from the demolished College, which was burned in 1923 and replaced by a much smaller structure in 1926.
Maurice F. Hurley, Lower House, Mallowgaton, Bandon, Co. Cork.

88. IROTEC LAB LTD, LITTLE ISLAND, WALLINGSTOWN
No archaeological significance
98E0089
Expansion of the existing premises of the Irotec Laboratories Ltd plant on an IDA industrial site in Little Island, Cork, led to monitoring of the development site before construction. The extension lies to the south of the existing production facility in a low-lying, undulating area that provides extensive views over the Lee Valley estuary. Apart from the recovery of a single sherd of post-medieval ware and two struck lithics, nothing of archaeological significance was noted during groundwork disturbance at the site.
Margaret McCarthy, Archaeological Services Unit, University College Cork.

89. 1–2 SOUTH MAIN STREET, YOUGHAL
Urban
21070 07810
98E0190
Three test-trenches were excavated in advance of an extension to an existing building, in an area next to the town wall, which forms the north boundary of the property. The stratigraphy to the north-east consisted of a 0.8m-thick limestone rubble layer, in a sandy soil matrix, with occasional animal bones and oyster shells. This overlay a purple shale deposit, 0.2m deep. Beneath this was a sterile, yellow boulder clay, 1.2m below modern ground level.

The foundations of the town wall were exposed at the north-west end of the trench and lay on the boulder clay. They were composed of uncoursed sandstone bonded with earth and lime-mortar. There was no trace of a foundation trench in this area. A 19th-century cobbled surface was the only feature revealed in the test-trench 6m to the south-west. There were no archaeological features to the rear of the property (south-west end), where a layer of sterile, purple shale, 0.75m deep, was found to overlie bedrock.
Tony Cummins for Archaeological Services Unit, University College Cork.

90. 2–3 SOUTH MAIN STREET, YOUGHAL
Urban
98E0163
Site testing was carried out to fulfil a request for information from Youghal UDC in relation to an application for planning permission to construct a dwelling-house at the rear of No. 3 South Main Street. The town of Youghal may have originated as a Hiberno-Norse port in the 9th century. It was walled in the early 13th century. The walled area of Basetown, or Irishtown, conjoined the main walled town of Youghal to the south and may have been walled after 1462. The development site lay at the south-western corner of Basetown.

The site was bounded to the south-west and north-west by stone walls that may have been built on the line of the original town walls. There was a level bank in the south-western portion of the site, 5.2m wide and 1.8m high; the remainder of the site sloped to the north-east.

Four trenches were opened on the proposed line of the house foundations. Trenches 1 (4m x 1.5m x 1.2m) and 2 (3m x 1.5m x 1.2m) were opened on the surface of the level bank. In each trench loose, voiding, dark brown silty sand with 60% stone was found directly under the sod. There were a number of modern inclusions within it.

Trenches 3 and 4 measured 5m x 1.5m and 1m² respectively, both yielded black, silty sand with occasional modern inclusions under the sod. The black sand varied from 0.4m to 0.6m deep and overlay the natural. No archaeological stratigraphy, features or artefacts were uncovered in any of the trenches excavated.
Jacinta Kiely, Eachtra Archaeological Projects, Clover Hill, Mallow, Co. Cork.

91. 19 SOUTH MAIN STREET, YOUGHAL
Urban
21068 07746
98E0403
Two test-trenches were excavated in advance of the construction of an apartment building in the back garden of a property facing onto South Main Street, Youghal. The town wall is to the north of the development area. The stratigraphy in both trenches was similar, with between 0.4m and 0.9m of dark, humic topsoil lying on a rubble layer containing both post-medieval and modern pottery, fragmented brick and animal bones. This rubble layer varied from 0.4m deep in the west half of the site to over 0.8m deep in the east. It overlay a sterile, yellow/brown, silty clay subsoil in all areas. No archaeological features or artefacts were uncovered in these test-trenches.
Tony Cummins for Archaeological Services Unit, University College Cork.

DERRY/LONDONDERRY

92. BALLYARNET
18th-century racecourse?
C446215
The trench for the pipeline was to be excavated through an area of very boggy land between two areas of more elevated dry land in Ballyarnet townland, Co. Derry, on the outskirts of Derry City. The site lies in a field along the Springfield Road, which is off the Racecourse Road, the name of which refers to the local racecourse that was in use from the later 17th through to the 19th century.

In 1996, during the construction of an earlier pipeline, a gravel-packed platform, apparently above wooden stakes and planks, was discovered by Declan Hurl (*Excavations 1996*, 14). A number of pieces of Neolithic pottery were found in the platform.

During the excavation of the main trench for the pipeline, which was *c.* 8m wide, a large deposit of packed gravel material, similar to the main constituent of the platform material discovered in 1996, was encountered. This was identified as probably being the same platform material, and construction work was temporarily halted until excavation of portions of the platform could take place.

The platform was *c.* 17m north-east by south-west. At right angles to this Declan Hurl had measured the platform as being *c.* 20m long. The dimensions of the platform appeared, therefore, to be *c.* 20m x 17m.

Given the positioning of the platform in a very boggy area it seems reasonable to conclude that its purpose was to provide some sort of dry, solid surface.

Based on the presence of Neolithic pottery in the previously investigated section of the platform it had been suggested that the platform was probably Neolithic, possibly part of a roadway or working area. In the aftermath of the excavation, in which no artefacts were recovered, this must be reconsidered. It is possible that the platform is later than the Neolithic period and that it disturbed some localised Neolithic archaeology during its construction. The platform is near the old Ballyarnet racecourse, which changed its route on a number of occasions since first being constructed in around 1700. It is known that the racecourse was 17m wide (J. Thompson, pers. comm.), the north-east/south-west dimension of the platform. It is possible that the platform was in fact a part of the racecourse that was laid down over a boggy stretch of land to give firm footing for the horses.

Cormac McSparron, Northern Archaeological Consultancy Ltd, Unit 6, Farset Enterprise Centre, Springfield Road, Belfast.

93. 20 CASTLE STREET, BELLAGHY
Post-medieval village
H953966

Excavation was undertaken at the cleared site of No. 20 Castle Street, Bellaghy, Co. Derry, from 3 to 19 August 1998 to try and find the archaeological remains of Plantation houses and property boundaries illustrated on the 1622 Thomas Raven map of the village. A school and yard, built in 1898, most recently occupied the site.

A trench, oriented north-east/south-west, was excavated from between halfway along the street frontage to approximately halfway along the wall of the adjoining property (No. 22 Castle Street). In this way it was hoped to pick up both the front and back walls of any surviving structures, as well as to reveal as whether the street frontage and plot boundaries in this part of the village had changed significantly since the 17th century.

The excavated trench had a maximum length, north-east/south-west, of 14.5m, and width, north-west/south-east, of 2m. A maximum of 1.16m of stratigraphy was encountered within the trench. At least two phases of post-medieval activity were encountered. The first phase took the form of several large pits cut into the subsoil in the east of the site. The second, and later, phase took the form of a rough cobbled surface overlying the earlier pits and a brick setting in the west of the site.

Finds were predominantly ceramic and 18th–20th century in date. Clay pipe, iron nails, bottle glass, red brick and slate were also uncovered.

No evidence of the original 17th-century Plantation village was uncovered during the excavation. Not even evidence of robbed-out building foundation trenches was found. Local people who visited the excavation informed the archaeologists that the subsoil on the site was different from that encountered elsewhere in the village, which, it was said, consisted of compact clays and gravels. It may be that early in the history of the settlement this particular area of ground was found to be unsuitable for the erection of buildings and that, instead, the sand was exploited for construction elsewhere (borrow pits).

Alternatively, it may be that the original street frontage has been altered considerably since the early 17th century and that the original line of the street lies further to the east in the site, perhaps under the 19th-century school.

Ruairí Ó Baoill, Archaeological Development Services Ltd, Unit 48, Westlink Enterprise Centre, 30–50 Distillery Street, Belfast BT12 5BJ/EHS: Archaeological Excavation Unit.

94. BISHOPSGATE, COLERAINE
Urban medieval
C84663230
SMR 7:19

The site is bounded to the north by Bridge Street, to the west by Hanover Place, to the east by Abbey Street and to the south by a modern housing development.

Excavations have revealed the basal remains of a substantial stone structure, running north–south, in the western area of the site. It can be assumed that the structure is part of St Mary's Dominican Priory, founded in the 13th century. Human burials have been excavated along the eastern and northern areas of the site.

Testing in the north-western corner of the site, along the junction of Hanover Place and Bridge Street, uncovered a wooden structure 5–6m long, most probably a short quay or jetty. Small areas of wicker were also uncovered, suggesting the location of fish traps. Pottery recovered from the riverine clay adhering to the timber dates to the early medieval period. Upslope, to the east of this along Bridge Street, a small portion of a ditch has survived and may have been part of the ecclesiastical enclosure. Excavations are still ongoing.

Cia McConway, Archaeological Development Services Ltd, Unit 48, Westlink Enterprise Centre, 30–50 Distillery Street, Belfast BT12 5BJ.

95. DERRY CITY: 1
Urban
C436167
SMR 14:35

An assessment of the site for the construction of the Millennium Theatre was required owing to its proximity to the city walls.

A series of 17th-century house frontages and associated cellars was uncovered in a series of three trenches.

Nick Brannon, Built Heritage, EHS, 5–33 Hill Street, Belfast.

96. THE MILLENNIUM COMPLEX, EAST WALL, DERRY
17th-century cellars and tunnel
C436167
SMR 14:34

This project took place inside the walls in the south-east corner of Derry in late December and early January and was necessitated by the proposed

Derry

construction of a theatre on the site, which lies between the city wall to the east and north, Bank Place/Linenhall Street to the west and Newmarket Street to the south.

Five test-trenches were sunk. Trench 1, the easternmost, lay *c.* 10m from the city wall. It ran approxmately north–south for 11m. The northern half was excavated to a depth of 1.2m, as the construction would be to a depth of only 0.9m. The southern half of the trench was excavated to a depth of *c.* 4m. Nothing of archaeological significance was noted.

Trench 2 lay to the west of Trench 1, 20m from the city wall. It was 2.5m wide and 5m long.

Trench 3 lay 3m to the east of the steps at the west of the site. It was 2.2m wide and 8m long and ran upslope beside the steps. The stratigraphy was composed of modern and 19th-century building rubble and wall footings that appeared to directly overlie the subsoil. Nothing of archaeological significance was noted.

The topsoil in Trench 4 was underlain by a layer of rubble *c.* 0.9m thick. This contained modern debris. Under this in the northern half of the trench was a concrete slab *c.* 0.2m thick, which formed the roof of a tunnel, 1.95m high, and 1.5m wide, walled with concrete blocks. It ran for *c.* 9 m and was blocked by rubble at each end. Where visible, the floor of the tunnel was composed of rough stone slabs, possibly the original flooring of the cellars. The concrete slab was not penetrated, nor was the walling disturbed. This slab formed the northern end of Trench 4.

The southern portion of the trench was extended at right angles to the main trench. In the south-western corner of the extension a layer of sand 0.5m deep was uncovered under the topsoil and on top of rubble. This portion of the trench was bounded on the south by a well-built, mortar-bonded brick wall. At the eastern end were the remains of a brick-built vault. The wall was *c.* 2m high and over 6m long. It was built on a stone-and-mortar foundation on the bedrock and was *c.* 0.5m deep. The material between these two walls consisted of a series of layers of rubbish. Modern material was noted at least 2m below the surface. At the base of the stone walling there appeared to be a more coherent silty layer. This also contained stones and brick, and may have been the floor of the structure. The face of the exposed wall was the internal facing of the southern wall of the structure (remains of the vaulting were visible). It is probable that the wall represents the surviving portion of a range of cellars or tunnels in the basements of 17th-century buildings.

The construction of the cement block tunnel would have destroyed the northern side of the cellar.

Trench 5 uncovered a very thin layer of topsoil over a very unstable mass of rubble. This was bounded on the north side by the carpark wall. At this point it is a composite wall made of mortar, the remnants of two brick vaults and cement. The southern side of these arches appears to have been shuttered with planks and filled in with mortar. Only part of the vaulting and the upper portions of the support pillars are visible. On the northern side the wall appears to be brick, spacer built and rendered. From what remains it appears that the roof was cross- (groin-) vaulted, i.e. composed of two

barrel vaults intersecting at right angles in each bay.

To the south of this wall was a mass of rubble. On removal, at a depth of *c.* 1m, a brick and stone wall, the eastern boundary of a room with the remains of vaulting, running approximately north–south, was uncovered at the east. The wall was broken by an entrance/fireplace in its centre, through which access to the modern tunnel was gained. At a distance of 2.8m to the south of the long wall was another, running parallel to the first. This was also brick with remains of matching vaulting, and was built on a stone footing, as in Trench 4. There were gaps in it, and it was in a much poorer state of repair than in Trench 4. The room extended at least 6.1m to the west and was filled with a great deal of rubble, both ancient and modern. It appears to have been deliberately destroyed and filled in relatively recently. There was no sign of a western end.

It was recorded by Dudley Waterman that a 17th-century tunnel was exposed during rebuilding at the YMCA (demolished in 1979). It extended from Linenhall Street to the back of the city wall and consisted of twelve brick-vaulted bays. This network of tunnels/cellars under the city was surveyed but the army confiscated the survey. Their function may have included facilitating the unobserved movement of troops, food and ammunition to the walls and acting as a place of refuge and an escape route (two of the passages went through the walls).

The passages are pre-Siege, and it is likely that they were constructed before 1629 'for sinking 22 cellars under sundry of the houses not done at first at 20 pounds per cellar, one with another 440 pounds' (OS of Derry 1875, 42).

It appears that much or all of the original settlement in this area has been destroyed by the subsequent occupation. This is particularly true in Trench 3. The other two trenches appear to be garden or yard areas of the 17th/early 18th century. Nick Brannon noted this in his trial-trenching in the carpark (No. 95 above)

The archaeological material recovered was predominantly animal bone. There were also some fragments of hand-made brick, possibly 17th century in date. Some pottery was also recovered, mostly sgraffito and brownware.

What appears to have been uncovered in Trenches 4 and 5 are the remains of a line of cellars of 17th-century date. They are in a poor state of repair, and it seems that they were known of at least as recently as the 1970s, judging by some of the material in them and the probable age of the cement block tunnel. The only real archaeological features appear to be the walls and associated features. It appears that they were used over a long period and were kept relatively clean. Upon their destruction the remains were collapsed and filled with rubbish. They were later further disturbed by modern construction.

Stephen Gilmore, Northern Archaeological Consultancy Ltd, Unit 6, Farset Enterprise Centre, Springfield Road, Belfast.

97. SHANTALLOW, DERRY
Neolithic trackway?
C44542150
SMR 14A:20
The excavation of a trench to accommodate a

pipeline adjacent to an earlier trench that exposed a Neolithic site, possibly a trackway, necessitated archaeological mitigation.

Cormac McSparron, Northern Archaeological Consultancy Ltd, Unit 6, Farset Enterprise Centre, Springfield Road, Belfast.

98. LOUGH ENAGH
Neolithic settlement
SMR 14:12, 14:65

Before the construction of a housing development at Enagh, Co. Derry, *c.* 2 miles from the city centre, close to the River Foyle, monitoring was carried out. Three sites were identified and excavated.

Site 1 lay *c.* 250m east of Lough Enagh West (C46761983). It was at a height of *c.* 10m OD. It consisted of a number of post-holes and pits cut into subsoil along the route of the proposed road and an area of charcoal and stone settings a few metres to the south of these. Pottery of probable Bronze Age date was recovered from the pits/post-holes and from hill-wash material deposited around the stone settings to the south. Only the northern pits/post-holes were under threat, so only these were fully excavated. The other features were planned and then covered in plastic and fine gravel. It seems reasonable to suggest that the features excavated to the north of the site were part of one or more buildings.

Site 2 lay *c.* 650m west-north-west of Site 1 (C46242030), 650m north-west of Lough Enagh West, on the western side of a high ridge over-looking the River Foyle, which is only *c.* 200m to the west. The site is *c.* 32.5m OD. It was a Neolithic house of rectangular shape, *c.* 6.2m x 4.3m. The wall foundations were stone-packed slots, which appeared to contain post-holes. At two corners large stone-packed post-holes were found, and it can be presumed that similar post-holes would have existed at the other corners. There was one small, internal post-hole fairly close to centre of the structure's interior, and this was likely to have been a roof support. There was no evidence of a hearth or an entrance, probably because of disturbance caused by deep ploughing over many years, which truncated the archaeological features. Some Western Neolithic pottery was found in the construction slots, and a flint knife was found in one of the external post-holes.

The developers agreed to move their service trenches in order not to disturb the archaeology, so the house was not totally excavated. But a complete plan of the surviving archaeology and cross-sections of the wall slots and corner post-holes was made before the site was covered in gravel and plastic.

Site 3 (C46412029) lay *c.* 300m to the east of Site 2, *c.* 41m OD. It was a large pit, 3m x 2.6m, filled with ash and loam. It contained some Western Neolithic pottery. This site also was not under further threat and so was planned, sampled and cross-sectioned before being covered.

A full report of this excavation, including site drawings, photos and finds illustrations, can be found on the Internet at homepage.virgin.net/na.c/index.html.

Cormac McSparron, Northern Archaeological Consultancy Ltd, Unit 6, Farset Enterprise Centre, Springfield Road, Belfast.

99. MAGHERAMENAGH
Souterrain
C860389

An assessment of the site of a souterrain was carried out ahead of housing development. Nothing of archaeological significance was uncovered.

Alan Reilly, Northern Archaeological Consultancy Ltd, Unit 6, Farset Enterprise Centre, Springfield Road, Belfast.

100. GLENONE, PORTGLENONE
No archaeological significance
C97350398

Proposed housing development in an area along the River Bann, which had produced numerous early finds, though few known monuments, prompted monitoring of the topsoil-stripping. No finds or features of archaeological significance were uncovered.

Alan Reilly, Northern Archaeological Consultancy Ltd, Unit 6, Farset Enterprise Centre, Springfield Road, Belfast.

DONEGAL

101. BALLYMACAWARD
Multi-period burial cairn: prehistoric/early medieval
1835 3627
97E0154

This monument was originally the subject of an investigative rescue excavation instigated by *Dúchas* The Heritage Service undertaken over a period of four weeks in May–June 1997 (*Excavations 1997*, 16). Following on from this a further season of excavation was undertaken for six weeks in May–June 1998 on an additional area, 80–90m east of the burial cairn. It was investigated because a geophysical survey had revealed anomalies suggestive of a possible destroyed circular enclosure.

Primary monument
The primary burial monument consists of a cairn, which was built around a natural rock outcrop by placing a layer of water-rolled boulders, similar to those found on the nearby beach, onto a sand-covering on the surface of the rock. The presence of uneven depressions (probable stone/boulder sockets) indicates the probability that the cairn-like structure also had a smaller cairn (now destroyed) on the summit. The presence in the cairn of a short cist of Bronze Age type (and a further destroyed example) implies that the monument was constructed in the Bronze Age. Over a period of about a millennium part of the monument became buried in sand and vegetation but was apparently still partially visible in the 2nd/1st century BC.

Excavation in 1998 revealed that this visible portion was augmented by the addition on the northern side of the mound of a level layer of stones interspersed with a mixture of charcoal and cremated bone and bounded by a low revetment. Also within this area were remains of a possible skull burial and one piece of cattle bone. The two small, bowl-shaped pits with cremated bone/charcoal (dated to the 2nd/1st century BC) found near the summit of the mound in 1997 appear to be contemporary with this secondary extension.

A further slab-lined grave containing an extended inhumation was recovered, bringing to four (possibly five) the number of such graves (all female) that were inserted into the monument in the 5th century AD. The remaining seven extended inhumations in unprotected dug graves (also female), recovered in 1997, have been dated to the 7th century AD. It is a noticeable feature that all the burials avoid the central area, a further indication of the probable presence of a central small cairn.

It is concluded that, because of the important historical background to the area in which this monument lies, it represents a Bronze Age cairn that became an ancestral boundary *ferta* (burial place) into which burials were then inserted at crucial historic periods.

Secondary excavation

Three cuttings were inserted through areas of positive and dipolar anomalies, possibly indicative of an enclosure, as revealed by the geophysical survey, *c.* 80–90m west of the burial cairn. All three cuttings revealed layers of blown sand interspersed with thin layers of vegetation, below which iron panning, varying in density of discoloration, in sand was encountered. The water table was reached immediately beneath the iron panning at a depth of *c.* 1.2m. It was concluded that the positive anomalies may be the result of iron panning and that the dipolar anomalies probably represent a reservoir of underground water. There was no evidence of a man-made enclosure, but, as the area regularly becomes water-logged in wet seasons, this could result in the formation, over an extended period, of a depression that would have the surface appearance of a destroyed enclosure.

Elizabeth O'Brien, 121 Barton Road East, Dundrum, Dublin 14.

102. KILBARRON, BALLYSHANNON

No archaeological significance

G852651

98E0148

Testing took place on 26 March 1998. All but one of the eight trenches were machine-excavated down to undisturbed natural without revealing anything of archaeological significance.

In the southernmost trench an area of flagstone paving was uncovered directly beneath the sod. It ran approximately parallel to the line of the laneway that defines the southern boundary of the development area. No dating evidence was recovered; however, the close proximity of the early church of Kilbarron adds to its significance. It is recommended that further investigations take place in this area.

Apart from this confined area, nothing of archaeological significance was uncovered elsewhere during the assessment.

Eoin Halpin, Archaeological Development Services Ltd, Unit 48, Westlink Enterprise Centre, 30–50 Distillery Street, Belfast BT12 5BJ.

103. CHURCHLAND QUARTERS, CARNDONAGH

Early ecclesiastical

2464 4448

SMR 11:61

98E0511

Test-trenching was undertaken at the site of the proposed shelter for the Carndonagh Cross to comply with a condition of planning permission. The work was undertaken initially by H.A. King, and R. Crumlish carried out subsequent testing and monitoring.

This is one of the most important Early Christian sites in Donegal; it was founded by St Patrick and gives the nearby town its name. It had erenaghs associated with it until the 16th century. The cross associated with the site is of national importance and, only for the strong will of a number of local people, might have never returned from a proposed journey to Dublin for a *Rosc* exhibition over twenty years ago. The cross is usually dated to the 7th or 8th century and originally stood in the field on the other side of the road, from where it was moved during road-widening works a number of years ago. Two small, decorated pillars (steles) flank the cross. The site of the early ecclesiastical foundation is currently occupied by a modern graveyard in which stands a Church of Ireland parish church built in the 18th century. Beside the entrance to the church, which consists of a reused 15th-century door, is a carved lintel, possibly from an earlier church. Also within the graveyard is an upright decorated pillar known as the Marigold Stone.

The site of the cross shelter consists of a small field 22m east–west by 10m, on the roadside immediately west of Donagh church. Five slit-trenches were opened, one long trench across the length of the field and four small trenches along the roadside on the line of new underground ESB cabling. The small trenches were *c.* 0.6m deep, and no archaeological stratigraphy was encountered. The long trench in the middle of the field consisted of brown ploughsoil to a depth of *c.* 0.5–0.6m, overlying yellow boulder clay. At the eastern side of the trench was evidence of a shallow ditch running north–south. Although there was no evidence of occupation in the field and the ditch had all the appearance of a recent field ditch, it was decided to undertake further testing when the site was being reduced before building works. It was also recommended that a watching brief be maintained on the demolition of the perimeter wall in case there were any worked stones incorporated in it.

Two further test-trenches were excavated by mechanical digger between 16 and 18 November. Test-trench 1 was dug 1.3m south of the long slit-trench excavated by Heather King during initial testing of the site and 0.5m west of the east site boundary. Test-trench 2 was dug 2.4m north of Ms King's trench and 1m west of the east site boundary. Both were orientated roughly east–west. Test-trench 1 was 6m long, 0.8–0.9m wide and 0.5–0.6m deep at its west end (2m max. depth at east end). Test-trench 2 was 5.8m long, 0.6–0.8m wide and 0.6m deep its west end (1.8m max. depth at east end). The monitoring involved the reduction in the level of the site by up to 1m.

The site measured 16m east–west by 10m. The excavation also involved the removal of a drystone wall along the north and east boundaries of the site.

The stratigraphy encountered in Test-trench 1 consisted of topsoil below which was yellow boulder clay over a 2m section at the west end of the trench. The final 4m of the trench at its east end revealed a different stratigraphy. Here, below the topsoil, was a light brown subsoil, 0.2m thick. Below the subsoil was a dark grey/black, stony deposit, 0.1–0.3m thick. Below the deposit was a soft and sterile, mottled yellow/grey deposit, which was 0.1–0.7m thick and was not fully excavated. Below the mottled deposit at either end were revealed the upper sections of two sides of a ditch feature that was not fully exposed. The ditch was 3.2m wide within the trench (its east side was not fully uncovered within the trench) and at least 1.4m (west side) deep and was cut into the boulder clay. The trench was not excavated below 2m (in total depth) owing to reasons of safety.

The stratigraphy encountered in Test-trench 2 was the same as in Test-trench 1. The stratigraphy over the remainder of the site to the west of the ditch feature consisted of topsoil above yellow boulder clay. The topsoil contained a small number of modern artefacts.

The three test-trenches produced evidence of a ditch feature in the general area where one would expect to find evidence of an enclosure associated with an ecclesiastical site. There is also a slight curve in evidence from north–south to north-north-east/south-south-west; however, nothing was recovered from the fills of the ditch that could date the feature. The stone facing around the perimeter was found to comprise rubble.

Heather A. King and Richard Crumlish, c/o National Monuments, Dúchas, 51 St Stephen's Green, Dublin 2.

104. CROCKAHENNY (INISHOWEN)
No archaeological significance
C460332 (centred on)
98E0003

The proposed site of Crockahenny Wind Farm lies around the summit of Crockahenny Hill (OD 326m) and stretches across the col between it and the lower slopes of Leamacrossan (OD 392m) to the east.

There are no known archaeological sites recorded in the immediate vicinity of the hill. Field-walking took place on 10 September 1997. No sites of archaeological interest were identified in the area of the wind generators, four of which are positioned close to the 1000ft contour.

The proposed access road traverses the southern flank of the hill, running approximately west to east. About a third of the way along, its line crosses that of a series of relict field boundaries. Four examples were noted, two of which ran downslope at right angles to the contours. The northern, upslope end of the westernmost example revealed evidence of a joining cross-wall. These features do not appear on the OS 6-inch map of the area and were in extremely poor repair, with the surviving stones deeply embedded in the subsoil. Taken together they may indicate a prehistoric field system, and, if so, it is possible that the upper slopes of Crockahenny Hill also have traces of this system surviving under the peat.

Nothing of archaeological significance was noted in the area of the switch-gear and control building.

Owing to the complex nature of the field system discovered during the field-walk phase, an EDM survey was undertaken to record its extent. Two distinct systems were recorded, the first on the western flank of the hill and the second centred on the area where the initial field walls were noted. The remains on the western flank consisted of a roughly circular enclosure some 170m in diameter and defined from north-west through north to east by the remains of a substantial stone wall. From east to the intersection with the trackway the enclosure appears to be preserved in the line of a broad, shallow, water-logged ditch. Its south-west arc seems to survive on the southern side of the trackway as a stone bank. However, the construction of the track has disturbed this area considerably, and therefore what is visible on the ground may be a by-product of the track construction rather than the original line of the enclosure. No trace was noted for a distance of some 70m to the north of the track on the west side.

The enclosure appears to be divided in half by a cross-wall that runs from north-north-west to south-south-east. However, it was not traced beyond half distance. A subrectangular enclosure, measuring some 6m by 5m, was noted on the west side of this cross-wall.

The north side of the enclosure revealed evidence of radial walls, the first running due north for some 85m. The second, to the north-east, ran for a distance of 30m before turning south-east and running up to a steep-sided rock outcrop, with a third wall running 20m from the enclosure to the rock outcrop.

At a distance of some 100m to the south-east of the enclosure a possible hut circle was recorded. It was situated on the 270m contour and consisted of a level platform, backed on the upslope side by an outcrop of rock and to the front and sides by the curving arc of a bank. These features defined an oval area measuring 25m east–west by 20m transversely. A possible break in the line of the bank to the south-east appeared to be the remains of an entrance.

Further to the east the line of a field wall was recorded running south-west to north-east perpendicular to the slope of the hill. It consisted of large boulders protruding from the grass- and peat-covered ground and was easily traceable for a distance of some 130m. Its northern end abutted an outcrop of bedrock. To the north of this the wall reappeared, arcing around roughly at a right angle and running for a further 40m to abut against another rock outcrop. The possible remains of a further wall were noted running across the corner created by Walls 1 and 2; however, this was not clear on the ground. A fourth wall was recorded to the south of the east end of Wall 2 and, as with Wall 1, ran perpendicular to the slope of the hill.

The line of the fourth wall marked a change in the vegetation cover on the hillside. To the west, where the hill was exposed to the prevailing south-westerlies, the cover was grass, reeds and exposed bedrock. To the east, the leeward side was covered in a blanket of peat, heather and sphagnum, which has the effect of masking any further evidence of archaeology along this flank.

Some bog probing took place, concentrating on two areas: at the apparent southern termini of the Walls 1 and 4 and along the proposed line of the access route up the hillside. The northern termini of Walls 1, 2 and 4 were examined, but each of these was found to run into outcrops of bedrock and was not seen to run beyond.

Donegal

The probing of the access route was carried out at 1m intervals starting at the upslope eastern end. The depth of bog cover was recorded, and, where rock was encountered, detailed probing took place to ascertain whether it was part of a larger, possibly archaeological feature. The termini of Walls 1 and 4 were likewise examined with detailed probing both across and along their projected lines.

The probing of the field walls showed that their downslope ends more or less terminated where they were visible on the ground, with their upslope ends disappearing into natural rock outcrops.

A proposed area of rock extraction was also examined and revealed nothing of archaeological significance.

Finally monitoring of the open-area stripping of the switch-gear building and of the access roadway and generator pads took place. Nothing of archaeological significance was found.

Eoin Halpin, Archaeological Development Services Ltd, Unit 48, Westlink Enterprise Centre, 30–50 Distillery Street, Belfast BT12 5BJ.

105. DOE CASTLE
Tower-house
20871 43198
SMR 26:02301

Doe Castle, situated on a small promontory in Sheephaven Bay, comprises a tower-house with adjoining buildings and is enclosed by a bawn wall. It has been undergoing restoration work for a number of years. Monitoring was undertaken in December 1998.

Two trenches were opened in the north-west quadrant of the bawn. One trench for electrical wiring ran from the window on the north wall of the tower-house in a westerly direction, immediately adjacent to the tower-house wall, and then across the bawn in a south-westerly direction to the projecting gate-tower. The second trench, for a drain outlet, was opened from the east side of the window on the north wall of the tower and ran northwards to exit under the loop in the bawn wall. The trenches showed that the castle is built on rock outcrop with small deposits of soil in the rock fissures. Nothing of archaeological interest was noted.

Heather A. King, National Monuments, Dúchas, 51 St Stephen's Green, Dublin 2.

106. SITE 9, DRUMHINNY LOWER
Prehistoric
G946775
97E0356

This site was revealed during the stripping of the topsoil for the Donegal Bypass. Initial assessment of the site revealed a possible hearth and areas of burning.

Three main cuttings were opened. The site had been severely disturbed by tree roots, making the identification of archaeological features difficult. However, a linear feature, identified as a shallow ditch, ran in a north-west to south-east direction across the southern portion of the site. This feature was 1m wide and had a total length of 6.2m, with a depth of 0.55m. The fill of the ditch was completely sterile, with the exception of a piece of timber 0.6m long and supported at either end by a stone and a piece of wood, placed deliberately underneath the

timber. To the east and west of the ditch was a series of stake-holes and small pits, 21 in all, possibly representing the remains of windbreaks, or a light wooden covering over a portion of the ditch. Several areas of charcoal were obvious to the immediate south-east of the ditch, and a small pit was revealed under one charcoal spread. Further to the north of the ditch a rough metalled surface was revealed measuring 2.2m x 2.6m.

A hearth was revealed within the central area of Cutting 2, measuring 1.6m x 1.4m, consisting of a semicircle of stones, resting on a bed of charcoal and peaty soil.

Three field drains were revealed in the northern section of the site running in a north-west to south-east direction and resting on the natural subsoil. It should be noted that the northern portion of the site was covered by peat before the excavation and that the whole site was extremely wet.

Three phases of activity appear to be represented on the site. The earliest phase may be the large spreads of charcoal, associated with the linear feature, together with the stake-holes, pits and nearby metalled surface. These features appear to represent a possible semi-industrial or domestic activity. A second phase of activity appears to be represented by the hearth, which rests on a thin layer of peat, and the final phase appears to be the insertion of the three stone field drains.

No dates have yet been ascertained for the site as radiocarbon dating is still being carried out, and no finds were recovered from the site; however, it may be possible to suggest that the differing periods of activity date from prehistoric up to post-medieval times.

It is important to note that the above site is just one of over twenty, the majority prehistoric, revealed during the stripping of the topsoil for the Donegal Bypass. All of these sites are concentrated in an area of only 7km.

Sylvia Desmond, 25 Rowan Hall, Millbrook Court, Milltown, Dublin 6.

107. SITE 11, DRUMHINNY LOWER
Prehistoric
G946776
97E0441

This site was revealed during the stripping of the topsoil for the Donegal Bypass during 1997 and had extensive areas of burning and charcoal spreads.

Three cuttings, each 9m x 8m, were opened. All of the topsoil had been removed by machine, revealing three main features on the site. Feature 1 was a rectangular feature, 1.65m north–south by 2.5m. It was delimited for the most part by a band of burnt, red subsoil 0.1m wide and 0.05m deep, with a high concentration of carbonised wood at the eastern end. It appears that the pieces of wood were laid down deliberately in an overlapping manner. Patches of burnt, red soil and high concentrations of charcoal, together with carbonised wood, constituted the fill of this feature. The red soil appears to be the natural subsoil, burnt red by the intense heat. A piece of unburned chert was recovered from this feature. During the initial discovery of the site fragments of bone (possibly human) and a struck flint were also recovered from this feature.

Feature 2 consists of a charcoal spread, 1.8m x 2.2m, *c.* 3m to the south of the above feature. Patches of burnt subsoil, evidence of intense heat, were also revealed within this spread. When the spread was removed a linear feature was revealed, running north–south for 2.5m, with a width of 0.2m and a depth of 0.8m.

Feature 3 was very similar, consisting of a linear cut 2.5m long and 0.5m wide and situated to the immediate south of Feature 2. Only 0.7m separated the two features. The redeposited fill of both features consisted of a grey, marl-like clay, with charcoal flecks, distributed throughout.

Feature 1 appears to be the most significant on the site. The very shape and size, together with the presence of burnt, red soil and wood, when combined with the burnt bone (possibly human) and struck flint and chert suggest that it may be a possible cremation pyre, but this has yet to be confirmed. [14]C dating is currently being undertaken, but it may date to the Neolithic or Early Bronze Age. Features 2 and 3 are rather enigmatic. Whether they had any connection with the possible cremation pyre is uncertain, and the absence of any finds makes it difficult to suggest a purpose or date for them. However, dates may be forthcoming from charcoal samples.

Like Site 9 (No. 106 above), this site lies within an area of intense prehistoric activity, all revealed during the monitoring of the Donegal Bypass. Both of the above sites are in close proximity to a Neolithic house/structure, a *fulacht fiadh,* a large wetland site and Drumrat Court Tomb. Many of these sites may be interrelated in time and space, and they appear to form part of a rich and diverse archaeological landscape.
Sylvia Desmond, 25 Rowan Hall, Millbrook Court, Milltown, Dublin 6.

108. GLENFINN TO GLENMORE (R252) ROAD IMPROVEMENT SCHEME
Burnt mound, pit
C060970 (Centred on)
98E0232

The borrow pit field, which is under improved grassland, slopes moderately steeply down from the present R252 road line. It then levels out into a long, undulating terrace, which runs from west to east, roughly parallel to the course of the River Finn. This terrace has two pronounced but relatively flat-topped hillocks, which together form the crest of a very steep slope that falls down to the river valley bottom. It was these hillocks that, during initial survey, presented themselves as possible areas of archaeological potential, particularly as on a similar terrace (albeit slightly upslope) lies a good example of a rath.

Using a 4ft-wide blade bucket six trenches were excavated. The first was opened along the crest of the ridge, angled to cross the summit of each of the hillocks. Nothing of archaeological significance was noted. Ploughsoil rested directly on natural that varied from yellow/brown, sandy gravel to yellow/brown, stony gravel. It was apparent that the hillocks were the product of local undulations in the underlying bedrock.

Four trenches were opened running perpendicular to the main east–west trench. Nothing of interest was noted in three of the four. The exception was the extreme eastern trench. The topography at this end of the field was different, consisting of a shallow depression open to the south. The base of this depression was relatively flat, and the test-trench was aligned to run across this level area.

The depth of ploughsoil at the southern end of the trench was consistent with that noted elsewhere, some 0.3m. However, as the trench progressed northwards, the depth of soil overburden increased, presumably owing to the process of hill wash. Close to the point where the subsoil started its natural rise upslope an area of grey clay, overlain by a stony, charcoal-blackened soil, was noted. Many of the stones within the black soil were heat-shattered, and it was immediately apparent that the vestiges of a burnt mound had been uncovered. A small trench was opened from the apparent centre of the concentration westwards. The burnt material in these two trenches was noted, therefore, to extend in an approximately circular area, some 10m in diameter.

Using the same-sized bucket three long trenches were opened roughly along the centre line of the proposed new roadway. Nothing of archaeological significance was noted in any of the three segments tested.

Only one minor piece of archaeology was uncovered. At the extreme western end of the westernmost trench along the road line a small area of *in situ* burning was noted. It appeared as the basal remains of a 1.5m-wide, circular, flat-bottomed pit. At most, the pit was 0.1m deep, with charcoal overlying red, oxidised clay. Nothing datable was noted in association, and its function remains unknown.
Eoin Halpin, Archaeological Development Services Ltd, Unit 48, Westlink Enterprise Centre, 30–50 Distillery Street, Belfast BT12 5BJ.

109. FISHERY COTTAGE, MAGHERACAR
Midden
505 010
98E0256

The site lies in the extreme south-west of Donegal, about 3km west of Bundoran. It lies on the south side of a small island at the mouth of the Drowes River, about 40m to the south of the site of Bundrowes Castle. No surface traces of this castle have been visible for at least the last 150 years. It is possible that the stones were used for the construction of buildings currently occupying the site.

Test-trenching was required owing to a holiday home development on the site. Monitoring of service trenches and foundations was previously carried out by J.C. McSparron. A shelly deposit containing two small pottery sherds of either Western Neolithic or everted-rim ware was uncovered in the north-east section of the trench to the west of the old building. They were too small and worn to identify properly. everted-rim ware in western Ulster dates to the period around AD 1500, so this may relate to the period of occupation at Bundrowes Castle or it may date to the Neolithic. As the derelict cottage was to be removed, test-trenching was considered essential as it seemed likely that the archaeology would continue to the north-east, under the house, which was reputed to be of 17th-century date.

Test-trenching began on 1 June 1998. Four trenches were excavated, partially by mechanical excavator and partially by hand.

The stratigraphy in Trench 1 corresponded with that in the north-eastern end of the pipe-trench. The 0.3m-deep topsoil contained much relatively recent material. It overlay a compact, yellow- and grey-laminated, lime-rich, stone-filled, sandy clay, 0.25m deep. Below this was a layer of fine, soft, beach sand up to 0.1m deep, which filled the interstices of the cobbled layer below and appears to have been a deliberate deposit. The well-laid cobbled layer was composed of beach stones up to 0.2m in diameter. It may represent an old farmyard or a roadway and was laid in a 0.35m-thick layer of grey clay/silt, which contained red brick. This lay on top of the subsoil. Also encountered in this trench was a 19th-century wall. This respected the cobbling and appears to have formed its north-western edge.

Objects found in these layers included willow pattern pottery, animal bones, glass and brick. Nothing pre-dating the 19th century was found.

Trench 2 was in front of the cottage. Topsoil, *c.* 0.3m thick, overlay a brown, silty clay up to 0.4m thick, which contained stones and modern rubbish. At the east of the trench this directly overlay the subsoil. Below this, at the west, was a coarse, shelly, sand layer, less than 0.1m thick. This petered out about 5m from the eastern end of the trench. It was no more than 0.5m wide. Underlying this was a brown, sandy clay layer up to 0.2m thick, which overlay a grey, charcoal- and shell-rich, sticky clay. This extended about 6m east–west and *c.* 3m north–south, was up to 0.3m thick, and overlay the subsoil. It appeared to be midden material of some sort. A piece of animal bone and a tooth were recovered. Shell types found were periwinkles, mussels and limpets. The only artefact found was a curved piece of rusty iron, 60mm long, possibly the remains of a knife. The deposit may be derived from Bundrowes Castle; radiocarbon dates for this site are pending.

Trench 3 was excavated close to the west gable of the house. The house's foundations were very shallow and were not in any sort of trench. Inside the house the topsoil was visible below the foundations. Finds were all modern or 19th-century.

Trench 4 was excavated inside the western end of the house. The sub-floor of the house was composed of a mortar-like material up to 0.2m thick, made from sand and limestone. It appeared to be laid directly on the subsoil except in one place. This was an organic, dark grey, charcoal-rich patch *c.* 0.8m in diameter and up to 0.2m thick.

Finds included two pieces of hand-moulded, badly fired or burnt brick. This suggests that this was no older than the 18th century. No material or strata of archaeological significance were uncovered

Some of the stones that composed the walls of the cottage appeared to be well dressed and not just rubble or brick. This could partially explain the disappearance of Bundrowes Castle.
Stephen Gilmore, Northern Archaeological Consultancy Ltd, Unit 6, Farset Enterprise Centre, Springfield Road, Belfast.

110. FORTSTEWART, RAMELTON
No archaeological significance
C27452030
98E0098
On 9 March 1998 an archaeological assessment was carried out at Fortstewart, Ramelton, Co. Donegal, on the site of a proposed domestic dwelling, in response to planning conditions. The site is close to a National Monument, Fort Stewart Bawn (SMR 46:11). Excavation was by mechanical digger using a toothless bucket, along the line of the foundations, septic tank, soak pit and driveway.

In all cases the removal of sod and ploughsoil revealed naturally deposited subsoil. Nothing of archaeological significance was uncovered.
Audrey Gahan, Archaeological Development Services Ltd, Unit 48, Westlink Enterprise Centre, 30–50 Distillery Street, Belfast BT12 5BJ.

DOWN

111. JORDAN'S CASTLE, ARDGLASS
Tower-house
J56013713
SMR 45:20
Two trenches were opened up, one upslope (west) of the tower-house and one downslope of it. The former found the area to have been disturbed in the last century by the construction of drains, although there were indications that an early road ran east–west adjacent to the north side of the structure. The downslope trench exposed the remains of a medieval wall separating the grounds from the road to the north. Nearby was a substantial pit, which was filled with stone chippings and mortar, as well as part of a scalloped piscina.
M. Gardiner, Department of Archaeology, Queen's University, Belfast.

112. NEWARK CASTLE, ARDGLASS
Tower-house
J56153710
SMR 45:21
The excavation within Newark Castle was intended to determine whether the original structure was a late medieval warehouse.

The east side was found to have been disturbed by the repeated construction and removal of light modern buildings. In the north a 19th-century coach entrance had been cut down into the bedrock. Around it, however, were sands pre-dating the structure and within which medieval pottery and a bone gaming piece were found. A shell-filled pit was cut into the sand.
Tom McNeill, Department of Archaeology, Queen's University, Belfast.

113. OLD BRIDGE COURT, BALLYVALLEY, BANBRIDGE
Ringfort
J12154559
SMR 27:89
The site lay in the Old Bridge Court development on the Ballygowan Road on the outskirts of Banbridge, in the townland of Ballyvalley, Co. Down. The site was a fragmentary remnant of a ringfort that had been nearly totally levelled in the 1960s. OS maps indicated that it had an internal diameter of *c.* 25m. A remnant of the bank has been incorporated into a hedge. This was particularly obvious from the south-west side of the hedge, outside the development site, where it could be seen as a distinct arc (*c.* 16m long). The bank was

1.3m high and 4m wide. Unmonitored restripping and levelling during the current development may have further truncated any ditch remains.

A 4m-wide strip between the house foundations and the south-western boundary of the site was machine-stripped but produced no trace of the ditch. The straightening and cleaning of the south-western boundary section revealed the base of the ditch a few centimetres above the present site level, so no trace of the ditch survived. The only surviving trace of the ringfort was the section of ditch in the south-western boundary of the development. This section was straightened with a view to drawing it.

The original ditch cut was roughly 1.5m deep by 3m wide. It was an irregular V-shape in profile. At some recent date a broad, shallow, U-shaped pipe-trench had cut through the earlier ditch. This cut removed the eastern edge of the older cut and the eastern part of the original upper fills. The original stratigraphy of the ditch fill could only be seen in the western, lower half of the ditch. It appears that minor silting had occurred, emanating from the external (eastern) edge of the ditch, represented by inspilling lines. After the deposition of these fills there seems to have been a large deposit that emanated from the internal (western) side of the ringfort ditch. This was probably slump from the internal bank of the ringfort.

The lower silts of the ditch have been sampled and submitted for radiocarbon dating and environmental analysis.

Alan Reilly, Northern Archaeological Consultancy Ltd, Unit 6, Farset Enterprise Centre, Springfield Road, Belfast.

114. IDB DEVELOPMENT SITE, BELFAST ROAD, DOWNPATRICK

Multi-period
J47204645
SMR 30:39

Archaeological investigations within the townlands of Inch and Ballyrenan began in November 1997, ahead of an 80-acre industrial estate development in Downpatrick, Co. Down, which was funded by the IDB. Over a period of ten months eight areas of archaeological significance have been identified, ranging in date from the Neolithic (5500–3500 BC) to the Early Christian period (AD 600–1100). This work was completed over two phases.

Phase 1: pre-development

Three areas of archaeological significance had been found as part of the pre-development phase of works. Area 1 was identified through aerial photographs, while Areas 2 and 3 had been identified through geophysical testing.

Area 1

One of the first areas investigated within Inch townland was the site of an Early Christian defended farmstead, or rath, on the north facing slope of Drumlea Hill (*Excavations 1997*, 20–1). It survived as a ditched enclosure, some 38–40m in diameter, with an entrance to the north-east. Within the enclosure two structures were uncovered. The first was a rectangular house structure, *c.* 9m long and 5m wide, surviving as a series of substantial bedrock-cut post-holes. The second was a circular hut structure *c.* 3.5m in diameter. Finds from the site included large sherds of souterrain ware pottery from the ditch fills, and a fragment of a lignite bracelet. There was also evidence of pre-rath activity on site, in the form of both an earlier hearth feature and other random post-holes, which produced fragments of Neolithic pottery.

Area 2

Near the base of a drumlin in the adjacent townland of Ballyrenan an area of random pits and post-holes was uncovered, along with a series of long gullies that contained charcoal-rich soil and burnt stones. This site was interpreted as a possible cooking/working area, which contained temporary hut structures. The gullies, which were situated along the junction between glacial till and grey gley clays, may have represented cooking-pits. The junction between the two soils was interpreted as an old water edge. Pottery sherds found on site suggest that this area dated to the Bronze Age (*c.* 4000–2500 BC).

Area 3

A large spread of stone material some 24m x 15m was found near the top of the above-mentioned drumlin. This later proved to be the remains of two stone platforms, one 15m x 14m, the other 14m x 16m, their long axes both aligned north–south. Around these platforms was evidence of further activity in the form of post-holes and pits. Finds from this area included Neolithic pottery, flint flakes and a scraper, and two blue glass beads.

Phase 2: Monitoring

The second phase of works involved monitoring topsoil-stripping, when a total of five further areas of archaeological significance were identified, in both Ballyrenan and Inch townlands.

Area 4

A fourth area of activity was roughly 400m from the Belfast road. This area produced evidence of a possible rectangular Neolithic house structure in the form of a series of post-holes and a badly truncated house slot. A large pit associated with the structure produced small fragments of Neolithic pottery.

Area 5

Archaeological activity in this area survived as a substantial pit cut into the hill from which prehistoric pottery, dating to the Bronze Age, was recovered. Under a spread of soil associated with this pit and to the east of it two post-holes were found

Area 6

This area produced evidence of a Bronze Age house structure. This survived as the remains of a circular slot, roughly 12m in diameter, containing internal post-holes. Finds from this site included Bronze Age pottery sherds and a flint scraper.

Area 7

A shallow pit containing charcoal-rich soil and burnt stones was uncovered at the base of the east slope of Drumlea Hill. This lay at the edge of an old water line, possibly the same as in Area 2, and was similarly interpreted as the remains of a cooking-pit.

Area 8

An extensive area on a ridge at the base of Drumlea Hill revealed an abundance of archaeological activity, which included a Bronze Age house structure and cemetery.

The cemetery survived as a collection of eight cremation burials, three of which had been enclosed by small ring-ditches. These three ring-ditch burials were orientated along a north-east/south-west line and ranged from *c.* 3m to 5m in size, each with a cremation pit burial in the centre. The largest of these had a setting of post-holes around the outside of the ditch, as well as a palisade slot on the inside of the bottom of the ditch, and may represent the most important burial on site. The second-largest ring-ditch burial also had a ring of post-holes around the outside of the ditch. The cremation pit in this second burial produced a number of sherds of Bronze Age pottery, which suggest that the cremated remains may have been deposited into an urn before being placed into the ground.

To the south-west of these burials was a group of three individual cremation burials, without any associated ditch. One of these produced evidence that the cremated remains may have been put into a bag before being deposited into the ground, as the burnt bone was firmly concentrated in the middle of the pit.

Further south of these burials were a further two ring-ditches, neither of which had any burials associated with them. The largest of these contained a substantial amount of large boulders within the ditch fill, which suggests that there may have been a stone mound or an earthen mound with stone facing inside the confines of the ditch.

A further 4–5m to the south of the latter, two ring-ditches and a house structure, similar to that in Area 7, were found. This house survived as the remains of a circular foundation slot *c.* 10m in diameter, with internal post-holes possibly representing roof supports. Pottery sherds from a pit associated with this house suggest that the structure is Bronze Age in date.

Summary

There has been a substantial amount of archaeological evidence of past settlements and associated activity provided by large-scale developments such as at the IDB development site in Downpatrick. In this case there is apparent evidence of occupation in the area spanning a 6000-year period. It is clear that the high ground afforded by drumlins was a prime settlement location for both prehistoric and historic communities, who no doubt would have utilised the resources provided by the surrounding rich landscape and nearby River Quoile. We have also been given an insight into the ritual and ceremonial practices of prehistoric societies through the discovery of the Bronze Age cemetery.

It is hoped that the evidence collected during these recent excavations, once viewed in conjunction with our existing knowledge, will further our understanding of past settlement patterns in the area of both Downpatrick and the rest of County Down.

I acknowledge both the IDB and DOE-EHS for their support and cooperation during both phases of archaeological works.

Ciara Mac Manus, c/o Archaeological Development Services, Unit 48, Westlink Enterprise Centre, 30–50 Distillery Street, Belfast BT12 5BJ.

115. CATHEDRAL HILL, DOWNPATRICK

Multi-phase landscape
J48534457
SMR 37:73

The granting of planning permission to construct a tourist and heritage centre on the slopes of Cathedral Hill in Downpatrick necessitated archaeological mitigation.

A sizeable ditch was found running downslope (south) and cutting two lower curving ditches; their fills contained souterrain ware. At the bottom of the hill was a Bronze Age industrial complex consisting of numerous small pits and stake-holes filled and surrounded by charcoal-rich soil; considerable quantities of bronzeworking slag were recovered from the area, which had been disturbed by a larger, shallow, medieval pit.

Further medieval pits were uncovered in the west of the site. One was stone-lined and *c.* 1.5m in diameter and depth and had a connecting stone-lined channel running south; neither the features nor the fill showed any signs of heating. Further east was a stepped pit, sheer-sided and *c.* 2m in diameter at the top, levelling suddenly before dropping down again.

Many of the features exhibited disturbance from the terracing prevalent on the slope.

Eoin Halpin, Archaeological Development Services Ltd, Unit 48, Westlink Enterprise Centre, 30–50 Distillery Street, Belfast BT12 5BJ.

116. CASTLE MILL GARDENS, NEWTOWNARDS

Post-medieval garden
J49137376
SMR 30:39

On 15–18 June 1998 a watching brief was undertaken of a geotechnical and contaminant survey of the walled Castle Mill Gardens at Newtownards and of land to the south of the walled garden. Twenty-six trial-pits were excavated within the walled area of the former 17th-century gardens. The trial-pits were positioned across the Castle Garden site so that a complete cross-section could be attained along both axes of the garden. A further sixteen pits were excavated across the land to the south of the walled garden.

A small trench had been excavated in 1992 by Declan Hurl in front of one of the pre-existing blocked gateways into the northern part of the Castle Gardens (*Excavations 1992*, 13), which uncovered evidence of two phases of path and gateway. The earlier path sealed a post-medieval ditch with a stone-lined drain at the bottom, thought to be related to the initial reclaiming of the area of the gardens. In addition medieval pits and gullies were found, which were possibly associated with the priory to the north. The drain and early path were thought to be associated with the Montgomery garden (early 17th century), and the later path and gate were thought to be related to the Colville period (late 17th century).

During the watching brief, no identifiable medieval deposits were found in any of the test-pits. In general the post-medieval deposits occurred *c.* 0.3–0.5m below the modern topsoil/disturbance and were *c.* 0.6–1m deep in the north of the Castle Gardens and shallower in the south-east of the walled area—*c.* 0.2–0.5m, although these depths did vary. The post-medieval deposits represented the build-up of soils for the reclamation of the area and garden soils. In the east of the site, where a series of 19th-century factory buildings had been constructed, survival of the post-medieval deposits was variable, with truncation occurring in areas disturbed by these later foundations. A number of drainage channels were discovered (similar to the stone-lined drain found in 1992) associated with the original reclamation of the walled area. The area of the former pond, first indicated on the 1830 map, was uncovered, although this proved to be of simple construction with no stone lining or clay lining evident.

Unfortunately no finds were recovered that could produce a definitive date for the creation of the garden and the redeposited layers of made ground. However, it was clear from the uniformity across the garden that it was created in a single event. This probably included the construction of the canal, walls and the underground drainage channel parallel to the northern wall. Even so, it does not solve the question of whether the garden was in existence during the Montgomery period or was created by Colville, as has been assumed in the past.

No medieval or easily identifiable post-medieval deposits were encountered in the test-pits outside the Castle Gardens. Later build-up on top of the natural was encountered in some of the test-pits, but these deposits appeared to be 19th–20th century in date. The average depth of these deposits was *c.* 1.8m (from below the topsoil), and they contained waste material such as broken bricks, rubble, ash and coal. Only Victorian willow pattern pottery was recovered from these layers. Most of the test-pits, however, showed only the topsoil (0.2–0.3m) lying straight on top of the natural silts/sands.

Steve Lawrence, Oxford Archaeological Unit, Janus House, Osney Mead, Oxford OX2 0ES, UK.

117. AIRPORT–BALBRIGGAN/NORTHERN MOTORWAY BYPASS

No archaeological significance
98E0479

Archaeological monitoring of borehole sample collection took place along the route of the Airport–Balbriggan/Northern Motorway Bypass between 5 and 16 October 1998. This involved examination of the cores for signs of archaeological activity, such as artefacts, charcoal etc. A record of any such finds and the depth at which they occurred was then taken.

As there were up to 300 boreholes scheduled to be dug along the route, monitoring was concentrated around those going through known archaeological sites and sites of archaeological potential. Up to sixteen such sites along an 11km stretch were previously identified through paper survey and field inspection.

Borehole investigations produced no evidence of archaeological activity. No specific archaeological layers or finds were observed. Occasional sherds of modern pottery were noted in the topsoil and ploughsoil layers, along with a small iron nail, also modern. Occasional small pieces of flint were also observed, but there was no evidence that these had been worked, and it is likely that they were naturally occurring.

Hilary Opie, 103 Cherrywood Drive, Clondalkin, Dublin 22.

118. THE ROYAL DUBLIN SOCIETY, SIMMONSCOURT ROAD, BALLSBRIDGE

Urban post-medieval
O183322
98E0016

An archaeological assessment followed by a stage of archaeological monitoring took place at the site of the proposed Four Seasons Hotel at the Royal Dublin Society at the corner of Merrion Road and Simmonscourt Road, Dublin 4. The assessment was carried out on 14–15 January 1998, and monitoring of groundworks was undertaken from 6 to 26 May 1998.

Both the assessment and monitoring episodes failed to reveal soils, features or deposits of archaeological potential. The initial stage of monitoring, along the Merrion Road side, revealed several post-medieval or early modern features, including red brick wall foundations and dump deposits comprising slag, cinder, iron fragments, patterned ceramics, glass bottles and butchered animal bone.

Three post-medieval features were uncovered in the northern corner of the eastern portion of the development area fronting onto Merrion Road. F1, 0.65m east of the north-west corner of the development area, consisted of a flat-based feature 0.5m wide and 0.68m deep, filled with black, humic soil containing a sherd of blackware. F2, 4m east from F1, was a large trench-like feature 1.8m wide and 1.7m deep containing red brick rubble and fragments of iron. F3, 3m east of F2, comprised a wall foundation of a structure (fronting onto Merrion Road) 2.7m wide and surviving to 0.65m high (situated *c.* 0.68m below old ground level). The wall foundations were constructed of red and occasionally yellow brick and were on average 0.35m wide and 0.65m high.

A large area comprising 19th- and early 20th-century waste was revealed within the eastern half of the development area. The deposit measured at least 25m north–south by 35m and was up to 2m deep. It seems likely that gravel quarrying had taken place in this area, which ultimately led to the filling in of the quarry pit(s) with locally generated domestic waste.

Ground reduction works within the south-west and south-east areas of the development did not reveal features, soils or artefacts of archaeological significance. There was a notable fall off in the number and quantity of post-medieval or early modern features, with the exception of modern drainage channels.

Malachy Conway, Margaret Gowen & Co. Ltd, 2 Killiney View, Albert Road Lower, Glenageary, Co. Dublin.

119. BALLYCULLEN

Two mounds
O126265
98E0076, 98E0077

In advance of construction of the Southern Cross Route Motorway testing was carried out on two features observed by aerial photography. A rectilinear mound, 27m x 25m, was tested under licence 98E0076. A circular mound, 10m in diameter, lay 60m to the south-east. This was tested under 98E0077.

Between 10 and 20 February trenches were dug in areas where the proposed motorway passed closest to the sites. Excavation showed that they had been largely destroyed by large-scale dumping from an adjoining housing estate. No archaeological features were discovered; however, fragments of a 13th-century belt-buckle were found in one trench near the rectilinear mound but were not associated with any feature.

Colin D. Gracie, 8 Abbeydale Close, Lucan, Co. Dublin, for Valerie J. Keeley Ltd.

120. BALLYFERMOT UPPER
Graveyard
30956 23322
SMR 18:31-04
98E0367

Archaeological test excavation was carried during October 1998 at the corner of Le Fanu Road and Raheen Road, Ballyfermot, Co. Dublin. The site lies in the townland of Ballyfermot Upper, within the registered area of three archaeological sites (SMR 18:31-01/03/04). These sites include Ballyfermot Castle, and Ballyfermot Church and Graveyard.

The castle, church and graveyard lie within Le Fanu Park. The park has been landscaped, and no standing remains of any of the monuments survive above ground, with the exception of a rectangular mound at the site of Ballyfermot Church. The foundation of the church dates to the 13th century, and it appears to have gone out of use in 1660 (Ball, *A history of County Dublin*, vol. 4, 101–6. 1906).

The test excavation was carried out in response to a proposed development that partially overlies the eastern fringes of Ballyfermot Graveyard. It uncovered the graveyard wall and articulated and disarticulated human remains within the boundary of the graveyard, which was used from the medieval period through to the beginning of this century (Johnston, *The ruins of the Church of St Laurence*, unpublished report held in the Ballyfermot Public Library, 1974), but no clear date was established for the burials uncovered. A wall was identified in Trench 1. Its location corresponds to the graveyard wall that surrounded the church. It appears that this boundary (the graveyard wall) turns sharply to the west between Trenches 1 and 2 and defines the extent of the burials on site. Trenches 2 and 3 appear to lie on the eastern side (outside) the graveyard wall. The deposits identified in Trench 3 record the landscaping of the graveyard in the 1970s.

Edmond O'Donovan, Margaret Gowen & Co. Ltd, Rath House, Ferndale Road, Rathmichael, Co. Dublin.

121. SOUTHERN CROSS MOTORWAY ROUTE, BALROTHERY/FIRHOUSE/SCHOLARSTOWN/ BALLYCULLEN/NEWTOWN/EDMONSTOWN/ TIBRADDEN/MARLEY GRANGE/TAYLOR'S GRANGE
Hearth, *fulacht fiadh*, bowl furnace
98E0206

Monitoring of topsoil removal was carried out between 23 April and 14 July 1998 along the route of the proposed motorway. Four features were discovered.

A hearth-type feature was excavated 10m from the site of Scholarstown 'Fairy Fort' (O117266). This was *c.* 0.8m in diameter and contained a number of granite stones, which had been burnt.

The second feature (O116266), a spread of burnt material containing black silt, burnt stone and charcoal fragments, was revealed to be a *fulacht fiadh*. A rectilinear pit 1.1m wide and 0.48m deep had been cut by a subcircular pit 2m long, 1.4m wide

and 0.6m deep. Beside this were the remains of a hearth and two linear concentrations of stake-holes—94 in total. The linear arrangement of stake-holes ran on either side of the rectilinear pit, and a number were clearly angled to form a tent-like structure over the pit.

The third site was another burnt spread also in Scholarstown townland (O119265). At the time of writing, this has yet to be excavated.

In the Tibradden townland a bowl furnace was found (O143257). It was 0.4m in diameter and contained numerous fragments of iron slag, as well as charcoal and burnt clay. Two saucer-shaped furnace bottoms of slag were discovered, one *in situ*, suggesting at least two phases of use. A fragment of copper was also found on the top of the feature.

Gaspipe-laying took place near the 'Brehon's Chair', Taylor's Grange, as part of the road scheme. Two fragments of flint were found during monitoring of this work.

Colin D. Gracie, 8 Abbeydale Close, Lucan, Co. Dublin, for Valerie J. Keeley Ltd.

122. SOUTHERN CROSS MOTORWAY ROUTE, BALROTHERY/BALLYCULLEN/EDMONDSTOWN/ KILMASHOGUE/TAYLOR'S GRANGE/ KELLYSTOWN
Pit
0311227 0316225
98E0206

From 17 August to 4 September 1998 monitoring of groundworks at Firhouse, at Ticknock and at College Road took place. One archaeological pit feature, in the same field as 'The Brehon's Chair' megalithic tomb, Taylor's Grange, was excavated, producing a sherd of coarseware pottery. The fill was burnt, and it is possible that some burning did occur within the pit. Two soil samples are to be analysed for possible seed remains.

Martin Reid for Valerie J. Keeley Ltd, 29/30 Duke Street, Athy, Co. Kildare.

123. 'THE BUNGALOW', ARDS, CABINTEELY
Cemetery site
SMR 26:119
98E0582

It is proposed to construct a rear extension and front porch to an existing dwelling, 'The Bungalow', Ards, Cabinteely, Co. Dublin. This bungalow rests on a registered cemetery site.

An excavation by Malachy Conway beneath the neighbouring Esso service station revealed *c.* 1500 human burials, ranging in date from the 5th/6th century to the 12th century (No. 124 below) The excavation also revealed that the cemetery had been enclosed by a succession of three ditches. Mr Conway projected that the inner ditch may have continued under the proposed extension and that the middle ditch may have crossed under the proposed porch.

The test excavation took place between 8 and 11 December 1998. The excavation comprised four hand-cut trenches (A, B, C and D), which failed to reveal any primary burial activity, suggesting that burials may be confined to the area south of the bungalow. In all, only three main features were exposed: a large ditch, a gully-like cut and part of a large cut feature.

Dublin

The origin and function of the ditch were unclear. It did not appear to follow the projected line of any of the three ditches uncovered during Mr Conway's excavation. The only find was a rotary quern fragment. The ditch cut into a series of sterile, orange/brown clays and sands. The gully-like feature appears to have been contemporary with the ditch but produced no finds. The test excavation failed to pick up the line of the inner ditch, but the large cut feature exposed in Test-trench D, at 0.8m below ground level (50.59m OD), may have been part of the cemetery's middle ditch.

Kenneth Hanley, 44 Eaton Heights, Cobh, Co. Cork.

124. MOUNT OFFALY, CABINTEELY
Early medieval enclosed cemetery
O233242
SMR 26:119
98E0035

The site, known locally as Mount Offaly, lies along the Dublin-bound carriageway of the N11, some 700m south-west of Cabinteely village. The topographic files of the National Museum of Ireland contain numerous references to the discovery of human remains from both the Mount Offaly site and adjacent properties. Two previous rescue excavations, at locations to the north and north-west of the site, recovered extended inhumations. The first was in 1957 when the NMI excavated a long cist containing an adult male inhumation with some additional female bones, and the second was by Raghnall Ó Floinn in 1991 when an unprotected inhumation was recovered from the root ball of a tree (*Excavations 1991*, 17). A pre-development assessment undertaken by Margaret Gowen in 1995 revealed at least fourteen *in situ* burials of early medieval date, as well as a sherd of Leinster cooking ware (*Excavations 1995*, 27–8).

The excavation of the site in advance of the construction of an Esso service station was undertaken from February to August 1998. This revealed a complex sequence of burial beginning at least in around the 5th or 6th century, culminating sometime in around the 11th or 12th century. At least 1553 individual burials were uncovered, along with numerous deposits of disarticulated remains and two charnel pits. Six broad phases of burial are at present proposed for the cemetery.

Phase 1 burial consists of at least twenty individuals, seven of which had associated grave-cuts, and two of which were in wood-lined (elm) graves . All Phase 1 burials were cut directly into the subsoil surface (sand to the south and gravel to the north of the site). In general these burials were well spaced and with clearly defined grave-cuts.

As the exact date of the Phase 1 burials has yet to be established it is unclear whether the cutting of the first enclosure ditch on the site took place before or after these burials. What is certain is that the inner ditch was filled in to facilitate the extension of the cemetery during Phase 3.

Phase 2 burial comprised at least 48 individuals, of which only three had surviving grave-cuts, while a fourth burial was contained within a grave comprising stone features. Phase 2 was also accompanied by a stone-lined socket, which may represent the position of a cemetery marker or grave alignment stone.

Phase 3 saw the filling in of the inner ditch and the excavation of a new enclosure ditch between 4.5m and 2m to the east. At least 120 individuals, of which five were interred in lintel graves and one in a stone-lined grave, represent this phase. The remaining burials were in earth-cut graves, and within this group four were accompanied by ear-muff stones and one had a stone component in the grave.

Phase 4 burial comprises at least 262 individuals and represents a marked increase in both the number of burials and the size of the area utilised within the enclosure. Several areas are, however, burial free, and these correspond with areas of stone cobble. Four of the lintel graves of Phase 3 were reopened and used for secondary burial. Eleven burials were found utilising ear-muff stones, and a further three had a stone feature or component to their interment.

Phase 5 represents another marked development in both the number of interments and the size of the enclosure. The middle ditch was filled in, and a third and final ditch was excavated 8.5m to the east of the former. At least 424 burials are represented for this phase, and of this number 33 burials had ear-muff stones and four had a small stone box or cist around the head. Only one of the head-cist burials contained a pillow stone (a large, flat, quartz pebble). As with the preceding phases, few clearly defined grave cuts survived (only eleven). A unique stone-lined charnel pit was uncovered, containing the remains of three individuals. The base of the charnel pit comprised an intact millstone.

Features within this phase included several areas of cobbles from which two bronze rings were recovered and, from the middle ditch, a furnace with associated hearth and dump deposits of metalworking debris, as well as a significant deposit of butchered animal bone, domestic waste and small finds.

Phase 6, the final phase, is characterised by the filling in of the outer ditch and the formation of a large cobbled surface, partly overlying the inner edge of the outer ditch. Test excavation immediately south of the surviving cobble failed to reveal any further continuation of the feature. However, as most of the archaeological deposits and burials from this area had been disturbed and/or removed during construction of the original garage in the 1930s, it is reasonable to assume that the cobble surface extended south. It is clear that the cobble forms a perimeter to the burial area; however, the reason for the filling in of the outer ditch and the utilisation of a cobbled area as the cemetery boundary is unclear.

Phase 6 consists of at least 450 burials of which over half are infants. Within Phase 6 sixteen grave-cuts survived, and of the total number of burials 57 have associated ear-muff stones and two have head cists. It may be possible to subdivide Phases 3 to 6 further. If successful, this may provide evidence that the site was used primarily as a kileen during its final phase.

Burials of Phases 1–2 and 4–6 were exclusively in earth-cut graves, which in many cases were not clearly visible owing to the numerous recuts and disturbance caused by successive interment. Many of the burials in earth-cut graves from Phase 3 through to Phase 6 had stones surrounding the head (ear-muff stones) or had the head surrounded by a stone setting resembling a head cist. In only one instance was a pillow stone used. Burial posture suggests that most of the interments were shrouded, and at least three large shroud-pins were recovered (although only one was directly associated with a burial).

Generally the burials were laid in the extended supine position with the head to the west; however, a number were aligned with the head to either the north or the east, and this group also included several prone burials and at least one crouched (cut into the middle ditch fill). Two female burials contained full-term foetuses, one of which was in the breach birth position. Other unusual burials include an adult male from Phase 3 with body in an extended supine position but with the skull turned around to quite literally face west.

At the time of writing, post-excavation analysis is ongoing, and so the results of the skeletal analysis to date have not been included in this summary. However, during excavation pathologies were noted when obvious, and these included a number of fractures, some showing signs of healing, dental and bone abscesses and compression fractures of the vertebrae. During post-excavation analysis a number of interesting features have become known, including at least one case of trepanation. A number of weapon injuries have been noted, in the case of one individual the nature of the attack can be illustrated. A diagonal 'sword' cut to his back extends from the upper vertebrae downwards and across the back of the left ribs. A fracture to the left arm was most probably incurred when the individual held it up to protect himself from a further blow, from either the left side or the front, by a blunt weapon, possibly the broad side of the sword or bladed weapon.

A large assemblage of small finds was recovered from the site. This includes ferrous and non-ferrous metal, stone, bone, glass and ceramic. A number of small finds were recovered directly associated with burials, e.g. three bone beads from separate infant burials, several pins including one iron shroud-pin and a number of iron knives. Most of the finds, however, were recovered from contexts within the burial horizon, and therefore some objects possibly represent material formerly associated with burials but disturbed by later recutting. Many artefacts of various types were recovered from contexts such as the enclosing inner and middle ditches. The finds assemblage includes shroud-pins, stick and possible ring-pins, iron knives, shears, gouges, D-shaped belt-buckles, nails, bone and blue glass beads, bone handles and double-sided bone combs, one of which retained both decorated panels (dot-and-circle) held in place by four iron rivets. The pottery assemblage includes fragments of Phocaean red slipware (which derives from a site/town in Turkey called Phocaea, from the late Roman period), Bi amphora, D-ware, E-ware and several perforated 'lids' of unknown origin. Sherds of locally made Leinster cooking ware, datable to the late 11th or early 12th century, were recovered from later site contexts.

In summary, the excavations have revealed a portion of an enclosed cemetery that, by the nature of the burial phases and succession of ditches, clearly reflects a sequential development or growth of the site. The large number of finds of funerary, domestic and industrial nature suggests that the site was not used exclusively for burial and religious practices. Along with producing objects interpreted as the mounts and fittings for possible shrines or reliquaries, it is suggested that the site had a dual religious and secular function. This is further highlighted by the large volume of butchered animal bone from the inner and middle ditches and the large (used) millstone derived from the base of the stone-lined charnel pit, as well as features such as the furnace and hearths. This clearly shows that agricultural and industrial activities were undertaken on (or very close to) the site. During at least two stages the area was possibly discontinued as a cemetery, and during these times cobbled surfaces were constructed (there is also tentative evidence of a structure) before the site reverted back to a burial-ground.

What is certain is that the range and type of objects recovered from the site, especially the imported pottery of 6th–7th-century date, suggests that the site is of considerable status and importance. The exact dimensions of the enclosure may only be estimated; however, it is reasonable to assume that within the boundary of the site lies evidence of perhaps a church, ancillary buildings, possible workshops and certainly further burials. The ongoing post-excavation work is expected to be completed by summer 1999, at which time samples will be submitted for radiocarbon determination in an effort closely to date the burial and site sequences.

Malachy Conway, Margaret Gowen & Co. Ltd, 2 Killiney View, Albert Road Lower, Glenageary, Co. Dublin.

125. CARRICKMINES–BRAY GAS PIPELINE, CARRICKMINES GREAT/LAUGHANSTOWN/ TIKNICK/RATHMICHAEL/SHANKILL/BALLYMAN
Wedge tomb, *fulachta fiadh*
98E0445

A number of sites were identified and excavated during the construction of a *Bord Gáis Éireann* pipeline in September–November 1998. The proposed route of the pipeline ran roughly north–south from Carrickmines to Bray. The townlands that the pipeline passed through included Carrickmines Great, Laughanstown, Tiknick, Rathmichael, Shankill and Ballyman in County Dublin, and Fassaroe, Kilbride, Kilcroney, Wingfield, Hollybrook and Ballywaltrin in County Wicklow.

Previously testing had been carried out by Eoin Sullivan on field systems (Dublin SMR 26:71) identified in Laughanstown/Tiknick townlands (*Excavations 1997*, 24–5, 97E360). As much of the area contained a stand of mature conifers any potential archaeological remains appear to have been disturbed during ground preparation and the planting of the trees.

In a number of areas narrow (less than 1m wide) roadside trenches were dug for the pipes, while on cross-country sections a *c.* 10m-wide corridor was stripped for construction. The roadside trenches were generally dug through deposits disturbed during the original road construction. There was no evidence that archaeological remains were disturbed by these sections of the pipelines. Pipes were laid alongside the roadway in Rathmichael townland and for practically all of the County Wicklow sections of the route.

On the cross-country sections six discrete archaeological sites were identified along with a number of early modern field drains. There had been no previous surface expression of any of the sites, which were identified during topsoil removal and then excavated to the limits of the pipeline corridor. The sites included four *fulachta fiadh*, a hearth of unknown date and a multi-period site that saw three phases of use including one that involved the construction of a wedge tomb.

Other areas of potential archaeological interest were two road crossings over the upper portion of Heronsford Lane (in Laughanstown/Tiknick townlands). As this runs to Tully Church, it may follow the line of an earlier road. It has been suggested that the upland (cross-country) portion of Heronsford Lane (which the pipe-trench cuts) dates to this period. Much of the surface had been eroded in the area of the road crossing and had been subsequently damaged by agricultural machinery. There appeared to be little chance of recovering any information from the two damaged sections.

Carrickmines Great
Fulacht fiadh
32134 22345
The site was originally identified during topsoil-stripping as a 7.5m (north–south) by 6m spread of burnt stone and charcoal in a loose, silty clay matrix (F1). It had been truncated by a field drain running north–south through the middle of F1. A pit (F3) was identified below the eastern portion of F1. It measured 0.95m (south-east/north-west) by 0.7m and was up to 0.42m deep. The pit was full of a deposit of burnt material that could not be distinguished from F1. A flake of struck flint was recovered from the interface between F1 and the subsoil, just east of F3.

Site 1, Rathmichael
Hearth site with associated post-holes
32290 22186
Just downslope from Site 2 in Rathmichael a hearth and a number of possible post-holes were identified alongside a French drain.

An irregularly shaped deposit of charcoal-rich topsoil overlay the hearth, which was up to 0.15m deep and measured *c*. 2m x 1.3m. A small number of granite boulders marked the area of the hearth itself. The natural clay in this area indicated that intense burning had taken place. This area of burning, as delineated by the stones, measured 0.8m x 0.4m. The post-holes did not form to any particular pattern, and only one was deep (0.23m).

Excavation yielded no obvious indications of the date of the site.

Site 2, Rathmichael
Fulacht fiadh
32291 22177
This site was uncovered upslope and some 50m south of Site 1, Rathmichael. It was initially identified as a spread of burnt stone (mostly granite) and charcoal across an area measuring 4m x 3m, which extended beyond the limits of the pipeline corridor. This was at most 0.25m deep except where it overlay a rectangular pit.

The pit was just over 1.9m long, 0.8m wide and 0.6m deep. A number of stones had been set around the upper edge as a form of kerbing. This mostly survived on the eastern side. There were no other features associated with this site, although a later French drain lay 10m to the south.

Site 1, Shankill
Probable fulacht fiadh
32345 22006
This site was noted as a spread of burnt material extending from the western limits of the pipe corridor. This spread of burnt stone (shale and granite) and charcoal extended for at least 6m east, into the pipeline corridor, and was at least 9m long (north–south). It was up to 0.4m deep. The natural subsoil below the site was irregular and appeared to have been altered in the past. There was no indication of any other features associated with this spread of material. A second spread of burnt material (Site 2) was present 10m to the north of the site.

Site 2, Shankill
Fulacht fiadh
32345 22006
There was one apparent phase of activity on this site. During this a spread of burnt stone (shale and granite) and charcoal accumulated, part of which was present within the pipe corridor. It extended for at least 7m east, into the pipeline corridor, and was at least 8m long (north–south). This deposit was up to 0.4m deep. The natural subsoil below the site was irregular and appeared to have been altered in the past. There was a rectangular trough associated with this spread of material, lying down the slope to the east. A second spread of material (Shankill, Site 1, above) was present 10m to the south of the site.

The trough had been truncated by a field drain but originally measured *c*. 1.8m x 1.3m and was 0.5m deep. Two post-holes were identified in the surviving corners, suggesting that there had originally been a wooden lining that was deliberately removed in the past or had since rotted away.

Site 3, Shankill
Fulacht fiadh, wedge tomb
32399 22061
There were four phases of activity on site. The earliest probably saw the construction of a subrectangular hut, a cobbled area and a trough. Both the by-products from the firing of the trough and a layer of clay sealed these. The layer of clay that sealed the Phase 1 activity also formed the main construction element of the mound of the wedge tomb, built in Phase 2 of the use of the site. This was in turn buried by the debris from the firing of a second trough in Phase 3. This later trough lay just to the south of the earlier one. The final phase saw the insertion of field drains and the digging of a boundary ditch in the early modern period.

Phase 1, fulacht fiadh
Phase 1 was marked by an oval (1.5m x 1.1m x 0.3m deep) trough sealed by a deposit of clay (F14) that also sealed a number of deposits of burnt stone and charcoal, a cobbled area (F18) and a line of stake-holes.

A subrectangular hut site, identified at the

northern limits of the cobbled area, also appears to be contemporary with it. This suggests that this phase saw the use of a trough alongside a cobbled area and hut site. The stake-holes began parallel to the trough and may have acted as some form of windbreak or screen at the southern end of the cobbled area, shielding the site from the prevailing winds.

The trough had been excavated down to the local shale bedrock and appeared to fill freely with water, which percolated through the beds of shale. A sticky, grey clay, heavily stained with charcoal, filled the trough.

The area of stake-holes measured 3.6m (north–south) by 2.1m and was defined by an oval setting of stake-holes. There was no indication of the presence of an entrance, other than an ill-defined gap in the south-eastern corner. The presence of multiple lines of stake-holes in some places suggested that there were a number of phases of reuse of the site for some form of light hut or tent structure.

The cobbled area measured roughly 4.2m (north–south) by 2.4m and lay between the hut and the line of stake-holes. The cobbles were mainly pebbles and boulders of local shale, with some quartz and granite. A single large granite boulder sat at the middle of the eastern side of the cobbled area. A metal disc (20mm diameter) and a flint flake were found among the cobbles. The metal disc appears to be a coin, possibly of early date, and is likely to be intrusive.

The deposit of burnt stone and charcoal that overlay F18 measured 8m (north–south) by 3m and was up to 0.4m deep. This too had been sealed by F14 and was present below the gallery of the Phase 2 wedge tomb.

Phase 2, wedge tomb
Some time after the Phase 1 use of the site a megalithic structure was constructed incorporating a gallery into a mound, which covered the Phase 1 trough, the stake-holes, part of F18 and F16. The mound was a continuous deposit of silty clay, into which the orthostats of the gallery had been set. Its maximum identified dimensions were 14m (north–south) by 9m. In the area south of the gallery F14 had been heavily stained with charcoal, while north of the gallery it was mid-brown The mounded deposit of F16 had been sealed with the mid-brown clay (F14) to the north-east of the gallery.

Within the gallery a number of stones and the remains of the cairn had sealed the floor layer, which was a continuation of F14, containing a single irregular lens of charcoal. There was no indication of burials or artefacts. Within the gallery F14 sealed a thin remaining spread of F16.

The floor level of the gallery (F14) contained a small number of granite boulders, up to 0.4m long, although their significance could not be determined.

The ground level had been lowered at the rear of the gallery, suggesting that a pit had been excavated into which the back end of the gallery was inserted. This commenced level with the junction between the first and second easternmost orthostats on the opposing walls of the gallery. The back end incorporated the western closing slab. It is possible that the source of some of F14 was the material that had been excavated from the subsoil to enable the insertion of the tomb.

The main components of the megalithic structure are a gallery of roughly parallel side-walls, orientated on an east–west axis, and a closely set outer walling. The stones are set within an irregular mound (of F14) rather than sockets. Two buttress stones are present towards the eastern end of the gallery, where they rest against the outer walling. Neither could be definitely claimed to be functional. The gallery and the mound material around the orthostats were not excavated, leaving these features in their original position.

There was a gap in the mound at the eastern end of the gallery, identifying this end as the front of the structure. The western end of the gallery is sealed by a low orthostat, and the whole structure had been placed within an artificial depression. This had been excavated into sloping ground. The orthostats in the northern wall of the gallery were noticeably higher than those in the southern wall. Traces of a cairn were present around and within the western end of the gallery. There were no surviving traces of a capstone.

Externally the gallery is some 2.35m long and measures 3.4m across at the eastern end and 1.5m across at the western end. Internally it is 1.95m long, tapering from 1.42m across at the eastern end to 0.96m across at the western end.

The mound surrounding the gallery was not fully examined as the eastern end lay beyond the limits of the site, where it is likely to have been heavily disturbed by a field boundary ditch. Its maximum identifiable width was 14m, and it was at least 9m long. The gap in the eastern end of the mound was 2.14m wide and was at least 1.65m long. It was positioned directly in front of the opening at the eastern end of the gallery. The east-facing entrance is similar to those at nearby wedge tombs at Carrickgolligan and Laughanstown.

Phase 3, fulacht fiadh
The final prehistoric phase on the site saw the construction of a second trough, just south of that of Phase 1. There was also a 23m (north–south) by 12m spread of charcoal and burnt stone associated with the use of this trough. This spread of burnt material also sealed the gallery of the wedge tomb to a depth of 0.7m.

The trough was *c.* 1.9m in diameter, and the southern half of the edge had a kerbing of granite boulders. This trough was unlined, *c.* 0.3m deep and had been cut into a natural spring, which could still refill the trough within 30 minutes of its being completely emptied.

Phase 4, 18th- and 19th-century agricultural improvements
During the last two centuries a boundary ditch and field drains were added to the eastern end of the site. During or before this period ploughing across the site also disturbed the upper levels of the archaeological deposits and scored orthostats of the wedge tomb.
John Ó Néill, for Margaret Gowen & Co. Ltd, 2 Killiney View, Albert Road Lower, Glenageary, Co. Dublin.

126. CARRICKMINES AND JAMESTOWN
Pits, *fulachta fiadh* and Pale Ditch
O21352429, O21192400, O20502433
98E0119
Topsoil-stripping associated with a new foul sewer

outfall in the Ballyogan Tiphead area of County Dublin between 20 April and 8 June 1998 uncovered two new archaeological features and occasioned an assessment of the Pale Ditch.

The first feature lay in Carrickmines townland and comprised two small pits, one of which was associated with burnt bone (O21352429). The second feature, in the adjacent townland of Jamestown, was a *fulacht fiadh* (O21192400). Both sites were excavated. A sample of timber from the *fulacht fiadh* returned a dendrochronological date of 2852 BC±9.

A test-trench was opened across the Pale Ditch in advance of the sewer pipe that crosses it in Jamestown (O20502433). The boundary lay undisturbed below a modern laneway. It was subsequently fully excavated by Martin Reid under the same licence (see No. 204 below).

Niall Brady, 'Rosbeg', Ard Mhuire Park, Dalkey, Co. Dublin, for Valerie J. Keeley Ltd.

127. SCIENCE AND TECHNOLOGY PARK, CHERRYWOOD

Multi-period
32425 22322
SMR 26:27
98E0526

This work was carried out at the location of part of the proposed Science and Technology Park at Cherrywood, Co. Dublin. An enclosure had previously been identified on the site from an aerial photograph. As part of pre-development assessment of this area of the site, geophysical survey and testing was carried out to identify the location of this enclosure.

Five test-trenches were opened across a number of anomalies identified in a magnetometer survey, which was carried out by GeoArc Ltd. These anomalies were almost all geological or modern in nature. There was no evidence of an enclosure such as that identified on the aerial photograph.

Ten discrete archaeological features and sites were examined in the area subsequently stripped for construction. These were numbered Cherrywood 1 to Cherrywood 10. Two were non-archaeological in nature (Sites 1 and 9). Four were isolated features, mostly of unknown date. The four other sites included two *fulachta fiadh*, two burials within an enclosing ditch, and a group of post-holes probably representing a structure. The sites were mainly identified during topsoil-stripping, although Sites 2 and 3 were revealed in a test-trench. Many of the archaeological sites, such as Sites 5, 6, 7 and 10, were probably too small to have shown up on the geophysical survey.

The area examined focused on a low hill overlooking the N11 and the Shanaganagh River to the east and the eastern side of a narrow glen down to the Loughlinstown River to the west. The area to the north had been developed previously and had been examined by Linzi Simpson (*Excavations 1995*, 27, 94E201) and Ed O'Donovan (*Excavations 1997*, 25, 97E279). The area to the south is bounded by the Loughlinstown River.

Geophysical surveys and testing are to take place in 1999 in other areas of the Science and Technology Park.

Site 2: prehistoric round house?
Site 2 was discovered during manual test-trenching in the western part of Test-trench 2. Three post-holes were revealed under the topsoil, and the trench was expanded to the south, south-west and north, where eighteen more post-holes were found. The structure measured 8m x 6m, at 36.3m OD. The eastern part of the structure proved to have been destroyed by later disturbance, leaving three truncated post-holes. An elongated and irregularly shaped pit lay to the east of the semicircle of post-holes. A deposit of stones disturbed the northern part of the structure, where no further post-holes could be found. The remaining post-holes form a semicircle around a central post-hole, with a gap between two post-holes in the south-east, possibly indicating an entrance into the structure. No evidence of date or finds were recovered from the features associated with this site.

A number of finds were recovered from the topsoil, mostly burnt and unburnt flint (no artefacts), as well as two fragments of prehistoric pottery and a broken rubbing stone. Some modern sherds of pottery and nails were also found in the vicinity of the site.

Site 3: fulacht fiadh
On a west-facing slope in the south-western corner of the field a 24m (north–south) by 9m *fulacht fiadh* was identified along with features relating to the Loughlinstown military camp. The site was immediately west of geophysical anomaly D, initially identified as a linear feature, which may have been a shadow image of the eastern limits of the site. The site was disturbed along its western side by a former lane dating back to at least the 1790s, when the military camp was in use. The site lay between *c.* 34.2m and 35.82m OD.

An 8ft by 6ft rectangular platform was uncovered just to the east of the *fulacht fiadh*. The platform had been dug into the slope, and only two shale flagstones and a narrow gully at the rear remained of what may have been a timber guard-post. This would have been an outpost along the lane leading into the camp, which is supposed to have lain further north of the development. The sunken base of the platform had been backfilled with topsoil that contained some fragments of animal bone and a 1792 Duke of Lancaster halfpenny token.

The mound of the *fulacht fiadh* had been levelled at this time, as a midden of material, including animal bone, was scattered amongst material that overlay a deposit of topsoil, sealing parts of the *fulacht fiadh*. This included another 1792 halfpenny token, from Camac, Ryan and Camac.

The main deposit of burnt material, F81, overlay a series of features related to the use of the site as a *fulacht fiadh*. Two deposits below F81, F82 and F83 (below F82) were also identified, although they were no more than a few centimetres deep. A number of other features were recorded below F81, including a series of lines of stake-holes, and post-holes and a shallow gully. It is unclear whether any of these should be seen as structural. It is likely that F83 and F82 were the same layer, with F83 only occurring at the interface between F82 and the natural. The area around the site appears to have been stripped of topsoil at the time of use, so these deposits are likely to be contemporary with the use of the site, as is F81.

Eight troughs were identified on the site, along with two possible troughs disturbed by the lane. All were circular or subcircular and unlined. The diameters ranged from 1.2m to 2m, and they were 0.3–0.8m deep. Several appeared to have been cut into natural springs. Hearths were identified as a number of circular areas of burnt clay beside the troughs.

Two field drains had been dug through the site (north–south), removing any direct stratigraphic relationship between F81, F82 and F83 and the troughs. Most of the trough had been backfilled with material indistinguishable from F81.

A series of finds was recovered from F81, F82 and F83. Only undecorated coarseware (Lough Gur Class II) was recovered from the lowest level (F83). Both decorated and undecorated pottery was recovered from F82, along with some worked flint. The pottery was mainly Lough Gur Class II-style undecorated coarseware with simple rims, a tulip-shaped profile and flat bases (Knockadoon variant). A single sherd of decorated (Beaker?) pottery was recovered at this level. The main deposit of burnt material (F81) contained a number of sherds of AOC comb-incised Beaker pottery, along with more of the Lough Gur Class II ware.

Flint flakes, debitage and hammerstones were also recovered from this deposit. A number of flint artefacts were recovered from the disturbed area of the lane and the interface between F81 and the natural at the north of the site. These included three intact javelinheads (62mm, 78mm and 118mm long), a broken and unfinished one and a leaf-shaped arrowhead (45mm long). A side-scraper and a double-ended scraper/hollow scraper were also recovered from this area.

Butchered animal bone was recovered from the upper (midden and topsoil) levels of the site. In only one instance could bone (an ovicaprid tooth) be associated with the *fulacht fiadh* phase.

Site 4: ring-barrow

This site was discovered during stripping of topsoil in the northern part of the site. It lies on the flat ridge, to the west of Site 5. The barrow is circular, while the width of the ring-ditch varies owing to the irregular outer edge of the ditch. It has an internal diameter of *c.* 8.5m. The site lies at 39.05m OD.

The barrow had been built by creating a mound (F71) in the centre of a ring-ditch (F51), probably using the material excavated from the ditch. The mound was up to 0.3m deep, and the ditch was up to 0.6m deep. There were no surviving traces of an external bank.

A rectangular cut in the ground surface below F71 was orientated north-north-west/south-south-east, measured 2.35m by 0.7m and was up to 0.3m deep. This was filled by the same material that had been mounded up in the centre (F71). Within the mound was a supine juvenile inhumation, lying alongside the rectangular cut and parallel to it. The burial was in poor condition, and there was no indication of a formal grave-cut.

A sub-square pit (F77) had also been dug into F71, measuring *c.* 0.8m² and *c.* 0.6m deep. At the base of this pit was a circle of stones containing five cattle teeth.

The central mound was capped with a layer of

clay that contained a pit cremation and a number of small spreads of charcoal. There was a small amount of fragmentary burnt human bone in the cremation, suggesting token deposition.

Within the ring-ditch the primary fill was a discontinuous lens of charcoal that also contained a large number of fragments of burnt bone, including some immediately identifiable skull and long bone fragments. The quantity of this material suggests that it may represent pyre debris.

Burnt human and animal bone and disarticulated animal bone was distributed irregularly but appeared in various densities throughout the ring-ditch. The faunal remains include cattle teeth and shed antler.

Pieces of struck flint were found (mainly at the four cardinal points), including two thumbnail scrapers, which suggest a possible Bronze Age date.

Site 5: Burnt pit

This site was revealed during topsoil-stripping on 20 November 1998 as a subcircular feature, 0.58m east–west by 0.5m. The depth was 0.18m, at 37.82m OD. The pit had shallow, sloping sides and a concave and irregular base, defined by fire-hardened/heated red clay, showing *in situ* burning. The fill contained dark brown/black, peaty clay with lumps of charcoal and staining. The fill was mottled with yellow/brown clay and particles of fired, red clay. Some unburnt limestone was also found in the fill. The date of the site is unknown.

Three pieces of flint were recovered, one of which had been burnt.

Site 6: burnt pit/cremation

This site was discovered during topsoil-stripping on 27 November 1998 and lies at the flat top of the gentle ridge. It is subcircular in plan, 0.15m in diameter and 0.09m deep, at 40.04m OD. The sides of the pit are shallow, and the base is concave. The fill contains a moderate amount of burnt bone in charcoal-stained, grey/black, silty clay and some small stones and grits. The stones appear unburnt.

Directly to the south of the pit is an area of fire-reddened clay as a surface spread, measuring 0.15m x 0.2m. The date of the site is unknown, although it is likely to be Bronze Age.

Site 7: pit with animal bones

Site 7 was discovered during stripping of topsoil on the flat ridge that forms the upper part of the field. A crescent-shaped pit was uncovered, which contained some disarticulated animal bone and charcoal.

The crescent-shaped feature measures 0.6–0.7m (north–south) by 2.7m and is 0.48m deep, cutting into natural. Occasional flecks of charcoal occurred in the top of the fill, which consisted of brown clay overlying brown/orange, silty clay. The date of this feature is unknown.

The fill contained a large amount of unburnt animal bone and teeth of mixed species, one piece of struck flint and one piece of worked chert.

Site 8: fulacht fiadh

Site 8 lies on a west-facing slope and appeared as an irregularly shaped deposit of burnt stone (100% granite, up to 0.25m long) and charcoal. The site was sealed by topsoil and overlies natural. The overall dimensions of the spread are 7.1m (north–south) by 3.6m; the depth was up to 0.23m at 33.95m OD. Later disturbance was apparent to the east of the site, and in the west a cobble-filled field drain cuts the site in a north–south direction.

A trough lay below the north-eastern corner of the burnt spread. It had been truncated in the north-eastern corner by original removal of topsoil for the drain-cut. The trough had two phases of use: the original trough and the later recut. The original trough measures 1.8m (south-west/north-east) by 0.5m and is up to 0.8m deep. It was filled with a deposit of sticky, grey clay, which contained burnt granite, charcoal and other burnt stone fragments. The stone was consistently <15–20% of the matrix. Four surviving post-holes appeared in the corners of the trough. The recut trough measured 2.05m (north-east/south-west) by 1.35m and was up to 0.6m deep. Post-holes from the original lining were visible along the long sides of the trough, five on each side.

A number of topsoil finds were recovered from the vicinity of the site, of which the cattle bone appeared to represent the most recent interment. There were no datable finds, but the site is probably Bronze Age in date.

Site 10: burnt pit/hearth
This single pit was discovered during topsoil-stripping. An oval feature was set into natural and appears to have been burnt *in situ*. It measures 2m (north-north-east/south-south-west) by 0.9m and 0.12m deep, at 38.54m OD. The base is concave, and the sides are shallow with a gradual break in slope. The fill was mixed, with grey/brown, silty clay, charcoal-rich clay and fired/heated, orange/red clay. A number of large burnt/heated stones (<0.2m), mostly granite and smaller fragments of rotted limestone, were found in the fill.

Fragments of burnt bone and a possible quernstone were found in the fill.
John Ó Néill, for Margaret Gowen & Co. Ltd, 2 Killiney View, Albert Road Lower, Glenageary, Co. Dublin.

128. CHERRYWOOD AND LAUGHANSTOWN
Prehistoric/post-medieval
O240235
97E0279
Archaeological monitoring was carried out on a 5ha site at Cherrywood and Laughanstown, Co. Dublin, in advance of topsoil-stripping associated with a housing development. Eleven sites were identified during the monitoring, in addition to those revealed during 1997 (*Excavations 1997*, 25–6). They ranged in date from the prehistoric to the post-medieval period and varied in function from cremation burials to hearths. The sites were identified through the presence of charcoal and dated by association or morphology. Intensive agricultural activity was carried on throughout the stripped area, and all of the sites were truncated by ploughing. The sites identified were all cut features, and no linear stratified deposits survived above the old ground surface, with the exception of Site O, which survived in a slight depression.

Prehistoric cremation burials: sites I, L, P and R
Four pits containing cremated human bone were

identified during monitoring. All of the sites lay along the spine of a ridge that runs north-west/south-east. Sites L and R contained a large quantity of cremated human bone. Sites I and P contained token cremated remains. Three of the sites (I, L and R) lay within 60m of each other at the south-eastern end of the ridge. Site P lay 320m to the north-west and was an isolated burial. The burials consisted of simple pits *c.* 0.5m in diameter and 0.4m deep filled with cremated bone and charcoal; no pottery or other finds were associated with the burials. Large areas surrounding the burials were cleaned back with a mechanical excavator, but no further burials were revealed.

Prehistoric pits: sites H, J, M, N and Q
These sites were identified as darker soils overlying the glacial boulder clay that covers the hillside. In all cases the soils contained charcoal and were deposited into features cut into the boulder clay. The features were initially dated to the prehistoric period by the association of worked flint, including debitage and work tools, such as the flint scraper found adjacent to Site N and the sherds of coarseware retrieved from the fill in Site H. The features found at Site N may be tree-root balls. Recent arable activity (ploughing) has removed the original ground surface; hence the features are all truncated.

Post-medieval hearth and cobbling: sites K and O
These sites were identified by the presence of dark soils overlying the boulder clay on the ridge. In all cases the soils contained burnt cinders surviving in features cut into the boulder clay. Ploughing had completely removed the original ground surface, with the exception of a small area in an infilled hollow on the hillside excavated at Site O.
Edmond O'Donovan, Margaret Gowen & Co. Ltd, Rath House, Ferndale Road, Rathmichael, Co. Dublin.

129. KILCARBERRY DISTRIBUTION PARK, NANGOR, CLONDALKIN
Monitoring
98E0572
The development is for the provision of infra-structural works to serve an industrial distribution park. Monitoring was requested as a condition to any planning permission. Reference to the SMR reveals the presence of a number of recorded monuments within the general landscape, although there are no known sites within the proposed development area.

Monitoring, ongoing at time of writing, has failed to note any archaeological features on the site, with the exception of one 1m-wide north–south modern field drain. Finds have been restricted to the north-west corner of the site but include only sherds of post-medieval pottery along with several sherds of modern pottery, all recovered from the topsoil.

Removal of topsoil has revealed limestone bedrock across the site, with occasionally a natural layer of friable, mid-grey, fine, silty clay with moderate stone inclusions sealing the bedrock layer and sealed by topsoil.
Dermot Nelis, Irish Archaeological Consultancy Ltd, 8 Dungar Terrace, Dun Laoghaire, Co. Dublin.

Dublin

130. 1–7 (REAR OF) ST AGNES ROAD, CRUMLIN
Medieval ditches and fields
O121317
98E0362

This assessment was carried out in August 1998. Eight trenches were opened by mechanical excavator in the open area to the rear of Nos 1–7 St Agnes Road. The site is adjacent to a medieval church, which sits within a round enclosure, suggesting that it could be of early medieval origin.

The assessment revealed a ditch outside and concentric to the boundary of the churchyard. No datable finds were recovered from it. Inside the ditch two pits containing burnt material were revealed. They are likely to be of medieval date.

Outside the ditch the trenching revealed the presence of poorly preserved medieval ridge and furrow cultivation. The furrows were spaced 2m or 4m apart, and their silty fills contained occasional sherds of locally made medieval pottery.
Alan Hayden, Archaeological Projects Ltd, 25A Eaton Square, Terenure, Dublin 6W.

131. CASTLE STREET, DALKEY
Urban medieval
O264268
98E0122

An archaeological assessment was requested by the developer before a planning application to develop the site, which lay to the south of the church park off Castle Street, Dalkey. Six trenches were mechanically excavated within the footprint of the proposed development on 9–10 March 1998.

Trench 1 ran along the western boundary of the site and revealed a small spread of white mortar that appeared to have been *in situ*. Trench 3, to the north-east of the site, ran north–south. It contained the remains of a compact mortar surface 7.1m long (0.9m from present ground level) and a small east–west-orientated granite field drain, 0.5m wide. Trench 4 lay to the south of Trench 3 and ran east–west. This contained a granite drain identical to that in Trench 3, associated with 18th/19th-century pottery, which cut the natural boulder clay.

Inspection of the stratigraphic profiles of all the excavated trenches indicates widespread modern disturbance across the whole site. The entire ground level of the site had been raised by modern deposition, with an average depth of *c.* 1.15m, increasing to the north. This dumping possibly occurred as a result of the construction of the carpark and the houses to the north.

All the soils immediately above the natural boulder clay appear to date, at the earliest, to the later post-medieval period. A light yellow/brown clay that occurred across the site appeared similar to some form of ploughsoil but contains later inclusions such as white ware and plastic.

With the exception of the mortar spread in Trench 1, only Trench 3 yielded any feature of archaeological interest, in the form of a compact mortar surface that may possibly have been associated with some form of structure. In the absence of any dating material first impressions suggest that it is probably post-medieval in date.
Rob Lynch, for M. Gowen & Co. Ltd, 2 Killiney View, Albert Road Lower, Glenageary, Co. Dublin.

132. CASTLE STREET/ULVERTON ROAD, DALKEY
Urban medieval
O263269
98E0182

This site, at the corner of Castle Street and Ulverton Road, is immediately adjacent to the recorded site of one of Dalkey's urban tower-house castles. The proposed development involved the refurbishment of a two-storey retail building and the construction of an extension covering its entire rear garden. The building survey found that the existing building was 19th century in date and incorporated no earlier fabric.

Two test-trenches revealed that undulating bedrock lay very close to the surface right across most of the site but that it shelved away quite steeply towards its eastern boundary. The garden had been created by filling the deep clefts in the rock with rubble and then raising the level (relative to the street level) by the introduction of garden soil. At the north-eastern corner of the site the bedrock surface lay 700–800mm below street level, rising sharply to just 300mm in a westerly direction; it broke the surface at the south of the site. The surface of the lower portion of rock exposed possessed the very scant remains of a highly compacted, yellow shell-mortar adhering to it. The mortar of the rubble fill was a sandy, grey/white mortar. With the similar Goat's Castle built on bedrock, and with no other evidence of any medieval activity whatsoever, this very thin layer of mortar was the only evidence on the site to suggest that a medieval structure (founded on bedrock—and completely cleared after demolition) may have extended into the north-eastern extremity of the site.
Margaret Gowen, 2 Killiney View, Albert Road Lower, Glenageary, Co. Dublin.

133. 21/22 ST PATRICK'S ROAD, DALKEY
Adjacent to site of castle
O266269
98E0002

Three test-trenches were opened in this small development site in Dalkey village.

The surface material related to modern demolition rubble sitting on the remains of a concrete floor. Underlying this a deposit of silty clay was revealed. Finds of a modern nature were associated with this deposit. Boulder clay was present below this silty clay.

No features or finds of an archaeological nature were revealed on the site.
Avril Purcell, Margaret Gowen & Co. Ltd, 2 Killiney View, Albert Road Lower, Glenageary, Co. Dublin.

134. MEÁNSCOIL IOGNAID RÍS CBS, DRIMNAGH CASTLE, DRIMNAGH
Vicinity of medieval castle
O11063176
SMR 18:36
98E0183

Test excavations took place over a number of days on the site of a proposed extension to the existing Scoil Iognaid Rís CBS, Drimnagh Castle, in response to a planning condition. The proposed extension will be *c.* 40m south-west of Drimnagh Castle in an area where a 17th-century bastion may have stood.

Two trenches were excavated in the areas of maximum anticipated disturbance. A stone-surfaced trackway of 17th/18th-century date, oriented south-west/north-east, was uncovered in Trench 1. Evidence of post-medieval ploughing was also uncovered. No earlier features were found within the test-trenches.

In view of the possibility of further archaeological remains surviving on the site of the proposed extension, archaeological monitoring of subsurface works associated with the development has been recommended.

James Eogan, Archaeological Development Services Ltd, Windsor House, 11 Fairview Strand, Fairview, Dublin 3.

135. ST PATRICK'S COLLEGE, DRUMCONDRA

Environs of 17th-century house
316000 236816
SMR 18:12
98E0604

A programme of archaeological trial-trenching was undertaken on 21 December 1998 for the Department of Education at the site of a proposed Education Centre in the grounds of St Patrick's Training College. The work was undertaken in compliance with conditions attached to the grant of planning in respect of the proposed development.

The area of development lies *c.* 100m south of the former Belvedere House, a 17th-century house with 18th/19th-century additions, which is now incorporated into the college. Three other sites of interest lie in the general environs of the development: Drumcondra House (SMR 18:14), an early Georgian house dating to *c.* 1725; a medieval church and graveyard site (SMR 18:13) associated with the Priory of All Saints and upon which the present St John the Baptist Church was erected in 1743; and a castle site dating to *c.* 1560. The first two sites lie in the College of All Hallows, and the last in St Joseph's School for Visually Impaired Boys.

Six trenches, ranging from 20m to 50m long, were mechanically excavated. No features were revealed, although two sherds of post-medieval pottery and a fragment of a possible 18th-century clay pipe bowl were recovered.

Martin E. Byrne, 39 Kerdiff Park, Monread, Naas, Co. Kildare.

136. AUGUSTINE STREET/16–17 JOHN STREET WEST, DUBLIN

Urban medieval
O148340
97E0343

Archaeological monitoring and subsequent excavation was carried out at Augustine Street, Block 1, from December 1997 for a period of nine weeks. A number of red brick-lined post-medieval pits and drains were found to overlie extended inhumations. These inhumations in turn overlay medieval pits.

A second season of archaeological excavations commenced in April 1998 and continued for twelve weeks. Post-medieval drains, possible tanning-pits, medieval pits and cobbled surfaces were identified, together with 168 extended inhumations.

The finds recovered included modern, post-medieval and medieval pottery, medieval floor tiles, flint, a wooden barrel, a possibly medieval wicker basket, animal bones, wood, shroud-pins, coins and miscellaneous iron and copper fragments.

The burial activity appears to be associated with St John the Baptist hospital site.

Una Cosgrave, Archaeological Development Services Ltd, Windsor House, 11 Fairview Strand, Fairview, Dublin 3.

137. BAGGOT LANE, DUBLIN

No archaeological significance
O183322
98E0212

The development site is in the immediate vicinity of SMR 6:38, a castle site that is thought to have stood close to 12 Pembroke Road (Kelly, D., *Four roads to Dublin* 1996, 35). The castle was the chief residence of the manor of Baggotrath and is believed to have been constructed in the early 14th century. It was partly destroyed in 1649 and was later attacked again. No attempt was made to restore the castle following these events, and the expansion of the city of Dublin in the 19th century required the removal of the castle remains.

Monitoring of groundworks was undertaken in May 1998 at the site of a proposed two-storey mews house at Baggot Lane, to the rear of 9 St Mary's Road. Four foundation trenches up to 1.5m deep were excavated, initially by hand and later by mechanical digger, within an area formerly used as a garden. The foundation trenches revealed a sequence of black soil containing red brick and cinder (0–0.4m), mottled, orange clay containing stones (0.4–0.9m), and grey-brown, compact clay (0.9–1.5m+). The development did not expose or remove any features or artefacts of archaeological significance.

Malachy Conway, Margaret Gowen & Co. Ltd, 2 Killiney View, Albert Road Lower, Glenageary, Co. Dublin.

138. CROPPIES ACRE, BENBURB STREET, DUBLIN

Possible graveyard
31418 23435
SMR 18:020447
98E0268

Testing was undertaken, on behalf of the Office of Public Works, to determine the impact that the groundworks associated with the proposed 1798 Commemorative Park at this site would have on any surviving remains, in particular on the documented mass burial-ground.

It is a commonly held tradition that in the aftermath of the 1798 rebellion courts martial were held at the Royal Barracks (now Collins Barracks) and that those who were subsequently executed were buried in an unmarked burial pit in what was to later become known as the Croppies Acre. There are two 19th-century accounts purporting to show the precise location of the Croppies Acre; these accounts were written at least 40 years after the executions took place.

In view of the sensitive nature of the site all cuttings were hand-excavated. Twelve test-pits measuring 2m x 2m were opened. The stratigraphy revealed in the test-pits was consistent, showing three distinct phases of activity. Phase I contained layers associated with the playing fields and the public park of the Esplanade. Phase II was layers associated with the levelling of previous buildings, the use of the area as a dump and the construction of the quay. Phase III contained organic/riverine deposits, identified at the base of all cuttings. These formed most likely because of flooding from the River Liffey.

There is no archaeological evidence to support the contention that the mass burial is within the area tested.

Rónán Swan, Arch-Tech Ltd, 32 Fitzwilliam Place, Dublin 2.

139. 15A BISHOP STREET, DUBLIN
Urban medieval
O155335
98E0441

An archaeological assessment was carried out in advance of lodging a planning application. Two trenches were opened by mechanical digger on 7 November 1998. The stratigraphy was uniform across the site, consisting of late building rubble over a yellow/brown, pure clay. There was no evidence of any archaeological material or finds.

Helen Kehoe, c/o Margaret Gowen & Co. Ltd, 2 Killiney View, Albert Road Lower, Glenageary, Co. Dublin.

140. 6–7 BOW LANE WEST, DUBLIN
Urban medieval
98E0129

Pre-development archaeological testing was carried out on this site in April 1998. Nothing of archaeological significance was identified.

Una Cosgrave, Archaeological Development Services Ltd, Windsor House, 11 Fairview Strand, Fairview, Dublin 3.

141. ST PATRICK'S HOSPITAL, BOW LANE/ STEPHEN'S LANE, DUBLIN
No archaeological significance
O136338
98E0363

The assessment was carried out in August 1998. Three trenches were opened by mechanical excavator. No deposits or features earlier then the 19th century were uncovered.

Alan Hayden, Archaeological Projects Ltd, 25A Eaton Square, Terenure, Dublin 6W.

142. IVEAGH HOSTEL, BRIDE ROAD, DUBLIN
Urban medieval
O152337
98E0218

The site lies to the rear of the Iveagh Hostel. Permission has been granted for the construction of an extension to the hostel. The site is within the zone of archaeological potential of Dublin; under a condition of the planning permission the Iveagh Trust was required to have test-trenching carried out in advance of construction. A single trench, 19m long, was excavated by mechanical digger to a maximum depth of 2.6m on the site of the proposed extension.

A charcoal-flecked, brown, silty clay was found over the northern 8m of the trench. Eight sherds of medieval pottery were found in this layer. The medieval layer has been cut away by 19th-century activity in the southern part of the trench. The layer containing the medieval pottery is 1m below the proposed finished floor level of the extension and will not be affected by the proposed development.

A small excavation will be carried out in early 1999 to further investigate the medieval soils found in this assessment.

James Eogan, Archaeological Development Services Ltd, Windsor House, 11 Fairview Strand, Fairview, Dublin 3.

143. BRIDE STREET, DUBLIN
Urban medieval
1475 1340
98E0013 ext.

Initial site testing was carried out by C. Newman in 1992; further testing and excavation was carried out by Beth Cassidy and R. O'Brien over two months (May and June) in 1998 under this licence. Archaeological monitoring and subsequent excavation was carried out at Bride Street, Block 2, from July 1998 for a period of seven weeks.

Testing carried out by Beth Cassidy revealed a well, together with post-medieval and medieval occupation soils.

The Block 1 excavations revealed a well containing architectural fragments, a possibly medieval stone-lined drain, metalled surfaces, large pits filled with domestic-type refuse of possibly medieval date and a possibly medieval wall running parallel to Bride Street.

The Block 2 excavations revealed a number of post-medieval red brick structures, possibly medieval clay-bonded walls, medieval pits, hearths, possible kilns and two possibly medieval wells, together with a series of medieval cobbled and metalled surfaces.

The finds recovered included modern, post-medieval and medieval pottery, medieval floor tiles, flint, architectural fragments, worked bone, animal bone, wood, shroud-pins, coins and miscellaneous iron and copper fragments.

Una Cosgrave, Archaeological Development Services Ltd, Windsor House, 11 Fairview Strand, Fairview, Dublin 3.

144. BRIDGEFOOT STREET/ISLAND STREET/ BONHAM STREET/MARSHAL LANE, DUBLIN
Urban
98E0358

The site of the assessment is a proposed development site bounded by Marshal Lane, Bridgefoot Street, Island Street and Bonham Street, Dublin 8. The site is owned by Dublin Corporation and contains social housing. It was developed in the 1960s and currently consists of complexes of flats. Dublin Corporation plans to demolish some of the existing flat complexes and to develop the site further. In advance of any development work on site an archaeological assessment was conducted on 16–17 September 1998. The assessment revealed archaeological stratigraphy on the northern portion of the site. The portion of the site bounded by Marshal Lane and Bridgefoot Street is archaeologically sterile.

The site of the proposed development is within a zone of archaeological interest as outlined for Dublin in the Sites and Monuments Record for the city. SMR 18:020313 is identified as the site of a school. On the Draft Dublin City Development Plan 1998 maps two designated archaeological sites bound the site of the proposed development. List 6, Site No. 136, is the site of the school of St Thomas Aquinas, and List 6, Site No. 137, is named as the site North of the Site of the Bridge. Rocque's map of 1756 indicates the area as being a dump, and the 18th-century nomenclature of the streets in the area is testament to this, i.e. Dunghill Lane.

The site is thus one of archaeological potential. To this writer's knowledge there have been no archaeological site investigations in the immediate vicinity, the nearest being at Island Street/Watling Street, where Claire Walsh found late 18th/19th-century tanning pits, with reclaimed soils in association. Excavations carried out on Usher's Quay by Leo Swan revealed evidence of a medieval revetment.

Six trenches were excavated across the site. Archaeological stratigraphy was revealed in three of the trenches at the northern end. In Trench 3 what appears to be 'natural ground' lay *c.* 4m below present ground level. It is not certain if this is 'natural ground' *in situ* or has been redeposited. All trenches were excavated with a 1m-wide bucket of a mechanical digger.

The southern portion of the site at Marshal Lane and the southern portion of Bridgefoot Street are devoid of archaeological soils, and no further archaeological response is deemed necessary in this area.

The northern portion of the site extending from Bridgefoot Street to Island Street contains archaeological soils. In places there is *c.* 2.5m of archaeological deposits. No features were ascertained in the testing, but the archaeological stratigraphy appears to be a homogeneous, black, organic fill.
Daire O'Rourke, Dublin Corporation, Civic Offices, Wood Quay, Dublin 8.

145. 89–93 CAPEL STREET/16, 17, 21 AND 22 GREEN STREET/195–196 NORTH KING STREET, DUBLIN
Urban
98E0300
O152346
Test excavation of this development site was undertaken on 25–26 June 1998. The site lies at the northern end of Capel Street. All standing buildings on the site had been demolished before testing; however, the adjacent buildings at Nos 88 and 95 Capel Street were propped with shoring that intruded onto the site and were in a precarious state. Consequently, the test excavations avoided the immediate vicinity of these buildings. Temporary builders' accommodation, site cabins etc., currently occupies most of the Capel Street frontage; as this area was extensively cellared it was not deemed necessary to move the cabins and to dig in this area.

Throughout the medieval period the area that is now Capel Street was part of the lands of St Mary's Abbey, founded in 1139. The site of the abbey buildings lies some distance south of the present development site, and the present development lies outside the extent of the former abbey precinct as illustrated on Speed (1610). To date, except for a localised area at the junction of Green Street and North King Street uncovered in test excavation by Frank Ryan in 1993 (*Excavations 1993*, 24, 93E0104), no areas of medieval stratigraphy have been uncovered at the northern end of Capel Street.

In the late 17th century Capel Street was developed and became a 'fashionable residential area'.

All trenches were excavated by mechanical

excavator. There were no deposits of archaeological interest. The underlying topography indicated a slope from north to south. A localised area to the south of the development site had a 0.6m-thick deposit of agricultural soil of post-medieval date remaining, and elsewhere all soils were removed by building foundations and deep cellars of red brick construction. These foundations are those of the small buildings illustrated on Rocque and the OS maps and are of buildings similar to those standing on 88 and 95 Capel Street.
Claire Walsh, 25a Eaton Square, Terenure, Dublin 6W.

146. 98–102 CAPEL STREET, DUBLIN
Urban post-medieval
O154340
97E0368 ext.
Test-trenching was undertaken at a site at 98–102 Capel Street, Dublin 1, on 21 January 1998 to fulfil a condition of the planning permission granted by Dublin Corporation.

A single trench was excavated by mechanical excavator across the rear of the site. The method statement had proposed the excavation of three trenches; however, the available ground was limited by the presence of standing buildings (to be retained) and extensive deep cellars, which projected for *c.* 6m to the west of Nos 99–100.

A soil horizon, *c.* 0.5m deep, which dates to the late 17th century, remained over a limited part of the development site, to the rear of Nos 101–102. The soil is quite heavy clay and, though classified by archaeologists as 'garden soil', bears no obvious indicators of agricultural derivation. A similar soil horizon was observed at a test site at nearby Green Street (*Excavations 1997*, 45, 96E0382). At that site the soil was dated to no earlier than the 18th century.

Elsewhere on the site considerable truncation by red brick cellars had occurred and no soil horizons, other than red brick demolition layers, remained.
Claire Walsh, 25a Eaton Square, Terenure, Dublin 6W.

147. 17–35 CARMAN'S HALL (ODD NOS ONLY)/ 1–7 ASH STREET/33–34 GARDEN LANE, DUBLIN
Medieval, post-medieval
O1485033650
98E0254
Test-trenching was carried out in May at this development site to fulfil a condition of the planning permission. The site lies outside the medieval walled town of Dublin but within an area that was well settled by the 13th century. Trenching revealed the presence of a deposit of 'garden soil' of medieval date, which overlay subsoil, across the entire site. This was overlain by a post-medieval soil layer and the demolition levels of recent buildings.

As a result of the test-trenching a condition was made that all clearance of deposits on the site be undertaken under archaeological supervision. The rubble overburden was cleared off initially, and the underlying strata were cleared by machine using a grading bucket. Site clearance continued to mid-June. Few features of archaeological interest were found, and, with the exception of a single gully of medieval date, all features encountered were post-medieval.

Medieval soil was present over the entire site, except where it was removed by late features. The soil varied from 0.3m to 0.6m deep. The 'garden soil' is extremely inorganic and contains a few small fragments of animal bone, marine shell and a few sherds of pottery. The lowest level of the soil was similar to subsoil, while the upper level was darker with a higher humus content. The colour difference may also be due to percolation of coal particles from the overlying post-medieval soil. No features were evident in the medieval soil, and there were no furrows, cultivation ridges or other evidence of tillage in the soil or in the surface of the subsoil.

A thick deposit of soil of post-medieval date overlay the medieval soil. This was up to 0.6m thick, formed a distinct, well-defined horizon and was generally consistent over the entire site. It evidently pre-dates any large-scale building in this area and contained sherds of post-medieval pottery and animal bone

Claire Walsh, 25a Eaton Square, Terenure, Dublin 6W.

148. 27–31 CHURCH STREET, DUBLIN
Urban medieval
O105344
96E209 ext.

A second phase of archaeological testing was carried out at the proposed development site on 8 and 9 April 1998 under an extension to the existing licence. Phase I of the testing, carried out by Dominic Delaney in 1996 (*Excavations 1996*, 21), revealed 2m of medieval and post-medieval fill under modern fill. Phase II of the archaeological testing followed the demolition of extant buildings.

Five trenches were opened in the north-west and southern half of the site. The stratigraphy was generally consistent throughout the site. A sticky, brown clay underlay late building rubble at marginally different depths and contained varying amounts of butchered animal bone, shell and charcoal fragment. Two sherds of medieval pottery were retrieved from this deposit. This was the extent of archaeological material retrieved from the assessment.

The site lies directly to the east of St Michan's Church (SMR 6:20-84). Church Street was formerly known as Oxmantown Street and was included within the medieval suburb of Oxmantown.

Helen Kehoe, c/o Margaret Gowen & Co. Ltd, 2 Killiney View, Albert Road Lower, Glenageary, Co. Dublin.

149. 102–108 CHURCH STREET/6–7 CATHERINE LANE, DUBLIN
No archaeological significance
O149348
98E0204

Three test-trenches were dug by mechanical excavator. No soils, features or finds of archaeological interest were encountered. This is in keeping with the negative results obtained from archaeological test-trenching of other sites in the immediate vicinity.

Alan Hayden, 25a Eaton Square, Terenure, Dublin 6W.

150. SISTERS OF THE HOLY FAITH, THE COOMBE, DUBLIN
Urban medieval
O149335
97E0004

Archaeological monitoring took place at a proposed redevelopment at the site of The Sisters of the Holy Faith Convent, The Coombe, Dublin 8. The site fronts onto the north side of The Coombe and is bounded on the west by Hanover Street West and on the north by a school fronting onto Mark's Alley West. The results of three previous stages of assessment and monitoring have been reported in *Excavations 1997* (38–9).

Stage 4 monitoring of ground reduction and excavation of strip foundations in the area north and east of the convent building were undertaken over January–February 1998. This revealed 18th- and 19th-century domestic refuse and occasional red brick wall foundations and stone-lined drains.

No further archaeological requirements were applicable to the development after Stage 4 monitoring works.

Malachy Conway, Margaret Gowen & Co. Ltd, 2 Killiney View, Albert Road Lower, Glenageary, Co. Dublin.

151. 57–58, THE COOMBE, DUBLIN
Urban
O148335
98E0170

Pre-development testing was carried out in the area of a proposed domestic dwelling between Nos 57 and 58, The Coombe, Dublin. Excavation was by mechanical digger, using a toothless bucket.

Owing to upstanding buildings on either side of the area, it was decided, for safety, to excavate a narrow trench centrally placed between the two buildings. The trench was excavated to a depth of 51.86m OD (1.7m below present ground surface) through modern overburden, to the top of an active sewer pipe. Excavation beyond this point was not possible.

Audrey Gahan, Archaeological Development Services Ltd, Unit 48, Westlink Enterprise Centre, 30–50 Distillery Street, Belfast BT12 5BJ.

152. 3–4 CRANE LANE/16–19 CRAMPTON COURT, DUBLIN
Urban
97E0483

An archaeological assessment was carried out on 23 January 1998 before the construction of a residential development complex to be built on a pile structure. The assessment was based on the examination of three slit-trenches opened by mechanical digger. Monitoring of the adjacent site at 2 Crane Lane in August 1997 revealed a section of a blackstone quay wall extending in a north–south direction (*Excavations 1997*, 39–40, 96E0222). It was intended to try to establish whether this wall extended into the present site as it appeared to do.

The initial 3m of rubble in all trenches was of an extremely loose nature and prone to 'collapse'. The remains of the quay wall found at 2 Crane Lane appeared to extend into the present site in Trench A; however, owing to continual trench collapse it was difficult to ascertain this precisely. It is most likely a continuation of the quay wall.

Remains of this quay wall were not found in Trench B, 8m north of Trench A. It may have been partly demolished during the construction of red brick cellars, which continued to a depth of 3.3m in this area. The underlying deposits were consistent with reclamation material, a soft, brown clay with shell and animal bone fragments.

Monitoring of substructural works was carried out between 26 November and 2 December 1998 under an extension to the same licence. Fourteen 900mm and 21 600mm augered piles were inserted throughout the site. The deposits yielded by the piling consisted solely of building rubble—mainly red brick cellar remains—and reclamation material identical with the stratigraphical profile recorded in the previous site assessment. The line of the Poddle culvert was accurately plotted, and a 2m x 2m trench revealed the top of the culvert at a depth of 2.1m from existing ground level. Piles in the vicinity of the Poddle culvert were positioned not less than 1m away from the culvert and from the remains of a blackstone wall uncovered in Trench A during the initial site assessment. The ground-beams were excavated to a maximum depth of 0.5m, remaining within the rubble material.

Helen Kehoe, 11 Norseman Place, Stoneybatter, Dublin 7.

153. BELVEDERE COLLEGE, DENMARK STREET GREAT NORTH, DUBLIN
Urban
O164353
98E0057

An archaeological assessment involving four mechanically excavated test-trenches took place on this site. The development was within Georgian Dublin, on the site of previously demolished Georgian houses. The rubble from the demolition of these houses composed the main deposit on the site. The material was backfilled into the remains of the contemporary cellars, sitting directly below the tarmac surface.

Boulder clay was revealed below the level of the backfilled cellars. No archaeological deposits were uncovered cutting this material.

No archaeological deposits or finds earlier than the demolished remains of 18th- and 19th-century buildings were identified on site.

Avril Purcell, Margaret Gowen & Co. Ltd, 2 Killiney View, Albert Road Lower, Glenageary, Co. Dublin.

154. 18 EARL STREET, DUBLIN
Urban
1450 3375
98E0380

Test-trenching was undertaken at 18 Earl Street South (on the corner of Earl Street South and Thomas Court) in advance of development. Three trenches were opened along the line of the proposed foundations. The maximum depth of the foundations was to be 1m below present ground level (*c*. 16.945m OD).

Trench 1 was excavated alongside the pavement of Earl Street and measured 5.5m x 1.2m. Below layers of landfill deposits containing modern debris and a 19th/20th-century wall, a greenish/brown clay containing some mortar fragments was uncovered at a depth of 0.7–1m below present ground level. At 1m depth a crude, partially metalled surface was also uncovered, but this had been very badly disturbed.

Trench 2 was excavated along the line of the foundation, which ran parallel to Thomas Court, and measured 4m x 0.5m. Below rubble landfill and

another late wall was the same brown/greenish, clayey soil, 0.5–1m+ below present ground level, which contained some stone, shell, animal bone and mortar fragments.

Trench 3 was dug along one of the proposed centre foundations of the two houses to be built on the site. It measured 4.8m x 1m. Below layers of landfill, another late wall and a disused sewer, was a dark brown/black, shelly deposit, 0.6–1m below present ground level. This deposit, which was heavily disturbed, contained pieces of animal bone, fragments of lime mortar and red brick fragments.

Nothing of archaeological significance was uncovered in section; however, the greenish, clayey deposit may represent a garden soil of unknown date. The dark brown/black, shelly deposit may also be archaeological in nature, but it had been very heavily disturbed.

As these deposits would not be impinged upon further, construction was able to proceed.

Dermot G. Moore, Archaeological Development Services Ltd, Windsor House, 11 Fairview Strand, Fairview, Dublin 3.

155. 35 ESSEX STREET EAST, DUBLIN
Urban medieval
O155341
98E0566

An archaeological assessment was carried out on 26 November 1998 at 35 East Essex Street (Bad Bob's Nightclub). The site lies at the eastern side of the original estuary of the Poddle/Liffey confluence. The Poddle culvert passes along the western limit of the existing building, which is undergoing extensive refurbishment.

One trench was opened in the basement area of the building, extending in a north–south direction. A 0.1m slab floor lay over *c*. 2m of a soft, grey material with some animal bone and shell remains, consistent with reclamation fill known to have been actively deposited by the early 1600s in the wide confluence of the Poddle and Liffey Rivers. The land was reclaimed by dumping deep deposits of organic refuse that was then held in place by timber revetments. No archaeological features were encountered.

Helen Kehoe, c/o Margaret Gowen & Co. Ltd, 2 Killiney View, Albert Road Lower, Glenageary, Co. Dublin.

156. THE PROJECT ARTS CENTRE, 37 ESSEX STREET EAST, DUBLIN
Urban medieval
O155341
97E0102

An assessment was carried out at the site of the now demolished Project Arts Centre. One trench was excavated north–south through the centre of the site on 7 December 1998.

The Poddle culvert circumnavigates the southern perimeter of the site, and all foundation layout was kept at least 1m away from its outer wall. This trench excavation concluded the final phase of site investigation of this development area (*Excavations 1997*, 40–1).

Red brick cellar remains up to 3m deep were uncovered at the northern end of the trench fronting onto East Essex Street. The remainder of the trench consisted of reclamation fill with shell, bone, antler

and leather scrap material, in keeping with extensive reclamation at the Poddle/Liffey confluence. There was no evidence of any archaeological structures.
Helen Kehoe, c/o Margaret Gowen & Co. Ltd, 2 Killiney View, Albert Road Lower, Glenageary, Co. Dublin.

157. 8–10 EXCHANGE STREET UPPER/ 1 ESSEX GATE, DUBLIN
Urban medieval
O147344
98E0198
The site lies at the north-east corner of the Viking town along the west bank of the River Poddle, close to its confluence with the River Liffey. In the modern town the site lies behind the Turk's Head pub (No. 27 Parliament Street) and extends as far west and north as the Exchange Street and Essex Gate street frontages respectively.

In early summer 1998 excavation of an area *c.* 20m east–west x 6m max. north–south, was carried out over a period of twelve weeks. The site was previously tested and partially excavated under Licence No. 96E040 (*Excavations 1996*, 23–4; *Excavations 1997*, 43).

A 3m-long north–south stretch of an earthen bank was uncovered. The bank, constructed on natural gravel deposits, was supported on its internal face by a post-and-wattle fence. Although no ^{14}C analysis has yet been undertaken, the bank is thought to be 10th century in date. A number of substantial post-holes and several stake-holes were the only surviving evidence of contemporary (or possibly earlier) structural activity on the site.

Part of a substantial stone pathway crossed the site and sealed the earlier activity. The pathway was relaid at least twice and appeared to have been in use for a considerable period. On either side of the path the deposits indicated that this was an area of open ground used predominantly for localised industrial purposes; hearths, ash spreads, shell middens and a complex accumulation of clay- and stone-working surfaces were exposed.

The finds assemblage suggests that the deposits ranged in date from the 10th to the 12th century. A selection of bone/antler, copper-alloy, iron (mainly nails) and stone finds (including flint flakes and nodules), amber and wooden objects was recovered. A range of 12th/13th-century pottery fragments was uncovered at the uppermost level, together with some pits of 16th/17th-century date. The surface deposits had been truncated by insertion of basements in the 18th century.

Outside the main area of excavation, an 8m-long north–south stretch of the Viking (*c.* AD 1120) town wall was identified beneath the existing party wall between No. 1 Essex Gate and No. 27 Parliament Street. (In *Excavations 1996* this wall was reported to be the 13th-century wall.) Abutting its external (eastern) face, the internal face of the later 13th-century wall was identified.
Georgina Scally, c/o 81 Upper Leeson Street, Dublin 4.

158. 7A FOWNES STREET, DUBLIN 2
17th-century reclamation
O15643411
97E0176
The site lay to the north of the 13th-century

Augustinian friary, parts of which (the east precinct wall, part of the south precinct wall, internal walls and a limekiln) were found in previous excavations (*Excavations 1996*, 20–1, 96E0003). The northern end or return of the east precinct wall was not found during those excavations, and it was thought it may have extended into the south-east corner of the site under discussion. However, no wall was found in this additional assessment (to that reported on in *Excavations 1997*, 43), the site forming part of the extensive reclamation in this area dating to *c.* 1600.
Linzi Simpson, Margaret Gowen & Co. Ltd, 2 Killiney View, Albert Road Lower, Glenageary, Co. Dublin.

159. 10 FOWNES STREET UPPER, DUBLIN
Urban
O15723418
98E0378
Two test-pits were hand-excavated in the basement of an upstanding 18th/19th-century building to provide information on the likely survival of archaeological remains before a decision on an application for planning permission for a mixed commercial and residential development on this site. The site is directly opposite that of the the Augustinian Friary of The Holy Trinity, part of which has recently excavated by Linzi Simpson (*Excavations 1996*, 20–1, 96E0003). Fownes Street was laid out in the 18th century.

The floor of the basement is *c.* 2m below street level. No archaeological remains were uncovered in the two pits excavated; undisturbed natural gravels were found in both. It appears that any archaeological remains that formerly existed on this site have been removed.

It is recommended that a watching brief be maintained during ground reduction for the proposed development.
James Eogan, Archaeological Development Services Ltd, Windsor House, 11 Fairview Strand, Fairview, Dublin 3.

160. 88 FRANCIS STREET, DUBLIN
Suburban medieval
O135335
95E0058 ext.
Pre-development archaeological assessments of the site were carried out in 1995 and 1997 (*Excavations 1995*, 19–20; *Excavations 1997*, 44), and the surviving archaeological deposits were excavated in 1997.

In November 1998 clearance of an area of the site at the rear (west end) of the property, which was not previously available for assessment, revealed an isolated human burial. This was excavated and removed. It is likely to have been of 16th- or 17th-century date.
Alan Hayden, Archaeological Projects Ltd, 25A Eaton Square, Terenure, Dublin 6W.

161. 23–27a GARDINER STREET MIDDLE, DUBLIN
Urban
O160350
98E0200
This was a pre-development assessment funded by the developer. Four mechanically excavated trenches were opened on 30 April 1998. The site was completely

taken up by 18th-century cellars, which had removed all earlier deposits to below the level of subsoil. Nothing of archaeological significance was found.
Alan Hayden, Archaeological Projects Ltd, 25A Eaton Square, Terenure, Dublin 6W.

162. 41–43 GEORGE'S STREET GREAT NORTH (REAR OF), DUBLIN
Urban medieval
97E0486

This assessment was carried out between 5 and 7 January 1998. The development site lies outside the medieval town of Dublin as illustrated by Rocque (1756). In 1719 St George's Church was founded on Hill Street, but in 1894 it was converted into an open area. The tower remains standing, and the graveyard is now a playground.

Examination of the site was based on inspection of three slit-trenches running north–south. There was no evidence of any early archaeological deposits; however, in Trench B, adjacent to the Hill Street frontage, a circular blackstone well was uncovered. The well's outer diameter was 1.2m, and it had a depth of 2.8m, but this did not represent the true base owing to rubble infill. Two large, squared timbers, which formed part of the water-drawing mechanism, were floating vertically in the well. A small section of a second, identical-type well and associated timbers were recorded 13m north of the first.

In all three trenches hard, stony, yellow clay was excavated to a depth of 3.5m, at which point boulder clay was found. The general purity of the trench stratigraphy revealed little disturbance of deep ground. The positions of the two wells, almost on the same alignment, suggested their construction in garden plots associated with early 18th-century house structures and indicated that their purpose was domestic.

A site assessment carried out at an adjacent site, Nos 36–37 Hill Street (*Excavations 1997*, 45, 97E0037), revealed no evidence of any archaeological features or deposits.
Helen Kehoe, Margaret Gowen & Co. Ltd, 2 Killiney View, Albert Road Lower, Glenageary, Co. Dublin.

163. 1–5 GREEN STREET, DUBLIN
Urban medieval
O152346
98E0100

An archaeological site assessment was carried out at a development site at the corner of Green Street and Little Britain Street, Dublin 1, on 30 March 1998. The 'Green' of St Mary's Abbey (founded 1139) originally extended to incorporate the area where Green Street now lies, and the original name of the street, Abbey Green (1558), reflects this.

Three trenches were mechanically excavated throughout the narrow site area. Trenches A and B extended north–south, and Trench C east–west. The stratigraphical profile of the site was similar in all trenches. It consisted of deep building/cellar remains over a loose, pure gravel material. There was no evidence of any archaeological features or deposits.
Helen Kehoe, c/o Margaret Gowen & Co. Ltd, 2 Killiney View, Albert Road Lower, Glenageary, Co. Dublin.

164. 6–10 HANBURY LANE/REAR OF 38 THOMAS STREET, DUBLIN
Urban post-medieval
O342142
98E0199

This site lies on the north side of Hanbury Lane. It was tested while occupied by standing buildings still in use (the 'Dublin Bazaar'). This severely restricted both access to the site and the scale of trenching that could be undertaken. The trenches were excavated using mini-mechanical excavators, whose reach was insufficient to allow all trenches to be excavated to subsoil. The narrow part of the site fronting onto Thomas Street was not available for assessment. The site is close to the eastern boundary of the medieval abbey of St Thomas. It was expected to encounter some evidence of this boundary in the trenches.

Seven trenches/pits were excavated; however, the excavation of two of these was abandoned at a high level owing to the presence of live cables and pipes. Two further trenches could not be excavated to subsoil owing to the restricted space and reach of the mechanical excavators.

All trenches contained a generally similar series of deposits. Subsoil, where it was reached, lay at between 0.5m and 2.7m below ground level. In Trench 3 it was overlain by a thin layer of cultivated soil that contained no finds. In all trenches a layer of organic silt, of later 17th-century date, occurred between 2.5–2.7m and 1.3–2.4m below ground level. This deposit was overlain by 19th-century fills of shallow cellars. These in turn were overlain by cobbled floors, by a possible laneway and finally by modern concrete floors.

No medieval deposits were noted in any of the trenches excavated. Further assessment, to be undertaken when the standing buildings are demolished, will determine whether a medieval wall stands on the western boundary of the site.
Claire Walsh, 25a Eaton Square, Terenure, Dublin 6W.

165. NO. 14 HANBURY LANE (SITE ADJOINING), DUBLIN
Urban
3146 2338
98E0053

A programme of testing was undertaken on the above site. A trench was positioned to intersect with the proposed foundations for the north and west walls. Five cellar walls were identified extending east–west, and two were identified extending north–south. They are positioned parallel to Hanbury Lane and at right angles to the western boundary wall. The cellaring was cut into the natural deposits and would have interfered with any archaeological contexts that may have survived in the areas exposed.
Rónán Swan, Arch-Tech Ltd, 32 Fitzwilliam Place, Dublin 2.

166. HILL STREET/PARNELL STREET, DUBLIN
Urban medieval
O016351
98E0351

An archaeological assessment was completed at a development site at the corner of Hill Street and

Parnell Street, Dublin 1. The site lies outside the medieval town of Dublin and outside the city as depicted on Rocque's Map (1756). Parnell Street and Hill Street were laid out in the latter half of the 18th century. St George's Church, constructed in 1719 on Hill Street, was demolished in 1894. Only the tower remains standing. The site on which it stood is now a playground, the southern end of which borders the development site.

Three trenches were excavated by mechanical digger. The stratigraphy was uniform and identical within the trenches opened, consisting of recent building rubble and cellar remains overlying a compact, light brown, stony natural. There was no evidence of archaeological features/finds.

Helen Kehoe, c/o Margaret Gowen & Co. Ltd, 2 Killiney View, Albert Road Lower, Glenageary, Co. Dublin.

167. 15–17 ISLAND STREET/33 WATLING STREET, DUBLIN
Urban
O140343
98E0147

Test excavation of a development site at Watling Street/Island Street, Dublin 8, was undertaken in March 1998. The site occupies the corner of these two streets, and measures *c.* 47m east–west by 24m north–south. It lies in a potentially archaeologically sensitive area, close to the River Liffey, near to the convergence of several watercourses and to a mill-race, depicted on Speed's map (1610). It lies outside St James Gate, the western limit of the medieval town. On Rocque's (1756) map Island Street was known as Dunghill Lane. Buildings and property walls then occupied part of the site.

The test excavation uncovered the remains of a group of hide-processing pits of Victorian date, which overlay a deep deposit of black, organic silt. Finds from the silt were primarily of 17th-century and later date. It is likely that the silt represents the clearance from stables and latrines in the town—this would account for the low level of artefacts present. A localised area of possible medieval silts was noted at the western part of the site; these silts may be related to the Limerick watercourse, an overflow from the City watercourse.

The hide-processing pits were excavated, and the underlying deposits were removed mechanically in a series of spits. Finds were retrieved, but no further archaeological features were recorded. This work was carried out over a further two-week period in April. The sole surviving evidence of the 19th-century industrial process from this site was the complex of stone- and brick-lined pits. These contained foul-smelling silts with hair, as well as lime.

There were no surviving contemporary levels from the Victorian period or other refuse deposits associated with the trade. The preliminary draft for the OS map of 1836 indicates the presence of skin manufacturers on the site. Skinners, tanners and neatsfoot oil manufacturers were prevalent in the Watling Street/Island Street area, as indicated in the Victorian trade directories. The industrial complex excavated was held by William Lowry of Watling Street in 1836.

Claire Walsh, 25a Eaton Square, Terenure, Dublin 6W.

168. JOHN DILLON STREET, DUBLIN
Medieval friary
O142338
98E0158

A test excavation was undertaken on a development site at John Dillon Street, Dublin 7, on 11 May, as part of a planning application to Dublin Corporation for permission to construct dwellings on the site.

This small plot, measuring 12.7–13m north–south by 11.8m, was formerly part of the landholding of the parish church of St Nicholas of Myra on Francis Street. The church in all likelihood occupies the site of the medieval friary of St Francis, founded in *c.* 1230. The holdings of the friary were never extensive, and the valuation of its property after the dissolution was very low. The house held a two-acre site in Francis Street, which by the 16th century was in a very bad state of repair. Part of the cemetery of the friary has been excavated at 34–36 Francis Street, by Declan Murtagh (*Excavations 1994*, 26, 94E0069), and this appears to lie on the northern side of the friary complex.

An east–west wall, with some evidence of rebuild, corresponds with the site of the south wall of a structure shown on Rocque's map (1756) as PMH (?Presbyterian Meeting House) and on the 1st edition of the OS map as an Independent Chapel.

The eastern wall is part of the modern precinct wall of the church lands, with a sizeable drop of up to 2.5m on the east side of the wall. A limestone calp wall, corresponding with the south wall of the Independent Chapel marked on the OS 1837 map, bisects the site east–west. A lobby for the chapel is shown on the south side; this corresponds with the southern side of the site. On the south side of the wall the ground level is 1.8m lower than on the north side and is up to 3.14m lower than the ground level outside the western boundary of the development site. This southern area is heavily overgrown.

A single trench was machine-excavated along the northern side of the existing wall that bisects the site. The trench was 1.6m wide, *c.* 5m long, and 1.8m deep. Topsoil, which was a heavily rooted, black loam, occurred to a depth of 0.3m. Some red brick rubble, limestone and a granite sill occurred in this soil. Over 1m of very loose, mortar-flecked soil, containing much red brick rubble, underlay the topsoil. The lowest level of soil, up to 0.5m deep, was a greenish 'garden soil', which contained mortar flecks and 18th-century pottery. Subsoil occurred at a depth of 1.8m below ground level in this area, which is *c.* 12.4m OD.

No deposits of medieval date were encountered in the trench, and these are unlikely to occur over the remaining area of the development site. The differing ground levels in this area may be due to a number of factors. When the last remnants of buildings on the south side of the site were demolished the area was evidently cleared to subsoil level. The considerable drop in ground level to either side of the boundary wall of the church land may be partly explained by the natural slope from west to east, which may have resulted in scarping and terracing the ground for the street. This factor, coupled with the build-up of demolition rubble from the mid-18th-century buildings that occupied this site, accounts for the ground difference of 2.5m to either side of the wall in this part of the church grounds.

Claire Walsh, 25a Eaton Square, Terenure, Dublin 6W.

169. 6–11 KEVIN STREET LOWER, DUBLIN

Urban medieval and post-medieval

O155334

97E0090 ext.

One trench was excavated running south from Kevin Street Lower, parallel to Liberty Lane to the east. A ditch, uncovered running east–west at the very north of the trench, dates to the early medieval period, as suggested by the pottery recovered from its fill. This ditch is most likely to be the continuation of the previous ditch uncovered at the corner of Kevin Street Lower and Church Lane South (*Excavations 1997*, 46) and is therefore part of the town ditch that enclosed medieval Dublin.

Along the south of the trench, several large, deep pits were excavated. From the nature of the fill and the pottery recovered, it can be determined that these were post-medieval cesspits.

Cia McConway, Archaeological Development Services Ltd, Windsor House, 11 Fairview Strand, Fairview, Dublin 3.

170. 1–3 KING STREET NORTH/62–63 BOLTON STREET, DUBLIN

Urban

O152348

98E0062

Testing was undertaken as part of planning permission on 14 July 1998. The standing buildings on the site were demolished, and it was apparent that deep cellars existed in the north-west corner and southern end of the site. Three trenches were dug. A localised area of post-medieval soil (0.6m deep) survived on site. The removal of this soil was monitored, and no features or artefacts of archaeological interest were noted.

Claire Walsh, 25a Eaton Square, Terenure, Dublin 6W.

171. 4–6 KING STREET NORTH, DUBLIN

No archaeological significance

31551 23391

98E0049

Planning permission was granted by Dublin Corporation for the construction of a five-storey over-basement building on the site. An assessment was required in advance of the development. Trial-trenches excavated in 1993 by Frank Ryan on the south side of North King Street revealed material of apparently medieval date (*Excavations 1993*, 24, 93E0104). The name 'King Street, Oxmantown' dates to at least 1552, but there was a 'Kings Lane' in Oxmantown in the early 15th century, which was possibly the same thoroughfare.

The three test-trenches, which were mechanically excavated, revealed backfilled basements overlying natural deposits. No archaeologically significant features or deposits were found.

Mary McMahon, 77 Brian Road, Marino, Dublin 3.

172. 189–194 KING STREET NORTH, DUBLIN

Graveyard

98E0098

The site lies at the eastern end of North King Street, on the southern side of the street, and extends along Halston Street and Green Street. Known originally as Abbey Green, 1558 is the first recorded usage of that name. The monastic buildings of St Mary's Abbey occupied an area bounded by Capel Street on the east, East Arran Street on the west, Little Mary Street on the north and the street called St Mary's Abbey. The wall surrounding St Mary's Abbey was encircled by a stream of water diverted into small rivulets. The River Bradogue ran on the west side, from which a branch appears to have entered the grounds on the north side, at about the present North King Street.

In the early 18th century land on the northern end of the Green was put aside to build a church and the decision was taken to cover in the river Bradogue. On Rocque's map of 1756 Green Street is called Little Green and the portion granted for the church is walled in. By the time of Rocque's map the present street pattern had been established and the medieval market place had moved northwards to the site of what is now St Michan's Park.

The site is currently owned by Dublin Corporation and is designated for a new community resource centre. Two phases of archaeological assessment were carried out on the site, pre- and post-demolition. A limited excavation was then carried out to facilitate some engineering test-pits. The initial assessment began on 19 March 1998. Two trenches were excavated and revealed disarticulated skeletal material overlying *in situ* extended skeletons, *c.* 1m below present ground level. Standing buildings, which have subsequently been demolished, then covered most of the rest of the site. On 8 September 1998 a further four trenches were excavated, which revealed *in situ* articulated skeletons across the site.

The site appears to be a burial-ground. The assessments revealed *in situ* articulated skeletons overlain by a rubble fill layer containing disarticulated human bone. Articulated skeletal material lies directly below a layer of rubble and overburden, at its shallowest *c.* 0.7m below present ground level and at its deepest *c.* 2.2m. Within the rubble layer is a large quantity of disarticulated human remains. The burials consist of adult male and female burials and infant burials. All are buried in an east–west direction, apart from two infant burials that were buried roughly north–south and lay just inside the site at the Green Street side.

A limited archaeological excavation was conducted in the autumn of 1998. The excavations revealed eighteen fully articulated skeletons. The skeletons consist of male and female adults and some children. Initial examination dates them to the late 17th/early 18th century. The site was once home to the city's gallows and is also close to the Debtor's Prison and other penal institutions that were in the area.

Daire O'Rourke, Dublin Corporation, Civic Offices, Wood Quay, Dublin 8.

173. KING STREET NORTH/CHURCH STREET/STIRRUP LANE, DUBLIN

Urban

O152344

98E0197

Archaeological monitoring of clearance of the southern side of the development site was undertaken in July 1998. The western half of the site was reduced by a depth of 0.7m below present ground level, and the eastern half was reduced by 0.5m. Test-trenches previously undertaken by Daire O'Rouke (*Excavations 1997*, 37, 97E0086) indicated that any material of archaeological interest (i.e., a stone-faced well and wooden pipes) occurred at a depth of 0.9m below present ground level. Owing to this fact the clearance carried out on site was not sufficiently deep to reveal anything of interest.

While clearance was being carried out in the south-west corner of the site, soil and rubble collapsed into an underlying stone well that contained occasional fragments of red brick in the facing. This well was probably contemporary with the one noted by Daire O'Rourke in her test-trench.
Conor McHale, c/o 25a Eaton Square, Terenure, Dublin 6W.

174. ABBEY MALL, NOS 13–15 LIFFEY STREET, DUBLIN
Urban medieval
O167344
98E0064
Monitoring of substructural groundworks, including excavation for lift shafts, was carried out on 9–10 March 1998 in accordance with a condition of the planning permission. Owing to the relatively shallow depth of the ground-beams and lift shaft bases excavation did not proceed beyond disturbed red brick rubble remains contained within a sandy, brown clay with late mortar inclusions. There was no evidence of any material of an archaeological nature.
Helen Kehoe, c/o Margaret Gowen & Co. Ltd, 2 Killiney View, Albert Road Lower, Glenageary, Co. Dublin.

175. 4–7 LURGAN STREET, DUBLIN
No archaeological significance
31521 23466
98E0242
An archaeological assessment, involving the mechanical excavation of four test-trenches, was undertaken in advance of development, which involved the construction of a three-storey building. This area began to develop with the building of Henrietta Street in the 18th century. The Linen Hall was built in 1716 in the immediate vicinity of Lurgan Street to accommodate the rapidly increasing linen trade. Part of the gateway survives at the entrance to the DIT Bolton Street School of Trades. As the street name implies, there was a close association with the linen trade in Ulster.

The four test-trenches revealed that cellars occurred over most of the site, and loose modern fill overlay natural deposits in all of the trenches. No archaeologically significant features or deposits were found.
Mary McMahon, 77 Brian Road, Marino, Dublin 3.

176. MARSHAL LANE (REAR OF 138–141 THOMAS STREET), DUBLIN
Urban
O141340
98E0274
Marshal Lane is marked as 'Crockers St' on the map of medieval Dublin published by the Friends of Medieval Dublin, thus suggesting that the area may have been occupied by pottery kilns in the medieval and/or the post-medieval period; *vicus pottorum* appears to have been in existence by 1190. There was a gate at the west end of the street, although this lies some metres to the west of the development site. This gate is shown on Speed's map of 1610, but no houses are shown on that map

on what would have been the line of Crockers Street. The area is shown as being built up on Rocque's map of 1756 but with no particular structures in the immediate area. The Four Courts Marshalsea Prison was built to the north-west of the development site in 1775.

In testing this site special attention was paid to evidence of kilns, i.e. kiln structures, evidence of burning, waste pottery, kiln furniture etc. Two warehouses stood on the site until recently. They appeared to have been 19th or 20th century in date and were built of brick. Two properties had been amalgamated into one. Four trenches tested the site.

Boundary walls and dividing walls within the two sites bottomed out at 2.8–3m below the modern site level. On the eastern half of the site the fill comprised grey, silty material containing brick fragments etc., while on the western half of the site the fill comprised loose, black garden material, again with brick fragments. These fills abutted the walls, down to their foundations.

There was no evidence in any of the trenches or in the fill of the survival of material associated with pottery manufacture.
Rosanne Meenan, Roestown, Drumree, Co. Meath.

177. 51–52 MARY STREET, DUBLIN
No archaeological significance
315535 234620
98E0251
An archaeological evaluation was undertaken at a development site at 51–25 Mary Street, Dublin 1, on 3 and 6 July 1998. The work was undertaken in compliance with a condition attached to the grant of planning in respect of the proposed development of the site.

The site lies in the general environs of St Mary's Abbey, a Cistercian establishment that dates to 1139 and that appears to have been affiliated to Savigny in Normandy. This abbey had lands in its immediate vicinity, but there is no evidence to indicate that the present site lies within the boundaries of such lands.

Five trenches were mechanically excavated. No features, structures or finds of archaeological interest were uncovered during the course of the evaluation, although it is possible that such material may have existed on the site before the construction of the existing basements.

Given the archaeologically sterile nature of the site, it was recommended that no further archaeological involvement was required in respect of the development.
Martin E. Byrne, 39 Kerdiff Park, Monread, Naas, Co. Kildare.

178. 22 MARY STREET LITTLE, DUBLIN
Urban
O152354
98E0546
Testing took place in the backyard of this property in advance of development on 29 November 1998. The test-trench was excavated to the depth of the foundations proposed in the planning application; however, the developer subsequently considered changing this application to include a basement, which would increase the area affected from 1m to 2.5m deep. As it was not safe to excavate the test-trench to the increased depth archaeological

monitoring of the clearance was recommended. The adjacent property (No. 23) had put a basement in place in early spring of this year, and it showed entirely rubble infill deposits.

Martin Reid, 37 Errigal Road, Drimnagh, Dublin 12.

179. 61–63 MEATH STREET, DUBLIN

No archaeological significance
31016 23608
98E0110

An archaeological assessment, involving the mechanical excavation of three test-trenches, was undertaken in advance of planning permission. The planned development involved the construction of a ground-floor shop and overhead apartments. The site lies outside the core of medieval Dublin but is in the vicinity of the 12th-century Augustinian Abbey of St Thomas the Martyr. Meath Street was developed between 1690 and 1710, and John Rocque's map of 1756 shows a fully developed street pattern in the area.

No archaeologically significant features or deposits were uncovered. The earliest evidence from the site was a body sherd of blackware, indicating possible late 17th- or 18th-century activity in the area.

Mary McMahon (for Arch-Tech Ltd), 77 Brian Road, Marino, Dublin 3.

180. THE HOUSES OF THE *OIREACHTAS*, MERRION SQUARE, DUBLIN

Urban medieval
O163336
98E0373

Archaeological monitoring of plant excavations at the Houses of the *Oireachtas*, Merrion Square, Dublin 2, was carried out as part of an advance contract before the construction of an extension to the north of the existing *Oireachtas* building. The excavations consisted of trenches dug to facilitate the laying of a new, redirected sewer and surface water drain. The main area of excavation extended from the east side of the *Oireachtas* buildings to an existing culvert under the road at Merrion Square West. A second series of excavations took place at Leinster Lane, to the north of the proposed development.

In the main area of excavation an east–west trench, 140m long, was opened by mechanical excavator. The trench was 2.2m wide with a maximum depth of 4.1m. A stone wall was recorded in this trench, 0.8m below existing ground level. The wall, an earlier (mid-18th-century) boundary wall, was in line with the existing boundary wall/fence of the *Oireachtas* on Merrion Square West. It was 0.4m wide and the remains stood to a height of 2.3m. The section of the wall in the trench was removed to facilitate the laying of the pipes. No other deposits of archaeological significance were recorded.

The excavations at Leinster Lane consisted of a 35m-long east–west trench, with a maximum depth of 0.6m. No deposits of archaeological significance were recorded.

Tim Coughlan, c/o Margaret Gowen & Co. Ltd, 2 Killiney View, Albert Road Lower, Glenageary, Co. Dublin.

181. RICHMOND HOSPITAL, MORNING STAR AVENUE, DUBLIN

No archaeological significance
O148346
97E0466

This assessment was carried out in January 1998. Five trenches were open by mechanical excavator. These suggested that the area existed as open fields until its development in the 18th century.

Alan Hayden, Archaeological Projects Ltd, 25A Eaton Square, Terenure, Dublin 6W.

182. PARKGATE STREET, DUBLIN

Urban
O132343
98E0188

Testing took place on 16 and 17 April 1998. Five trenches were machine-excavated, down to undisturbed natural where possible, without revealing anything of archaeological significance. At the extreme east end of the site, a subsurface layer of 0.3m-thick concrete was uncovered. This precluded close examination of the layers in this area; however, the evidence from the other trenches nearby strongly suggested that nothing of significance survived in this area.

The results suggest that beneath the present surface and associated hard-core post-medieval layers lie directly on natural riverine silts and clays. In the south-western corner over 2.5m of made ground lies directly on river gravels.

Nothing of archaeological significance was uncovered during the assessment.

Eoin Halpin, Archaeological Development Services Ltd, Unit 48, Westlink Enterprise Centre, 30–50 Distillery Street, Belfast BT12 5BJ.

183. 19 PARLIAMENT STREET, DUBLIN

Urban medieval
O154342
98E0451

Monitoring took place during November and December 1998. Thirty-eight no. 200ml piles were inserted, and the site area was then reduced by 0.4m. The material removed by mechanical digger consisted of red brick/mortar remains in a loose, brown clay with some shell fragment. There was water ingress at 3m depth from the present street level. The material excavated for ground-beams (0.7m x 0.6m deep) consisted of identical redeposited rubble remains.

There was no evidence of material of an archaeological nature, and excavation works yielded no finds.

Helen Kehoe, c/o Margaret Gowen & Co. Ltd, 2 Killiney View, Albert Road Lower, Glenageary, Co. Dublin.

184. 1–4a RED COW LANE/62–63 and 67–76 NORTH KING STREET/71–72 BRUNSWICK STREET NORTH, DUBLIN

Urban, post-medieval
O145346
98E0255

Test-trenches dug by mechanical excavator uncovered no deposits of archaeological interest. Deep red brick cellars occur along the North Brunswick frontage and also along most of the North King Street frontage available for testing. Elsewhere wall foundations of late 17th/18th-century date penetrate to a depth of between 0.6m and 1.8m below present ground level. A deposit of green soil, up to 0.4m deep, overlay subsoil in a limited area of the site.

The soil had no datable finds and was sterile. It may be subsoil disturbed from the construction of walls or may represent the former agricultural land and be of post-medieval date.

Claire Walsh, 25a Eaton Square, Terenure, Dublin 6W.

185. NEW PHYSIOTHERAPY BUILDING, ST JAMES'S HOSPITAL, DUBLIN

Unknown
O136360
98E0235

The development comprised an extension to an 18th-century building on the campus of St James's Hospital. The building dates to *c.* 1750 and formed part of the workhouse complex here, which was founded at the end of the 17th century. The programme of work consisted of the demolition of existing outhouses and the construction of a two-storey, 5m-wide concourse running along the length of the pre-existing building on the west side. Ground reduction and the excavation of foundation trenches was monitored.

A slight plinth for the building was exposed. A layer of brick and stone, 2m below the level of the surrounding yard, was exposed. This layer appeared to lie at the base of a deposit of soft, brown clay that appeared to have been cut into the natural boulder clay. The brick deposit and the soft, brown clay probably formed part of a large pit (*c.* 2m wide north–south, unknown width east–west), which had been dug at this point for unknown reasons but was probably associated with the construction of the 18th-century building.

Rosanne Meenan, Roestown, Drumree, Co. Meath.

186. ST MARY'S CHURCH, SAINT MARY'S STREET/WOLFE TONE STREET, DUBLIN

Urban medieval
O155345
98E0085

St Mary's Church of Ireland Church is reputedly one of the earliest galleried churches in Ireland and dates to the late 17th century. The building was in use until recently as a retail unit but retains many of its original features, including a decorated wooden organ casing dating to *c.* 1700 and an oak, break-fronted gallery. Other original features include staircases in the west tower and door casings. The church also has stone memorial plaques hanging on the walls. An appraisal of the building was carried out by Linzi Simpson in November 1997 (report lodged with Dublin Corporation and *Dúchas* The Heritage Service). The graveyard of the church lies on the southern side and now forms Wolfe Tone Park. The church is currently being redeveloped as a commercial unit.

A preliminary assessment was carried out in advance of the redevelopment. Four trenches were opened by mechanical excavator outside the north and west walls of the church. No archaeological deposits were identified in these trenches. A further six test-pits were opened by hand, one in each of the six under-ground crypts. Various remains were found within the crypts. These consisted, for the most part, of bits of timber coffins and disarticulated human remains but also included several articulated skeletons.

On the basis of the evidence revealed during the assessment an excavation was carried out in the crypts to record and remove the human remains and to clear the crypts to boulder clay levels.

All of the *in situ* remains were uncovered on an *in situ* soil level sealed by a deep deposit of loose soil. It is not clear why there was such a large amount of loose bone scattered throughout the crypts above the articulated remains, particularly in Crypt 4, as much of this bone was evident within the debris layer. Some of the bones were obviously disturbed by recent vandalism, as modern debris was associated with them.

The table below shows the minimum number of individuals (MNI)* identified in the crypts of the church. The figures show substantial differences between individual crypts, with Crypt 1 containing the highest number of *in situ* remains and Crypt 4 containing the largest quantity of loose bones.

Crypt no.	No. of burials	Loose bones (MNI)*	Total (MNI)*
1	22	5	27
2	6	4	10
3	1	5	6
4	5	26	31
5	0	3	3
6	0	3	3
Totals	34	46	80

An additional assessment was requested by the developer in advance of a further planning application to extend the basement to include the area between the church and Wolfe Tone Park. The assessment took place between 11 and 14 December 1998 and was based on the excavation of five test-pits, opened by mechanical digger.

It is clear from the additional test-pits that the area between the railings that surround the church and its south wall was used to inter human remains, as several *in situ* human skeletons were found, orientated east–west. The main graveyard, however, lay to the south, in the area now known as Wolfe Tone Park. Most of the remains recorded during the assessment lay *c.* 1.8m below existing ground level and were sealed by an infilled brown soil with red brick inclusions. However, it is possible that there are graves surviving at a higher level in the areas not covered by the test-pits.

Tim Coughlan, c/o Margaret Gowen & Co. Ltd, 2 Killiney View, Albert Road Lower, Glenageary, Co. Dublin.

187. ST STEPHEN'S GREEN, DUBLIN

Urban medieval
31602 12337
98E0542

Archaeological monitoring of a series of geotechnical boreholes was carried out on 9 and 10 November 1998. The boreholes were inserted at intervals into the footpath surrounding the Green to establish the nature of the ground profile before a planned project to upgrade and repave the footpath area. The boreholes ranged from 0.22m to 0.57m deep, with a circumference of 0.1m. The sample fill yielded by the bores consisted mainly of late material associated with groundworks over previous years.

Helen Kehoe, c/o Margaret Gowen & Co. Ltd, 2 Killiney View, Albert Road Lower, Glenageary, Co. Dublin.

188. SHIP STREET (PHASE V)
Urban medieval
O154337
97E0093 ext.

A fourth phase of archaeological testing was carried out on a development site bounded by Ship Street Great and Stephens Street, Dublin 2, between 21 and 23 September 1998. Twelve mechanically excavated trenches were opened during the three phases of testing, ten by Linzi Simpson in 1996 (Phases I and II, *Excavations 1996*, 30–1, 96E170) and two by this writer, completed in April 1997 (Phase III, *Excavations 1997*, 51–2).

The fourth phase involved the mechanical excavation of two trenches (14 and 15) extending east–west from the Ship Street Great frontage. The stratigraphy of both trenches was similar to the overall ground profile established in the previous phases of testing. Deep rubble and cellar remains were uncovered along the street frontage, overlying a uniform, yellow clay over stony natural. In Trench 15 a section of a red brick culvert was revealed, orientated north–south, uncovered 9m eastwards along the trench. It was 3.5m wide and 2m deep, set on a two-course blackstone foundation on either side of the red brick arch. There were no archaeological remains revealed in either trench.

Excavations carried out by Kieran Campbell in 1981 (*JIA* **V**, 1989–90, 74) immediately north of the site under review revealed the remains of the church and round tower belfry of St Michael le Pole and associated burial-ground. While the burial area appeared to extend southwards into the adjoining property, there was no evidence of any burials in the portion of the site under review.

Helen Kehoe, c/o Margaret Gowen & Co. Ltd, 2 Killiney View, Albert Road Lower, Glenageary, Co. Dublin.

189. 13–15 SPITALFIELDS, DUBLIN
Urban medieval
O149336
98E0054

An assessment was carried out at a site bounded by Spitalfields and Mark's Alley West. It extends more than halfway through the block towards Francis Street, with access from Carmen's Hall. The site was investigated in two phases. Phase I was completed in February 1998, when three trenches were opened by mechanical excavator, and Phase II in September 1998, when four trenches were excavated.

The site lies immediately outside the medieval walled town of Dublin. Francis Street takes its name from the Friary of St Francis (founded 1233), which stood on the east side of the street, close to or on the site of the modern Catholic church of St Nicolas of Myra.

The initial 2m of stratigraphy consisted of loose late building remains infilling red brick cellars over a brown clay deposit. A post-medieval refuse pit,

uncovered at a depth of 2.2m in Trench B, yielded two sherds of post-medieval, red-glazed eastern ware and one medieval body sherd of local ware. There was no evidence of any archaeological features.

Helen Kehoe, c/o Margaret Gowen & Co. Ltd, 2 Killiney View, Albert Road Lower, Glenageary, Co. Dublin.

190. TEMPLE BAR WEST
North-east corner of Viking town
O154341
96E0245

The fourth and final phase of excavation commenced in Temple Bar West in January 1998 at the western (Fishamble Street) side of the site. The previous excavations had uncovered early evidence of habitation and ploughing, as well as mid- to late 9th-century Viking habitation superseded by industrial activity, which continued into the Anglo-Norman period (*Excavations 1997*, 41–2).

The west side of the site also produced evidence of ploughing followed by early habitation in the form of three small, well-preserved, sunken structures clustered together. These were sealed by a phase of infilling and levelling-up of the slope, which was followed by the creation of three large properties, orientated north–south and delineated by post and wattle fences. These properties contained wattle pens and at least one dwelling, thought to date to the mid- to late 9th century. The early 10th century saw reorganisation of the area and the division of the three early properties into six property plots, each of which contained a house (Type 1 after Wallace), wattle path and sub-buildings. At the upper levels the paths were of stone. In all at least seven levels were identified, with over 100 buildings in total. These included one small, sunken house with a well-preserved wattle floor, thought to date to the 11th century.

Linzi Simpson, Margaret Gowen & Co. Ltd, 2 Killiney View, Albert Road Lower, Glenageary, Co. Dublin.

191. ST CATHERINE'S CHURCH, THOMAS STREET, DUBLIN
Urban medieval
O147339
98E0236

St Catherine's was a parish church in medieval Dublin, and the original building is thought to have occupied much the same site on Tomas Street as the present church, which dates to *c.* 1707. It is a fine example of a galleried church, a type common in Dublin from the late 17th century. The main façade, which survives intact, is of granite. In the interior the timber-fronted gallery survives relatively intact. It consists of superimposed Doric columns that hold the continuous galley above. There are also the remains of an organ. The church was substantially renovated in the recent past but was later badly vandalised, with many of the timber fittings removed. In the crypt at the east end of the church there are up to nine lead-lined coffins, some highly decorated. The remains include those of the Earl and Countess of Meath, Lord and Lady Brabazon.

Archaeological monitoring of excavations, which formed part of refurbishment works at the church, was carried out between February and July 1998. The excavations consisted of a general reduction of

Viking house (Site A) at Temple Bar West.

ground level in the nave and in an annexe at the south-east corner of the church, the excavation of a pit in the centre of the nave to facilitate the construction of a new baptismal font, and the excavation of a trench for drainage pipes at the rear of the church.

Archaeological deposits were recorded in the pit in the centre of the nave. These indicated that there was considerable infilling of soils and rubble before or during the construction of the church. Large dumps of disarticulated human bones recorded in some of these layers suggest that a number of earlier human graves, probably associated with the medieval church, were disturbed during the construction of the church. However, there was no evidence of *in situ* medieval deposits or any human burials in any of the excavated areas.

Tim Coughlan, c/o Margaret Gowen & Co. Ltd, 2 Killiney View, Albert Road Lower, Glenageary, Co. Dublin.

192. TOWNSEND STREET/LUKE STREET, DUBLIN
17th-century river revetment
O163343
97E0484

Archaeological excavation of a development site at Townsend Street/Luke Street, Dublin 2, was undertaken over a five week period from 22 January 1998. Occupying a position on the corner of Townsend Street and Luke Street, the site was until recently that of the Countess Markievitcz Swimming Pool.

The site lies outside the medieval walled town of Dublin, between the lands of Trinity College and the River Liffey, in an area known in the medieval period as Lazar's Hill, in the vicinity of the hospital or hostel of St James, built in *c.* 1216.

Alan Hayden undertook archaeological assessment of the site on 29 and 30 December 1997 (*Excavations 1997*, 54–5). Following the results of the assessment it was deemed by the planning section of Dublin Corporation, in association with National Monuments, that all timber structures on the site be excavated.

Hand-excavation of the underlying deposits followed machine clearance of overburden. The archaeological assessment had uncovered the remains of timber revetment structures and *c.* 1.4m depth of associated 17th-century river silts. Two phases of buildings post-dated these archaeologically significant structures: the Hospital of the Incurables, built in *c.* 1753, and the Countess Markievitcz Swimming Pool, constructed in the 1950s. All of the remaining silt deposits within 4–6m of the timbers were hand-excavated to subsoil.

The 17th-century silts to the north of the site, and to the extreme east and west of the site, were removed in a series of machine spits, in order to remove the artefacts and to determine the presence of further timber structures. The site measures 45m north–south by 36m; in total, an area measuring 27m east–west by 23m was excavated by hand. Timber revetments, invariably of oak, measuring a total length of 52.5m were uncovered on the site.

Although several sherds of medieval pottery were recovered, there were no medieval occupation levels on the site.

The timber structures on the site comprise six separate elements. All of the wood used was oak, except for two minor elements, which were probably of pine. No nails were used in the construction, and the dowels were almost exclusively of oak. There is no evidence of rebuilding of the structure, and it

Plan of timber revetments at Townsend Street, Dublin.

appears to have been relatively short-lived. Several of the timbers have some evidence of reuse; interestingly, no ships' timbers were used.

Two parallel lines of revetments, 5.5m apart, extended for 15.5m north–south into the bed of the Liffey. The line of each revetment turned, perpendicular to the main line, to form two revetments extending east–west, parallel to the main Liffey channel. All of these lines of revetment were of similar construction, in that baseplates were scarfed end-to-end, upright posts were tennoned into mortises cut into the baseplates, and horizontally laid planks were pegged onto the uprights.

The revetments were constructed in what appears to have been open riverbed and were braced from the rear at irregular intervals. Most of the soils on the site were deposited by the river. Artefacts recovered from the lowest levels of the silts were of mid- to late 17th-century date. Dendrochronological dates from some of the timbers yielded a felling date of AD 1656.

Documentary research on the site by Frank Myles indicates that the revetments were constructed by Henry Hicks, a brewer and member of a cartel of Dublin businessmen who were granted a 90-year lease in 1659 on this stretch of the shore. They were charged with repairing breaches, protecting the highway from the sea and reclaiming new ground.
Claire Walsh, 25a Eaton Square, Terenure, Dublin 6W.

193. 109 TOWNSEND STREET, DUBLIN
Post-medieval
O169317
98E0213
Archaeological test excavation was carried out on a

development site at 109 Townsend Street, Dublin 2. The site, a single property on the south side of the street, lies towards the eastern end of Lazar's Hill, a gravel ridge that was probably occupied by houses from the 16th century onwards. In 1659 there is a mention of a 'forte' on Lazar's Hill, which de Courcy (*The Liffey in Dublin*, 1996, 164) suggests was probably on the junction of Lazar's Hill and Sandwith Street. This structure is likely to be the one depicted on Petty's (1654) map as 'Andrew's Folly' and may have been a customs post. The likelihood of uncovering remains of any archaeological significance on this plot was considered slight. The test excavation was carried out in tandem with site clearance.

Subsoil, which comprised a relatively soft, yellow/brown boulder clay, lensed with coarse gravel, was reached at 1.6m below street level. The intervening material was a loose rubble and red brick fill, which probably represents the demolition of the last standing building on the plot. This building had a semi-basement but did not appear to have had a formal flooring.

The foundations of the standing buildings to both sides rest on subsoil.

There was no evidence of any late medieval or post-medieval activity on the plot. A small yard area at the rear of the building was also cleared of soil. The garden soil, averaging 0.75m deep, contained 19th-century crockery sherds, directly overlying subsoil.

There was no trace of any deposits of archaeological interest on the plot.
Claire Walsh, 25a Eaton Square, Terenure, Dublin 6W.

194. BERKLEY LIBRARY BUILDING EXTENSION, TRINITY COLLEGE DUBLIN

Urban medieval

O163339

98E0361

An archaeological assessment was carried out at Trinity College Dublin before the building of an extension to the present Berkeley Library. The area under investigation extended from the south of the Berkeley Library/Arts Block building to the Nassau Street boundary of Trinity College.

Nassau Street, which forms the southern boundary to Trinity College, was originally known as St Patrick's Well Lane, from a 12th-century well or fountain that lay within the grounds of the college.

Four trenches were opened, three of which consisted of topsoil over compact, brown, stony clay. Initial deposits in Trench 4 consisted of late red brick wall remains, including the original blackstone boundary wall that enclosed the Provost's garden. There was no evidence of any earlier archaeological features or finds.

Helen Kehoe, c/o Margaret Gowen & Co. Ltd, 2 Killiney View, Albert Road Lower, Glenageary, Co. Dublin.

195. LIBRARY SQUARE, TRINITY COLLEGE, DUBLIN

Site of All Hallows Priory and early College

O061341

98E0150

In March 1998 pipe-laying in Library Square, TCD, uncovered articulated, stratified, skeletal remains in a 'graveyard' deposit *c.* 0.6m deep. The remains were orientated east–west and, at the lowest level, lay in shallow pits cut into the boulder clay. They are presumed to relate to the Priory of All Hallows, the forerunner of the College, which was founded by Diarmait Mac Murchada in *c.* 1166 (or before). The priory is thought to have stood in the south-east corner of Front Square, which would place the cemetery to the west of the original quadrangle. On inspection of the pipe-trench the cemetery appears to be bounded on the north and west by the present buildings of Library Square (the Rubrics and the Old Library). The east and south extent is not known.

A series of walls was also exposed in the pipe-trench. As well as several later walls, the walls of the original early 18th-century ranges were uncovered on the north and west side of Library Square (the only surviving range is the Rubrics on the east side). These walls were not removed but were neatly drilled through by Hole Masters.

Linzi Simpson, Margaret Gowen & Co. Ltd, 2 Killiney View, Albert Road Lower, Glenageary, Co. Dublin.

196. SCIENCE OF MATERIALS BUILDING, TRINITY COLLEGE, DUBLIN

Urban medieval

O164341

98E0601

An archaeological assessment was carried out before the construction of a new Science of Materials Building, Trinity College Dublin, on 11 and 14 December 1998. The area under investigation lies within the north-eastern area of the campus, south of the Luce Hall and west of the O'Reilly Institute building.

The site of the proposed development is outside the original College footprint at the corner of Pearse Street and Westland Row. Before 1710 an area of about 2ha at the intersection of Westland Row and Pearse Street was a brickfield; neither of these streets existed at the time.

Five trenches were opened by mechanical digger. The stratigraphy of the site consisted mainly of modern foundation remains over a soft, grey clay that contained some shell fragments. There was no evidence of any archaeological deposits.

Helen Kehoe, c/o Margaret Gowen & Co. Ltd, 2 Killiney View, Albert Road Lower, Glenageary, Co. Dublin.

197. 15/16 WERBURGH STREET, DUBLIN

Urban

98E0081

An assessment was conducted at 15/16 Werburgh Street, Dublin 8, over three days in March 1998, before development. The medieval town wall and the River Poddle run through the site. The objective of the assessment was to ascertain the exact line of the wall and Poddle culvert. Two trenches, both oriented north–south, were excavated by a 1m-wide bucket of a mechanical digger.

The assessment was inconclusive as there is over 3m of rubble, overburden and friable soils on the site. The trenches were unsafe and continually collapsed. The assessment was abandoned. It is proposed to undertake further assessment in 1999.

Daire O'Rourke, Dublin Corporation, Civic Offices, Wood Quay, Dublin 8.

198. 22–31 WOLFE TONE STREET, EXTENDING TO JERVIS LANE, DUBLIN

Urban

O150351

98E0027

The site occupies an area measuring a maximum of 70m north–south by 40m and fronts onto Wolfe Tone Street to the east and Jervis Lane Upper to the west. Four trenches were excavated to subsoil using a mechanical excavator.

Large cellars up to 4m deep occurred beneath the demolished building that had formerly fronted onto Wolfe Tone Street, while cellars up to 3m deep occurred beneath the buildings that formerly fronted onto Jervis Lane. All of the cellars were cut deeply into subsoil and were backfilled with 19th- and 20th-century material.

In the areas between the former buildings subsoil occurred at 2–2.5m below modern ground level and was overlain by layers of loam and rubble containing 18th- and 19th-century pottery, bricks and other refuse.

Claire Walsh, 25a Eaton Square, Terenure, Dublin 6W.

199. ST MICHAEL'S HOLY FAITH CONVENT, WELLMOUNT ROAD, FINGLAS

Stone wall

98E0123

An assessment was carried out on the site of proposed development (an oratory) at St Michael's Holy Faith Convent, Wellmount Road, Finglas, Dublin 11. The site was within the zone of archaeological potential for Finglas, as identified by the Urban Archaeological Survey. One trial-trench was excavated on 9 and 10 March 1998. Before excavation the site had been a lawn.

Dublin

The test-trench was 8m long and 2m wide on the north-west/south-east axis. Excavation was halted at a depth of *c.* 0.9m when the uppermost remains of a wall were exposed. This wall was *c.* 0.6m wide and survived to a height of *c.* 0.5m. It consisted of three courses, and its exposed top was heavily mortared. It was recommended that the wall remains not be interfered with.

On 30 June and 1 July 1998 the foundation trenches for the proposed oratory were dug. As expected the wall was again uncovered; contrary to expectation, however, it did not run in a north–south direction but rather east–west, thereby running at right angles to the remains of the wall uncovered during the testing. Once the remains of the wall had been uncovered the developer requested that the foundation trench for the oratory be dug to a further depth of 0.5m on each side of the stone wall remains. This was considered necessary in order to consolidate the foundations and was agreed.

As advised in the archaeological testing programme the stone wall remains were covered with terram in order to protect them from the development work.

Eoghan Moore for Arch-Tech Ltd, 32 Fitzwilliam Place, Dublin 2.

200. HOLY FAITH CONVENT, GLASNEVIN
Medieval
98E0299

Archaeological monitoring was carried out on an extension for a residential care centre in the Holy Faith Convent grounds, in response to a condition of planning. The work took place on 7–15 July and 4–6 August 1998. No archaeological features were uncovered. A fragment of a line-impressed floor tile and a late medieval green-glazed jug handle were recovered from the topsoil.

The floor tile had a six-foil in circle pattern, identical to Type L38. Only one other tile fragment has been recorded from Glasnevin, also line impressed. As the tile fragment was recovered from the topsoil its context was disturbed. However, its presence is probably connected to the local medieval Church of St Mobhi.

Richard N. O'Brien, Archaeological Development Services Ltd, Windsor House, 11 Fairview Strand, Fairview, Dublin 3.

201. CORR CASTLE, HOWTH ROAD, HOWTH
Tower-house
3268 2395
SMR 15:25
98E0349

Testing took place at this site for a period of six weeks, commencing on 3 August 1998, to determine the interface between the undisturbed deposits on the rise and the backfill deposits of the surrounding quarry, and also the nature and extent of archaeological deposits in the vicinity of the castle. It was undertaken in compliance of An Bord Pleanála planning conditions. This development is being undertaken in the vicinity of Corr Castle, which is intended for use as the focal point within the development.

For the past 150 years this site has been used as a limestone quarry, and it has been backfilled within the past twenty years. An aerial photograph shows that the quarrying activity avoided the castle itself and an area 10m around it.

Five cuttings were excavated initially, positioned to identify the limit of the archaeological area, while a test-pit was positioned to determine the existence of a bawn wall (at the north-western corner). It was decided to extend the scope of the testing programme as a cobbled layer was found to the front of the castle, a garderobe chute found on its south-eastern corner and a limekiln identified to the north-east of the castle. As a result of extending the cuttings the entire area to the north of the castle was exposed.

The area of cobbles extended across the entire area to the north of the castle. This surface seems to be contemporary with the castle, as the layer extends into the ground floor and is at the same level as the base of the jambstones. The eastern edge of the cobbling is aligned to the eastern edge of the castle and stair tower. Also uncovered was a cobbled driveway leading from the east onto the rise. This driveway is defined on the northern side by a setting of boulders and on the southern by a setting of roughly cut stone. These cobbles appear to be set directly upon natural deposits. Artefacts recovered from above the cobbled layer included sherds of gravel-tempered ware.

There was no evidence of a bawn wall; however, there was evidence of a one-course, mortared plinth that may have been used to support a gallery-type feature to the front of the castle.

To the east a cutting was positioned from the base of the castle to the edge of the quarry. There was evidence of the deposition of a layer of stone chippings to provide a level surface for the castle's construction, beneath which was a layer of burning on the surface of the bedrock.

A single cutting extended to the south of the castle. As with the eastern trench, fissures in the bedrock were filled with stone chippings to provide a level surface for the construction of the castle. At the southern end of the cutting sherds of 13th/14th-century medieval pottery were recovered, but they were not associated with any archaeological features or structures.

A cutting was positioned to the west leading from the base of the castle to a recent boundary wall. This area had been used on several occasions for the dumping of charcoal and ash from fires, which were probably associated with the occupation of the castle itself. However, at the eastern end of the cutting an area of burning was identified that extended under the castle. A stone setting was evident at the base of the garderobe chute. It seems that this setting was designed to collect the effluent, which could be subsequently dumped elsewhere.

The aim of this testing was to define the extent of the archaeological area around the base of the castle. To the north the limit of the archaeological area is a maximum of 13m from the base. The quarry deposits are 11m from the western wall of the castle, just on the far side of the western boundary wall. On the eastern side the quarry deposits are within 5m of the base of the castle, while the quarry did not extend to the south of the castle.

Historically, Corr Castle is believed to have been built during the 16th century—the first record of the castle refers to the White family living here in 1550.

However, the architectural features of the castle may place its construction a century earlier, while the areas of burning to the west and east of the castle and the 13th/14th-century pottery that has been found throughout the site, but particularly to the south of the castle, suggest an earlier phase of activity, pre-dating the construction of the castle.
Rónán Swan, Arch-Tech Ltd, 32 Fitzwilliam Place, Dublin 2.

202. 28–31 CONYNGHAM ROAD, ISLANDBRIDGE
No archaeological significance
O130343
96E0026 ext.
The site at Conyngham Road, Islandbridge, lies on the north bank of the River Liffey, a short distance east of Islandbridge village and Sarah Bridge. Phase 1 of the test excavation was undertaken in 1996 (*Excavations 1996*, 34, 96E026), and Phase 2 in 1998. In all, twelve trenches were excavated by mechanical digger, and in no trench were finds or features of any archaeological significance uncovered.
Georgina Scally, c/o 81 Upper Leeson Street, Dublin 4.

203. BALLYOGAN ROAD, JAMESTOWN
Pale Ditch
O320224
SMR 26:1
98E0119
All aspects of ground disturbance in the development of a sewage outfall at Ballyogan Road, Jamestown, Stepaside, Co. Dublin, were monitored from 23 March to 23 April 1998, when sewage pipe-laying was undertaken over *c.* 150m. The licence was transferred to Martin Reid for the remainder of the works (see No. 204 below).

A section of the Pale Ditch runs east–west, parallel to the proposed development, and is manifest as a linear earthen bank with an internal and external fosse. The Pale boundary was constructed under an act of Poyning's Parliament in 1494 to defend the rapidly receding Anglo-Irish heartland against increasing encroachments from the Gaelic Irish. The Pale Ditch survives as an interrupted linear earthwork, and archaeological investigation has shown that it also varies morphologically.

Development works on this site commenced on the northern side of the Ballyogan Road. The topsoil was stripped with a track machine using a flat grading bucket. No archaeological features, deposits or artefacts were recorded. Trench excavations for the sewage pipe commenced at the eastern end of the field, on the southern bank of the Ballyogan Stream. In general the trench was 3.5m deep, and no archaeological stratigraphy, features or artefacts were recorded. The stratigraphy consisted of grey/brown and orange/brown, sandy clays that in places overlay granite bedrock.
Laurence Dunne, Eachtra Archaeological Projects, 43 Ard Carraig, Tralee, Co. Kerry.

204. BALLYOGAN, JAMESTOWN
Pale ditch
O320224
SMR 26:1
98E0119
An archaeological investigation was carried out in tandem with the laying of sewage pipes along a laneway within the Ballyogan tiphead on 24 and 25 June 1998. The excavation was undertaken as a part of the overall monitoring for the Ballyogan Sewer Outfall Project. The laneway crosses the line of the Pale Ditch.

The investigation involved a topographic survey and the controlled excavation of the sewer trench. The profile of the base of the Pale Ditch was revealed in the section of the sewer trench and was 1.6m wide and up to 1.2m deep. The bank was less clear as construction disturbance had taken place in the area of the laneway. No finds were recovered from the clay ditch fill.
Martin Reid for Valerie J. Keeley Ltd, 29/30 Duke Street, Athy, Co. Kildare.

205. KELLYSTOWN AND TICKNOCK
Monitoring
O15702560–O16662560
98E0206
Transfer of the licence from Martin Reid (No. 204 above) permitted a continuation of monitoring the topsoil-stripping along the Southern Cross Route, for a stretch that runs from within the grounds of St Columba's College, across the Little Dargle River and through Kellystown to Ticknock. It also covered a small extension of ground disturbances at Ballycullen (O12102650). The monitoring took place between 7 and 24 September. No archaeology of significance was observed.
Niall Brady, 'Rosbeg', Ard Mhuire Park, Dalkey, Co. Dublin, for Valerie J. Keeley Ltd.

206. BOW BRIDGE HOUSE, BOW LANE WEST, KILMAINHAM
Urban post-medieval
O135338
97E0435 ext.
A pre-development archaeological assessment was carried out during 12 and 13 January 1998 in advance of a proposed apartment development close to the west bank of the River Camac at Bow Bridge House, Bow Lane West, Kilmainham, Dublin.

The Bow Bridge crosses the river Camac at Kilmainham. It appears to have been erected on the edge of Dublin City sometime after AD 1200. The Downe Survey of 1655–6 shows 'Bowe Bridge' on the 'Cammock River'. It is also illustrated on Taylor's fire survey of Kilmainham in 1671 and on subsequent maps.

The site had been cleared to modern ground level before the assessment took place. Six trenches were excavated across the site to undisturbed estuarine levels, roughly between 2.5m and 3.5m below modern ground level, but significant archaeological deposits were not encountered. In fact nothing was observed during the investigation to suggest that there was any significant archaeological activity on this site before the post-medieval era. Thick deposits of organic clay found to be lying directly over the undisturbed estuarine silts within the excavated trenches were clearly the result of river action over a considerable period of time.

After the assessment was completed, and on the recommendation of the City Archaeologist, provisional permission was given for the development to commence.

Archaeologists will have to look elsewhere in the Kilmainham area for the elusive Viking longphort.
Ruairí Ó Baoill, Archaeological Development Services Ltd, Unit 48, Westlink Enterprise Centre, 30–50 Distillery Street, Belfast BT12 5BJ.

207. (SITE ADJOINING) 7 ROWSERSTOWN LANE, KILMAINHAM

Post-medieval
O128335
98E124

The site adjoining No. 7 Rowserstown Lane, Kilmainham, lies along the River Camac between the old medieval village of Kilmainham to the south and the medieval priory and the 17th-century Royal Hospital to the north. Phase 1 of the test excavation was carried out in March 1998, Phase 2 will be carried out subject to demolition of No. 7 Rowserstown Lane and the granting of planning permission for the proposed development.

The site measured 15m east–west x 7m north–south max. Three trenches, 6.5–4.5m long and 2–1.3m wide, were excavated by hand. The earliest features uncovered were a stone-lined flue and firebox, together with deposits of clinker or slag, of probable late 18th/early 19th century date. A cobbled surface contemporary with the flue was also identified. These features were probably associated with the remains of some sort of localised industrial activity on the site, possibly a forge. The remains of mid- to late 19th-century cottage foundations sealed this activity; the cottages were demolished in the 1960s.

At the eastern end of the site, a stone wall stands *c.* 3.6m high. This wall is part of the rear wall of one of the 19th-century buildings situated on high ground, north of the development site, fronting onto Kilmainham Lane.
Georgina Scally, c/o 81 Upper Leeson Street, Dublin 4.

208. KINGSTON

No archaeological significance
O316225
98E0407

Topographic and geophysical surveys covered two areas, one on either side of the south end of the Ballinteer Road, in advance of development associated with the South-Eastern Motorway. These identified a number of possible archaeological features, and eight trenches were excavated to assess their archaeological potential. The evidence from the test excavation showed that the areas in question had been cleared of topsoil and used as a dump for adjacent housing estates in the 1960s. The topsoil was subsequently replaced, and the fields were reinstated as grazing on the east side of the road and as a public amenity on the west side.
Martin Reid for Valerie J. Keeley Ltd, 29/30 Duke Street, Athy, Co. Dublin.

209. LAMBAY ISLAND

Neolithic axe production site with associated activity
O317508
93E0144

The site shows evidence of two related activities: the working of the porphyritic andesite outcrops that form the sides of the valley for stone axe production; and the occurrence of a number of related features on the valley floor, under and partially truncated by a cultivation soil resulting from 19th-century spade cultivation.

The primary objectives of the 1998 season were:

(1) To evaluate the extent and nature of the pits and associated features in the main area of excavation on the valley floor (Test-pit 2 and associated areas, Cuttings 3 and 5–8). Several additional test-pits were excavated to determine the condition of survival and the extent of archaeological features.

(2) To continue and complete the excavation of the cross-section (Cuttings 1, 1W, 4, 9 and 10) across the valley from the working area out from the west-facing rock face to the low bank forming the east-facing side of the valley at this point. The excavation of Cuttings 1 and 1W had been completed in 1997 (*Excavations 1997*, 57–9).

(3) To examine spatial variability in the working of the porphyritic andesite by excavating a series of test-pits along the bank of porphyry build-up against the west-facing porphyritic andesite outcrop.

(4) In 1997 a series of test-pits had been dug in the small valley immediately to the west of the valley that has been the focus of the excavation project. One of these (Test-pit 3), close to the west-facing porphyritic andesite outcrop, had revealed the edge of a build-up of porphyritic andesite debitage and associated grinding stones, with little signs of disturbance by cultivation activity. To look at the nature and character of the exploitation an excavation cutting 7.3m (east–west) x 2m in extent (Cutting 11) was opened, with Test-pit 7 lying immediately to the north-west of the cutting.

The main area of excavation on the valley floor
As in previous years, all the cultivation soil that was excavated was removed in spits 0.1m deep and finds were recorded in 1m x 1m units. A distinct difference can be seen in the stratigraphic sequence beneath the cultivation soil within the excavation area. In the western part it was possible to recognise a very thin interface between the cultivation soil and the underlying subsoil. It appears that this interface represents the base of disturbance/truncation of the original palaeosol. In the eastern part of the area underlying the cultivation soil is a brown to dark brown, sandy loam (C707) over subsoil. This appears to be the surviving portion of the palaeosol. The sandy subsoil also slopes down to the east and has numerous rabbit burrows cut into it. It was hoped that C707 would have greater preservation of Neolithic features, and a number had been identified (F8–10, 14 and 15).

In 1998 a further two features were identified in the Cutting 7 area. F16 appeared to be a small segment of a trench with a distinct, loam-textured fill containing occasional charcoal flecks. In the north-east corner of Cutting 7 was a dense spread of stones (F21). Excavation of this feature exemplified the problems of recognising features in this context: there was no sign of a cut or edge and yet it appeared to be a definite feature. C707 had been churned up by rabbit-burrowing activity, and this has resulted in the destruction of the cuts of archaeological features. The stone fills of what appear originally to have been pits (F14, 15 and 21) are all that have survived to a

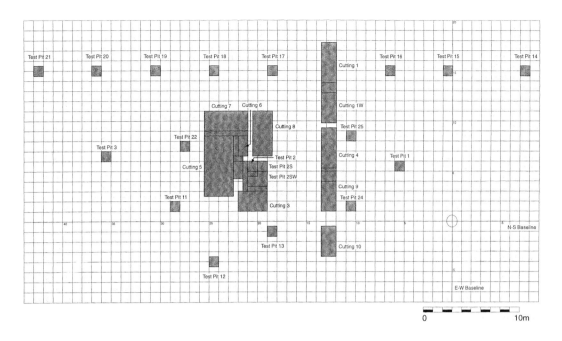

Plan of the main area of excavation at Lambay Island with current excavation areas indicated.

greater or lesser extent intact. In Cutting 8 a dark yellowish/brown, loose, sandy loam with numerous pieces of porphyry underlay C707/807 and overlay the subsoil.

To the west of the edge of C707 Neolithic features only survive as truncated cuts in the subsoil or as spreads of stone above pit features. In Cutting 5 a segment of a very shallow trench, *c.* 0.8m in surviving length, was discovered cut into the subsoil. In the fill was a small sherd of Neolithic pottery and a flint flake.

At the end of the 1998 season excavation of much of this main area was completed. What remains to be worked on is a 3m x 4.5m strip running north-east to south-west, centred on F11, F2, F7, F8 and F10.

A series of test-pits was excavated to the north and west of this main area of excavation. Test-pits 11 and 22 were immediately to the north, 12 and 13 to the west, and 26–28 at the northern end of the valley in the lowest of the three modern cultivation terraces, or small fields, east of Cutting 2. The character of the stratigraphy was similar in all these pits with the exception of Test-pit 12, which is immediately adjacent to the east-facing outcrop of porphyritic andesite forming the western side of the valley. Here was debitage immediately below the sod and above the subsoil. In all the other test-pits there was clear evidence of intensive spade cultivation. There was Neolithic flint in all, but no surviving archaeological features. The presence of Neolithic pottery and a large projectile point or javelinhead in Test-pit 13 suggests that the southern end of the valley was the main focus of Neolithic activity.

Cuttings 4, 9 and 10
In Cutting 4 what was left to excavate was the major basal layer of the porphyritic andesite material, C408, overlying a palaeosol, C409, which has some smaller porphyritic andesite pieces impressed into the surface. The basal slabs in C408 are quite large and appear to have been deliberately placed to level

up the original ground surface, which may have been quite uneven. The build-up over this surface includes non-porphyritic andesite lithic material, such as hammerstones, rubbers and struck flint flakes, some with retouch. Further west in this cutting 19th-century cultivation has truncated the stratigraphic sequence almost to the top of the palaeosol. In addition running east to west through the cutting is a series of intrusive rabbit burrows. On the south side of the main burrow run and truncated by it is a small cut feature, F13 (0.23m x 0.1m with a depth of 0.14m), cut into the palaeosol and subsoil. In this were a number of flint blades and flakes that appear to be part of a cache. This cache was sealed by C408. Excavation in 1998 revealed more disturbed flakes from the cache.

About 0.75m to the north-west of F13 on the north side of the east–west-trending burrow and cut into the subsoil was a roughly circular pit, F00, measuring 0.7m at the mouth and with a depth of 0.3m, which appears to have been sealed by the palaeosol, C409. The top of the pit seems to be disturbed on the southern side by rabbit activity. There was a large stone in the top of the pit, which was lined by small slabs on the southern side. The fill was a homogeneous, soft, dark yellowish/brown loam, with charcoal flecks. There were a number of structured deposits in the pit. In this regard F00 appears to be related in some way to the pits in the main area of excavation to the north.

Excavation revealed what appears to be the top of another pit feature (F19) in the north-west corner of Cutting 4. Here there was a setting of stones with a distinct, curved outer edge, suggesting that it is a segment of what may be a larger feature. On the surface large quantities of flint flakes and beach nodules are visible.

In Cutting 9 the cultivation soil was relatively shallow and was underlain by a compact build-up of porphyritic andesite. This context (C904) is an intact Neolithic surface with spreads of pottery and lithics,

Test Pit 14

Test Pit 15

Test Pit 16

Test Pit 17

Test Pit 18

Test Pit 19

Test Pit 20

Test Pit 21

South-facing section faces of Test-pits 14–21, showing the stratigraphic sequence in the 'bank' of porphyritic andesite debitage.

apparently corresponding to C408 (and C111) and overlying F19. C904 continues into Cutting 10, where the edge of the context can be seen running in a north–south line close to the eastern edge of the cutting.

Two test-pits (25 and 24) immediately to the south of Cuttings 4 and 9 confirm that the stratigraphic sequence seen in these areas continues to the south. It appears that C904 has a considerable surface expression and that there is a definite modern cultivation cut or truncation into the porphyritic andesite build-up along a north–south line at the east end of Cutting 4.

Test-pits 14–21
Eight test-pits were dug along the north–south line 14.5m east of the site baseline to test the stratigraphy and the character of the porphyritic andesite build-up along the bank abutting the west-facing outcrop, to the north and south of Cutting 1. Test-pit 17 was excavated down to the bottom of the build-up to see how the stratigraphy compared with the stratigraphic sequence found in Cutting 1 to the south.

The results show that there is a recognisable build-up of porphyry debitage stretching from Test-pit 14 to Test-pit 20. Test-pit 20 appears to be close to the northern terminal of this build-up, and in plan the surface of the porphyry debitage deposit curves to the east. In Test-pit 21 there was no sign of the porphyry debitage deposit. The test-pits show that along the line of the bank the porphyry debitage has been disturbed. Test-pits 15 and 17–20 all show signs of a truncation of the surface of the porphyry build-up. However, the stratigraphy in Test-pit 16, with a weathered, compact, porphyry-rich layer over the actual debitage surface, suggests that in this location the debitage build-up is undisturbed. At the southern end of the bank of debitage in Test-pit 14 it appears that what remains of the debitage is all sitting in cultivation soil. Immediately to the east of this test-pit there are also indications of modern quarrying of the porphyry outcrop in the form of what appears to be a well-defined, wedge-shaped cut into the bedrock.

Looking at the character of the surface of the debitage build-up in the test-pits and examining the components of this build-up in Test-pit 17 it seems clear that the bank of debitage is not of uniform composition and is varied along its length. It may be that the apparent regularity of the bank on the field surface is the result of modern clearance and cultivation activity and that before this it was much more amorphous, reflecting debitage from a series of quarrying and production episodes, perhaps spread over a considerable period of time during the Neolithic.

In Test-pit 21, while there is no sign of porphyry debitage, the surface of the bedrock has a ground surface with multiple, parallel, fine striae orientated north–south. These striae are the result of glacial smoothening. The implication of this is that the exposed outcrop surfaces in the valley would all have been striated. It may well be that part of the original attraction of the valley was that it had porphyritic rock outcrop that already had an apparently polished surface.

Cutting 11
In the small valley to the west of the one that has been the focus of the excavation project a cutting 7.3m (east–west) x 2m was opened up, with Test-pit 7 immediately adjacent to the north-west of the cutting. The higher, eastern end of the cutting is actually on the porphyry outcrop.

Removal of the sod revealed a compact, weathered, porphyry debitage surface. Excavation to date suggests that there are a number of distinct layers or contexts representing episodes of quarrying and production. A major spread of debitage forms the current excavation surface. Towards the western end of the cutting a rabbit burrow disturbed the surface of this context, but further west is a zone with a concentration of pieces of porphyry with ground surfaces and small sandstone rubbers.

Within the excavated layers of the debitage are small flakes and chips of flint, some burnt, occasional pieces of rock crystal and small sherds of Neolithic pottery. Most of the last seems to resemble the decorated bowl pottery found elsewhere on the site, but there are also sherds of thin-walled, fine pottery that may come from carinated bowls (Western Neolithic pottery).

Radiocarbon dating
A sample of *Prunus* charcoal from one of the fill contexts in the large excavated pit feature (F1) on the valley floor was submitted to the Radiocarbon Laboratory, Department of Experimental Physics, UCD. The sample dates to 4930±175 radiocarbon years BP (rounded to the nearest five years). Calibration of the date was carried out using the CALIB programme of Stuiver and Reimer (1993) and was based on the decadal calibration of the dating using the intercept method. The 1-sigma calibrated age range for the sample is estimated as 3965–3383 BC. This provides an indication of the date of activity on the site. Further samples from other contexts are being dated.

The final season of excavation will take place in 1999. Excavation in 1998 was grant-assisted by funding from *Dúchas* The Heritage Service, Department of Arts, Heritage, Gaeltacht and the Islands, on the recommendation of the National Committee for Archaeology of the Royal Irish Academy.
Gabriel Cooney, Department of Archaeology, University College Dublin, Belfield, Dublin 4.

210. 10 MAIN STREET, LUCAN
Medieval borough
303361 235445
98E0416
Archaeological trial-trenching was undertaken at a proposed development to the rear of 10 Main Street, Lucan, on 6 September 1998. The work was undertaken in compliance with a request from the Planning Authority for additional information in respect of the proposed development.

The site lies within the medieval manorial borough of Lucan, which is believed to have been established a short time after the Anglo-Norman invasion. The street-plan of the borough was essentially linear, and the modern Main Street is on the site of its medieval predecessor.

Three trial-trenches were excavated by hand. Two cobbled surfaces were uncovered, separated by a layer of silty sand that had a maximum thickness of 370mm. The upper cobbled surface is clearly associated with the existing premises. Investigation of the lower cobbled surface indicated that it was not truncated by the foundations associated with the present structure, indicating that it was also associated with the existing premises. It appears that the garden area was raised at some time in the past, and this is demonstrated by the fact that the present yard surface is *c.* 300mm above that of the internal ground-floor level of the existing building.

No features, structures or finds of archaeological interest were uncovered during the testing.
Martin E. Byrne, 39 Kerdiff Park, Monread, Naas, Co. Kildare.

211. MAIN STREET/THE SQUARE, LUCAN
Urban
30332 28331
Archaeological monitoring took place, in advance of the building of a commercial premises, on the site of a demolished building on the corner of Main Street and The Square, Lucan. Because the area was within a zone of archaeological potential there were several conditions attached to the planning permission issued by *An Bord Pleanála.*

The previous buildings had already been demolished before commencement of monitoring, and most of the floors had been removed. The sub-floor had been laid directly on a natural deposit of sand and gravel. This deposit was dug through to a depth of 3.4–3.5m below the modern floor level. No archaeological deposits, features or artefacts were found across the area of the development.
Jim Higgins, 'St Geralds', 18 College Road, Galway.

212. 'THE ORCHARD', OLD LEIXLIP ROAD, LUCAN
No archaeological significance
98E0149
An archaeological assessment was carried out on the site of proposed development (a block of apartments) at 'The Orchard', Old Leixlip Road, Lucan, Co. Dublin. Part of the site was within the zone of archaeological potential for Lucan, as identified by the Urban Archaeological Survey.

Three trial-trenches were opened by mechanical excavator on 23 March 1998. Each was excavated to natural subsoil.

Trench 1 was 43m long and 0.6m wide on a south-west/north-east axis. It was *c.* 0.4–0.8m deep and was made up of redeposited topsoil and three horizons of stone deposits, which formed the foundations of a gravel pathway. No archaeological remains were found.

Trench 2 was 35m long and 0.6m wide on a south-east/north-west axis. It was *c.* 1m deep and was made up a homogeneous layer of redeposited topsoil. No archaeological remains were uncovered.

Trench 3 was 21m long and 0.6m wide on a south-west/north-east axis. It was *c.* 0.9–1m deep and was made up of two layers of gravel, a layer of redeposited topsoil and a layer of natural clay intermixed with small to medium-sized stones. No archaeological remains were uncovered.

This assessment did not uncover any archaeological remains on the site of proposed development.
Eoghan Moore for Arch-Tech Ltd, 32 Fitzwilliam Place, Dublin 2.

213. POST OFFICE ROAD, LUSK
Possible Early Christian/medieval
322115 253413
98E0116

An archaeological assessment took place at a proposed residential development at Post Office Road, Lusk, Co. Dublin. The site was thought to be within the enclosure of an early monastery founded by St MacCuillinn in the 5th century. Six trenches were excavated along the proposed foundations and bio-cycle unit. Trenches were dug to 1–1.35m deep and revealed sod, ploughsoil and boulder clay.

Trench One revealed a black layer at a depth of 0.9m. This layer contained shell, burnt animal bone and fragments of iron slag but no datable artefacts. It was 0.2m thick and overlay boulder clay. Proposed house foundations will not extend beyond 0.75m below the surface and will not truncate archaeological deposits.
Deirdre Murphy, Archaeological Consultancy Services Ltd, 15 Trinity Street, Drogheda, Co. Louth.

214. QUARRYVALE, PALMERSTOWN UPPER
Area of burning
307000 234580
96E0178 ext.

In June 1998 further topsoil removal was monitored, the initial work having been carried out during 1996 (*Excavations 1996*, 37).

An area of burning was identified, and subsequently an area 2m x 5m was excavated. Although the feature had been disturbed by deep ploughing, prehistoric pottery (one sherd of decorated, coarse Beaker ware and one sherd of either undecorated Beaker ware or Late Bronze Age coarseware (R.M. Cleary, pers. comm.)) and a flint flake were found. These early finds were associated with modern pottery as a result of the ploughing.

The discovery of evidence of prehistoric occupation, albeit limited, shows the value of on-going monitoring on a site that has already had four phases of topsoil clearance with negligible results.
O. Scully with C. Kelleher and C. Gleeson, 7 Bayview, Tramore, Co. Waterford.

215. SCHOLARSTOWN
Possible *fulacht fiadh*
O311227
98E0518

This site was identified as a series of burnt spreads by Colin Gracie during monitoring of topsoil-stripping of the South-Eastern Motorway (see No. 121, above). A two-week excavation was conducted at the beginning of November, and the spreads were defined more fully. They consisted of deposits of burnt stone with some charcoal and several pits also filled with burnt stone and clay. No archaeological materials were recovered, and there was no indication of a trough. Several soil samples were taken for analysis, and results are awaited.
Martin Reid for Valerie J. Keeley Ltd, 29/30 Duke Street, Athy, Co. Kildare.

216. PHOENIX STREET/STABLE LANE, SMITHFIELD
Medieval
98E0398

Eoin Halpin carried out pre-development testing on this site in September 1998. Organic deposits of possibly medieval date were identified under post-medieval deposits.

This writer commenced excavation on the site in November 1998, and work is ongoing. Four areas (8m x 8m, 11m x 24m, 6m x 11m and 15m x 8m) representing *c.* 48% of the site are currently being resolved. The archaeological material is being predominantly hand-excavated but where practical is being machine-excavated. A metal-detector has scanned all possible medieval soils, at the request of the National Museum.

To date, a series of medieval and post-medieval ditches has been identified underlying post-medieval industrial activity. Two post-medieval wells have also been identified, and a post-and-wattle fence has been noted within one of the medieval ditches.

The post-medieval finds include pottery, tiles, clay pipes and coins. The finds of possibly medieval date recovered include fabrics, leather, pottery, coins, nails, floor tiles, shroud-pins, a silver finger-ring and a possible silver ingot.
Una Cosgrave, Archaeological Development Services Ltd, Windsor House, 11 Fairview Strand, Fairview, Dublin 3.

217. STEPASIDE
Bronze Age/medieval
O193238
97E0467

This licence originally for testing (*Excavations 1997*, 24) was extended to cover a rescue excavation in advance of construction at a housing estate. The excavation covered an area measuring *c.* 38m x 32m. With the exception of features cut into the subsoil, most deposits had been affected by ploughing. Nevertheless, the excavation did identify a series of activities including settlement, the construction of field boundaries, agricultural cultivation and quarrying.

Evidence of settlement was based on a series of post-holes and wall slots. Soil samples contained charcoal, and oak, ash and hazel species were identified from these. One of these charcoal samples (oak) was sent to Groningen for ^{14}C dating and produced a date of 3670±50 BP.

Settlement was also represented by pottery, as well as struck and worked flints, which were found across the site. The flint assemblage was examined by Nyree Finlay of UCC, who concluded 'the chronological affinities of the assemblage are Neolithic–Bronze Age with a post-EBA date preferred for most of the material'. The pottery was identified as Leinster cooking ware, a 13th- to early 14th-century ware.

Field boundaries were represented by a linear north-east/south-west-oriented ditch, which also served as a drainage channel. Several fragments of the medieval pottery were found in the fill. Analysis of a soil sample from the ditch identified charred grains of oat (*Avena* sp.) and a possible rye grain (*Secale* sp.).

Agricultural cultivation was identified in a whole series of regularly spaced furrows, which were oriented at an approximate right angle to the drainage ditch/field boundary. While it is thought that most of the furrows were contemporary with the boundary, some cut through the backfill, thus indicating a later date.

Evidence of quarrying was seen where a large quarry-pit truncated the east side of the site, including one side of the area of post-holes.

Martin Reid for Valerie J. Keeley Ltd, 29/30 Duke Street, Athy, Co. Kildare.

218. CHURCH LANE, SWORDS

Urban medieval

98E0082

This site lies within the town of Swords and is bordered on the south-east by the Ward River, on the north-east by the Old Vicarage and on the north-west and west by Church Lane, on the other side of which is the medieval church and round tower. During the renovation of the Old Vicarage building human skeletal remains were uncovered after the removal of floorboards. The remains consisted of one partly articulated skeleton and scattered bone fragments over a previously disturbed ground level. Before further work the remains of an estimated further six skeletons were removed. Subsequent archaeological work (by Geraldine Dunne, *Excavations 1997*, 61) revealed five more partly articulated skeletons, the line and orientation of which indicate that they were Christian burials pre-dating the vicarage, at least part of which was built in the 17th century, and were disturbed by its foundations.

The original line of the monastic enclosure is unclear, although it is possible that the stream formed one of its boundaries. The present ground levels are not a reflection of their previous height, as the garden of the Old Vicarage is up to 5.5m higher than the level of the site under investigation, with a stone wall set on exposed bedrock separating them. At the north end of the site Church Lane is *c.* 6.25m higher than the area bordering the stream. The ground level at the stream seems to have been built up, as the stream banks are quite steep at this point. Local history refers to the site as having been used as a quarry, and this is borne out both by an engineer's report and by the depth of disturbance found in the northern part of the site. Bedrock is also exposed beneath the stone wall that borders Church Lane.

Work was carried out over two days of very overcast and wet weather.

Test-trench 1 was set on average 2m from the boundary wall with the Old Vicarage and ran parallel to it, north-west/south-east. It was 21.7m long and was disturbed along the greater part of its length up to a point 8m from its south-eastern end. Over the first 14m of the trench the general profile was humus (100) averaging 0.2m deep, followed by a dark, stony soil, a balanced clay/sand (101a), averaging 0.15m deep. At the junction between Trenches 1 and 2, 3m from the west end of Trench 1, was an area of dumped material containing mortar, brick, modern china and glass, and also the remains of a modern drain or wall footing. There were also some fragments of human bone in the layer (103) that contained the mortar. This layer overlay 102, a light-coloured clay that appeared to be redeposited at this point. Layer 103 occurred at two other points along this trench and may coincide with foundations of one of the glasshouses that had stood on this part of the site; the wall footing was most likely part of such a structure as well. Layer 101a 8m from the west end became much less stony and had the appearance of a rich, modern garden soil, termed 101b.

About 7.5m from the east end of the trench bedrock and undisturbed boulder clay (104) began to appear on the north side. Over the last 7m of the trench at a depth of 0.6m below the surface was a layer (105) of mid- to dark brown, friable, silty loam with a large quantity of shell inclusions. These consisted of mostly intact mussel, limpet and oyster shells. This layer deepened at the east end and was at least 0.5m thick. It lay below a thicker (0.25m) spread of the dark, stony soil (102). Further west, at 6.5m from the east end, was a cut (F101) in the boulder clay that ran into the face of the bedrock. It was almost vertical, running diagonally across the trench from bedrock southwards, and cut from the north-west side, but no opposite side occurred. The fill was the shell-filled layer 105, and no finds occurred. It was known that peach trees had been planted at this point, and the cut may relate to modern gardening activity or to quarrying.

Finds from Test-trench 1 included the head and part of the neck of two possibly human femurs, flower pot fragments, modern and bottle glass and two sherds of medieval pottery, both local ware.

This mortar-bearing layer (103) occurred at different points over the site and usually contained post-medieval and modern material; only in Trench 1 did human bone occur.

Test-trench 2, 44.65m long, was aligned north-east/south-west roughly along the centre of the proposed building. As in Trench 1, no attempt was made to find natural in the areas that clearly had been quarried (i.e., the first 15m from the junction with Trench 1). The material uncovered was broadly similar, with significant stretches of 103 at an average depth of 0.8m below the surface. At a distance of 10.2m from the junction of Trenches 1 and 2 the remains of a wall or foundation projected into the cutting from the east side. This was 0.6m below the surface, and a spread of 103 occurred to either side. Within this to the south of the foundation walling were pieces of slag (iron) and fragments of pantile. A pale, mottled clay (102/4) was revealed beneath 103, but it was not obvious whether it was redeposited. To the south of the remains of the foundation the clay had a less disturbed appearance. From a point *c.* 20m from the north end of the trench layer 103 overlay a layer (106) that was initially similar to 101b but contained some charcoal, abundant small stones and shell flecks and had more of a clay content. This was less than 0.1m thick, and then 104 resumed. This layer 106 was noted for the remainder of the trench.

Finds from Test-trench 2 included pantile fragments, iron slag, modern china and a sherd of post-medieval slip ware.

Test-trench 3 projected for 4m west of Trench 2 and continued for 10m to the east. For the first 6m from west to east the stratigraphy was as for the southern end of Trench 2. This changed 6m from the west end of the cutting, and the remaining 8m contained *in situ* medieval deposits with a rather enigmatic stone feature. The layers 100, 101b and 106 were present; 103 did not occur.

Below 106, now 0.3m deep, and at a distance of 9.6m from the west end of the cutting, a dark brown soil with abundant small stones and occasional shell, bone and charcoal was uncovered (107). This also produced four sherds of medieval pottery (13th/14th century). This layer, 0.15m thick, overlay a layer of yellow marl (108), which projected into it from the east side. This partly overlay and partly abutted a layer (109) of broken stones, some of which had a burnt appearance, all angular and *c.* 60–80mm long. Beneath this were large, irregular, flat stones that formed a rough paving (F102), gently sloping from the west to the east. The stones were between 0.2m and 0.4m long. Only a part of the paving was exposed, for a distance of 1.5m, but it continued further east than this point. Layer 107 continued part way over this sequence of 108 and 109 and rose slightly towards the east. It abutted a layer of similar texture but lighter colour, which contained a very large quantity of shells. It was the same material as found in Trench 1, layer 105. This layer was *c.* 0.3m thick and directly overlay 109. At a distance of 2.3m from the beginning of the paving two rough courses of large stones occurred, running north–south and set into 105. This possible wall was, like the paving, unmortared, and was contained within 105. It is not certain that it is an actual feature as opposed to a dump of stones.

Test-trench 4 (7.1m long) was set 4.8m to the north of Test-trench 3 and ran parallel to it. Its stratigraphy was as follows: 100, 101b humus and topsoil, 0.4m deep. Brown, silty clay, high mortar content, 103, depth 0.25m. Grey-brown clay silt with charcoal and organic inclusions, 106, 0.1m thick. Dark brown soil, friable, silty clay with bone, charcoal and medieval pottery, 107, 0.3m thick, followed by the shell-rich layer 105, which was 0.4m thick. Below this was a similar layer with fewer shells, 105a, and this extended for another 0.4m. There was a pale clay on the bottom, but directly overlying it in 105a were many pieces of charcoal up to 15mm long. The trench was excavated to this depth, 1.85m, at one point only. There were two finds from this cutting, both from 107: a possible line-impressed tile, very abraded and possibly cut, and a body sherd of probable local ware.

Test-trench 5 was 3m long, and, as the upper layers contained a lot of later rubble, it was decided to attempt to find natural. A grey/green clay, very compact, became greyer and wetter and was seemingly devoid of finds. It was attempted to find the depth of bedrock at this point, and a stony, gravelly layer was reached at 3m. The material above this was the grey clay, but at this depth a large portion of a Victorian creamware plate was found. As this cutting did not coincide with the engineer's test-trenches as recorded, it is possible that this is the result of backfill into a quarried area.

The site has been altered from its original topography by quarrying, possibly in the late 18th and early 19th centuries. Its subsequent use as a garden has further modified it. It is possible also that the riverbank was raised. It is clear that the site was a quarry and that this affected the northern sector. This activity would have removed archaeology in this area. As the bedrock rises towards both Church Lane and the Old Vicarage the depth of the overburden correspondingly decreases.

The presence of human bone at the junction of Trenches 1 and 2 within a layer containing significant amounts of mortar and rubble is probably best seen in the context of modifications carried out to both the Old Vicarage and its gardens, which were terraced, at various stages in the past. The shell layer (105) uncovered at the east end of Trench 1 would by analogy with that in Trenches 3 and 4 pre-date the layers that produced the medieval pottery. Given that the pottery is in an abraded condition, with two possibly late medieval sherds and an abraded/ reworked tile, and that this shell layer appears to contain the paved area and adjacent possible wall, it is most likely also medieval in date. The paved area in Trench 3 may relate to some semi-industrial rather than domestic activity, although what type is not clear. There are some 0.5m of deposits containing medieval/late medieval material above it.

Finola O'Carroll, Greenanstown, Stamullin, Co. Meath.

219. MAIN STREET, SWORDS
No archaeological significance
O182470
98E0165

Fingal County Council relaid a sewer along the length of Main Street. The work was monitored. No undisturbed ground was encountered, owing to the considerable number of existing trenches, and rock was encountered at an extremely high level. In most areas the bedding for the road surface overlay rock. No archaeological deposits were noted.

Claire Walsh, 25a Eaton Square, Terenure, Dublin 6W.

220. THE STAR BAR, MAIN STREET/CHAPEL LANE, SWORDS
Possibly medieval
3183 2468
98E0443

A single test-trench, 15.5m long by 1m wide, was opened along the front of an extension to the premises. This was undertaken with the agreement of *Dúchas* The Heritage Service as a compensatory measure after the developer had failed to adhere to the archaeological condition contained in his planning permission.

The excavated trench revealed deposits of 'garden-type' soil containing 18th/19th-century fill, overlying natural deposits. The fill contained post-medieval pottery including blackware and transfer ware. However, two sherds of medieval pottery (Dublin glazed ware) were also found in this soil, indicating medieval occupation in the vicinity.
Mary McMahon (for Arch-Tech Ltd), 77 Brian Road, Marino, Dublin 3.

221. THE OLD SCHOOLHOUSE RESTAURANT, SWORDS

No archaeological significance
O179464
98E0317

Testing took place on 22 July 1998. Two trenches were machine-excavated down to undisturbed natural. The results suggest that the construction of the schoolhouse, allied to localised quarrying, removed any significant archaeology from the area of the proposed restaurant extension.

The ground to the north, the location of extra carpark space, appeared to be devoid of any archaeological remains, although the presence of mature trees and dense undergrowth precluded an extensive examination of this area. Its location, close to the course of the River Ward, may be significant.

It was not possible on this occasion, owing to difficulty of access, to test the area to the south of the restaurant, where it is proposed to construct an extension to the existing carpark.
Eoin Halpin, Archaeological Development Services Ltd, Unit 48, Westlink Enterprise Centre, 30–50 Distillery Street, Belfast BT12 5BJ.

222. 'THE BREHON'S CHAIR', TAYLORSGRANGE

Multi-period
O130265
SMR 22:33
96E0091

An extensive programme of archaeological monitoring and excavation was carried out between 15 April and 19 June 1998 in advance of a housing development adjacent to the south and east of the Brehon's Chair portal tomb, Taylorsgrange, Rathfarnham.

Four seasons of excavation by Valerie Keeley to the north of the tomb had revealed a wide scatter of features accompanied by fine and coarse pottery and a wide range of lithic artefacts dating to the Neolithic to the Early Bronze Age (*JIA* **V**, 1989–90; 74, *Excavations 1985*, 23–4; *Excavations 1986*, 18; *Excavations 1987*, 14–15). In 1996 work by Tim Coughlan involving two archaeological assessments and a geophysical survey in the area of the proposed development revealed a number of features of archaeological potential (*Excavations 1996*, 39).

Despite the fact that much of the archaeological material discovered in the course of the excavation was fragmentary and highly truncated by later agricultural activity, the site yielded evidence of Neolithic, Beaker, Early Bronze Age, Iron Age and Early Christian activity in the form of hearths, postholes and pits.

After the removal of topsoil the site was divided into three areas, A, B and C.

Area A lay 35m east of the Brehon's Chair. It was highly truncated by post-medieval agricultural activity, which removed virtually all horizontal stratigraphy, leaving only an incoherent series of negative features.

It showed evidence of two phases of use, although these were not clearly distinguishable between all the features recorded. It was cut by a number of stake-holes most of which had no coherent pattern, although several may have represented the truncated remains of small fences. There was also evidence of three hearths, F11, F26 and F69, across the area, all of which survived as small areas of fire-reddened clay over natural. F26 was surrounded by a series of three double stake-holes, which probably functioned as some form of hearth furniture, possibly a tripod. A small burnt pit 5m to the north of F26 produced a calibrated date of 3620–3356 BC. There was an almost complete absence of diagnostic artefacts from Area A, a burnt hollow scraper being a notable exception.

Those features that can be reasonably linked to Phase 2 activity consisted of several spreads of charcoal-flecked clay, which sealed earlier stake-holes, and a linear spread of stone, F40, some 5.8m long, which had been badly disturbed by later activity. The function of F40 was unclear. Two highly weathered Beaker sherds were found adjacent to it; it was not apparent whether this pottery was *in situ* or redeposited as a result of later disturbance.

Although no clear pattern could be placed on the features within Area A, it appears that they represented some form of small-scale or marginal activity adjacent to the monument, perhaps the tail end of the more substantial activity discovered by V.J Keeley to the north.

Area B, 14m south of Area A, contained the only evidence of *in situ* and coherent archaeological stratigraphy across the site.

The earliest phase consisted of a Beaker hearth-pit, F231, which was surrounded on one side by two concentric lines of stake-holes forming windbreaks. Roughly 1.2m to the north-west of the hearth lay a small burnt pit that contained flecks of cremated animal bone. This was surrounded by an almost continuous ring of small stake-holes, which again appeared to act as some form of windbreak around the pit.

To the north of the hearth was evidence of three small, east–west-orientated fences running across Area B. The maximum surviving length of any of them was 2m. Their proximity to each other suggested that they were not contemporary. It was likely that they acted as windbreaks, sheltering the area around the hearth.

Phase 2, Level 1, consisted of a layer of dark brown/purple, sod-like, humic clay, F101, which probably represented the remains of an old ground surface. This sealed the Beaker features and contained a number of decorated vase urn fragments, several of which had carbonised material on their inner surface. Although no cut features or structural elements were discovered, six pieces of baked clay, interpreted as daub, suggest the possibility of adjacent features. The carbonised material on the interior of the vase urn also suggests domestic activity.

A layer of compact, brown clay, F102, which acted as the working surface for Phase 2, Level 2, sealed F101. The central feature of this level was a rough stone surface, F124. The surface was orientated north-west/south-east, an axis of orientation that ran directly through the Brehon's Chair to the north-west. The entrance to the south-eastern end of the surface was formed by two large boulders, which were tightly hugged by the cobbles.

At the north-western end of F124 lay a small burnt pit containing fragments of cremated animal bone. Much of F102 was sealed by a compact, burnt, black clay, which appeared to have accumulated as a result of the activity associated with the use of the pit.

Phase 3 dated to the early part of the Early Christian period and was represented by a series of three successive large burnt pits, all in a small area measuring 3m x 1.5m. These pits lay 3m to the west of the Beaker hearth and had been heavily truncated by a trial-trench dating to 1996.

Black, charcoal-rich clays, some of which contained charred cereal remains, filled what remained of the pits. The bases of the pits, where they survived, had been reddened through intensive burning. It has been suggested that these pits may have functioned as areas where grain was dried out/ processed before consumption; the validity of this interpretation should become clearer following post-excavation analysis.

A date of AD 540–647 was obtained from the fill of F93, the latest in the series of pits. The fact that the two earlier pits were identical in form, and located directly below F93, suggested that they were broadly contemporary.

Area C was heavily disturbed by post-medieval activity, and only isolated stake-holes survived. Despite this, 52 sherds of Beaker pottery, representing at least seven vessels, were retrieved from the ploughsoil covering the area.

Monitoring of soil-stripping for house foundations and for the site access road also revealed a number archaeological features, including two possible hearths, scatters of stake-holes, several large post-holes and three large burnt pits.

Two of the burnt pits, F182 and F236, lay within 1.2m of each other and 15m south of Area B. They were similar in form and size to the Phase 3 pits in Area B, and their bases were also fire-reddened. They contained no evidence of cereal remains and were somewhat earlier, with F182 yielding a date of 160 BC–AD 58.

F143 lay 15m south-west of F182 and F236, was shallower and contained fragments of cremated animal bone. F143 was dated to between AD 238 and AD 392.

The function of these pits is uncertain. F182 and F236 may have had a similar function to the pits in Area B and may represent a form of cereal processing that was carried out in the area over a period of 500–600 years. F143, on the other hand, may have functioned as a cooking-/roasting-pit.

Phasing and interpretation of most of the archaeological features excavated was extremely difficult owing to the high level of later agricultural disturbance and to the fact that within the confines of the development many of the features occurred in relative isolation. Despite this, we can speculate that the area was occupied through the prehistoric period up to at least the Early Christian period.

The Neolithic evidence discovered suggests that the main settlement was concentrated to the north of the monument, with more peripheral activity occurring to the east in Area A. The available evidence suggests that the Beaker occupation was centred on the higher ground to the south of the monument. Although no coherent structural elements were found associated with the Beaker hearth F231, it is likely that it was domestic in function. Beaker house sites are rare in the Irish record, with many 'domestic' sites being represented by pottery scatters and hearths. Despite the truncated and fragmentary nature of the surviving evidence, the spread of Beaker pottery across Areas A, B, C and in some of the areas monitored to the south of these suggests widespread Beaker activity across the site.

The Early Bronze Age material again appears to be domestic in nature. Sherds of vase urn have been known to occur in habitation contexts, for example in Dalkey Island. This level appears to have been deliberately sealed by the clay F102. The orientation of the stone surface F124 with the monument may suggest a possible ritual function.

Wood identification of the charcoal filling the Early Christian pits indicates a managed landscape, with hedgerow species being identified along with cereals, straw and weeds that grow alongside cultivated species. Although this evidence implies that the area was inhabited, no such features were identified.

Thus despite the fragmentary nature of the archaeological evidence it is apparent that the Brehon's Chair remained a landmark for the inhabitants of the area throughout the prehistoric and early historic period.

Rob Lynch, Irish Archaeological Consultancy Ltd, 8 Dungar Terrace, Dun Laoghaire, Co. Dublin.

223. TAYLOR'S GRANGE
No archaeological significance
O130265
98E0078
Trial-trenching was carried out in advance of construction of the Southern Cross Route Motorway in an area close to the site of a possible tower on the Kellystown Road (an area mostly taken up by the Grange Lodge Hotel). Nothing of archaeological significance was observed

Colin D. Gracie, 8 Abbeydale Close, Lucan, Co. Dublin, for Valerie J. Keeley Ltd.

224. TEMPLEOGUE, HOUSE, TEMPLEOGUE
Precinct of castle
3127 2288
SMR 22:10
98E0221
Testing and monitoring were undertaken at the above site on behalf of South Dublin County Council to determine whether there were any surviving archaeological features in the immediate vicinity of Templeogue House.

Previous archaeological and historical research suggests that Templeogue House was built in the middle of the 16th century. A castle was initially built at this site, which, in the early years of the 18th century, was renovated as a Queen Anne House. It was during this period that Sir Compton Domville built an elaborate water garden. The next major transformation Templeogue House underwent was in the early years of the 19th century, when the house was entirely rebuilt. The most recent transformation took place in the late 1980s, with the demolition of the entire western wing to facilitate the construction of St Michael's House. One of the main effects of this cycle of construction and demolition has been the severe disturbance of the surrounding area.

Three trenches were positioned to the north and east of Templeogue House. A consistent stratigraphy was apparent in the cuttings, reflecting the construction works that had taken place. In the course of testing, a ditch was identified to the north of Templeogue House. This ditch is most likely to have been constructed in the 18th century, as part of Sir Compton Domville's water garden.

Rónán Swan, Arch-Tech Ltd, 32 Fitzwilliam Place, Dublin 2.

225. WOODSIDE
Tree ring, possible ringfort
O325218
SMR 22:69
98E0074

A site topographic survey of this monument at Woodside, Sandyford, including contour plans and hill-shaded models, was carried out by Barry Masterson and Paul Sinnott of the Discovery Programme. This showed the earthwork to have an internal diameter of 24m and an external diameter of *c.* 28.5m.

Three test-trenches were excavated in February 1998, two across the bank and ditch and one in the interior of the circle. Trench 1, excavated across the east side of the feature, uncovered a U-shaped ditch (2m wide, 0.5–0.65m deep) and internal bank (0.5–0.7m high). The similarity of proportions indicates that the bank was formed from material upcast from the ditch. A 'Paris Vase' or 18th–19th-century stoneware base sherd was recovered from the ditch, along with an iron coal shovel, iron horseshoe and nails. Trench 2, a small trench excavated to a depth of 0.25–0.3m in the middle of the ring, consisted of a profile of rooty humic soil over boulder clay. Trench 3 was excavated across the bank and ditch in the south-west. In this area the ditch was 1m wide and only 0.25m deep. The bank was 0.6–0.7m higher than the external ground level here, which is partially accounted for by the prevailing slope. An iron-link chain, a horseshoe and further iron nails were found in this section of the ditch.

The survey illustrates that the earthwork is circular in plan, which is one of the more distinctive criteria for recognition of a tree ring. The lack of any clear entrance gap and the planting of ornamental trees including beech on the ring-bank also point to its being a tree ring. The lack of finds that clearly

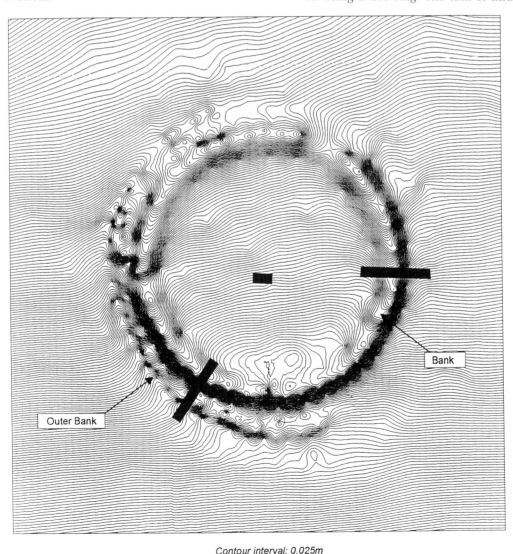

Contour interval: *0.025m*

0m   10m   20m   30m   40m

Contour plan indicating excavated areas at Woodside, Co. Dublin.

pre-date the 17th century, when the earliest tree rings were constructed, also points to this category of monument.

Archaeological monitoring of groundworks was recommended; however, the National Monuments Service may require further archaeological investigations before this goes ahead.

Martin Reid, 37 Errigal Road, Drimnagh, Dublin 12.

FERMANAGH

226. MOLLY MOUNTAIN, MOLLY

Prehistoric burial

H23752801

SMR 259:1

The site lay on a limestone plateau on the north-western slopes of Molly Mountain at an altitude of *c.* 180m. Upon initial inspection it resembled a raised platform with remnants of a circular enclosing bank, *c.* 42m in diameter, partially incorporated into the existing field boundaries.

Full excavation revealed a centrally located cinerary urn cremation adjacent to a cremation cist surrounded by smaller pits containing fragments of pottery, burnt bone and worked flint. One of these smaller pits also produced fire-cracked stone, which was similarly present in a *fulacht fiadh*-like trough 3m south of the main pit concentration.

Two clusters of stake-holes were uncovered to the north and south of the site. These stake-hole patterns were not easily identifiable as discrete structures; however, both patterns contain arcs of four to five stake-holes amid the apparent random distribution.

The structure of the site was predominantly natural, with the exception of a stone and earth bank running across the south of the site linking natural rock outcrops to the east and west, thus forming an enclosure. The internal face of the bank was well finished, with local limestone slabs set on their sides. The southern bank appeared to post-date the lowest layers of internal stratigraphy. Several scatters of pottery were recorded within the natural bedrock fissures.

A single east–west inhumation lay outside the site to the east. This inhumation occurred within a shallow, stone-lined grave that truncated an earlier circular pit with evidence of intense burning at its base.

Photographs, plans and descriptions of finds and features at this site are available on the Internet at: http//ourworld.compuserve.com/homepages/JChanning/.

John Channing, 17 Rowan House, Sussex Road, Dublin 4.

227. REYFAD

Earthwork enclosure

H1124 4613

SMR 210:72

Set on a small eminence that lies a short distance to the east of the Reyfad cup-and-ring marked stones (SMR 210:13), the monument lies in the Reyfad hills overlooking the Sacred Heart Church in Toneel North townland, where an Early Christian cross-shaft and base are situated (SMR 210:14).

First recorded in 1987 during fieldwork by Brian

Williams of the Environment and Heritage Service, DOE NI, the earthwork consists of a small, subrectangular, earthen platform defined on three sides (east, west and south) by scarps but level with the ground surface on the northern side. The monument measures *c.* 22m north-west/south-east by 27m. The enclosing bank is most prominent along the east section, while in the south-east corner there is a gap some 2m wide, which may mark the position of an original entrance. In the north-west sector of the enclosed space is a raised area, some 0.5m high, which displays evidence of a rectangular line of overgrown stone footings, which may mark the location of an artificial platform. A short distance downslope to the north is what appears to be the opening into a natural cave in the limestone bedrock.

The proximity of the earthwork to the cup-and-ring marked stones offers the possibility that the earthwork is of prehistoric date. Alternatively, it may be a rath of irregular form or a late medieval settlement site. Clearly this is an enigmatic monument, and, as such, the objective of the excavation was to ascertain an understanding of its date, morphology and function.

The excavation was undertaken during a two-week period in August 1998. The Environment and Heritage Service, DOE NI, provided material assistance.

Two trenches were opened. Trench 1 was 1m x 12m, orientated north-east/south-west and bisected the earthen bank and the artificial platform in the north-west sector of the monument. Trench 2 was opened in the interior of the earthwork and consisted of a 2m x 2m trench orientated east–west.

In Trench 1 the topsoil, containing a number of post-medieval artefacts, was removed to a depth of *c.* 0.1–0.2m. In the central area of the trench an outcrop of limestone bedrock was revealed, which acted as a division in the trench. In the north-east end the topsoil lay directly above a layer of clay that contained small to medium-sized stones loosely deposited throughout. Two lines of boulders aligned north–south formed the outer edge of the artificial platform, and a paved surface abutted the eastern face of this revetment. The paving consisted of angular slabs embedded in a brown clay to provide a level surface, and a cereal grain was recovered from the clay bedding.

Removal of topsoil from the south-west end of the trench revealed that a foundation cutting had been dug into the natural land surface. The cutting had subsequently been filled with large, angular boulders, bedded in a sticky, orange clay and forming a foundation raft that abutted the south-western edge of the outcrop of bedrock. A cattle astralagus was discovered on the surface of the foundation raft. This has been submitted for radiocarbon dating. A heavily compacted bank of gravelly soil had then been deposited over the central area of bedrock, and this cap sloped down to cover the north-east-facing edge of the foundation raft.

The removal of topsoil in Trench 2 revealed a single archaeological feature cut into the natural surface at the northern end of the trench. This comprised a circular stain of grey clay delineated by four medium-sized stones. It is not intended that any future excavation be undertaken in this section of the site.

The enigmatic nature of the earthwork has been further highlighted during this initial period of investigation, and it is intended that a second season of excavation will be undertaken during August 1999. *Colm J. Donnelly and Eileen M. Murphy, 24 Lille Park, Finaghy, Belfast BT10 0LR.*

228. SILLEES RIVER
Dredgings
H120500
A metal-detecting investigation was carried out on the dredgings from the Sillees River. The material located had no archaeological significance.
M. McDonagh, Built Heritage, EHS, 5–33 Hill Street, Belfast.

GALWAY

---

229. ABBEYLANDS SOUTH
No archaeological significance
98E0073
This project involved monitoring the excavation of foundation and service trenches at Dunmore School, Abbeylands South, Dunmore, Co. Galway. Nothing of archaeological significance was revealed.
Fiona Rooney, Archaeological Consultancy, Ballydavid South, Athenry, Co. Galway.

230. ATHENRY HOUSE, ATHENRY
Urban medieval
15022 22771
SMR 94:1
98E0432
Test-excavation was undertaken in advance of planning, from 28 September to 8 October 1998. The site lies immediately south of the modern town and comprises *c.* 8.5 acres of unenclosed pastureland. The ruins of the imposing early 19th-century Athenry House and its associated coach-house and outbuildings lie towards the north-west end of the site. The site is within the bounds of the Anglo-Norman town, which was founded by Meiler de Bermingham in around 1235. A 75m stretch of the medieval town wall forms the south boundary of the site, and the site of the Spitle Gate, a postern into the medieval town, lies in the southern corner of the site. It has been suggested that the gate probably gets its name from a hospital that must have stood in this area, away from the inhabited part of the town. There is no evidence to suggest that this part of the town was settled in the medieval period.

Ten test-trenches were excavated at locations corresponding to the footprint of the proposed development. The trenches were 1m wide and varied from 40m to 100m long. The main features of archaeological significance were linear cuts in Trenches 1 and 3 and a curvilinear cut in Trench 3. The linear cuts appear to be associated and probably form part of a continuous feature. This feature is orientated north-east/south-west and averages 0.75m wide. The upper fill consists of a grey, silty clay containing pebbles, cobbles, boulders and flecks of charcoal. In Trench 1 this deposit overlies an organic, mid-brown, silty clay with inclusions of cobbles, oyster shell, animal and bird bone, flecks of charcoal, burnt wood fragments and occasional boulders. A similar deposit of dark brown/black, organic material was encountered nearby and appears to be associated with the linear cut. This deposit yielded a fine rim/spout sherd of Saintonge pottery, suggesting a medieval date for this feature.

The curvilinear cut in Trench 3 is 0.9m wide, and the upper fill comprises a dark grey, sandy clay with frequent inclusions of pebbles, cobbles, shell, bone and flecks of charcoal. No finds were recovered from the fill, but it appears to represent a feature of archaeological interest, possibly an enclosure ditch. In addition to these features several areas of archaeological potential were identified during testing, and some of the trenches yielded unstratified sherds of medieval and post-medieval pottery wares.
Dominic Delany, 31 Ashbrook, Oranmore, Co. Galway.

231. CROSS STREET, ATHENRY
Urban
98E0553
Pre-development testing in the form of trial trenches took place to establish the nature and extent of any archaeological features or deposits at Cross Street, Athenry, Co. Galway. Three trenches were mechanically excavated, with nothing of archaeological significance uncovered.
Martin Fitzpatrick, Archaeological Consultancy, Ballydavid South, Athenry, Co. Galway.

232. NORTH GATE STREET, ATHENRY
No archaeological significance
98E0131
This project involved the monitoring of foundation trenches at North Gate Street, Athenry, Co. Galway. No features, deposits or artefacts of archaeological significance were revealed during monitoring.
Fiona Rooney, Archaeological Consultancy, Ballydavid South, Athenry, Co. Galway.

233. NORTH GATE STREET, ATHENRY
Urban
98E0141
This project involved the monitoring of ground disturbance associated with the development of three apartments on first-floor level with parking and toilet facilities at ground-floor level, at North Gate Street, Athenry, Co. Galway.

The removal of a modern concrete surface revealed a cobbled stone surface at the north end of the site. Measuring 7.5m long and 3m wide, these cobbles indicated the original ground surface of a shed. The cobbles comprised rounded limestone laid on a bed of sand. A 20th-century date for this surface was confirmed by the discovery of pottery underneath the cobbles. No further features or artefacts of archaeological significance were encountered during monitoring.
Martin Fitzpatrick, Archaeological Consultancy, Ballydavid South, Athenry, Co. Galway.

234. D.H. BURKES, NORTHGATE STREET, ATHENRY
Urban
15022 22771
SMR 84:1
98E0599
This work was undertaken on 15 December 1998. The proposed development involves the construction of a number of commercial and residential blocks, with

carparking facilities. The proposed site, currently being used as a carpark, lies within the medieval town of Athenry, to the west of North Gate Street opposite St Mary's Collegiate church, and is bordered on its north and north-west by the medieval town wall. The North Tower, in ruins, stands in the north-west corner of the site. Testing involved the mechanical excavation of three trenches.

Trench 1, 30m x 1m and 0.7m deep, was orientated west-north-west/east-south-east and was positioned to run through the centre of the site. In general, hard-core lay above the grey, sandy subsoil. At 3m from the eastern limit of the trench a dark brown, compact, silty material with frequent small stones was found. It contained fragments of red brick and glass sherds and lay above the subsoil.

Trench 2, 10m x 1m, had a similar stratigraphy to Trench 1.

Trench 3, 30m x 1m, contained the brown, compact layer seen in Trench 1, as well as, in the west of the trench, a friable, orange/brown clay layer, 4.5m long and 0.8m deep. It overlay natural.

Judging from the extant medieval features it is possible that the present ground surface has been considerably reduced in recent years. It appears on the evidence of the test-trenches that the proposed development poses no threat to the immediate archaeological environment.

Billy Quinn, 1c The Market, Ennis, Co. Clare, for Archaeological Services Unit Ltd.

235. BALLYNABUCKY
Adjacent to ringfort
14377 21787
98E0570

This work was undertaken on 7 December 1998. The proposed development involved the construction of a single serviced dwelling in the townland of Ballynabucky, Kilcolgan, Co. Galway. The site is in close proximity to a ringfort (SMR 103:18). Testing involved the mechanical excavation of four trenches, three on the site of the proposed dwelling-house and one on the proposed percolation area.

The trenches were excavated down to natural. All four had a similar stratigraphy, and all were archaeologically sterile. On the evidence of the trenches it appears that the proposed development posed no threat to the immediate archaeological environment.

Billy Quinn, 1c The Market, Ennis, Co. Clare, for Archaeological Services Unit Ltd.

236. CAHERWALTER
Adjacent to medieval church
98E0001

Excavations took place at Caherwalter townland, Loughrea, during January 1998 in advance of a proposed housing development for which permission had been granted.

The site consisted of two large fields, deemed to be of archaeological potential because of their proximity to a medieval parish church and modern cemetery dedicated to St Bridget. The church, a single-cell structure, is in ruins. A single sherd of 17th–18th-century German Westerwald pottery was found on trodden ground outside the south doorway of the church during fieldwork.

In all, some thirteen trenches were opened in the development area using a mechanical digger, and these were examined for archaeological artefacts and features, none of which were found apart from artefacts of 19th–20th-century date and a drainage ditch feature of the same date.

Jim Higgins, 'St Gerards', 18 College Road, Galway.

237. CASTLEGAR
Adjacent to souterrain?
14382 21870
SMR 103:104
98E0498

Archaeological testing involving the mechanical excavation of three test-trenches on the site of a proposed house in the townland of Castlegar, Kilcolgan, Co. Galway, took place on 15 October 1998. Galway County Council provided funding for the work.

The site lay at the rear of an existing farmhouse. According to the Galway Archaeological Survey, a souterrain lay to the north-east of the farmhouse. It was examined by Professor Etienne Rynne in 1967, on behalf of the National Museum of Ireland. Also mentioned in the report is the discovery of a number of skeletons nearby.

Three trenches were sited to archaeologically resolve the areas that were to be directly affected by the development. Trench A measured *c.* 17m x 1m and was excavated to a depth of 0.35m. A sod and topsoil layer of dark brown silt with small stones, maximum depth 0.17m, with finds of a modern nature (crockery sherds and glass fragments) overlay a compact, orange-brown silt, 0.2m thick. This overlay natural limestone bedrock.

Trench B was positioned to traverse the site of the proposed dwelling-house. It measured *c.* 20m x 1m and was excavated to a depth of 0.8m. Its south-west end crossed over the supposed line of the souterrain as indicated by Professor Rynne's coordinates. Sod and topsoil overlay the orange-brown, silty layer, which here was on average 0.35m thick. Below this a natural, light grey, gravelly clay, with a moderate amount of limestone boulders and an average thickness of 0.4m, overlay bedrock.

Approximately 7m from the south end of the trench the stratigraphy was interrupted by a cut, backfilled with a limestone rubble deposit. The cut was *c.* 0.9m wide and 0.5m deep with straight edges visible in the section face. The fill contained a single modern pottery sherd

Trench C, which measured 30m x 1m and ran parallel to Trench B, was designed to investigate the proposed driveway area. According to the landowner, this trench crossed the area most likely to contain the souterrain. The sod and topsoil layer overlay a dark, silty deposit. This was moderately compact, had an average thickness of 0.25m and contained a moderate amount of cobble-sized stones and occasional boulders. Below was the natural clay.

Testing of the site failed to reveal the souterrain or indeed any archaeological material. Extensive land clearance work in recent years seems to have destroyed or concealed any trace of archaeological remains.

Billy Quinn, Archaeological Services Unit Ltd, Purcell House, Oranmore, Co. Galway.

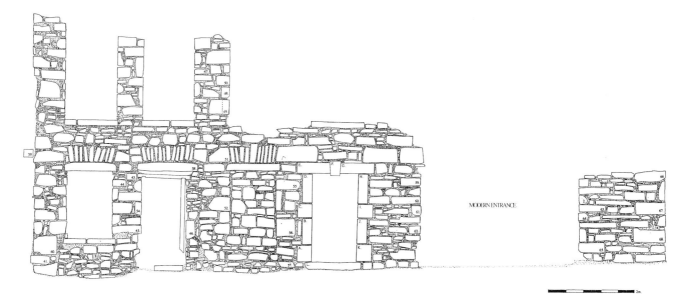

Elevation of 19th-century facade at Abbeygate Street Lower, Galway.

238. DRUMACOO

Penitential station

98E0231

Pre-development testing in the form of trial-trenches took place in advance of proposed development at Sites Nos 1 and 2, Drumacoo, Co. Galway. The proposed development was to be in the area where there were once the remains of two penitential stations, possibly associated with the early ecclesiastical remains at Drumacoo. These monuments were marked on the 1st edition of the OS map in 1838 and named as 'Station Monuments'.

In Site No. 1 two trenches were mechanically excavated in the area of the proposed development. The stratigraphy encountered revealed nothing of archaeological significance.

In Site No. 2 two trenches were mechanically excavated in the course of pre-development testing. In Trench A outcropping bedrock was found directly below the sod. It appeared that the natural rock was utilised to form a station monument.

Fiona Rooney, Archaeological Consultancy, Ballydavid South, Athenry, Co. Galway.

239. ABBEYGATE STREET UPPER, GALWAY

Urban medieval

12986 22525

SMR 94:100

98E0154

The site lies to the rear of several properties at Abbeygate Street Upper and contains several derelict cottages and ruinous buildings, some of which were in serious danger of collapsing. A building's survey was undertaken by this writer in December 1997, and it was established that the large, three-storey building that dominates the site preserves substantial remains of a late medieval structure. Archaeological monitoring of the demolition of all other buildings was undertaken from 23 February to 6 March 1998, and several reused late medieval stones were retrieved.

The second phase of work was carried out between 9 and 27 March 1998 and comprised a reassessment and survey of the large three-storey building. Portions of the north-west wall and south-west gable were late medieval in date, but it was also

clear that the north-east gable and south-east wall were of 19th-century construction. The north-east gable was demolished immediately as it was in an extremely dangerous condition. Several late medieval stones were recovered from this phase of demolition and it was noted that the east corner of the building was almost entirely built with reused late medieval stones (corbels, sills, jambstones etc.). A scaled elevation drawing of the outer face of the south-east wall was undertaken, and all reused late medieval stones and the fine 19th-century doorway were numbered, in order to facilitate retrieval. During the subsequent demolition of this wall all numbered stones and numerous other reused late medieval stones were recovered. These are stored on site.

Following the completion of demolition works the north-west wall and south-west gable were scaffolded, cleared of ivy growth and stripped of the modern plasterwork. The exposed south-west gable was almost entirely faced with red brick, indicating that it was extensively rebuilt or refaced as part of the 19th-century refurbishment of the building. The ground floor of the north-west wall contains two, possibly three, late medieval slit opes set in deeply splayed embrasures.

A test excavation was undertaken from 30 March to 3 April 1998. Four test-trenches were excavated. No archaeological stratigraphy was encountered, but important and complex late medieval structural remains were identified in the above- and below-ground fabric of the large, late medieval/19th-century building. It is extremely difficult to interpret the findings without further excavation, but the evidence from Trench 1 suggests that there are at least three phases of medieval construction preserved in the existing structural remains.

Dominic Delany, 31 Ashbrook, Oranmore, Co. Galway.

240. 26 ABBEYGATE STREET UPPER, GALWAY

Urban medieval

1296 2252

98E0287

The rescue excavation of a small area to be used for the laying of a sewer pipe, at No. 26 Upper Abbeygate Street, Galway, was carried out on 15 June

1998. It was undertaken during development works at the premises and on recommendation of the National Monuments Service, following a site assessment prepared by this writer in May 1998.

The site lies within the original city walls, in an area that contains a number of architectural features dating to the 16th and 17th centuries. Nos 26 and. 28 (to the north-west) were originally the one late medieval building, containing 16th-century window fragments and a 17th-century armorial fireplace, divided up in the 19th century.

A single trench was excavated by hand at No. 26. It was orientated north-east/south-west and was 6.4m long, 0.5–0.6m wide and 0.4–0.45m deep. It was begun at 1m from the north-west boundary wall and 0.5m from the north-east boundary wall.

The stratigraphy encountered consisted of a rubble fill, to a depth of 0.25–0.4m, below which was a ceramic sewerage pipe. Below the pipe at its north-east end were Liscannor flags, 30mm thick, within the rubble fill. Also found below the rubble fill, along a small number of sections of the trench towards its south-west end, was natural subsoil and boulder clay. These were visible in the base of the trench.

No artefacts were recovered, and no features were in evidence. The stratigraphy encountered was completely disturbed because the trench lay along the line of an older sewerage pipe, probably dating to earlier this century.

Richard Crumlish, Archaeological Services Unit, Ltd, Purcell House, Oranmore, Co. Galway.

241. 50 ABBEYGATE STREET UPPER, GALWAY

Urban medieval and post-medieval

98E0045

Archaeological testing in advance of development took place in the backyard of the Panache Hair Studio at No. 50 Abbeygate Street Upper, Galway, in February 1998.

Before excavation the top of a very badly destroyed wall (Wall A) was visible in the north-eastern (back) boundary wall of the site. In this an incomplete relieving arch of roughly worked limestone voussoirs was visible, protruding just above modern ground level. The wall was tied into and contemporary with a further corner of walling that projected from beneath a modern boundary wall on the west side of the site. This segment of walling (Wall B) was partially exposed in Cutting 1 and projected some 0.2–0.22m out from the base of the modern wall built on top of it. The top of the footings of a further wall (Wall C), set at right angles to Wall A, was also visible. This protruded towards the eastern side of the site.

A fourth, much better built wall footing was also visible and ran more or less parallel to Wall A. This wall (D) bisected the site. Fragment of a further putative wall (Wall E) extended from the corner at the end of Wall D and under the modern eastern boundary wall of the site. This latter wall seemed to have been relatively late in date as it clearly incorporated one piece of 18th–19th-century red brick.

Cutting 1 was excavated inside the north-eastern boundary wall of the site in an attempt to elucidate the relieving arch and the extent of the wall that contained it.

Below the concrete was a layer of mixed material containing late 19th and 20th-century artefacts with very large quantities of animal bone. The animal bone was associated with the site being a butcher's premises between *c.* 1900 and 1980. Also occurring were many thick pieces of Liscannor slab and the occasional naturally rounded stone, which appeared to have been cobblestones but was invariably *ex situ*. Below this was a mortar floor, 60–90mm thick.

At the north-west end of the cutting, just beneath the low relieving arch, lintels of a drain were uncovered at the same level as the mortared floor. Wedged between the lintels were a piece of roofing slate, a piece of decorated 17th-century(?) glazed ridge tile and some red and yellow bricks. The bricks may date to any time from the 18th to the early 19th century and were clearly building bricks.

The drain was between 1.2m and 1.28m wide and a short stretch of between 0.46m and 0.67m. It was only partly exposed and excavated, and the contents included finds of 19th–20th-century date. Just below the base of a large, mouth-blown wine bottle of green glass occurred, of a type generally datable to between the end of the 16th to the early 18th century. The neck of a wine bottle of similar form was also found embedded in the mortar of the wall above the drain. The drain was contemporary with the mortared floor found throughout Cutting 1 and extending into Cutting 2, where the lime mortar overlay large yellow bricks of late 18th–19th-century type.

The only finds from the mortared floor were a piece of 17th–18th-century North Devon gravel-tempered ware and a clay pipe bowl of Dutch origin of a late 18th-/ early 19th-century date. Both of these finds were found in Cutting 2 among small stones and a very thin deposit of light, organic soil inside Wall C and directly on the mortar floor.

It is clear that the drain and the mortared floor are of post-medieval date, as is the back wall and relieving arch under which the drain flowed.

Cutting (1A) was made into the mortared floor. Below it was a mixture of small stones, building rubble and 18th- and 19th-century glazed pottery and clay pipe stems. There were also fragments of 18th/19th-century ridge tiles. Some animal bone and oyster shells were also found. At *c.* 0.2–0.22m below the mortared floor was an irregular, cobbled floor of large and sometimes elongated limestone cobbles, generally between 0.15m and 0.22m thick, which post-dated the back wall. These cobbles were much larger than those found at a higher level in Cuttings 1 and 2. They were bedded in a brown clay containing post-medieval pottery and ridge-tiles, North Devon gravel-tempered ware and various 17th-century smoothware and clay pipe stems.

This clay varied considerably, from 0.25m to 0.55m, and gave way gradually to silt and boulder clay, which incorporated builder's spoil from the construction phase of the back wall of the building. This material quickly became water-logged, which made excavation difficult. The lower layer of material extended under the back wall, which was clearly built on estuarine silts and boulder clay.

The north-east wall of the excavated building complex had no plinth, and the maximum depth of the wall below the mortared floor was between 0.65m and 0.79m. At the base of the wall were numerous lumps of limestone. These were hammer-marked spalls derived from waste stone that had been trimmed by masons, possibly those who built the wall. Also found were numerous pieces of trimmed slate, some of which were possibly used in stone-wall building, where spalls were used as pinnings between the facing stones of the wall. Slate also occurred in the layer above but was mainly blue, whereas more friable, schisty slate occurred at this level.

Late medieval pottery found at this level included North Devon smoothware and gravel-tempered ware, Staffordshire plates with red and yellow patterns, white-glazed ware of English origin, imported German stoneware and clay pipe fragments of late 16th- to early 17th-century type. Some lime mortar was also found. Animal bone and oyster shell also occurred. It seems likely that the late medieval back wall of the site was built into deposits of late 16th/17th-century date and that the stone and slate spalls were part of its construction phases.

Later material was also found in an apparent cut made for the foundation of the north-east wall.

Cutting 2, at right angles to Cutting 1, was cut to examine some wall footings, the top of which had been visible before the excavation began. The wall footings that occurred along the middle of the cutting (Wall C) were later than and abutted the back wall. At a later stage the join in the north-north-east corner of the building was plastered over with lime mortar where one of later floor levels (the mortared floor) was laid down. This cutting provided many more details on the various late floor levels found than did Cutting 1.

Below the modern floor the accumulation of late rubbish was of the same type as found in Cutting 1. There was a certain amount of Liscannor flooring still *in situ*. This was 19th century in date, as some late yellow brick of 18th–19th-century type was found embedded between the slabs. In the cross-section of this cutting a further piece of Liscannor slab was visible at a lower level, which seems to have been bedded in a spread of lime mortar. This in turn overlay the mortar flooring found in Cutting 1.

In places in Cutting 2 it was clear that the lime mortar of the mortared floor overlay a well-preserved setting of red brick. This only occurred in some places and was not encountered in Cutting 1.

On the eastern side of Cutting 2, to the east of Wall C, a series of large granite boulders was partly bedded in hard, mid-brown subsoil and angled slightly from the north-east and towards the south-west. This gave the general impression of an irregular line that may have been an old foundation course of a wall. Much of the line extended beneath a modern boundary wall forming the eastern side of the yard; the line of Wall C seemed to have been built partly on top of the dispersed or partly displaced stones of this wall, and little attempt was made to remove them when Wall C was being built. A 17th-century clay pipe was found at the same level of the boulders, suggesting perhaps that the line belonged to a 17th-century context and may have been a building foundation.

Jim Higgins, 'St Gerards', 18 College Road, Galway.

242. 44 DOMINICK STREET LOWER (REAR OF), GALWAY
Urban
1296 2250
98E0423

The test excavation of a site, in advance of development, at the rear of No. 44 Lower Dominick Street, Galway, was carried out on 22 September 1998. The development consisted of the construction of sixteen apartments on the site. Although planning permission was granted for the development without any conditions relating to the preservation of potential archaeology, this testing was undertaken because of recommendations by the National Monuments Service.

The site lay outside the original city walls in a suburb that probably began to develop before 1500. The River Corrib is adjacent to the south-east site boundary.

The single trench, excavated by machine, was orientated north-west/south-east and was 55.3m long, 1.1–2.4m wide (average width 1.2m) and 1.5–2.5m deep. It was begun at 5.9m south-east of the boundary wall of the existing premises and 5m from the north-east boundary of the site. At the north-west end of the trench the water table was encountered at 1.2m deep. Therefore the excavation ceased at 2.5m along the length of the trench and moved a further 2m to the south-east before resuming.

The stratigraphy encountered consisted of a rubble fill (0.2–1.2m thick) below which was topsoil (0.5–1m thick) and a black, organic deposit (0.2–1.5m thick). Below the topsoil along the final 9m of the trench at its south-east end was found a second rubble fill (1m thick). Below the black, organic deposit was a sterile, yellow marl/clay and bedrock, visible at the base of the trench.

The rubble fill and topsoil contained modern artefacts. The black, organic deposit contained animal bone fragments, oyster shells and a small number of modern and post-medieval pottery sherds. The second rubble fill contained red/yellow brick. Six modern wall foundations of a building just demolished on site crossed the trench.

The stratigraphy encountered during this test excavation was indicative of modern and post-medieval use of this site. The artefacts recovered testify to this. No features were in evidence.
Richard Crumlish, Archaeological Services Unit, Ltd, Purcell House, Oranmore, Co. Galway.

243. 47 DOMINICK STREET LOWER, GALWAY
No archaeological significance
98E0017

This project involved the monitoring of ground disturbance associated with the development of a two-storey extension to the rear of the existing property at 47 Dominick Street Lower, Galway. The removal of a modern concrete surface revealed a brown, clayey silt, 0.2m deep. Underlying this was a dark, humic layer (1.3m deep) with occasional shells throughout. Extensive disturbance in the form of pipes and cables was evident throughout this layer. Eleven boreholes, for piling of foundations, were then drilled.

No artefacts or features of archaeological significance were encountered during the course of monitoring.
Martin Fitzpatrick, Archaeological Services Unit Ltd, Purcell House, Oranmore, Co. Galway.

244. 65 DOMINICK STREET LOWER (FORMERLY 'THE GALWAY ARMS'), GALWAY

Urban

98E0223

Archaeological investigation at the site of a proposed development at 65 Dominick Street Lower, Galway, revealed previously unrecorded structural remains. Two existing buildings were demolished, and pre-development testing was carried out on 5 May 1998. Full excavation of the site was undertaken from 15 June to 10 July 1998.

The excavation revealed several phases of activity at the site. The most recent involved the construction of and adjustments to the recently demolished premises. The remains of walls and foundations and a drain date to this phase.

At an earlier stage the site was occupied by a building that appeared to broadly follow the line of the recently demolished buildings, facing along Dominick Street and Mill Street. The walls and foundations indicated that the building was rectangular. An external end wall on the Mill Street side and a rear wall on the Dominick Street side were not uncovered in the course of the investigation, and therefore an estimated size of this structure cannot be accurately given.

Underlying all other structures on the site were the remains of a broad wall. This wall and an associated stone facing and rubble fill appeared to represent the earliest activity on the site. The cartographic evidence suggests that the site was not occupied by domestic buildings until after 1691 at the earliest, and it is possible that the rectangular structure on the site forms a part of the streetscape as it is represented on the 1818 map. The wall is of impressive width, 2.8m across, and, although only a small portion of the structure was exposed, it is likely that this structure was part of a fortification strategically positioned to protect the west entrance to the city, currently the William O'Brien Bridge. Such a fortification may date to as early as 1625, when the presence of a fort in the general area to the west of the bridge was recorded on the Plot of Galway map. Alternatively, it could form a part of the triangular fort marked on the 1651 Pictorial Map. An insufficient area of the features has been exposed to allow a more detailed assessment of this earliest phase of activity on the site.

Anne Connolly, Archaeological Services Unit Ltd, Purcell House, Oranmore, Co. Galway.

245. 65 DOMINICK STREET LOWER, GALWAY

Urban

12986 22525

98E0223 ext.

Monitoring of groundwork took place at the site of a proposed development at 65 Dominick Street Lower, Galway. The site consists of a roughly rectangular area, 11.2m north–south by 14.5m. The proposed development involves the construction of a public bar and guesthouse, including the installation of a basement. The site had been the subject of a full archaeological excavation by Anne Connolly (No. 244 above). The excavation revealed a complex of wall foundations showing several phases of activity. The earliest structural features, which may be part of a 17th-century fortification, were deemed archaeologically significant.

The basement design as presented in the original planning application would have destroyed these structural remains. *Dúchas* recommended that the fortifications be preserved *in situ*, and a conservation strategy was agreed upon to do this. This involved covering the fortifications with a protective sheet of terram membrane and then filling the cavity between the wall and the shuttering with a polystyrene material.

Monitoring of the work began on 12 August 1998. A mechanical digger was used to remove the late walls and the surrounding fill. The archaeological brief, although allowing for full provision to record exposed archaeological material, could not be safely carried out owing to difficulties encountered during excavation. Flooding on site, as well as the depths being excavated, restricted access to the fortifications. Recording of the fully exposed wall, C14, and the surrounding material layers was limited to taking general dimensions and photographs.

Mechanical excavation began to the east of the broad wall, C14. Contexts 7, 8, 9, 12 and 13 were all removed to below the proposed development level. C14's east face was then exposed and cleaned back 3m to the site's northern limit on Mill Street. The wall's composition and construction were as revealed by Ms Connolly, i.e. roughly hewn, random, uncoursed blocks of granite, heavily mortared, with an internal rubble fill. C14 had an even east face and varied between 1.3m and 1.5m deep. The foundation below the wall C14 was very rough. At the northern end was a rubble base of granite boulders, while towards the south the wall seemed to sit directly on a compact, dark, stony layer. Boulder clay appeared *c.* 3m below ground level.

On the western side of the site, excavation was delayed owing to safety concerns. The western boundary attached to Mill Street Garda Station rested on a loose foundation. Further excavation at its base might have had a destabilising effect. After consultation with *Dúchas*, it was decided to underpin the foundation with concrete. As excavation recommenced it became apparent that the west face of C14 was uneven and splayed out to 3m on the southern side. The west face of C14 was *c.* 1.5m deep and also rested on a rubble foundation.

Excavation under C16, the rubble facing, exposed a lower, uncoursed foundation below which was a dark layer with frequent shell inclusions. Digging continued to a depth *c.* 3.8m below street level.

After the walls were recorded the conservation strategy as agreed upon was fully implemented.

The monitoring of groundwork at 65 Dominick Street Lower further exposed the broad wall, C14, and confirmed that it did indeed continue further to the south. Standard recording of the archaeological layers removed was not possible for safety reasons, but no associated cut for the broad wall was evident. The site was excavated to boulder clay to the east and the west of C14.

Billy Quinn, Archaeological Services Unit Ltd, Purcell House, Oranmore, Co. Galway.

246. 13 EYRE SQUARE, GALWAY

Urban

1301 2254

98E0548

Testing of a proposed development at No. 13 Eyre

Square and Nos 3 and 5 Forster Street, Galway, was undertaken on 25 November and 1 December 1998. The testing and monitoring programme was undertaken in compliance with a recommendation made by *Dúchas* The Heritage Service following an archaeological building survey conducted by Richard Crumlish.

Richard de Burgh founded Galway City in the late 13th century. In 1333 the city became independent, and a royal charter in 1361 granted permission to erect defensive walls. By the early 17th century it was completely enclosed by walls, with fourteen gates and two forts. The Pictorial Map of Galway (1651) shows suburbs that grew up outside the walls to the north-east (Eyre Square), north-west (Mary Street) and in the Claddagh (Dominick Street). Their foundation date is unknown; however, they may have begun to develop before 1500. The site at No. 13 Eyre Square is represented on the Pictorial Map as a two-storey building.

It is proposed to demolish No. 13 Eyre Square and Nos 3 and 5 Forster Street, with the exception of the wall along the south-east of the hallway on the ground floor of No. 13 Eyre Square. The proposed development will also entail the excavation of a new basement level and the construction of a new four-storey building.

Testing of the site involved the mechanical excavation of a trench measuring 20m x 1m, orientated north-east/south-west and running across the middle of the site. Before testing, the site was strewn with rubble and building debris.

The surface deposit, a mixed, grey, multi-composite and rubble layer, had an average thickness of 0.2m. This overlay a mid-brown, sandy clay layer, with occasional inclusions of disarticulated animal bone and modern pottery sherds. It was 0.12–0.2m deep. Below this was a natural, orange/brown, sandy clay layer. This softly compact subsoil was 0.3–0.4m thick and contained no finds. Directly under this was a grey boulder clay with occasional limestone.

This stratigraphic sequence was interrupted by three wall foundations along the trench's section face. The three foundations corresponded to wall foundations associated with the recently demolished building and were of relatively modern construction. All were built of randomly coursed limestone rubble with occasional red brick.

Piling around the perimeter and under the supporting walls of the site began on 5 January 1999. The piling was monitored at its initial stages, but, owing to the nature of the piling, nothing was visible. Therefore it was decided to cease the watching brief.
Billy Quinn, Archaeological Services Unit Ltd, Purcell House, Oranmore, Co. Galway.

247. 5–7 EYRE STREET, GALWAY
Urban medieval
SMR 94:100 (in vicinity of)
98E0174
Archaeological test excavation was undertaken in advance of a proposed residential and commercial development in response to a condition of planning. The site comprises two adjoining properties, which lie *c.* 50m outside the north bastion of the medieval walled town. A building survey was undertaken

before demolition. The property at 6–7 Eyre Street contained a derelict two-storey dwelling-house, which was in a very unstable condition. Galway Corporation had placed a demolition order on the building some years ago. The property at 5 Eyre Street contained a large three-storey 19th-century house, which had a fine doorway fronting onto Eyre Street. Several medieval stones, including a decorated window spandrel, were retrieved during monitoring of demolition works at these sites.

Two test-trenches (16.5m north–south) were excavated at 6–7 Eyre Street on 16 and 23 May 1998. The stratigraphy was best preserved at the north end of Trench 1, where a deep, silty clay deposit overlay a compacted, grey, medium sand and gravel. The silty clay deposit was cut by an 18th-century clay-lined pit (2.7m north–south), which contained frequent inclusions of brick, slate, red earthenware roof tile fragments, animal bone, shell (mainly oyster) and occasional pottery sherds and glass fragments. The sand and gravel deposit yielded a couple of post-medieval finds and may represent the remains of an east–west watercourse. The natural, yellowish/brown clay was encountered at 1.5m.

A single test-trench was excavated at 5 Eyre Street on 20 June 1998. A substantial wall face formed the east edge of the trench at the south end of the site. The wall face extended north–south and was a two-phase structure. The upper wall face (height 0.35m) was built of randomly coursed, rounded and angular cobbles and was built directly on top of a wall face (height 1.2m) composed of roughly coursed, large, unhewn limestone and occasional migmatite boulders. This wall face rested on a foundation of rounded boulders, which formed a rough plinth at its base. The ground was almost entirely composed of redeposited soils. A sterile, dark brown, silty clay deposit was encountered at 1.85m below the existing ground level, and outcrops of bedrock were encountered at a depth of 2m.

Substantial remains of a large 19th-century stone-arched 'cellar' were encountered under the site of the demolished house at the north end of the site. The walls were faced with rubble limestone masonry, and the arch is built of roughly hewn, rectangular, limestone blocks. The arch was in very poor condition and collapsed upon exposure. A disused modern sewer pipe was encountered at the base of the trench.
Dominic Delany, 31 Ashbrook, Oranmore, Co. Galway.

248. FLOOD STREET/NEW DOCK STREET, GALWAY
Urban
97E0377
The site at Flood Street/New Dock Street lies inside the town walls of Galway and falls within the zone of archaeological potential as depicted in the Urban Archaeological Survey.

Pre-development testing in the form of trial-trenches was undertaken, and numerous wall foundations and cobble levels of possible archaeological significance were revealed. Based on these findings, it was recommended by *Dúchas* The Heritage Service that full excavation be carried out in the areas where there was a high concentration of piles.

The excavation revealed a number of archaeological features, the remains of the town wall along the south-east boundary of the site being the most significant. The area where the wall was revealed was excavated to a depth of 1.3m. It was constructed of roughly coursed limestone masonry, with a solid core of rubble and mortar. The wall sloped from a maximum height of 1m at the north-east to 0.5m at the south-west. It was 1.24m wide, although it is likely to have extended further below the wall of the adjacent building.

Abutting this wall the foundations of a further wall were revealed, which may have represented a medieval/post-medieval structure. The town wall and the associated features, foundation walls and cobble surfaces, were not fully excavated as consultations with *Dúchas* The Heritage Service resulted in the foundation layout being changed to facilitate the archaeological features uncovered. A 300mm buffer zone comprising a layer of terram, covered with hard-core, was placed between the bottom of the ground-beam and the ground surface, to facilitate preservation *in situ*.

Fiona Rooney, Archaeological Consultancy, Ballydavid South, Athenry, Co. Galway.

Town wall at Flood Street/New Dock Street, Galway, taken from west.

249. CONVENT OF MERCY, FRANCIS STREET, GALWAY
Late and post-medieval
98E0192
Excavations in the grounds of the Convent of Mercy were undertaken when an 18th/19th-century building, containing a fine armorial doorway dated to 1624, was being demolished and the doorway removed and incorporated in the new structure.

Stripping of the interior walls of the building resulted in the discovery of reused cut stone architectural fragments and late medieval timbers, the latter used as lintels to doorways and windows. The building was constructed in the early 19th century on the site of an 18th-century building. The present Convent of Mercy lies partly on the site of the Franciscan foundation established by William Liath de Burgo in 1296 on St Stephen's Island. A large number of medieval and late medieval architectural fragments relating to that foundation are displayed in the grounds of the convent.

A cutting made outside the end of the building produced evidence of a cellar that seems to pre-date the present building, appearing to belong to an 18th-century building constructed on much the same line. The finds from the cutting, all of 18th/19th-century-

date, include numerous pieces of stained glass with floral patterns, along with pottery and bottle glass.

A large, deep, U-shaped ditch, which must originally have run across the site of the 19th-century building and continued into the grounds of the present Franciscan cemetery, just across the wall from the present grounds of the convent, was encountered. It seems to correspond to one partially excavated by this writer in 1997 (*Excavations 1997*, 69–71, 97E0223). The feature may represent one of the large canalised streams that ran through the gardens of the Franciscan Abbey, shown on the Pictorial Map of Galway of 1651.

The finds from this feature included the usual range of late and post-medieval pottery, including North Devonshire graffito and gravel-tempered ware, a Spanish olive jar, Weltcruwald stoneware, clay pipes and small copper-alloy shroud-pins. Quantities of mortar, slate and animal bones also occurred.

Jim Higgins, 'St Gerards', 18 College Road, Galway.

Renaissance-style doorway dated 1624 at the Convent of Mercy, Galway, after its reconstruction (photograph by Jim Higgins).

250. LOUGH ATALIA ROAD/FORSTER STREET, GALWAY
Urban medieval
SMR 94:100 (in vicinity of)
98E0272
Test excavation was undertaken from 16 to 23 September 1998 in response to a condition of planning. The site comprises three large green-field areas and forms part of a glacial ridge that extended north-east/south-west along the Lough Atalia shoreline. The site covers an area of *c.* 1500m² and represents one of the last remaining green-field sites in close proximity to the city centre. It lies *c.* 500m east of the medieval walled town and 350m north-east of Forthill Cemetery, the site of a strategically important early 17th-century star-shaped fort. The

1651 Pictorial Map of Galway depicts it as unenclosed pastureland, and there is no evidence to suggest that this area was settled in the medieval period. However, there is a tradition of 16th- and 17th-century military encampments along the high ground at Lough Atalia Road, and there have been stray finds of musket balls etc. in the area. Logan's Map of Galway (1818) names this area 'East Fort Hill', which appears to confirm the tradition of military activity in this area.

Ten test-trenches (average length 50m north-west/south-east) were excavated, and the stratigraphy was consistent across the site area. The topsoil comprised a grey/brown silt with moderate inclusions of pebbles, cobbles, bone, shell (mainly oyster) and flecks of charcoal, and occasional inclusions of boulders, burnt bone, slate and red brick fragments. The topsoil had an average thickness of 0.35m and frequently overlay the naturally occurring, light brown, sand and gravel glacial deposit. Occasionally the topsoil overlay a yellowish/brown, silty subsoil (0.2m thick), which in turn overlay the light brown sand and gravel. Almost all of the trenches yielded occasional sherds of late and post-medieval pottery types as well as numerous modern pottery sherds.

A linear cut, 0.7m wide and orientated east–west, was encountered in Trench 4. It contained a fill of mid-brown, clayey silt with moderate inclusions of angular cobbles, animal bone, shell and flecks of charcoal. A couple of late and post-medieval pottery sherds were recovered from this deposit. Two subrectangular features, measuring *c.* 2.7m x 1.7m, were encountered on the north-west brow of the glacial ridge in Trench 8. The features are cut into the natural, light brown sand and gravel and contain a fill of mid-brown silt with moderate inclusions of cobbles, pebbles, animal bone, shell and flecks of charcoal. Two sherds of late medieval pottery were recovered from the fill of one of these features. Considering the tradition of military activity in this area, it is possible that the subrectangular features represent small military entrenchments. It was recommended that all of these features be excavated in advance of the proposed development. *Dúchas* The Heritage Service had already indicated that all topsoil removal at construction phase should be archaeologically monitored.
Dominic Delany, 31 Ashbrook, Oranmore, Co. Galway.

251. NAUGHTON'S CARPARK, MARKET STREET, GALWAY
Urban medieval
12986 22525
SMR 94:100
98E0243
Test excavation was undertaken in advance of planning between 10 and 19 June 1998. The site lies almost directly opposite the medieval church of St Nicholas and comprises an open rectangular area measuring *c.* 60m north-west/south-east x 40m. Examination of the 1651 Pictorial Map suggests that the medieval town wall extended across the north-west end of the site. It was also noted that the late medieval townhouse known as 'Athy Castle' may have been close to the south end of the site. The map also depicts a line of dwelling-houses fronting onto

North Street (now Market Street), with large rear gardens extending back to the medieval town wall. In 1749 the Lombard Barrack was erected on this site, and the barrack buildings were subsequently reused to house the Patrician Brothers' School, which was founded here in 1826. The site was cleared in the 1970s.

Three test-trenches were excavated. The trenches extended north-west/south-east and averaged 40m long and 1.25m wide. The medieval town wall was encountered at the north-west end of Trenches 1 and 3. It is built of angular migmatite boulders facing a mortared rubble core and is 1.7m thick. Substantial remains of the 18th-century barracks were also uncovered. The barracks appear to have consisted of a main north-west block flanked by opposing wings at the north-east and south-west. The excavated barrack walls are 0.85m thick and are built of coursed, roughly hewn limestone masonry. A late medieval/post-medieval garden soil deposit was encountered at an average depth of 0.45m in all three trenches. It consisted of a grey/brown, silty clay containing moderate inclusions of pebbles, cobbles, mortar, slate, animal and fish bone, shell and flecks of charcoal. Finds from this deposit included post-medieval pottery sherds, glass fragments, clay pipe fragments and occasional medieval pottery sherds.
Dominic Delany, 31 Ashbrook, Oranmore, Co. Galway.

252. HYNE'S CARPARK, MERCHANT'S ROAD/DOCK ROAD, GALWAY
Urban medieval
SMR 94:100 (in vicinity of)
98E0018
Archaeological test excavation was undertaken in January 1998 at the request of Galway Corporation. The site comprises an open carpark area measuring *c.* 57m north-west/south-east x 67m. It lies south-east of the walled town in an area that must have formed part of the tidal flood-plain in the medieval period. The 1651 Pictorial Map of Galway depicts enclosed garden plots in this area.

Six test-trenches, averaging 50m north-west/south-east, were excavated. The modern rubble landfill was 1.7m deep and overlay a dark grey/brown, clayey silt, with infrequent inclusions of pebbles, cobbles, organic matter, shell, bone and flecks of charcoal and mortar. Two sherds of post-medieval pottery were recovered from the upper level of this deposit in Trench 3. The deposit was 0.4m thick and overlay the natural ground, which varied from a grey, coarse sand and gravel to a light brown, sticky boulder clay. Occasional large migmatite boulders and outcrops of bedrock were also encountered.

A wall was encountered 7.5m from the north-west boundary wall in Trenches 1 and 2. It extended north-east/south-west and ran parallel to the north-west boundary wall. The wall is 0.8m thick and is built of roughly coursed limestone masonry. It rests on a foundation plinth of large limestone boulders, which overlies the natural boulder clay.

A substantial stone-lined drain (north-north-west/south-south-east) was encountered in Trench 6. The drain is faced with large, roughly worked limestone boulders and angular cobbles and is capped and floored with large limestone flags. The wall and stone-lined drain appear to date to the period following extensive land reclamation in this area in the early 19th century. No archaeological deposits or features were encountered.

Dominic Delany, 31 Ashbrook, Oranmore, Co. Galway.

253. ST NICHOLAS'S SCOLLEGIATE CHURCH, GALWAY
Medieval church and cemetery
98E0428

Emergency archaeological work was carried out at St Nicholas's Collegiate Church, Galway, in September 1998 because of some unlicensed disturbance by mechanical digger. The area is bounded by Market Street, Church Lane, Lombard Street and Church Yard Street. During the course of laying a French drain human bones and other archaeological material had been encountered. Most of the trenches had been backfilled, and in only a few could the stratigraphy be recorded.

The archaeological team sieved all the remaining spoil from several trenches that had not yet been dumped and retrieved large amounts of human bone along with numerous artefacts. The trenches were on average 0.4–0.45m wide and 0.8–0.9m deep; in segment F the trench was 0.9–1m wide.

Segment E, 0.4m wide, had been partly infilled but was photographed and drawn. The spoil was sifted, and human bone, along with mainly 19th-century pottery and some glass, was recovered. It is clear that the area had been disturbed in relatively recent times. The crushed and broken nature of the bone seems to suggest that the soil either contained a residue from burials that had been extracted from it or had been redeposited from elsewhere in the vicinity.

Some distance below the gravel and the mixed, brown, stony layer that occurred beneath it in Cutting 2 was a disturbed layer of cobblestones. It seems likely that a cobbled layer originally extended as far as the South Porch (or certainly the entire length of the present cutting). The cobblestones were generally set in a matrix of grey to greyish/brown soil, which contained grits, some small stones and the occasional piece of bone.

Below this was a deposit of stone of various sizes that had been introduced to raise the ground level considerably; 18th- and 19th-century pottery came from this context. This layer gave way to a second layer of cobblestones. These were substantially larger but less disturbed than those above and extended across most of the length of the cutting. The cobbles were generally edge set with their long axes set flat in the ground towards the south end of the cutting. Further towards the north the cobbles tended to be smaller and were set in the ground along their vertical axes. They may have had several phases of setting and resetting.

Context 7 consisted of what may have been a disturbed area. There were stones here that may have been disturbed cobbles, but generally the stone was cruder. They were set in a layer of material that varied from mid-yellow to grey, and the soil had obviously been mixed as a result of disturbance. Some disturbed human bone was also found in this context. The bone, however, was not *in situ*.

The finds included three sherds of green-glazed Saintonge pottery, large quantities of 18th/19th-century pottery and glass and some 17th–19th-century clay pipe fragments. Also found were ridge-tile fragments and modern bottle glass, along with some scraps of iron and lead and some lengths of copper-alloy wire. Also recovered was part of a bone handle from a late medieval piece.

Jim Higgins, 'St Gerard's', 18 College Road, Galway.

254. 4 SHOP STREET, GALWAY
Urban
29850 25800
SMR 94:100
98E0409

Dúchas The Heritage Service requested an archaeological assessment of the proposed development, as the site is within the zone of archaeological potential for Galway City. Neil O'Flanagan undertook a building survey with the production of scaled plans and elevations of any medieval fabric. Intrusive fieldwork took the form of four hand-excavated test-pits, along with the recording of seven previously machine-excavated engineering test-pits in the basement of the building.

Archaeological excavation and recording revealed an 18th/19th-century made ground layer sealing natural clays and sealed by a modern cement layer. One small pit was recorded in the west-facing section of Test-pit C, which lay in the middle of the site, although it failed to reveal any datable material. No further archaeological features or finds were recorded.

Dermot Nelis, Irish Archaeological Consultancy Ltd. 8 Dungar Terrace, Dun Laoghaire, Co. Dublin.

255. 36 SHOP STREET, GALWAY
No archaeological significance
98E0462

Monitoring of one trench associated with the development at 36 Shop Street, Galway, took place. Nothing of archaeological significance was revealed.

Fiona Rooney, Archaeological Consultancy, Ballydavid South, Athenry, Co. Galway.

256. HIGH ISLAND
Early Christian monastery
SMR 21:26C
L501572
95E124 ext.

In summer 1998 a fourth season of excavation was carried out at the Early Christian monastery on High Island, Co. Galway, with funding from *Dúchas*, The National Monuments and Historic Properties Service of the Department of Arts, Heritage, Gaeltacht and the Islands.

Following on from previous years' excavations, the partially collapsed central section of the east wall of the church and the stone altar inside the church were dismantled. Excavation of the deposits beneath revealed remains of an earlier altar. This altar, its later replacement and the church were constructed over an extensive burnt deposit, which has so far yielded Iron Age dates. Based on dating evidence as revealed from radiocarbon analysis of burials adjacent to the church, the church is late 9th–10th century in date.

Outside the north and south enclosure walls a *c.* 2m-wide strip was cleared of rubble and soil and a paved surface exposed. Remains of an earlier enclosure wall were identified on the north side.

Beyond the north enclosure wall the entrance to Cell A, the smaller of the two partially intact beehive cells, was excavated. The cell was entered directly from the paved area around the enclosure. Excavation of the cell interior was completed. A paved floor with remains of an occupation deposit was exposed. Two decorated slabs were found incorporated into the floor.

Further to the east excavation in the larger cell, Cell B, was 90% completed. A substantial stone-floored hearth with associated hearth debris covered most of the cell interior, suggesting that this building may have functioned as the monastic kitchen. It appears that this cell (and not Cell A as suggested by G. Petrie in 1820) was linked to the enclosure by means of a covered passage; further excavation is required to confirm this.

The wall chamber in the cashel wall was partially excavated. Only a shallow build-up of an organic-type deposit remained *in situ* at the base of the chamber, the remaining depth being composed of fragmented rubble and collapsed lintels from the chamber roof. Excavation in the dog-legged trench, which extended from the wall chamber as far as the west wall of the enclosure, continued. Remains of the collapsed cashel wall were identified at the west end of the trench, while at the east end several layers of a stone-paved surface, contemporary with the paved area around the south enclosure wall, were exposed. In the central part of the trench, and contemporary with the earliest of the paved surfaces, a number of stone-built features (one possibly being a drain) were identified but not excavated.

Georgina Scally, c/o 81 Upper Leeson Street, Dublin 4.

257. CHURCH STREET, LOUGHREA
1622 2164
98E0552

The test excavation of a site at Church Street, Loughrea, Co. Galway, in advance of its development and in response to a planning condition, was carried out on 21 September 1998. The development consisted of the demolition of an existing modern building on the site and the construction of a townhouse with separate living unit on the ground floor.

The site, which lay within the medieval town founded by Richard de Burgh in the 13th century, was very small, measuring 7.7m east–west by 4.4m, and contained three walls of a modern roofless building.

The single trench, excavated by machine, was orientated east–west and was 7.4m long, 0.8–1.1m wide and 1.2–1.9m deep. It was begun at 0.6m from the interior face of the west wall of the existing building (i.e. the wall facing onto Church Street) and 1.5m from the interior face of the north wall.

The stratigraphy encountered consisted of a concrete floor (50–100mm thick) found over the entire surface of the trench, below which were a rubble-built foundation and a fill. The fill consisted of a soft, grey/brown clay, 0.3–0.7m thick, and was found over the entire length of the trench except where the rubble foundation crossed the trench, at 1.2m from its east end. The rubble foundation was 1m wide and 0.6m thick and was related to the now removed east wall of the modern building on the site. Below the soft clay fill was a dark brown, friable, organic fill within a U-shaped cut, which was 1.6m long and 1.3m thick and lay 1m from the

west end of the trench. Boulder clay was found below this cut, at the base of the trench.

The soft clay fill contained a small number of modern artefacts. The organic fill contained occasional to moderate amounts of animal bone fragments, flecks of charcoal, oyster shells, red brick fragments and one clay pipe stem.

The stratigraphy encountered was indicative of modern use of this site.

Dave Pollock, 33 Woodlawn, Cashel, Co. Tipperary.

258. MOANMORE, LOUGHREA
No archaeological significance
98E0220

This involved the monitoring of ground disturbance associated with the development of a dwelling-house at Moanmore, Loughrea, Co. Galway. Nothing of archaeological significance was found in the course of monitoring.

Martin Fitzpatrick, Archaeological Consultancy, Ballydavid South, Athenry, Co. Galway.

259. MAINISTIR CHIARÁIN, OGHIL, (INIS MÓR)
Early Christian/medieval monastery
L810120
96E0081

A third season of excavation was carried out at Mainistir Chiaráin, Inis Mór, Co. Galway, over seven weeks between late June and mid-August 1998. Previous summaries can be found in *Excavations 1996* (44–5) and *Excavations 1997* (77).

Owing to the partial collapse of the north-east corner of Building A at the start of the 1998 season, it was necessary to step back from its walls, thus reducing the area excavated. Adjacent to the church wall excavation was restricted to two 1m-wide trenches parallel to the church on either side of Wall 028. Inside Building B the area excavated was also reduced in the northern half of the cutting, in order to step back from the walls. A second cutting, 6m x 6m in extent, was opened to the east of Cutting 1, 3m south of the church.

Inside Cutting 1 a cobbled surface was identified underlying Wall 028, the west wall of Building B. Incorporated within this cobbled area was a narrow, well-constructed drain of small dolomite slabs, running east–west. The cobbled area was delimited to the south and west by a wide, L-shaped drain, which was constructed of limestone slabs and covered at its north-western end by a large, broken capstone. The upper fill of this feature contained burned organic material and produced a number of finds, including some bone points, a bone pin with a bronze ring, fragments of worked jet and a bronze pin with a silvered shaft and terminal loop. The context directly overlying the fill of the drain also produced a decorated bronze pin with double scroll terminals and a fragment of a jet bracelet. Three radiocarbon dates of 1190±60 BP, 1250±60 BP and 1280±50 BP were recorded for the fill of this feature, the surface overlying it and on either side of it. The function of the feature remains unclear at present.

Excavation was not completed in the interior of Cutting 1; the drain and surrounding surfaces remain to be excavated in 1999. Adjacent to the church layers rich in charcoal and organic material were identified underlying the cut for the church wall.

In Cutting 2 a shell-rich soil underlay the topsoil. Cultivation furrows were evident above the shell midden. A rich garden soil of considerable depth underlay the spread of shell. The cultivation in this area of the site has led to extensive disturbance of archaeological strata. The east wall of Building B appears to have been completely robbed, but the line of the wall was suggested by a number of stone-holes running north–south along the west baulk and by a spread of occupation material. The bases of a number of gullies and possible stake-holes were cut into clay underlying the garden soil.

The construction level of the church was identified lying directly on the clay subsoil. Evidence of activities related to construction included a large pit, possibly dug to extract clay and backfilled with stoneworking debris, a lime-pit and a spread of partially worked and unworked limestone blocks.

This excavation is funded by the Heritage Services, Department of Arts, Heritage, Gaeltacht and the Islands, on the recommendation of the National Committee for Archaeology of the Royal Irish Academy, and by the University Research Expeditions Program, Berkeley.
Sinéad Ní Ghabhláin, 3262 San Helena Drive, Oceanside, California 92056.

280. ORANMORE SEWERAGE SCHEME
Various
98E0375
A preliminary archaeological assessment of the areas likely to be affected by the Oranmore Sewerage Scheme was compiled by Diarmuid Lavelle in January 1995. Subsequent fieldwork by Mr Lavelle, along with a search of the cartographic and literary sources, resulted in the identification of a total of fourteen sites. Of these, five were previously listed in the SMR for County Galway and nine were new sites of potential archaeological significance.

Gerry Walsh (*Excavations 1996*, 45, 96E388) carried out some pre-development testing and excavation.

In order to avoid confusion, the sites excavated by this writer have been given Roman numerals to distinguish them from those sites listed by Lavelle and tested by Walsh.

In 1998 this writer undertook monitoring along the route of the pipe-laying, and a number of smaller sites were resolved under that licence. Work is ongoing at several of the larger sites, for which separate licences have been applied, and will continue during 1999.

Site I: Oranmore, midden
This was immediately visible under the scraw and humus as a circular spread of burnt stone measuring 2.5m x 2.8m in maximum dimensions, at a depth of 0.35–0.45m below ground level. The material seemed to be a heap of lime and burnt stone 0.28–0.3m deep, which lay on yellow/grey subsoil (natural). There were no finds apart from some oyster and periwinkle shells. Several pieces of what appear to be burnt peat were also found.

Site IA: Oranmore, shell scatter
This was a thin scatter of shell, much of it broken, in a matrix of yellow/brown subsoil. There were no finds. The maximum extent of the spread was 2m x 1.8m.

Site II: Oranmore, shell spread
This large, thin spread of shell, 0.1–0.2m deep, occurred over an area of roughly 3.5m x 4.5m. The shell was concentrated in three clusters, but excavation showed that a more or less continuous deposit was present throughout the area. Oyster and periwinkles predominated and were sometimes deposited in distinct, separate, small caches. There was some animal bone.

Site III: Oranmore, midden
An irregular and thin spread of midden material (shell with some animal bone) showed on the surface, over an area with maximum dimensions of 2.3m x 2.6–2.8m. The surviving material was an average of 50mm thick.

Site IV: Oranmore, stray find
This was the suspected site of a possible hearth that had been previously identified in field-walking. Excavation showed that the reddish/orange staining and black staining in the soil were natural deposits in a superficial deposit of estuarine mud. Some nodules of chert occurred, but these were natural and unworked.

About 1.8m south-south-west of this suspected site a piece of chert was discovered lying on the surface of the estuarine mud. This find seems to have been chipped or retouched.

Site V: Oranmore, midden
This was an irregular spread of midden material, most of it badly disturbed by machine tracks, originally 8m x 9–9.8m. Most of the deposit consisted of shell, mainly oyster and periwinkle, and some bone. The scraw and grass had previously been stripped but had averaged 0.2–0.25m deep. The lower deposits of humus beneath the scraw had survived and averaged 20–50mm deep over parts of the midden material. The deposit was not continuous, and two midden layers separated by a brown soil level could be discerned in places in one of the long faces of the cutting.

Site VI: Oranmore, middens
Stripping of the topsoil led to the discovery of a number of continuous and discontinuous spreads of midden material consisting of shell with smaller quantities of bone. The total area of the spreads was *c.* 8m x 12m. On the first day of monitoring a flint, leaf-shaped arrowhead, a struck piece of chert and a possible chert core were found. These were all among exposed shells of the midden in an area less than 1.8m across. They suggest that the midden may be of prehistoric date, and as a result an area 3m x 5m of the main, apparently undisturbed deposit, which occurred around an outcrop of limestone, was excavated.

It was concluded that the deposits consisted of two core areas, one on each side of the outcrop, with the occasional cluster of shell and bone and unworked chert occurring between the natural grooves in the outcrop.

Two cuttings were made down to the boulder clay. One tooth found in Cutting 1 was possibly human. A lump of chert, which may have been a struck core, was found at a depth of 0.22–0.25m between the grikes in the limestone outcrop. One piece of ferrous material (rusted iron) came from the black, humic material just beneath the scraw. Large quantities of naturally occurring chert were found.

Site VII: Oranmore, shell scatter
This was a small scatter of oyster shells. The maximum extent was 1.1m x 0.65m. The layer was no more than 60mm thick and mixed with small stones. It lay directly on limestone outcrop and produced no artefacts.

Site VIII: Oranmore, shell spread
This was a spread of oyster shells over an area of 3.5m x 3.5m. The midden material was 0.1m deep.

Site IX: Oranmore, midden
This was a spread of midden material including oyster shell, periwinkles and much bone. Most of the upper levels of the midden seem to have been removed during soil-stripping. The spread was 1m x 0.5m and 0.15m deep. Some small pieces of charcoal and a tooth were found, as well as a sherd of pottery of a grey fabric with some white grits, which seems to be from the base of a vessel.

Site X: Oranmore, midden
This was a small spread of midden measuring *c.* 1.28m x 0.6m, including cockles, oysters and periwinkles. There was a small quantity of bone.

Site XI: Oranmore, midden
This was a truncated spread of midden material that was undoubtedly thicker before soil-stripping. The maximum spread of material visible before excavation was 2m x 1m. It consisted mostly of oyster shells and some periwinkles. One animal tooth was found. The midden material was 0.22m thick.

Site XII: Oranmore, walled garden
The walled garden through which the pipeline passed proved to be of 18th-century date. Two wide pathways (of a series of pathways that divided the area internally) were kerbed with limestone and contained red brick. English 18th-century red-ware pottery of a type copied from Chinese originals, with machine-made patterns of grooves and lozenges, occurred beneath the path. A worn coin of Charles II was found on the pathway but in a disturbed context.

Site XIII: Innplot, gravel spread with post-medieval pottery
Resolved.

Site XIV: Innplot, non-antiquity
Resolved, proved to be a 19th-century soak-pit.

Site XV: Innplot
As Site XIV, resolved.

Site XVI: Innplot
As Site XV, resolved.

Site XVII: Millplot, mill (site of)
This included wall footings, millpond flooring and millpond wall along with millstones still extant (Gerry Walsh's site 11). As well as the mill site

(resolved by G. Walsh), a wall of a millpond and several other non-related features were found. This new millpond wall proved to be fragmentary. It will be left, and the pipeline will be diverted elsewhere.

Cleaning around the base of a peat deposit on what appears to be natural riverine gravels resulted in the discovery of a human male skull, some animal bone and several groupings of boulders. Also discovered were wattle-like pieces of wood. These are frequently worked, and as well as withies and stakes, some charred timbers, pegs and larger pieces of worked timber occurred.

The site is more extensive than hitherto suspected and appears to be a habitation area of some complexity that will require some further work. Among the smaller finds were some crudely worked but undiagnostic pieces of bad quality grey/blue chert, some hazelnut shells, periwinkle and mussel shells and roughly half of a jet or lignite bracelet. Some crude cobbling occurs in the area in which the boulders have been placed or dumped, and some of these boulders appear to sit on top of some of the pieces of charred wood.

The site is enigmatic, and its structural features are poorly preserved. There is, however, good organic material present. The wattle 'walling' may represent a fish weir, a property boundary or part of a building. A separate licence has been applied for to excavate this site.

Site XVIII: Oranmore, midden of shell and bone with kiln-like structure beneath
This midden, on cleaning, looked to be fairly confined and small. Below is a small, two-chambered structure linked by a low lintelled passage. Some worked chert, possibly prehistoric, occurred in the midden material. A separate licence has been applied for to complete this site.

Site XVIX: Oranmore, pathway outside walled garden
This was found to be of 18th/19th-century date and produced pottery of that period.

Site XX: Oranmore, midden spread with 19th-century pottery
Excavated and resolved.

Site XXI: Oranmore, midden spread
Contained modern pottery and clay pipe fragments. Excavated and resolved.

Site XXII: Oranmore, small midden spread
This probably prehistoric(?) spread contained mostly periwinkle shells. Excavated and resolved.

Site XXIII: Oranmore, spread of post-medieval rubble
This was formerly thought to have been associated with the demolition of a 17th-century Jacobean style mansion, shown in an 18th-century engraving, but it is now thought to be associated with the 1950s renovation work on the nearby Oranmore Castle. A field wall at the seaward side of the site is modern and incorporates pieces of concrete and 19th-century cut stone. Post-medieval pottery, slates, ridge-tiles etc. occurred.

Galway

Site XXIV: Oranmore, spread of midden material
This site has been archaeologically resolved. It produced a glass bead of uncertain date, midden material (bone, shell) and some struck chert.

Site XXV: Oranmore, clay 'floor' that produced some struck chert
This site has yet to be cleaned to establish its extent and whether a red area is a hearth and habitation. Prehistoric worked chert occurs. Some possible areas of cobbling may occur. This site will be returned to under separate licence.

Site XXVI: Oranmore, a possible lintel grave or industrial 'furnace'
This area, with an area of dense burning around it, has been cleaned but not yet fully excavated. The site has produced burnt bone and prehistoric chert to date.

Site XXVII: Oranmore, truncated embankment
This seems to be a field embankment attached to (and later than) a nearby ring-barrow. A pair of ditches flank the embankment. Only 2.8m of its length occurs within the way-leave. It has produced a barbed-and-tanged arrowhead, thumbnail scrapers, chert debitage and other prehistoric material and will be returned to under a separate licence.

Site XXVIII: Oranmore, field-wall system or possible enclosures with possible 'lintel graves'
This is a complex of sites that extends across the way-leave and includes field walls and hut-like features. It lies close to Gerry Walsh's Site 9, which produced a thumbnail scraper and other worked chert artefacts. The site extends the entire width of the way-leave and beyond it. Work is to continue here under separate licence.

Site XXIX: Oranmore, burnt stone spreads and midden material
Burnt stone and midden material occurs in several irregular spreads. It is suggested that this material should be archaeologically resolved. A separate licence has been applied for.

Site XXX: Oranmore, cobbled area, midden material, possible pit
A small midden spread is visible, and machine tracking has partially exposed and damaged a cobbled surface. Cleaning of this surface has produced a spindle whorl, debitage from chert working, half of the butt-end of a polished stone axehead and the front end of another that was later cut down and reworked. A stone flake may have come from a further axehead.

A separate licence to fully resolve this site has been applied for.

Site XXXI: Oranmore, field embankments and a series of field clearance cairns
The site consists of a series of field embankments and clearance cairns. These appear (from finds of glass and pottery) to be 18th and 19th century in date. The extent to which this site impinges on Site XXX is as yet unknown, and it is suggested that the intervening area, some 10m wide, should be test-trenched to resolve this issue. Recently about half of

a Mesolithic Bann flake was found nearby in a disturbed context. A separate licence has been applied for for this site.

Site XXXII: Oranmore, midden
In the road leading to Oranmore Castle a small midden spread was found. It has been archaeologically resolved.

Site XXXIII: Roscam, midden spread and slight embankment
To date, this site has produced post-medieval pottery. Its extent and features are still to be established. It seems to be modern and has produced pieces of late milk crocks. The site is to be resolved next year.

Site XXXIV: Roscam, midden
Thin deposit, no finds; archaeologically resolved.

Site XXXV: Oranmore, spread of chert artefacts and stone-kerbed feature
The small kerbed feature seems to be too small to be a hut-site and may be field clearance or possibly a very unusual burial mound. The adjacent area has been stripped of topsoil and cleaned. Apparent deliberately laid 'cobbling' occurred between areas of limestone bedrock; some of this may have been due to field clearance or agriculture. Much evidence of chert working including thumbnail scrapers and other side-scrapers occurred.

Part of the stone-kerbed area is artificial, the rest is deliberately kerbed by linear groupings of small stones. A separate licence to excavate these sites was applied for.

Site XXXVI: Oranmore, chert debitage
This area on the outcrop was stripped by hand. Chert debitage from lithic manufacture occurred within the crevices between the outcrop.

Site XXXVII: Oranmore, as XXVI
A further area like Site XXVI was hand-stripped. Examination of the soil between the rock outcrop produced no artefacts whatsoever.
Jim Higgins, 'St Gerard's', 18 College Road, Galway.

261. ORANMORE
No archaeological significance
13804 22452
SMR 95:114
98E0525
The monitoring of groundwork at the site of St Mary's Church and graveyard, Oranmore, took place on 12 November 1998.

The church is being redeveloped into a community office, with ancillary alterations and accommodation, funded by the local Community Development Association. Development work involved the excavation of two service trenches and a box area to accommodate an ESB cable and a foul sewer connected to a holding tank (all groundwork is to take place outside the building). With the exception of the area to the rear of the building, which was dug by hand, all the excavation work was carried out by mechanical digger using a toothless bucket.

Trench A was *c.* 27m long, 0.6m wide and 0.9m

deep and ran from the now office entrance at the north-west of the church to the front gates of the site. The sod and topsoil layer was 0.13m deep and contained two sherds of modern pottery and broken glass. The tarmacadamed driveway directly overlay a brown, silty sand, 0.21m deep. Under this a dark grey/brown, stony layer was 0.23m thick, above natural.

Trench B ran alongside Trench A and extended from the rear of the church around to the toilets in the community office. It had an overall length of 38m, was excavated in two sections and had the same stratigraphy as Trench A. The only finds retrieved were two disarticulated pieces of animal bone found under the tarmac layer. The trench had a maximum depth of 0.9m and an average width of 0.6m, widening to 3m to accommodate the holding tank.

At the rear of the church the hand-dug trench was more narrow and shallow, measuring 0.4m and 0.45m respectively. A thin topsoil with a brown silt sod, 0.8m thick, overlay a coarser sand with a moderate amount of small stones, 0.12m thick. Below this was a dark brown, silty layer, similar to the bottom layer in Trench A. This stratigraphic sequence was interrupted at the north-east corner of the church by a yellow/brown clay that was found below the dark brown, silty layer. This layer may be associated with a nearby grave-cut.

Monitoring of the groundwork at St Mary's Church revealed no archaeological levels or finds. Both trenches were deliberately sited to cause as little disturbance as possible to the surrounding grave sites. This aim was achieved successfully.
Billy Quinn, Archaeological Services Unit Ltd, Purcell House, Oranmore, Co. Galway.

262. PORTUMNA CASTLE, PORTUMNA
Post-medieval castle
N040853
SMR 127:18
95E0074

Another season of archaeological excavation took place at Portumna Castle during 1998. Archaeological investigation has been ongoing since 1995 (*Excavations 1995*, 37–8; *Excavations 1996*, 46; *Excavations 1997*, 77–8) alongside the restoration work by the National Monuments Section of *Dúchas* The Heritage Service.

Work in 1998 concentrated on the east side of the castle and on the south garden. The test-trenches excavated in the south garden confirmed the presence of bawn walls on both the east and west sides of the garden. In addition, an early ditch running north–south was uncovered midway across the garden. This ditch was backfilled before 1791 and probably represents an original 17th-century garden feature. A stone-lined ditch was uncovered further to the east, also running north–south. This feature is still visible along its full length and may be associated with one of the late drains exiting the south-east corner tower. The stone-lined ditch appears to take water away from a square, stone-lined pit in the wooded area to the south-east of the castle, which has not been investigated to date.

Further excavation took place beside the west wall of the medieval abbey in the area of what would have been the main entrance to the 17th-century castle. A rock-cut channel with stone-lined sides was exposed, 2.4m wide and 2m deep. It was stepped and sloped gently towards the east. The side walls were battered inwards, and the feature has the appearance of a stone-lined ditch. The feature is relatively early in date and clearly pre-dates the

Excavation of Portumna Castle showing drain and 19th-century annexe.

17th-century avenue. It is possible therefore that the feature is medieval in date, and it may be part of the original boundary of the medieval abbey or associated medieval borough. The rock-cut channel ran east–west and returned to the south, just outside the west wall of the medieval abbey.

Archaeological excavation on the east side of the castle revealed the presence of a 19th-century annexe to the castle itself. This consisted of a rectangular building measuring 14.2m north–south by 7.1m. The building consisted of two rooms either side of a central stairwell leading from the courtyard on the east side of the castle down towards the central spine of the castle basement. This building is probably connected with the work done by the architect George Papworth in the early 1820s, shortly before the castle was destroyed by fire. This 19th-century annexe was originally three storeys high, as can clearly be seen from the plaster on the east wall of the castle.

In addition to this building a small 19th-century toilet block was uncovered immediately to the east of the north-east corner tower. This consisted of two cascades leading from ground level down to the main drain below, which runs through the castle basement and out under the south-west corner tower. The main conduit was also exposed just outside the north-east corner tower. It was of similar construction to the main conduit exposed below the castle basement itself and consisted of mortared stone walls with large lintels. It appears that this main conduit originally commenced just outside the north-east corner tower of the castle and that at some stage during the late 18th century a red brick culvert was constructed, which brought water from a well in the middle of the courtyard to the east into this main conduit. Restoration work is currently continuing on the castle.
Donald Murphy, Archaeological Consultancy Services Ltd, 15 Trinity Street, Drogheda, Co. Louth.

263. PORTUMNA SEWERAGE SCHEME, PORTUMNA

Post-medieval brick kiln
M039852
98E0386

Monitoring of the outfall lines for the Portumna Sewerage Scheme in 1998 uncovered the remains of a partially destroyed brick kiln in the woods to the south-west of Portumna Castle and within what would have been the 17th-century demesne.

The kiln measured 8.5m east–west and 6m north–south but continued beyond the east baulk so that its full extent is not known. It consisted of rows of bricks placed 0.4m apart, which formed channels or flues through which the heat could travel in order to circulate around the bricks so that they would be properly fired. Only the bottom two courses, and in places only the bottom course, of bricks survived, with the feature having been very badly disturbed by the trees that had been planted on top of it during the last 200 years.

Although no substantial dating evidence was retrieved from the feature, the bricks themselves are consistent with the 17th-century bricks found in Portumna Castle itself. It is highly likely therefore that the brick kiln was constructed for use at the nearby castle.
Donald Murphy, Archaeological Consultancy Services Ltd, 15 Trinity Street, Drogheda, Co. Louth.

264. RAHEEN

No archaeological significance
98E0117

This project involved the monitoring of ground disturbance associated with the development of a dwelling-house at Raheen, Athenry, Co. Galway. Nothing of archaeological significance was encountered in the course of monitoring.
Martin Fitzpatrick, Archaeological Consultancy, Ballydavid South, Athenry, Co. Galway.

Brick kiln found during Portumna Sewerage Scheme excavations.

265. RINVILLE WEST
Environs of possible souterrain
M358230
97E0351
This third and final phase of archaeological assessment and examination of the site, incorporating the site of a possible souterrain identified in the Environmental Impact Survey prepared for the development, revealed no trace of any archaeological features or soils (see *Excavations 1997*, 78–9, for previous assessments).
Margaret Gowen, 2 Killiney View, Albert Road Lower, Glenageary, Co. Dublin.

KERRY

266. *AN RAINGILÉIS*, BALLYWIHEEN
Early Christian monastic site
Q352035
98E0371
Reinstatement of topsoil in an area of unauthorised groundworks within the zone of a registered National Monument at Ballywiheen, on the Dingle Peninsula, Co. Kerry, necessitated prior archaeological excavation. Investigation immediately outside the wall of an Early Christian monastic enclosure revealed evidence of activity, some of which may be contemporary with the original occupation of the site.

The earliest archaeological feature identified was the remains of an infilled soutcrrain aligned north-west/south-east and 10m long. While the full extent of the souterrain could not be ascertained within the excavated area, it is presumed that it is contemporary with the original use of the monastic site. The basal courses of a stone wall 3.98m long overlay the south-eastern edge of the souterrain. The nature and purpose of this wall are uncertain. A portion of a small pit-like feature was found at the northern end of the trench, but this had no stratigraphic relationship with other features at the site.

The partial remains of a human burial represented the latest phase of activity. Two fragments of the lower limbs of an adult were visible in the upper layers of the exposed section face. The available evidence indicated that the burial may have been contained within a stone-lined grave.

Material finds included a fragment of a stone lamp and a flint scraper, both of which may have derived from the occupation of the monastic site.
Margaret McCarthy, Archaeological Services Unit, University College Cork.

267. BRAY HEAD (VALENCIA ISLAND)
Early medieval farmhouses
V344737
97E0278 ext.
Excavation was undertaken over a four-week period in August and September 1998. This is the sixth season of excavation undertaken on Bray Head. This year's work concentrated on the group of early medieval houses revealed in 1997 (*Excavations 1997*, 81–2). To date, nine early medieval buildings have been uncovered, superimposed on each other in at least five phases. Five rectangular houses overlay four round houses. One of the round houses

was found to contain a souterrain, as well as evidence of internal divisions and other features that rarely survive in buildings of this period.

Not all the buildings could be fully excavated in the time allotted, and it is hoped to return to the site in 1999 to complete the excavation and to try to determine whether the settlement was enclosed or unenclosed.

^{14}C dates are awaited for the structures, but the latest has been previously dated to the 11th century. Samples retrieved from the floors of the structures indicate that wheat, barley and oats were being consumed and probably grown in the area in the early medieval period.

The work was funded by *Dúchas* The Heritage Service.
Alan Hayden, Archaeological Projects Ltd, 25A Eaton Square, Terenure, Dublin 6W.

268. CAHERLEHILLAN
Early ecclesiastical enclosure
V572835
SMR 70:43
93E0073
Excavations at this site, which are being undertaken as part of UCC's Department of Archaeology undergraduate training programme, continued during June 1998.

The investigation of Area 1, in which two early adult graves, both of dug-grave type, were uncovered during 1997 (*Excavations 1997*, 82), continued. A stone-lined and lintel-covered grave, which was partially truncated by the cut of one of the dug graves, was uncovered and will be investigated fully in 1999.

Further work on Area 2, which lies towards the centre of the enclosure, revealed further stake-holes; it now appears that the many post- and stake-holes in this area represent the former existence of two conjoined circular structures.

Evidence of another post-hole structure is emerging in Area 3, in the south-west quadrant of the site, where evidence of metalworking continues to emerge.

Excavations in Area 7, located between Areas 2 and 3, revealed that the subsoil C8 overlies the present top of the site's enclosing wall. The charcoal-rich soil spread C28, which has revealed large quantities of imported pottery in Area 3, has now been found in Area 7.

Area 8, which centres on the shrine structure in the north-east quadrant of the site, was opened in 1998. All four sides of the structure, formed by upright slabs laid on end, were revealed, as was its top, which is formed of three large slate slabs. Overlying the top was a mounded deposit of quartz pebbles within which was contained at least one *ceallúnach*-type burial.
John Sheehan, Department of Archaeology, University College Cork.

269. TAILOR'S ROW, CASTLEGREGORY
Castle site
6217 11337
SMR 27:8
98E0090
This test excavation was undertaken following a planning application to construct a dwelling in close

proximity to the supposed site of Castlegregory Castle. No upstanding remains of the castle are visible, but a number of architectural fragments survive in various locations around the village. The original castle was possibly built by Gregory Hoare, a tenant-in-chief of the Desmonds, most likely in the 16th century.

The site had been levelled and cleared in the recent past. Four areas were selected for excavation. The trenches were opened by mechanical digger and completed by hand. Trench 1 was 3.7m x 1.5m and excavated to a depth of 1.8m. The loose fill consisted of a build-up of dump material to a depth of 1.5m below a thin sod cover. Finds included modern pottery sherds, shells (predominantly periwinkles) and other modern domestic rubbish, most likely associated with the site clearance.

Trench 2, 4.5m x 1.5m, was excavated to a depth of 2m and aligned east–west. A ditch feature was exposed running in a general north–south direction. The ditch was 3.8–4m wide and had a flat base. The upper fill of the ditch consisted of a shell midden layer predominantly of cockles and periwinkles, with mussels and oysters also represented. The layer also contained some beach cobbles, but no artefacts or charcoal were present.

Trench 3, 6.5m x 1.5m, was excavated to a depth of 0.9–1.5m. A large boulder, 1.5m x 0.9m, was exposed just below the surface and was set in natural material. Overlying the natural was an organic deposit that produced three sherds of glazed earthenware from the late 19th/early 20th century.

Trench 4 was 3.5m x 0.9m and 0.9m deep. Topsoil overlay natural, which occurred at 0.4m. Modern domestic rubbish, including two sherds of modern pottery, was found in the topsoil.

Laurence Dunne, Eachtra Archaeological Projects, 43 Ard Carraig, Tralee, Co. Kerry.

270. 'THE CANON'S GARDEN', GREEN STREET, DINGLE

Town wall
SMR 43:224
98E0262 and ext.

Monitoring of the site of a proposed housing unit for the elderly on Green Street, Dingle, began on 18 May, and continued intermittently until the beginning of July. The name 'The Canon's Garden' derives from the site's use as a garden for some time, and it was still undeveloped when the present work commenced. The site measures 40m north-east/south-west x 20m and lies within the area of archaeological potential for Dingle town. It was possible that the line of the town wall had extended onto the site, which is bounded by the grounds of the Presentation Convent/*Díseart* to the north-west (in property possibly occupied by the Sisters since 1829) and by an 18th-century building to the north-east. St Mary's Catholic Church (commenced 1812) is to the south-west. The site is shown as open ground on both editions of the 6-inch map, but the extreme south-western portion is shown on the 1st edition as containing part of a girls' national school. The site originally sloped very steeply to both the south-east and south-west.

The boundary with the street consists of a high stone wall, neatly faced externally, but internally the lower *c.* 1.3m is quite rough. This is consistent with it not being visible while the area was used as a garden. This wall was to be retained in the new development, apart from the entrance area, but its poor condition meant that it had to be taken down and rebuilt for much of its length. This was not necessary for the south-western stretch, however, where it may incorporate part of the town wall.

Clearance work began before an archaeologist was contacted, but some of the initial soil removal, to bring the ground down to present street level (it having been on average 1.7m above it before work commenced) was monitored and nothing of archaeological significance noted. In an area where soil removal had not been monitored, along the north-eastern boundary of the site, were some layers of possible interest in the eastern end, running for a length of 4.9m from the street front, where two stony layers not noted elsewhere were seen in section. Their rough nature was not consistent with a structure, although it is possible that they are the remains of a demolition layer.

Further south within the site the amount of soil removed was less, consistent with the downhill slope of the land. Here, only *c.* 1m of soil was removed, particularly in the area adjacent to the street front.

After the site was cleared down to present street level an obvious change in wall construction in the area where it might be expected that the town wall would be present was noted, and some stones of a long-demolished wall protruded inwards from the street wall, up to 1.3m above cleared ground level. A change in structure is also visible on the external (street) face of the wall. On cleaning the loose soil at the base of this feature, a line of stones was noted. It was 1.15m wide, and was exposed for a length of only 0.6m max. As this was consistent with the probable location of the town wall, investigations ceased as an excavation licence had not been obtained for this work, which was only intended as monitoring.

The original intention of the architect had been to dig foundation trenches in the area of this newly discovered wall, which would have destroyed it. On the recommendation of *Dúchas*, plans were redrawn so that the building could proceed without any further excavation having to take place in that area and the wall would remain undisturbed. The area around it was to be covered with hard-core, with a terram protection for the actual wall. Archaeological excavation of the area was therefore no longer necessary, but the exposed portion of the wall was cleaned, photographed and drawn, before it was again covered.

It is impossible to say how much deeper the wall remains, nor could one be sure how much of it remains underground crossing the site—it certainly did not seem to be present at the north-western boundary wall, although it was possible to make out where it should have been. Here again the site had been cleared to well below natural, and, with the confusion of walls in this area, it was difficult to say which, if any, may have been town wall.

Monitoring of foundation digging in the south-western portion of the site took place on 2 July. The maximum depth of foundations was 0.5m below the previously cleared (street) level. In some areas the natural was exposed, otherwise, particularly in the extreme south-western (downhill) portion of the site, a dark brown soil was present, similar to that removed already from the site. Three sherds of pottery, two of medieval date, were found in the soil or lying on the already cleared surface.

There was no evidence of the town wall being present at this level in any of the foundation trenches dug at the north-western end of the site.

Also noted on the site was a lintelled drain, 0.8m to the south-west (outside) of the town wall and running in line with it. Its line could be followed for at least 2.6m from the street into the site. It was at least 0.32m deep, but may have silted up, and was 0.55–0.6m wide. It may have been part of an already known, probably 19th-century, culvert system.

Isabel Bennett, Glen Fahan, Ventry, Tralee, Co. Kerry.

271. GARVEY'S SUPERMARKET, HOLYGROUND, DINGLE

Monitoring

SMR 43:224

Unlicensed monitoring of ground disturbance works during the construction of an ESB sub-station at the back of Garvey's Supervalu Supermarket, Holyground, Dingle, Co. Kerry, took place on 8 June. Nothing of archaeological significance was noted, with only recently disturbed ground being dug into.

Isabel Bennett, Glen Fahan, Ventry, Tralee, Co. Kerry.

272. JOHN STREET, DINGLE

Monitoring

The site, on the western side of John Street, Dingle (a continuation of Main Street), is within the zone of archaeological potential for the town as recognised by the Urban Archaeological Survey. It may lie within the area defined by the town wall, if it corresponds to the suggested line as shown in the *Dingle Peninsula Archaeological Survey*. The actual line of the wall is uncertain in most parts of the town, as there are no upstanding remains. The site in question *may* lie within the town wall, although this is unlikely, and it probably stands some distance outside it.

The development had commenced before an archaeologist was informed, and any ground disturbance that was to take place had already done so.

The site was inspected on 2 March 1998, and it was noted that an extension had been constructed to the rear of the existing street-front buildings (whose foundations were not disturbed) and a smaller structure had been erected on the site of an earlier one in the backyard area. The ground level had been trunked up, so no original ground level, before the commencement of the construction, was exposed. Any foundations that had been inserted were *c.* 0.45m deep below present ground level and, according to the builder, were dug into previously undisturbed soil.

As no archaeologist was present when ground disturbance work took place, comment cannot be made on any archaeology that may have been present. On the evidence of the builder, and knowing the lack of material found at a nearby site also in John Street (*Excavations 1997*, 84), and at most of sites investigated so far in Dingle town, it is likely that there was nothing of archaeological significance at this site.

Isabel Bennett, Glen Fahan, Ventry, Tralee, Co. Kerry.

273. MAIN STREET, DINGLE

Town wall site

4470 10103

98E0152

This test excavation and licensed monitoring was a condition of planning permission granted to P&T Fitzgerald for a major development at the rear of their supermarket on Main Street. The first phase of the development was previously reported (*Excavations 1997*, 85, 97E0153). This second phase was undertaken in proximity to the line of the medieval town wall and within the archaeological zone of Dingle town.

The town of Dingle was most likely built on virgin ground in the Anglo-Norman period. It is likely that it was walled towards the end of the 16th century. Traces of the town wall were recorded in the mid-19th century by Richard Hitchcock, and the 1st and 2nd editions of the OS maps (1841; 1896) also show the line of the town wall. The coherent footprint of the medieval town comprising the linear layout of main street and rear burgage plots remains virtually intact today.

Test excavation work concentrated on the extreme south-western corner of the site, where upstanding rubble-built walls, exposed by the demolition of sheds, were locally believed to be the remnants of the original town walls. The walls displayed at least two distinct building techniques in the excavation area. It was obvious at the outset that the level of the development site had been greatly raised in the past. Indeed the external ground level was some 2m below current ground level.

A hand-dug trench measuring 6m x 1.3m was opened at the base of the walls in the south-west limit of the site. The main fill consisted of introduced loose stones and other dump material, consistent with the raising of the ground level in the 18th and 19th centuries. Sixteen contexts were recorded, including the basal remains of two sandstone rib walls, each abutting the southern boundary wall. Clay pipe fragments, sherds of post-medieval and modern pottery, shells and occasional faunal remains were recovered. A degraded sherd of medieval pottery was recovered. The subsurface sections of the boundary wall confirmed differing construction techniques; however, it was not found to be earlier than the 18th century.

Monitoring of all disturbance on site was undertaken. Over forty pads were excavated by mechanical digger to an average depth of 1m. Most of these contained fills of sandstone trunking with little or no organic material, although at two pad locations the same sequence of deposits and fills that was recovered in the excavation trench was present. In some areas the trunking overlay sterile natural, and this was consistent with the findings from the previous year's excavations. In more pads the trunking overlay a dark brown, mixed fill, which produced post-medieval and early modern pottery sherds, shells, slate fragments and some small faunal remains. The service trenches likewise consisted mainly of sandstone rubble fill. It was obvious that the level of the development site was raised in the 18th/19th century.

Most of the finds indicate that early 19th- and possibly late 18th-century activity destroyed earlier levels. Medieval pottery sherds were recovered, but these were found in introduced fill.

Laurence Dunne, Eachtra Archaeological Projects, 43 Ard Carraig, Tralee, Co. Kerry.

Kerry

274. MAIN STREET, DINGLE
Urban
SMR 43:224
98M0016

Planning permission was granted to demolish existing buildings and erect a new premises to the rear of that already existing at Main Street, Dingle, Co. Kerry, with a condition attached that all topsoil removal and ground disturbance aspects of the development be monitored. The site lies on the south-western side of and about halfway up the street and backs onto the line of the town wall.

Monitoring took place on 7 September 1998, and the site was also visited on 9 September, as the concrete foundations of the building that formerly stood on the site were being removed. The site is within a burgage plot, of long burgage form, typical of Anglo-Norman towns in Ireland, and there is documentary evidence that the town of Dingle was in existence certainly from the later part of the 13th century.

Foundations were dug to an average depth of 0.5m. On the uphill portion of the site (the north-west) they were dug almost immediately into undisturbed subsoil, as it became apparent that the site must have been levelled off before the erection of the earlier building. But on the downhill portion of the development up to 0.3m of rich, dark soil lay above the subsoil.

Apart from a couple of sherds of modern, glazed pottery, and some fragments of red brick, no finds were retrieved. Apart from the modern concrete foundation of the previous building on the site, no features were apparent.

Isabel Bennett, Glen Fahan, Ventry, Tralee, Co. Kerry.

275. GARRANEBANE
Children's burial-ground/ringfort
4601 7868
SMR 79:40
98E0522

Monitoring and subsequent excavations were carried out to fulfil conditions of planning permission to construct a new VEC community college at Garranebane, Caherciveen. Work focused on the recorded monument classified as a 'Children's Burial Ground'. This monument had been virtually destroyed in the recent past, not least as a result of a concrete farmyard that covered much of the site and its environs, the continuous use of the monument as a dump and the density of growth on the site. The site lies on the seaward lower slopes of Bentee Mountain at the south-eastern limits of Caherciveen and commands extensive maritime views over the Valentia River estuary, Beginis and Valentia Islands and Doulus Head.

Children's burial-grounds often occur associated with pre-existing archaeological monuments. This one appears to have the remains of a ringfort as its host monument. The site was so heavily overgrown and disturbed that an accurate survey was impossible before a clean up. The site was bounded to the west and east by field boundaries and to the south and south-west by the possible embanked remains of a ringfort. Measurements of the extant remains of the ringfort bank and from the 1st edition OS map showed that the host monument was circular in plan and *c.* 33m in internal diameter. No *in situ* grave-markers were found. A provisional 10m buffer zone was established around the proposed limits of the *ceallúnach.*

Monitoring of topsoil removal by machine throughout the main body of the site was carried out in October 1997. No artefacts, deposits or stratigraphy of an archaeological nature were identified.

Before any archaeological excavations it was necessary to remove the concrete that extended into the monument and beyond. This revealed that the north and north-east areas of the site had been heavily disturbed. However, in the south-east area of the site a subcircular arc of discoloured soil was revealed, possibly relating to the remains of an infilled ditch. An upper portion of a rotary quern was recovered here.

Two trenches were opened. Area 1 lay in the east of the site, orientated east–west; Area 2 lay in the north, where the concrete intruded on the monument.

Area 1 was subdivided into two cuttings, 1 and 1a. Cutting 1 was 4m north–south x 3m. Removal of the surface material revealed a complex of drainage channels and concrete girder pads. All earlier archaeological deposits had been destroyed, and no artefacts or stratigraphy of an archaeological nature were found.

Area 1a measured 2m north–south x 1.7m. It was positioned to reveal the possible remains of the host monument. Removal of modern rubble exposed a white, clayey natural. A grey, gravel natural was also exposed, into which a ditch 3.7m wide x 1.5m had been cut. This proved it to be the remains of the ringfort ditch, which had been deliberately backfilled and in more recent times utilised as a field drain. The ditch was subcircular in plan with a graduated break of slope. The sides were slightly concave in the east and steeply inclined towards the base. The break of base is concave, and the base is predominantly flat and U-shaped. No artefacts or other dating material were recovered from the ditch.

Area 2 measured 2m x 2m. Removal of topsoil exposed a stony shale layer. A small box-like setting of stones was encountered towards the south-west of the trench. Cleaning of this feature produced a number of small quartz nodules, supporting the

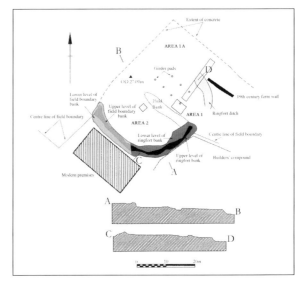

Overall layout plan of excavations and monument.

interpretation that this may have been the remains of a child burial associated with the use of the monument as a *ceallúnach*. However, additional cleaning failed to produce any evidence of an associated grave-cut. The lack of burials encountered may be due to the nature of the division of the original monument by field boundaries and by the level of destruction.

Owing to the extent of the destruction and the amount of modern dump material no soil or charcoal samples were recovered. A number of organic samples were taken from the lower levels of the ditch fill, and specialist reports on these are pending.

A burial-ground clean-up took place concurrently with the excavations, and this enabled a detailed contour survey to be undertaken. Conservation work on the surviving remains of the monument will be carried out in the near future.
Laurence Dunne, Eachtra Archaeological Projects, 43 Ard Carraig, Tralee, Co. Kerry.

276. SKELLIG MICHAEL (MONKS' GARDEN), GREAT SKELLIG
Monastic site
02453 06042
SMR 104A:001
Work this year concentrated on a recently discovered entrance through the southern wall of the inner monastic enclosure. This proved that the entrance and the part of the wall immediately to the west of it pre-date all standing structures within the inner enclosure and ignore the present layout of the monastery. The entrance lies beneath the large oratory and pre-dates both it and the graveyard immediately to the east of it. Ground level in the inner enclosure at the entrance would have been at least 2m below present ground level, although the area opened was too small to reveal any structures associated with the entrance.

By the time that the large oratory was built this entrance had gone out of use, and traces of stone revetment both for the foundation of the large oratory and for the blocking of the entrance were revealed by the excavation. At a later stage a series of rough steps and a pathway around the oratory and past the entrance were constructed. After this had gone out of use the ground was raised again, probably in the 1870s, and in the uppermost layers of this backfill some redeposited human bones were found. These may have been retrieved from the partial collapse of St Michael's Church in the last century and reburied by the workmen. Work in this area is set to continue in 1999.
Edward Bourke, Dúchas, 51 St Stephen's Green, Dublin 2.

277. KILLARNEY SEWAGE SCHEME
Urban
97E0429
Monitoring of Phase 2 of the Killarney Sewage Improvement Scheme was undertaken from October 1997 to May 1998. Groundworks involved the mechanical excavation of fifteen trenches in and around the vicinity of Killarney town. Despite extensive groundworks very few features or finds were recorded. This lack of archaeological evidence is because most of the trenches followed old, previously disturbed pipelines. Features that were exposed and investigated included a number of culverts, stone wall foundations, boulder sockets and a limekiln, all of which were subsequently found to be of relatively modern construction. No stray finds of archaeological significance were retrieved.
Billy Quinn, Archaeological Services Unit Ltd, Purcell House, Oranmore, Co. Galway.

278. CASTLECONWAY, KILLORGLIN
Tower-house
7774 9640
SMR 56:25
98E0319
This excavation relates to a planning application for the renovation and extension of the Castleconway Arms public house and restaurant, Killorglin. The eastern end of the development site is bounded by the western wall of the upstanding remnant structure of Castleconway. The castle of Killorglin was burnt or razed a number of times since Maurice Fitzgerald built the first one in 1215. The current remains are possibly the fifth structure to be built and, according to Windele (1848), date to the late 17th century.

The proposed area of development comprises the current backyard and shed at the rear of the Castleconway Arms. The shed is built against the substrata of the castle, some 3m below the very basal stones. The exposed foundation levels consist of an undressed, coursed, sandstone-built wall, clearly visible 2.6m above the shed floor. This comprises the south-west external corner of the monument, from which all the quoins have been robbed.

An L-shaped trench running 5m east–west and 5m north–south x 1.5m wide was excavated at the base of the monument and inside the shed. The concrete floor lay directly on the sterile subsoil. The dismantled traces of an 18th/19th-century structure consisting of the foundations of two walls were evident. This whole area had been scarped out in the late 18th or 19th century to construct the adjoining crushing mill (now a furniture store) and ancillary buildings, and later, in more recent work associated with the public house. This resulted in the total removal of all archaeological remains and deposits along a section of the exterior of the south-west side and corner of the castle.
Laurence Dunne, Eachtra Archaeological Projects, 43 Ard Carraig, Tralee, Co. Kerry.

279. KILLOUGHANE CHURCH, KILLOUGHANE
Medieval church site
SMR 65:58
98E0309 and ext.
Archaeological excavation took place over two days, 27 July and 24 August 1998, at the proposed siting of a septic tank and an extension to an existing dwelling-house in a field immediately to the east of the remains of Killoughane medieval church, Killoughane, Beaufort, Co. Kerry. The developer had been refused planning permission for a new house on this site but was now proposing to apply for permission to extend slightly the existing dwelling, subject to the archaeological resolution of any areas to be disturbed.

Initially it was proposed that any areas to be disturbed be hand-excavated. The area of the proposed extension (5.6m east–west by 2.6m) was investigated. The subsoil was reached at an average depth of 0.4m, and nothing of archaeological significance was found.

Owing to the archaeologically sterile nature of this portion of the site, permission to use a mechanical digger to excavate the septic tank area, which was to be *c.* 11.6m to the south of the south-eastern corner of the existing house and *c.* 20m to the east of the site of the medieval church, was obtained. Subsoil was encountered here at an average depth of 0.3m. Nothing of archaeological significance was encountered.

Isabel Bennett, Glen Fahan, Ventry, Tralee, Co. Kerry.

280. KILMANIHEEN WEST
Possible hillfort?
R084216
98E0478

Test excavations were recommended by the National Monuments Service following the submission of an archaeological assessment of the proposed route of the N21 realignment, between Headley's Bridge and Feale Bridge, Co. Kerry.

The test excavations were carried out on the west-facing slope of a low hill *c.* 1km south of the River Feale. The hill rises from the floor of the Owveg River valley and affords great views in all directions. It overlooks the river valley to the west and south and the modern crossing of the River Feale to the north. The views into north Kerry and south Limerick are expansive.

The assessment noted at this point three separate bank-like terraces on the west-facing slope of the hill and traces of possible ditches inside the two upper-most terraces; the excavation was concerned with testing these features.

The excavation took place between 13 and 16 October. It was proposed initially to place two trenches across the bank-like terraces of the hill; however, given the poor results from the first two trenches, three further trenches were dug.

No archaeological features or strata were encountered; however, there is substantial evidence that the lands have been the subject of intensive drainage and improvement works over a long period. There is no known archaeological impediment to the proposed road at this point; however, given the level of disturbance noted in the test-trenches, there is a possibility that archaeological evidence of a now destroyed site may be encountered during the stripping of the route. Therefore, all ground disturbance relating to the construction of the road should be closely monitored.

Michael Connolly, Kerry County Museum, Tralee, Co. Kerry.

281. LISTOWEL CASTLE, LISTOWEL
Castle
9880 13353
SMR 10:59
98E0293

Dúchas intends to build a metal stairway at the back of Listowel Castle to allow access to the upper floors of the two surviving towers. A substantial portion of the front of the castle remains, the fabric of which probably dates to the 15th century. The bulk of the structure, however, no longer survives. An area corresponding to the footprint of the stairway was excavated to see whether any archaeological material was present.

This revealed a series of modern rubble layers and three late pits. The fills of these contained ash, charcoal, animal bone, limestone blocks and redeposited subsoil. All of these continued into the baulks. The largest was 1.95m x 0.85m and 0.65m deep. The northern edge of the trench abutted the castle wall. In the section face could be seen a part of the base of the foundation of the western wall. This indicates that the demolition of the remainder of the castle was quite thorough and that the front was deliberately left in place. The amounts of ash found in two of the pits suggest that parts of the castle may have been set on fire in order to break up the fabric of the structure. Beneath these pits and deposits was the foundation cut for the castle wall. It was best preserved nearest the upstanding structure. Further away from the castle it was shallower or not present. It is 2.7m wide and 0.25m at its deepest. Along part of its southern side its edge is very compact, probably owing to contact with the mortar used in the foundation. The cut is flat bottomed and straight sided.

The bulk of the castle was demolished in the 18th/19th century, when much of the stone was used to build a nearby mill, as well as several of the houses in the town. All of the finds from the site were post-medieval in date, mostly modern. The oldest date to the late 18th century.

Florence M. Hurley, 8 Marina Park, Victoria Road, Cork.

282. LISSYVIGGEEN
Stone circle
9974 9060
SMR 67:20
98E0178

In April 1998 a limited excavation was carried out at Lissyviggeen, Killarney, Co. Kerry, to recover radiocarbon samples from the enclosing element to assist in the dating of this monument. The site consists of a small stone circle, surrounded by a low earthwork bank with two massive outlier stones 11.5m to the south of the enclosure. It was also hoped to explore the chronological and cultural relationship to Beaker period settlement in the Killarney area and specifically to the copper mining at Ross Island.

The strategy was to excavate a 2m-wide trench from the stone circle northwards through the enclosing earthen bank but not to excavate inside the circle. This cutting was placed to investigate a possible inner ditch feature, the presence of which was suggested by electrical resistivity survey. Excavation in the southern half of this area, close to the stone circle, revealed a natural soil profile with no archaeological stratification or finds. Excavation at the northern end revealed the upper fill of a ditch lying directly inside the earthen bank enclosure. Ten sediment deposits were excavated from the ditch, mostly of a sandy texture with a high incidence of rounded field cobbles and small boulders. No artefacts or other cultural material were recovered.

The ditch has a steep-sided profile and narrow, flat bottom, ranging in width from *c.* 3m at the top to about 1m at the base. The maximum central depth is estimated at 2.05m from the top of the cut profile, or

2.5m below the modern ground surface. The position of the ditch with respect to the adjacent bank suggests that there is unlikely to be any intervening berm.

There are only two chronological markers in this ditch sequence. The first relates to the discovery of white china pottery near the base of the humic A-horizon that overlies this ditch fill. Within the latter the only dating evidence is provided by a single radiocarbon date for charcoal from a sediment in the upper fill sequence. This result (Grn-23973: 1940+15BP) can be calibrated to AD 27–75 (68.3% certainty) or AD 20–80 (95.4% certainty) calibration (I am grateful to Jan Lanting for providing this result). This charcoal date provides a very broad *terminus ante quem* for the accumulation of sediments in the lower part of the ditch. It is not possible to assess the interval of time between the digging of this ditch and the fire event represented by the radiocarbon charcoal.

In the light of these results and to minimise damage to this unique site it was decided not to excavate through the adjacent bank, where the recovery of dating evidence was considered unlikely.

The discovery of a substantial ditch inside the bank enclosure at Lissyviggeen adds to speculation that this monument has affinities with the Neolithic henge tradition in Ireland. However, no artefacts or other archaeological remains were discovered that would confirm that this is indeed a circle-henge. Possible connections with later prehistoric barrow traditions cannot be ruled out. A radiocarbon date obtained from the upper ditch fill does confirm that this earthwork enclosure is prehistoric in date and raises interesting questions about the secondary use of these monuments in the Iron Age.

William O'Brien, Department of Archaeology, National University of Ireland, Galway.

283. MEANUS
Cropmark enclosure
8171 9410
SMR 57:93
98E0372

An archaeological assessment was undertaken at Meanus, Killorglin, following an application for planning permission to construct a dwelling-house. The proposed development site lies near a recorded monument identified as a cropmark by aerial photograph in 1971 and classified as an enclosure. The monument stands on the lower slopes of Ardraw Hill, which rises out of the vast flood-plain of the Laune River. Examination of the aerial photograph seems to indicate a coherent circular cropmark, with possibly the remnants of an outer earthwork in the south-eastern and south-western quadrants.

A series of machine-dug trenches was opened in the general area of the proposed dwelling. Further investigations were continued by hand in areas of potential.

A ditch-like feature was uncovered in the north-western limits of the trenches at the intersection of the adjoining north–south trench, *c.* 9m from the proposed location of the house foundations. Excavation revealed it to be much wider and deeper than modern land drains. The ditch bisected the trench at about 45°, more or less consistent with the approximate location of the outer earthworks identified in the south-eastern

quadrant of the cropmark enclosure. The ditch lay *c.* 0.35m below ground surface and was 3.8m wide on top. The western edge of the ditch was further removed to a depth of 0.9m, at which it was still coherent. The ditch was composed of two fills: a bluish/black, water-laid material with a heavy clay content, overlain by a dark brown, organic material with some small stone content. No artefacts were recovered. The ditch feature was not bottomed out. No further archaeological features were uncovered.

John Tierney, Eachtra Archaeological Projects, Curragh East, Ardmore, Co. Waterford.

284. SCRAHANE 1
Enclosure and smelting site
SMR 66:75
9637 8979
96E0153

The site at Scrahane lies approximately half a mile south of Killarney town centre. The denuded remains of a circular enclosure were present in the north-west corner of the site, and, because of planning regulations for a housing development in the field, the site was the subject of ongoing archaeological activity from 1996 (*Excavations 1997*, 87). This work revealed evidence of smelting activity, including hearths, charcoal spreads and ash pits, in areas both inside and to south of the cropmark enclosure.

The cropmark site itself was the subject of an excavation carried out over seven weeks from March to May 1998. The eastern perimeter of the enclosure ditch lay within the proposed green area of the development and was not uncovered.

Excavation revealed that there was a second curvilinear ditch inside the line of the main enclosure. It is likely that these are contemporary, although this could not be demonstrated archaeologically. Both were stratigraphically earlier than the smelting phase, and the inner ditch in particular had almost completely filled up before metalworking activity. No internal archaeological features were found relating to the earlier ditches, and there was no evidence of a bank.

The outer ditch: F10
The outer enclosure was circular in plan and measured 38m in external and 32m in internal diameter. A total circuit of 22.5m of the ditch was excavated, and it had a broad U-shaped profile with a flat base. It varied from 2.35m to 3.66m wide and from 0.69m to 1.13m deep. The entrance to the enclosure appeared to be on the west side of the site and had apparently been formed by leaving a portion of the ditch undug.

The excavated sections of the northern half of the ditch showed that it had been almost completely filled before the smelting phase, which was represented in the upper ditch fills as deposits of ash and spreads of charcoal. It was clear that there had been very little fill in the southern part of the ditch before extensive deposits of ash and charcoal containing metal slag were discarded into the base.

The inner ditch: F100
The inner ditch enclosed a subcircular area 25m north–south x *c.* 22m. In total *c.* 24m of the ditch was excavated. It had a well-defined, narrow V-shaped profile with a flat base, ranging from 0.62m to 1.39m

wide and from 0.42m to 0.89m deep. It lay inside the outer ditch, but as it was not completely circular it did not respect the curvature of F10 and the distance between the two ditches varied. The circuit of the ditch was broken in two places within the area of excavation, both towards the northern end of the site. The shorter, northern section of ditch was 19.2m long and had rounded terminals at both ends. The southern section was 35.4m long and also had a rounded terminal at its northern end. The gap between these two sections was 2.4m. A fourth terminal should have been apparent in the north-eastern part of the site, but no definite evidence of the inner ditch could be found in that area, possibly as a result of intense cultivation. The inner ditch had partially filled before the beginning of metalworking at this site and, as with the outer ditch, had been used as a convenient dump for waste material from the firing process.

The smelting phase

Two main concentrations of smelting activity were noted within the enclosure, and many isolated smelting-related features were scattered throughout the southern end of the excavated area. In most areas the activity was of a single phase, although there was evidence of two separate phases of activity in Smelting Area 1 at the south-eastern end of the site.

Smelting Area 1 lay in the south-east corner of the site, and two main phases of metalworking activity were recognised. The primary phase consisted of a furnace around which was a semicircular arrangement of stake-holes. The stake-holes may represent the remains of a superstructure or a screen around the furnace. Three large ash pits to the south and west of the furnace had apparently been dug to contain smelting waste.

An extensive layer of very compact, white, sandy ash containing a few small stones and occasional metal slag sealed the features associated with the primary smelting phase. This layer measured 4.2m x 3.7m and varied in depth from 0.04m to 0.07m. A reuse of the hearth and the construction of a smaller superstructure/screen represented the second phase of smelting. More extensive spreads of charcoal were also noted at this level.

Smelting Area 2 lay close to the centre of the site. The main focus of activity was a hearth around which numerous small pits and stake-holes were dug. The underlying soil in this area had been oxidised red from intense burning, and the surface over time became covered by a layer of charcoal containing pockets of white ash. A large pit lay *c.* 1.5m to the south of the hearth and may also have been associated with the smelting activity. Two charcoal-filled pits to the west of the smelting area were also associated with this phase.

A small number of isolated smelting features were noted and recorded during the course of the excavation. Most of these were concentrated in the southern area of the enclosure.

Conclusions

Excavation of the cropmark site at Scrahane, Killarney, revealed a double-ditched enclosure (of an as yet unknown date) and a later phase of metal smelting. No features or deposits associated with the original use of the ditches survived, and as a result it was not possible to obtain absolute dates for the site. The morphology of the site indicates that it is unlikely to be a ringfort.

It will be possible to obtain ^{14}C dates from the smelting phase of activity, and as the enclosure is earlier than the smelting this will be useful in establishing a *terminus post quem* for the ditches. The type of metal slag found at Scrahane 1 has been found at only one other Irish site, at Ross Island, just a few miles away. In advance of obtaining the results of the ^{14}C analysis it seems likely that the smelting activity at Scrahane 1 is contemporary with the later phase at Ross Island, which has an Early Christian date (O'Brien, pers. comm.)

Mary O'Donnell, Archaeological Services Unit, University College Cork.

285. BALLYVELLY, TRALEE
Flat cemetery and crematoria
8300 11420
98E0240

Licensed monitoring and subsequent excavation were undertaken in relation to the development of a large housing estate at Ballyvelly in the western urban district of Tralee, Co. Kerry. The development lies close to two recorded monuments: SMR 28:112, a hillfort, and SMR 28:117, classified as an enclosure. The site lies on the lower southern slopes of a small but prominent hill that has unimpeded views of Tralee Bay and the Slieve Mish Mountains that form the spine of the Dingle Peninsula.

Monitoring of topsoil-stripping revealed eight areas of archaeological potential, all subsequently excavated, and also produced a complete saddle quern. Work on this site took place in stages during 1998, and post-excavation analysis, dates and other specialist reports are at a preliminary stage. Initial results seem to indicate the presence of a large prehistoric flat cemetery and possibly also unique crematoria.

Area 1, 12m x 5m, at the extreme southern limits of the development site, consisted of three linear features, five cremation pits and a number of stake-holes. The saddle quern and a tiny fragment of a copper/bronze object were found here during initial soil-stripping. Of the linear cut features, the northernmost extended for 4.1m x 0.95m and was 0.23m deep. However, its full length was not determined, as it continued under the eastern baulk. It contained one major fill that consisted of much burnt shattered stone, dark black material, charcoal and cremated bone. It appears that this was primarily dump fill, as no *in situ* burning had taken place. The two other, slightly smaller linear features were of the same general size, orientation, fill and fill inclusions. The three features were cut parallel to one another and virtually contiguous.

Six small oval pits containing varying quantities of cremated human bone and charcoal were found immediately to the south of the linear features. All of the bone recovered consisted of very small crushed fragments; this was consistent throughout the entire excavation. The largest pit measured 0.54m x 0.49m x 0.13m, and the smallest 0.16m x 0.2m x 0.18m. Other, similar pits were also excavated, but no bone was recovered. No other artefacts were recovered from the pits. A number of stake-holes were also excavated, two of which produced stone mauls.

Area 2, 12m north–south x 16m, lay *c.* 70m upslope from Area 1, to the north-east. Topsoil-stripping had revealed three linear burnt cut features (possibly crematoria), two linear features, five cremation pits and a number of stake-holes, two of which also contained cremated human bone. The linear cut features averaged 2.85m long, 0.62m wide and 0.23m deep. Two lay in the south-west of Area 2, abutted one another and were aligned north–south. The other lay in the north-east of Area 2 and was aligned north-east/south-west. The two furnaces/crematoria in the south-west displayed the same general characteristics: shape; intensity of burning; red/brown, sandy loam fill with occasional inclusions of charcoal and burnt bone. The third furnace/crematorium, in the north-east, was more regular in shape and wood-lined, and its fill produced large quantities of charcoal and *in situ* burnt wood. Fragments of cremated bone were also recovered.

Up to ten possible cremations were recovered from Area 2. Six of these were in small pits, and four others were components of larger linear cut features. The pits were concentrated in the north of Area 2, measured on average 0.4m in diameter and 0.17m in depth and were generally circular in plan. The fills of the pits consisted of a dark brown, sandy loam with high charcoal and pebble content. The linear cut features measured on average 2.25m east–west x 0.96m and were 0.14m deep. They displayed a metalled base of carefully set (and often burnt/shattered) stones.

A number of other random pits, post-holes and stake-holes were also investigated.

Areas 3–8 reflect smaller discrete archaeological find spots in proximity to Area 2 revealed in the course of monitoring. In general they consist of dark burnt spreads, pits, post-holes and stake-holes. Six further cremations were recorded in these areas.
Laurence Dunne, Eachtra Archaeological Projects, 43 Ard Carraig, Tralee, Co. Kerry.

286. CLOGHERS, TRALEE
Neolithic house
98E0238
Monitoring of a house construction project in the townland of Cloghers on the southern side of the River Lee and Tralee town was divided into six phases. Licensed monitoring of Phases V and VI was undertaken in June 1998. No archaeological stratigraphy was recorded during the monitoring of Phases IV and V; extensive archaeological stratigraphy was recorded during the monitoring of Phase VI.

An area of burnt stratigraphy lay on the northern side of a limestone reef, which forms the south-western boundary of the site. An area 12m north–south by 27m was excavated. A Neolithic house was uncovered in the western section of the trench. A series of pits and stake-holes was found in the eastern section of the trench. The archaeology was truncated by a series of cultivation furrows aligned north–south. They were *c.* 2m apart, 1–1.5m wide and 0.2m deep. There were five pits and a number of stake-holes in the area to the east of the Neolithic house. A small faunal assemblage was recovered from the deepest of the pits. To date, the bones of cow and small perching birds have been identified.

The rectangular Neolithic structure measures 7.5m north–south by 12.5m. It is orientated east–west, with a possible entrance to the east. The bedrock in the north-western corner is high, and the line of the structure is incomplete in this area. The remains suggests that the walls of the structure, including the two internal divisions, were constructed with vertical split planks set in bedding trenches, supported by corner posts and intermittent posts located on the line of the walls. Sherds of pottery, fragments of polished mudstone axes, burnt hazelnut shells, mudstone scrapers and flint were recovered from some of the substantial post-holes. The eastern and central room of the structure is 3.5m wide; the western room is 4m wide. No hearth had survived. A fence line lies 0.8m to the south of the southern wall of the structure. It was constructed of small stakes set within a wider bedding trench.

To date, around 100 sherds of pottery have been examined by Helen Roche. It is estimated that a minimum of nine vessels is represented. They are round-based, modestly carinated bowls, typical of the early Western Neolithic-type pottery dating to the early part of the third millennium.

Assemblages of mudstone, flint, chert, quartz and sandstone were recovered. Post-excavation work is ongoing.
Jacinta Kiely, Eachtra Archaeological Projects, Clover Hill, Mallow, Co. Cork.

287. CLOUNALOUR HOUSE, TRALEE
Monitoring
Q842149
98E0359
A programme of archaeological monitoring was undertaken within the grounds of Clounalour House, Tralee, Co. Kerry, in order to identify and record any deposits and finds that would be encountered during building construction. Nothing of archaeological significance was noted during excavation works at the site.
Margaret McCarthy, Archaeological Services Unit, University College Cork.

288. DROMTHACKER, TRALEE
Ringfort
Q154837
SMR 29:95
97E0022
Excavation of the eastern line of the ditch surrounding the ringfort at Dromthacker was carried out in the spring of 1998. This area will be under a pedestrian access to the new campus of the Institute of Technology, Tralee, and the ground surface will be built up over the ringfort ditch infill.

Excavation had previously been carried out at the ringfort (*Excavations 1997*, 85–6), and the results of the 1998 season showed that the infill history of the ditch was the same as that recorded the previous season. The plan of the excavated ditch showed that it had an elliptical curvature and varied in width from 2.5m to 3m, with a U-shaped profile. The fill of the ditch was continuous, and there was no evidence of an entrance. Excavations in 1997 indicated that a section of the ditch on the southern side of the ringfort had been backfilled with stone, and this may have been the location of an entrance, albeit not the

Kerry

original entrance to the site. The infill layers showed that the bank began to slip soon after the material was excavated from the ditch, as there was no evidence of naturally occurring silt in the base of the ditch. The ditch was subsequently infilled with a layer of redeposited boulder clay, suggesting a deliberate infill. Once the ditch was excavated it was recorded and backfilled.

Rose M. Cleary, Department of Archaeology, University College Cork.

289. LOWER ABBEY STREET, TRALEE
Dominican priory
8345 11430
98E0263

This test excavation was carried out in advance of the construction of a commercial unit at Abbey Court, Lower Abbey Street, Tralee. The site lies within the zone of archaeological potential for Tralee and is near the site of the Dominican Priory. This priory was established in 1243 and was suppressed sometime before 1580. There are no above-ground remains surviving today.

Recent test excavations by Martin Byrne, in the UDC (Abbey) carpark area that adjoins this development site, revealed *in situ* human skeletal remains, possible church foundations and fragments of masonry (*Excavations 1997*, 87, 97E0232).

Two areas were selected for excavation within the proposed development site. The work was carried out with the aid of a mechanical digger and by hand. In Area 1 a trench 4m east–west x 1.6m was opened in the western section of the site. A very substantial wall, possibly dating to the medieval period, running north-east/south-west and *c.* 1.2m wide, was recorded in the base of the trench. The trench was not excavated any further upon exposure of the wall. The wall consisted of medium and large unhewn pieces of limestone laid horizontally and set in clay; no mortar was recorded. Two layers of silty clay, which included fragments of bone and charcoal, had accumulated above the remains of the wall. A layer of cobbles dating to the 18th/19th century had been laid on the surface of the silty clay. The layers above the cobbles were all modern deposits.

A trench 5m north–south x 2m was opened in Area 2 in the eastern section of the site. A number of structural features were uncovered in the trench. Two 18th/19th-century wall sections exposed in the trench were left *in situ*. A third, more substantial wall, running north–south, was exposed at the base of the trench. This wall consisted of medium and large pieces of limestone laid horizontally, similar in fabric and construction to the wall in Area 1. However, the wall was only partially exposed to a maximum width of 0.8m, as it ran under the baulk of the trench. It appears that this wall runs at right angles to the wall in Area 1 and may be its return. Layers of silt overlay the wall and underlay 18th/ 19th-century demolition fill/deposits.

The walls probably represent the basal or lower remnants of the south-east range of the Dominican Abbey. As the two exposed sections are running at right angles to one another, it is likely that they reflect the same structure. No batter or dressed architectural fragments were recovered or revealed. No human remains were found. Archaeological

stratigraphy is present at a minimum of 1.1m in the test excavation areas. However, it is possible that further archaeological remains are present in the development site at higher levels.

Laurence Dunne, Eachtra Archaeological Projects, 43 Ard Carraig, Tralee, Co. Kerry.

290. MONAVALLY, TRALEE
Pit burials
Q842154
98E0127

Monitoring of topsoil-stripping before a housing development was carried out in March–April of 1998. Seven shallow pits were uncovered, cut into the yellow boulder clay. These were arranged in a linear fashion, separated by an average distance of 1m. These pits were truncated by agricultural activity, the upper fill being somewhat disturbed. Small fragments and flecks of cremated bone were recovered from the fill of five of these pits. These were too small to positively identify as being human (B. Ó Donnabháin, pers. comm.) Charcoal recovered from the upper fill of two of these pits was deemed to be unreliable for dating purposes, as it may have come from nearby modern bonfire remains, being dragged towards these pits in the course of ploughing. No associated structures were uncovered.

Frank Coyne, Aegis Archaeology, 24 Castle Court, Clancy Strand, Limerick.

291. CLOCH AN OIGAIR, (CARRIGEENDANIEL TOWNLAND), MOUNT HAWK, TRALEE
No archaeological significance
97E0456 ext.

Unlicensed monitoring of an access road initially took place on this site during March 1997, and licensed monitoring of further road construction took place during December 1997. Nothing of archaeological interest was noted during either exercise. Further monitoring of another road through the as yet undeveloped portion of the site, now to be known as *Cloch An Oigair* (the previously developed area now being known as *Árd na Sídhe*), was undertaken in 1998.

As a condition of the planning approval granted to the developer it was required that an archaeologist monitor ground disturbance aspects of the proposed development at the time of construction, owing to proximity to SMR site Nos 29:111, 114, 115 and 116 (three enclosures and a standing stone), which lie at least 250m to the south of the development, with the Tralee Livestock Mart situated inbetween.

Soil-stripping and the laying of a foundation for the road took place on 28 September 1998. Nothing of archaeological significance was noted. An initial 0.1m of topsoil was stripped, and the only finds noted were a small number of sherds of modern pottery and clear glass. The second level of stripping was down into the undisturbed natural (or limestone bedrock in the southern third of the area).

The maximum depth of the soil removed was 0.45m, although in places where the limestone bedrock was close to the surface it was as little as 0.2m. Topsoil was generally 0.35m deep above the yellow natural.

Isabel Bennett, Glen Fahan, Ventry, Tralee, Co. Kerry.

Kerry

292. MOUNTHAWK 2, TRALEE

Cultivation furrows
8250 11566
97E0212 ext.

Ground disturbance works were monitored in 1997 (*Excavations 1997*, 88) in the townland of Mounthawk, within the area of the Old Tralee Golf Club, in compliance with a planning condition of the proposed housing development. No extant archaeological sites lie within the development site; however, a complex of Late Bronze Age sites was excavated in the adjoining field (*Excavations 1997*, 87–8, 96E0390). During the course of last season's monitoring of the excavation of the site roadways a small number of possible archaeological features were recorded and excavated, but no datable material was recovered.

The second phase of the development took place in July 1998. Testing on the footprint of the foundations of each of the house sites was undertaken, the angle and orientation of each of the test-trenches being as varied as possible. Each of the test-trenches was on average 12m x 10m x 2.5m wide. The topsoil was stripped by track machine using a flat bucket. Differences in the soil stratigraphy were noted in nine of the trenches. Each of these was trowelled and recorded. A series of cultivation furrows, averaging 0.6–0.8m wide and orientated north-east/south-west, was recorded in Trenches 1, 2, 4 and 6–9. A field boundary marked on the 1st edition OS map was recorded in Trenches 1, 5 and 6. A drain was recorded in Trench 3. No other archaeological stratigraphy, features or artefacts were recorded.
Laurence Dunne, Eachtra Archaeological Projects, 43 Ard Carraig, Tralee, Co. Kerry.

KILDARE

293. ST JOHN'S LANE, ATHY

Urban medieval
268074 193967
98E0411

An archaeological evaluation was undertaken at Pettit's Supermarket, St John's Lane, Athy, on 16 September 1998. The work was carried out in compliance with a condition included in the grant of planning in respect of extensions to the western side and southern front of the existing supermarket. The foundations on the western side of the building had been excavated before archaeological involvement and could not be inspected because they had been filled with concrete. Consequently, construction works on the site had been halted until the required archaeological assessment had been carried out, the report submitted to the relevant authorities and written authorisation to proceed given by the NMHPS, *Dúchas*.

The site lies on the western bank of the River Barrow and on the northern side of Duke Street, in the vicinity of the postulated location of the town wall and close to the site of the Priory of St Thomas and Hospital of St John, a *Fratres Cruciferi* establishment dating to the early 13th century. Furthermore, there is a possibility of medieval industrial activity on the immediate area in the form of milling. A mill-race, shown in the 1st edition OS 6-inch map, ran from St John's Lane to the river, and other streams also existed in this area, all having been filled over

the last hundred years or so. Accordingly, the development site lies within the designated zone of archaeological potential for Athy.

Three trenches were excavated by machine. In general a number of layers of rubble and gravel were uncovered that had been dumped during efforts to reclaim the area from the flood-plain of the river. The combined depth of these layers ranged from c. 1.7m to 2.1m below the present ground surface. Following their removal, the surface of a 'peat-like', silty clay was revealed at 53.128–53.638m OD. The surface of this material falls to the east and south. Similar material was revealed during the excavation of archaeological test-trenches associated with the nearby St John's House (*Excavations 1995*, 43), the investigation of which led to the recovery of animal bone, shell and twigs. The material uncovered during the present evaluation was not investigated, and it is speculated that it is of archaeological interest, given the results from the nearby St John's development.

Four fragmented clay pipe stems and one clay pipe bowl were recovered from the rubble layer, the nature and form of which indicate a probable 19th-century date.

The foundations, both previously inserted and proposed, have a maximum depth of 0.4m below the present ground surface. Therefore, they will have no physical impact on the peat and their relatively shallow depths should have little or no impact on the existing level of ground water. Consequently, it was recommended that no further archaeological involvement was required at the site in respect of the current development.
Martin E. Byrne, 39 Kerdiff Park, Monread, Naas, Co. Kildare.

294. CHURCH ROAD, BALLYMORE EUSTACE

Urban medieval
287138 201662
SMR 15:16
98E0413

Monitoring of groundworks associated with the reconstruction of a house and extension was undertaken at a site at Church Road, Ballymore Eustace, from 14 to 16 September 1998. Archaeological involvement with the development was carried out in compliance with the grant of planning.

The site lies at the base of Garrison Hill, and a reduction of existing ground levels by up to 3m in the area of the rear extension was required. It was also necessary to strip the topsoil in a section of the garden area in order to reduce the severity of the existing slope.

Removal of the topsoil revealed a layer of mid-brown, clayey sand, which appeared to be relatively undisturbed, and a number of sherds of medieval pottery were recovered from this layer. No features or structures of archaeological interest were uncovered during the course of the work.
Clare Mullins, 39 Kerdiff Park, Monread, Naas, Co. Kildare.

295. BALLYSHANNON DEMESNE

Medieval/post medieval
73175 113082
SMR 28:58/32:3
98E0345

An archaeological evaluation was undertaken at a

proposed development site at Ballyshannon Demesne, Kilcullen, on 29 July 1998. The work was undertaken in compliance with recommendations issued by The National Monuments and Historic Properties Service, *Dúchas*, in respect of a pre-planning enquiry.

The site lies in the immediate environs of an archaeological complex comprising a motte, earthwork and church. Colonel John Hewson, who was with Cromwell's army, described Ballyshannon in 1650 as a strong garrison with double works and wet moats with a mount with a fort upon it.

Ten trial-trenches were excavated by mechanical excavator fitted with a 'ditching' bucket. No features or structures were revealed, and fifteen sherds of medieval/post-medieval pottery were recovered scattered over the entire area, with a higher percentage found to the south.

It was expected that parts of the outer defensive system associated with the 17th-century fortifications of 'Ballyshannon Castle' would be revealed. However, given the locations, lengths and orientations of the trial-trenches, together with the negative results, it can be implied that such features lie to the west of the tested area.

Martin E. Byrne, 39 Kerdiff Park, Monread, Naas, Co. Kildare.

296. BARREEN
Vicinity of church
N889346
98E0559
Five trenches tested the area of the proposed development, which comprised the construction of horseboxes with an access road near a church and graveyard at Barreen, Kilcock, Co. Kildare.

Trench 1 produced evidence of dumping of different layers of clay, presumably to raise the level of the ground surface. A small pit-like feature cut into natural subsoil was exposed. The peat-like fill produced medieval pottery and animal bones. The pottery dates to the 13th–15th centuries and suggests activity in the area at that time, although its nature and extent are not known and there were no other finds in the remainder of the trench.

Nothing of archaeological significance was exposed in the other trenches.

Rosanne Meenan, Roestown, Drumree, Co. Meath.

297. BAWNOGUE/TIPPERKEVIN/WALSHESTOWN
No archaeological significance
23657 21830
97E0081 ext.
Four phases of topsoil-stripping were monitored in advance of a proposed development at Bawnogue, Tipperkevin and Walshestown, Naas, Co. Kildare. The site lies in an area of undulating topography (OD 150–165m) on the western edge of the foothills of the Wicklow Mountains. The proposed development comprises the extraction of sand and gravel from an area of 42.5 acres on an overall site of 44.6 acres. The monitoring took place on 28–9 January, 6 February, 14 May and 3 June 1998. The stratigraphy was consistent across the stripped areas. The topsoil consisted of a light greyish-brown, silty clay with inclusions of roots, pebbles, cobbles, flecks of charcoal and occasional modern pottery sherds. It had an average thickness of 0.3m and overlay a

yellowish-brown, silty clay subsoil. No archaeological features or deposits were encountered.
Dominic Delany, 31 Ashbrook, Oranmore, Co. Galway.

298. BOHERHOLE
Earthwork
2867 3009
98E0550
The monument is a semicircular ditched enclosure: it may have originally continued across the road to form a full circle. Its maximum diameter is 200m, and the ditch is *c.* 4m deep. It is known to have been affected by gravel extraction.

A cutting 95m long and 1.5m wide was excavated in the area to be affected by road widening. Some traces of ridge-and-furrow cultivation were found in the enclosed area but no structural remains or finds. What appeared to be a fosse, 7.3m wide, was found at the outer edge of the enclosed area, but as this continued below the area to be affected by the road it was not investigated further. Beyond this, more directly in line with the visible fosse, was a possible further ditch, but this area had been the entrance to the gravel pit so it was not possible to be certain. No artefacts were found.
Thaddeus C. Breen, 13 Wainsfort Crescent, Dublin 6W, for Valerie J. Keeley Ltd.

299. ATHY ROAD, CASTLEDERMOT
Urban medieval
98E0225
An archaeological evaluation was carried out at a site at Athy Road, Castledermot, Co. Kildare, from 28 October to 2 November 1998, in response to a request for further information by the planning authority regarding an application to construct a housing development.

The proposed development site is roughly triangular in outline, occupying most of the area of land between Athy Road on the west, Barrack Road on the east and Carlow Gate Street on the south. The south-west corner of the site abuts the site of Carlow Gate, while the intersection of Carlow Gate Street and Barrack Road, beyond the eastern corner of the development site, is the site of a castle. The known line of the town wall runs through the development site from Carlow Gate north-eastwards to Barrack Road, and the line of this wall can still be made out in part of the site.

Seven test-trenches were inserted, based along five trench lines, distributed approximately evenly over the entire site. Two of the trenches were designed to transect the line of the town wall and to permit the comparison of the stratigraphy on the external and internal sides of this feature.

The test-trenches were generally dug to a depth of 0.5–1m below the present ground surface. Several features of archaeological significance were identified, including the remains of the town wall, which was indicated by the linear concentrations of stone and rubble uncovered on both the eastern and western sides of the site.

On the western side of the site a number of features were noted on the internal side of the town wall. These included a number of small linear cut features as well as at least two possible ditch features, which ran roughly parallel with the line of the town wall. A number of sherds of medieval pottery were found within the fills of these features.

On this side of the site the remains of the town wall appeared to be indicated by a band of uncut stone of various sizes, mixed with mortar, which occurred precisely on the line of the town wall as indicated by the Urban Archaeological Survey. This band of stone was 5.2m wide and appeared to run in a north-east to south-west direction. It occurred at a depth of 0.5m beneath the ground surface. Nothing was noted on the external side of the town wall on this side of the site.

On the eastern side of the site three distinct bands of stony material, which ran parallel to the line of the town wall, were noted in the known vicinity of this structure. They measured, respectively from south to north, 3.8m, 1.8m and 3m wide and, combined, covered an extent of almost 13m. They occurred between 0.2m and 0.4m beneath the ground surface. These features may indicate a complex structure to the town wall in this area.

No features were observed north of the line of the town wall on this part of the site. Other features noted on the internal side of the town wall in this area included a number of possible medieval drains, which may emerge from a habitation area in the vicinity of the street front and run northwards towards the town wall. One of these features produced a medieval iron arrowhead.

The area of the site outside the known line of the town wall was largely free of archaeological remains. However, a number of non-specific features also occur in this area. A layer of brown, sandy silt was noted immediately outside the line of the town wall in the central area of the site. This layer produced a single sherd of medieval pottery and a medieval bronze ring-brooch. The occurrence of two medieval finds within this layer, together with the absence of modern inclusions, strongly suggests that this represents a medieval soil horizon.

One feature of particular interest occurred in the north-western area of the site. It consisted of a curving band of red and black material. This continued for a distance of at least 1.5m. The material inside this curving band contained fragments of a white material that appeared to represent burnt stone. This may represent a phase of activity pre-dating the medieval occupation of the area.

A number of modern stone water conduits and other drains were found in the north-western part of the site.

Clare Mullins, 39 Kerdiff Park, Monread, Naas, Co. Kildare.

300. CASTLEFARM
Prehistoric complex
252779 200006
SMR 32:28
95E0209 ext.

Test-trenching was carried out on the site of a proposed development at Castlefarm, Narraghmore, Athy, in August 1995. This revealed the existence of a large ditch running north–south along the western side of the development site. A bowl-shaped feature filled with ash and charcoal was also identified within the site (*Excavations 1995*, 44–5).

Monitoring of groundworks associated with the

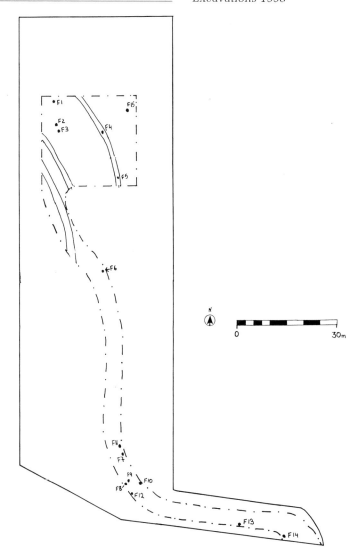

Plan of Castlefarm Td, Co. Kildare, indicating position of features.

development was carried out during February 1998. This revealed the curving line of the ditch that had previously been identified during testing over a distance of *c.* 30m at the northern end of the site, as well as the existence of two further ditches that were external to the first. In addition to this triple-ditched structure fifteen discrete charcoal-rich deposits were identified within the development site.

The inner ditch, identified during testing, was the largest of the three, measuring up to 3.2m across and up to 1.5m deep. The ditches appeared to become progressively less substantial towards the periphery, for while the central ditch measured 1.5m across, the outer ditch measured only 1.2m across. The outer ditch was only 0.35m deep (a section through this was excavated where it lay in the path of a proposed wall), but there was no indication of the depth of the central ditch. A distance of 4–5m separated the inner and central ditches, but the distance between the central and outer ditch was approximately four times this figure. These ditches appeared to curve concentrically, from north-west to south-west, down the western side of the development site, and the estimated diameter of a circular enclosure, based upon a projection of the observed curves, suggests a diameter of more than 100m for the external ditch. However, there is no direct evidence that the ditches do continue to form an enclosure of any shape.

Fifteen discrete features, formed by deposits of charcoal-rich material that occupied cuts within the natural, were also identified. Some of these were positioned inbetween or over the ditch features, but others appear to be positioned external to the ditch complex, on the basis of the projected curve. One of these features (F2) was damaged during the course of the development and was therefore excavated. It represented a pit that was broadly bowl-shaped in profile, with a depth of 0.2m, and subcircular in plan, measuring 0.6m x 0.4m. The fill consisted mainly of charcoal mixed with silty clay, and there was slight oxidisation of the soil at the edge of the feature.

If these curving ditches represent some kind of enclosure it is clear that the centre of such an enclosure would lie outside and to the west of the development site, in the adjacent field. If an actual enclosure is not represented it would also seem likely that the focus of activities on the site should lie on the western side of the curving line delineated by the ditches. It is clear that the features uncovered during testing and monitoring represent a large complex, and the apparent location of many of the discrete features outside of the ditch complex indicates that its extent is by no means well defined. It is also possible that a fourth ditch lies beyond that which is currently being identified as the external ditch.

The size of the ditch features and the considerable distance between them suggests that they were not defensive in concept. The location of some of the charcoal-rich deposits over the backfill of these ditches indicates that the enclosing element was backfilled in antiquity, and this again suggests a ritual function for the site. Tiny fragments of burnt bone were noticed within the fill of some of the discrete features, and this may indicate that they functioned as cremation pits.

A sample of charcoal from F2 returned a radiocarbon determination of 3970–3710 BC (95% confidence level).

The original reason for archaeological involvement in this development was the depiction of a castle on the site in Taylor's map of 1783. No trace of this castle was found during testing or monitoring, and local tradition places this castle on the opposite side of the road in the 'castle field'. The discovery of this complex therefore appears to have been entirely coincidental.

Clare Mullins, 39 Kerdiff Park, Monread, Naas, Co. Kildare.

301. CASTLEREBAN SOUTH
Proximity to various sites
264738 197084
98E0166
Monitoring of groundworks was undertaken on 24–5 August 1998 at a site at Castlereban South, Athy, Co. Kildare. The work was undertaken in compliance with a condition attached to the grant of planning to develop a playing field and associated structures by Castlemitchell GAA. The site measures *c.* 130m x 140m, and groundworks associated with the development included the stripping of topsoil in the area of the proposed buildings and carpark, the removal of a field boundary and the reduction of ground levels over a high area of the proposed playing field.

No features of archaeological interest were discovered during the course of this work, but several sherds of medieval pottery were recovered from the topsoil.

Clare Mullins, 39 Kerdiff Park, Monread, Naas, Co. Kildare.

302. NEW MEDICAL COMPLEX, MAIN STREET, CELBRIDGE
Urban
2974 2331
98E0568
Testing was undertaken at the above site in December. No deposits or features of archaeological significance were identified.

Rónán Swan, Arch-Tech Ltd, 32 Fitzwilliam Place, Dublin 2.

303. CLANE
No archaeological significance
N875277
97E0345
The works associated with *Bord Gáis Éireann* and Kildare County Council's Urban Renewal scheme in Clane (*Excavations 1997*, 92) continued into February 1998. Activities focused on pipe-laying along the footpaths on Main Street and within Park View Estate to the south-west of the town. No further discoveries of note were made.

Niall Brady, 'Rosbeg', Ard Mhuire Park, Dalkey, Co. Dublin, for Valerie J. Keeley Ltd.

304. CLANE
Urban medieval
N870280
97E0345
No archaeological features were uncovered during monitoring of gas pipe-laying over three weeks during May 1998. This period of monitoring was undertaken as a licence transfer from Neil Brady at the end of the project (see No. 303 above).

Martin Reid for Valerie J. Keeley Ltd, 29/30 Duke Street, Athy, Co. Kildare.

305. JONES's PUB, MAIN STREET, CLANE
No archaeological significance
N876276
98E0510
The site of the development at Jones's Pub, Main Street, Clane, lies within the zone of archaeological potential highlighted in the recent Medieval Urban Survey. The village is also the location of the early Irish monastery of Clane, or *Cloenath*, founded by St Ailbe at *Cluain-damh* on the River Liffey. Owing to the potential archaeological sensitivity of the development area, pre-development testing was requested as part of the planning conditions. This was carried out on 27 October 1998.

Two test-trenches were machine-excavated. The first was opened along the approximate centre line of the long axis of the development, with the second placed perpendicular to the first. Nothing of archaeological significance was noted.

Eoin Halpin, Archaeological Development Services Ltd, Unit 48, Westlink Enterprise Centre, 30–50 Distillery Street, Belfast BT12 5BJ.

306. CORBALLY, BROWNSTOWN AND SILLIOT HILL
Neolithic structures and prehistoric activity
N850130
97E0449

In November 1997 work commenced on a large-scale development near Kilcullen, Co. Kildare. A sand-and-gravel extraction pit was opened in a green-field location straddling three townlands: Corbally, Brownstown and Silliot Hill. Planning permission had been received for the phased extraction of the sand deposits over a period of several years. Monitoring of topsoil removal was required under the terms of the planning regulations.

The first stage of the development involved monitoring of topsoil-stripping in three separate areas: the access road, an overburden storage area and the quarry. An account of the preliminary work (the excavation of several archaeological deposits in the townlands of Corbally and Silliot Hill) was reported in *Excavations 1997* (91). These included deposits located on the access road and in part of the extraction area.

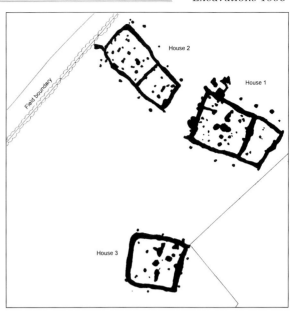

Preliminary site plan of excavation at Corbally, Co. Kildare.

Corbally townland
In January/February 1998, when soil-stripping recommenced in the remaining small portion of a pasture field in Corbally townland, a number of significant, well-preserved archaeological features were revealed. The foundations of three Neolithic houses were uncovered. These were surprisingly well preserved and were fully excavated. Several other areas of archaeological activity were revealed within this same field, including separate features containing Beaker pottery and possible grooved ware.

The post-excavation phase is ongoing. The final report on the Neolithic houses will be completed in 1999.

The Neolithic houses
Three Neolithic houses were uncovered in the south-western corner of a field. House 1 was centrally placed, 3m south-east of Structure 2 and 12m north-east of Structure 3. The remains of substantial foundation trenches were revealed in all three, as well as internal features including post-holes, stake-holes, pits and hearths. External post-holes and pits were also found. The three houses were constructed of post-and-plank walls.

A significant quantity of finds was recovered from the site, including sherds of Western Neolithic, round-bottomed, shouldered bowl and worked stone, including flint, chert, quartz, serpentine, saddle querns, hammerstones and broken fragments from polished stone axes.

House 1 was the largest of the three, measuring 11.07m x 6.73m. It was orientated north-west/south-east and was trapezoidal in plan, narrowing at the south-eastern end, where the doorway appears to have been. A large, continuous foundation trench divided this building into two chambers, and small, discontinuous trenches subdivided a third, smaller chamber.

The foundation trenches were very substantial, with post-holes dotted at regular intervals along their length. Large, substantial internal post-holes were present, which acted as roof supports, and two large, substantial hearths were centrally placed in the large chamber. There is the suggestion of two phases of

activity within the house, as well as two phases of pre-house activity. Finds from this building were particularly rich. Only one radiocarbon date has been obtained to date, placing the house in the early fourth millennium BC, 3995 BC (5220±80 BP).

House 2 measured 10.77m x 5.29m and was again orientated north-west/south-east. This structure was slightly trapezoidal in plan, although this was not as obvious as was House 1. The narrower end of the trapezoid was at the south-east end, where the entrance appears to have been. A large, continuous foundation trench divided the house into two chambers.

The foundation trenches were substantial but slightly smaller than in House 1. Post-holes were found in the foundation trenches. Pairs of internal post-holes divided the house into aisles, which supported the roof. Several additional post-holes appear to have been added during the lifetime of the house, presumably to augment the support provided by the original post-holes. The house dates from the fourth millennium BC, 3685 BC (4910±80 BP).

House 3 was the smallest of the three buildings, measuring 7.37m x 6.45m. The structure was orientated north-west/south-east and was subrectangular in plan. Discontinuous foundation trenches subdivided the building into two chambers.

The foundation trenches were very substantial, with post-holes dotted regularly along them. The house was divided into aisles by roof-supporting post-holes. A large central hearth was present.

Discussion
These three structures were very similar to previously excavated Western Neolithic houses, and the radiocarbon dates indicate that they were constructed from the early to mid-fourth millennium BC. Peripheral archaeological activity was identified near the houses. Additional radiocarbon dates may cast further light on the contemporanity of this activity.

Peripheral archaeological activity
A subcircular pit lay less than 100m to the east-north-east of the Neolithic houses. Occasional tiny

fragments of burnt bone, several burnt worked flints and a considerable amount of Beaker pottery were found in the pit. It measured 1.18m north–south by 1.25m and was 0.23m deep.

Archaeological deposits were also found *c.* 100m to the north-east of the Neolithic structures. A series of post- and stake-holes was revealed. Seven of the larger holes formed a rough arc *c.* 9m in circumference. Most of the smaller stake-holes were clustered together to the north-east, inside this arc. Further north-east of these deposits the ground had been disturbed by machine activity during soil-stripping, where it had been partially scarped away. Although many of the recorded features were very deeply cut and would have survived such disturbance, no trace of additional features, truncated or otherwise, was found. No finds were recovered from these deposits.

A pit lay 20m from the arc of post-holes. This measured 4m north–south by 2.24m. It was oval in plan but very irregular. One piece of worked chert and one tiny sherd of decorated pottery, possibly Beaker ware, were found in it.

Approximately 235m to the north-east of the arc of post-holes another small pit was found. It measured 1.44m north–south by 0.94m and was 0.54m deep. It contained a large quantity of early prehistoric pottery, possibly grooved ware, as well as worked stone. This feature was at the edge of the sand-pit. Similar features may lie adjacent to it outside the development area.

Brownstown townland
Further monitoring was carried out 800m south of the Neolithic houses, on the side of a gently rising hill, where limited soil-stripping was undertaken. During the course of this work three small pits, one post-hole, and part of a large curvilinear feature were uncovered.

The pits were small, charcoal-rich features *c.* 0.6–0.8m in diameter. Cremated bone fragments were present in one of these, and a flint thumbnail scraper in another.

A section was put through the curvilinear feature to reveal a V-shaped ditch, 0.5m deep and 2m wide. The feature was traced over 23m. Both ends continued under the surrounding topsoil, suggesting that it is part of a larger circular enclosure. It probably represents the ploughed-out remains of an enclosure, with a shallow ditch surviving. It is likely that the remainder of the feature survives under the surrounding ploughsoil. The topsoil was backfilled after the section had been dug, and no development works were undertaken in this area.

These features appear to represent a phase of Bronze Age activity, not unusual given the large amount of previously recorded Bronze Age activity in the surrounding parts of north Kildare, as well as the presence of upstanding monuments.
Avril Purcell, Margaret Gowen & Co. Ltd, 2 Killiney View, Albert Road Lower, Glenageary, Co. Dublin.

307. CORBALLY
Peripheral activity associated with Neolithic settlement
N850130
98E0094
A geophysical survey was conducted in advance of

the expansion of a sand quarry at Corbally, Co. Kildare. The geophysical survey was carried out adjacent to the site of three Neolithic houses, uncovered by excavation (No. 306 above). A 20m x 40m area was surveyed; four test-trenches were subsequently opened to calibrate the results.

The geophysical surveying was conducted in June and July 1998, while the Neolithic structures were still under excavation. Both magnetic susceptibility and magnetic gradiometry surveys were conducted. A series of positive anomalies was identified by the magnetic susceptibility survey, and a series of positive and negative anomalies was identified by the magnetic gradiometry survey. However, these anomalies did not suggest the presence of coherent archaeological deposits consistent with the Neolithic houses. The test-trenches revealed several isolated post- and stake-holes. However, most of the anomalies highlighted by the geophysical surveys proved to relate to subsoil changes and not to archaeological deposits.

When the area was fully stripped of topsoil this pattern of isolated ephemeral small features continued. In spite of its close proximity to the Neolithic houses, no large-scale archaeological deposits were revealed.
Avril Purcell, Margaret Gowen & Co. Ltd, 2 Killiney View, Albert Road Lower, Glenageary, Co. Dublin.

308. THE CURRAGH
Prehistoric and later
97E0418 ext.
As previously reported (*Excavations 1997*, 92, 97E0418), inclement weather conditions caused the postponement of the completion of the required trenching for the Bord Gáis Éireann, Newbridge–Kildare Gas Feeder Pipeline until 1998. Work was resumed in late February 1998 on a stretch of pipeline trench extending from Herbert Lodge adjoining the Naas–Newbridge Bypass north-westwards to Collaghknock Glebe in the vicinity of Mountjoy Lodge, traversing terrain in the vicinity of three listed archaeological sites. The trench was routed a minimum distance of 15m from each site.

A second stretch of pipeline trench was mechanically excavated in late February to early March to extend a gas pipeline from its existing function near Ballymany Roundabout northwards to the Standhouse Hotel.

No material or features of archaeological interest came to light in the course of this work.
Breandán Ó Ríordáin, Burgage More, Blessington, Co. Wicklow, for Valerie J. Keeley Ltd, Duke Street, Athy, Co. Kildare.

309. THE CURRAGH
Enclosure/ringfort
N750128
98E0593, 98E0594
A topographic survey was conducted along the line of the proposed M7 Motorway/Kildare Bypass in the area of The Curragh. A contour map, a 3D surface map and a shaded relief map of the area were produced. An archaeological aerial survey was also conducted for the area of the bypass.

Two sites were considered for testing, based on the assessment.

Kildare

Site A (98E0593)
This was described as a circular embankment and
'the bank surrounding a hollow [that] spreads out to
a width of ~20m in parts' in the assessment report.
Two test-trenches laid out at right angles to each
other were excavated at this site. Topsoil lay directly
over boulder clay at a depth of 0.2–0.3m below the
sod. There was no evidence of archaeological activity.
It was concluded that this hollow was a natural
undulation in the landscape.

Site B (98E0594)
The outer bank of a multivallate ringfort lay *c.* 25m
away from the road take, where it was proposed to
excavate two test-trenches. Topsoil lay directly over
boulder clay at 0.2–0.3m depth. As time allowed, and
with the permission of the National Monuments
Service, a further four test-trenches were excavated
with the same lack of archaeological features resulting.
*Martin Reid for Valerie J. Keeley Ltd, 29/30 Duke
Street, Athy, Co. Kildare.*

310. DOWDENSTOWN GREAT
Adjacent to enclosure site
SMR 24:25
292108 213653
98E0368
An archaeological evaluation was undertaken at a
proposed development site at Dowdenstown Great,
Co. Kildare, on 15 August 1998. The work was carried
out in compliance with a condition included in the
grant of planning in relation to the construction of a

private house. The general landscape in the immediate vicinity of the site is hilly pastureland, some of
which has been subjected to quarrying activities.

The site is adjacent to an enclosure site known as
'The Ring.' This was partially destroyed before 1837
and is marked on the OS 6-inch maps as C-shaped. It
appears from cartographic sources that the site was
subcircular, with a minimum diameter of *c.* 200m.
This indicates that it may have been a hillfort,
although it is impossible to determine its exact
function without archaeological investigations.
Much more of the site has been destroyed by
quarrying in recent years, an activity that has now
ceased, although it is still possible to identify the
remains of the external bank feature. There are no
definite indications of an external fosse.

Six trial-trenches were excavated by means of a
mechanical excavator fitted with a ditching bucket.
No features, structures or finds of archaeological
interest were uncovered. It was therefore recommended that no further archaeological involvement
was required at the site.
*Martin E. Byrne, 39 Kerdiff Park, Monread, Naas,
Co. Kildare.*

311. GRANGE CASTLE, GRANGE
Late medieval/post-medieval tower-house
26209 23646
SMR 2:7
98E0228
A few small trenches were opened to the south of the
tower-house at Grange Castle, Carrick, Co. Kildare, to

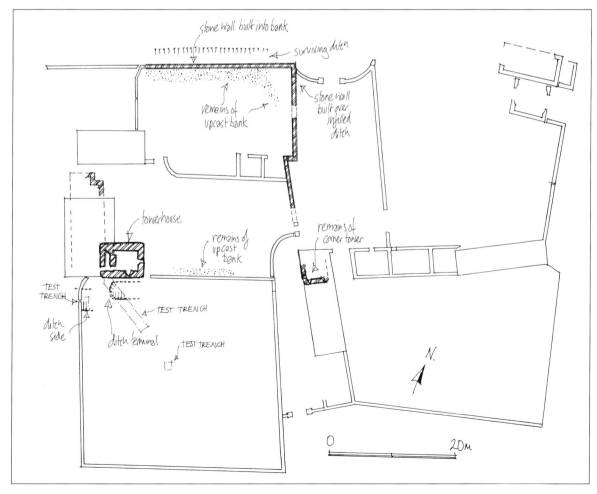

General plan of Grange Castle.

assess the presence and/or survival of early garden remains and to look for signs of the bawn.

The original tower-house (15th-century?) was set against one side of a banked and ditched bawn enclosure, partly a defence and partly a drain, which probably meshed into a pattern of small drained fields. (Two slices of ditch were uncovered but were not emptied.) The ditch at the foot of the tower-house was infilled in the early 17th century, when an elegant new top was set on the building and lengths of the rustic enclosure bank were replaced in mortared stone. A cluster of stone buildings and walled enclosures (standing today) was built around the tower in the 17th, 18th and early 19th centuries. *Dave Pollock, 33 Woodlawn, Cashel, Co. Tipperary.*

312. HARRISTOWN
Medieval borough
282891 198176
98E0482

Archaeological trial-trenching was undertaken at a proposed dwelling-house site in the townland of Harristown, *c.* 8.5km south of Naas, on 10 October 1998. Harristown lies *c.* 3 miles east of Kilcullen, beside the River Liffey.

Six trenches, ranging from 38m to 110m long and *c.* 1.5m wide, were opened by mechanical excavator. They were not confined to the development area of the site, given that the entire plot lies within the defined area of archaeological potential. The topsoil, which was 285–390mm deep, overlay a layer of fissured rock and/or bedrock.

No features, structures or finds of archaeological interest were uncovered during the course of the archaeological testing.
Martin E. Byrne, 39 Kerdiff Park, Monread, Naas, Co. Kildare.

313. MAIN STREET, JOHNSTOWN
Urban medieval
98E0113

On behalf of *Bord Gáis Éireann*, and within the zone of archaeological potential recognised in the Urban Archaeology Survey for Johnstown, a gas pipe was laid along the main street and parallel to the site of the medieval church, font fragment and graveyard. The installation of the gas pipeline over a distance of 100m in this area was carried out using the trenchless technology system of the compressor-driven mole type. This system necessitated the use of a small number of narrow trench slits (1800mm long, 800mm wide and 900mm deep) in the roadway, to allow the insertion and later removal of the mole rods. No archaeological deposits or features came to light in the course of this work.
Breandán Ó Ríordáin, Burgage More, Blessington, Co. Wicklow, for Valerie J. Keeley Ltd, Duke Street, Athy, Co. Kildare.

314. KILDARE
Urban
N72801230
98E0376

Eight test-trenches were excavated at seven sites within the historic core of Kildare town in advance of large-scale pipe-laying on behalf of *Bord Gáis Éireann*. The positioning of seven trenches was to ascertain whether the gates, town wall and monastic enclosure would be revealed at the depth of the proposed works (*c.* 1m). The eighth trench was excavated on the north-west side of Market Square in the centre of the town beside the cathedral and within what would have been the monastic enclosure.

Significant archaeological levels were observed at the latter site only. An amount of animal bone was recovered from a dark clay layer directly underlying the surface tarmacadam. No artefacts were observed. The thickness of the deposit was not ascertained, although it reaches below the 0.4m depth of the excavated trench.

A short stretch of pipe was laid along Station Road and Lourdesville. No archaeological deposits were noted.
Niall Brady, 'Rosbeg', Ard Mhuire Park, Dalkey, Co. Dublin, for Valerie J. Keeley Ltd.

315. KILDARE
Urban medieval
27250 21260
98E0020

On behalf of *Bord Gáis Éireann*, and within the zone of archaeological potential recognised in the Urban Archaeological Survey for Kildare town, a gas pipe was laid in a trench in the roadway immediately west of the cemetery adjoining the White Carmelite Friary. The trench was 500mm wide and was mechanically excavated in the road to an average depth of 900–1000mm. No materials or structures of archaeological interest came to light in the course of this work.
Breandán Ó Ríordáin, Burgage More, Blessington, Co. Wicklow, for Valerie J. Keeley Ltd, Duke Street, Athy, Co. Kildare.

316. KILDARE
Urban medieval
98E0574

Monitoring of *Bord Gáis Éireann* pipeline laying, within the zone of archaeological potential for Kildare town, commenced on 30 November 1998. This is scheduled to continue into 1999. At the time of writing, *c.* 500m of pipe had been laid, out of a total length of *c.* 2500m. This involved the mechanical excavation of trenches 0.4–0.45m wide and 0.7–1.1m deep. A combination of open and keyhole trenching with associated moling was used. At the time of writing no finds or features of archaeological significance had been uncovered.
Hilary Opie, 103 Cherrywood Drive, Clondalkin, Dublin 22.

317. MARKET SQUARE, KILDARE
Urban medieval
98E0239

Monitoring and excavation took place in advance of an extension of the 'Carnoisseur' shop at the corner of Claregate Street and Market Square in Kildare town on 21–2 May 1998. An area measuring 4.6m east–west x 5.1m was stripped of overburden, and three 1m-wide strip foundation trenches were machine-excavated. Archaeological features were subsequently hand-excavated within the trenches to the required foundation depth of 800mm.

One edge of a drain/gully feature running south-west/north-east was revealed in the south and east trenches. This was filled with a light brown, charcoal-flecked, organic clay. A small portion of this clay had a darker, more heavily charcoal-flecked consistency. Both clays contained disarticulated animal bones, slate fragments, unworked wood fragments and sherds of medieval pottery.

At the south-west edge of the drain a cobbled/ metalled stone surface was revealed. This was partially covered by a layer of stones, perhaps collapse from a wall fronting Claregate Street? The cobbled surface may have acted as a footpath along the side of the drain. Further excavation was not required, and the features were covered with terram.

Richard N. O'Brien, Archaeological Development Services Ltd, Windsor House, 11 Fairview Strand, Fairview, Dublin 3.

318. ST BRIGID'S SQUARE, KILDARE
Environs of early monastic and medieval urban centre
272619 212093
98E0322

An archaeological evaluation was undertaken at a proposed development site at St Brigid's Square, Kildare, on 28 July 1998. The work was undertaken in compliance with a condition of the grant of planning pertaining to the development. The site lies within the designated zone of archaeological potential associated with Kildare town, to the south of the proposed line of the outer early medieval monastic enclosure and the later medieval defences.

The archaeological trial-trenching consisted of the mechanical excavation of five trenches within the confines of the development site. The results indicated that much of the site had not been disturbed before the commencement of the evaluation. However, the foundation remains of a building illustrated in the 1908 map of Kildare were uncovered on the northern end of the site.

One single sherd of medieval pottery was recovered from a disturbed context.

Given that no deposits, structures or artefacts in an undisturbed context were recovered during the course of the work, it was recommended that no further archaeological involvement was required at the site.

Martin E. Byrne, 39 Kerdiff Park, Monread, Naas, Co. Kildare.

319. KILHILL, KILL
Environs of archaeological complex
294162 222907
98E0179

Archaeological monitoring was carried out at the site of a housing development at Killhill, Kill, Co. Kildare, on various dates from February to August 1998. The development site lies just outside the zone of archaeological potential for Kill and is surrounded by several other archaeological sites. A large enclosure, SMR 20:1, encompasses the base of Killhill, which is situated a short distance to the east of the development site. Monitoring was conducted of topsoil-stripping within the housing area and of trench digging for the laying of service pipes from the housing development into the centre of Kill village.

During monitoring of the pipeline no archaeological features or artefacts were noted. Some unusual deposits were identified in one area, just east of the junction between the old Dublin road and the motorway access road, along a stretch of several metres of the pipeline. These deposits consisted of deep, silty sediments with occasional timber inclusions. A secondary deposit, which contained frequent timber inclusions, occupied a depression within the more generalised layer of silty material. In section this secondary deposit appeared to represent the fill of a ditch or pit that was 2.5m wide and 1m deep, but such an interpretation must remain speculative given the limited nature of the evidence.

Topsoil-stripping for the housing development was carried out using a toothless bucket. Topsoil was stripped just to the surface of the natural over an area of approximately twelve acres. No archaeological features were identified. Several fragments of burnt bone and a few tiny fragments of charcoal were found during the course of soil-striping, but in no instance did any of these appear to be associated with structural features within the ground. Several of the bone fragments appeared to derive from a relatively localised area within the general site. On this basis, and as an added precaution, the reduction of levels into the natural for the creation of a roadway through this area was also monitored. This linear strip was treated as a test-trench, and its sides and base were inspected. No features of archaeological significance were noted within the trench. Another test-trench, inserted through an apparently disturbed area, also failed to reveal evidence of archaeological material.

Several fragments of flint were also found during the course of soil-stripping. These mainly comprised unworked pieces, but two represented struck flakes and one appeared to represent a core from which flakes had been struck. A single sherd of medieval pottery was also recovered.

Clare Mullins, 39 Kerdiff Park, Monread, Naas, Co. Kildare.

320. KILL
Urban
98E0014

On behalf of Bord Gáis Éireann, and within the zone of archaeological potential recognised in the Urban Archaeological Survey for Kill, archaeological monitoring was carried out on the gas pipeline trench mechanically excavated along Main Street and the Glendara Estate. The Glendara Estate lies in the vicinity of a motte and bailey.

The trench, on average 1000mm deep and 400mm wide, was laid along the southern side of Main Street, with the exception of the site of the bridge over the Kill River, where the pipe trench was diverted to the northern side of the street. Throughout the course of monitoring, both in the Main Street and in the Glendara Estate, no archaeological features or artefacts came to light. However, it should be noted that in the Urban Archaeology Survey it is recorded that two sherds of 13th/14th-century pottery were picked up by Survey staff in a cutting opposite the Parochial House, i.e. on the south side of the street adjacent to the bridge over the Kill River.

Breandán Ó Ríordáin, Burgage More, Blessington, Co. Wicklow, for Valerie J. Keeley Ltd, Duke St., Athy, Co. Kildare.

321. MAIN STREET, LEIXLIP
Urban medieval
300559 235836
98E0103

Test-trenching was carried out at a site at Main Street, Leixlip, on 5 March 1998 in response to a planning condition for the construction of a small, two-storey block of apartments. The site consists of a plot of land, approximately 25m by 25m, to the rear of the street-frontage properties.

Three test-trenches were inserted to examine the stratigraphy near the greatest impact of the development. There was no evidence of surviving archaeological stratigraphy from any of the test-trenches, nor was there any evidence to indicate destroyed or disturbed archaeological remains. A sherd of medieval pottery and a sherd possibly of medieval lustre ware were found in the topsoil of Trench 3.

Clare Mullins, 39 Kerdiff Park, Monread, Naas, Co. Kildare.

322. 18 MAIN STREET, LEIXLIP
Urban medieval
300529 235699
98E0173

An archaeological evaluation was undertaken at the rear of 18 Main Street, Leixlip, on 4 April 1998. The work was carried out in compliance with a planning condition in respect of a rear extension to existing commercial premises.

Three trenches were opened by machine. Similar stratigraphy to that uncovered by Clare Mullins (pers. comm.) in the adjoining development site (No. 321 above) was exposed.

No finds, structures or deposits of archaeological interest were uncovered, and it was decided that no further archaeological involvement was required at the site.

Martin E. Byrne, 39 Kerdiff Park, Monread, Naas, Co. Kildare.

323. MAYFIELD
Fulacht fiadh
266375 211216
98E0288

Archaeological monitoring of topsoil-stripping during the drainage phase of ancillary works relating to the Kildare Town Bypass in the area of the proposed Mayfield Interchange, a part of the Monasterevin–Kildare Motorway Scheme N7, resulted in the identification of the site of a *fulacht fiadh*. Archaeological excavation of the site was carried out from 11 August to 14 September 1998.

The site initially consisted of a burnt area *c.* 30m^2 and 0.1–0.15m deep. Features uncovered included stake-holes, some charcoal and a small quantity of burnt limestone. The main feature of the site was a trough/pit exhibiting a 50–80mm-thick wood lining, which extended throughout half of the trough. Five bone fragments, three of them charred, were found in the fill of the pit. It is suggested that there were three periods of use of the pit as a trough. However, the dimensions and shallowness of stratigraphy suggest that the site was used over a short period.

Breandán Ó Ríordáin, Burgage More, Blessington, Co. Wicklow, assisted by Niall Gregory, for Valerie J. Keeley Ltd, Duke Street, Athy, Co. Kildare.

324. MAIN STREET/MILL STREET, MAYNOOTH
Urban
N935375
98E0060

Monitoring of Telecom and cable TV duct laying was carried out between 14 January and 4 February 1998. Trenches were dug on both sides of Main Street and Mill Street. Outside the 'Leinster Arms' some 18th-century pottery sherds were found, but nothing of archaeological significance was observed.

Colin D. Gracie, 8 Abbeydale Close, Lucan, Co. Dublin, for Valerie J. Keeley Ltd.

325. MONASTEREVIN
No archaeological significance
97E0445

Nothing of archaeological significance was discovered during monitoring of the construction of the Kildare Bypass drainage works in this area.

Carmel Duffy, Umberstown Great, Summerhill, Co. Meath.

326. MOONE ABBEY, MOONE
Early Christian monastery
S789926
SMR 36:31
98E0276

The excavations, funded by *Dúchas* The Heritage Service, were carried out in advance of conservation, from 22 June to 7 August 1998. The site is the Early Christian monastery reputedly founded by St Colmcille in the 6th century.

Investigations confirmed that the eastern end of the church was Early Christian, probably dating to the 10th or 11th centuries. The small church with antae had internal dimensions of 9.5m east–west by 5.6m. In the cutting (7.5m x 7m), 6.5m from the east end, the remains of the Early Christian west wall were discovered. The wall (*c.* 0.8m wide) survived at both ends and was best preserved at the south, where five courses in height were extant. Numerous sharpening marks were revealed on the stones at the south-west corner of the Early Christian church. The south-west anta could be traced in the masonry.

The Early Christian church was converted into the chancel when a long nave (internal length 23.2m) was built. Architectural features did not survive that would provide definitive dating, but the 13th century is suggested for this construction phase. A chancel arch was inserted that necessitated the demolition of most of the west wall. The base of the south jamb of the chancel arch was preserved, which was supported on the Early Christian foundation and was built up against the remains of the west wall. The chancel arch would have had a span of 3.7m, and a sketch by Austin Cooper in 1784 depicts a semicircular-headed arch.

In the lowermost layer investigated a silt mixed with sand, charcoal fragments and 13th–14th-century artefacts was found in the south-east corner of the nave. The finds comprised pottery, a single-sided composite antler comb and a copper-alloy strap-tag.

Three adjoining cuttings (total area 4.34m^2) were opened at the north wall of the nave, *c.* 12m from the west end. In the cutting outside the nave a grave containing an adult had cut into undisturbed levels

(1.1m deep). The overlying deposit of silty sand had human skull fragments. A second grave was discovered above, in which the articulated leg bones of an adult were present. It appears that this latter burial pre-dates the nave and that the proximal skeletal remains were disturbed when the wall was built.

A small pit (0.35m x 1m and 0.47m deep) was revealed beside the nave wall, which had cut through the underlying stratigraphy into the undisturbed levels. The pit fill contained fragments of human bone and charcoal. Undisturbed layers were not reached in the cutting inside the nave (1.02m deep). A deposit of sand contained large unhewn stones, scattered human bone fragments and charcoal flecks.

A crypt was discovered beneath the north-west of the chancel, which has yet to be investigated. A small hole in the roof enabled two coffins to be observed inside. The blocked entrance to the crypt was outside the cutting to the east. In the north-west corner of the chancel the plinth for the memorial monument associated with the crypt was uncovered. The plinth consisted of worked limestone blocks, one of which had an inscription — IACOBUS SHERGOLD ME INSCRIPTS IT. Other fragments of the monument, commemorating Walter Archbold (of Timolin), who died in 1629, and his wives Elizabeth Eustace and Amie Ussher, are preserved at Moone Abbey.

A cutting (2m x 3m) was investigated 9m south of the church in the graveyard, where the tall granite high cross was erected in the mid-19th century. No evidence was found to indicate that this was the original site of the cross. Undisturbed sand layers were reached at a depth of *c.* 1.3m. A small oval pit (0.68m x 0.87m and 0.27m deep) had cut into the sand. In the pit fill were human bone fragments and a complete adult tibia. The overlying deposit was graveyard soil (1.2m maximum depth), and three adult burials with associated coffin remains were excavated. In the mid-19th century these burials were partially removed when a large, irregularly shaped pit (*c.* 1m deep) was dug. The pit was filled with stones and sand to provide a firm foundation for the high cross.

Miriam Clyne, Templemartin, Craughwell, Co. Galway.

327. NAAS

Urban
97E0151

Additional monitoring of mechanical cutting of trenches to accommodate *Bord Gáis Éireann* pipe-laying in certain areas in Naas was carried out in the period between 9 and 14 June 1998 (see *Excavations 1997*, 96–8, for 1997 season of work).

A trench in Dara Court ran along the course of a now obsolete watermain in disturbed material, including rubble and bricks, and underlying boulder clay excavated to a depth of 0.8m and a width of 0.4m. A short length of trench was also cut in the southern part of Corban's Lane. A main sewer runs north–south through Corban's Lane to South Main Street. This, together with electricity service cables, had given rise to totally disturbed strata.

Although a ditch and 12th–14th-century pottery sherds had been uncovered at a development site running parallel to Corban's Lane, no material of

archaeological interest came to light here in the course of this project.

A stretch of the southern end of New Row close to the west side was mechanically excavated. The soil consisted of boulder clay and many large and small water-rolled stones under tarmacadam dressing. No archaeological material was present.

Subsidiary gas pipe connections were laid in John's Lane and Poplar Square adjoining Lawlors Hotel and Butt Mullins Restaurant and at the southern side of the junction between North Main Street and Sallins Road, and in South Main Street. The strata in all cases had been disturbed in earlier years through the laying of other services and development works. No material of archaeological significance came to light.

The laying of a gas pipeline along the southern side of part of Friary Street had been proposed. However, owing to traffic hazards and other considerations this was not proceeded with.

Breandán Ó Ríordáin, Burgage More, Blessington, Co. Wicklow, for Valerie J. Keeley Ltd, Duke Street, Athy, Co. Kildare.

328. ABBEY STREET/CANAL STREET, NAAS

Urban medieval
289060 219316
98E0237

An archaeological evaluation was undertaken at a proposed development site at Abbey Street/Canal Street, Naas, Co. Kildare, on 18–19 May 1998. The work was carried out in compliance with a condition of the grant of planning in relation to a mixed apartment and office development.

The development lies within the zone of archaeological potential of Naas, and it is postulated that a portion of the town defences ran through part of the site. Furthermore, it is generally believed that a friary existed at or near the junction formed by Canal Street and Abbey Street, near where human skeletal material was uncovered by Martin Reid in 1995 (*Excavations 1995*, 47, 95E0042). Patricia Lynch (*Excavations 1996*, 53, 96E0011) recovered similar material from Abbey Street during 1996.

Twelve test-trenches were opened with the use of a mechanical excavator. Part of the site fronting onto the canal had recently served as a builder's machinery yard, and evidence of the surface of such was uncovered during testing. Furthermore, there were indications that the levels of this area of the site may have been raised at some time in the past, possibly linked with construction works associated with the canal from 1786 to 1789. A wet, organic material uncovered in this general area of the site may indicate that the area was generally waterlogged in antiquity. Evidence of such waterlogging still exists in lands beyond the site of the Dominican Priory to the north of the development and downslope from the motte. This material produced a number of sherds of pottery, which generally date to the latter half of the 18th and the 19th century, as well as a number of undatable clay pipe stems. One sherd of medieval pottery was also recovered from this material.

A wall on the western side of the Abbey Street plot is believed to preserve the line of the medieval town wall. However, no evidence of such was revealed, with the present wall, which has a plinth foundation, most likely dating to the mid- to late 18th century, as the material upon which it is constructed produced pottery and clay pipe fragments that generally date to this period.

In terms of topography the natural subsoil sloped gently down to the west in the lower area of the site. A similar but much steeper gradient was noted on the northern quarter of the site. Furthermore, the natural subsoil was found to be of differing materials, with that found in the northern quarter indicative of the gravel ridge upon which the medieval town was constructed.

No evidence of a town wall, enclosing earthen bank, or structures and burials associated with the Dominican(?) Priory was uncovered. It is concluded that, given the results from this and other sites, the priory is most likely situated between Abbey Street and the eastern boundary of the development site, most of which lies within the present Telecom Éireann complex. Furthermore, it is possible that the slope of the gravel ridge formed part of a defensive system, below and beyond which was soft, wet ground.

Martin E. Byrne, 39 Kerdiff Park, Monread, Naas, Co. Kildare.

329. FRIARY ROAD, NAAS

Urban medieval

64798 121819

98E0468

An archaeological evaluation was carried out at a site on Friary Road, Naas, Co. Kildare, on 19 October 1998. Planning permission had been granted for the construction of three two-storey apartment blocks on the site.

The development site consists of a rectangular property, *c.* 53m east–west by 17m, fronting onto Friary Road. Most of the site has been vacant in recent years. A single structure stood in the northwestern corner of the site along part of the street front, and this was demolished before testing.

Three test-trenches were inserted over the development area. The stratigraphy was generally quite simple over most of the site, consisting of topsoil to varying depths, over natural gravel. A number of features, which consisted of cuts into the natural filled with a material almost indistinguishable from the topsoil, were noted within Trenches 1 and 2. F2–4 and possibly F5 appeared to represent pits or linear cuts, but neither their form nor fills provided evidence to permit a more precise interpretation. The occurrence of a sherd of medieval pottery within F5 may indicate a medieval origin for this feature, and the general absence of any modern or early modern contamination in the fills of these features militates strongly against an argument that they are of modern origin. Indeed, while a couple of sherds of modern pottery were found within the topsoil that covered most of the site, the general absence of modern material within this topsoil was noteworthy and suggests little disturbance in recent centuries.

One feature, identified at the rear of the site, was of particular interest. While only the western edge of this feature was uncovered during testing, the exposed sections of the cut are suggestive of a linear ditch of substantial dimensions. The location and direction of this feature would be consistent with the line of the town wall as suggested by Bradley in the *Urban Archaeological Survey*. An antiquity for the feature is suggested by the apparent absence of inclusions of modern origin and by a sherd of medieval pottery, found on the base of the trench, which may have originated from its fill.

Subsequent monitoring of level reductions in this area confirmed that this feature continued across the site and under the northern boundary wall. It could be seen to measure 3.4m wide in this area. Monitoring also revealed the base of what may be an early south boundary wall on the eastern end of the site. This feature lay over the backfill of the ditch.

Further monitoring of groundworks associated with this development is to take place in 1999.

Clare Mullins, 39 Kerdiff Park, Monread, Naas, Co. Kildare.

330. MAIN STREET, NAAS

Post-medieval

98E0070

Monitoring took place at the site of Moloneys Bakery, North Main Street, Naas, Co. Kildare, in advance of it being developed as a new McDonalds fast-food outlet.

The foundations of the structural walls of the new building were monitored once all of the buildings (apart from the façade and part of the shell of the structure fronting onto the main street) had been demolished and most of the concrete flooring had been removed. The rest of the site was to remain undisturbed, and the area was to be raised above the present floor level.

Cutting 1, which was 6m long, 0.9–1.05m wide and 1.6–1.8m deep, was to the rear of the site and at right angles to a stone boundary wall. Below several modern layers were found Contexts 7 and 8, which are fundamentally the same. Context 7 was a black, organic deposit with oyster and mussel shells (some small fragments of limpet shell were also noted, and, while animal bone also occurred, it was less common than in Context 8). It contained post-medieval pottery fragments, the occasional piece of twig, many pieces of limestone, stone and numerous pieces of crushed slate, mainly greyish-blue. Some very small pieces of schist also occurred.

Context 8 was a thick deposit of dark, organic material very rich in animal bone, including the remains of cattle, sheep and pigs. Again small stones and a large amount of broken slate also occurred. Among the finds was a variety of post-medieval pottery, some pieces of mortar and a fragment of ridge-tile. Also occurring was some imported German stoneware (?Raeren), a fragment of a stoneware 'Bellarmine' or 'Grey beard' jug and some pieces of wood. A piece of wine glass also occurred. Below this was boulder clay.

Cutting 2 was made along almost the entire length of the site. It produced little of archaeological consequence. In only two areas was there any undisturbed stratigraphy. One section produced a short segment of cobbled flooring. This was undoubtedly late, as a piece of willow pattern plate was found in the gravel beneath the cobbles and a clay pipe stem fragment was also found in this context.

The stratigraphy in Cutting 3 was similar to that in Cutting 1.

As the foundations of the new building were

designed not to extend more than 0.2m below the present surface, and as no archaeological deposits would be disturbed, it was recommended that the building work should proceed as planned.

Jim Higgins, 'St Gerard's', 18 College Road, Galway.

331. SOUTH MAIN STREET, NAAS
Urban medieval
289059 219313
98E0030
Archaeological monitoring of groundworks associated with an extension to the rear of premises on South Main Street, Naas, was carried out from 19 to 22 January 1998. The work was undertaken in compliance with a condition of the grant of planning. The groundworks associated with the development required a reduction of the existing ground levels within the area of the extension, partial demolition of the northern boundary wall and the excavation of foundation trenches.

Two distinct features of archaeological interest were noted during the course of the work. One was a layer of black, organic silt that was uncovered along the northernmost edge of the development and ran into the adjacent property to the north. This layer was 0.56m wide and 0.1–0.12m thick; it lay directly upon the sterile subsoil. This layer had been truncated by the foundation trench associated with the original northern boundary wall, which was partially demolished as part of the development. No trace of this layer was uncovered in any of the other foundation trenches, as many disturbances, associated with previous developments, had taken place down to, and into, the natural.

The other feature was a well situated in the central area of the extension. The structural integrity of the well was not endangered by the development, and it was covered over with slabs.

No finds of archaeological interest were recovered during the course of the work. Apart from the features described above, only one mixed layer was encountered above the natural. This consisted of a moderate, mid-brown, silty clay with many stones. This material also contained a quantity of modern material including glass bottles, brick, ceramic pipe fragments etc.

Clare Mullins, 39 Kerdiff Park, Monread, Naas, Co. Kildare.

332. OLD KILCULLEN
Environs of ecclesiastical remains
282625 206805
SMR 28:49
98E0019
An archaeological evaluation was undertaken at a proposed development site at Old Kilcullen, Kilcullen, Co. Kildare, on 15 January 1998. The work was undertaken in compliance with a condition of the grant of planning in relation to the construction of a private dwelling with associated driveway and septic tank.

The site, which is roughly wedge-shaped in plan, lies south-south-west of Old Kilcullen ecclesiastical remains, on the western side of the Old Kilcullen–Halverstown road. Seven trenches were excavated by machine.

No features or structures of archaeological interest

were uncovered during the course of the evaluation, and the only find of note was a single sherd of probable medieval pottery, recovered from the topsoil layer. Consequently, it was recommended that no further archaeological involvement was required at the site.

Martin E. Byrne, 39 Kerdiff Park, Monread, Naas, Co. Kildare.

333. BALLYSAX ROAD, OLD KILCULLEN
Environs of Dún Áillinne archaeological complex
281145 20750
SMR 23:68
98E0385
Monitoring of groundworks associated with the construction of a private house at Ballysax Road, Old Kilcullen, was carried out on 24 August 1998, in compliance with a condition within the grant of planning. The development site lies on the periphery of a large area of archaeological potential, while the hillfort of Dún Áillinne lies a short distance to the north-east. Stripping of topsoil for the house and driveway, as well as the excavation of three pits for the construction of the septic tank, had already been carried out without archaeological monitoring. The groundworks that were monitored consisted of the excavation of foundation trenches and the extension of one of the pits for the septic tank.

No archaeological finds or features were observed during the course of this monitoring.

Clare Mullins, 39 Kerdiff Park, Monread, Naas, Co. Kildare.

334. GLEBE NORTH, OLD KILCULLEN
Early monastic and medieval centre
SMR 28:49
77130 115414
98E0344
Test-trenching was carried out on 5 August 1998 at the site of a proposed development in Glebe North, Old Kilcullen. Testing was in compliance with a condition within the grant of planning for the construction of a private house, driveway and septic tank. The development site lies within the zone of archaeological potential for Old Kilcullen. The western site boundary coincides with the suggested western line of the town defences as defined in the Urban Archaeological Survey, and a low earthen bank, which appears to act as a field boundary, at present defines this western site boundary.

Four test-trenches were inserted within the area of greatest impact from the development. No archaeological deposits or artefacts were recovered during the excavation of these trenches. A feature visible on the ground surface as a shallow, linear depression running in a north-east to south-west direction, parallel to the western site boundary, proved to represent a field drain.

It was recommended that no further archaeological involvement was required at the site.

Clare Mullins, 39 Kerdiff Park, Monread, Naas, Co. Kildare.

335. OLDTOWN/AGHARDS
No archaeological significance
2963 2335
98E0104
A testing programme was undertaken to address the

impact that the proposed development would have on three distinct areas:

The area closest to St Mochua's church

Three trenches were positioned to determine whether there was any evidence of an outer enclosure. These trenches were opened by machine to an average depth of 0.85m. The stratigraphy revealed a heavily disturbed ploughsoil overlying natural deposits and bedrock. There was no indication of any archaeological features or deposits in this area.

The area of the townland boundary between Oldtown and Aghards

The purpose of these trenches, the average depth of which was 0.9m, was to determine the nature of this townland boundary. A disturbed ploughsoil overlying a woody deposit and natural deposits was revealed. This woody deposit appears to be the only surviving evidence of the townland boundary, which would probably have been a hedge. There was no indication of an associated ditch or bank. Likewise with the curving boundary, this does not seem to have had any particular archaeological significance.

The roadway

The proposed final trench was not cut, as it was apparent that this was a continuation of the right of way, which is identified on maps of the area. This roadway extends from the present end of the right of way (as identified by a wire fence) 275m to the north-west. The ditch on the southern side is still evident, while the northern ditch has been eroded by agricultural activity. This roadway is depicted on both Noble and Keenan's map of 1753 and Taylor's map of 1783, leading to Oldtown.

Before any development work takes place the shrubbery and undergrowth should be cut back and removed to enable a detailed topographical/contour survey of the roadway to be completed. It will then be possible to determine whether further testing is required.

Rónán Swan, Arch-Tech Ltd, 32 Fitzwilliam Place, Dublin 2.

336. PUNCHESTOWN LITTLE
No archaeological significance
2917 2159
98E0031

It was a condition of planning permission that monitoring be carried out during alterations at the north end of Punchestown Racecourse stadium complex, in that area of the development in closest proximity to a ring-barrow (SMR 24:10). The groundworks were associated with a new entrance structure and the realignment of a pre-existing road. Groundworks extended as far north as 35m south of the ring-barrow.

Once the tarmac and an underlying foundation layer of gravel were removed a mixed glacial till was exposed, consisting of orange-brown, silty clay and grey-brown sand. There was no evidence of an earlier sod layer that may have been removed during the construction of the tarmac surface. There were no archaeological features cut into this boulder clay.
Christiaan Corlett, 88 Heathervue, Greystones, Co. Wicklow.

337. RATHMORE WEST
Burials
295801 219308
SMR 20:9
98E0135

Monitoring of groundworks associated with the construction of a private house in Rathmore West, Naas, Co. Kildare, was carried out in March 1998, in compliance with a condition of planning. The development site lies *c.* 200m south of a motte.

The site lies on sloping ground, and this necessitated the reduction of levels into the subsoil over a considerable part of the development area before foundation trenches could be excavated. During the reduction of levels towards the rear of the proposed house two areas that showed a high concentration of charcoal were identified. Further groundworks in this immediate area were halted pending investigation of these features.

Feature 1 proved to be a bowl-shaped pit that had been cut into the subsoil and filled to about half level with a series of layers of charcoal, red oxidised earth and ash. The pit had an original depth of *c.* 0.6m, but the upper half of the pit was filled with redeposited natural, a fact that may have hindered identification of the feature had development plans not required reduction of levels well into the natural in this area. A considerable quantity of burnt bone was found throughout the various fills of the pit.

Feature 2 consisted also of a bowl-shaped pit and was *c.* 0.5m deep. The fill was less spectacular than that of Feature 1 and consisted mainly of redeposited natural with a terminal deposit of charcoal and ash in the centre of the pit. It produced only a small number

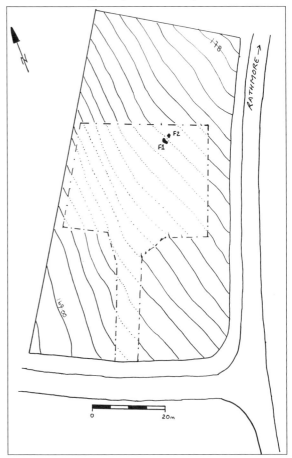

Plan of site (98E0135) at Rathmore West, Co. Kildare.

of tiny fragments of bone and a few larger pieces, while small flecks of charcoal occurred as occasional inclusions within the fill of redeposited natural.

The occurrence of these features, considered in conjunction with the discovery, at the end of the last century, of some inhumation burials beneath the motte, may indicate that the general area held some ritualistic importance in the late prehistoric period.

Subsequent monitoring of level reduction near these features did not reveal any further evidence of archaeological material.

Charcoal samples from Feature 1 returned a radiocarbon date range of AD 230–420 (95.4% confidence level).
Clare Mullins, 39 Kerdiff Park, Monread, Naas, Co. Kildare.

338. RATHMORE WEST
Medieval
SMR 20:9
98E0145
Test excavation was carried out as part of a pre-development impact assessment before the construction of a house. The site, the boundaries of which preserved the outline of a burgage plot, was a landscaped garden at the rear of an existing dwelling-house in the centre of the village of Rathmore and to the east of the motte and church. The site, before being made into a garden, was occupied by a farmyard and associated outbuildings.

Four trenches were excavated, and a series of medieval and post-medieval features was uncovered, overlain by two major phases of disturbance. The most recent phase of disturbance was the redeposited remains of the levelled farm outbuildings. The second and earlier phase of disturbance, a matrix of dark brown, friable, sandy clay, contained occasional pieces of red brick, mortar, coal and charcoal. Finds included several sherds of modern china and blackware, as well as a few sherds of North Leinster cooking ware and a local ware of probable 13th/14th-century date. There was also a broken chert nodule and a multi-planar chert core.

This disturbance extended down as far as the natural sand, into which the medieval and post-medieval features had been cut and hence preserved. However, they were clearly significantly truncated by the later disturbance. The first feature, effectively located in the centre of the site, was a simple, clay-bound, north–south-orientated wall made from whole and broken limestone cobbles. There was a thin gravel deposit abutting it on the east side, and a clay pipe stem found on the surface of this gravel deposit provided a date somewhere between the late 17th and mid-19th century. The other features, which occurred at the eastern end of the site, were the vestiges of a number of truncated medieval refuse pits, ranging from 0.08m to 0.2m in depth and 0.4m to 0.6m in diameter. Finds from the fill, a friable, sandy loam ranging from brown to dark brown, included sherds of both North Leinster cooking ware and the local ware of probable 13th/14th-century date, as well as a few fragments of both pig and avid bone.

Monitoring, following from the impact assessment, was carried out under an extension to the same licence. The stripping of topsoil and the excavation of the foundations for the four external walls of the dwelling-house were monitored. On the eastern side of the site the foundation trenches extended down to and impinged upon the areas of the natural, sandy subsoil previously exposed. However, on the western side they did not penetrate the modern disturbance. No further archaeological material or deposits were discovered in these areas.

On the east side of the site, where the foundation trenches were widened by *c.* 0.5m for a chimney breast, and on the south side, where the foundations were stepped out to accommodate the rear porch, further archaeological deposits were uncovered. In the area of the chimney breast another small truncated refuse pit, measuring 0.25m in diameter and 0.06m in depth, was uncovered, and in the area of the rear porch a second pit, measuring 1.4m in diameter and 0.45m in depth, was also revealed. There were two finds: a single sherd of medieval pottery and a small animal bone.
Emmet Byrnes for Cultural Resource Development Services, Campus Innovation Centre, Roebuck Castle, Dublin 4.

339. TULLY EAST
Medieval
273537 210902
98E0288
Archaeological monitoring of topsoil-stripping in connection with the construction of a coach park and new roadway adjacent to the Irish National Stud and Japanese Gardens, part of the Kildare Town Bypass project, revealed some material of archaeological interest. Excavation was therefore carried out from 1 to 8 October 1998.

The main feature discovered was a deposit of over one hundred glazed potsherds of medieval date, some animal bones, molluscs and other domestic refuse. This deposit is considered to have been in a secondary position and used as infill on marshy ground. The finds were probably originally associated with a Commandery of the Knights Hospitallers established at nearby Tully House in the early 13th century.
Breandán Ó Ríordáin, Burgage More, Blessington, Co. Wicklow, assisted by Eoghan Kieran, for Valerie J. Keeley Ltd, Duke Street, Athy, Co. Kildare.

KILKENNY

340. GREEN STREET/MILL STREET, CALLAN
Graveyard
SMR 26:10
98E0512
The site comprises a yard to the rear of a small hotel that adjoins the graveyard and medieval church of St Mary's. One test-trench was opened to a depth of 300mm in the yard close to the graveyard on 4 November 1998. Some disarticulated and broken human bones were found. The trench was closed, and the developer was advised that no further disturbance should take place in that area. Following this, foundation trenches for an extension to the building were monitored. Some broken human bones were recovered in the trenches and were reinterred in the south-east corner of the development site.
Sheila Lane, 1 Charlemont Heights, Coach Hill, Rochestown, Cork.

341. CALLAN CO-OP, WEST STREET, CALLAN
Urban medieval and post-medieval
24149 14355
98E0280

Test excavations were carried out at the site of a proposed filling station at Callan Co-op in June 1998, in response to a planning condition. The site lies beside West Street, immediately west of Skerry's Castle, a tower-house originally protecting one of the town gates. A stone wall standing 2.5m high forms the boundary between the site and the site of the tower-house (the wall was surveyed as part of the site assessment). A mill lies on the west side of the site, and King's River flows to the north.

During initial test excavations a late 17th-century wall (keyed into the boundary wall) was uncovered overlying earlier deposits in the area of the fuel tanks. As a result another test-trench was excavated towards the rear of the site to find an alternative location for the fuel tanks.

A number of walls were recorded and roughly dated. Two appeared to date to the late 17th/early 18th century (contemporary with the boundary wall between the site and Skerry's Castle?), and a clay-bonded wall pre-dated the site boundary wall. It is probably contemporary with the early years of Skerry's Castle.

Otherwise the trenches cut through late 17th/18th-century garden soils and garden features, which appeared to be the earliest surviving remains this far from the street front. The construction trench at a right angle to the east boundary wall revealed no evidence of a town fosse.

Groundworks associated with the development have not disturbed structural remains close to the street front. The ground level over the site has also been raised with rubble and hard-core, by between 0.25m and 0.75m, since the last generation of buildings on the site was demolished. Because of this and because the site drops almost 2m from front to rear little archaeological damage has been caused to surviving archaeological deposits.
Jo Moran, 33 Woodlawn, Cashel, Co. Tipperary.

342. DUNGARVAN
No archaeological significance
SMR 24:68
98E0450

The area for proposed redevelopment lay within the zone of archaeological potential for the village of Dungarvan, Co. Kilkenny. Archaeological assessment in the form of test-trenches was requested as a planning condition for a redevelopment of a dwelling-house adjacent to the street frontage. Twelve trenches were opened. There were no indications of archaeological material within the designated areas.
Cathy Sheehan, Hillview, Aglish, Carrigeen, South Kilkenny.

343. ST MARY'S CHURCH, GOWRAN
Medieval church
26325 15345
98E0112

Service trenches associated with the refurbishment of the chancel of Gowran parish church were cut by hand through the present graveyard.

On the north side of the church a stump of mortared stonework was found set into a hard medieval surface, perhaps the market area. The surface appeared to overlie graves, and to the east, beside the chancel, the surface was covered with an imported soil and the ground used again for (late medieval/early post-medieval?) burial.

A medieval mortuary building was identified beside the chancel (attached to the medieval chancel), and a medieval kiln (grain-dryer?) found at the west end of the present graveyard, presumably outside the medieval precinct.
Dave Pollock, 33 Woodlawn, Cashel, Co. Tipperary.

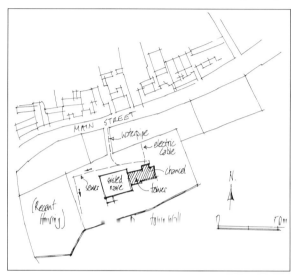

General plan of St Mary's Church, Gowran.

344. MAIN STREET, GRAIGUENAMANAGH
Urban medieval
SMR 29:18
271907 143129
98E0387

An archaeological evaluation was carried out at a site at Main Street, Graignamanagh, Co. Kilkenny, on 24 August 1998 in response to an archaeological condition within the grant of planning for the construction of a two-storey dwelling-house on the site.

The development site consists of a narrow property fronting onto Main Street and backing onto the River Duiske and lies to the north of the Abbey and on the periphery of the zone of archaeological potential as defined by the Urban Archaeological Survey.

Four test-trenches were inserted in the area of greatest impact from the development. No archaeological deposits or artefacts were identified during the investigation, and it was therefore decided that no further archaeological involvement was required.
Clare Mullins, 39 Kerdiff Park, Monread, Naas, Co. Kildare.

345. 'ABBEY HOUSE', JERPOINT ABBEY
Environs of deserted settlement and abbey
256966 146790
98E0554

A programme of trial-trenching was undertaken at a proposed development at Abbey House, Jerpoint Abbey, Thomastown, Co. Kilkenny, on 19 November 1998. The work was undertaken in compliance with conditions attached to the grant of planning in respect of a rear extension to the existing building.

The site lies *c.* 16km south-south-west of Kilkenny City and *c.* 2km from Thomastown, on the main Dublin–Waterford road (N9). It lies to the immediate north-west of Jerpoint Abbey, across the above-mentioned road. It consists of a mid-18th-century house with a modern rear extension, with a number of outbuildings situated to the north and north-west. One of the outbuildings is a dilapidated cornmill with an associated mill-stream, which runs in a north–south direction, parallel to the Little Arrigle River. The ground surface falls noticeably towards the mill-race and river. However, in the area of the proposed extension the ground surface has been built up to be level with the existing house area. This work was done when the existing extension was constructed a number of years ago.

The proposed development site lies on the eastern boundary of an archaeological complex, listed in the Recorded Monuments for County Kilkenny as 28:62 and classified as a deserted settlement (i.e. Newtown Jerpoint).

Three trenches were excavated by machine. In general the original ground level was raised when the existing extension to the rear of the house was undertaken. Indeed, there was evidence that the original topsoil horizon was disturbed in the northern part of the development area, and it is probable that such disturbance is associated with the existing services. It appears that the ground surface was raised by up to 800mm above the original. Furthermore, evidence from Trench 3 indicated that the original ground surface fell gently towards the river.

No features, structures or finds of archaeological interest were uncovered, and consequently it was recommended that no further archaeological involvement was required.

Martin E. Byrne, 39 Kerdiff Park, Monread, Naas, Co. Kildare.

346. ABBEY STREET, KILKENNY
Urban
25050 15603
SMR 19:26
96E0047

A 4m-diameter circular shaft for a manhole was excavated in Abbey Street, Kilkenny, 0.6m to the north of the medieval walls and close to the 13th-century Franciscan Abbey, known as the Black Abbey. The Black Freren Gate, the only remaining medieval gate in Kilkenny, stands 25m to the east of the site. Martin Reid previously carried out excavations in the immediate area under the same licence number (*Excavations 1996*, 56).

The manhole formed part of the Kilkenny Main Drainage Scheme and was excavated down to a final depth of 4.5m below present ground level. In order to restrict any possible ground movement and subsequent damage to the nearby city wall and its foundations it was decided to construct the manhole by means of segmented concrete rings, placed on top of each other and bolted together. A bracing structure and monitoring system were constructed on the city wall in order to monitor any movement.

Below the modern concrete road surface and hard-core an east–west wall spanned the width of the shaft on the north side. An east–west drain,

formed by cobbles, ran parallel to this wall, and it was apparent that this drain skirted a cobbled roadway, of which only the northern edge remained. Below this cobbled road a metalled surface was revealed containing animal bone, post-medieval pottery and one sherd of medieval pottery. The archaeological strata were severely disturbed on the southern side of the shaft by the insertion of three modern drains.

However, the northern portion of the manhole revealed varying layers of rubble, some containing medieval pottery, together with a quantity of animal bone, all underlain by a black, sterile layer. The east–west wall appeared to be resting on the foundations of an earlier wall. When these two walls were removed a layer of redeposited soil was uncovered. A layer of large, roughly quarried stones, which filled the northern section of the shaft, underlay this. On removal of these stones large wooden piles were revealed, closely packed together and averaging 2m long. All of the piles had a slight diagonal angle and lay in a north to north-east direction. The piles were concentrated in the northern section of the shaft and ran into the northern side of the manhole. The piles, with well-pointed tips, had been inserted into a very peaty, bog-like soil, which was very dense. This peaty soil came down to mid-brown, natural gravel at a depth of 3.8m.

It is thought that the walls may be the remains of 18th/19th-century houses that fronted onto the north side of Abbey Street and that the cobbled drain and road may be contemporary with the upper wall. The layer of large stones and the wooden piles appear to be attempts to consolidate a wet, boggy area. The Bregagh River currently lies only 20m to the north of the site. A dendrochronology date from the 12th century has been received in relation to the wooden piles, which are of oak, and it appears that they may be contemporary with the initial Anglo-Norman presence in Kilkenny from 1172 onwards.

Sylvia Desmond, 25 Rowan Hall, Millbrook Court, Milltown, Dublin 6.

347. EVAN'S LANE, KILKENNY
Urban medieval
S504560
96E363 ext.

An archaeological assessment took place in October 1998 for a proposed development at Evan's Lane Kilkenny, in the northern sector of the medieval city, to the rear of Rothe House. The proposed development involved the construction of two houses on the site, covering an area 16m x 6.5m. No demolition of existing walls is planned.

Three linear test-trenches were opened and revealed no early standing walls or significant archaeological deposits. However, the presence of finds dating to the late medieval/post-medieval period, in a disturbed ditch, suggested the presence of archaeological layers or features close by.

Archaeological monitoring of foundations was recommended by *Dúchas* and took place in November 1998. No archaeological soils or features were observed during monitoring.

Paul Stevens for Margaret Gowen & Co. Ltd, 2 Killiney View, Albert Road Lower, Glenageary, Co. Dublin.

Kilkenny

348. 14 HIGH STREET, KILKENNY
Urban
SMR 19:26
98E0603

An L-shaped test-trench was excavated in the cobbled yard to the rear of 14 High Street, Kilkenny, to comply with a planning condition. The area of the proposed development lies within the walled medieval city. Access to the yard is gained from a medieval laneway, running at a right angle from High Street. The gable of the 'Hole in the Wall' forms the northern boundary of the yard. It is a late 16th-century building, identified as Site 50 by the Urban Archaeological Survey of Kilkenny. John G.A. Prim (*JKEIAS* 1862–63, 169–77) describes the 'Hole in the Wall' as 'the great supper house of Kilkenny at the end of the last and beginning of the present century and [it] was particularly patronised by John Butler, Earl of Ormonde', and he quotes:

> If ever you go to Kilkenny,
> Remember 'The Hole-in-the-Wall'
> You may there get blind drunk for a penny,
> Or tipsy for nothing at all

The test-trench measured 5.5m north–south by 4.5m and was 2m wide. It was excavated to a depth of 2m (51.026m OD). Five layers were recorded. C1 was a sandy clay with inclusions of brick, slate and modern pottery. C2 was a sandy clay with inclusions of mortar, shells, charcoal and animal bone. C3 was a clay with inclusions of charcoal and post-medieval pottery. C4 was a clay with inclusions of brick, slate, post-medieval pottery and animal bone. C5, a layer of gravel, was the basal layer in the trench. It was excavated to a depth of 0.7m and appears to be natural.

The layers C1–4 included sherds of post-medieval pottery and fragments of brick and slate. No archaeological features or artefacts, with the exception of the post-medieval pottery, were recorded or recovered from the trench.

Jacinta Kiely, Eachtra Archaeological Projects, Clover Hill, Mallow, Co. Cork.

349. 5–7 JAMES'S STREET, KILKENNY
Urban medieval
S504559
98E0427

An assessment took place in September/October 1998 for a proposed shopping arcade development site fronting James's Street, Kilkenny, in the centre of the city within the town walls. The proposed development site extends from James's Street to High Street, where the existing 1960s shopping arcade will be refurbished.

Three linear test-trenches were opened across the site, which revealed an archaeological deposit crossing its northern half. This medieval garden soil was truncated at the southern side and also partly truncated by the floors of the Edwardian houses. It sealed a number of medieval occupation features including a post-hole, an irregular feature and two wall trenches parallel to the street. The garden soil and the features beneath it contained green-glazed medieval pottery and cut limestone fragments. The southern half of the site was heavily truncated by recent activity, and no medieval soils survived.

The development site was thought to lie along the line of the early Anglo-Norman town wall; however,

no remains of the wall were revealed in the trenches opened, therefore the wall may lie immediately to the north under or north of James's Street.

Paul Stevens for Margaret Gowen & Co. Ltd, 2 Killiney View, Albert Road Lower, Glenageary, Co. Dublin.

350. 10 JOHN STREET, KILKENNY
Urban
25054 15600
SMR 19:26
98E0050

A site assessment consisting of one test-trench was carried out on 7 February 1998. The trench was dug to the rear of the building where it was proposed to build an extension. It was opened to the depth of the foundation trenches, 0.6m. Loose rubble fill was noted to 0.3m; brown mud interspersed with brick, bone and charcoal was noted to a depth of 0.6m. No finds or features of archaeological significance were noted.

Sheila Lane, 1 Charlemont Heights, Coach Hill, Rochestown, Cork.

351. BRIDGE HOUSE, JOHN STREET, KILKENNY
Urban medieval
S503576
95E0053

The final phase of an archaeological assessment was carried out on a development site in Kilkenny in February 1998. Five test-trenches were excavated. The site lies on the eastern bank of the River Nore adjacent to and immediately beside St John's Bridge. The suburb is an extension of the main medieval town (Hightown) on the western side of the Nore. This suburb grew up around St John's Priory, which moved to its present location in 1325.

John Street is the central axis from which the suburb was laid out (Lanigan, K. and Tyler, G., *Kilkenny, its architecture and history*, 1987). This continued into the Tudor period, when large stone houses were built. With the redevelopment of the street over the past 400 years many of these buildings have been removed or altered. However, Nos 78/81, the 17th-century residence of a branch of the Fitzgeralds and Shees, survives, as well as Nos 88/89 (Bridge House, the Dower House of the Ormond family).

The earliest recorded mentions of town walling around the suburb of St John's occur in the early 16th century, when there are references to a stone and lime wall, with reference to a turret in 1570 (Thomas, A., *The walled towns of Ireland*, 1992). The suburb is mentioned in Cromwell's account of the siege of Kilkenny in 1650: 'Having possessed the Irishtown, and there being another walled town on the other side of the river (St John's); eight companies of foot were sent over to possess that'. The town wall was evidently in existence from at least the mid-16th century and continued in use through to the end of the 17th century.

The line of the town wall has been discussed in detail by J. Bradley (*The town wall of Kilkenny*, Old Kilkenny Review, parts I and II, 1975–6) and A. Thomas (*The walled towns of Ireland*, 1992). They both speculated, based on Rocque's map, that the town wall ran along the eastern boundary of the development site. The wall has been positively identified at the north-eastern corner of the suburb. It extends from a small mural tower on Maudlin Street, along the rear property plots of John Street, where it stood at the rear of Nos 68/69 (O'Donovan, E., Unpublished archaeological assessment report, 1997).

A section of wall enclosing the suburban precinct of St John's was identified in Trench D. It stood 24m south of and parallel to John Street, was 0.43m wide and lined the western edge of a ditch. The wall was 0.19m deep on its western side and 1.7m deep on its eastern side, where it displayed a characteristic basal batter. The ditch outside the wall was 2.5m wide, 0.8m deep and cut into natural boulder clay. The basal 0.3m of the ditch was filled with poorly humified organic material, containing occasional fragments of red brick. A deposit of grey clay, 0.5m thick, sealed this. A thick mantle of demolition rubble made up of mortar, red brick and stone sealed all of the features in the trench.

Throughout the assessment a significant number of trenches were excavated in the rear gardens of Nos 85–89 John Street. It was thought that the town wall ran along the south-eastern property boundary of the site (Thomas, *ibid.* and Bradley, *ibid.*); however, owing to the identification of the town wall in Trench D, it now appears that the wall is significantly further north-west. The soil profiles recorded in all of the archaeological trenches (apart from Trench D (this assessment) and Trenches 12, 13i and 13ii (previous assessment by Margaret Gowen, *Excavations 1995*, 49–50) are modern and insignificant. This area can be considered as a river flood-plain that acted as a fallow area outside the town wall in the medieval period, which could be readily defended from the town wall.

Edmond O'Donovan, Margaret Gowen & Co. Ltd, 2 Killiney View, Albert Road Lower, Glenageary, Co. Dublin.

352. 10–13 KIERAN STREET, KILKENNY
Urban medieval
2507 1559
98E167

A four-part archaeological assessment was carried out at 10–13 Kieran Street, Kilkenny, before the proposed extension and development of the existing Dunnes Stores. The assessment involved a building survey of the existing houses; test-trenching within the house basements and the adjacent carpark; full excavation to the rear of the houses; followed by monitoring of the house demolition, the piling process and the digging of the ground-beam and service trenches. The project was carried out between 23 March and 2 October 1998.

A full internal and external inspection of the houses was carried out. None of the structures incorporated any surviving medieval fabric or features, although two reused cut and chamfered stones were noted in the basement wall of No. 12. Two more reused cut stones were observed in the yard wall separating Nos 11 and 12, while others were noted lying loose in the yard of No. 11. This suggested that there may have been an earlier structure on the site, with some of the stones being reused in the construction of the later houses. Examination of the houses also indicated that No. 11 was the earliest of the four.

Test-pits were dug in the basements of Nos 10–12.

Nos 10 and 11 produced no evidence of medieval activity. In No. 12 a wall was observed, running in a north-east/south-west direction along the section face of the pit and under the present foundations of the house. This was post-medieval in date but was sitting on a number of clay deposits, three of which contained medieval pottery sherds. A test-trench was also dug in the carpark of Dunnes Stores. This produced no pure medieval layers, although an Elizabethan coin and occasional medieval sherds of pottery turned up in a disturbed context.

Open excavation was carried out to the rear of the houses. The site was dug to a predetermined level of 43.37m OD, designed to create a buffer zone between the archaeology and the formation level of the new structure. Consequently, it was not dug to a uniform archaeological level, or to undisturbed subsoil levels.

Post-medieval activity was noted across the site. This consisted of a large working surface of clay and cobbles. Two walls of a stone structure were noted on this surface. Two culverts and a continuation of the wall noted during test-trenching were also picked up, running beneath the houses. Two wells were also uncovered—these too were post-medieval in date.

Medieval activity was noted in the south-west of the site, closest to the houses. This consisted of dumps of clay and organic material, containing sherds of medieval pottery. Two pits were uncovered in the far south of the site, and a well and associated stone structure (possibly a trough or overflow feature) were partially uncovered in the west of the site. These features were not bottomed but clearly continued below the 43.37m OD level.

Monitoring uncovered further archaeological features of significance. The piling process suggested that the medieval deposits continued up to 1m below the excavated depth of 43.37m OD, based on the material brought up by the piling auger. Digging of the ground-beam trenches produced evidence of the original doorway for No. 11, which was uncovered in section, along with an early relieving arch at basement level. Further evidence of the wall noted during test-trenching and excavation was also found. More of the culverts and part of an earlier boundary wall were also uncovered during the monitoring phase. It was also clear that the construction of the basements of the houses had removed virtually all archaeological layers and features.

Hilary Opie, 103 Cherrywood Drive, Clondalkin, Dublin 22.

353. MAUDLIN STREET, KILKENNY
Urban medieval
S510560
98E0346

An archaeological assessment took place in August 1998 for a proposed development of an apartment block on a site in the centre of the city on the north bank of the River Nore. The assessment consisted of a detailed photographic record of the extant upstanding walls and three linear test-trenches

In Trench 1 a large medieval ditch was found, aligned approximately east–west and 1.1m deep. It lay up against the street frontage in the southern portion of the site and probably represented part of the town defences of the medieval walled city. The southern edge of the ditch and several deposits filling the ditch were identified, the lowest containing medieval pottery and bone. An upper fill was also recorded containing later medieval/post-medieval finds. This layer was also revealed in the second trench to the north, where it was cut by a limestone well.

Post-medieval layers were revealed at the east of the site, associated with a substantially truncated and reworked building fronting the street and a second building fronting the alley to the east. The foundations of the latter were found to rest on boulder clay. It appeared that all stratigraphy associated with the floor of this building had been removed. A possible third building stood in the northern corner of the property.

The eastern corner of the site revealed natural sands and gravel at a high level sealed by a thin layer of garden soil. The walls to the rear and east of the property were post-medieval and early modern in date.

Further excavation and detailed building recording were recommended.

Paul Stevens for Margaret Gowen & Co. Ltd, 2 Killiney View, Albert Road Lower, Glenageary, Co. Dublin.

354. NEW BUILDING LANE, KILKENNY
Urban medieval
25037 15608
98E0051

Two test-trenches were opened on the site in February 1998 in advance of development to fulfil planning conditions. Both an archaeological assessment and an architectural survey of buildings on the site were carried out in 1997 by Edmund O'Donovan (*Excavations 1997*, 101–2, 97E0028) and Malachy Conway (*Excavations 1997*, 102, 97E0166).

The test-trenches were dug in areas that were still occupied by buildings during the previous assessments. Each trench was 1.2m wide and ran inside the line of the buildings parallel to New Building Lane. Trench 1, the more easterly of the two, was on the line of a car service pit, and therefore much of the underlying stratigraphy was disturbed. The trench contained loose fill, which yielded a fragment of 19th-century glass, to a depth of 1.3m, at which point natural gravel was reached. The foundation of the eastern wall of Building 3 (recorded by O'Donovan) was dug into the level of the loose fill. Trench 2 contained a layer of cobbling to a depth of 0.22m. Below this was brown, sandy soil with mortar, stones and bone fragments to a depth of 1.2m. No evidence of walls or late medieval structures or layers was noted.

Sheila Lane, 1 Charlemont Heights, Coach Hill, Rochestown, Cork.

355. NEW STREET LOWER, KILKENNY
Urban
25050 15603
97E0382 ext.

Initial monitoring of development works on this site was previously reported (*Excavations 1997*, 101). Further monitoring of the groundworks associated with the preparation of the carpark area was carried out in March 1998. A large area of topsoil was cleared, and a series of foundation trenches was cut for a perimeter wall. All groundworks were carried out by mechanical means.

The removal of topsoil involved the cutting of an arbitrary level into the ground, which cut through the garden topsoil and partially into a subsoil, different in colour and content. The topsoil was a loose, dark brown silt, typical of garden soil in urban locations; it contained occasional fragments of mortar and red brick and frequent flecks of charcoal. Ceramic finds from this were all post-medieval in date. A compact, mid-brown/green clay subsoil, containing frequent flecks of charcoal and occasional fragments of red brick and mortar, underlay the topsoil. Finds from this layer were similar to those from the topsoil but less frequent.

Some features were found at the arbitrary level of topsoil removal. There were three areas of burning, which were linear in form, shallow in profile and equidistant in plan. They were filled with a dark brown clay/silt, which included charcoal and fragments of broken glass. A series of deeper pits of similar fill and composition was also revealed at this level. Both of the features were cut into the subsoil. They align with the existing property boundaries to the north-east of the site. It was hypothesised that these features represent potting holes for boundary hedges.

All trenches for the perimeter wall were excavated into the boulder clay. The sections of these trenches revealed no archaeological features.

Jacinta Kiely, Eachtra Archaeological Projects, Clover Hill, Mallow, Co. Cork.

356. 26–29 PATRICK STREET, KILKENNY
Urban medieval
98E0092

The site consists of the back gardens of 26–29 Patrick Street, Kilkenny, along with the house currently standing at No. 26. The development (by Jeto Properties Ltd) consists of a hotel and office complex. All of the areas of the site to be affected by the development have been excavated. On the south-east of the site archaeological layers were exposed but will not be damaged and have been covered by a layer of geo-textile.

The excavation on the site was a condition of planning as a result of the trial-testing in February 1998.

Patrick Street is first recorded on William Petty's 17th-century map of Kilkenny and was a main thoroughfare of the medieval town in the 17th century. It was flanked by tall stone houses. On the west side (where the site lies) these houses have marked garden plots. Plots corresponding with the stone boundary walls upstanding on the site appear on John Roque's 18th-century map of Kilkenny. It had originally been suggested by archaeologists carrying out trial-trenching at the site that these walls corresponded with the boundaries of medieval burgage plots. However, upon excavation many pits and trenches of probable 12th–16th-century date did not respect these boundaries and ran directly under the foundations of the surviving walls.

The excavation took place over an area *c.* 50m x 35m from 9 March to 27 April 1998. Earlier building activity and the demolition of existing structures had already heavily damaged the eastern end of the site, so that in part no archaeological level survived. The excavation produced considerable evidence of both medieval and post-medieval activity. Analysis of the pottery and other finds from the site has yet to take

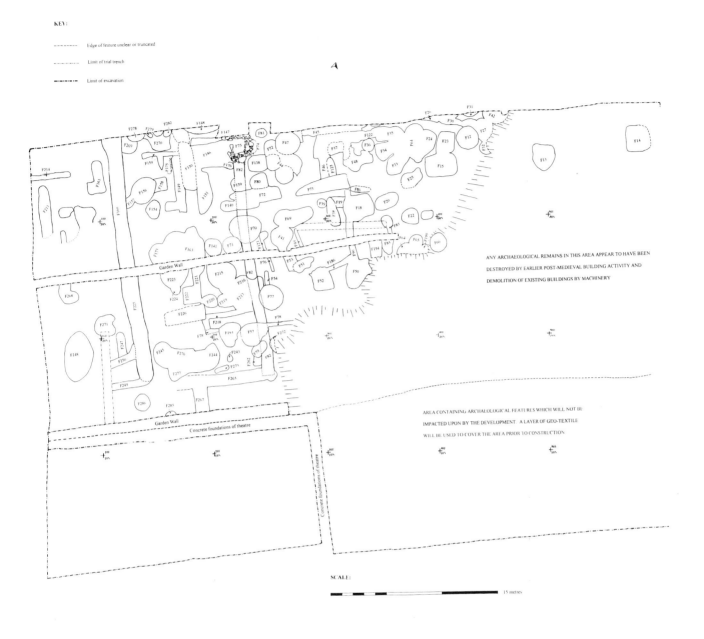

Site plan of 26–29 Patrick Street, Kilkenny.

place, so remarks on the dating of features on the site are provisional.

The site is characterised by a dense concentration of pits. Most of the features appear to be medieval in date, probably 12th–16th century, although there were also some post-medieval pits. A substantial linear palisade trench divides the area of pits and other features from a less archaeologically rich area. This palisade trench (F160) continues in the area of excavation to the north (No. 358 below). It appears to be contemporary with the pits in this area, as it produced medieval pottery (probably late 12th–14th century in date) similar to that from the pits. The palisade trench may be a boundary between the original medieval burgage plots and more open agricultural or common land; none of the pits on the site cut it. Most of the pits to the west of the trench appear to be post-medieval in date, and one in particular produced a large and varied amount of

17th-century pottery and glassware.

The earliest feature on the site seems to be F82, a ditch that runs north–south across the site. It is cut by a series of pits, some of which are medieval in date. At the northern end of the ditch was a stone structure that seems to relate directly to it. F82 may be an earlier enclosure pre-dating F160 and most of the pits, although its precise purpose and function are as yet unclear.

It had been thought that the stone garden walls upstanding on the site before excavation may have related to the boundaries of medieval burgage plots. However, this has not been borne out by excavation. Many medieval features run under the walls, and the only features that appear to respect them are post-medieval in date. Many of the houses on Patrick Street were built or refurbished during the Georgian period, and these walls probably relate to this phase in the development of Patrick Street.

It is intended that detailed post-excavation analysis of the material from the excavation will take place in conjunction with work on the material from the adjacent site at Patrick Street/Pudding Lane, Kilkenny (No. 358 below).

Judith Carroll, Pine Forest Art Centre, Pine Forest Road, Glencullen, Co. Dublin.

357. 33 PATRICK STREET, KILKENNY
Urban medieval
98E0402
The site of No. 33 Patrick Street lies within a large area of current development and archaeological excavation. Excavation has taken place at the 26–29 Patrick Street to the south (No. 356 above) and Patrick Street/Pudding Lane to the north, north-west and west (No. 358 below). The development of No. 33 Patrick Street comprises a three-storey extension with basement to the immediate rear of the premises, currently operating as a hotel.

The excavation of the site was a condition of planning permission as a result of the trial-trenching investigation that took place on 10 September 1998.

Also part of the assessment was a request for further information regarding the upstanding walls surrounding the site. In response to this a drawn survey of three of the walls, including a 16th/17th-century wall to the south-east of the site, which contained, amongst other features of note, a small ogee-headed window, was carried out by Ben Murtagh.

The development site lies within the medieval city walls in an area that also preserves the medieval layout of streets and land divisions. Pudding Lane to the east and Pennyfeather Lane to the north retain their original narrow shapes, and houses of medieval date would be expected to have fronted onto these lanes. The long, narrow plots of land, which extend back from the properties fronting onto Patrick Street, reflect typical medieval burgage plots. Habitation evidence dating from the medieval period is thus likely to be found in the grounds of the houses fronting onto Patrick Street.

Patrick Street is first recorded on William Petty's 17th-century map of Kilkenny, and was a main thoroughfare of the medieval town at that time. It was flanked by tall stone houses. A plot corresponding to the stone boundary walls upstanding on the site appears on John Roque's 1758 map of Kilkenny.

A substantial amount of trial-trenching and excavation has already taken place in the area around the site since 1990. This was carried out by Heather King and John Bradley (Archaeological trial excavations in Kilkenny, *Old Kilkenny Review* **4** (4), 973–87 and *Excavations 1990*, 40–1), Christine Grant (96E0007), Margaret Gowen (*Excavations 1995*, 50–1, 95E0224) and this writer (*Excavations 1997*, 104), and Nos 356 above and 358 below). Full excavation by this writer in all areas around the site has shown that the remains of undisturbed medieval habitation, mainly in the form of medieval pits, as well as foundation trenches and other features, are likely to be found on all areas of all sites fronting onto Patrick Street.

The excavation took place from 21 September to 13 November 1998 over an area *c.* 25m x 14.5m. Demolition of existing structures to the rear of No. 33 Patrick Street, the removal of an iron security fence

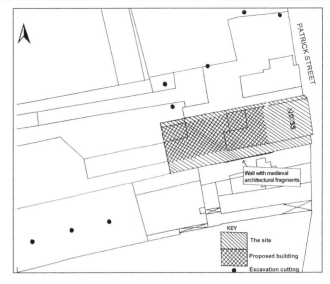

Site, proposed building and excavation cutting at 33 Patrick Street, Kilkenny (after Valerie J. Keeley Ltd., Archaeology Consultancy).

and gate and the complete removal of the wall to the north were carried out before the full extent of the site was exposed. Before this an L-shaped area comprising three cuttings within the carpark was excavated. The excavation produced considerable evidence of medieval activity in the form of pottery but evidence also for post-medieval occupation in the form of foundations for a rectangular building following the line of the northern wall and also ground disturbance in the extreme north-eastern corner. Analysis of the pottery and other finds from the site has yet to take place, so any remarks on the dating of the features on site are purely provisional.

At the eastern end of the site was a rectangular arrangement of stone foundations forming two distinct cells of a dwelling, which possibly corresponds to a building shown on John Rocque's 18th-century map of Kilkenny.

Beneath the 0.02–0.05m-thick layer of tarmac was a 0.1–0.24m thickness of levelling layers, above a single layer of water-worn cobbles of up to 0.15m diameter. These layers also included the bases for the concrete buttresses supporting Wall B to the south. Below the cobbles a 0.25–0.35m-thick layer of rubble (F5) contained fragments of red brick, mortar, slate and lenses of gravel and sand. This lay directly above the first stratified soil layer, F6, which contained inclusions similar to F5, in addition to occasional lumps of charcoal and coal. This layer was 0.22–0.35m thick and occurred at 51.71– 50.965m OD. Below F6 and sealing the upper level of archaeological features was a layer of dark, organic but homogeneous soil between 0.5m and 0.75m thick. This was evident across the whole of the site.

The site is characterised by a fairly dense concentration of deep pits, similar to those found at the neighbouring 26–29 Patrick Street excavation (No. 356 above) and parts of the Patrick Street/ Pudding Lane excavation (No. 358 below). Most of these pits were exposed at the two lowest levels. A circular stone-built well, a rectangular stone-built pit feature, metalled surfaces and wall foundations all appear to represent the next phases of activity, with a deep (0.5–0.75m) build-up of rich garden soil (F7) being the final phase of activity in the medieval period, sealing all other features. To judge from the pottery, medieval activity seems to have taken place between the 12th and 16th centuries.

As the footprint of the development does not come within 1.5m of the upstanding walls to the south of the site the relationship between these and the excavated features could not be ascertained.

Excavation of the site was completed on 13 November 1998. It is intended that detailed post-excavation analysis of the material from the excavation will take place early in 1999, in conjunction with work on the material from the neighbouring sites at 26–29 Patrick Street (98E0092) and Patrick Street/Pudding Lane (97E0468).

Judith Carroll, Pine Forest Art Centre, Pine Forest Road, Glencullen, Co. Dublin.

358. PATRICK STREET/PUDDING LANE/ PENNYFEATHER LANE, KILKENNY
Urban medieval
97E0468
The site lies between the old city walls at the west and the medieval streets of Patrick Street and Pudding Lane at the east. The excavation was a condition of planning as a result of trial-trenching in December 1997 and January 1998 (*Excavations 1997*, 104).

The development was initially restricted to Areas 1–4, but during the course of the excavation of these areas, from 29 April to 5 November 1998, the developer acquired an additional plot of land (Area 5), formerly belonging to the Franciscan friary. This necessitated an additional programme of trial-trenching and assessment, based on which the Heritage Service recommended an additional programme of monitoring and further excavation.

The site lies in the south-west of the medieval town, within the city walls, in an area that preserves the medieval layout of streets and land divisions. Patrick Street is shown on William Petty's 17th-century map of Kilkenny as a main thoroughfare of the town, lined with tall stone houses. Long plots of land typical of medieval burgage plots are shown in the area of the present site, running from the rear of these houses towards, but not reaching, the city wall.

John Rocque's map of 1758 shows similar plots, extending as far as the sconce that ran inside the city wall and in places apparently abutting the wall itself. Most of the wall lines shown on Rocque's map were still extant until very recently, some having been demolished as part of the present development. It had been suggested that these walls corresponded with the boundaries of the medieval burgage plots. However, excavation at this site and the preceding work on Nos 26–29 Patrick Street (see No. 356 above) identified many pits and trenches of probable 12th-16th-century date, running under the foundations of the extant wall, suggesting that the original burgage plots had somewhat different lines. The wall at the western end of the site was built between 1240 and 1440, with further work carried out in the 17th century.

Summaries of the results of excavation in each of these areas are presented here in the order in which work was carried out.

Area 4: main hotel area (29 April–27 July 1998)
Area 4 was completely excavated. It runs from the south-west edge of site No. 356 above to the edge of the area of preservation around the group of upstanding structures tentatively identified as a sallyport bastion and guardhouse/stables once attached to the now demolished Myler's Tower.

A number of shallow drainage channels of probable medieval date were identified adjacent to the area of preservation in front of the sallyport bastions. At the other end of the area a larger number of small pits and narrow trenches were excavated, some seeming to extend into the area excavated under the licence to the east (No. 356 above). Between these two areas no medieval features were identified, adhering to a pattern of distribution that is also visible in the other areas.

Two very large post-medieval pits of greater than 2m depth were excavated close to the sallyport bastion. Other, smaller post-medieval pits were also excavated in this area. A more dense concentration of post-medieval pits and shallow trenches was present at the eastern end of the area.

Area 2: main hotel area (29 April–27 July 1998)
Area 2 was completely excavated. As with Area 4, features tended to be concentrated at the east and west ends, with a much lower density of features in the central area.

The most notable feature of Area 2 is a well-defined trench, tentatively identified as a palisade ditch, running roughly north-north-west/south-south-east across the eastern end of the area. This is the continuation of the palisade trench excavated in the preceding excavation (98E0092), carried out at the rear of Nos 26–29 Patrick Street, to the south of Area 2 (No. 356 above). As noted below, this feature seems to continue into Area 5 to the north. It was observed during excavation that there was a notably higher concentration of medieval features lying to the east of this ditch than was evident to the west. This pattern was borne out in Areas 2 and 5 as well as in the previous excavation.

Several other substantial medieval ditches were excavated in Area 2, including a steep-sided trench that runs east-north-east/west-south-west for half the length of the northern part of this area. Also of apparent medieval date is a pair of shallow, carefully cut, sub-square, flat-bottomed pits with a deliberate lining of small, well-sorted stones, which appears to be linked to shallow drainage channels. A large number of more substantial medieval pits was excavated to the east of the palisade ditch, many of which continue into the unexcavated section face under the north–south access road that links the 26–29 Patrick Street site to the present development.

Post-medieval features include several large, deep pits, one of which produced an intact pot, and some small, well-defined drainage channels that run east-north-east/west-south-west across the site. A substantial post-medieval feature (or series of merged smaller features) runs across the western end of the site, extending into the area of preservation. As this feature lay predominantly outside the zone of impact, only limited investigation took place.

Also identified were the foundations of plot walls shown on Rocque's map but subsequently demolished, including the western end-walls of the plots that occupied Area 2.

Area 2 with palisade(?) trench F210, running north–south under excavation.

Area 3: leisure centre (27 July–8 September 1998)
Area 3 was completely excavated, with the Area of Preservation along the line of the city wall forming its western border. A small number of pits were identified in the west of the area. Of these, one was of probable medieval date and the rest appeared to be post-medieval. Two shallow, flat-bottomed ditches running roughly east–west were identified, both quite disturbed but of a probable medieval date.

Four partially intact human burials were excavated, three lying along a rough north–south line with a fourth at right angles to this alignment. Additional disarticulated human bones were recovered from soil in their vicinity, suggesting at least one further individual. The disarticulated partial remains of an adult female had been recovered from a post-medieval pit in the western portion of this area during a previous phase of trial-trenching (Keeley and Grant 1996, Trial-trench 1, 96E0007). The remainder of this pit was investigated during the present excavation, and further disarticulated remains were identified, possibly belonging to the same individual. The date of these burials has not yet been firmly established.

Nearly all features in Area 3 were cut into by a superimposed criss-cross system of shallow, narrow, post-medieval ditches, probably the remnants of cultivation ridges or temporary drainage channels.

Area 1: multi-storey carpark and retail units (27 July–23 October 1998)
On the recommendation of the Heritage Service Area 1 was excavated to formation levels only. Where features extended below formation levels they were not excavated below that depth, except in the south-east corner of Area 1, which was substantially completed before this recommendation. In addition to these partially unexcavated features it is extremely likely that significant archaeological layers still remain in any areas that were not affected by the present development. Most of Area 1 was excavated, and it was characterised by a very high density of features, both medieval and post-medieval.

Area 1 contained a large number of medieval features, including a high density of pits, as well as

hearths, structural trenches, stake-holes and evidence of metalworking. Three large hearths of likely medieval date were identified, two of which showed evidence of multiple phases of intense use on successive earthen floor surfaces. Both are close to the probable street front of Pudding Lane. In addition there is extensive evidence of metalworking in the medieval period, with large volumes of slag coming from several apparently medieval pits.

A number of substantial ditches or trenches of probable medieval date were identified, with three running east-north-east/west-south-west and one running north-north-west/south-south-east. A more narrow and shallow, L-shaped trench suggested a truncated house foundation, but most of the feature was below formation levels, and it was not possible to investigate this possibility further.

As well as ordinary pits producing large amounts of medieval pottery (including a near-complete pot, cup and jug from separate features), two very large and two smaller stone-lined pits appear to be medieval in date, with very finely set intact dry-stone walling.

Post-medieval features consisted mainly of numerous pits (some very extensive), walls and several drainage features. A badly truncated, brick-lined linear feature filled with material apparently vitrified *in situ*, as well as quantities of post-medieval pottery and tile, suggests ceramic manufacture on the site.

A fine brick-walled drain capped with substantial stone lintels runs east-north-east/west-south-west for nearly the whole length of the area before turning off at right angles to the north-west at its western end. This feature cuts into and overlies several of the more significant medieval features, and despite its relatively modern fabric its location may reflect an established medieval drain line. Multiple near-parallel lines of deep stake-holes run almost exactly parallel to this drain, just to the south of it, but these have yet to be dated.

Probably dating to the 19th or early 20th century, but worthy of note, is a series of three iron-hooped wooden vats of 3m diameter set into the ground, running roughly east–west down the approximate centre of Area 1. Similarly, three substantial iron-banded mill-wheels, one intact and two broken, were recovered from the overburden in the south-west of the area.

Excavation of stone-lined pit F829 in Area 1.

Area 5: multi-storey carpark (extension) (25 September–5 November 1998)

A low density of features was noted here, in keeping with the character of the central band of the site as a whole. Two shallow trenches of a probable medieval date were identified, both running roughly north–south. One of these ditches appears to be the northern continuation of the palisade ditch from Area 2 and No. 356 above. Several pits of post-medieval date were also investigated. The excavation of potential features impinged upon by one remaining undug foundation trench in Area 5 has been deferred, as access is currently prevented by ongoing construction works. This investigation will take place when access becomes available.

Judith Carroll, Pine Forest Art Centre, Pine Forest Road, Glencullen, Co. Dublin.

359. ST FRANCIS ABBEY, SMITHWICKS BREWERY, KILKENNY
Medieval
25060 15620
98E0069

This work was undertaken beneath the footprint of a small extension to the existing fermentor block. The structure rests on a piled foundation. Pre-development inspection and excavation of test-trenches (related to the relocation of services) revealed no medieval remains. Study of two previous phases of extension to the fermentor block had revealed an organic silt deposit, thought to be of possible medieval date, sealed by fill and below the formation level of the new structures (by this writer, *Excavations 1996*, 58, 95E0242, and by Edmond O'Donovan, *Excavations 1997*, 105, 97E0099).

Two 600mm-wide masonry wall foundations of post-medieval date, crossed through by services, were revealed within the development area, but these could not be identified with any particular phase of the site's history. Beneath fill and cut by these walls the organic silt deposit recorded in the previous investigations was found to continue into the extension area at the same depth as before.

For future development purposes a general historical study of the brewery site, incorporating existing archaeological records, is due to be undertaken in 1999.

Margaret Gowen, 2 Killiney View, Albert Road Lower, Glenageary, Co. Dublin.

360. 8 WILLIAM STREET, KILKENNY
Urban medieval
S505558
96E0155

Phase II of the monitoring of the excavation for foundations of the more easterly of two blocks of townhouses took place on 2 March 1998. (For Phase I, excavated by Jo Moran, see *Excavations 1996*, 60). No archaeological features were uncovered during this phase of monitoring.

Martin Reid, 37 Arrigal Road, Drimnagh, Dublin 12.

361. 21 WILLIAM STREET, KILKENNY
Urban
S50535582
98E0014

This work took place in response to a condition of the planning permission granted for the construction of a dental surgery to the rear of 21 William Street, a late 18th-century street. The site is within the area of the medieval town of Kilkenny and is bounded on its northern side by Guard Lane, a probable medieval laneway. Cartographic evidence suggests that there were no structures on this site in the mid-18th century. In the late 18th to mid-19th century three buildings were erected on the site, two facing onto Guard Lane and the extant No. 21. The Guard Lane buildings were demolished in the late 19th to early 20th centuries and the properties were amalgamated.

Four test-trenches were excavated to the rear of 21 William Street within the footprint of the proposed new building. They were excavated with a mini-digger and reached a maximum depth of 1.4m below present ground level. Nothing of archaeological significance was uncovered.

No further archaeological work is required on this site in advance of development.

James Eogan, Archaeological Development Services Ltd, Windsor House, 11 Fairview Strand, Fairview, Dublin 3.

362. LOUGHBOY
Ringforts
SMR 19:40, 19:41
98E0219

Testing and subsequent full excavation were carried out on foot of archaeological conditions imposed on a grant of planning permission by Kilkenny County Council to IDA Ireland for the construction of an industrial and business park at Loughboy, Co. Kilkenny. The conditions were necessary because of two circular enclosures shown in the area on the 1st edition 6-inch OS map but not now visible above ground. A report in the files of the National Museum of Ireland refers to the destruction of the two ringforts in the area in 1937, as well as the discovery of human remains. Test excavations were carried out under this licence in May 1998 by Sarah McCutcheon, during which archaeological features were uncovered. Full excavation followed in November 1998.

The enclosures lay on two low knolls on undulating ground with a general northwards slope towards Kilkenny City, which lies *c.* 1.5km to the north and is clearly visible from the site.

Despite extensive exploratory trenching no definite trace was found of the more easterly of the two sites (SMR 19:41). The depiction of this area in the 1945 edition of the 6-inch OS map suggests that the landscape had been modified, possibly by gravel quarrying. This is borne out by the evidence of landfill in the area in the form of extensive deposits of loose stone in a dark brown, loamy matrix containing fragments of brick and modern earthenware pottery.

The surviving remains of the most westerly site (SMR 19:40) comprise the base of a circular fosse enclosing an area *c.* 30m in diameter, with an entrance facing north. The fosse varied from 1m to 1.2m wide and from 0.53m to 0.65m deep, with a steep-sided V-shaped profile. The fill of the fosse contained a considerable quantity of animal bone. A secondary 'loop' ditch was also present, forming a subrectangular extension to the main site on the south, south-east and east sides.

Kilkenny

The only original features that survived within the ringfort were three charcoal spreads in the southern half of the enclosure. These contained some slag and molten metal, and close to one a fragment of a decorated bone comb was recovered. The latter compares well with Dunlevy's class C1, which she dates to the 4th–7th centuries AD.

In addition a number of human skeletons were found, concentrated in the south-east quadrant of the site. These were uncovered immediately below the topsoil. Many were in a fragmentary condition, probably because of the destruction of the site in 1937, but it appears that at least nineteen individuals were represented. Several of the skeletons were interred in the fill of the fosse, indicating that they post-dated the ringfort. The exact date of the skeletons is not yet known.

Eamonn Cotter, Ballynanelagh, Rathcormac, Co. Cork.

363. LOUGHBOY
Adjacent to ringforts
S505548
98E0282

The site lies in the townland of Loughboy in St Patrick's Parish, Co. Kilkenny. Two enclosure sites (SMR 19:40 and 19:11) are marked on the area of the proposed development. Test excavation by Sarah McCutcheon and later full excavation by Eamonn Cotter (see No. 362 above) established the presence of these features in the subsoil. This monitoring licence was for the stripping of topsoil in the south-east and north-east of the site, away from the enclosures. Initially work was carried out by Joanna Wren and John Purcell, and then Martin Reid took over the work and the licence.

No archaeological features were uncovered during the soil clearance work. Incidental finds included a clay pipe bowl, one sherd of post-medieval pottery and one sherd of late 13th/14th-century Leinster ware, like that found at nearby Kilferagh (Hurley 1987).

Reference
Hurley, M.F. 1987 A corn-drying kiln at Kiferagh, Co. Kilkenny. In R.M. Cleary, M.F. Hurley and E. Twohig (eds), *The archaeology of the Cork–Dublin gas pipeline.* University College Cork.

Joanna Wren and Martin Reid, c/o The Mile Post, Waterford.

364. MARKET STREET, THOMASTOWN
Urban medieval
25850 14187
98E0080

Three trenches were excavated in the area of a proposed extension behind 5 Market Street, Thomastown.

Trench 1 uncovered a late 17th/early 18th-century roughly paved surface, potentially associated with the early years of the building still standing. Trench 2 intercepted a wall likely to have been part of an early extension to the rear of the building (and replaced by the recently demolished kitchen). Floor level associated with the wall was 0.9m below present ground level. Trench 3 intercepted a length of the wall formerly running beside a lane between the two gables of the standing building beside Market Street.

A box 1m² was excavated a further 0.4m by hand in Trench 1, through the paving at the west end of the trench, onto a 12th/13th-century occupation level. An earlier series of clay and midden layers was separated from the 12th/13th-century occupation deposits by a band of sand and gravel. A significant amount of Ham Green sherds, probably from a single vessel, were found pressed into the earlier occupation deposits. Early surfacing in Trench 2 is likely to be of similar date. The flooring and midden deposits may belong to structures built against the north boundary wall.

The standing building was probably in use by the late 17th century (dating from pottery recovered in the test-trenches). It is currently two-storeyed, but the slightly irregular arrangement of the first-floor windows and door suggests an original single-storeyed building. The credit union building immediately to the north has been dated to the 17th century in an architectural survey.

Jo Moran, 33 Woodlawn, Cashel, Co. Tipperary.

365. MILL STREET, THOMASTOWN
Urban
25850 14187
SMR 28:40
98E0176

Testing was carried out in advance of the construction of a two-storey dwelling-house. The site lies on the eastern bank of the River Nore. There is a very substantial drop, *c.* 4m, from the site's present ground level to the river.

Two test-trenches were opened with the aid of a mechanical digger. Testing on the site had to be abandoned, and all site works have been deferred to mid-1999. This was due to the depth of built-up material (building rubble and debris) that had been imported onto the site. It was not possible to extend beneath the level of this material (it was at least 3m deep) or to determine whether archaeological remains survived beneath the rubble fill or the level of natural subsoils.

It is the intent of the owner of the site to carry out further pre-construction testing work with a larger machine and to establish the soil profile beneath the rubble fill. Further archaeological investigative work will be carried out sometime during 1999.

Mary Henry, 1 Jervis Place, Clonmel, Co. Tipperary.

LAOIS

366. BROOMVILLE GARDENS, BALLYROAN
No archaeological significance
248047 199176
98E0460

Archaeological trial-trenching was undertaken at a proposed housing development in the townland of Ballyroan, on the eastern outskirts of Portlaoise, in compliance with a condition included in a grant of planning. The work was undertaken on 3 October 1998. The development site lies in the general environs of a holy well (SMR13:43) and an enclosure site (SMR13:44).

Seven trenches, ranging from 38m to 110m long and *c.* 1.2 m wide, were opened by mechanical excavator. All were confined to the construction areas of the site.

No features, structures or finds of archaeological interest were uncovered, and it was therefore recommended that no further archaeological involvement was required.

Martin E. Byrne, 39 Kerdiff Park, Monread, Naas, Co. Kildare.

367. CARLOW NORTHERN RELIEF ROAD, GRAIGUE
Burnt spreads
27053 17720 (Site 1), 27048 17707 (Site 2), 27139 17770 (Site 3)
98E0382
Sites 1 and 2 were spreads of dark grey-brown soil, with some patches of charcoal, and black, charcoal-rich soil. They were 11m and 8m long, respectively, and at least 4m wide, but each continued beyond the take of the road. Deep ploughing had disturbed both, and Site 1 had been further disturbed by a drain. The only finds were modern bottle glass. Site 3 was a smaller spread of similar material, measuring 1.2m x 0.8m. A fragment of burnt bone was found here.

Thaddeus C. Breen, 13 Wainsfort Crescent, Dublin 6W, for Valerie J. Keeley Ltd.

368. KILMURRY
Vicinity of medieval/post-medieval church
98E0466
Archaeological monitoring was necessitated by the planned extension at the eastern end of a bungalow a short distance (6.5–7m) from the north-western corner of the apparently post-medieval (possibly late 16th/early 17th-century) church at Kilmurry.

An area measuring a maximum of 1.9m x 2.5m was opened directly in front of the front door of the house, to a maximum depth of 0.9m. Nothing of archaeological significance was noted.

Ten trenches of various sizes were machine-excavated and cleaned by hand in an area of *c.* 11m x 10m. No finds or archaeological deposits were present.

Jim Higgins, 'St Gerard's, 18 College Road, Galway.

369. SPA BRIDGE, PORTARLINGTON
Underwater survey
25425 21264
Laois County Council commissioned an underwater inspection to be carried out in the River Barrow in advance of construction works on the Spa Bridge, Portarlington. The survey area extended from *c.* 10m upstream of the bridge to a point *c.* 40m downstream of the bridge. A visual search and a licensed metal-detector survey revealed only one artefact of archaeological interest: a bronze ring of possible Later Bronze Age date. It was recovered from an upstream location and outside that of the proposed works.

Niall Brady, 'Rosbeg', Ard Mhuire Park, Dalkey, Co. Dublin, for Valerie J. Keeley Ltd.

370. PORTLAOISE GAOL AND COURTHOUSE, PORTLAOISE
Graveyard, 18th-century buildings
2470 1984
96E365 ext.
Archaeological testing and monitoring were carried at the courthouse and old gaol, Portlaoise, Co. Laois,

from December 1997 to February 1998. Thaddeus Breen had investigated three areas under this licence in 1996 (*Excavations 1996*, 62–3). Two areas were investigated during this current phase.

Trench 3 was dug in the south-west corner of the courtyard. It produced evidence of cellars associated with the courthouse and a cobbled area (pre-dating the present courthouse). The cobbled area was found to be quite extensive, as cobbles were found during monitoring in the courtyard area of the site to the south.

Trench 1 was dug outside the north-east gable of the gaol. A building had been recently demolished here. It produced a cobbled area that may be associated either with the building or with the other cobbles on the site previously mentioned.

During monitoring of foundation trenches in the courtyard six skeletons were discovered. They were orientated roughly north–south, and all but one had their heads to the south. All skeletons were supine, with evidence of coffins. Skeletons 75 and 81 were complete. Skeleton 73's feet were truncated by a wall to the south. Skeleton 79 had been disturbed by the foundation trench to the east. Skeleton 77 was truncated from the pelvis up. Skeleton 91 was truncated from the patellae up.

From the location of the surviving nails it can be suggested that the coffins were built of several pieces of wood tacked onto a frame. The coffin of Skeleton 75 seems to have had a thin iron band down the centre of the lid, which may have served to keep the coffin together or may have been a decorative strip. Evidence in support of the latter was found when, on closer examination of the metal, an impressed flower motif and swirls were noted. This gives the impression that some care was taken in the construction of the coffin. This is contrary to the impression given by the feet (they were squashed into the coffins) and the incorrect orientation. Perhaps the metal band was reused. It can be suggested that the coffins were built to a standard size as consideration was not given to individuals' dimensions.

The fills produced post-medieval pottery sherds, glass and animal bone. The only directly associated finds were a copper-alloy shroud-pin on Skeleton 73 and the coffin nails and metal.

Further monitoring did not reveal anything of archaeological significance.

Fiona Reilly, Wood Road, Cratloekeel, Co. Clare, for Valerie J. Keeley Ltd.

371. OLD GAOL/COURTHOUSE, PORTLAOISE
18th-century building
2470 1984
96E0365
Archaeological monitoring was carried out in October 1998 on the final phase of ground disturbance works associated with the upgrading of Portlaoise Courthouse and the redevelopment of the old gaol into a new arts centre. The courthouse was built in 1789 and replaced an earlier structure destroyed by fire. The gaol was built at around the same time and remained in use until 1830, from when it functioned as an RIC barracks, until the 1860s. It was converted into a public library in the 1950s.

Two phases of trial-trenching and monitoring preceded this programme of monitoring and were carried out between December 1996 and February 1998 (by Thaddeus Breen, *Excavations 1996*, 62–3, 96E0277, and Fiona Reilly, No. 370 above). These investigations found the remains of a graveyard in the courtyard of the old gaol, a cobbled surface that pre-dated part of the gaol and the remains of a structure outside its eastern wall.

Five service trenches were excavated as part of the development, three in the courtyard on the eastern side of the courthouse (Trenches 1, 4 and 5) and two outside the eastern wall of the old gaol (Trenches 2 and 3).

Trench 1 (22m long, 1.2m wide) revealed two phases of activity. Phase 1 consisted of a small pit cutting the natural clay at the southern end of the trench, which was filled with organic material containing 18th-century pottery. To the north of Trench 1 a large feature cutting natural was revealed. This was filled with heavy clays containing animal bone and occasional sherds of 18th-century pottery. This feature was cut by a large north–south-orientated limestone wall, 14.85m long, which also extended into Trench 4 (9.77m long, 2.65m wide), to the south.

This feature was one of two walls making up Phase 2; the second was orientated east–west and ran off at a right angle from the first. It is likely that these walls formed part of ancillary structures associated with the courthouse.

To the east of the old gaol Trench 2 (44.2m long, up to 1.7m wide) exposed two phases of archaeological activity. Phase 1 consisted of a large east–west-orientated pit, which extended into Trench 3 to the west, giving it a minimum length of 4.6m. It was 1.87m wide and 0.95m deep. The pit was lined with organic waste and backfilled with heavy clays. It also showed evidence of having been recut. Phase 2 consisted of the remains of a north–south-orientated limestone wall exposed for 4.1m in section, which was abutted by an east–west-orientated wall to the west of it. This wall continued into the adjacent Trench 3, where the remains of a disturbed cobble and flagstone surface were exposed 1.6m to the south of it. These two walls formed part of the boundary wall enclosing the gaol precinct.

To the north of Trench 3 sections of the southern and eastern walls of a previously identified structure were revealed. These walls enclosed the remains of a cobbled surface. The surface was sealed in places by a compact layer of cess and overlay the earlier pit described above. It is likely that this structure functioned as a stable, possibly associated with the RIC barracks.

Rob Lynch, Irish Archaeological Consultancy Ltd, 8 Dungar Terrace, Dun Laoghaire, Co. Dublin, for Valerie J. Keeley Ltd.

LEITRIM

372. CARRICK-ON-SHANNON
Post-medieval urban
194456 300018
98E0248
Archaeological assessment took place at the site of a proposed commercial development at Carrick-on-Shannon, Co. Leitrim. The town was a former post-medieval borough. Three trenches were excavated on the site in the south of the town. Large quantities of modern rubble were excavated to depths of 3m, below which was the natural peaty soil of the riverbank. No archaeological features or objects were recovered.
Donald Murphy, Archaeological Consultancy Services Ltd, 15 Trinity Street, Drogheda, Co. Louth.

373. WATER STREET, MOHILL
Urban
N089976
98E0201
Testing took place on 28 April 1998. Three trenches were machine-excavated down to undisturbed natural, without encountering anything of archaeological significance. Bedrock was encountered at *c.* 47m OD, although it sloped down along the eastern edge of the site, where a small stream flows.

The results suggest that beneath the present grass-covered surface and associated turf line post-medieval layers lie either on till or directly on bedrock.

Nothing of archaeological significance was uncovered during the assessment.
Eoin Halpin, Archaeological Development Services Ltd, Unit 48, Westlink Enterprise Centre, 30–50 Distillery Street, Belfast BT12 5BJ.

LIMERICK

374. ADARE MANOR GOLF CLUB, ADARE
Part of historic town
R470469
SMR 21:32
This site lies to the north-east of the graveyard and within the zone of archaeological potential. The development consisted of two extensions to the existing clubhouse, one to the north and another to the east, and the construction of a new road on the north side of the building. A single condition attached to the planning permission was that an archaeologist be present to monitor all digging. When the site was visited it was found that construction was at an advanced stage, with all foundations cut, block-work in progress and the proposed new access in place.

In the eastern extension, where, at the time of inspection, the block-work was two courses high, what appeared to be spoil from the cuts was piled into the centre. It consisted of mixed, brown, clay-type soil, with a high stone content. Two small sherds of post-medieval brownware were recovered. To the north of the carpark near the main road was a long pile of spoil, which, it was assumed, originated from the site. A single sherd of medieval pottery was recovered from its north-eastern end. Also noted along the length were oyster shells, animal bone, 19th-century crockery, red brick and glass.

The presence of the medieval sherd suggests that there was evidence of archaeological activity that should have been identified earlier and handled in the proper way.
Celie O Rahilly, Limerick Corporation, City Hall, Limerick.

375. ADARE MANOR, ADARE
Medieval borough
R468461
SMR 21:32
It was proposed to carry out percolation testing in the grounds of Adare Manor in the area of a proposed treatment plant within the zone of archaeological potential as defined by both the Urban Survey and the Recorded Monuments Map. Unlicensed monitoring of the work was carried out.

Initially an area measuring 2m east–west by 1.7m and 0.6m deep was opened. Eleven sherds of medieval pottery were recovered from the spoil, and the work was stopped. Also noted in the southern section of the cutting were a possible pit or ditch and a deposit of possible ash, charcoal, animal bone and some stones.

A second attempt was made to do a cutting *c.* 80m south of the first. This was 1.9m north–south by 0.8m and was 0.2m deep. On removal of the sod two sherds, one broken base and one glazed body sherd, were recovered. The work was stopped.

Between the two cuttings and in the area around is a series of low mounds, which may reflect features relating to a medieval settlement. A possible barrow noted during the field-walking lay to the north-east, and a medieval building (?tower) is to the north-north-west.
Celie O Rahilly, Limerick Corporation, City Hall, Limerick.

376. ASHFORT
Ringfort or ringwork
SMR 13:76
R550512
97E0285 ext.
An archaeological assessment was carried out at this site during the summer of 1997, before the construction of the proposed N20/N21 Adare–Annacotty road scheme (*Excavations 1997*, 110). The line of the road will remove approximately half of the ringfort, and therefore further excavation was required during the summer of 1998.

The monument is *c.* 30m in diameter, with a still extant bank measuring in places more than 1m above present ground surface. Five sections were manually excavated through the external, enclosing ditch. These showed the ditch to be roughly U-shaped and on average 4.2m wide and 1.5m deep. The remainder of the ditch was removed by a mechanical digger. The ditch was filled to a large extent by slippage from the bank, and no organic remains were uncovered. The only datable artefact from the fill was a sherd of medieval pottery, most probably of local production.

The bank was composed of redeposited subsoil, almost certainly upcast from the ditch construction. Within the bank, two whetstones and part of a rotary quern were recovered. Internal features consisted of a scatter of post-holes, which indicated no apparent structure. Also revealed were the upper torso and skull of a small child, within a roughly cut, shallow pit. The cut of the pit was evident in the later build-up of material, indicating that the deposition belonged to a period after the use of the monument and was not associated with it. Most probably the child was interred here during the post-medieval period.

While no evidence of any real internal structure could be identified, either during excavation or previously during assessment, it may be suggested that this monument was not for domestic habitation. Further, the location of the medieval pottery, as well as a silver coin found during assessment, may indicate that the site dates to the medieval and not the Early Christian period and may be a ringwork rather than a ringfort. However, this assumption remains tentative as insufficient evidence exists to offer conclusive proof.
Audrey Gahan, Archaeological Development Services Ltd, Unit 48, Westlink Enterprise Centre, 30–50 Distillery Street, Belfast BT12 5BJ.

377. ASKEATON
Historic town
R340505
SMR 11:92
98E0585
Groundwork for the construction of a feed store/shop on land at the northern end of the town of Askeaton was monitored between 17 December 1998 and 13 January 1999. The stripping of topsoil and the digging of foundation and service trenches revealed that the site was used for quarrying limestone until relatively recently and then restored with sand and gravel, redeposited boulder clay and topsoil. No archaeological features were noted.
Kenneth Wiggins, 17 Vartry Close, Raheen, Co. Limerick.

378. ATTYFLYN
No archaeological significance
15164 14901
97E0476
Assessment excavations were undertaken at this site on 28–9 January 1998. The area to be investigated lay along the route of the proposed Adare–Annacotty Bypass, between two known archaeological sites. These were both probable *fulachta fiadh* (AR8 and AR8A), and the excavation was undertaken to assess the possibility of there being further archaeological evidence in the area. A previous geophysical survey identified an anomaly to the west of AR8. This was orientated north-west/south-east for a distance of *c.* 24m and had a maximum width of 1m.

The site lay in two adjacent fields, close to the N20 Cork–Limerick road, in Attyflyn townland, Co. Limerick. The field to the south of the main field boundary was designated Area 1, while the field to the north was termed Area 2. Both fields sloped gently to the east and contained areas of wet ground.

Ten trenches encompassing 610m^2 were excavated by machine. All were *c.* 2m wide and varied from 15m (Trench 1) to 45m (Trench 6) long. Area 1 contained three trenches (Trenches 1–3), and Area 2 contained seven (Trenches 4–10).

Two trenches were excavated across the line of the geophysical anomaly in Area 1, but nothing of archaeological significance was uncovered. The anomaly can most likely be attributed to readings created by a band of orange-pink clay in Trench 2 and a patch of very stony subsoil in Trench 1. Both the clay and the stones were naturally occurring and therefore do not represent archaeological features.

Nothing of archaeological significance was uncovered in any of the other eight trenches.

Paul Logue, Archaeological Development Services Ltd, Unit 48, Westlink Enterprise Centre, 30–50 Distillery Street, Belfast BT12 5BJ.

379. ATTYFLIN
Burnt mound
15164 14901
SMR 21:122
97E476 ext.

During 1997 Cia McConway carried out an assessment at this monument (*Excavations 1997*, 110–11, 96E379) that showed the site to be a burnt mound with possible later activity. The proposed Adare–Annacotty N20/N21 road, while not directly removing the mound itself, will pass very close to it. Therefore, it was decided that topsoil in the affected area be removed under archaeological supervision.

An area of *c.* 22m (roughly north–south) by 11m was stripped by mechanical digger using a toothless bucket. Removal of the topsoil revealed evidence of a random scatter of small pits or post-holes. In all, 23 features of this nature were excavated. Although no artefacts that could date the features were uncovered, it is most probable that they relate to one or both of the two phases of activity on the site.

Audrey Gahan, Archaeological Development Services Ltd, Unit 48, Westlink Enterprise Centre, 30–50 Distillery Street, Belfast BT12 5BJ.

380. ATTYFLIN
Burnt mound
R520491
97E0291 ext.

This site was previously tested at the assessment stage of the Adare–Annacotty N20/N21 road scheme (*Excavations 1997*, 111). It was identified as a burnt mound. As the road will destroy the site, full excavation took place during the summer of 1998.

The mound measures *c.* 15m x 13m and is slightly crescent-shaped. It was constructed of layers of heat-shattered stone, within charcoal-stained soils. Within the hollow area of the crescent, roughly on the northern side of the mound, a trough was uncovered. This measured *c.* 4m east–west and was 3.2m at its widest north–south. The trough was shelved or stepped, being 0.4m below present ground level, dropping to 0.7m at its deepest.

The area surrounding the burnt mound, along the line of the road, was mechanically stripped of topsoil to investigate whether there were any associated structures. A random scatter of post-holes or small pits was uncovered, which did not appear to form any structure or pattern. It is most likely that they belong to the phase of activity of the burnt mound.

No artefacts that could date the site were uncovered, but it is most likely of Bronze Age date.

Audrey Gahan, Archaeological Development Services Ltd, Unit 48, Westlink Enterprise Centre, 30–50 Distillery Street, Belfast BT12 5BJ.

381. BALLYCLOGH
Circular depression
98E0490

Commissioned by Limerick County Council, this work involved the investigation of a number of possible sites in advance of the Limerick Southern Ring Road.

The site was first identified by Celie O Rahilly during the course of fieldwork for the archaeological impact assessment for the road, and she recommended testing to establish the archaeological merit of the site.

The site consisted of a circular, almost flat-bottomed depression, in an area of poor-quality grassland. It measured 12m in diameter with possible traces of an enclosing bank on the east side. Two test-trenches were manually excavated to determine the archaeological potential of the site. Both revealed boulder clay directly below topsoil. No features or artefacts of archaeological significance were encountered.

Martin Fitzpatrick, Archaeological Consultancy, Ballydavid South, Athenry, Co. Galway, in conjunction with Aegis Archaeology Ltd.

382. BALLYCUMMIN
Pits, post-holes
R546521
98E0108

Excavations were undertaken at this site during the periods 2–20 March and 12 May–2 June 1998. The work was carried out in advance of road construction, on behalf of the Road Design Office, Limerick County Council. The site lies in former grounds of Roche Castle, Raheen, Co. Limerick, *c.* 1km south of the existing N20/21 Limerick–Cork road.

The excavation consisted of two large trenches, Areas 1 and 2, measuring 100m x 10m and 65m x 11m respectively. Area 1 contained twelve features of archaeological significance. The largest of these was a curvilinear gully measuring 6m north-west/south-east x 1.1m with a maximum depth of 0.5m. The other features uncovered in Area 1 had an average diameter of 0.2m and maximum depth of 0.15m. They most likely represent the remains of truncated post-holes. No artefacts were recovered during the excavation of this area.

Area 2 contained seventy features of archaeological significance. A line of three subcircular pits and a grouping of larger subrectangular pits seemed to divide the central part of the area, with groupings of smaller pits and post-holes to the east and west of them. The three subcircular pits had an average diameter of 0.75m and maximum depth of 0.7m, with the larger pits having average excavated dimensions of 2.5m x 1.5m and depths of 0.5m.

To the east of this division was a grouping of thirteen post-holes, one shallow gully and three stake-holes. The post-holes were all subcircular in plan and had an average diameter of 0.3m. The fills of these post-holes were similar, mainly being a mottled brown, charcoal-flecked, loam soil. Despite these similarities and an even spacing between the features no definite structural pattern could be defined from the outline of the post-holes.

To the west of the division was a grouping of fifteen post-holes and five shallow pits. Within this grouping the partial remains of one likely structure could be discerned. It was formed by an arc of six post-holes containing similar fills and possibly associated with a seventh post-hole 0.3m outside the arc to the north-east. Adjacent to the eastern edge of the structure an arc of four shallow pits was exposed. The positioning of the pits respected the arc of the structure and as such may relate to it in some way.

A penannular-shaped gully was uncovered in the southern part of Area 2 at a distance of 14m from the partial structure. This had a maximum width of 0.6m and a maximum depth of 0.3m. It partially enclosed an area measuring 3.9m north–south x 3.8m, with the open end to the south. The upper fill of the cut contained the remains of at least two charcoalised timber planks, possibly indicating a structural purpose for the cut. Two large, paired post-holes were uncovered 0.5m to the north of the penannular cut, with a second set of paired post-holes 1.1m east of the cut.

The artefacts recovered from Area 2 include one spindle whorl, several saddle quern fragments and many sherds of coarseware pottery. All the finds are likely to be of Bronze Age date.
Paul Logue, Archaeological Development Services Ltd, Unit 48, Westlink Enterprise Centre, 30–50 Distillery Street, Belfast BT12 5BJ.

383. BALLYCUMMIN
Prehistoric
R148292
98E0504 and ext.
The Loughmore Link represents a stretch of *c.* 750m of the proposed N20/N21 Adare–Annacotty road scheme, within the townland of Ballycummin, Co. Limerick. Removal of topsoil along this part of the road was monitored for archaeological material. Five areas of archaeological significance were identified and excavated. In all cases the features survived only where they cut subsoil, the result of generations of farmland development.

Area 1 consisted of an arc of small pits and post-holes filled with charcoal-rich soils. It is possible that the site, which was *c.* 7m in diameter, represents the heavily truncated remains of a circular hut, of probable prehistoric (Bronze Age?) date.

Area 2 was adjacent to an area previously excavated by Paul Logue (No. 382 above), where substantial evidence of Bronze Age activity was uncovered. Most likely this area was an extension of that activity. The site itself consisted of around 40 post-holes and pits. No discernible structure could be identified, and a saddle quern, within one of the pits, represented the only artefact from the site.

The remaining three areas investigated consisted of random scatters of pits and post-holes. Truncation in the area means that no discernible structures could be identified. No artefacts that could conclusively date the sites were recovered, but, as with the rest of the archaeology within this area, it appears most likely that they date to the prehistoric period.
Audrey Gahan, Archaeological Development Services Ltd, Unit 48, Westlink Enterprise Centre, 30–50 Distillery Street, Belfast BT12 5BJ.

384. BALLYGRENNAN
Possible settlement
R552590
SMR 5:39
98E0321
The site, on the north-eastern side of the Old Cratloe Road, was bordered to the south-east by Galtee Avenue, originally a road leading to a farm, now defining the western limits of a housing estate. To the north-western side it was defined by the townland boundary, and to the north-eastern by a field boundary. On the earlier maps there was a north-east by south-west subdivision of the field. The eastern field was slightly elevated; the western one, low-lying and prone to flooding, was, along the western and northern boundaries, permanently marshy. A possible settlement (Down Survey maps) was marked partly on this side of the western boundary.

The topsoil-stripping of the area of the proposed development was monitored. With the exception of a localised spread of burnt stone and a pit/ditch, which it was not possible to date, there was no trace of any activity pre-19th century, and this consisted mainly of attempts to drain the land. The area where the 'possible settlement' was allegedly situated was particularly prone to flooding. The level ground on this part of the site, together with the high level of the impermeable clay, has resulted in a total lack of natural soakage. If there had been a settlement it is more likely that it was either on the higher ground to the east or outside the area of the proposed development, i.e. to the west or south.
Celie O Rahilly, Limerick Corporation, City Hall, Limerick.

385. BALLYMACKEOGH–MULKEAR CERTIFIED DRAINAGE SCHEME
Riverine sites
R643577
97E0350, incorporating Metal-Detection Licence 97R0030
This project was carried out by the engineering services of the OPW and involved the embanking of a portion of the Mulkear River and its tributaries, from its confluence with the River Shannon near Annacotty, Co. Limerick, northward to Newport, Co. Tipperary. The scheme began in May 1997 and continued until December 1998.

During the scheme all bridges were repaired, new sluices were constructed, drains were deepened and widened, the rivers were embanked at places prone to flooding and a stretch of the Newport River was dredged. During this time all the works were monitored by the project archaeologist, who was appointed to the scheme in August 1997.

An Environmental Impact Survey (EIS), which detailed all features of archaeological and cultural heritage significance along the route of the scheme, was carried out in 1996. These included fording points, limekilns, bridges and enclosures. During the scheme the works came close to the EIS sites, but none was negatively affected by it. Several of the sites identified in the EIS document, such as the fords, were found to have been replaced with modern bridges, and none of the limekilns was encountered. An underwater survey of a bridge at Bunkey and a weir at Annacotty, Co. Limerick, was undertaken before their demolition.

The portion of the Newport River that was dredged and embanked during the scheme was monitored, with the spoil being deposited and spread on the banks and metal-detected before being made into embankments.

During the monitoring of the scheme and the metal-detection survey, despite the works being in

Limerick

close proximity to several known archaeological sites, nothing of an archaeological nature was discovered. It was noted during the scheme that a sandstone trough and the upper portion of a rotary quernstone were in the possession of a farmer at Killeenagarriff, Co. Limerick, and were reported to the National Museum of Ireland.
Tracy Collins, Aegis Archaeology Ltd, 1 Ardara, Fairies Cross, Tralee, Co. Kerry.

386. BALLYSIMON I
No archaeological significance
16219 15505
SMR 5:71
98E0484
The site investigated as part of pre-development testing in advance of Limerick Southern Ring Road was thought to be a possible hut site. It transpired that it was a modern dump of stones, barbed wire etc., with occasional finds of modern pottery and glass. It was of no archaeological significance.
Frank Coyne, Aegis Archaeology, 24 Castle Court, Clancy Strand, Limerick.

387. BALLYSIMON II
Possible enclosure
16201 15517
SMR 5:70
98E0485
This site was identified in the Environmental Impact Survey of the Limerick Southern Ring Road (1994) as a possible circular enclosure, on the right bank of the River Groody. Two hand-dug test-trenches were opened to investigate it.

Trench A, 7m x 1.5m, was cut in a north–south direction to ascertain whether there was an enclosing element around the enclosure. It lay in the south-western quadrant of the site. Trench B, 6m x 1m, was cut in a north-east to south-west direction in the north-eastern quadrant of the site, to investigate the nature of the enclosure and to reveal any enclosing element.

The test-trenching concluded that the site was of no archaeological significance and may have been naturally created from the flooding waters of the adjacent river. Finds were two fragments of clear bottle glass and one sherd of modern willow pattern pottery, both from the topsoil of Trench A.
Tracy Collins, Aegis Archaeology Ltd, 1 Ardara, Fairies Cross, Tralee, Co. Kerry.

388. BALLYSIMON III, AR23
Possible mill?
16173 15507
SMR 5:42
98E0486
This site was investigated as part of pre-development testing in advance of the Limerick Southern Ring Road. Four trenches were inserted to ascertain whether an earlier building, most likely a mill, had stood on the site.

The first trench showed that a stretch of walling along the right bank of the Groody River probably functioned as a revetting wall, holding back the high ground to the north. Finds of pottery and glass from this trench showed that the wall was constructed in relatively modern times. The remaining trenches did not reveal an earlier structure, the natural boulder clay being encountered immediately below the topsoil. It is possible that this site was the headrace for Ballysimon mill, which lies further to the north-east.
Frank Coyne, Aegis Archaeology, 24 Castle Court, Clancy Strand, Limerick.

389. BALLYSIMON III
Water mill
16149 15543
SMR 5:41
98E607
This site is marked as a mill on the 17th-century Down Survey Map of the area. There is a small building *c.* 5m x 7m) at this location, of undressed limestone of roughly coursed rubble construction.

The building was investigated to see whether this was the 17th-century structure or there had been an earlier building at this site. Owing to the recent usage of the site as a creamery and later a farmyard the only available position for a trench was in the interior of the extant structure. Because of the unstable condition of much of the remains, a trench, 1.5m x 3.5m, was hand-excavated in the south-east corner of the building.

The mill had been filled with a large amount of modern debris, such as household refuse and loose masonry (no architectural features were noted). The original floor surface was of rough cobbles and a reused limestone flag. The floor was set in a bed of gritty, white mortar with a brick, stone and mortar mix below as a foundation. The walls of the structure rested on the underlying red boulder clay material, with the east wall being partially strengthened by the addition of a plinth, 0.1m wide, along its base. This strengthening, it is assumed, would have made the wall more secure, as it was the wall that would have held the original overshot wheel. It would also have guarded against the wall being undermined by the lapping of the mill-race water.

The investigation did not reveal any artefacts of archaeological significance and proved that an earlier building did not exist on the site of the extant mill structure.
Tracy Collins, Aegis Archaeology Ltd, 1 Ardara, Fairies Cross, Tralee, Co. Kerry.

390. BALLYSIMON
D-shaped enclosure
98E0487
Funded by Limerick County Council, this work involved the investigation of a number of possible sites in advance of the Limerick Southern Ring Road. This site was first identified by Celie O Rahilly during the course of fieldwork for the impact assessment for the road. The area was interpreted as having a series of possible cultivation ridges to the north of the church and graveyard at Ballysimon.

From a study of the aerial photographs a possible D-shaped enclosure was identified. Four trenches were excavated, and in two of these the remains of a ditch were revealed, which was 3.5m wide and 1.4m deep. Finds included one fragment of medieval pottery and a fragment of lead, possibly part of a lead mount.
Fiona Rooney, Archaeological Consultancy, Ballydavid South, Athenry, Co. Galway, in conjunction with Aegis Archaeology Ltd.

391. BOHEREEN
Sub-circular enclosure
98E0524

Funded by Limerick County Council, this work involved the investigation of a number of possible sites in advance of the Limerick Southern Ring Road. This site was first identified by Celie O Rahilly during the course of fieldwork for the archaeological impact assessment for the road. She identified the feature as an enclosure with a possible associated bank and recommended testing to establish the archaeological merit of the site.

Two test-trenches were manually excavated. No features or artefacts of archaeological significance were encountered.

Fiona Rooney, Archaeological Consultancy, Ballydavid South, Athenry, Co. Galway, in conjunction with Aegis Archaeology Ltd.

392. CAPPAMORE
Monitoring
777 515
98E0313

Construction of a diversion channel and flood-relief works at Cappamore, carried out by the Engineering Section of the OPW, were monitored from July to September. No archaeological remains were encountered during the initial topsoil-stripping phase of the development. As part of this development entailed the widening and deepening of the Bilboa River, it was necessary to test all dredged material with a metal-detector. One artefact was recovered, an iron salmon spear of possible post-medieval date, although spears of this type have continued in use into this century.

Frank Coyne, Aegis Archaeology, 24 Castle Court, Clancy Strand, Limerick.

393. CROMWELL'S ROAD, CASTLECONNELL
Late medieval roadway
SMR 32:7
98E0429

Testing was carried out on the 'Track of Cromwell's Road', Castleconnell, Co. Limerick, in advance of gasworks from Limerick to Ballina, Co. Tipperary, via Castleconnell, Co. Limerick. The road name appears to derive from the activities of General Ireton (Cromwell's son-in-law) in 1651.

Two test-trenches, A (1m x 4m) and B (1m x 5m), were tested to a depth of 1m and revealed a similar stratigraphic sequence but no finds. At *c.* 0.47m below the modern road surface iron panning occurred over a compacted, sandy clay surface. This may represent an original dirt track or road. If this was a dirt track there is no evidence that it was manipulated or altered in any way but was merely used as a routeway. The underlying strata appeared to be sterile natural deposits. The first road surfacing occurred with the insertion of a crude layer of cobbling or metalling, set into a bed of fine sand, probably in the 19th/20th century. Above this was a series of modern tarmac road surfaces. The gas pipeline was monitored through the rest of the roadway (although some areas were drilled), which revealed a similar array of sterile clays.

If this was the route taken by Ireton's forces their presence appears to have been marked by name only.

Kenneth Hanley, 44 Eaton Heights, Cobh, Co. Cork.

394. CLOGHACLOKA
Fulacht fiadh
R534504
98E0159

Excavations were carried out from 2 March 1998 to 14 April 1998. The work was undertaken in advance of road construction, on behalf of the Road Design Office, Limerick County Council.

The site, a *fulacht fiadh*, measured 24m north-east/south-west x 18m and lay in marshy, low-lying land close to the canalised remnant of a small stream. It contained two main phases of activity, the earliest of which consisted of a low mound of burnt stone fragments in a grey-green, loam clay matrix. This phase was associated with a trough 1.8m north-east/south-west x 1.2m and 0.2m in maximum depth. The trough was cut into the subsoil from the north around clockwise to the south. The south-western through to north-western sides of the trough were formed by the building of a wall of stones and redeposited clay subsoil. Evidence was also uncovered to suggest that the trough was deepened by the continuation of the clay wall around its entire circuit. Internally the trough contained nine large stake-holes, most likely to support a wooden lining. A contemporary stone surface extended from the trough west to the stream.

The early surface and trough were both overlain by a second, similar stone surface associated with a second trough 7.4m to the north. This second cut measured 3m east–west x 1.35m. The base was lined with clay and stones, and overlying this the sides of the cut were lined with a second deposit of clay and stones. This deposit was thickened and heightened above the old ground level, creating a wall similar to that surrounding the earlier trough. The clay wall was most likely supported on the exterior by stakes. Evidence of these was found around the circuit of the cut as stake-holes adjacent to the outer face of the wall. This method of construction formed a trough measuring 2.8m east–west x 0.7m and 0.55m in maximum depth. The trough was contemporary with two small hearths to the north and east.

A third trough was uncovered adjacent to the south-west. It measured 1.58m north–south x 1.6m and had a maximum excavated depth of 0.4m. The cut contained seven large stake-holes, most likely providing the framework support for a wood-lined trough. Excavation suggests that the trough was deepened by the addition of a clay wall from the south-west clockwise around to the north-west. This trough cut the stone surface that serviced the secondary trough and was associated with one small hearth to the north and also the reuse of part of the secondary trough as a hearth.

Both the second and final troughs were filled by material from the upper phase of the mound, a mix of burnt stone and loose, black soil.

All features were cut into the compact, orange clay subsoil. The clay was maximum of 0.4m deep and overlay a gravel subsoil. The clay subsoil formed a capping on top of the gravel layer, with the base of the clay dictating the level of the water table. Any feature cutting below the base of the clay would immediately flood with water. Hence the three troughs were given the required depth by creating a shallow cut into the clay and raising the sides with the excavated subsoil as a water-tight clay wall.

Paul Logue, Archaeological Development Services Ltd, Unit 48, Westlink Enterprise Centre, 30–50 Distillery Street, Belfast BT12 5BJ.

395. CUSH
Enclosure
16990 12587
SMR 48:03406
98E0392

Dúchas The Heritage Service acquired a site within the large field system SMR 48:03401, which contains the remains of 23 other monuments. One of these, the enclosure 48:03406, lay within the new site. Owing to its location within a known archaeological site, the erection of permanent fencing around the site was monitored. No evidence of archaeological activity was uncovered.

Mary O'Donnell, Archaeological Services Unit, University College Cork.

396. GARRAUN
Subcircular enclosure
98E0489

Commissioned by Limerick County Council, this work involved the investigation of a number of possible sites in advance of the Limerick Southern Ring Road.

The site consisted of a central hollow that measured 22m and was partially enclosed by a low bank 0.4m high. Two test-trenches were manually excavated. Both revealed the natural layers directly below topsoil. No features or artefacts of archaeological significance were encountered.

Fiona Rooney, Archaeological Consultancy, Ballydavid South, Athenry, Co. Galway, in conjunction with Aegis Archaeology Ltd.

397. GARRYGLASS/TOWLERTON I
Linear earthwork
16106 15568
SMR 5:67
98E0488

This site was identified as a trackway in the Environmental Impact Survey attached to the development of the Limerick Southern Ring Road (1994). Testing was recommended to establish the archaeological merit of the site. It consisted of a raised linear trackway running north-east to south-west in an otherwise flat field.

One trench, 1m x 8.5m, was dug by hand across the feature, orientated north-west to south-east. It was found that the track was modern in date, as large amounts of modern pottery and stone had been used as metalling for the track surface. It was not of archaeological significance.

Tracy Collins, Aegis Archaeology Ltd, 1 Ardara, Fairies Cross, Tralee, Co. Kerry.

398. GORTADROMA
Holy well
R220432
SMR 18:93
98E0467

An archaeological assessment took place in October 1998 for a proposed extension to a landfill site at Gortadroma, Co. Limerick. The development lies south of the town of Foynes and the River Shannon. It was proposed to develop north of the current landfill in an area measuring 415m east–west x 360m, incorporating the site of a holy well. The holy well could not be found during the field inspection for an Environmental Impact Survey, so test-trenching within a 20m zone around the suggested location of the monument was recommended.

Four linear test-trenches were opened, 10m long, 2.5m wide and 0.3m–1m deep. The soil profile suggested that the area had been quarried of sand before disturbance by the current development. The assessment revealed no evidence of surviving archaeological deposits or features associated with the holy well. The suggested location of the well, marked on the 1st edition OS map, places the site within an area of the site already quarried before assessment.

Paul Stevens for Margaret Gowen & Co. Ltd, 2 Killiney View, Albert Road Lower, Glenageary, Co. Dublin.

399. AR2, GORTEEN
Rectangular moated enclosure
14996 14781
SMR 21:17
97E0339 ext.

Excavations at AR2, at Gorteen, Co. Limerick, began on 4 November 1998, in advance of road development on the N20 Limerick Bypass scheme and were completed on 15 January 1999. Audrey Gahan uncovered the site, marked in the OS Memoirs as a possible ringfort, through trial-trenching the previous summer (*Excavations 1997*, 114–15). Only part of the monument lay within the line and take of the road, thus only this portion of the site was to be excavated.

Audrey Gahan had opened a trench, roughly 60m x 15m, along the take of the road in the area of the monument. This revealed part of a rectangular ditched enclosure. The north-west corner of the enclosure, along with its west-facing line running south-west for a distance of 13.5m and the north-east-facing line running south-east for a distance of 31.5m, had been uncovered. Other activity within this trench included two earlier gully features and a number of shallow, pit-like features external to the enclosure.

The ditch itself was fairly uniform in construction, ranging from a V-shaped to U-shaped cut and 3.72m in diameter at its widest point and 2.38m at its narrowest. The depth ranged from 1.43m to 0.2m. At a distance of 20m along the west-facing line of the enclosure from the corner the base of the ditch rose to a depth of 0.2m to form a step, some 3.25m long, before dropping back to the V-shaped cut ditch.

The fill of the ditch was fairly uniform throughout, showing evidence of silting over time. However, portions of the ditch were particularly stony in nature and may have represented the slump of an associated bank with stone facing. The fill also produced a quantity of animal bone and seashell material, along with a sherd of medieval pottery. Parts of the inner face of the ditch had been revetted with stone. This occurred in areas where there had been earlier activity and the edge of the ditch was structurally unsafe. At a distance of *c*. 9.5m south-

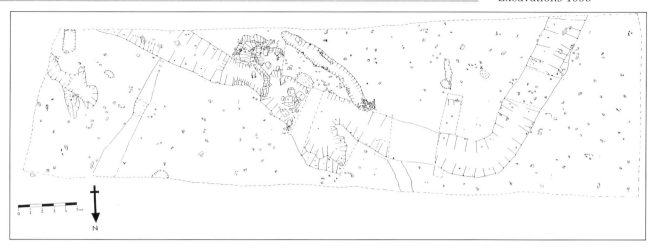

Post-excavation plan of the medieval ditched enclosure at Gorteen, Co. Limerick.

east of the corner of the ditch an earlier drain was uncovered running north-west/south-east. Here the inner face of the enclosure ditch was revetted with a dry-stone face, 2m long and 0.42m deep. This earlier drain was V-shaped in section, 1.1m wide and 0.5m deep, containing a stony fill. At a distance of *c.* 31m south-east of the north-west corner another stone facing was uncovered in an area where another earlier ditch had been. This ditch again ran north-west/south-east and was *c.* 13.5m long, 3.5m wide and 0.86m deep, becoming shallower (0.44m) at its north-west terminal.

That parts of the inner face of the enclosure's ditch were revetted, along with the large quantities of stone within the ditch fill, is evidence that the enclosure may have had an inner bank.

The only features found within the enclosure were two very shallow, truncated pits with no obvious function.

Externally in the east end of the trench a number of features were found. The first of these was a small pit, 9m to the north of the ditch, which contained a charcoal-rich fill with burnt stone. This feature may represent a rubbish pit. The other features in this area were two elongated gullies. The earlier (which was cut by the later) ran north–south and measured 4m x 0.98m x 0.3m. The later feature ran north-east/south-west for a distance of *c.* 5m into the east section of the trench and was 1.15m wide and 0.4m deep. Approximately 1.5m south of these two gullies was another shallow, elongated pit, running into the south section of the trench. This was filled by a dark, peaty, silty material, which contained a number of stones. To the west of this group of features was a furrow, which had been subsequently cut by the enclosure's ditch.

The results of excavations at AR2 further proved the existence of a rectangular moated enclosure of medieval date. This would have consisted of a rectangular ditch and possible inner bank. However, no evidence was produced from the excavation of an inner raised platform, nor was there any evidence of any internal structure. This lack of evidence, however, is probably due to the fact that not enough of the inside of the enclosure was included in the area of excavation.

The evidence of earlier activity on site was limited to a series of gullies and an earlier ditch,

none of which produced any dating evidence.
Ciara MacManus, c/o Archaeological Development Services Ltd, Windsor House, 11 Fairview Strand, Dublin 3.

400. GORTNASCARRY
Possible barrow and associated features
R780513
98E0196
Test-trenching in advance of the construction of a diversion channel by the Engineering Section of the OPW was carried out in April–May 1998. Three areas were tested: an enclosure of possible archaeological significance and two stretches of townland boundary between Gortnascarry and Knocknacarrige townlands.

Test-trenching of the enclosure revealed it to be a large barrow 85m in diameter. Timber settings were encountered in the ditch area, from where a blue glass bead of Iron Age date was recovered. A worked flint flake was recovered from the top of the central mound area. In the light of these discoveries the developers decided to redesign the route of the diversion channel.

Two test-trenches were cut into each stretch of the townland boundary. The first set showed the boundary to be a bank constructed from one deposit, with a single accompanying ditch. The second two trenches showed that the character of the boundary had changed closer to the Mulkear River. Here the earthen bank was constructed of six separate layers, the bank itself being flanked on either side by a ditch. No artefacts were recovered from any of the trenches, nor was any suitable dating material encountered.

Three mounds were also investigated before the redesign of the diversion channel in June 1998. These proved to be natural features.
Frank Coyne, Aegis Archaeology, 24 Castle Court, Clancy Strand, Limerick.

401. GRANGE
Supposed line of ancient trackway
98E0437
Five test-trenches in the area of a proposed new bungalow development revealed no features of archaeological interest.
Brian Hodkinson, Annaholty, Birdhill, Co. Tipperary.

Limerick

402. GREENMOUNT AND LOGAVINSHIRE
Charcoal spreads
15305 14886
98E0252

Monitoring uncovered two previously unrecorded sites, both of which consisted of spreads of charcoal associated with shallow pits. The sites were ephemeral in nature and of limited archaeological significance. In addition two potential sites (COR Sites 22 and 23, highlighted during the Environmental Impact Survey) associated with the proposed development proved not to be archaeological. The landscape surrounding Greenmount consists of gently rolling open grassland. The soil is fertile and rich and is surrounded by a dense distribution of archaeological field monuments. The site lies on two glacial ridges orientated north-west/south-east. The ridges converge to the south forming a natural, U-shaped hollow.

Site A, Greenmount townland, was identified during the monitoring of topsoil-stripping, as a spread of charcoal in a hollow between the two ridges. The site initially appeared as a dense black staining immediately under the topsoil. A cutting measuring 4.2m north–south by 2.5m was opened on the spread. Four small extensions to the cutting were added to define the extent of the activity on the eastern, western and southern sides.

Site B, Logavinshire townland, was identified during monitoring as a spread of charcoal and fire-reddened clay immediately under the topsoil on the slope of the south-western ridge. A cutting measuring 3.5m north–south by 2.4m was opened. Two larger areas measuring 10m x 10m were then opened on the site's southern and eastern sides to establish whether the feature extended beyond the cutting. This proved not to be the case.

The excavation revealed an arc-shaped linear feature 2.95m long and 0.7m wide. The trench varied from 0.19m to 0.28m deep and was U-shaped in profile. It was filled with bands of compact, redeposited, burnt tan boulder clay and grey, charcoal-flecked clay. A dense oval deposit of charcoal measuring 0.26m east–west by 0.48m and 0.07m deep was present centrally in the feature.

A bronze ring was retrieved from the loose residual topsoil over the surface of the feature. The ring was oval and was between 26mm and 28mm wide. It was solidly cast, with a facetted section measuring 30–40mm in diameter. The ring's original function and date are uncertain; however, it may have formed part of a brooch (where the pin is missing).
Edmond O'Donovan, Margaret Gowen & Co. Ltd, 2 Killiney View, Albert Road Lower, Glenageary, Co. Dublin.

403. ABBEYFARM, KILMALLOCK
Urban medieval
SMR 47:22
16084 12786
98E0538

The proposed development is an urban renewal scheme. An archaeological assessment recommended that a series of test excavations be carried out to ascertain the remains and to allow for advance mitigation.

Test-pits 1–4 were excavated where the proposed works were breaching the line of the medieval defences. The excavations were undertaken to ascertain how much, if any, of the medieval wall survived and to pinpoint the location of any gate structures so that the impact of the scheme could be mitigated in advance. Test-pits 5–7 were excavated in the area of the proposed carpark within the medieval town. Test-pits 8–10 were incorporated into this testing strategy in an area that may be developed in the future outside, but adjacent to, the town wall.

At the northern limit of the town (Test-pit 1) it appears that existing services and road widening had removed all traces of the town wall at the eastern side of the street. At the postern leading to the Dominican Priory (Test-pit 2) modern backfill extends below the proposed level of the surface water sewer by *c.* 0.9m. At the eastern Watergate no trace of the wall was found in the test-pit (3), and modern backfill had accumulated over the natural gravel to a depth of 1.5m.

At the southern gate (Ivy Gate, Test-pit 4) remains of the town wall and possibly the gate-tower were established. These consisted of the basal courses of a wall 1.3m wide that extended 3.1m into the street. A stone setting to the south-east, at right angles to the town wall, may represent a second wall and possibly the base of a gate-tower. Both walls were abutted by a cobbled surface.

In the green-field site boulder clay was generally established at 0.6–0.7m below existing ground level. Above this was a homogeneous 'garden soil'/silty clay, which contained pottery from a wide date range (13th–19th century). Some of this layer may have accumulated in medieval times; however, in the test-pits excavated no upstanding features were recorded. The remaining features (pits and drains) were cut into the boulder clay and were only recognisable at this level, given the similarity of the overlying strata. In the area closer to the street it appears that accumulated layers have been scarped and only features (pits) cut into the boulder clay remain, at a depth of 0.35–0.54m below ground level.

In the area proposed for future development the town wall was revealed below the existing ground level. Some layers of silt and charcoal were established *c.* 20m from/exterior to the town wall. Elsewhere in the field there was an accumulation of 'garden soil'/silty clay lying above undisturbed boulder clay. Sherds of medieval pottery were found in this layer, but it was featureless in the areas excavated.
Sarah McCutcheon, Limerick County Council, PO box 53, County Buildings, 79/84 O'Connell Street, Limerick.

404. BROAD STREET/GEORGE'S QUAY, LIMERICK
Urban
1575 1575
98E0581

Monitoring of pre-development engineering site investigations associated with Limerick Main Drainage was carried out from 7 to 9 June 1998 by John Ó Néill and this writer. Three test-trenches were opened in areas where their location corresponded to the supposed location of the town defences. Two were dug at both ends of Baal's Bridge on Broad Street and George's Quay. The final trench was excavated at the foot of Creagh Lane on George's Quay.

All three trenches yielded evidence of the

survival of masonry structures between 0.45m and 1.3m below the existing street level, under surviving road surfaces. At Baal's Bridge the masonry structures were interpreted as being portions of the gates on either side of the bridge. The trench at the foot of Creagh Lane on George's Quay revealed the location of the town wall running parallel to the river along the centre of the present road.

The trench depth never exceeded 1.4m below the present ground level, the specified depth limit in the engineering site investigations contract. Therefore, it was not possible to fully identify evidence of archaeological deposits, as there is a distinct potential for archaeological deposits to occur both inside and outside the town wall at a level below the bottom of the trial-pit trenches.

Eighteenth-century fill was identified outside (Abbey River side) of the 'town wall' along George's Quay. This suggests that an area of relatively low archaeological potential may lie outside the town wall, between it and the present quay.

Test excavations were carried out at Nos 4–5 George's Quay (C. O Rahilly, pers. comm.) A single trench was excavated into the deposits on the site, where 0.8m of demolition rubble was identified over two layers of black, sticky, silty clay. The clay and silt deposits are highly likely to be archaeologically derived. These deposits give an indication of the type and nature of the archaeological deposits inside the 'town wall' on George's Quay.

Edmond O'Donovan, Margaret Gowen & Co. Ltd, 2 Killiney View, Albert Road Lower, Glenageary, Co. Dublin.

405. CREAGH LANE, GEORGE'S QUAY, LIMERICK

Urban medieval/post-medieval
R579575
97E0453 ext.

Monitoring of the development on this site, which lies within the zone of archaeological potential for Limerick, was carried out in February–March 1998.

Clearance of the overburden uncovered two stretches of walling of post-medieval date. Several sherds of sgraffito were also recovered from this phase of monitoring, as well as a stoneware sherd and a basal sherd of a green-glazed Saintoinge vessel, attesting to the disturbed nature of this site. Test-trenching carried out here in 1997 by Celie O Rahilly (*Excavations 1997*, 121) had uncovered medieval remains. This development did not excavate to a deep enough level to encounter these remains. However, during piling of the site some scraps of shoe leather of possible medieval date were recovered. No medieval structures were encountered.

Frank Coyne, Aegis Archaeology, 24 Castle Court, Clancy Strand, Limerick.

406. ISLAND ROAD, LIMERICK

Historic town
R578580
SMR 5:17
98E0026

This site lies at the northern end of the Englishtown to the east of the Island Gate, between Island Road to the north-east, Old Dominick Street to the south-west and the new Northern Relief Road to the south-east. It was partly within the walled area of the

medieval town, in an area known as the Orchard, which was part of the grounds of St Mary's Convent before being separated from it by the construction of the Northern Relief Road. Testing was carried out to ascertain the location of the town wall, which, according to cartographic evidence, crossed the site.

In 1989–90 B.J. Hodkinson carried out excavations on the line of the proposed road to the south-east of the site and traced the line of the wall across it (*Excavations 1990*, 42, E471). All that remained of the wall, apart from a small tower to the south-east, was a shallow cut with traces of rubble and mortar, crossing the site. Also uncovered was an external ditch.

The 1840s OS shows two angled stretches of wall marked 'Town Wall'. William Eyers's map, dated to 1752, shows a similar arrangement of angled wall area, with the notation: 'That Part of the Wall between N, O, is extremely bad, and very narrow in many places between Island Gate and Thomond Bridge'. There is also a section showing a profile of the town wall with the ditch some distance outside it. The Civil Survey describes three large plots and a few buildings in this area, to the north of St Domninic's Abbey.

Five cuts were made. They were positioned in such a way as to pick up the line of the wall based on the information from both of the maps and from the work on the adjacent site. There was no evidence of any masonry, or even of the base of the wall trench, as was identified on the adjacent site in 1995 (*Excavations 1995*, 54, 95E0064). The western side or internal face of the ditch was, however, identified. The distance between this edge and the line of the town wall as represented on the 1840 OS plan decreased at the northern end, near the Island Gate.

Celie O Rahilly, Limerick Corporation, City Hall, Limerick.

407. KING JOHN'S CASTLE, LIMERICK

Castle
R577577
9300E82

Limited archaeological work took place at the castle during April–May 1998, in advance of reopening on completion of its 'Phase 2' development. Phase 2 comprised the Castle Lane commercial properties along the southern curtain wall; the provision of a new exhibition in the visitor centre; a completely redesigned 'forecourt' area in front of the visitor centre, including a new entrance ramp, courtyard gates, paving and trees etc.; as well as partial restoration of the courtyard itself.

The monitoring of the construction of the ramp did not reveal any archaeological material; the location coincided with ground previously opened during excavations at the castle in 1990/1 (*Excavations 1990*, 43–4). A series of pits was opened for the planting of the trees. Limestone foundations in TP1 were consistent with rooms of the extended infantry barracks constructed in the 19th century. In contrast limestone foundations revealed in TP3 were not connected with the barracks and must represent evidence of a building of broadly 18th-century date fronting onto Nicholas Street.

In the courtyard the serious problems of conservation and visitor access to the medieval undercroft in Cutting 2 were largely ignored by

Shannon Heritage and SFADCO, although the corridor masonry was recorded. It is expected that a final decision on the fate of the structures here will be made in 1999. In the meantime some of the ground peripheral to Cutting 2 was restored by backfilling the extension to the east of corridor wall F3035 and levelling the yard to the south of corridor wall F3026.

Before the extension was backfilled a small sub-cutting was excavated. The purpose of this was to try and pinpoint the location of the ringwork bank from 1175–6 and the continuation of its limestone facing, first revealed in 1990 (see cover of *Excavations 1990).* The cutting revealed a steep cut in the natural clay and redeposited boulder clay, which were consistent with the ringwork, but no sign of the limestone revetment. It is possible that the latter was dug out in the 18th century during work on the construction of the foundations of the barracks square.

Kenneth Wiggins, 17 Vartry Close, Raheen, Co. Limerick.

408. WIDOWS' ALMS HOUSES, NICHOLAS STREET, LIMERICK

Urban

R577578

98E0047

This site lies along the southern side of the Castle Lane development next to King John's Castle. The alms houses were built in the 19th century in the former grounds of St Nicholas's parish church, which was demolished in the second half of the 17th century. The Castle Lane architectural consultants, Murray Ó Laoire Associates, suggested that a combined gas/ESB service trench be dug on the site as part of the groundwork in connection with the construction of Castle Lane. Approval to dig the trench was granted by Limerick Corporation, owners of the alms-house terrace. Work began without archaeological consultation in the garden nearest Nicholas Street on 9 January 1998 but was quickly suspended when some human bone remains were uncovered, denoting the presence of burials relating to the graveyard of the church.

Following this discovery arrangements were made to have the digging of the trench archaeologically monitored. However, owing to objections from the residents and other problems, the contractor opted to lay the services along the southern side of the Castle Lane site itself. Therefore the limited area already disturbed at the eastern end of the garden was backfilled and no further work on the site took place.

Kenneth Wiggins, 17 Vartry Close, Raheen, Co. Limerick.

409. VERDANT PLACE/ISLAND GATE, LIMERICK

Historic town

R576581

SMR Part of 5:17

E433, 98E0026 and 98E0557

This site was tested before development for local authority housing, with an additional area at the northern end where the proposed pumping station for the Main Drainage Scheme will be built. The site lies at the northern end of the Englishtown, just outside the town walls, and is within the zone of archaeological potential as defined by the Urban Archaeological Survey. It is defined on the western side by the River Shannon and by Verdant Place (north–south). To the south is a lane (also called Verdant Place but running east–west) linking the former with Dominick Street. On the east side at the southern end is the continuation of Dominick Street, now called Island View Terrace; at the northern end are the back gardens of Nos 6 and 7. To the north is a row of north-facing structures, now in use as a garage.

Today the site consists of a walled enclosure or paddock to the north-west (A) and a central section that was the site of two cottages, Victoria and Albert (B), with open ground at the southern end (C). Some low perimeter walls are still *in situ*, but no buildings remain. As the site lies outside the town wall, there is very little written history. There is, however, a considerable amount of information provided by the cartographic evidence. Two adjacent sites were also tested, Verdant Place (E433), and the Orchard site (98E0026).

Town wall

The standing remains of two turrets survive on Verdant Place (north–south). There is evidence that the wall survives behind these. The wall along Verdant Place (east–west) may also be a rebuild, with the original wall surviving south of it (see 1840s plan). At the eastern end it also curves but is of a different build. This was thought to be the remains of another turret/tower. Testing in the Orchard site, on the eastern side of Old Dominick Street, provided evidence that the ditch external to the town wall extended to just north of the kink in the boundary wall opposite the Villiers building.

Island Gate

This presumably stood on the line of Dominick Street, between the two stretches of town wall. All of the cartographic evidence, pre-1800, supports this. The maps show the gate as a square tower, which is in conflict with the curving section of wall on the west side of the street. On the 1840s plan Island Gate is marked to the west of the street and north of the town wall line. The later OS maps do the same with the addition of 'Site of' and a cross *pommée.* The gate served as access to the northern end of the King's Island, but this was not a main thoroughfare to the hinterland. It was rebuilt in 1685 by Mayor Robert Smyth (Lenihan, *A history of Limerick*, 210).

The external ditch lay in the Orchard site at the north-western end, where it was *c.* 3m from the remains of the town wall.

Two property entries in the Civil Survey (1654–6) presumably refer to the areas to the east of the road extending north from Dominick Street and to the east of the Island Road. Judging by both the 1752 and the 1840 OS plans the ground between the road and the riverbank was open.

After 1800 land to the north of the Island Gate was developed following the demolition of the town walls in the 1760s. By 1827 Franklin's Quay was in place, fronting the riverbank. By 1840 there were buildings fronting Franklin's Quay. By 1870 there was a row of eleven houses fronting the east side of the site. The Quay was replaced by two residences: Victoria Cottage to the north and Albert Cottage to the south. These fronted eastwards onto a narrow lane at the rear of the houses mentioned above with gardens onto the riverbank and survived to 1941, but the houses on the street had undergone some change. Verdant Place (north–south) was put in place sometime between 1840 and 1870.

Five cuttings of varying lengths were made across the site. They were 1.2m wide except where collapse occurred and in Cut 5, which was widened to expose the masonry.

Area (A), 'Paddock': Cuts 1/A, 1/B, 2/A and 2/B
This walled area was, presumably, a garden with a layout of thin concrete paths. None of the maps available showed the paths, but neither do they identify any separate structure with which the garden could be associated. It is, therefore, presumed to have been part of the northern cottage (Victoria). The surface was a very soggy, black soil, supporting no growth. In three of the cuttings, 1/A, 2/A and 2/B, was a very similar fill: garden soil, debris and mixed fill, overlying a mixture of brick and stones associated with severe flooding. In all three cases the work was abandoned.

In 1/B, to the east side of the area, was evidence of an accumulation of dumped material that produced a sizeable assemblage of sherds etc., of late 17th/early 18th-century date. This, together with the cartographic evidence, implies that this area was reclaimed somewhat later than that to the south, (B) and (C).

Area (B), Victoria Cottage and Albert Cottage: Cut 3/A–G
No structural evidence of the buildings fronting Franklin Quay survived in the cut; presumably they were destroyed by the construction of the cottages. Of these, two walls were noted: Wall (45) was probably the remains of the west wall, and Wall (53) the remains of the east. The insubstantial Wall (35) is probably one of the garden walls. It is unclear what the brick layer in 3/B and D was. Given that the bricks were not bonded together but just set in the sand, they may have served as an anti-tidal sealing layer.

Below the level of the walls and the various deposits of overburden and debris was an extensive accumulation of dumped material across the cut, in which no structural features were noted. The lowest level of this was superimposed on the original foreshore, identified by sand and gravel deposits and occasional decayed vegetation and mud. This began close to the eastern limit of the site and sloped down towards the west.

Area (C), open area: Cut 4/A–E and Cut 5
No structural remains were identified in Cut 4/A–E. There was a similar accumulation of dumped material and sloping foreshore as identified in Cut 3. At the eastern end, in 4/E, a natural clay was noted, as opposed to sand/gravel and rock.

Judging by the various distinct differences in the dumped material in both Cuts 3 and 4 it appears that the dumping occurred in stages, as it was not a homogeneous layer. There was obviously time for the sand and gravel, presumably by tidal/river action, to become incorporated into the layers and even separate them; some of what appeared to be pure, natural layers of sand and gravel had finds

filtered through. It is reasonable to assume that the area west of the access to the Island Gate was gradually reclaimed by using it as a 'town dump' from the mid-17th century, just as the area around St Francis's Abbey was used in the medieval period. By the early 19th century, however, the reclaimed area was built on, with the quay in place.

As structural remains were identified 0.6m below the surface, possibly of the gate or a building associated with it, further work in Cut 5 was deferred until a larger area could be opened up and investigated.
Celie O Rahilly, Limerick Corporation, City Hall, Limerick.

410. NEWTOWN
No archaeological significance
16237 15578
SMR 5:68
98E0493
Test-trenching at this site, in advance of the Limerick Southern Ring Road, showed it to be a naturally occurring hollow, with no trace of an enclosing element or any archaeological stratigraphy being encountered.
Frank Coyne, Aegis Archaeology, 24 Castle Court, Clancy Strand, Limerick.

411. RIVERS
Enclosure
16416 15715
SMR 6:19
98E0539
The surface water drainage scheme was close to an enclosure. *Dúchas* requested an assessment of the impact of the scheme on the known and potential archaeology of the site. On foot of this assessment all topsoil-stripping was monitored.

The scheme was sited in the fields to the north and east of the enclosure, which slope gently towards the Mulcair River. They consist of poor waterlogged ground that is under pasture with reeds and generally marshy growth.

The corridor was on average 12m wide to incorporate the trench and a drag road. A track machine with a toothed bucket carried out the topsoil removal. Sod and topsoil were thin, less than 0.1m. The subsoil was light brown with flecks of oxidised clay that appears to originate in the topsoil, as there was no evidence of *in situ* burning. This flecking was concentrated to the east and west of a fence line. Modern china and fragments of red brick occurred, which became more frequent closer to the road and the farmyard.

No archaeological remains were uncovered or disturbed during the course of the works.
Sarah McCutcheon, Limerick County Council, PO box 53, County Buildings, 79/84 O'Connell Street, Limerick.

412. TOWLERTON II
Circular mound
R609559
98E0608
This site was identified during the rewalking of the route of the Limerick Southern Ring Road. It consisted of an almost perfectly circular mound, with no extant evidence of any enclosing feature.

One trench was opened by hand, measuring 1m by 5m, orientated east–west. The investigation concluded that there was no archaeological activity in the centre of the mound and no enclosing element around its perimeter. Several sherds of modern pottery and a modern horseshoe were retrieved during the digging.

Tracy Collins, Aegis Archaeology Ltd, 1 Ardara, Fairies Cross, Tralee, Co. Kerry.

413. WOODSTOWN I
Circular depression
98E0491

This work, commissioned by Limerick County Council, involved the investigation of a number of possible sites in advance of the Limerick Southern Ring Road.

The site was first noted during the course of fieldwork for the Archaeological Impact Assessment for the road by Celie O Rahilly, who recommended testing to establish the archaeological merit of the site.

The site consisted of a kidney-shaped depression measuring 20m north–south by 12m. It had gradually sloping sides. Along the south edge a mixture of earth and stone was exposed. A trench measuring 5m east–west by 1m was manually excavated to ascertain whether any enclosing element existed and whether any archaeological remains existed in the interior. The trench revealed boulder clay directly below topsoil. No features or artefacts of archaeological significance were encountered.

Martin Fitzpatrick, Archaeological Consultancy, Ballydavid South, Athenry, Co. Galway, in conjunction with Aegis Archaeology Ltd.

414. WOODSTOWN II
Circular depression
98E0492

Commissioned by Limerick County Council, this work involved the investigation of a number of possible sites in advance of the Limerick Southern Ring Road. The site was first noted during the course of fieldwork for the Archaeological Impact Assessment for the road by Celie O Rahilly, who recommended testing to establish the archaeological merit of the site.

The site measured 18m north–south by 17m. It had steep sides and a flat bottom. Along the edge of the enclosure a mixture of earth and stone was exposed, with faint traces of a possible bank. A trench measuring 8m east–west by 1m was manually excavated to ascertain whether any enclosing element existed and whether any archaeological remains existed in the interior. The trench revealed boulder clay directly below topsoil. No features or artefacts of archaeological significance were encountered.

Martin Fitzpatrick, Archaeological Consultancy, Ballydavid South, Athenry, Co. Galway, in conjunction with Aegis Archaeology Ltd.

LONGFORD

415. BALLINALEE
Post-medieval
98M0005

One day's monitoring took place at the Longford County Council OAPD Scheme at Ballinalee village on 29 July 1998. The site is known locally as both 'The Croppie's Acre' and 'Bully's Acre'.

Preliminary archaeological assessment of the site followed by trial-testing was carried out by Judith Carroll in 1995 (*Excavations 1995*, 56, 95E0095), and excavation of a large area of the site followed in 1996 (*Excavations 1996*, 72, 96E0196). In 1998 the removal of a stone structure or 'folly' of stone slabs and the excavation of the area beneath and adjacent to it was also completed by Ms Carroll (see No. 416 below).

In May 1998 Ms Carroll was contacted about the discovery of human bones in an area of the site where a former boundary wall of the cemetery was removed, and she prepared a report. This writer then carried out monitoring of the site on 29 July 1998.

Eight holes had been dug to insert a fence on the site. The subsoil into which the holes were dug was a hard, light brown to grey, compacted subsoil with many small stones. This gave way to natural limestone outcrop in four of the post-holes. The only finds from the holes were three fragments of 19th/early 20th-century clay pipe stems, some sherds of 19th/20th-century pottery, modern clear glass and eight small pieces of bone. Of these, at least half were pieces of animal bone and three bore saw or knife marks. The cut bone came from the two holes dug nearest to the old stables, All finds came from the churned up topsoil and from introduced topsoil. A worn counterfeit of an Irish halfpenny coin of George II, dated 1760, was found.

The archaeological work consisted of monitoring the digging of the post-holes only, and no archaeological deposits or features were encountered in them.

The topsoil brought to this part of the site from elsewhere on the site was searched, but nothing other than 19th–20th-century glass was noted in them.

Jim Higgins, 'St Gerards', 18 College Road, Galway.

416. BALLINALEE/SAINT JOHNSTOWN
Stone structure
96E0196 ext.

The purpose of this excavation, carried out on 26–7 January 1998, was to have an anomalous stone structure of no known archaeological significance removed from a site being developed by Longford County Council. The site lies in Ballinalee village between the disused graveyard and the Longford road. Before development in 1996 the site had been extensively excavated (*Excavations 1996*, 72). During those excavations cuttings were brought up very close to the stone structure, but, apart from 18th/19th-century garden features, nothing of archaeological significance was found in the area of this feature.

The stone structure stood at the western end of the site and consisted of four large, thin, stone slabs, forming three sides of a rough box (*c.* 1.5m high and 1.05m wide), with one slab acting as a capstone. At the foot of the structure was a rough, slightly corbelled portion of stone wall. The feature has no parallels in any known monument type. It was surveyed and photographed before removal. The feature was then dismantled and the ground beneath it brought down to natural subsoil. No remains of archaeological significance were found.

Judith Carroll, Pine Forest Art Centre, Pine Forest Road, Glencullen, Co. Dublin.

417. KILSALLAGH, EDGEWORTHSTOWN
Vicinity of ringfort
22856 27000
SMR 20:15
98E0449

Archaeological assessment took place at Killsallagh, Edgeworthstown, Co. Longford, in advance of a proposed residential development. The site lies within a destroyed ringfort. The area of the driveway, septic tank and house site was stripped, and natural, grey, sandy soil was exposed below sod and ploughsoil in all areas at between 0.3m and 0.6m. All traces of the ringfort seem to have been destroyed.

Deirdre Murphy, Archaeological Consultancy Services Ltd, 15 Trinity Street, Drogheda, Co. Louth.

418. FORGNEY
Vicinity of ringfort
22128 25511
SMR 27:39
98E0394

The site of the development of a private dwelling was *c.* 30m south of a ringfort. Owing to the close proximity of the monument, *Dúchas* The Heritage Service recommended that archaeological test-trenching be requested as a condition of any planning permission granted.

Four trenches were opened with a mechanical excavator. All revealed modern topsoil sealing a relict ploughsoil deposited over a natural, silty, gravel subsoil. No archaeological features or finds were recovered from the excavated area.

Dermot Nelis, Irish Archaeological Consultancy Ltd, 8 Dungar Terrace, Dun Laoghaire, Co. Dublin.

LOUTH

419. CARLINGFORD
Urban
J1811
98E0161

Test-trenching, rescue excavation and monitoring in and around Carlingford has been ongoing since the end of March 1998. The test-trenching was necessitated by the installation of a new drainage and sewerage scheme in and around Carlingford by Louth County Council and by the laying of Telecom cables.

Thirty-five test-trenches were excavated. The programme of test-trenching followed from the results of a series of slit-trenches excavated for engineering purposes in November 1996, supervised by Beth Cassidy, which uncovered metalled roadways, possible early street frontages and a substantial wall immediately to the south of Taaffe's Castle. As works are still in progress, this report is of a preliminary nature.

Trenches were opened in Market Street, Newry Street, Back Lane, Dundalk Street, Old Quay Lane, Station Road, Shore Road and vicinity, Greenore Road, Liberties and Fair Green. Several trenches produced archaeological remains. In the field adjacent to the present Ghan House a large rectangular structure was uncovered measuring 12.9m x 6m. It was constructed of stone and lime mortar and may have functioned as a warehouse,

possibly associated with the present canal. The present southern field boundary used the southern wall of this building. No finds were associated with this structure, but a quantity of red brick rubble was uncovered in the northern foundation trench, suggesting a post-medieval date. The pipe-trench was relocated to the north of the structure so as not to damage it.

Nothing of archaeological significance was uncovered in the test-trenches either along the Shore Road and its vicinity or along the Greenore Road, with the exception of a sleeper 'bed' dating to the time of the railway construction (1876).

Along Old Quay Lane and Fair Green nothing of archaeological significance was uncovered, with the exception of the area immediately to the east of Taaffe's Castle, where a possible metalled slipway(?) and possible mooring posts were discovered. The slipway lies at approximately the same level as the original floor of the barrel vault of Taaffe's Castle (*Excavations 1995*, 57).

At Station Road, immediately to the south of Taaffe's Castle, test-trenching and monitoring necessitated a rescue excavation in advance of pipe-laying when two north–south-running walls were uncovered at the western and eastern ends of the street. The easternmost large masonry wall was uncovered at the remains of the present arch on the south-east corner of the building. This wall had an intact height of 1.3–1.5m and a maximum width of 2.2m. It was constructed of stone and lime mortar with very tight joints on its eastern (seaward) face and had a very solid, mortared interior.

It appears that this wall was partially built before the laying of the castle foundations and then the walls were constructed together to form the arch. This wall had been breached at its southern, excavated end, possibly during the post-medieval period, and a later wall had been inserted. This later wall appears to be similar to the upstanding warehouses along Old Quay Lane.

The second wall, also running north–south, was of cruder construction, although its eastern face had the tight jointing evident in the eastern wall. The wall was 0.93m wide with an intact height (including stone footings) of *c.* 2m.

These two walls appear to form the bawn of the castle, although both appear to have been exposed to the sea at one time. It is suggested that the western wall was constructed first and then the eastern wall was constructed when the castle was being built to enclose a courtyard. Both walls appear to have served the dual function of bawn- and sea-walls.

Nothing of archaeological significance was uncovered in the three trenches excavated along Dundalk Street, although it was expected that the southern portion of the town wall might have crossed the street to join the present wall, on the west side of the town, to the Tholsell.

The trenches in Market Street uncovered nothing of archaeological significance as there was severe disturbance by insertion of services.

Of the two trenches excavated along the northern end of Back Lane, only one produced archaeological remains. This was a ditch or very large pit 6.2m in maximum width and *c.* 0.7m deep. At the base of this feature some early medieval pottery was recovered along with a few fragments of animal bone.

The five trenches excavated in Newry Street produced remains of the original roadway in the form of cobbled and metalled surfaces overlying deposits containing medieval pottery.

At the top of Newry Street, at what is known as Castle Hill, test-trenching uncovered two walls and part of a cobbled roadway. A rescue excavation was undertaken at this area as the line of the pipe-trenches could not be changed. The excavation uncovered the original boundary ditch (running east–west), *c.* 3.5m wide, cut into the natural gravel. Sometime later a wall and gateway were built slightly off the line of the ditch. The wall (*c.* 0.1m below the present level of tarmac road) was constructed of stone and lime mortar, set on large stone footings, and had an intact height of 2.2m and a varying width of 1–1.05m at its top. The width of the gateway is 2.15m.

Set into the south side of the wall is a set of steps that may have led to an upper room or wall-walk. At the eastern portion of the wall a relieving arch was revealed 0.65m below the top of the wall (width *c.* 1.45m, height *c.* 1.45m). It had been constructed through the wall, possibly to allow the flow of spring water under it.

Through the gateway ran a cobbled roadway bounded on its eastern edge by a line of large boulders. Overlying this line and abutting the masonry wall was a stone-and-clay wall (*c.* 1.5m wide at its base and 1m at its top) running approximately north–south for a distance of *c.* 6.5m, which may have been a later boundary wall.

Only a small number of pottery finds were retrieved from the ditch, suggesting a 13th/14th-century date for the ditch infilling. The wall and gateway were also probably of this date as infill deposits containing similar pottery lay against the wall on its southern side.

Work is continuing with the monitoring of the pipe and service insertions.

Dermot G. Moore, Archaeological Development Services Ltd, Windsor House, 11 Fairview Strand, Fairview, Dublin 3.

420. KILCURRY, CARRICKEDMOND
No archaeological significance
302640 312670
98E0442
SMR 4:100

Archaeological assessment was undertaken at Carrickedmond, Kilcurry, Dundalk, Co. Louth, at the site of a proposed residential development. The site lies within an archaeological complex that contains stone alignments, stone circles and a possible hut site. The entire area to be affected was stripped of its topsoil to determine the presence/absence of archaeological features.

Ploughsoil was identified at 0.2–0.4m, and boulder clay at 0.5–0.9m. No features of archaeological significance were identified.

Deirdre Murphy, Archaeological Consultancy Services Ltd, 15 Trinity Street, Drogheda, Co. Louth.

421. CARSTOWN
Fulacht fiadh
O11627945
SMR 22:37
98E0042

The assessment took place at Carstown, Co. Louth, in advance of a proposed dwelling-house. The site was previously recorded as a burnt mound in the Archaeological Survey of County Louth (site 1245).

After stripping of the topsoil an area of burnt material covering 10m east–west by 6.75m was

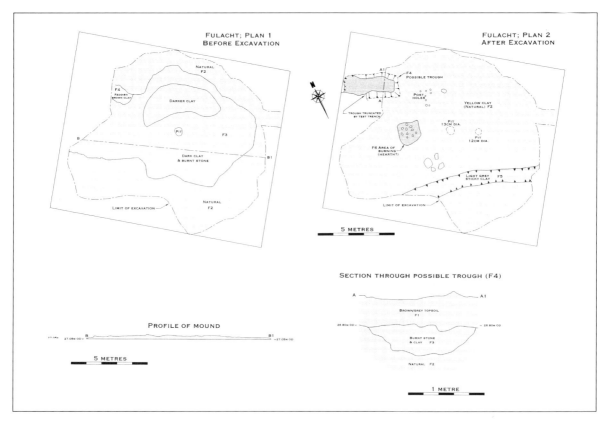

Before and after site plans of excavated fulachta fiadh at Carstown, Co. Louth.

revealed. The burnt material was composed of fire-cracked sandstone and charcoal-stained clay that was up to 0.24m thick. This rock type is not local to the area. The mound did not have the classic horseshoe shape and was probably damaged by ploughing.

A number of features were cut into the yellow/brown natural boulder clay. A U-shaped gully up to 0.43m deep ran across the south of the site and may have been a deliberately cut ditch to carry water to the site. An oblong trough lay in the north-west of the site and was 3.6m east–west by 1.6m and up to 0.36m deep. There were no traces of a lining, and the feature was filled with burnt stone. Eight post-holes close to the trough may have been some form of screen.
Donald Murphy, Archaeological Consultancy Services Ltd, 15 Trinity Street, Drogheda, Co. Louth.

422. CASTLELUMNY
Vicinity of castle site
303799 285381
SMR 21:2
98E0354
Archaeological assessment took place at Castlelumny, Dunleer, Co. Louth, in advance of a proposed residential development. The site lies close to the probable site of a castle first mentioned in 1301, on the south side of the 'castle field'.

Six trenches revealed orange boulder clay at between 0.26m and 0.44m from the surface underlying ploughsoil. No archaeological features or objects were found, and locals suggest that the castle site stood on the summit of the hill to the north.
Donald Murphy, Archaeological Consultancy Services Ltd, 15 Trinity Street, Drogheda, Co. Louth.

423. CHARLESTOWN
Vicinity of medieval church
295065 294860
98E0247
SMR 14:31
Archaeological assessment was carried out at a proposed residential site at Charlestown, Ardee, Co. Louth. The site lies close to the remains of a medieval church and the site of a barrow identified by ploughmarks. Four trenches were excavated along the foundations and bio-cycle of the site. The trenches were excavated to the natural, grey subsoil at 0.3m and 0.4m. No archaeological features or objects were recovered.
Donald Murphy, Archaeological Consultancy Services Ltd, 15 Trinity Street, Drogheda, Co. Louth.

424. CLONMORE
Vicinity of Early Christian monastery
O11208815
SMR 18:20
98E0005
A site at Clonmore, Dunleer, Co. Louth, was excavated in advance of a proposed residential development. The site lies close to that of a monastery founded in AD 551 and of a tower-house. Four trenches were excavated, one east–west and three north–south. No archaeological features or objects were recovered, with the natural boulder clay lying between 0.4m and 0.7m below topsoil.
Deirdre Murphy, Archaeological Consultancy Services Ltd, 15 Trinity Street, Drogheda, Co. Louth.

425. BACHELORS LANE, DROGHEDA
Urban medieval
O091754
SMR 24:41
97E0433
Pre-development testing and subsequent limited archaeological excavation, in response to a planning condition, took place at the site of a proposed apartment and office complex on the north side of Bachelors Lane, Moneymore, Drogheda, Co. Louth. Excavation took place from 28 January to 6 February 1998. The earliest documentary references to the lane occur in the early 14th century, and previous excavations (*Excavations 1996*, 75–6) in the lane uncovered medieval stratigraphy. The site was within the town walls, near the 'Blind Gate' and just outside the proposed precinct of the Franciscan friary, founded *c.* 1245. A series of 18th-century coach-houses stood on the site immediately before excavation. These were demolished to make way for the development. A total area of 143m^2 was excavated.

The earliest features uncovered were two compacted gravel surfaces dating to the 13th–14th century. The function of these was unclear, although there was slight evidence of industrial activity associated with one of the deposits. No structural features connected with the surfaces were found. Garden soil was subsequently dumped in three separate episodes from the 13th to the 16th century. These deposits contained large quantities of local and imported medieval pottery and animal bone. A small amount of kiln waste material was also recovered. Only the earliest deposit of garden soil extended throughout the site to the lane.

Post-medieval activity on the site was represented by the construction of the coach-house complex, which scarped out some 2m of the garden soil deposits. The pottery assemblage associated with the construction phase suggests that it dated to *c.* 1700–1800. No further archaeological work was required.
Donald Murphy, Archaeological Consultancy Services Ltd, 15 Trinity Street, Drogheda, Co. Louth.

426. 2 BESSEXWELL LANE, DROGHEDA
Urban medieval
O091753
98E0086
The site lies at the west end of Bessexwell Lane, on the south side. The lane runs into Shop Street, which was one of the major thoroughfares in medieval Drogheda. The lane is known to have existed at the beginning of the 14th century (Bradley 127), when it was recorded as the 'lane to the Friars minor', i.e. the Franciscan friary that is known to have been built east of Mayoralty Street. There is also a record of a property plot owned by Martin Johan in 1363 (*ibid.* 113) immediately to the west of the development site. One trench tested the very small site.

The remains of a stone wall ran east–west across the site. It was abutted on the south side by building rubble and on the north side by a mixed deposit of gravel, yellow clay and silt, the function of which was not clear. These three features were post-medieval in date. They all overlay the grey, mottled silt layer, which, when found in adjoining 3–4 Bessexwell Lane No. 427 below), was interpreted as a medieval layer.

Reference:
Bradley, J. 1978: The topography and layout of medieval Drogheda. *Co. Louth Archaeological and Historical Journal* **19** (2), 98–127.

Rosanne Meenan, Roestown, Drumree, Co. Meath.

427. 3–4 BESSEXWELL LANE, DROGHEDA
Urban medieval
O091753
97E0455

The development site, at the west end of Bessexwell Lane, is known to have existed at the beginning of the 14th century (Bradley 127), when it was recorded as the 'lane to the Friars minor', i.e. the Franciscan friary that is known to have been built east of Mayoralty Street. There is also a record of a property plot owned by Martin Johan in 1363 (*ibid.* 113) immediately to the west of the development site.

Three test-trenches were dug following demolition of the 19th-century buildings that stood on the site. These buildings do not seem to have caused disturbance to the underlying material.

A layer of mixed brown gravel, sand and clay underlay the thin layer of demolition rubble. Deposits of ash could also be seen within it. This layer was 1.5–1.6m deep. In Trench 1 was evidence of a layer of cobbles within the layer. No finds were seen in this material, but it was probably post-medieval in date.

The underlying layer of mottled grey, brown and black clay was *c.* 2m deep. It was very plastic in texture and was probably naturally deposited by the river. It also contained small lenses of black vegetable material. There was evidence to suggest a wattle fence within it. The deposit resembled other riverine deposits exposed in medieval excavations in Dublin and elsewhere. Natural, grey-blue sand lay underneath.

No evidence of structures was exposed.

Reference
Bradley, J. 1978: The topography and layout of medieval Drogheda. *Co. Louth Archaeological and Historical Journal* **19** (2), 98–127.

Rosanne Meenan, Roestown, Drumree, Co. Meath.

428. BLIND QUAY/MERCHANT'S ROW, DROGHEDA
Urban post-medieval
O092751
98E0101

The site comprises a block that stretches between North Strand and the Quays along the Boyne, with Blind Quay as its western boundary. It was occupied by 19th-century stone buildings, which functioned in more recent times as a corn store and a warehouse. The development also encompassed a stone building at the north end, which will be retained.

Five test-trenches exposed evidence of reclaiming of ground and of dumping of material, dating from the 17th into the 18th century. A major element of the dumping was building rubble, presumably derived from elsewhere in the town. The dumping may have been carried out with the aim of reclaiming ground in the bed of the River Boyne. Where this material was bottomed it was 3m deep. The remains of an east–west stone wall, probably associated with the construction of the warehouse, were exposed.

Medieval structures or layers were not observed.
Rosanne Meenan, Roestown, Drumree, Co. Meath.

429. CHORD ROAD/NORTH STRAND, DROGHEDA
Unknown
O09657549
98E0046

A medieval church (SMR 24:30) and graveyard stand to the north-east of the development site. Bradley identifies the church as that of the hospital of St Laurence, established *c.* 1206 (Bradley 117).

Five trenches tested the site. The area along the frontage of Chord Road might have been expected to produce material associated with the church or with the medieval hospital that existed there. No such material was observed.

Reference
Bradley, J. 1978: The topography and layout of medieval Drogheda. *Co. Louth Archaeological and Historical Journal* **19** (2), 98–127.

Rosanne Meenan, Roestown, Drumree, Co. Meath.

430. SIENNA CONVENT, CHORD ROAD, DROGHEDA
Urban medieval
310263 275918
SMR 24:41
97E0149

Archaeological assessment of a proposed residential development took place at Sienna Convent, Chord Road, Moneymore, Drogheda, Co. Louth. The site lies outside St Laurence's Gate and the medieval town walls. The area may well have been a medieval suburb of the town, and the name 'Chord Road' may apply to a particular trade practised in the area. The road led to the medieval leper hospital of St Laurence.

Fourteen trenches were excavated. Trenches 1, 5, 7, 11 and 13 contained no archaeological features.

Trench 2, in the west garden, revealed yellow/orange boulder clay at 0.65m deep. Two pits, one medieval and the other of 17th/18th-century date, were cut into the natural.

Trench 3, east of Francis Street, revealed 0.8m of topsoil. Two pits of early post-medieval date were cut into the boulder clay.

Trench 4 was dug perpendicular to Trench 3. Boulder clay was encountered at between 0.7m and 1.2m deep, and a single course of a stone wall running north–south was revealed midway along the trench. While dating is inconclusive, it may be late medieval in construction.

Trench 6, in the south-west of the site, consisted of modern gravel overlying dark brown garden soil to a depth of 0.67m, at which point brown clay loam containing post-medieval pottery was encountered. This overlay a thin layer of light brown clay containing animal bone, which in turn overlay natural boulder clay.

Trench 8, in the eastern area of the site, exposed a layer of dark brown post-medieval clay 0.3m thick underlying topsoil, which in turn overlay boulder clay.

Trenches 9, 10 and 12 encountered post-medieval clay layers at depths of between 0.22m and 0.33m, which ranged from 0.6m to 0.75m thick and overlay natural boulder clay.

Trench 14, in the north-west of the site, revealed a cobbled pathway of 18th/19th-century date underlying topsoil. In the remainder of the trench topsoil overlay post-medieval dark brown clay, which in turn overlay natural boulder clay.

Deirdre Murphy, Archaeological Consultancy Services Ltd, 15 Trinity Street, Drogheda, Co. Louth.

431. FAIR GREEN, DROGHEDA
Medieval town
309267 275944
SMR 24:41
Archaeological monitoring of a proposed commercial development took place at Fair Green, Drogheda, Co. Louth. Ground level was lowered by between 0.3m and 2m and revealed modern deposits lying directly over boulder clay.

Donald Murphy, Archaeological Consultancy Services Ltd, 15 Trinity Street, Drogheda, Co. Louth.

432. HAYMARKET/JOHN STREET, DROGHEDA
Urban medieval
O009075
98E0250
Test excavation was carried out on a proposed development site in Drogheda in June 1998. The site straddles both sides of the River Boyne, at Haymarket on the north side of the river and at John Street to the south. The purpose of the excavation was to create a surface contour model of the archaeological deposits on the site. Trenches 1–10 were excavated at the Haymarket, Trenches 11–14 at John Street.

The Haymarket site appears to have been crossed by an early (medieval) quay wall, *c.* 15m inside the present quay wall. Two distinct soil profiles were evident on either side of the wall alignment. Post-medieval garden soil overlying medieval organic deposits was evident in the northern portion of the site, fronting onto Dyer Street (i.e. inside the medieval quay wall). The organic deposits appeared to represent medieval reclamation fill. A deep deposit of post-medieval (17th/18th-century) fill occurred to the south of the medieval quay (i.e. outside it) and inside the present quay wall. The post-medieval deposits appear to represent a second major phase of reclamation behind the existing quay front. The medieval quay wall formed the boundary between these two deposit sequences. The early quay wall appears to be substantially robbed out, and it was difficult to identify during the assessment. However, there was a suggestion of a masonry structure abutting the southern edge of the post-medieval garden soils and medieval organic material in Trench 7.

The successive reclamation of river frontage is a feature of the organisation of medieval towns. It is consistent with the picture emerging from urban excavations, such as those at Essex Street West in Dublin (Simpson, L., *Excavations at Essex Street West, Dublin*, 1995) and at Wood Quay (Wallace, P., *Dublin's Waterfront at Wood Quay: 900–1317*, CBA report 1981). A similar sequence of reclamation can be tentatively proposed for the Haymarket site.

The line of the supposed medieval quay structure identified in Trenches 7 and 10 was also evident in the excavation carried out by Donald Murphy (pers. comm.) in 1997 at the foot of Stockwell Street in advance of the Drogheda Main Drainage Scheme. A 'circular structure and wall' were identified at Site B along the Haymarket pipe-run. This circular structure is likely to be the foundations of a mural/quay-front defensive tower on the riverbank. A wall running east from the 'circular structure' is aligned with the medieval quay front identified during this assessment.

At John Street the line of the town wall and ditch bisects the proposed development site. The position of the town wall can be estimated by the superimposition of the 25-inch map (1862) of the town on the existing street plan. The town wall remained intact up to 1837. A large tannery was developed on the site in the middle of the 19th century, when the wall is likely to have been substantially altered. However, the line of the wall remains evident within the tannery (it can be identified on the 1862 OS map). The tannery and any remaining upstanding fragments of the wall were demolished with the construction of the new Drogheda inner relief dual carriageway along John Street.

A substantial wall was uncovered in Trench 12. A circular masonry structure was identified in Trench 11. These features are interpreted as forming portions of the medieval defences of the town. The 'town wall' terminated with a circular tower at its junction with the river. Medieval clays and pits were identified at the eastern end of Trench 12. This activity is likely to be associated with domestic settlement within the town. Organic deposits were identified on the western side of the town wall; these would be consistent with a ditch or moat. A portion of this ditch was uncovered during the excavations carried out in advance of the Drogheda Main Drainage Scheme by Donald Murphy (pers. comm., and see *Excavations 1996*, 76–7, and *Excavations 1997*, 127–9)

Edmond O'Donovan, Margaret Gowen & Co. Ltd, 2 Killiney View, Albert Road Lower, Glenageary, Co. Dublin.

433. 30 MAGDALENE STREET, DROGHEDA
Urban post-medieval
308940 275445
SMR 24:41
98E0323
Archaeological assessment was carried out on a proposed commercial development at 30 Magdalene Street, Drogheda, Co. Louth. The site is within the medieval town and lies to the north of St Peter's parish church.

Two trenches were excavated. Trench 1 ran north–south across the site and was 4m long and 0.8m wide. Under the 19th-century garden soil a layer of light brown, compact clay was exposed that was 18th century or later in date and contained residual medieval pottery. This layer pre-dated the boundary wall of the site. A number of small pits were cut through this layer. At the south end of the trench a thin layer of compacted burnt pebbles underlay the garden soil and overlay a compacted mortar, stone and brick path up to 0.12m thick. A pit was cut through the light brown clay and contained medieval and early post-medieval pottery. The clay overlay natural, orange boulder clay, which the pit also truncated to 25.933m OD.

The second trench was orientated east–west and

was 6m long and 1m wide. On removal of the garden soil, up to 0.42m deep, a layer of light brown clay with an 18th-century date was encountered and overlay natural boulder clay at 26.035m OD. The mortar feature found in Trench 1, interpreted as a pathway, was also found in this trench, running to its northern limit, and was up to 0.3m wide.
Donald Murphy, Archaeological Consultancy Services Ltd, 15 Trinity Street, Drogheda, Co. Louth.

434. MILL LANE, DROGHEDA
Vicinity of medieval town
308404 275733
SMR 24:41
98E0004
A site on Mill Lane, Drogheda, Co. Louth, was excavated in advance of a proposed residential development on 7 January 1998. Mill Lane runs south towards the river from Trinity Street and was outside the medieval walled town.

Two trenches were excavated. Trench 1 was 9.2m long and 1.4m deep. A layer of brown clay and rubble was excavated to 0.3m, after which natural gravel was exposed. Trench 2 revealed the natural gravel at 0.3m. No archaeological features or objects were recovered.
Deirdre Murphy, Archaeological Consultancy Services Ltd, 15 Trinity Street, Drogheda, Co. Louth.

435. 9/10 MILL LANE, DROGHEDA
Vicinity of medieval town
308405 275735
SMR 24:41
98E0404
A site on Mill Lane, Drogheda, Co. Louth, was excavated in advance of a proposed residential development. Mill Lane runs south towards the river from Trinity Street and was outside the medieval walled town.

Three trenches were excavated. Trench 1 was 6m long and 1.1m deep. A layer of brown rubble was excavated to 1m, after which a layer of rich, humic garden soil containing red brick, glass fragments and animal bone was exposed. It extended to a depth of 2.2m and directly overlay a sterile, grey/brown loam.

Trench 2 ran east–west and was 5m long and 1.5m wide. Red brick and rubble was excavated to 1.2m, below which humic garden soil with red brick fabric was revealed. It overlay natural, orange boulder clay at 2m.

Trench 3 was excavated from the north-west corner of the site and was 6m long, 1.5m wide and 2m deep. It contained the same stratigraphy as Trench 2.

No archaeological features or objects were recovered.
Deirdre Murphy, Archaeological Consultancy Services Ltd, 15 Trinity Street, Drogheda, Co. Louth.

436. DONAGHY'S MILL, MILL LANE, DROGHEDA
18th-century mill
308395.62 275223.46
SMR 24:41
98E0115
Archaeological assessment took place at Donaghy's Mill, Mill Lane, Drogheda, Co. Louth, in advance of a proposed residential/commercial development. The site lies outside the medieval walled town of

Drogheda; however, there may have been suburban development in this area in that period.

Two trenches were excavated in the interior of the mill. Trench 1 was excavated in a north–south direction between the mill walls. It recovered north–south-running walls, which acted as foundations for roof supports. Orange boulder clay was encountered at 0.55m OD. Trench 2 revealed more roof supports cut into boulder clay but no other features of archaeological interest.
Deirdre Murphy, Archaeological Consultancy Services Ltd, 15 Trinity Street, Drogheda, Co. Louth.

437. MILLMOUNT, DROGHEDA
Urban post-medieval
309007 274782
SMR 24:25
98E0194
Archaeological assessment was undertaken at the Millmount, Lagavooren, Drogheda, Co. Louth, in advance of conservation and restoration work by Drogheda Corporation on the Martello tower at the summit. The site is a large motte with attached lower bailey, which was subsequently used as a windmill in the later medieval period, and featured in the Cromwellian siege of the town. Since then it has been used as a military barracks and is currently a museum.

Three trenches were excavated. Trench 1 ran from the southern face of the tower to the surrounding modern stone wall on the perimeter. A layer of black loam containing limestone rubble, red brick and 19th-century pottery was encountered below the sod line. This layer was up to 0.5m thick and abutted the dressed stone plinth of the Martello tower. This overlay a layer of brown clay with red brick flecks up to 0.33m thick, which also abutted the tower. Under this was a layer of orange daub up to 0.23m thick and extending 1.44m wide from the tower, abutting the plinth and overlying the roughly built stone footing. A mortared limestone wall running south seems to have been cut during the construction of the tower and was up to three courses thick. The wall was abutted by a mid-brown clay with brick fragments. Excavation ceased at this point.

Trench 2 lay to the south-east of Trench 1. A thin layer of black clay loam was removed, up to 0.6m deep, and a large mortared stone wall was encountered at 46.056m OD. The wall extended throughout the entire trench and was bonded with a compact, white mortar that contained red brick fragments. Excavation ceased at this point.

Trench 3 was excavated on the north side of the tower. A layer of black clay loam under the sod contained glass fragments, red brick fragments and coal, continued to 46.626m OD and was identical to the uppermost layer in Trench 1. This overlay a layer of mid-brown clay containing red brick fragments and coal that was also identical to that in Trench 1. Under this a red brick structure at least two courses high, which abutted the lower footing of the Martello tower, was revealed at 46.346m OD.

Development of a viewing deck for the Martello tower is expected to be restricted to above these earlier structures, which may be associated with the 18th-century barracks below in the bailey.
Donald Murphy, Archaeological Consultancy Services Ltd, 15 Trinity Street, Drogheda, Co. Louth.

438. SHOP STREET/BESSEXWELL LANE, DROGHEDA

Urban medieval

SMR 24:41

30902 27506

97E0430

Archaeological testing was carried out in advance of a proposed commercial development at the southern junction of Shop Street and Bessexwell Lane, Drogheda, Co. Louth. The site lies in the heart of the medieval town.

Two trenches were dug. Trench 1 was oriented north-west/south-east and was 4m long, 1.9m wide and 1.3m deep. The top 0.8m was very disturbed and consisted of red brick rubble. This overlay a light brown, sticky clay with charcoal flecks. This extended to 0.94m below ground level, where a grey, silty loam was evident. This contained shell, bone and late medieval pottery. It extended to 1.04m deep and overlay a fine, green, compact sand. This overlay a further grey, silty clay, which contained medieval pottery.

Trench 2 was excavated in an east–west direction parallel to Bessexwell Lane. It was 4.8m long, 1.4m wide and 1m deep. Red brick rubble extended to 0.8m below and overlay a brown, sticky clay loam. This extended to 0.94m below the surface. This overlay a grey, sticky silty clay similar to that in Trench 1 and containing medieval pottery.

No further excavation took place.

Deirdre Murphy, Archaeological Consultancy Services Ltd, 15 Trinity Street, Drogheda, Co. Louth.

439. 12/13 SHOP STREET/DYER STREET, DROGHEDA

Urban medieval

309844 275333

SMR 24:41

98E0229

Archaeological assessment was undertaken at a proposed commercial and residential development at 12/13 Shop Street, Moneymore, Drogheda, Co. Louth. The site is directly to the north of the excavations along Dyer Street (*Excavations 1996*, 75,

96E0160), which uncovered the remains of two sides of a medieval house constructed in the 13th century. The north-western corner of the property, facing Dyer Street, incorporates a stone returning wall with sandstone jambs. A portion of the upstanding stone wall of the property to the south, which was demolished in the course of the Drogheda main drainage scheme, remained attached to the property and appeared to be in line with the west wall of the medieval house mentioned above. Stripping of plaster and building survey revealed a patchwork of walls including a stone returning wall some 14.5m from the afore-mentioned corner. Testing was undertaken alongside the north wall of the property to elucidate the structural sequence.

A trench 1.85m east–west by 1.7m was opened. Nineteenth-century cobbles were uncovered at a depth of 2.95m OD. Directly under these was a stone wall jutting out 0.84m from the base of the northern upstanding wall of 12/13 Shop Street. On excavation a footing was recovered and the wall matched the dimensions of those for the medieval wall. A rectangular feature within the thickness of the wall with a sloping north wall is probably the remains of a garderobe chute, and the deposit in front of the wall suggested the presence of a drain or a pit leading away from it. A single piece of Saintonge from the footing suggests a *terminus post quem* in the mid-13th century. This clearly puts the upstanding wall later, except for the north-west corner, which appears to be medieval to a height of 5.06m.

Further testing within the existing building before demolition revealed a substantial wall 1.4m thick fronting onto Shop Street, which incorporated two thresholds of former entrances. A similar limestone mortared wall was found at the west of the building. No wall was found along the northern edge of the building. Medieval layers abutted all these walls. Full excavation of the building is to be undertaken.

Donald Murphy, Archaeological Consultancy Services Ltd, 15 Trinity Street, Drogheda, Co. Louth.

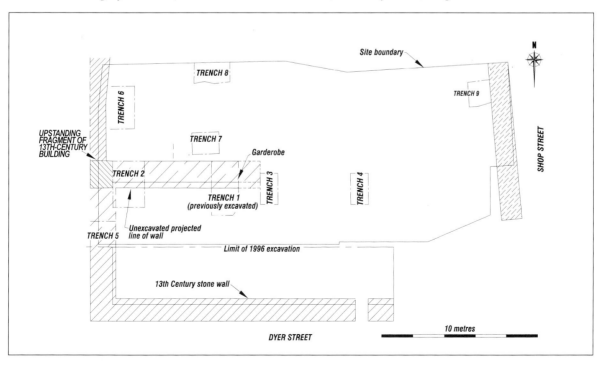

Medieval structures at Dyer Street, Drogheda.

440. WELLINGTON QUAY, DROGHEDA

No archaeological significance

308642 275059

SMR 24:41

98E0096

Archaeological testing took place in advance of a proposed residential development at Wellington Quay, Drogheda, Co. Louth. The site is outside the town wall, close to the present Dominican church. Previous testing on the street (by Christiaan Corlett, *Excavations 1997*, 129, 97E0172) has suggested that the whole site is composed of built-up ground dating to the 18th/19th century.

Two trenches were excavated. Trench 1 ran north–south and was 10m long and 1m deep. A small section was excavated to a depth of 1.5m. A layer of brown clay loam containing frequent lumps of animal bone, red brick rubble and mortar extended under concrete to the bottom of the trench.

Trench 2 was 6m long, 1m wide and 1m deep. A blackened stone surface, perhaps the footing of an earlier building, overlay a layer of brown clay loam identical to that in Trench 1. This extended to the limit of the trench.

Deirdre Murphy, Archaeological Consultancy Services Ltd, 15 Trinity Street, Drogheda, Co. Louth.

441. 78/79 WEST STREET, DROGHEDA

Urban medieval, post-medieval

O08257519

SMR 24:41

98E0396

Five trenches were excavated at the rear of 78/79 West Street in advance of a proposed commercial development. West Street was one of the earliest streets founded in the medieval town, and burgage plots are likely to run north–south on both sides. The street and defences were expanded in the 13th century to incorporate the Abbey of St Mary D'Urso.

Trenches were placed along the lines of foundations and on the positions of reinforced concrete columns. The remains of an 18th-century building were found at 9.11m OD towards the western boundary of the site underlying a layer of red brick, mortar and other demolition waste in a matrix of mid-brown clay up to 0.62m deep. The structure consisted of a small, rectangular, cobbled room measuring 2.5m north–south by 2m east–west, which abutted a further eastern room with a clay floor the extent of which was not determined owing to the limitations of the trenches required.

Below this structure and over the remainder of the site was a deep layer of homogeneous, soft, mid-brown clay containing post-medieval and medieval pottery. At the southern end of the site bedrock was encountered at 8.6m OD, under a thin patchy layer of green-grey gravel. A cut had been clearly made into the bedrock and was filled with brown clay containing horn cores and post-medieval pottery to a depth of 8.6m OD. To the north the bedrock had been clearly cut away and the mid-brown layer was dug to 7.84m OD without reaching bedrock. At the north end of the site bedrock occurred again at 8.9m OD and rising, presumably following the rise to Fair Street, where OD levels stand at 19m OD. The drop in OD levels in the plot is suggestive of medieval and post-medieval quarrying, which has been seen elsewhere in the town.

Deirdre Murphy, Archaeological Consultancy Services Ltd, 15 Trinity Street, Drogheda, Co. Louth.

442. GLEESON'S LOUNGE, WEST STREET, DROGHEDA

Urban medieval

308556 275274

SMR 24:21

98E0611

Archaeological assessment was undertaken at Gleeson's Lounge, Narrow West Street, Drogheda, Co. Louth, in advance of a proposed extension. Three trenches were excavated.

Trench 1 was dug in the south-west corner of the vaulted cellar to establish its antiquity. Under the brick floor a layer of brown loam up to 0.21m thick and containing 19th-century artefacts overlay a layer of mid-brown loam containing a large percentage of shell and 15th/16th-century pottery. The wall of the cellar had been cut into this layer, which continued beneath it. The trench was dug to 6.94m OD.

Trench 2 was excavated in the north-east corner of the building. It was 1.8m north–south by 1m. A concrete floor up to 0.12m thick overlay a dark, sandy clay containing 19th-century pottery and underlay the cellar walls. The layer overlay bedrock that sloped westwards at 7.28m OD. The bedrock had evidently been scarped out for the cellar's construction in the 19th century.

Trench 3 was excavated in the yard at the rear of the premises and was 5.3m long and 1.85m thick. A concrete floor up to 0.12m thick was removed by machine. Underlying this was a cobbled floor made from water-worn limestone up to 0.2m wide and 0.1m deep. This layer sloped upwards from south to north and had been truncated by a modern ceramic watermain. This lay over a layer of compacted, mid-brown clay, which contained red brick and coal inclusions and was up to 0.23m thick. This overlay a thick layer of loose rubble consisting of sandy, mid-brown clay, whole and partial red brick fragments and lumps of mortared limestone and containing sherds of 19th-century pottery.

At the west this layer abutted a north–south-running wall, and at the east an east/west-running wall. The north–south wall was encountered in the north of the trench and was up to six courses high (1.1m). It evidently ran southwards; however, it could not be exposed for the full length of the trench owing to the overhead watermain. It was bonded into the east–west wall at the northern end of the trench. It was composed of roughly squared blocks of limestone bonded with a compact, white mortar, which contained small fragments of coal and red brick. The north–south wall was of similar construction and was intact up to just below the concrete floor of the yard down to 10.08m OD.

A layer of water-worn limestone cobbles extended throughout the trench just above the base of both walls. This overlay a layer of silty, grey-brown clay, which contained red brick fragments as well as manganese mottled ware and tin-glazed earthenware. This layer was up to 0.32m deep and ran under both walls. On removal of this layer a thick deposit of sandy clay and red brick rubble was encountered. A depth of 0.51m of this layer was excavated to 9.46m OD, at which point excavation ceased owing to the proximity of standing buildings.

This building was probably the remains of a cellar that ran southwards to connect with the existing cellars. The north wall of the existing cellar looks like it may have been blocked up in the past.
Deirdre Murphy, Archaeological Consultancy Services Ltd, 15 Trinity Street, Drogheda, Co. Louth.

443. DROMISKIN
Vicinity of Early Christian monastic site
O04789732
SMR 12:04301
98E0316

Archaeological assessment took place at the site of a proposed residential development at Dromiskin, Dundalk, Co. Louth. It lies close to an Early Christian monastic site, which includes the remains of a round tower, high cross and church, as well as evidence of souterrains and an enclosure. SMR 12:04301 is an earthwork associated with a complex of sites associated with a series of souterrains.

Four trenches were excavated along the foundations and proposed septic tank. Trenches were dug through sod, ploughsoil and then natural, yellow boulder clay. No archaeological features or objects were recovered.
Donald Murphy, Archaeological Consultancy Services Ltd, 15 Trinity Street, Drogheda, Co. Louth.

444. 49 ANNE STREET, DUNDALK
Medieval town
J04550680
SMR 7:119
98E0370

A single trench was excavated in advance of a proposed commercial development at 49 Anne Street, Dundalk, Co. Louth. The trench was orientated north-west to south-east and was excavated to a depth of 0.6m. The fill of the trench consisted of red brick rubble contained within a brown clay loam matrix. No features or objects of archaeological interest were recovered.
Donald Murphy, Archaeological Consultancy Services Ltd, 15 Trinity Street, Drogheda, Co. Louth.

445. CASTLETOWN CROSS, CASTLEBLAYNEY ROAD, DUNDALK
No archaeological significance
SMR 7:118
98E0461

An extension was being built onto an existing house within the boundaries of the medieval settlement of Castletown. The site had been part of the garden at its northern end, and at the southern side the topsoil and part of the subsoil had already been scarped to level the site for the existing house and associated yard.

Nothing of archaeological interest was noted during the digging of the foundation trenches for the extension and the soil removal for the new driveway.
Finola O'Carroll, Greenanstown, Stamullin, Co. Meath.

446. CASTLETOWN, DUNDALK
Urban
Unlicensed monitoring of topsoil-stripping along Line 1 of the Dundalk Sewerage Scheme began on 12

November 1998 and continued until 14 December. Monitoring was recommended as the general area forms part of the zone of archaeological potential recognised by the Urban Survey and the Urban District Council and contains a wide variety of archaeological remains, from an Early Bronze Age cist burial to a 15th-century tower-house.

To date, only one site of archaeological significance (a *fulacht fiadh*) has been exposed in the course of topsoil-stripping. This was excavated in December 1998 (see No. 447 below). Soil-stripping is due to recommence and be completed in early 1999.
Rob Lynch, Irish Archaeological Consultancy Ltd, 8 Dungar Terrace, Dun Laoghaire, Co. Dublin, for Valerie J. Keeley Ltd.

447. CASTLETOWN, DUNDALK
Fulacht fiadh
98E0573

A subrectangular pit filled with burnt clay and stone was revealed during monitoring of topsoil-stripping along Line 1 of the Dundalk Sewerage Scheme (see No. 446 above). Full excavation was carried out between 30 November and 4 December 1998.

The site was on low-lying ground (4.41m OD), roughly 300m west of the Castletown River, with the natural topography sloping gently from west to east. A local person said that *c.* 40 years ago the whole area to the south of the Castletown Road was boggy marginal land, before being stabilised during the construction of Marion Villas to the east.

The excavation revealed a subrectangular trough, cutting a heavy, yellow, alluvial clay. It was orientated north–south and measured 1.6m x 0.85m and 0.29m deep. The trough was filled by a burnt, black clay with frequent inclusions of heat-shattered sandstone, which contained one fragment of cremated bone.

A layer of burnt, black clay with burnt stone, 2.94m long, lay 0.85m north of the trough. It had been truncated by machine while the archaeologist was monitoring elsewhere on site. This layer sealed a small pit 0.28m wide and 0.23m deep.

Three small, irregular pits cutting the alluvial clay lay 2.75–3m south of the trough. These ranged in size from 1.4m x 0.41m to 0.63m x 0.6m and averaged 0.14m deep. All of these features had two identical fills: a primary fill of redeposited alluvial clay with occasional inclusions of charcoal flecks and fragments of burnt stone, and a secondary fill of dark grey, sticky clay with charcoal and burnt stone.
Rob Lynch, Irish Archaeological Consultancy Ltd, 8 Dungar Terrace, Dun Laoghaire, Co. Dublin, for Valerie J. Keeley Ltd.

448. CHAPEL STREET, DUNDALK
Urban medieval
J048076
97E0124

The development lies south of the junction of Chapel and Yorke Streets. The site of the Seatown Gate in the town wall is marked by Gosling (1991, fig. 13) at the junction, possibly in the middle of Yorke Street, where Chapel Street turns westwards to meet it. The line of the town defences also approaches the site from the south-west.

One test-trench was excavated. A layer of loose, black clay with stone and rubble formed the uppermost layer in the trench, overlying a silt layer and another loose, black clay layer. These were post-medieval in date and together were *c.* 1.5m deep.

A possible ditch was exposed at the east end of the trench, part of it remaining unexposed under the footpath. It was at least 800mm deep and was filled with a very hard-packed material that did not produce finds. Another possible pit or ditch was exposed to the west; it was 9m wide east–west, but, as it was not excavated out, its depth was not recovered. This may have been the uppermost level of the town ditch as suggested for this eastern side of Dundalk by Gosling (1991, 289). Crude remains of a stone wall (max. 1m wide) were exposed west of the latter feature. While it may have run on the line of the town defence here, it was considered unlikely that the stone deposit represented remains of a town wall and more likely the remains of a modern stone wall footing.

Reference:
Gosling, P. 1991: From Dun Delca to Dundalk: the topography and archaeology of a medieval frontier town, AD *c.* 1187–1700. *Journal of the Co. Louth Archaeological and Historical Society* **22** (3), 227–353.

Rosanne Meenan, Roestown, Drumree, Co. Meath.

449. AIB BANK, 96 CLANBRASSIL STREET, DUNDALK
Urban
3047 3075
98E0456
This site lies at the southern end of Clanbrassil Street, in close proximity to the area of Warren's Gate at the edge of the medieval town, but with the expansion of the town during the 17th century the area would have become part of the core of Dundalk.

Testing was undertaken at this site in October 1998, followed by an excavation in January 1999. During the testing programme a layer of cobbles had been identified at the base of the cuttings (25.9m OD). However, no artefacts were recovered that could date this layer. An excavation was undertaken to determine the nature of this cobbled layer. Owing to safety requirements and a modification in the layout of the building, an area 4m x 8m was available for excavation.

Once the overburden had been removed the cobbled layer was shown to extend across the entire area, from which five sherds of medieval pottery were recovered. However, the layer had been extensively damaged by modern drains and pipes. The cobbled layer was cut into a compact, blue-grey clay, which appears to be the original marl deposit.

This cobbled layer also overlay three features cut into the natural marl: a semicircular pit, a linear trench and a shallow pit. These features were filled with a pink/brown clay with a mottled, black mix. They also had a high proportion of organic material, which includes fragments of wood and occasional pieces of shell.
Rónán Swan, Arch-Tech Ltd, 32 Fitzwilliam Place, Dublin 2.

450. CROWE STREET/DEMESNE, DUNDALK
Medieval town
304903 307313
SMR 7:119
98E0310
Testing took place at the site of the demolished public conveniences, Crowe Street and Demesne, Dundalk, Co. Louth, in advance of the proposed construction of new facilities.

Trench 1 was excavated at Crowe Street and was 2.5m long and 1m wide. Under concrete a layer of grey/brown, stony loam with red brick inclusions was encountered. The trench was dug to 1m, which was the required depth for the development.

Trench 2 was dug at Demesne, into a flowerbed. The topsoil was 0.3m deep and overlay a sand deposit 0.3m deep. This in turn overlay a grey/brown, sandy clay loam with inclusions of red brick.
Donald Murphy, Archaeological Consultancy Services Ltd, 15 Trinity Street, Drogheda, Co. Louth.

451. 69 DUBLIN STREET, DUNDALK
Urban
J050070
98E0534
Testing at this site, before the construction of an extension to a dwelling-house, produced nothing of archaeological significance.
Rosanne Meenan, Roestown, Drumree, Co. Meath.

452. 2A EARL STREET, DUNDALK
Urban medieval
J04840717
98E0397
A single trench tested the line of a proposed new wall at the rear of the existing building. Nothing of archaeological interest was exposed.
Rosanne Meenan, Roestown, Drumree, Co. Meath.

453. 19 JOCELYN STREET, DUNDALK
Urban medieval
305211 307384
SMR 7:119
98E0410
Archaeological testing was carried out at the rear of 19 Jocelyn Street, Dundalk, Co. Louth, in advance of a proposed extension to commercial premises. Three trenches were excavated by hand along the proposed footprint of the building. Layers of post-medieval rubble and garden deposits were encountered to a depth of 1m, at which point the natural glacial till was encountered. No features or deposits of archaeological interest were found.
Cóilín Ó Drisceoil, Archaeological Consultancy Services Ltd, 15 Trinity Street, Drogheda, Co. Louth.

454. LAURELS ROAD, DUNDALK
Urban medieval/post-medieval
30472 30776
98E0102
The site consists of an area of cleared ground measuring 26m east–west by 19m, on the north side of Laurels Road, a side street running west from Church Street, which was on the axis of the main street of the medieval town. The exact date of the foundation of Dundalk is unclear, but there is evidence of a developing town in the second quarter of the 13th century.

Laurels Road as a public street dates to the first half of the 20th century; previously it was an entranceway to the demesne of the Clanbrassil Estate. On the OS 6-inch map of 1836 there are buildings along the northern and western perimeters of the site. The building on the western edge of the site was a five-storey grain store, demolished fifteen to twenty years ago.

Five trenches were dug using a mechanical digger and hand-excavation where necessary. The depths of the deposits were measured from the existing ground surface. Demolition rubble overlay the whole site to a maximum depth of 0.75m, bringing the site to the level of the present-day footpath. Beneath this on the western side was a solid concrete floor, visible in Trenches 1 and 2, a foundation wall for the grain store, visible in Trench 3, and a cobbled surface, visible in Trench 5. This cobbled surface was found to occur in Trenches 2, 4 and 5 and was associated with the grain store. Various fills associated with this phase of activity occurred beneath the level of the cobbles, and all were lying on a garden soil that varied from dark greyish-brown to greyish-brown to a grey, friable soil.

The test-trenches show that the old floor levels of the demolished buildings, concrete and cobbles, were at a lower level than the existing level of Laurels Road. This drop in level is still apparent in a yard to the east of the site. Foundation material and rubble fills are present to depths of 0.9–1.65m and everywhere overlie a greyish-brown soil of reasonably homogeneous appearance. The sparse datable finds recovered from the dark soil are of medieval to early 19th-century date. Two medieval pottery sherds from Trench 1 were at the same level as a clay pipe stem. The wide date range of the finds would be consistent with a garden soil. The grain store is shown on the 1836 OS 6-inch map but does not feature on the 1785 Clanbrassil estate map. The site was apparently open garden before the construction of the store sometime around the turn of the 19th century.

Finds included medieval local ware, tin-glazed earthenware, fragments of clay pipe, a fragment of a 17th-century roof ridge-tile and a body sherd and attached handle of a skillet of North Devon gravel-free ware, late 17th-century in date.

Finola O'Carroll, Greenanstown, Stamullin, Co. Meath.

455. MARKET SQUARE, DUNDALK
Urban medieval
30485 30733
98E0532
An archaeological assessment of a proposed office building was carried out at Market Square, within the medieval town of Dundalk, Co. Louth. The site of the proposed development consisted of an overgrown open space at the street front measuring 15m east–west x 9m. It was proposed to construct a three-storey office building to occupy most of the site.

Two trenches were excavated on the site, and the natural boulder clay was exposed at a depth ranging from 1.1m to 1.6m. The ground above this consisted of a fill material containing red brick fragments and industrial waste pipes. No archaeological stratigraphy was exposed, and no features or finds were recovered from the trench.

Deirdre Murphy, Archaeological Consultancy Services Ltd, 15 Trinity Street, Drogheda, Co. Louth.

456. MILL ROAD, CASTLETOWN, DUNDALK
No archaeological significance
30308 30857
SMR 7:118
98E0191
The site lay on the east side of Mill Road and consisted of the northern part of a large garden attached to an existing house. Test-trenches were excavated by machine and were continuous along the lines of the proposed house. Natural glacial till was exposed under 0.25–0.4m of sod and topsoil. No archaeological features were evident, and no artefacts of archaeological interest were found.

Finola O'Carroll, Greenanstown, Stamullin, Co. Meath.

457. MILL ROAD, CASTLETOWN, DUNDALK
18th-century mill-race
J029088
98E0278
The development site (of a single dwelling) fronted onto the Mill Road, with the site of a mill-race, associated with an 18th-century mill, extending through the rear. Test-trenching, however, revealed that the site had been scarped at the Mill Road side and infilled to a depth of *c.* 2m, sealing the mill-race beneath. Consequently no archaeological features were found.

Linzi Simpson, Margaret Gowen & Co. Ltd, 2 Killiney View, Albert Road Lower, Glenageary, Co. Dublin.

458. 66–67 PARK STREET, DUNDALK
Urban medieval
304890 307036
SMR 7:119
98E0033
The site at Park Street underwent archaeological assessment in advance of a proposed commercial development. The site lies within the former walled area of Dundalk.

Two test-trenches were excavated. Trench 1 was 13.8m long and was orientated north-west to south-east, perpendicular to Park Street. At the north-west end of the trench concrete 0.1m thick overlay sandy gravel in the base of the trench at 1.4m below ground level. At *c.* 6m south-east of the footpath a layer of sandy, red brick rubble containing 19th/20th-century pottery extended to a depth of 0.8m. This overlay a grey-green, silty clay with shell, animal bone and local medieval pottery.

Trench 2 was parallel to Trench 1 and was 15m long and 1.2m wide. A layer of red brick rubble 0.2m thick overlay brown loam with red brick fragments. This overlay a layer of yellow, sandy gravel, which contained large quantities of stone and was sterile. This extended to the base of the trench at 1.2m deep.

Deirdre Murphy, Archaeological Consultancy Services Ltd, 15 Trinity Street, Drogheda, Co. Louth.

459. 66–67 PARK STREET, DUNDALK
Medieval town
305402.67051 307408.93978
SMR 7:119
Monitoring was carried out during the construction of factory units at 66–67 Park Street, Dundalk, Co. Louth. Foundation trenches ranged from 0.23m to 0.75m deep and revealed no archaeological deposits.

Deirdre Murphy, Archaeological Consultancy Services Ltd, 15 Trinity Street, Drogheda, Co. Louth.

460. CREDIT UNION, RAMPARTS ROAD, DUNDALK
Medieval town
304557 306561
SMR 7:119
98E0139

Archaeological assessment was carried out at Ramparts Road, Dundalk, Co. Louth, in advance of proposed Credit Union offices. Three trenches were excavated across the site.

All trenches revealed consistent stratigraphy: 0.4–0.42m of topsoil followed by 0.4m of brown loam containing 18th-century pottery, overlying a 0.3m-thick layer of gravel, followed by a sterile, brown, silty clay that continued to 2m below the top of the trench and was first encountered at 3.8m OD.

No datable finds were recovered, and the development proceeded without further archaeological investigation.

Deirdre Murphy, Archaeological Consultancy Services Ltd, 15 Trinity Street, Drogheda, Co. Louth.

461. DUNDEALGAN ATHLETIC CLUB, SEATOWN, DUNDALK
Urban medieval
J05260752
SMR 7:110
98E0436

Archaeological assessment took place at Dundealgan Athletic Club, Seatown, Dundalk, Co. Louth, in advance of a proposed leisure development. Three trenches were dug.

Trench 1 was 4m long, 0.8m wide and 0.9m deep. Topsoil to a depth of 0.4m overlay stony natural. Trench 2 was 3.6m long, 0.8m wide and 1.04m deep. Sod and topsoil extended to 0.2m, under which a layer of 19th-century garden soil was excavated. The layer was 0.08m thick and overlay natural gravel. Trench 3 was 3.9m long, 0.9m wide and 1.2m deep. Sod and topsoil extended to 0.25m, below which a layer of post-medieval garden soil containing much rubble, interpreted as debris from cottages demolished in the 1950s, was excavated, which in turn overlay natural gravel.

Deirdre Murphy, Archaeological Consultancy Services Ltd, 15 Trinity Street, Drogheda, Co. Louth.

462. DUNLEER
Vicinity of ecclesiastical enclosure
30581 28808
98E0348

An archaeological assessment was carried out before the commencement of the Dunleer Sewerage Scheme, at the site of the sewage treatment works and along the line of the pipelines both in and on the outskirts of the town. Dunleer is an Early Christian foundation dating to the 6th or 7th century.

Three test-trenches were excavated, two of them in Main Street, to test for the possible survival of an Early Christian enclosure, and the third to test for the survival of burials at the point where the scheme comes closest to the churchyard.

Evidence of disturbance caused by insertion of sewerage and water pipes was exposed in Main Street, to a maximum depth of 3m in the case of Trench 2 but at a higher depth in Trench 1. The third test-trench exposed natural subsoil under garden soil.

Nothing of archaeological interest was exposed in the three trenches.

Rosanne Meenan, Roestown, Drumree, Co. Meath.

463. FARRANDREG
Souterrain
J03000800
95E0109 ext.

Construction work at Farrandreg, Castletown, Dundalk, Co. Louth, revealed the dry-stone air vent of a souterrain on top of a prominent, flat-topped rise east of Farrandreg House. Ten souterrains lie within a one-mile radius of the site.

Archaeological assessment uncovered a dark stain marking the line of a backfilled souterrain against the yellow, compact, natural, sandy clay. A trial-trench revealed a dark, soft, humic deposit, which contained lenses of charcoal, ash and stone. The walls of the souterrain were recovered at 0.96m below the surface. They were built from large, irregular blocks of limestone, which were corbelled towards the top, standing up to 1.04m high. A thin layer of redeposited natural underlay the fill and in turn overlay a large stone lintel. It was evident that further passages existed below. Full excavation then took place.

The souterrain was entered through a narrow creep that ran east and west. The eastern section led to a large, rectangular chamber, up to 2.8m wide, 4.4m long and 1m high, with a central wall for supporting lintels. The western passage led to the substantial oblong chamber first discovered in testing. From this, two lower chambers were entered through a semicircular drop-hole. The first was 8.5m long, up to 1.3m wide and between 1.04m and 1.5m high. It was the terminal point of the air vent. The second was entered through a semicircular drop-hole. Four rectangular slots were positioned over the drop-hole and contained charcoal, suggesting a trap-door entrance. The lower chamber was partially cut from bedrock and opened substantially towards the west. It was 7.5m long, between 1.1m and 2m wide and up to 2.1m high. Lintels had been robbed from all the upper chambers, while the latter two were intact and had evidently not been entered. The upper chambers were filled with occupation debris, i.e. black loam with frequent lenses of ash and charcoal, evidently settlement debris from occupation above.

Finds included stick pins, souterrain ware, a fragmentary rotary quern, bone needles, a bone comb, worked flint and animal bone. It appears from the stratigraphical record that the lintels were robbed in antiquity, owing to the lack of any finds datable to later than the 12th century. Post-excavation work is ongoing, and the souterrain has been backfilled.

Deirdre Murphy, Archaeological Consultancy Services Ltd, 15 Trinity Street, Drogheda, Co. Louth.

464. KNOCKLORE
Circular enclosure (site of), cemetery (site of)
N92759240
98E0126

Plans to improve the nearby N2 road included realigning it through this site. Trial-trenching, carried out in 1996 by Martin Fitzpatrick, showed that bulldozing of the site in 1964 had removed all traces of the monument (*Excavations 1996*, 82,

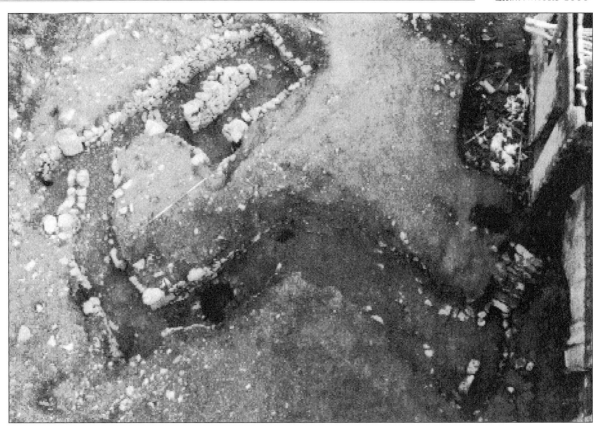

Overall shot of souterrain at Farrandreg, Co. Louth.

96E0162). A request by the National Museum of Ireland was made for the hand-excavation of a 10m x 10m area in the centre of the site. This was carried out from 12 to 20 March 1998. No archaeological remains or strata were found.

Colin D. Gracie, 8 Abbeydale Close, Lucan, Co. Dublin, for Valerie J. Keeley Ltd.

465. KNOCKNAGORAN
Earthwork site
31384 31682
SMR 5:5
98E0318

This site is listed in both the *Archaeological inventory of County Louth* and the *Archaeological survey of County Louth*. The same entry appears in both volumes: 'Earthwork (site) Marked as an antiquity on the current OS 6-inch map and known locally as "O'Hagan's Fort". No visible surface trace except curve in field fence to S (C *c.* 50m).'

The curving field fence is composed of a bank faced with granite boulders and surmounted by a hedge, similar to the other field fences in this area. The northern circuit of the site is defined by a scarp as shown on the OS maps. The topographical setting and placename evidence suggest that the site is that of a levelled ringfort.

The proposed development consisted of a small housing estate built to the west of the earthwork, which was to be retained as a landscaped feature but would have an access road pass beside it. Trenching in the areas closest to the earthwork that will be disturbed by house building did not reveal any archaeological material.

A trench was dug to the north of the monument along the line of the proposed access route. Natural stony clay was exposed under topsoil at a depth of 0.1–0.3m for 19m at the eastern end of the trench. Westwards, closer to the earthwork, a deposit of grey soil overlying stones was uncovered for a distance of 17m along the trench. The grey soil had a maximum thickness of 0.2m and was a soft, sandy, silty clay that contained no stones and only occasional charcoal inclusions. The stones below were mostly of grey-green shale, with occasional granite, and had an average size of 100mm, with some up to 300mm. No artefacts were observed in either the soil or stone layers. These petered out at the western end of the trench, where topsoil, 0.3m thick, covered natural, orange, sandy clay.

Two further trenches were dug, which indicated that the grey soil spread upslope towards the earthwork for 5m and for a distance of 1m from the line of Trench 1. The stony layer spread further to the north than the grey soil.

In the western part of Trench 1 a short gully crossed it running east–west. This was 0.5m wide and 0.25m deep. It had a fill of soft, dark grey/brown, sandy loam with small to medium-sized (200mm) stones. No finds were recovered from it.

The deposits of grey soil and loose stones are of unknown date. They follow an approximate north-east/south-west course in a hollow at the base of the slope from the earthwork. They are 15m from the top of the scarp defining the earthwork and are therefore unlikely to represent the filled-in ditch of a ringfort. Also, the stones appear to be deliberate dumping rather than a gradual accumulation. As a spring is marked on the map but is not now visible, they may represent a reclamation of wet ground. If so, the materials used to reclaim the hollow may have derived from the banks of the ringfort, of which there is now no trace.

The small gully is a possible archaeological feature.

It was recommended that these features be further investigated if the road layout could not be altered to avoid them.

Finola O'Carroll, Greenanstown, Stamullin, Co. Meath.

466. PRIORSTATE, LOUTH
Medieval borough
295218 301429
SMR 11:115
98E0227
Archaeological assessment was undertaken at the site of a proposed commercial/residential development at Louth village, Co. Louth. The site lies within the area of archaeological importance occupied by the Early Christian monastery and the medieval borough. Two trenches were excavated along the footprint of the proposed house. Boulder clay occurred under sod at a depth of 0.3–0.4m. No archaeological features or objects were recovered.

Donald Murphy, Archaeological Consultancy Services Ltd, 15 Trinity Street, Drogheda, Co. Louth.

467. RICHARD TAAFFES HOLDING, LOUTH
Urban medieval
296260 301030
SMR 11:115
98E0413
Archaeological assessment was undertaken at the site of a proposed commercial development at Louth village, Co. Louth. The site lies within the area of archaeological importance occupied by the Early Christian monastery and the medieval borough. Six trenches were excavated along the footprint of the building. Boulder clay occurred under sod and modern sandy clay at a depth of 0.5m. No archaeological features or objects were recovered.

Deirdre Murphy, Archaeological Consultancy Services Ltd, 15 Trinity Street, Drogheda, Co. Louth.

468. MULLAGHARLIN AND HAGGARDSTOWN
Enclosure
J05250438
98E0440
Pre-development testing was undertaken in an area of approximately 100 acres, designated Site B, near the Finnabair Industrial Estate, Dundalk, Co. Louth. Within the area to be investigated there was one known archaeological site, a horseshoe-shaped, ditched feature, SMR 7:95. In the surrounding area there are a number of souterrains and an enclosure, suggesting that the landscape has a very high potential for sites dating to the Early Christian period.

Of the 28 trenches examined, only three produced archaeological remains. Trench 1 was dug at the horseshoe-shaped enclosure. A 2m x 24.4m trench was excavated from the centre of the enclosure southwards across the open area of the site to a maximum depth of 2.3m. Within this the continuation of the line of the enclosing ditch was uncovered. The ditch was 5.3m wide at its top and had an excavated depth of 1.8m. It had been cut through the slaty boulder clay on its southern edge and through what appeared to be a peat-filled natural hollow (containing wood remains) on its northern (interior) edge. The fills of the ditch comprised a peaty clay fill at its base with overlying shaly clay deposits, which may have been part of the original bank.

This enclosure may have been a small ringfort, although no internal features were uncovered, with the exception of a small area of charcoal and burnt stone measuring 1.8m x 0.6m.

It must be noted that with the enclosing ditch and external bank the interior of the site would have been quite small when compared with other known ringforts and crannogs.

Trench 7, orientated approximately north–south, measured 66m x 5m, with a 6m x 10m extension at its southern end. In this southern area of the trench, at the break in slope between a natural hillock and ridge, two areas of burnt and heat-shattered stones were uncovered sitting on the clayey gravel subsoil. The first measured *c*. 5m x 4.5m, and the second 2m x 1m. No finds were recovered from either area of burning, which had both been severely disturbed by later plough action.

Trench 13 measured 95m x 5m and was oriented north-west/south-east. Below the topsoil, at the southern end of the trench, another small area of burnt stone and charcoal-rich soil was uncovered sitting on the natural. This measured 1.1m x 1.4m. No finds were recovered from this area, which also had been disturbed by plough action.

Work is currently continuing in this part of Site B, and a buffer zone has been delimited around the horseshoe-shaped enclosure.

Dermot G. Moore, Archaeological Development Services Ltd, Windsor House, 11 Fairview Strand, Fairview, Dublin 3.

469. MULLAGHARLIN AND HAGGARDSTOWN
Possible ringfort
J052504338
SMR 7:95
98E0440 ext.
Archaeological testing of the proposed Xerox Industrial Park was carried out by Dermot Moore (No. 468 above). Further testing was carried out by this writer, under an extension of the original licence, in the vicinity of a horseshoe-shaped enclosure.

Three trenches were excavated, to the north, east and west of the monument, extending from the ditch edge, to ensure that no archaeological remains existed within a proposed 10m buffer zone around the site. The trenches were mechanically excavated by a digger fitted with a toothless bucket and on average measured 2m x 20m.

A small area of charcoal-stained soil lay within the northern trench, *c*. 6m from the monument. It lay directly above subsoil. This was not investigated further as it lies within the buffer zone. All of the trenches were excavated to subsoil, but no further evidence of archaeological material was identified.

Audrey Gahan, Archaeological Development Services Ltd, Unit 48, Westlink Enterprise Centre, 30–50 Distillery Street, Belfast BT12 5BJ.

470. PHILLIPSTOWN
Vicinity of holy well
O010863
98E0584
There is a record of a holy well in the townland of Phillipstown (Mosstown Parish), Dunleer, Co. Louth, with the tradition that it lay 'by the roadside to N. of RC church' (notes from SMR files for SMR 17:64). Its

precise location is not noted. A dwelling-house was planned for the side of the road *c.* 80m north of the Catholic Church.

Four trenches were excavated to test the location of the proposed well, in the gateway and driveway of the development, as these all lie by the side of the road, as well as in the locations of the house and of the percolation area. A continuous shallow trench was cut along the line of the driveway.

A grey, loamy sod and ploughsoil, 200–300mm deep, overlay a mixed, natural glacial deposit. This varied from grey to brown and also in stone content. Nothing of archaeological significance was observed.
Rosanne Meenan, Roestown, Drumree, Co. Meath.

471. TATTYBOYS/KNOCKLORE/COOKSTOWN/ RAHANNA/HARRISTOWN/GLEBE
Group of *fulacht fiadh*-type features
292150 295600 to 295920 291580
Included site of SMR 14:14
98E0125

Monitoring was carried out of topsoil-stripping on the 5.5km-long line of the widening and other improvements taking place on the N2 running north-east from Ardee. Nine spreads of burnt material were found and excavated (Sites A–I). No other archaeological features were found.

Sites B, C, D and E were thin spreads of grey soil, some with flecks of charcoal.

Site F (Td Knocklore; 29265 29527) was similar to these but contained some cremated human bone, along with some fragments of cattle bone. It was approximately circular, with a diameter of *c.* 0.9m.

Site G (Td Knocklore; 292847 295189) consisted of three circular, dish-shaped hollows filled with burnt stone and black, charcoal-rich soil. There were no finds.

Site A (Td Tattyboys; 292348 295504) was a spread of burnt stone and charcoal-rich soil covering an approximately triangular area measuring 9m x 5m. One side was cut away by a pipe-trench before the commencement of excavation. The average depth of the burnt spread was 0.25m, and it overlay hard yellow clay. Four features were dug into the clay. Two parallel furrows 0.2m wide and 60mm deep were also cut through the burnt material and were filled with the brown soil that overlay it. The burnt material at this point was 70mm thick. A shallow post-hole (oval in plan, 0.28m x 0.21m in diameter and 0.11m deep), an oval pit (0.8m x 0.55m in diameter and 0.3m deep) and a rectangular pit (2.26m x 1.27m and 0.5m deep) were all filled with burnt stones and charcoal-rich soil. Three flat stones lay on the base of the latter at one end. A few whole fragments of charcoal were found in the fill. Apart from these the charcoal was comminuted, and there were no artefacts at all found on this site.

Site I (Td Cookstown; 293107 294920) was a spread of burnt stones and charcoal-rich soil measuring 11m x 9m at least (to the north-west it extended beyond the take of the road and so could not be investigated further in that direction). The depth ranged from 0.1m to 0.3m, except at the edges, where it tapered off. It lay on top of yellow/grey clay with many stones, and in places the bedrock was exposed. The surface was very uneven in places, with numerous hollows of various sizes, but all apparently natural. Part of the area, however, appeared to consist of a flat platform, and it was here that a rectangular pit was found cut into the surface. The 'platform' was bounded on two sides by hollows that may have been artificially deepened but appeared to be primarily natural. The rectangular pit measured 2.5m x 1.2m and was *c.* 0.3m deep. A piece of stone with incised lines was found near the base of the layer in one of the hollows, and a few pieces of cattle bone (some burnt) and teeth were also found.

Site H (Td Cookstown; 292934 295028) consisted of a spread of burnt stones covering an area measuring *c.* 8m x 6m. Charcoal-rich soil was present in the upper 0.1m. Adjoining the deposit was a pond, part of which had been reclaimed by filling it with stones. This, and the presence of a modern coin in the burnt layer, suggests that it was a similar site to A and I but was subsequently disturbed.
Thaddeus C. Breen, 13 Wainsfort Crescent, Dublin 6W, for Valerie J. Keeley Ltd.

472. CREDIT UNION, BIG STREET, TERMONFECKIN
Vicinity of Early Christian monastery site
31415 28044
SMR 22:24, 25
98E0075

Archaeological assessment took place at the Credit Union, Big Street, Termonfeckin, Co. Louth, in advance of a proposed extension. Termonfeckin was the location of an early monastic site of which a possible enclosure, church foundations and cemetery, two souterrains, a high cross, a well and a grave slab remain. It is also the site of a later medieval borough that included two late medieval tower-houses.

Three trenches were excavated. Trench 1 was north–south in orientation and 11m long, 1m wide and 1.5m deep. Sod was 0.1m deep and overlay a sandy, brown loam 0.4m deep, which produced no finds. This lay over the boulder clay, which was cut by two pits measuring 1m and 0.6m in diameter, filled with dark brown clay and stone, but produced no finds.

Trench 2 was 5m long and was excavated to a depth of 1m. The boulder clay was exposed at 0.5m under topsoil.

Trench 3, 12m long, 1m wide and 1m deep, was excavated in the south end. Boulder clay was encountered at 0.6m deep. A pit, 0.9m wide and 0.7m deep, cut into the natural clay, contained stones but no diagnostic finds.
Donald Murphy, Archaeological Consultancy Services Ltd, 15 Trinity Street, Drogheda, Co. Louth.

473. STRAND ROAD, TERMONFECKIN
Vicinity of Early Christian monastic site
O14148044
SMR 22:24, 25
98E0406

Archaeological assessment was carried out at Strand Road, Termonfeckin, Co. Louth, in December 1998 in advance of a proposed residential development. The site lies immediately south of the known location of the Early Christian monastery, the remains of which consist of two souterrains, a high cross and possible church foundations. Termonfeckin was also a major ecclesiastical centre in the later medieval period, and a borough was founded at this location.

Nine test-trenches were excavated in the areas to be disturbed. Trenches 1–3 and 5 in the south-east corner of the site revealed medieval loam layers at between 0.6m and 0.81m below the sod. Trench 4, in the north-east corner of the site, revealed three roughly equally spaced cuts into natural, between 0.6m and 1m in diameter, filled with dark brown, silty clay containing medieval pottery. These were interpreted as medieval plough furrows. Part of a small cut filled with a mid-brown loam and a high percentage of shell was encountered in the east of this trench. All of these features lay under 0.69m of sod and ploughsoil.

Trench 8 in the north-eastern corner revealed three linear cuts of medieval date, which were interpreted as plough furrows, a part of a pit containing loam and a large quantity of shell at 0.6m below sod.

Trench 6 contained a layer of redeposited natural underlying 0.53m of sod and ploughsoil. This overlay a setting of unmortared stones. The trench was excavated down to 1m below the sod.

Trench 7 in the south-west of the site uncovered sod/topsoil up to 0.52m thick. It overlay a layer of mid-brown loam containing a large percentage of shell and animal bone. No datable artefacts were found in the 0.28m of this layer that was excavated. A spread of charcoal and fire-reddened clay underlay this layer and was not excavated further.

Trench 8 was excavated close to the western boundary of the site. Sod and ploughsoil were up to 0.44m thick. They overlay a layer of mid-brown loam between 0.18m and 0.41m thick, containing a large percentage of shell. The orange boulder clay lay under this. A portion of a cut into natural was encountered at the northern end of the trench. This was filled with a mid-brown loam containing a large fragment of local medieval pottery. A linear cut was visible at the western end of the trench cut into natural and a hard, silty grey-brown clay.

Trench 9 revealed a cut into natural underlying up to 0.65m of sod and ploughsoil. This was filled with a sticky, dark brown clay containing a high percentage of shell and animal bone.
Donald Murphy, Archaeological Consultancy Services Ltd, 15 Trinity Street, Drogheda, Co. Louth.

MAYO

474. AGHTABOY
Rath
SMR 81:29
98E0505
This proposed development, of a house and shed at Aghtaboy, Knock, Co. Mayo, was allowed within 6m of a univallate rath, situated in the adjacent field to north. The rath is enclosed by an earthen bank, with no indication of a fosse.

Four trenches were opened on 22–3 December 1998. Within those trenches closest to the monument the outside of a fosse was encountered. Although only a short stretch was encountered, it was at a distance of *c.* 4m parallel to the bank of the fort. It has been cut into the boulder clay, and, while no width measurement could be obtained from the cutting, it is at least 0.8m deep into the boulder clay. A stony, dark clay layer fills much of the upper part of the fosse, with a yellowish mixture of clay and daub beneath.

In other trenches, beneath the topsoil was a light brown, fine clay, in which was a good scatter of unworked chert and white quartz.

In the light of the findings the house is in the process of being repositioned
Leo Morahan, James Street, Kiltimagh, Co. Mayo.

475. AHENA
Cemetery
1285 2745
98E0177
A rescue investigation took place at Ahena, Co. Mayo, after the discovery of human remains during gravel quarrying. An enclosure, not recorded in the SMR, was uncovered 148m south of the burial site. The remains of nine individuals were recovered from the site. Orientation suggests Christian burial. One of the nearby fields is known as the 'Coilean field', which may be a corruption of *Cillín*.
Deirdre Murphy, Archaeological Consultancy Services Ltd, 15 Trinity Street, Drogheda, Co. Louth.

476. BALLA
No archaeological significance
98E0289
Nothing of archaeological significance was found during monitoring of foundations at this site.
Gerry Walsh, Rathbawn Road, Castlebar, Co. Mayo.

477. HIGH STREET, BALLINROBE
No archaeological significance
SMR 118:22
98E0391
Pre-development testing was undertaken on the site of a proposed development of eight houses in High Street, Ballinrobe, Co. Mayo, in August 1998.

Six test-trenches, 12m x 2m and 15m x 2m, were excavated by machine. In general the sod/topsoil layer directly overlay a natural, light brown boulder clay. No archaeological features or finds were recovered from any of the trenches,
Gerry Walsh, Rathbawn Road, Castlebar, Co. Mayo.

478. BALLYHAUNIS SEWERAGE SCHEME
Urban
61599 274159
98E0032
Monitoring of groundworks associated with the Ballyhaunis Sewerage Scheme Project was undertaken on various dates from late January to early October 1998. It had been recommended by NMHP, *Dúchas*, that all ground disturbance associated with the development be monitored, under licence, by an archaeologist. However, the area encompassing the proposed wastewater treatment plant, site compound and access road were subjected to topsoil-stripping and general ground-surface reductions in September 1997 without archaeological involvement.

The project provided for the construction of a new sewage pumping station and storm storage tank on Clare Street, a new wastewater treatment works at Abbeyquarter, sewers to direct flow to the pumping station and a rising main to the wastewater treatment works. The project also included the construction of surface water sewers, watermains and ducts on Clare Street, Main Street, Knox Street and Bridge Street. The construction of an advance section of the Ballyhaunis

Water Supply Augmentation Scheme was also included in the project brief.

All streetworks were to take place on the western side of the town, with the treatment works situated on the southern side.

In general both the rising main to and the outfall from the treatment works were laid in green-field contexts, with the remaining works situated along existing roads and streets. The groundworks were generally confined to the required width of the pipeline trenches. However, a layer of peat, with a maximum thickness of c. 1.4m, was revealed by trial-trenching along the length of Clare Street and in the area of the pumping station. It was subsequently decided that the peaty layer would be removed along the entire street, footpath edge to footpath edge, from its junction with Bridge Street/Main Street to the outermost extent of the scheme. In all other areas it was revealed that previous roadworks had truncated the surface of the subsoil.

The only features of note uncovered during the scheme were stone culverts running south-east across Clare Street and down Main Street. No other features or finds of interest were revealed during the course of the work.

Martin E. Byrne, 39 Kerdiff Park, Monread, Naas, Co. Kildare.

479. CARROWBEG

Rath
SMR 62:45
97E0474

Monitoring of soil removal was carried out on 11 April 1998 in advance of the erection of a horse exercise unit at Carrowbeg, Swinford, Co. Mayo. The site lies just north and north-north-west of a univallate rath, which is situated on a drumlin, at least 3.8m above the level of the field at north.

Removal of soil, to a maximum depth of 0.65m, showed stony clay of varying thickness overlying gravel.

Nothing of archaeological significance was revealed in the monitoring.

Leo Morahan, James Street, Kiltimagh, Co. Mayo.

480. KNOCKACROGHERY, CASTLEBAR

Urban
SMR 78:3
98E0071

Pre-development testing was undertaken on the site of proposed developments in Knockacroghery, Castlebar, Co. Mayo, in February 1998. Half of the proposed development site lies within the designated archaeological area of Castlebar town.

It appears that over the years some topsoil has been removed from the development site and that some modern rubble and fill has been dumped onto it.

Eight test-trenches were excavated by machine. No archaeological features or small finds were recovered from any of the trenches.

Gerry Walsh, Rathbawn Road, Castlebar, Co. Mayo.

481. CASTLEGAR

Burnt spread
SMR 101:25
98E0454

As part of the assessment of the ongoing Knock/

Claremorris Bypass archaeological testing was undertaken in the road corridor adjacent to an enclosure. The eastern (outer) edge of the levelled enclosure is 20m from the acquisition line of the proposed bypass.

The sod/topsoil layer, 0.7m thick, directly overlay a natural, orange boulder clay. A small spread of burnt soil and charcoal, measuring 1.5m x 1m and 30mm thick, was uncovered in the northern end of the area tested. No finds were recovered. A chert end-scraper was recovered from the topsoil adjacent to it.

Gerry Walsh, Áras An Chondae, Mayo County Council, Castlebar, Co. Mayo.

482. CLARE

Fulacht fiadh
98E0412

A rescue excavation was carried out when a *fulacht fiadh* was revealed during topsoil removal for the Knock/Claremorris Bypass. The site lies on the outer edges of a tract of bogland, south-east of Claremorris town.

Already disturbed by land reclamation, it was seen directly below the sod as a level spread of burnt and heat-fractured stone covering an area of 8.2m north–south by 11.3m. A cutting placed centrally through the burnt material revealed a sub-oval, wooden trough, aligned north–south and held in place at each end by a series of short stakes hammered into the underlying boulder clay. A narrow wooden causeway facilitated access to the trough, extending from its southern extremity for a distance of 3m. The causeway was composed largely of a single felled tree. Both the trough and the causeway had been set into boulder clay.

A further deposit of wood, consisting of individual branches and brushwood, was noted adjacent to the west of the causeway and seemed to be contemporary with it. The branch and brushwood layer was randomly placed and would have provided a suitable working surface in an otherwise wet, low-lying area.

Post-dating these features and lying diagonally across the causeway 0.3m above it was a subrectangular wooden platform 1.2m long and 0.7m wide. It consisted of six split, branch-trimmed timbers, laid down to form the base of the platform, with a shorter closing timber at each end.

A multi-platform chert core was found amongst a concentrated deposit of hazelnut shells, animal bone and charcoal. This was the only artefact uncovered. More information concerning activities on the site as well as their time-frame will be revealed with the results of analysis of the wood and environmental samples.

Suzanne Zajac, 1 Chapel Lane, Killala, Co. Mayo.

483. CLARE

No archaeological significance
98E0412

Set stone and large split timbers were uncovered during topsoil removal on the Knock/Claremorris Bypass. They were found a short distance north-east of a *fulacht fiadh* (No. 482 above) and were investigated under the same licence. Once uncovered the set stones were seen to be a stone-built culvert. The accompanying timbers were thought to have originat-

ed from the building of the adjacent railway during the last century. A small flake of waste flint was found in the disturbed topsoil overlying these features.
Suzanne Zajac, 1 Chapel Lane, Killala, Co. Mayo.

484. COOLROE

Fulachta fiadh
98E0389

This site was identified by Gerry Walsh during the site assessment of the main treatment works for the Claremorris Sewerage Scheme. Three adjacent *fulachta fiadh* were fully excavated. Each consisted of a mound of burnt stone in a matrix of charcoal-rich clay, with one or more troughs cut into the subsoil. Associated finds included cut wooden stakes, several struck flakes of chert, one flint scraper and some antler and bone.

The first to be excavated was discovered while digging a drain to the east of Site 5 (a *fulacht* identified during the original site assessment, see below). It consisted of a mound of heat-fractured stone in a matrix of charcoal-stained, black, silty clay. It was roughly oval in plan, measuring 19m x 9m, reaching a maximum thickness of 0.6m. The main features were a rectangular trough measuring 1.9m x 1.3 and 0.2m deep and a pit/trough roughly circular in plan with a diameter of 0.9–0.55m and a depth of 0.26m. Another, less definite rectangular trough was also identified.

Several wooden stakes were recovered from the vicinity of the site but did not appear to form any part of a regular feature or structure. Small finds included one flint end-scraper and several flakes of struck chert, including a number of chert blades. Some bone and fragments of at least two antlers and a poorly preserved skull with antlers still attached were recovered adjacent to the mound.

The second to be excavated was Site 5. The mound had a horseshoe-shaped plan above the surface but was oval at its base, measuring 12m north–south x 17m and 0.7m in maximum thickness. Two troughs occurred below the mound.

The central trough measured 3.5m x 2.3m and was 0.1m deep. It had an almost circular recut to the south-east, with a diameter of 1.6m, and had a maximum depth of 0.3m. The recut had been dug down as far as a natural layer of marl in the subsoil. At this level several stakes were visible at or near the sides of the trough. There were about 34 stakes, some surviving as small fragments and others as long as 0.4m, with cut ends. The second trough was almost square in plan with sides 1.6m long and a depth of 0.2m. Other features include a post-hole, a drain and some hollows.

Small finds from this site include some struck chert flakes, antler fragments and some worked wood.

The third *fulacht* was discovered during soil-stripping of the surrounding area, 3m east of Site 5. The mound was roughly horseshoe-shaped, measured 11.2m east–west x 7m and was 0.3m in maximum thickness. The trough was to the south of the mound within the horseshoe. It measured 1.6m north–south x 0.95m and was 0.2m deep. Finds included one struck chert waste flake, some bone and one piece of worked wood. A cut through the north-west quarter of the site probably represents a later drain, and a hollow filled with mound material

and redeposited natural to the west of it may also represent later disturbance.
Richard Gillespie, Moneen Roundabout, Castlebar, Co. Mayo.

485. CORIMLA SOUTH

Enclosure
SMR 31:54
98E0388

Pre-development testing was carried out on a levelled enclosure to ascertain whether any subsurface features remained intact before the proposed construction of a dwelling-house. The enclosure had been extant until 1958, and based on cartographic evidence and topographical location it had been tentatively classified as a possible barrow.

The development site is rectangular in plan and covers 0.462ha. The archaeological site is contained within this, just east of centre. Vague traces of a shallow, curving depression were evident from east clockwise to south-east, which may have been the remains of a ditch. Other than this the area consisted of level grassland.

Four areas were tested. None of the areas examined revealed evidence of archaeological material. The shallow, curving depression noted before testing appeared to be a natural fall in the ground. Local information suggested that extensive reclamation and deep ploughing had previously occurred within this area.
Suzanne Zajac, 1 Chapel Lane, Killala, Co. Mayo.

486. DOOGORT (ACHILL ISLAND)

No archaeological significance
97E0473 ext.

Monitoring took place of pipe-laying trenches under the road surface and through areas of peat. No archaeological features or small finds were identified.
Richard Gillespie, Moneen Roundabout, Castlebar, Co. Mayo.

487. FARRANOO/GARRANKEEL/
BELLEEK/KILMORE–MOY

Fulachta fiadh
98E0284

Before the commencement of the development the site, an area of *c.* 100 acres, consisted of undulating, well-drained pastureland and pockets of water-logged peat. The removal of topsoil by bulldozers and mechanical diggers was monitored.

Two spreads of heat-fractured stones, each with an associated trough, were identified at the south-west area of the development. The spreads were positioned at a distance of *c.* 20m apart, at the edge of a low-lying, waterlogged area. The ground level rose to the west and south of the sites.

The spreads were excavated by hand. Spread 1 was subrectangular in plan. It measured 13.5m north–south by 11.5m and ranged from 0.2m to 0.5m high. It was composed of a combination of heat-fractured sandstone (80%) and limestone (10%) in a charcoal-rich matrix. Two modern field drains and a horse, buried in a machine-dug pit, cut the spread.

A trough underlay the north-east edge of the spread. It was oval in plan and measured 1.55m along its long axis and 0.55m deep.

Spread 2 was sub-oval in plan. It measured 8.2m

east–west by 4m and reached a maximum height of 0.26m. Modern agricultural activities and topsoil-stripping had truncated the northern edge. The primary components were heat-fractured sandstone (80%) and limestone (20%).

A trough was sealed and partly filled by the burnt mound material. Its northern end had been removed by recent agricultural activity. It survived for a length of 2.75m and ranged from 0.6m to 0.76m wide. The sides were straight, and its base was flat.

The excavation retrieved no small finds of archaeological significance.

Paula King, Patrician Park, Newport Road, Castlebar, Co. Mayo, for Margaret Gowen and Co. Ltd.

488. FRENCHGROVE

Crannog

E000996

During the summer of 1997 a newly discovered crannog was reported to National Monuments, and the IAWU was requested to carry out an assessment of the site. An area 8.5m long, 4.5m wide and up to 0.9m deep had been machine-excavated within the palisade, and as a result a two-day project to reinstate the site was undertaken and reported in *Excavations 1997*, 208.

A further week's work was carried out from 20 to 24 April 1998 to complete the reinstatement, recover artefacts and carry out palaeoenvironmental sampling. This involved trowelling and limited wet sieving of the upcast spoil and recording and protection of timbers.

The disturbance of the site had upcast 22 large worked trunks and five split timbers, three of which had extremely long tenons at each end. These timbers were recorded in 1997, and the records were updated in 1998. All of the trunks and two of the less well-preserved split timbers were reburied at the site, and the remaining three timbers have been put in storage on site, awaiting their removal for conservation.

The upcast spoil heaps were divided into transects and trowelled so that any patterns in the distribution of artefacts or palaeoenvironmental samples could be identified. All artefacts and animal bones were retrieved, as well as samples of stone types, burnt stone and dating samples.

The overall number of artefacts recovered was small; however, a range of domestic artefacts was represented, including whetstones, grinding stones and a spindle whorl, and fragments of querns, of a glass bead, of a wooden vessel and of a copper-alloy object. Preliminary analysis of the animal bone indicated a predominantly domesticated assemblage.

A dendrochronological date of after AD 733 has been returned for a timber from a disturbed context.

Conor McDermott, Irish Archaeological Wetland Unit, Department of Archaeology, University College Dublin, Belfield, Dublin 4.

489. GARRANKEEL

19th-century tree ring

125901 321179

98E0214

Archaeological assessment was carried out at Garrankeel, Ballina, Co. Mayo, in advance of a proposed industrial development. The site consisted of two low banks at right angles to each other,

identified in the course of an Environmental Impact Statement.

Two trenches were excavated. Trench 1, 3.5m x 1m, was placed across the eastern bank. Sod was found to overlie naturally derived gravel, which overlay natural, yellow/brown boulder clay. No trace of a ditch was recovered, and the interior contained a layer of stony, brown clay in which were two iron handles of a bucket of probable 19th-century date. The feature appears to be a 19th-century tree ring, built as part of Belleek Castle demesne.

Donald Murphy, Archaeological Consultancy Services Ltd, 15 Trinity Street, Drogheda, Co. Louth.

490. TULRAHAN GRAVEYARD, KILDARRA

No archaeological significance

SMR 102:42

98E0595

Pre-development testing was undertaken on the site of a proposed extension to Tulrahan graveyard, Kildarra, Co. Mayo. The proposed extension lies within the zoned area of archaeological importance for the site of ecclesiastical remains.

Four test-trenches were excavated by machine on the site of the proposed extension. In general topsoil overlay boulder clay. No archaeological features or small finds were recovered from any of the trenches.

Gerry Walsh, Áras An Chondae, Mayo County Council, Castlebar, Co. Mayo.

491. LECARROW

No archaeological significance

98E0458

Pre-development testing was undertaken on the site of a proposed modern graveyard extension, west of Crossmolina, Co. Mayo. This writer had noted a previously unrecorded possible archaeological mound on top of a natural hill at the rear of the graveyard. Three test-trenches were excavated by machine adjacent to the mound.

In Trenches 1 and 2 the sod/topsoil layer overlay boulder clay or bedrock. In the southern half of Trench 3 the sod/topsoil directly overlay the limestone bedrock. At a point 15m from the northern end of the trench the stratigraphy changed. It appears that in the recent past some gravel had been extracted from the hill and some small stones, possibly collected from field clearance, were backfilled into the gravel pit. For a distance of *c.* 10m a stone fill layer, 0.65m thick, directly underlay the sod. Underlying this stone fill layer was a layer of brown clay 0.5m thick, which in turn overlay another layer of stone fill, 0.4m thick. This lower layer of stone fill directly overlay the bedrock. The layers of fill were backfilled and graded to coincide with the contours of the hill.

No archaeological features or small finds were recovered from any of the test-trenches.

Gerry Walsh, Áras An Chondae, Mayo County Council, Castlebar, Co. Mayo.

492. RUSHBROOK EAST

Mound

13436 27263

SMR 101:71

98E0193 ext.

The site, a roughly circular, flat-topped mound, was

on land owned by Claremorris Golf Club. It measured *c.* 29m in diameter. Preliminary testing by Gerry Walsh identified a ditch at the northern and western sides of the monument.

Further investigation entailed the excavation by hand of five cuttings. The cuttings were positioned to examine the ditch and the interior of the monument in detail. As the findings from the excavation of these cuttings were inconclusive, in consultation with *Dúchas* the remaining area of the site was stripped under archaeological supervision using a mini-digger.

It was found that the mound was a natural feature composed of gravel and boulder clay. A ditch encircled its base. The ditch averaged 3.2m wide and reached a maximum depth of *c.* 1m. It was filled primarily with deposits of rounded limestone mixed with brown loam. Evidence indicated that the ditch had been widened.

Rabbits had substantially disturbed the upper 0.75m of the ditch fill. Some landscaping attributable to the development of the golf course was also in evidence. Finds retrieved from the ditch were a number of pieces of iron slag, animal bones, golf balls and rabbit snares.

Cultivation furrows cut the subsoil in the interior of the enclosure. The furrows averaged 0.4–0.6m wide and reached a maximum depth of 0.1–0.2m. Finds retrieved from the furrows included modern pottery, glass and a 1955 sixpenny piece. Two relatively large sherds and a number of fragments of prehistoric pottery were also retrieved from the interior of the enclosure. Rose Cleary, UCC, has identified the sherds as being similar to Western Neolithic pottery. Unfortunately they were not retrieved from a secure context, and a date for the interior of the enclosure cannot be inferred from them.

In short the excavation revealed that the mound was a natural gravel rise encircled by a ditch. No features, finds or datable material were recovered that positively indicate the date and function of the monument.

Paula King for Gerry Walsh, Rathbawn, Castlebar, Co. Mayo.

493. SHRULE
Adjacent to church
SMR 122A:4
98E0567
Pre-development testing was undertaken on the site of a proposed development in Shrule, Co. Mayo, in November 1998. Part of the proposed development site lies within the designated area of a church.

The test-trench measured 96m x 2m. In general the sod/topsoil lay directly above the boulder clay. No human remains nor any other archaeological features were recovered.

Gerry Walsh, Rathbawn Road, Castlebar, Co. Mayo.

494. THE DESERTED VILLAGE, SLIEVEMORE (TUAR AND TUAR RIABHACH) ACHILL ISLAND
Multi-phase landscape
5918 30770
SMR 42:00802–42:010904
91E0047
The eighth season of survey and excavation at the Deserted Village, Slievemore, Co. Mayo, continued

over a seven-week period (29 June–15 August) in 1998.

Cutting A was extended northward to investigate the unusual mound, partially uncovered during the 1997 season (*Excavations 1997*, 135–6). An area 5m x 2m was de-sodded, joining Cutting A with the Test-trench F14. The mound of yellow clay was apparently cut into during the construction of House 36, with a layer of flat stones laid around it, situated close to the village pathway.

A drain west of House 36 was full of rotted organic material, the remains of the last thatch roof of House 36. Underneath this was a yellow clay with small stone inclusions, which is present over most of this cutting and into which two metalled surfaces are set.

Excavation south of the southern gable of House 36 uncovered a second mound of very red, oxidised soil with large stones and iron pan inclusions mixed within it. Lower down, the large stones disappeared, while the red, oxidised soil became much thicker and extremely hard, perhaps as a result of some sort of heat treatment. Underneath this was a layer of yellow clay, which extends over the whole cutting and which was cut into and redeposited to form the house platform. This is also borne out by the evidence of Trench F14 in Cutting B, where a spade cut was discovered in what is almost certainly this same yellow layer. Everything under this layer pre-dates the house.

Cutting B, in the garden to the north-east of House 36, was extended. This involved a northward extension of Test-trench F14. This enlarged the cutting by 3.5m x 3m. Under the sod were two long, rectangular deposits of orange ash, running in a north–south direction (F11). This appears to be a deposition intended to fill in the deep furrows of the lazy-beds to even out the ground surface. This is clearly shown in section and would explain the relatively flat surface of the garden. Interestingly, when House 36 was excavated very little ash was found near the hearth. What F11 almost certainly represents is that ash. It appears that no attempt was made to mix the ash into the soil as a fertilizer, and so it appears simply as a dump layer. Perhaps F11 represents an initial phase of occupation for the people who lived in House 36. There is evidence to suggest that before the house was built the land was cultivated, so in order to save the people having to redig and recultivate the lazy-beds they simply dumped ash down the furrows of the old lazy-beds. F11 runs the length of the garden in two strips. There is possibly a third deposit, but this does not appear as clean-cut as the existing two. Each strip was *c.* 1m wide and 0.3m deep. Both ran north–south and appear to correspond with the deep lazy-beds in the field immediately north of the garden wall.

F13, a previously unexcavated (control) area in the south-east corner of the cutting, was opened and produced a multitude of finds, mainly broken glass and pottery and also an iron shoe of a metal *gowl gob* in quite good condition with a nail hole near the top. The object is of quite crude construction and may have been 'home-made'. The sod layer ranged from 0.1m to 0.4m deep and produced numerous finds. Thickly matted roots extended very deep into the layers in this area. Directly under the sod was a thick layer, ranging from 0.2m to 0.5m deep, which consisted of a brown/grey, mixed soil, with lots of inclusions, e.g.

ash, charcoal, small stones and pieces of turf.

Work in Cutting C centred mainly on a pit (F27) found in 1997. The fill proved to be quite complex, with many layers sandwiched closely on top of each other, few being more than 40mm deep. It was dug into the area immediately east of the manure pit. Dug into the south-east corner of this pit was another pit, F41, covered over with a large boulder. F24, a small pit excavated in 1996, was 0.75m to the south of F27. In the north-east corner of Cutting C a later pit (F64) was shown to be cut into F27. South of F27 a narrow drain, slightly curved, was dug, running in an east–west direction and terminating where it met the wall of the oval manure pit east of House 36. Part of the manure pit wall is missing at this point and may be connected with this drain.

On plan, F27 appears to be quite irregular in shape, and it seems that it is made up of a couple of contemporary pits cut into one another. It is still clear, however, that F41 and F64 are both later pits cut into F27, although F41 was more or less contemporary with the use of F27.

F64 was not fully excavated and has been left for the 1999 season. Its fill was very mixed and loose, consisting mainly of yellow/red, oxidised sandy material mixed with grey, silty material and the odd large stone. The first 0.2m was removed, revealing cavities but no finds. It is thought that this pit continues down for a good depth and may even continue under the adjacent garden wall. The presence of horseshoes as well as slag in F27 and a piece of haemitite in F41 may suggest some sort of 'smithy' activity, and there is a nearby source of running water.

Two trenches were opened in the area of the Monk's Garden: Trench 1 in the garden itself, and Trench 2 c. 5m to north. A number of features appeared under the sod, which were planned. No further excavation was carried out here as, after removal to the sod in Trench 2, evidence of a structure began to appear. Trench 2 consisted of a rectangular cutting 5m x 1.5m, running in an east–west direction. It was decided to position the trench here as a large slab stone, F5, lying flat side down, was protruding and had a cavity underneath. Under the sod, and covering almost the entire area of the cutting, was a fill layer of loose stones F4 (0.05–0.1m) mixed in a silty clay. At the eastern end of the cutting tightly packed stones of the same size as in F4 appeared. F4 was removed, for the first 3m eastwards to a depth initially of 0.2m, until it crossed the protruding western wall of the souterrain, when it dived to c. 0.5m deep.

Two walls of a structure were revealed. Both were running in a north–south direction but were distinctly different in construction and appearance. The western wall was of orthostatic construction, while the eastern was dry-stone, with slight corbelling. Cairn material was packed tightly up against the eastern side of the east wall. Both walls ran up to the lintel stone F5 and appeared to support it.

The passageway between the two walls was a very mixed fill of odd stones jumbled together irregularly and mixed with soil and ashy material. The cutting was extended northward directly above F5, and an area 2m x 2.5m was opened and joined onto the existing cutting. More cairn material was uncovered here, and, while there was no positive evidence of a

cut, there was a demarcation in the size of stones, i.e. between this cairn material and the line of the village pathway running in the same direction.

A new extension running in a south-easterly direction was opened. It revealed that both the west and east wall 'kinked' off from a north–south direction towards the south-east. One metre to the east the passageway narrowed and the orthostatic wall terminated at what appears to be a blocked entrance. Eastwards, just under the sod in brown-earth soil, was found an oblong stone with abrasions at both ends that has been tentatively identified as a hammerstone. Its location close to the surface and within a jumble of other stones suggests that it is a stray find.

The structure described, despite some unusual features, e.g. the orthostatic wall and no clear evidence of a cut, may be a souterrain. The excavation will continue in 1999.

Theresa McDonald, St O'Hara's Hill, Tullamore, Co. Offaly.

495. STRADE ABBEY, STRADE
Medieval priory
M258976
97E0381

Excavations at Strade Abbey, Co. Mayo, were carried out from January to March 1998 in advance of the restoration of the Penal Church to house the Michael Davitt Museum. The Penal Church is attached to the south-west corner of the medieval friary church, and, in addition to the complete excavation of the interior of the church, several trenches were opened outside for the proposed services.

Excavation in the interior of the Penal Church revealed that it had been built on the line of the demolished west range of the medieval abbey. Two substantial medieval walls over 1m thick and at right angles to each other were exposed directly below the mortared floor of the Penal Church. The first of these walls, running north–south through the church, most

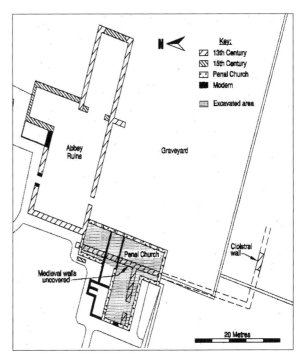

Excavated features at Strade Abbey, Co. Mayo.

likely represented the west wall of the west range of buildings. It continued northwards and southwards beyond the walls of the Penal Church and ran parallel to the west gable of the priory church.

Owing to the disturbance associated with the construction of the Penal Church, only the lowermost archaeological deposits survived. These consisted of a clay floor to the east of the north–south wall, which almost certainly represented a floor within the west range of buildings. A stone kiln was uncovered in the north end of the area excavated, which had been badly disturbed by the building of the Penal Church. A stone-lined and lintelled culvert was exposed in the western end of the church and came through what must have been a doorway or gateway in the wall. Two substantial post-holes were exposed, one on either side of the doorway.

To the south of the Penal Church part of what may have been an enclosing ditch was exposed running east–west through the cutting. Finds from the site included Saintonge pottery and a large fragment of a rotary quern. Further work remains to be done before the restoration of the church.

Donald Murphy, Archaeological Consultancy Services Ltd, 15 Trinity Street, Drogheda, Co. Louth.

496. TERRYDUFF

No archaeological significance
SMR 48:70
98E0036

Pre-development testing was undertaken on the site of proposed developments at Terryduff, Bofeenaun, Crossmolina, Co. Mayo, in January 1998. The proposed development sites lie within the constraints of a burial mound and standing stone.

Following discussions with the National Monuments Service, it was agreed to relocate the proposed driveway and site entrance in development Site No. 2 away from the burial mound and standing stone. The new driveway and entrance is to be built to the east of the proposed house.

Six test-trenches were excavated within the boundaries of the proposed development sites. No archaeological features or small finds were recovered from any of the test-trenches.

Gerry Walsh, Rathbawn Road, Castlebar, Co. Mayo.

497. WESTPORT–BELCLARE, R335 ROAD REALIGNMENT SCHEME

No archaeological significance
9813 2832
97E0417 ext.

Monitoring continued in relation to the scheme (see *Excavations 1997*, 136) in mid-October and early November. The work was confined to a *c.* 1.1km stretch of road running west from Carrownalurgan Bridge. All topsoil-stripping associated with the widening and realignment of the road was monitored. Groundworks along the southern side of the road were confined to a corridor 3–13m wide, and along the northern side a 4–17m-wide area. No features or finds of archaeological interest were uncovered during the course of the work.

Further monitoring in respect of the scheme will be undertaken during 1999.

Martin E. Byrne, 39 Kerdiff Park, Monread, Naas, Co. Kildare.

498. ABBEYLAND SOUTH AND BLACKCASTLE DEMESNE

Medieval/post–medieval
N86826815, N86866822
98E0463

A thin stratum of archaeological deposit was revealed below landfill deposits in Abbeyland South on the south bank of the River Blackwater in advance of the Navan Inner Relief Road 2A. The investigation of a 103.6m² area between 6 and 28 October 1998 uncovered the remnants of walls that would have belonged to substantial buildings of the post-medieval period. A large assemblage of potsherds and several other objects, including three copper coins and fragments of an inscribed finger-ring, suggest a date in the early/mid-17th century.

A small area of medieval activity was identified below one of the wall features. It constituted a patch of burning datable to the 14th/15th centuries on the evidence of associated ceramics. The inclusion of line-impressed tile fragments suggests an ecclesiastical association. The site lies *c.* 120m west of where St Mary's Priory is believed to have been centred, and it is likely that this represents part of the complex. The post-medieval activity occurred between the priory's dissolution and the building of a cavalry barracks *c.* 1700.

In the course of removing topsoil at the edge of the land-take on the north bank of the Blackwater in Blackcastle Demesne townland, part of a previously unrecorded *fulacht fiadh* was exposed on 16 October 1998. The section was recorded, and the site was reburied.

Niall Brady, 'Rosbeg', Ard Mhuire Park, Dalkey, Co. Dublin, Valerie J. Keeley Ltd.

499. ABBEYLAND/BLACKCASTLE DEMESNE

Corn-drying kiln
N86866825
98E0590

The buried remnants of a previously undiscovered corn-drying kiln were uncovered while removing topsoil deposits on the north bank of the River Blackwater, in advance of the Navan Inner Relief Road 2A. The site straddles the townland boundary between Abbeyland and Blackcastle Demesne. It lay beneath a later hedgerow and roadway that had truncated the site.

The kiln was excavated between 18 and 22 December 1998. It consisted of a single stone-built bowl and a stone-lined flue pit that was cut into the underlying boulder clay. The flue was oriented almost at right angles to the bowl and was set at a lower level. No artefacts were recovered. Soil samples were retrieved for further analysis.

Niall Brady, 'Rosbeg', Ard Mhuire Park, Dalkey, Co. Dublin, for Valerie J. Keeley Ltd.

500. ATHLUMNEY

Vicinity of castle and graveyard
N87656740

Monitoring was carried out during excavation for a Telecom Éireann service trench along the public road between Athlumney graveyard and Athlumney

Castle, using a very narrow bucket and to a depth of 1m. At all times the machine excavated through fill. At the eastern end, closest to the convent, the fill comprised crushed stone, but going westwards it comprised mixed layers of sand, gravel and clay. At the western end of the trench the level of the road rose substantially above the level of the fields on either side in order to bring it over the railway bridge. The layers of fill had presumably been laid down when the railway bridge and the road approaches on either side were being constructed.

Rosanne Meenan, Roestown, Drumree, Co. Meath.

501. BETTYSTOWN

No archaeological significance

31601 27413

98E0038

The site lies on the west side of the Bettystown/ Laytown road, close to the village of Bettystown. Its rear (western) boundary wall separates it from the small housing estate 'Brookside', where an Iron Age cemetery (SMR 21:10) was excavated by Eamonn Kelly in 1979 (*JIA* **4**, 1987–8, 75). The ground level of the housing estate is higher by *c.* 1m than that on the site, and this rise is artificially continued to the estate wall. Part of the area of the site closest to the wall may have been partially scarped before the erection of a building that stood there, but there is a noticeable, though gentle, ridge running north–south and extending northwards behind the village.

Seven trenches were dug by mechanical digger with a toothless bucket in the area of the main building.

Although a number of features were noted, these proved to be natural, resulting from the overlying of the old shoreline by a deposit of boulder clay and gravels.

Finola O'Carroll, Greenanstown, Stamullin, Co. Meath.

502. BETTYSTOWN (BETAGHSTOWN TOWNLAND)

Iron Age cemetery

O01607331

98E0072

The site was tested before construction of a large holiday complex. Eamonn Kelly found Iron Age burials in the area to the south of this site in the 1970s.

A total of 27 trenches were excavated over the area of the two fields comprising the development. Two of these produced human burials, while a third yielded evidence of a possible ditch. The burials were exposed underneath the ploughsoil, at the interface between the latter and the natural layers. Subsequently the site was excavated by James Eogan, who recovered Bronze Age and Iron Age burials and evidence of a Late Neolithic timber circle (see No. 503 below).

Rosanne Meenan, Roestown, Drumree, Co. Meath.

503. BETTYSTOWN

Prehistoric/multi-period site

O15607320

SMR 21:10

98E0072

This site is part of a low ridge overlooking the sea just south of the village of Bettystown. Excavations in the late 1970s by Eamonn Kelly on an adjoining site uncovered an Early Bronze Age cist and an inhumation cemetery of 6th-century AD date (*JIA* **4**, 1987–8, 75). A total of 27 test-trenches were excavated on this site by Roseanne Meenan, in response to a condition in the planning permission granted for a mixed residential and commercial development (see No. 502 above). Human remains were found in two of the trenches, and consequently the National Monuments Service required hand-excavation of two specified areas and monitoring of all groundworks associated with this scheme.

Three main phases of archaeological activity were identified on this site, the archaeological features being all concentrated on the top of the ridge.

Timber circle

A total of 27 post-pits formed a circular structure 7.6m x 6.5m (externally). There was an entrance defined by four large pits on the south-east side of the structure; four internal pits were found. Each of the pits held a single upright wooden post. Finds from the fill of the pits include a considerable amount of struck flint, the predominant artefact type being end-scrapers, grooved ware-type pottery, animal bone (burnt and unburnt) and seashells.

Early Bronze Age flat cemetery

Nine graves (two short, one polygonal and one rectangular cist, and five pits) were found *c.* 40m south-west of the timber circle. They contained nine inhumations and one cremation burial. Four of the inhumations (one teenage girl and three children) were associated with food vessels. The other burials were three children, a middle-aged female and two adult males, one of whom had been cremated, in the same grave. The burials were confined to an area *c.* 8m x 8m; no evidence was found of a covering mound or any other above-ground marker; there is stratigraphic evidence of at least two phases of burial.

1st millennium AD inhumation cemetery

A total of 55 inhumation burials were found in a linear cemetery that extended along the top of the ridge. Most were extended inhumations, oriented west–east (heads at the west), buried in simple, subrectangular, stone-lined pits that had been dug into the underlying sand and gravel deposits. Three of the burials were contained within lintel graves; six were found in slab-lined graves. None of the burials were accompanied by grave-goods. Apart from three cases the graves were not intercut; the timber circle had been cut by three of these graves.

Two crouched inhumations were found in simple pit graves. One, a child, was found within the timber circle, it cut one of the post-pits; the second, a young adult female, was *c.* 25m west of the other; a large rock had been placed on her abdomen during burial.

James Eogan, Archaeological Development Services Ltd, Windsor House, 11 Fairview Strand, Fairview, Dublin 3.

504. MOYNAGH LOUGH, BRITTAS

Late Mesolithic settlement site

N818860

E000377

Excavation work, financed by the National Committee for Archaeology of the Royal Irish

Academy, focused on an area of Later Mesolithic activity sealed beneath the early medieval crannog. The principal features were two subrectangular platforms arranged roughly at right angles to one another and separated, at their nearest point, by a distance of just over 2m. The platforms rose directly from a layer of brushwood-strewn, brown, open-water mud, with high concentrations of hazelnut shells. There was evidence of the presence of a third platform further to the west.

Platform 1

Three sides of a subrectangular platform were exposed. It averaged 5.5m wide, had a maximum exposed length of 8.3m and rose to a maximum height of 0.75m above the open-water mud. Excavation revealed that there were at least three levels of occupation, separated by thin layers of peat, suggesting that the site was returned to periodically. Only the uppermost level was investigated. A total of 56 post-holes and two pits were identified. The post-holes did not form any obvious, regular pattern, but at one point a group of at least fifteen were arranged in a C-shape with maximum dimensions of 3m x 1.2m. A series of timbers protruded from beneath the platform, but it has not been established whether these were foundation material or the result of natural growth. At the narrowest point between Platforms 1 and 2 patches of gravel and a group of timbers were present. These appear to have been deposited with the aim of creating a 'stepping-stone' between the two platforms.

Platform 2

Two sides were exposed of a subrectangular platform with maximum dimensions of 7m x 8m; it rose to a maximum height of 0.65m above the open-water mud. At least two phases of occupation were identified. Examination of the uppermost level revealed two post-holes. A sample of the charcoal-flecked mud from this platform provided a radiocarbon date of 5270±60 BP (*c.* 3320 bc, calibrated 4313–3980 BC; GrN-11443).

Platform 3

There appears to be a third platform *c.* 17m west of Platform 2. The evidence consisted of a thin, charcoal-flecked band, with maximum exposed dimensions of 4m x 3m and varying from 10mm to 20mm thick. One chert blade and two flakes were found in the layer, while ten additional pieces of chert, including four blades, lay in the open-water mud at the same level. It is likely that these derive from an occupation platform immediately to the west. No attempt was made to investigate this further.

Artefactual evidence

The artefacts included three polished stone axeheads, six spearheads of slaty sandstone, five elongated pebbles, nine hammerstones and two polishing stones. Approximately 2000 pieces of chert, flint and other stone were recovered. From a preliminary analysis roughly 200 are implements. The blades fit into a small number of well-defined types, leaf-shaped, pointed, parallel-sided, elongated and irregular, while among the flakes the most distinctive form is quadrilateral with an oblique distal end. One

bone point and an elongated wooden object were found. Among the animal bones, boars' tusks were noted, suggesting that pig was a source of meat.

John Bradley, Department of Modern History, NUI Maynooth, Co. Kildare.

505. CORSTOWN
Environs of archaeological complex
258978 276874
98E0417

Trial-trenching was undertaken at a proposed development site at Corstown, Oldcastle, Co. Meath, on 12 September 1998. The work was undertaken in compliance with a condition included in the grant of planning in relation to the construction of a private dwelling.

The site lies on the base of the southern slopes of the Slieve na Calliagh hills, where the Loughcrew Megalithic Cemetery and a number of other archaeological sites are found. Five cairns, six megalithic tombs, a standing stone and a stone cross are situated in the townland of Corstown alone.

Five trial-trenches were opened within the confines of the proposed development site. All were dug by a combination of machine- and hand-excavation. The topsoil consisted of a mid-brown with a dark orange hue, silty clay, with moderate angular/subangular pebbles and small cobbles dispersed randomly throughout. The undisturbed natural subsoil lay directly below the topsoil and had a similar matrix except that the soil was lighter in colour and contained more stone. No features, structures or finds of archaeological interest were recovered during the course of the work.

Martin E. Byrne, 39 Kerdiff Park, Monread, Naas, Co. Kildare.

506. MAIN STREET, DRUMCONRATH
Medieval borough
289340 290756
98E0157

This assessment took place in advance of a proposed residential development on Main Street, Drumconrath. The site lies in a zone of archaeological interest owing to the proximity of a medieval church site and two mottes, as well as being the location of a former borough.

Three test-trenches were excavated within the site. Trench 1, 7m long, revealed yellow boulder clay at 0.3m, above which were layers of hard-core and sand. The second trench was the same length and was excavated to 1m deep. It consisted of natural boulder clay underlying sand and hard-core at 0.2m. A few large stones, up to 0.2m in diameter, sitting on the boulder clay, may represent a cobbled surface. The third trench was 4m long and consisted of brown loam producing modern artefacts lying over boulder clay. This may have been a result of the construction of a lounge for the nearby public house.

Deirdre Murphy, Archaeological Consultancy Services Ltd, 15 Trinity Street, Drogheda, Co. Louth.

507. MAIN STREET, DULEEK
Medieval borough
O04686842
98E0208

Archaeological assessment took place at a proposed

commercial site at Main Street, Duleek, Co. Meath. The site lies within the area of archaeological importance attached to this early monastic settlement and medieval borough.

Two trenches were excavated along the lines of the foundations. Trench 1 was 7m long and 1m wide and was orientated east–west. The top 0.6m was a brown loam with stone and gravel, under which boulder clay was exposed. In Trench 2, which was 25m long and 1m wide running north–south, a brown, sandy clay some 0.9m thick overlay a thin layer of charcoal 0.2m thick. A layer of brown loam containing red brick fragments underlay this. At 1.6m below the surface boulder clay was visible.

Donald Murphy, Archaeological Consultancy Services Ltd, 15 Trinity Street, Drogheda, Co. Louth.

508. DUNSHAUGHLIN
Urban
SMR 44:33
29705 25270 to 29693 25175
98E0355

A gas main was laid from north to south through the town, partly in an open-cut trench and partly by boring between cuttings. Over most of the area the road surface had been laid directly upon the boulder clay. At two points disturbed deposits up to 1.25m deep were found, containing fragments of shell, charcoal and animal bone. No artefacts were found.

Thaddeus C. Breen, 13 Wainsfort Crescent, Dublin 6W, for Valerie J. Keeley Ltd.

509. IRISHTOWN, GORMANSTOWN
Early Christian
O165670
SMR 28:17
98E0025

An archaeological assessment was carried out on this site in two phases—initiated by Avril Purcell in February and concluded by Edmond O'Donovan in May 1998. Fourteen test-trenches were opened.

The stratigraphy in the trenches was remarkably similar. Three or four layers were revealed including sod, topsoil, occasionally grey/brown clay and, at the base of each trench, sand and gravel. Undulations were apparent in the some of the deposits.

No features or finds of an archaeological nature were revealed.

Edmond O'Donovan and Avril Purcell, Margaret Gowen & Co. Ltd, 2 Killiney View, Albert Road Lower, Glenageary, Co. Dublin.

510. KNOCKCOMMON
Medieval church site
298841 269605
98E0023

Archaeological assessment was carried out at Knockcommon graveyard, Donore, Co. Meath, in advance of a proposed extension to the graveyard. The present fabric of the church is probably late medieval in date. Four trenches were dug in the field east of the graveyard. They revealed sod, ploughsoil and finally boulder clay. No archaeological features or objects were present.

Deirdre Murphy, Archaeological Consultancy Services Ltd, 15 Trinity Street, Drogheda, Co. Louth.

511. KNOWTH
Multi-period
N995735
SMR 19:30
E0070

In association with the ongoing programme of conservation, excavation continued in the passage of Site 1, the Western Tomb. This involved extending the cutting inwards to the area between Orthostats 24 and 60 and 30 and 55, as well as a small area to the back of Orthostat 5, an area that had suffered considerable damage. The overlying mound consisted entirely of smallish, rounded loose stones; a number were water-rolled and would have originated in a post–glacial landscape or possibly from the bed of the Boyne. There were also some angular stones, mainly limestone, and these appear to have been quarried.

The cairn stones overlay the basal layer of the mound. This consisted of redeposited material. Some of this had an organic content and involved the use of sods, but there were also thin layers of shale. This basal layer, on average 1m thick on each side of the passage, extended across the top of the capstones, where it was 0.15m thick. The cross-section was hog-backed; the material to the sides was more compressed. The basal layer was placed directly on the old ground surface.

The mound material was examined by Brenda Collins. She reported that occupation and food debris was absent from the samples and that charcoal, which undoubtedly derived from episodes of burning, was present in very small quantities and could not be interpreted as the dumping of charred waste. Seeds associated with pasture, meadow and grassland were indicated, and the presence of annual weeds was noted.

In this particular section the passage was in a very poor state of preservation. Most of the stones had suffered structural damage. All the orthostats leaned inwards, the corbels had been displaced and a number, as a result of mound adjustment, had been pushed down on the outside of the orthostats. The straightening up of the orthostats involved the lifting of some corbels, and consequently a complete record of the structure was obtained. Over the floor of the passage was a spread of stones. Apparently these slipped in from the cairn when structural adjustment was taking place.

As part of the conservation work Corbel 5 (at the back of Orthostat 5) was lifted. Underneath was a deposit of cremated bone (identification pending). This was a primary feature. It backed on to the orthostat, but there was no formal edging on the other sides. The back of Orthostat 5 had megalithic art, consisting of large spirals. The cremation burial extended up to the orthostats at about the level of the upper spiral. As this decoration was 'associated' with the burial, it was probably of special significance. It should also be noted that the orthostat directly opposite (No. 81) also had hidden art, while the overlying capstone, No. 3, had decoration on its bottom surface. It is considered that these stones were reused from an earlier tomb (Eogan, *Antiquity* **72** (1998), 162–72). Further examples of megalithic art were discovered. These consisted of two capstones (Nos 23 and 24) and three corbels (Nos

24–26, 26–27 and 58–60).

Before the conservation work at Site 9 the already excavated surface around it was re-examined, but no new features emerged. Also in this area a cutting was opened to see if the palisade trenches continued and, therefore, constituted a circle (Eogan 1984, *Excavations at Knowth, Vol. 1*, 219–33). No features or finds came to light.

George Eogan, Knowth Project, University College Dublin, Earlsfort Terrace, Dublin 2.

512. LOUGHSALLAGH
Unknown
O029410
98E0295

Monitoring of excavation of part of the Clonee–Dunboyne sewerage scheme was carried out in June 1998 in the area of ridge and furrow and a tree ring, which had been recorded by Emmet Byrnes.

A 20m-wide strip was cleared of topsoil by a machine with a grading bucket. The trench for the pipe was then excavated to a depth of 3–4m and to a width of 2–3m, cutting through a ploughsoil and into very sandy material. The area of ridge and furrow stretched eastwards from the field fence east of the tree ring for *c.* 138m and north–south for *c.* 40–50m. The pipeline corridor cut the ridge and furrow. The ridges were flat-topped, with 4.5–5m between the top of each ridge; the furrows were *c.* 1.7m wide. The height of the ridges was *c.* 350–400mm from top of the ridge to the bottom of the furrow. No finds were recovered from the fill of the furrows.

Nothing of significance was noted during the rest of the soil-stripping and of the trenching.

Rosanne Meenan, Roestown, Drumree, Co. Meath.

513. MONKNEWTOWN
No archaeological significance
3004 2751
SMR 19:15
98E0424

A programme of archaeological monitoring took place at this site, which is in the vicinity of a known monument, during October 1998 and January 1999. No archaeological material was recovered.

Rónán Swan, Arch-Tech Ltd, 32 Fitzwilliam Place, Dublin 2.

514. NAVAN SEWERAGE SCHEME
Monitoring
98E0602

Monitoring of works associated with the Navan Sewerage Scheme commenced in late December. It is expected that monitoring will continue until mid-1999. Furthermore, a limited programme of test-trenching will be undertaken at the Boyne Road in January 1999.

Clare Mullins, 39 Kerdiff Park, Monread, Naas, Co. Kildare.

515. NAVAN INNER RELIEF ROAD (PHASE 2a), ABBEYLANDS SOUTH, NAVAN
Urban
98E0184

Testing was carried out in the townland of Abbeylands South, Navan, Co. Meath, in April–May 1998. The site lay to the west of the site of the Abbey of St Mary.

Seven trenches were investigated. The area of Trenches 1, 2, 6 and 7 had up to 6m of modern fill deposited in the mid-1980s, which made excavation difficult. Trenches 1–5 and 7 did not produce anything of archaeological interest.

Trench 6 produced evidence of a compacted road surface and two walls. It can be suggested that these represent the walls and lane marked on the 1st edition OS map. The lane ran to a mill by the river to the north-east. This lane (and presumably the mill it led to) had gone out of use by the 2nd edition map in 1882.

Fiona Reilly, Wood Road, Cratloekeel, Co. Clare, for Valerie J. Keeley Ltd.

516. THE LYRIC CINEMA, BREW'S HILL, NAVAN
Urban
2854 2662
98E0233

When the Lyric Cinema was built in the 1940s a basement down to a depth of 2.5-3m below the street level was excavated. The evidence of the excavation remained in the form of concrete foundations down to the depth described. The foundations had cut through a clay layer *c.* 500mm deep; this overlay a 2m-deep natural deposit of grey sand. The top of another clay layer was exposed at this level.

As such a large proportion of the site had already been removed during the construction of the cinema, there was little left to test. A mechanical digger with a 3ft bucket was used to pull a trench along the access ramp along the east side of the site.

The stratigraphy was shown to be very disturbed, even in this area. An earthenware sewage pipe ran along the east side of the ramp; this lay at 1.5m below the present street level, and there was redeposited clay underlying the pipe and overlying the natural sand layer. A concrete wall associated with the cinema was exposed along the west side of the ramp. It was as deep as the other cinema walls. It is clear therefore that there was major disturbance in this area to a depth of *c.* 2.5m.

Nothing of archaeological interest was exposed in the test-trench.

Rosanne Meenan, Roestown, Drumree, Co. Meath.

517. 40–42 CANON ROW, NAVAN
Urban
N859679
98E0121

As a condition of planning permission three test-trenches were excavated with a tracked mechanical excavator with a 3ft-wide bucket on this site, which is within the zone of archaeological potential of Navan town. The Civil Survey (1654–6) records houses outside West Gate on the north side of Canon Row.

Trench 1 was excavated on the Canon Row frontage. Nothing of archaeological interest was found.

Trench 2 ran south-west/north-east across the yard to the rear of 42 Canon Row. A series of gullies was found cut into underlying natural, with associated 18th- and 19th-century pottery. The upper levels of the trench related to the modern use of the site as a farmyard.

Trench 3 ran south-west/north-east down the middle of the site. Nothing of archaeological interest was found. Undisturbed natural was found to slope

gently towards the north-east end of the site.
James Eogan, Archaeological Development Services Ltd, Windsor House, 11 Fairview Strand, Fairview, Dublin 3.

518. 28 TRIMGATE STREET, NAVAN
Urban medieval
N866674
98E0162
The site lies just west of the line of the town wall. The wall crosses Trimgate Street in a curved line towards the north-east; it is considered possible that the east wall of Dunnes Stores incorporates the wall (Bradley, 99). One property, Dunnes Stores, separates the line of the wall from the development site, and therefore it was considered possible that a town ditch lay in the area of the development.

While it was not possible to carry out a detailed survey of the standing structures, there was no obvious evidence of medieval or early post-medieval fabric in them, and little disturbance was expected. One trench tested the back of the site for the proposed extension. An overburden of grey, stony material was exposed along the length of the trench; this layer was 0.6m deep and overlay a light brown clay, interpreted as natural boulder clay.

A pit had been dug into the boulder clay. It was at least 2.3m wide at the top and was 0.7m deep, with straight sides. The fill was organic, with wood chippings and fibrous material resembling horse manure. The pottery recovered from the fill was early 19th-century black-glazed ware, and some sherds of bottle glass were also found. The feature was interpreted as a pit into which rubbish had been thrown, probably sometime in the last century, most likely associated with the use of the building fronting onto Trimgate Street. No feature or object of an earlier date was observed during the testing.

Reference:
Bradley, J. *The Urban Survey for Co. Meath.*

Rosanne Meenan, Roestown, Drumree, Co. Meath.

519. THE KNOCKANS, TELTOWN, ORISTOWN
Linear earthwork
280940 274335
97E0301
The double-banked monument known as the Knockans at Teltown, Co. Meath, was partly destroyed in May 1997. Excavation (on behalf of the National Monuments Service) was undertaken there in 1997 (*Excavations 1997*, 143), and a second season, of nine weeks' duration, took place in July and August 1998.

The focus of this excavation was the eastern side of the southern bank, in order to complete the recording of the archaeological layers exposed by machine in 1997. Excavation revealed that there was a much greater depth of deposit in the central organic core (the burnt deposit) of the monument than the 0.8m recorded in 1997. The core, buried beneath 1–2m of redeposited gley, was made up of layers of deposited silts with some large stones revetting their southern side. Over these, and on the northern side, were many lenticular deposits of silt with pointed stakes driven into them.

Because of machine destruction the relationship of the organic core to what appeared to be a ditch between the two banks was not resolved in 1997, the old ground surface not being clearly identified. Excavation of a greater depth of this organic core in 1998 clarified this issue and demonstrated that the banks were constructed without an intervening ditch, the gap between them containing a considerable depth of silts and clay resting on the original ground surface. Although it was not possible to complete the excavation of this year's cutting to sterile ground across its entire length, it was possible to recover secure samples for dating and analysis from undisturbed contexts.

The reinstatement and grass planting of the northern bank was completed, but the final reshaping of the upper eastern slope of the southern bank was not finished as additional topsoil was required; the reconstruction of this small area will now have to wait until dryer weather in spring 1999.

Finds consisted of post-medieval pottery and modern material from the plough zone at the southern end of the southern bank. Flint and a fragment of bronze were recovered in the lower layers of the bank construction material, while fragments of leather, wood, a small amount of bone and one sherd of glass came from contexts within the organic core.
John Waddell and Madeline O'Brien, Department of Archaeology, National University of Ireland, Galway.

520. PRIORYLAND
Site of enclosure
O05496738
SMR 27:21
98E0083
A section of the Kilmoon–Drogheda road east of Duleek runs beside a site marked as 'Enclosure'. The enclosure comprises a raised platform 140m north–south by *c.* 50m, with the long axis running parallel to the road. It is not clear whether the feature is man-made or was created by natural processes associated with the river Nanny. Meath County Council intends to raise the level of the road and remove the field fence between the road and the field that contains the enclosure, thus encroaching on the site. It was felt that testing was required before the works commenced, and three trenches were excavated by mechanical digger.

Two gullies were exposed in the northernmost trench. They were exposed at *c.* 0.9m below the present sod layer. They were 0.8–1m wide, and the gully, which was excavated by hand, was 0.2m deep. Their function was not known, but it is possible that they had some kind of drainage purpose as the ground here is very low-lying and prone to flooding. The other trenches revealed nothing of archaeological significance.
Rosanne Meenan, Roestown, Drumree, Co. Meath.

521. CURRAGHA ROAD, RATOATH
Zone of archaeological potential
98E0360
The site lies close to the northern limit of the area of archaeological potential for Ratoath as defined by the Urban Survey. Four trenches tested the proposed location of a dwelling-house. Trench 1

exposed a layer of yellow clay within natural boulder clay at its west end; there were no inclusions within the yellow clay to suggest that it had been redeposited. The three other trenches exposed evidence of insertion of drainage channels around the development area. They were cut into the natural, dark grey-brown clay with much broken stone. No features of archaeological interest were exposed.

Rosanne Meenan, Roestown, Drumree, Co. Meath.

522. MAIN STREET, RATOATH
Urban medieval
O017519
98E0296

The development site lies on the north side of Main Street, which curves around the line of the motte. There are no recorded monuments in this part of the village, but presumably there was settlement here from the medieval period onwards. Eight trenches of varying lengths tested this large development site.

The frontage on Main Street was sealed by a concrete slab as a floor for horse stables. Contamination was caused here by a leakage of diesel oil, which mixed with ground water to produce a viscous sludge. This was present in Trenches 1–3. Trench 4 showed natural, brown clay underneath the slab and stone filling.

The other trenches further to the north showed evidence of dumping of modern rubbish and of redeposition of boulder clay in Trench 8.

Nothing of archaeological interest was observed in the trenches.

Rosanne Meenan, Roestown, Drumree, Co. Meath.

523. ROSSAN
No archaeological significance
26014 24512
98E0481

Monitoring of the N4–N6, 1km-long, Kinnegad Link Road was undertaken between 7 and 30 October 1998.

Monitoring in areas from within 60m of the Kinnegad River revealed a mixed layer of gravelly clay that sealed natural and was under topsoil. This has been interpreted as representing activity associated with river widening and diversion schemes undertaken within the last 150 years. In all other areas monitoring revealed topsoil sealing natural geology and failed to reveal the presence of either archaeological features or portable finds from within the development area.

Dermot Nelis, Irish Archaeological Consultancy Ltd, 8 Dungar Terrace, Dun Laoghaire, Co. Dublin for Valerie J. Keeley Ltd.

524. ROUGHGRANGE
Vicinity of archaeological complex
303097 272802
SMR 20:28

Monitoring took place at Roughgrange, Donore, Co. Meath, during the groundworks for the construction of a dwelling-house. The site lies close to the *Brú na Bóinne* archaeological complex. Nothing of archaeological significance was recovered.

Donald Murphy, Archaeological Consultancy Services Ltd, 15 Trinity Street, Drogheda, Co. Louth.

525. ROUGHGRANGE
Vicinity of archaeological complex
30247 27270
SMR 20:28
98E0537

Testing was carried out at Roughgrange, Donore, Co. Meath, in advance of a proposed extension to an existing dwelling. The site lies within the Boyne Valley complex of monuments. Five trenches were excavated across the extension and effluent treatment units. Boulder clay was uncovered under sod and topsoil at between 0.14m and 1.3m without encountering any archaeological features.

Donald Murphy, Archaeological Consultancy Services Ltd, 15 Trinity Street, Drogheda, Co. Louth.

526. SIMONSTOWN
Prehistoric burial/ritual site
285152 272439
98E0352

Outokumpo Zinc, Tara Mines Ltd, intends to excavate soil from two borrow areas (Simonstown and Randalstown) for the construction of the Randalstown tailings facility. Monitoring of topsoil-stripping at Simonstown revealed six sites of archaeological potential covering a total of *c.* 7 acres. Areas 1, 3, 1 and 6 contained c1 circular pits (c. 0.5m in diameter) dug into the subsoil and filled with charcoal and burnt sandstone, and a number were filled with cremated bone. Area 2 contained a linear charcoal deposit. Area 6 was a spread of charcoal and heat-fractured sandstone indicative of a *fulacht fiadh*. It was decided to excavate Areas 2 and 4, and test-trenches were excavated across three linear ditches in Area 3.

Area 2

Two principal features were excavated: a burnt subrectangular structure and a ditch that may enclose the structure. All archaeological features were exposed and recorded but not removed. The structure had maximum dimensions of 11.3m x 5.8m and was orientated east–west. It consisted of a subrectangular 'room' defined by a foundation trench that was filled with charcoal. No internal post-holes have been found. One small post-hole was found 2.4m away from the west wall of the structure. A leaf-shaped arrowhead of probable Neolithic date was found in the fill. The entrance may be in the north-east of the structure, although this area has not been fully investigated. Deposits of charcoal and ash were found directly outside the south 'wall' of the house. Radiocarbon samples were taken from the charcoal deposit, and results are awaited.

Six test-trenches were excavated to find the extent of the ditch. It was found running north-east/south-west to the north-east of the burnt structure. The ditch was traced for 15m of its length, after which it ran outside the limit of excavation, although it may return in the west of the site around the burnt structure. The ditch was excavated into the subsoil and had a maximum depth of 0.5m and a maximum width of 1.8m. In profile it was U-shaped. The ditch was truncated by a later field drain. The ditch was filled with a grey, sandy silt, which contained moderate amounts of burnt red sandstone. A deposit of charcoal and burnt stone was a

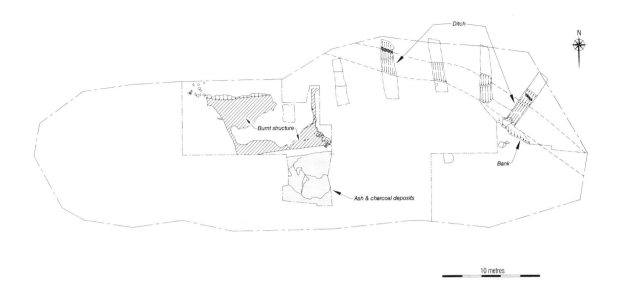

Excavations at Simonstown, Co. Meath.

secondary fill. Charcoal from this was collected for radiocarbon dating, and results are awaited. No artefacts were recovered from the fills. A small, stepped cut was found, excavated into the subsoil, outside the ditch. It was 0.1m deep and was traced for 6m in the east of the site. This may be interpreted as the remains of an external bank.

Area 3
One test-trench was excavated across each of three linear ditches. No artefacts were recovered. Charcoal from the fill of the ditch has been submitted for radiocarbon dating.

Area 4
All of Area 4 was investigated. The principal features discovered were a cremation pit, 'fireplaces', a post-pit, post-holes and cultivation furrows.

The cremation pit was excavated into the subsoil. It was subcircular and measured 0.31m x 0.27m and 8.5mm deep. A post-hole lay at the base of the pit, sealed under the fill, which consisted of very fragmentary burnt bone and charcoal in a matrix of black-brown, silty clay. The bone has been submitted for palaeopathological analysis. Radiocarbon results from the charcoal are also awaited. Five 'fireplaces' were excavated. All were similar and consisted of a simple pit excavated into the subsoil 0.3m x 0.2m and *c.* 0.1m deep. A fire was lit in the pit, leaving a deposit of ash and charcoal. Four 'fireplaces' lay around the south and west of the cremation pit. The fifth was to the south of the others, on top of a portion of the old sod. Radiocarbon results are awaited.

The post-pit was subcircular, 0.6m x 0.47m and 0.1m deep. Directly beside the post-hole that lay on its east side was a square deposit of orange, oxidised soil. There were a number of different fills of the post-pit. The lining of the base was a thin deposit of charcoal. This underlay a deposit of orange, oxidised

soil, which underlay a dark-brown, clayey silt. No artefacts were recovered from the post-pit. It is hoped to obtain a radiocarbon date for the charcoal lining the base.

Altogether six post-holes were excavated. Three were near fireplaces, the others have already been mentioned. One post-hole was isolated. No evidence of wood survived in the post-holes, and no artefacts were found.

Five linear features were excavated. These may be interpreted as cultivation furrows. Late medieval pottery was associated with one of the furrows. They were unevenly distributed throughout the site and showed signs of considerable disturbance.
Cóilín Ó Drisceoil, Archaeological Consultancy Services Ltd, 15 Trinity Street, Drogheda, Co. Louth.

527. ABBEY LANE, TRIM
Urban medieval
N80235690
98E0556
Archaeological assessment took place at Abbey Lane, Trim, Co. Meath. The site is close to two late medieval buildings and may have been within the precinct of St Mary's Abbey, founded in the 13th century. Four trenches were excavated.

Trench 1 was 17.4m long and 1.6m wide. A layer of light brown loam containing 19th-century pottery was encountered at the east end and underlay sod up to 0.42m thick. This overlay natural gravel. At the west end of the trench a layer of light brown clay, 0.22m thick, overlay a dark brown loam containing medieval pottery and fragmented shell. At 7.6m from the western corner of the trench sod overlay a layer of grey/brown, sandy clay containing an early post-medieval pantile fragment, which in turn overlay a substantial clay-bonded stone wall up to 0.9m high, with a rubble core. A roughly built stone wall/ foundation ran eastwards from this for 2.98m and overlay natural, orange boulder clay at 57.25m OD. A layer of rubble overlay this. A small area of reddened clay was visible overlying natural in the southern section.

Trench 2 was excavated south of Trench 1 and was 18.6m long and 1.5m wide. The sod was up to 0.22m thick. Underlying this was a layer of dark brown, soft loam. This layer contained oyster shell, large quantities of animal bone, occasional charcoal fragments and medieval pottery. It was excavated up to a depth of 0.6m.

Trench 3 was dug close to the eastern boundary, running north–south, and was 15.2m long and 1m wide. A layer of sod up to 0.28m thick was removed. This overlay a layer of rich, dark brown loam containing oyster shell, a large percentage of animal bone, occasional small charcoal fragments, fragments of late medieval and early post-medieval pottery and a small fragment of a clay pipe stem. Owing to the similarity of this deposit to those encountered in Trenches 2 and 3, a small portion of the trench was dug to 2m below the sod. More medieval pottery was recovered with no differentiation in this layer. At 1.7m below the sod a layer of orange/brown, silty loam was encountered. This layer contained no significant inclusions and yielded sherds of medieval and post-medieval date and a brick fragment. Boulder clay was encountered at 2.01m below the sod.

Trench 4 was dug at a right angle to Trench 3 and was 35.8m long running towards the laneway at the west. After stripping of sod up to 0.29m deep a layer of dark brown loam was encountered. This was identical in composition to that encountered in the other trenches and contained mostly medieval and a single sherd of post-medieval pottery. To determine a more precise date for this deposit a small portion of the trench was dug to 1.9m below the sod. This revealed a layer of orange-brown silt with no artefacts at 1.67m below the sod. Natural boulder clay was encountered at 1.9m below the sod. The organic layer remained undifferentiated.

Matthew Seaver, Archaeological Consultancy Services Ltd, 15 Trinity Street, Drogheda, Co. Louth.

528. BRIDGE STREET, TRIM

Urban medieval

279030 256148

98E0465

Trial-trenching was undertaken at the site of the former 'Dean Swift' pub on 17 October 1998. The work was carried out in compliance with a condition attached to the grant of planning in respect of a replacement licensed premises. Before the commencement of the trial-trenching the site was subjected to an architectural and archaeological assessment, following which monitoring of demolition works was undertaken. The site lies on the western side of Bridge Street, on the southern side of the town, overlooking the river and immediately adjacent to the bridge. It lies within the designated zone of archaeological potential of Trim, as defined by the UAS, OPW.

Six trial-pits were excavated by machine. All were excavated through layers of rubble, which extended to depths of 1.6–3.28m below the existing ground surface. Below the rubble the surface of a silty, organic deposit was exposed, which contained fragments of animal bone, shell and wood-chip.

Such material is similar to deposits uncovered in other urban areas, which proved to be of archaeological significance. However, no attempt was made to determine the nature and depth of such deposits as the rubble would have had to be removed from a large area in order for any hand-excavation to be undertaken in a safe manner. Subsequent geotechnical investigations at the site indicated that the depth of the organic material was up to 2.3m. The levels of the organic deposits, 50.77–52.79m OD, indicate that the surface falls towards the river, which is hardly surprising given the location of the site with respect to the Boyne.

Consequently, a piled foundation plan was prepared for the site, with the ground-beams/services a minimum of 0.6m above the highest recorded level on the surface of the organic layer. All piles were 0.25m in diameter, and a grid of 5.3m was proposed.

Martin E. Byrne, 39 Kerdiff Park, Monread, Naas, Co. Kildare.

529. HAGGARD STREET, TRIM

Urban medieval

N80285737

98E0111

The development comprised an extension to the Supervalu supermarket. The site lay just within the east–west line of the northern stretch of the town wall, which runs from the Athboy Gate eastwards before taking a southwards bend. The line of the town wall also forms the boundary of the supermarket site.

The site lies south of St Mary's Dominican Priory, which was founded in 1263. Stone footings and earthworks associated with the priory still survive on open ground. These were subjected to an intensive geophysical survey carried out in 1988 by Dr William Jerrard Kennedy of Florida Atlantic University (lodged in the National Monuments Service). This survey showed subsurface features, which Dr Kennedy identified as different parts of the monastic buildings.

The present supermarket building stands on ground south of the priory buildings. It is *c.* 2m lower than the ground on which the priory remains stand, and the ground must have been substantially reduced when the supermarket and its carparking area were being built, resulting in a steep slope down from the priory to the carpark.

One trench tested the line of the west wall of the proposed extension. The stratigraphy was consistent along the length of the trench. It comprised two layers of tarmac and hard-core to a depth of 0.5m, overlying a compacted, stony boulder clay. In places the boulder clay was sandier, and large erratic boulders were exposed at the bottom of the trench, which was *c.* 1m deep.

No material of archaeological interest was observed.

Rosanne Meenan, Roestown, Drumree, Co. Meath.

530. NEWTOWN, TRIM

Medieval borough

282365 257727

98E0265

Archaeological assessment took place at a proposed

residential development at Newtown, Trim, Co. Meath. The site lies within an area of archaeological importance incorporating the suggested area of a medieval borough and the lands surrounding the former episcopal seat of the Liberty of Meath, which comprised the church of SS Peter and Paul and an Augustinian priory.

Four long trenches were excavated and uncovered sod, ploughsoil and natural gravel and yellow boulder clay. No archaeological features or objects were recovered.

Deirdre Murphy, Archaeological Consultancy Services Ltd, 15 Trinity Street, Drogheda, Co. Louth.

531. PETERSTOWN, TRIM
Possible Early Christian cemetery
N81325752
97E0389 ext.
Further archaeological rescue excavation was carried out at Peterstown, Trim, Co. Meath, on 16 May 1998, after a human burial was uncovered during drainage works associated with a road improvement scheme by Meath County Council. The remains of four individuals, three males and one female, were discovered 75m north-west of here in November 1997 (*Excavations 1997*, 143–4). Skeletal analysis had produced tentative evidence of an Early Christian or early medieval date for these burials. A radiocarbon date of 1594±37 years BP (cal. AD 414–532) for Burial 2 confirmed this Early Christian date. There was no archaeological or historical evidence of a cemetery in this area before this.

The stratigraphy above the latest burial had been disturbed by modern cuts, and the feet had been truncated during the mechanical excavation of the pipe-track. A subrectangular grave-cut, 0.28m deep at the south and 0.36m at the north, had been dug into the natural at a depth of 1m from the modern ground level. It measured 1.38m east–west by 0.52m. The fill of the grave-cut was redeposited natural and sand.

The burial was of a standard type and consisted of a supine extended inhumation aligned north-east/south-west. It was 1.65m long. There was no evidence of a coffin or shroud. The skeleton was largely complete and well preserved, although the skull and feet were truncated by the machine. The skull was recovered but not the feet. The lower jaw was still *in situ* and was facing north, indicating that the skull originally faced this direction. The position of the arms was unusual. The right arm was flexed over the lower abdomen, and the right hand was extended over the left arm. The left arm was extended by the side. The legs were apart and fully extended.

Skeletal analysis revealed that the remains were that of a male between the ages of 17 and 25. The burial had numerous skeletal pathologies and anomalies, and there is evidence that death may have been caused by a severe tooth infection. No artefacts were recovered in relation to this burial (Burial 3), athough a radiocarbon date of 446±46 years (cal. AD 1425–1461) indicates a 15th-century date for it. No further archaeological work is required in this area.

Deirdre Murphy, Archaeological Consultancy Services Ltd, 15 Trinity Street, Drogheda, Co. Louth.

532. TRIM CASTLE, TRIM
Medieval castle
N202564
95E0077 ext.
Dúchas The Heritage Service is to construct a block of toilets inside the west gate of the castle. Monitoring of topsoil-stripping in January 1998 revealed the presence of medieval structures close to the intended location of the toilets. The buildings were excavated in June, when trenches were also opened adjacent to the inner side of the gatehouse, inside the curtain wall south of the gatehouse and in the ramp leading to the gatehouse from its outer side.

The remains of a stone-footed structure were uncovered beneath the gatehouse. It appears to have burnt down. It is possibly the remains of a timber gatehouse that defended the castle in the 1170s–1180s. The two-phase building of the late gatehouse was reflected in the deposits around it, and part of the now truncated curtain wall was revealed south of the gatehouse. A succession of road surfaces was also uncovered leading into the castle from the gatehouse.

The large earthen bank that stands inside the curtain south of the gatehouse was partly excavated and proved to be most probably of early 14th-century date. Two stone-walled medieval buildings that were reoccupied during the 1640s were cut into this earthen bank. These were fully excavated.

The proposed location of the toilets was altered to avoid all the surviving medieval structures in the area.

Three short trenches were also cut into the ramp leading up to the west gate from outside the castle. The ramp proved to be composed of dry-stone masonry that could not be dated but that may be of medieval origin.

The work was funded by *Dúchas* The Heritage Service.

Alan Hayden, Archaeological Projects Ltd, 25A Eaton Square, Terenure, Dublin 6W.

MONAGHAN

533. CASTLEBLANEY WATER SCHEME
No archaeological significance
98E0497
Monitoring associated with the Castleblaney Urban Water Supply Scheme was carried out from October to December 1998. The scheme is an extension to the existing Lough Eglish Regional Water Supply Scheme. It involved the laying underground of a pipeline running in a general north-east direction from Tossy Cross, *c.* 8km south-south-west of Castleblaney, towards the town, where it turned in a general north-westerly direction to a termination point on the Monaghan Road, adjacent to Corracloghan House. Furthermore, a water reservoir was constructed at Connabury Td, on the southern side of Castleblaney town, adjacent to the existing reservoir. This was linked to the new main water pipe by means of an extension/spur line running in a general westerly direction from the reservoir site. In all, *c.* 10km of pipeline was involved, as well as groundworks associated with

the reservoir site.

A 10m-wide way-leave existed along the length of the pipeline in all green-field areas (*c.* 7km). Sections of the pipeline route were laid along the existing roadways and roadway grass verges. Continuous monitoring of topsoil-stripping was undertaken in all green-field areas, while trench excavations along the existing roads were monitored on an occasional basis.

No features, deposits or finds of archaeological interest were uncovered during the course of the work. *Martin E. Byrne, 39 Kerdiff Park, Monread, Naas, Co. Kildare.*

534. CARA STREET, CLONES

Zone of archaeological potential
98E0245

An archaeological assessment was carried out on the site of a proposed development at Cara Street, Clones, Co. Monaghan. The site was within the zone of archaeological potential for the town as identified by the Urban Archaeological Survey and lay *c.* 50m from the boundary wall of a graveyard that contains a round tower and an Early Christian stone sarcophagus. One test-trench was excavated on 23 May 1998. Before excavation the site was used for carparking.

The test-trench measured 9m x 1.8m on a north-east/south-west axis. It was excavated to the top of the natural subsoil. At a depth of *c.* 0.7m the remains of a flat-bottomed ditch with its accompanying coarse, grey fill were uncovered. The ditch was *c.* 1.3m wide at the point where it was dug into the natural subsoil and *c.* 1.1m at its base. It had been cut into the natural to a depth of *c.* 0.3m. It was excavated by hand.

The stratigraphy of the test-trench consisted of a gravel layer *c.* 0.1–0.2m deep, which lay directly above a layer of redeposited, dark brown topsoil and a layer of redeposited, dark brown/black topsoil intermixed with redeposited, coarse, grey ditch fill. A pottery sherd with the remains of a green glaze on its inner surface and three clay pipe stem fragments were found at the interface of the undisturbed ditch fill and the redeposited dark brown/black topsoil intermixed with the redeposited ditch fill. These finds (in particular the clay pipe stem fragments) indicate that the ditch dates to the early modern period (perhaps the 17th century, when the town of Clones underwent considerable development).

Two rubbish pits, cut into the natural, were also uncovered towards the centre of the test-trench. They were found to contain only modern rubbish.

In view of what was uncovered at the site it was recommended that either the proposed development be excavated before planning permission being granted or that the foundations not disturb the ditch remains. The archaeological resolution of the site has yet to be completed.
Eoghan Moore, Prospect House, Dunsrim, Scotshouse, Co. Monaghan.

535. CORKEERAN

Vicinity of ringfort
264879 319480
98E0063

Archaeological assessment took place at Corkeeran, Co. Monaghan, in advance of the construction of a proposed dwelling-house. The site is near a ringfort. Three trenches were excavated, two north-east/south-west and a third north–south.

Trenches 1 and 2 had 0.3–0.35m of topsoil and sod, after which boulder clay was exposed to a depth of 0.85m. Trench 3 was 15m long, 1.2m wide and was excavated to 0.9m deep. Sod and topsoil were 0.3m deep and at the south of the trench overlay a layer of dark brown soil, which contained fragments of red brick and rubble to a depth of 0.45m, after which boulder clay was encountered.
Deirdre Murphy, Archaeological Consultancy Services Ltd, 15 Trinity Street, Drogheda, Co. Louth.

536. CORNAPASTE

Near the Black Pig's Dyke/Worm Ditch linear earthwork
98E0408 and ext.

Testing was carried out on the site of proposed development at Cornapaste, Scotshouse, Co. Monaghan, in order to fulfil conditions for planning approval. The site lay 50m west of the Black Pig's Dyke, or Worm Ditch, and is best described as a water meadow. Five test-trenches were excavated by mechanical excavator on 14–17 September 1998.

Trench 1 measured *c.* 9.8m x 1.6–1.7m on a north–south axis. At a depth of *c.* 0.9m numerous pieces of wooden twigs with associated possible wooden stakes were uncovered, lying immediately above white lake marl at the northern end of the test-trench. These were interpreted as constituting a brushwood surface, and therefore only their upper surfaces were exposed.

On account of this discovery it was decided to test the area immediately to the east of Trench 1 to ascertain whether the brushwood extended eastwards (the presence of an electrical pole militated against investigating the area to the immediate west of Trench 1). Two test-trenches (2 and 3) were excavated by mechanical digger. Trench 2 measured 9.5m x 2.3–2.5m, while Trench 3 measured 4.5m x 1.6–1.7m. No brushwood (or any archaeological) remains were uncovered in either of these trenches.

A further two test-trenches (4 and 5) were mechanically excavated on an east–west axis immediately to the north of Trench 1. Trench 4 measured 26m x 1.6–1.7m, while Trench 5 measured 9.8m x 1.6–1.7m. No archaeological remains were uncovered.

Further testing was carried out on 31 December 1998. Two test-trenches were mechanically excavated in accordance with a request from the Planning Section, Monaghan County Council. These test-trenches, measuring 6.2m x 1.6–1.7m and 6.6m x 1.6–1.7m respectively, on an east–west axis, were excavated in the southern area of the site for proposed development. No archaeological remains were uncovered.

It was recommended that before development took place on the site the area of Trench 1 should be fully excavated to determine the nature, extent and date of the possible brushwood surface and stakes. The archaeological resolution of this site has yet to be completed.
Eoghan Moore, Prospect House, Dunsrim, Scotshouse, Co. Monaghan.

537. DRUMLANE I
Environs of ringfort
276581 316106
SMR 24:23
98E0499

Investigations at this site were undertaken as part of the Castleblaney Urban Water Supply Scheme. Topsoil-stripping inside the way-leave area and within a 50m radius of the site was undertaken in compliance with the recommendations of the Archaeological Assessment Report. The work was undertaken before the commencement of the scheme in order that any archaeological features or deposits could be identified at an early stage so that appropriate protection measures could be implemented.

The site, *c.* 5.5km south-south-west of Castleblaney, lies on the south-western slope of a high north-west/south-east drumlin ridge, which is part of a very high east–west ridge further to the north. When originally surveyed in 1968 the site consisted of a circular, flat area (35m north-east/south-west x 37.5m) surrounded by a sharply defined, large earthen bank with a U-shaped fosse outside. The interior sloped gently from north-west to south-east. There was a large gap in the bank at the south-east, which may have been the original entrance, although at the time it was closed by a modern low bank. Furthermore, the outer face of the bank and surface of a possible causeway had been scarped, and the fosse was partly filled in at this point. A row of cottage plots extended from the south-east and south-west sides of the ringfort to the nearby laneway. There was also a large gap at the west, which was described as modern. A few modern field fences cut across the fosse at east-south-east and south, and a modern field fence was positioned at the outer tip of the fosse. A number of old cultivation ridges ran north-north-east to south-south-west through the interior of the site.

The present condition of the fort is somewhat different from that described above. The cultivation ridges both within and outside the fort had been levelled, and there are no surface traces in existence. Furthermore, much of the fort has been levelled, leaving only a faint trace of the bank on the ground surface running in an arc from south-south-east to north-north-west and no trace of the fosse. The remainder of the fort is as described above.

The area was slightly dog-legged in plan and measured 10m x 100m. No features, deposits or finds of archaeological interest were recovered.
Martin E. Byrne, 39 Kerdiff Park, Monread, Naas, Co. Kildare.

538. DRUMLANE II
Environs of ringfort
278114 316285
SMR 24:24
98E0500

Investigations in the environs of this site were undertaken as part of the Castleblaney Urban Water Supply Scheme. Topsoil-stripping within a 50m radius of the site and inside the way-leave was undertaken before the commencement of the scheme. The site, *c.* 350m north of Drumlane I (see No. 537 above), lies at the east-south-east end of a

long, high drumlin ridge, which rises to its summit well above the ringfort. There is a lot of rock outcrop visible to south and south-east.

When first surveyed in 1968 the site consisted of a circular area (38m east-north-east/west-south-west by 41m) surrounded by the remains of an earthen bank on a high embankment, with the partial remains of a fosse at the north-west. There was a broad rib running west-north-west/east-south-east through the interior, with the ground sloping a good deal to the south-west and north-east. The bank was best preserved at north-west and south-east; along the south-west and north-east sides there were only faint traces of the bank, but the embankment was quite high here. The fosse only existed at north-west across the neck of the ridge. Several field fences touched the ringfort, and at the south-west one continued as outer facing to the embankment. There were several gaps in the bank, but the original entrance was not identifiable.

The present condition of the fort is that it is heavily overgrown with blackthorns, and it appears to be very much as described above.

The area of evaluation was slightly dog-legged in plan and measured 10m x 100m. No material of archaeological interest was recovered during the course of the work.
Martin E. Byrne, 39 Kerdiff Park, Monread, Naas, Co. Kildare.

539. DUNMADIGAN
No archaeological significance
266046 346508
98E0260

Trial-trenching was undertaken at a development site in Dunmadigan Td, Emyvale, Co. Monaghan, on 20 June 1998. The work was carried out in compliance with a request for further information from the planning authority in respect of a planning application for the construction of a dormer bungalow at the site. The site lies within the general vicinity of two ringforts, SMR 3:41 and 3:42, both of which are over 100m from the development site, and it had been recommended by the NMHPS that no archaeological involvement was required.

Six trenches were opened by mechanical excavator fitted with a ditching bucket. It was determined that the topsoil had a general average depth of 0.6m and that it directly overlay the natural sterile subsoil. No material of archaeological or historical interest or significance was uncovered.
Martin E. Byrne, 39 Kerdiff Park, Monread, Naas, Co. Kildare.

540. ULSTER BANK, THE DIAMOND, MONAGHAN
Possible castle site
2673 3338
98E0175

Testing was undertaken at the above site to determine whether there were any surviving traces of Monaghan Castle. There is a tradition recorded in the Ordnance Survey Letters 'That the large house in the Diamond opposite Glaslough Street, is said to possess (occupy?) the site of a castle'. This suggests the possibility that the castle stood in the location of the present Ulster Bank, which is adjacent to the Church of Ireland church and has been in use as a bank for at least 100 years. The present building was built in the 1960s on the site of a previous one, which had extended the length of the entire yard.

Two trenches were positioned across the length and breadth of the site; they revealed a stratigraphy consistent with the extensive works that have taken place on the site over the past 150 years, which have effectively destroyed any archaeological evidence.
Rónán Swan, Arch-Tech Ltd, 32 Fitzwilliam Place, Dublin 2.

541. TEMPORARY BANK, GLASSLOUGH STREET CARPARK, GLASSLOUGH STREET, MONAGHAN

No archaeological significance
2673 3339
98E0144
Testing was undertaken at the above site on behalf of Ulster Bank Plc. No evidence of archaeological features or deposits was recovered.
Rónán Swan, Arch-Tech Ltd, 32 Fitzwilliam Place, Dublin 2.

OFFALY

542. BALLICKNAHEE

Cemetery
228971 234727
98E0286
Following an initial site inspection a limited rescue excavation was carried out in Ballicknahee townland near Clara, Co. Offaly, following the discovery of several burials during gravel extraction from an esker ridge. The excavation took place to allow the sides of the quarry to be graded back and thereby stabilise the surrounding ground to protect further burials from collapsing into the quarry. There had been no previous indication of burials on the site.

An area surrounding the top of the quarry was chosen for excavation. The remains of at least seventeen individuals were recovered, most of which had been disturbed by the machine during the extraction of the gravel from the esker ridge. All of the remains were recovered at a depth of *c.* 0.4m below modern ground level; however, only one of the burials (Burial 2) was undisturbed. This was orientated north-east to south-west and was placed in a shallow, simple grave cut.

Of the seventeen individuals recovered, thirteen were adults and four were juveniles. Only seven of the individuals could be sexed, five of which were male and two female. The complete female burial (Burial 2) was 40–55 years at time of death. There was also at least one young adult aged 18–21 years and a juvenile aged 14–16 years among the disarticulated remains.

No finds were recovered that would give any indication of date, and it was recommended that the site be entered in the Register of Historic Monuments as there was a high potential for further burials being uncovered. All of the burials appear to have been interred in simple pits and consisted entirely of extended inhumations.
Donald Murphy, Archaeological Consultancy Services Ltd, 15 Trinity Street, Drogheda, Co. Louth.

543. BALLYBURLEY

Adjacent to church and graveyard
255169 235181
SMR 4:13
97E0321 ext.
Test-trenching was carried out on 16 October 1997 at a site adjacent to the late medieval Ballyburley church and cemetery, near Rhode, Co. Offaly. Archaeological remains were uncovered during testing. These consisted of evidence of a ditch that possibly originally encircled the ecclesiastical site and disturbed human remains on the cemetery side of this ditch (*Excavations 1997*, 147)

Monitoring of groundworks associated with the development was carried out on various dates in February and June 1998.

Foundations for the house were dug just north-east of the apparent line of the ditch, as identified during the evaluation of the site, and therefore did not transect the line of this feature. Levels were also reduced over a larger area surrounding the house, but the fact that no further evidence of the ditch was identified during this process may be due to the generally low visibility of many forms of archaeological remains.

In the percolation trench on the northern corner of the site a considerable amount of generalised disturbance was observed at a depth that appeared to be slightly below the original level of the sterile natural in this area. Tiny fragments of charcoal, as well as a number of what appeared to be charred seeds, were also found within this disturbance. There was no obvious structural organisation to this material as it seemed to fill a series of irregular undulations in the surface of the natural, but the narrowness of the percolation trench served to inhibit any clear perspective of this material. No further human remains were found during monitoring.

While no clearly identifiable archaeological features were discovered during the course of monitoring, it certainly appears that some archaeological material exists over the general area of the site, particularly in the northern and western sides. This suggests that the archaeologically sensitive area is not confined to the cemetery side of the ditch and that the general environs of the site are also of archaeological significance.
Clare Mullins, 39 Kerdiff Park, Monread, Naas, Co. Kildare.

544. BANAGHER

Urban
SMR 21:3
97E0444 ext.
The construction phase of the sewerage works in Banagher was monitored. Initial monitoring of the scheme, undertaken in 1997, was previously reported (*Excavations 1997*, 146–7).

The trenches varied from 1m to 2m wide and from 1.5m to 3.5m deep. No archaeological stratigraphy, features or artefacts were recorded from the trenches on Cuba Avenue, Lusmagh Road, the area of the Marina, Crank Road or Main Street, or the areas of the pumping stations.

A limestone wall, recorded in the manhole K1, and the return of a wall, recorded in the sewer trench between N4 and N3, were uncovered in the area of the Constabulary Barracks. It is possible that these walls were associated with the 17th-century fort.

A ditch, 4m wide and 1.5m deep, was recorded in the rising-main trench between B3 (Main Street) and the Crank Road. Four fills were recorded in the ditch. No artefacts were recovered. The ditch may be the 17th-century town earthworks. It lies 15m south-west of the line of the town defences as proposed by the Urban Archaeological Survey of County Offaly. According to a plantation map of the town, which dates to *c.* 1629, the town was defended on three sides by an earthwork, linear in plan except to the north-east, where there was a projecting bulwark. No evidence of the earthwork was recorded in the area of M8, east of the Marina Pumping Station.
Jacinta Kiely, Eachtra Archaeological Projects, Clover Hill, Mallow, Co. Cork

545. KYLEBEG, BANAGHER

17th-century and later military fortification
N003155
SMR 21:2
98E0097

The fort, and later Royal Irish Constabulary barracks in which it is incorporated, has a long history. It was the site of the early 17th-century Fort Falkland and was used for many centuries as a military barracks. The fort was built in 1624. It was extensively remodelled in the 18th and 19th centuries, probably most extensively in 1807. It was in its latest para-military phase, a constabulary barracks, and is marked as such on the 1909 OS map. It was used as an RIC barracks until 1920, when it was burnt by the Irish Republican Army during the War of Independence.

The towers depicted on 17th-century maps are still extant, and these extend beneath the present front wall of the barracks. Further walls were found within the fort; one may also be of 17th-century date, while the other may be later. Some of the buildings that survive overground seem to be of late medieval date, others post-date 1807.

Recent archaeological monitoring of pipelines by Ken Ryan has shown that further 17th-century walls occur outside the middle of the front and outside the north-north-east corner of the barracks. This licence was first held by Dominic Delaney and was trans-ferred to this writer, who carried out test excavations in June 1998.

The developer wished to build thirteen holiday homes within the fort. An archaeological impact statement involving test-trenching was requested by the NMHPS. Planning permission was refused, and the applicant, before reapplying, at the request of Offaly County Council engaged an archaeologist to have test-trenching carried out. Previous test-trenching, in which no trace of the earlier fort had been found, was undertaken at the site by Beth Cassidy in 1990 (*Excavations 1990*, 50).

The current excavation, using a mechanical digger, established that a substantial number of walls occur within the fort. In Trench 4 Wall I is over 1m thick and may be late medieval. Two further wall segments are flimsier and may relate to walling that formed part of an L-shaped building shown as extant on the 1909 map.

In Trenches 5 and 5A the foundations of a partial-ly extant rectangular building were outlined. It may be pre-18th century.

In Trench 3A the footings of another wall (III), which does not appear on the 1909 map, were noted. This may be of late medieval date, and its footings may be extensive. It was sealed below 19th-century cobbling.

The walls of a massive gate-tower of 17th-century date was found in Trenches 6–8. This tower may be one of the pair of D-shaped bastions shown on a depiction of Fort Falkland by Nicholas Pynnar, dated 1624 (British Library Add. MS 24200). This shows a pair of towers flanking a round-headed gateway. The towers have square backs and rounded fronts and seem to relate to portions of the fort shown on two depictions of 1624. One of the towers found matches the features shown on the Pynnar drawing fairly well. The walling is 1.7–1.8m thick in places, and the rendered exterior of one curved bastion was clearly visible on excavation. The base of the tower had a steep base-batter. The tower runs beneath the present front wall of the barracks. Part of the rendered wall of this or a related feature has also been found in monitoring by Ken Ryan of pipe-laying .

Trenches 6–8 were not cut to great depth, but enough was uncovered to show that the plan of one of the gate-towers can be completely recovered. The other tower is likely to remain beneath the ground, which seems to have been raised deliberately in the 18th or 19th centuries, probably with the refortifica-tion of the site in *c.* 1807.

A large lump of late medieval masonry also projects from beneath the south-east wall of the site, and this too may be of 17th-century date. It lies in the yard of the nearby Vine House pub and restaurant.

It is clear even from preliminary archaeological testing that substantial remains of the early 17th-century fort, its internal buildings as well as its D-shaped towers, exist. Further excavation would reveal more traces of the early plantation fortress.

A 19th-century pump set into a subcircular well structure accessible beneath ground by a series of steps was also uncovered in Trenches 6 and 7. This may lie above the site of an earlier well, but it was not excavated to any depth. The upper fill contained 19th- and early 20th-century material.

A stone trough and 19th-century cobbling occur near the centre of the site, and the outlines of many of the later buildings are still marked by walls or portions of walls, as well as partly destroyed cobbled, concrete and other flooring of Liscannor stone. Evidence of the destruction of the fort (or part of it) by fire in the 1920s was seen in Trench 3, where a burnt floor and scorching of the walls was visible. It is clear that the north-north-east corner of the fort (into which a concrete munitions store has been built) incorporates earlier fabric.
Jim Higgins, 'St Gerards', 18 College Road, Galway.

546. MAIN STREET, BANAGHER

Urban
98E0301

This involved the monitoring of ground disturbance associated with the development of a shop extension at Main Street, Banagher, Co. Offaly. Nothing of archaeological significance was encountered in the course of monitoring.
Martin Fitzpatrick, Archaeological Consultancy, Ballydavid South, Athenry, Co. Galway.

Offaly

547. CLONMACNOISE
Early medieval wooden bridge
20068 23068
97E0243

Underwater archaeological excavations were carried out over a four-week period in June 1998 on an early medieval wooden bridge crossing the River Shannon at Clonmacnoise. The excavations were funded by the NMHPS. The bridge lies between Clonmacnoise townland, Co. Offaly, and Coolumber, Co. Roscommon, crossing a narrow part of the river west of the Anglo-Norman masonry castle.

Previous work on this site included both underwater survey and excavation. In 1994 a preliminary underwater survey in the River Shannon at Clonmacnoise identified a number of wooden posts and beams on the riverbed. A more detailed survey carried out in 1995 seemed to indicate that the timbers were the remains of a bridge, from which some 100 timbers seemed to survive. These included vertically set posts, longitudinal and transverse beams, planking, and complex carpentry. A dendrochronological sample from a post on the northern side of the structure yielded a date of AD 804. A series of dug-out canoes was also revealed, lying on the riverbed and among the structural timbers.

Underwater archaeological excavations in 1997 (*Excavations 1997*, 148–9) investigated the nature of the bridge's construction. This revealed that the structure was built using a complex method of sharpened and through-mortised posts with individual baseplates of beams and planks. There were also hints of the superstructure of the bridge in the occasional well-preserved vertical timber now lying on the riverbed. Finds from the survey and excavations included nine dug-out wooden boats; four early medieval, iron, woodworking axes; a large, early medieval, decorated bronze basin; iron slag; a whetstone; animal bone; and a Mesolithic chert core. These excavations also confirmed that the bridge spanned the river from bank to bank and that it was uninterrupted in its length.

In 1998 a third season of underwater investigations at Clonmacnoise was carried out. The project aimed to answer a number of unresolved questions about the preservation of the dug-out canoes, the status of a previously identified timber scatter lying downstream and the nature of the archaeology upstream of the bridge, which had hitherto been unexplored.

The first aim of the project was to lift, record and assess the erosion of the dug-out boats. There were concerns that those on the riverbed were the most subject to erosion of all the features, all of them having lost ends and sides to the constant erosion of the channel and the movement of mussel shell fragments. It was decided to lift and record these boats and move them to a safer location. Therefore, in the first two weeks of the excavations each boat was lifted and brought up to the riverbank. This task was accomplished using buoys and lifting slings. The boats were then drawn at 1:10 scale, with cross-sections and profiles completed. Each boat was also photographed in detail. It was clear that more information could be gleaned from the boat in the open air than underwater. At the close of the season each boat was transported back into the water and left at a known location downstream of the bridge. It is intended that some, if not all, of these boats will be fully conserved in the future.

The second aim of the project was to assess the archaeology of a scatter of timbers found 100m downstream of the bridge adjacent to the east bank. These timbers had been surveyed in detail during the 1995 season, so it was possible to return to their location. However, it had not been possible to record them any more closely during that survey season, as they were lightly buried in the river silts. It was suspected that they were the remains of the original early medieval bridge's superstructure and that they could therefore supply much useful information on the carpentry of bridge. However, during the 1998 season, after rapid exposure on the riverbed and timber recording, it became evident that all of these downstream scatter timbers were modern in origin. They were all of pine roundwood, sharpened at one end and heavily rotten from exposure to wetting and drying. These posts probably derived from the riverine end of a modern barbed-wire fence that runs down to the river from the west side of the Anglo-Norman castle. They therefore have no relationship of any kind with the early medieval bridge. Indeed, it now seems likely that little or no trace of the original bridge superstructure remains in the river.

A third aim of the project was to extend the underwater survey upstream of the bridge, bringing the investigated area up to the riverbank of the monastic site. A survey was carried out along the east bank, to a point 200m upstream of the bridge and out to the middle of the river channel. There was no evidence of any wooden structures in this area. A number of finds were made, including wooden objects, iron buckets and various other objects. Most importantly, the remains of two more dug-out boats were found on the riverbed. One example was unusual in that it had a flat bottom, with slightly raised ends, in the manner of river cots depicted on early modern maps of Ireland. This boat is at least 7.75m long and is the largest yet found. A remote-sensing survey of the riverbed was also carried out by Kevin Barton of the Geophysics Department, UCG, using differential GPS and a bathymetric sonar survey.

The present programme of underwater archaeological investigations of the early medieval bridge at Clonmacnoise can now be considered complete. The project has been high successful, accomplishing in a relatively brief period the detailed recording of a substantial 9th-century wooden bridge and the recovery and curation of eleven dug-out boats and various metalwork finds. However, there are serious concerns about the future preservation of this unique structure, as this stretch of the River Shannon is subject to an ever-increasing volume of boat traffic and large cruisers. This, as well as natural riverine erosion, may well be having a detrimental effect on the archaeology that lies only a few metres under the water.

Aidan O'Sullivan, Niall Brady and Donal Boland, Management for Archaeology Underwater Limited, Arden Road, Tullamore, Co. Offaly.

548. NEW GRAVEYARD, CLONMACNOISE
Early Christian settlement
2011 2308
SMR 5:58
E0558

The final season of excavation on this site took place

in June and July, with funding from the NMHPS and Offaly County Council (see *Excavations 1990*, 49; *1991*, 40–1; *1992*, 53–4; *1993*, 66–7; *1994*, 74–5; *1995*, 76–7; *1996*, 93–4 and *1997*, 149). Four small cuttings in the north-east end of Section 1 of the New Graveyard, i.e. 14–17, were excavated to natural.

Cuttings 14 and 15 were opened to determine the extent of the 'revetment' at the northern (Shannon) side of the site. This feature, consisting of a bank of marl faced on the settlement side by large boulders (see *Excavations 1997*), ran for *c.* 8m east–west across the north (Shannon) side of Cutting 13. Excavation in Cuttings 14 and 15 showed that the 'bank' of marl extended a further 4m to the north (the full extent of this feature has not been recovered as it extends northwards beyond the graveyard wall) and *c.* 2.5m to the east. It now appears to represent an introduced, impervious layer laid on the early (i.e. 8th–10th-century) deposits on the low-lying ground adjacent to the Shannon. It was faced on the settlement side with stones and on the east by a trench that may have held a wooden fence.

A burnt floor or collapsed roof, revetted on the east by a post-wattle-and-stone wall or fence and measuring 3m x 2m, was uncovered in Cutting 16 and may indicate an early post-and-wattle structure close to the Shannon. A second stone-lined well, very disturbed in the upper levels, was found in Cutting 17, with a number of medieval potsherds in an adjacent layer. The number of medieval pot-sherds found throughout the entire excavation has been extremely small; none were stratified, and they were only recovered through sieving the disturbed topsoil. The sherds found this season may indicate the construction of a well in the 13th century or, alternatively, the late use of an 11th/12th-century well. Evidence of settlement dating to the 8th–12th centuries in the form of pits, hearths and stake-holes was also uncovered.

A total of 153 artefacts were found this year. Material recovered from sieving the topsoil included half a Hiberno-Norse coin, bronze dress-pins, bronze toilet implements, worked bronze pieces, decorated bone comb fragments, crucible fragments, iron objects including a fish hook, a buckle and key, a small quantity of medieval and post-medieval pottery, a reused quernstone and other miscellaneous objects. Stratified material included medieval potsherds, some decorated scrap bronze, a stone ingot mould, a cross-slab fragment, bone points including a possible stylus, a range of iron objects, crucible fragments, mortar, slag and furnace bottoms.
Heather A. King, National Monuments and Historic Properties Service, Dúchas, 51 St Stephens Green, Dublin 2.

549. DEERPARK
Close to archaeological complex
249651 233608
98E0549
Archaeological monitoring of groundworks for the construction of a private house and driveway was carried out on 18–19 November 1998 in compliance with a condition within the grant of planning. The development site was a green-field site on the lower south-eastern slope of Croghan Hill, an area of immense archaeological significance.

No features of archaeological significance were identified during the course of this work.
Clare Mullins, 39 Kerdiff Park, Monread, Naas, Co. Kildare.

550. DERRYVILLA
Medieval
254758 214334
98E0315
An archaeological evaluation was undertaken during 20–31 July 1998 at the site of a burial-ground in Derryvilla townland, Co. Offaly. The area in question is the site of a sand quarry, and as a result of the quarrying activities human remains were exposed. There had been no previous indication of a burial-ground on the site. The area is a plateau forming the top of a hill. The land slopes steeply to the north and east, while the south side of the plateau corresponds with the edge of the quarry bowl. It can be presumed that this plateau originally extended southwards into the area now occupied by the quarry. Most of the exposed bones were found in the vicinity of an ESB pylon that stands on the north side of the quarry, and human remains could be seen protruding from the section face of the quarry in this area.

The purpose of the test excavation was to determine the lateral extent of the burial-ground and to give some indication of the concentration of burials within. A series of twenty hand-dug box trenches was inserted at intervals over the natural plateau that existed above and to the west of the ESB pylon. Three machine-cut trenches were also inserted outside the burials as defined by hand-testing. A fourth machine-cut trench was inserted on the south-west side of the quarry, where some fragments of human bone had been observed lying on the ground surface during the initial site visit.

The stratigraphy across the site consisted of topsoil to a depth of *c.* 0.3m, overlying a brown, humic sand that occurred to a depth of up to almost 1m in places. Within this brown sand lay the skeletons. Beneath the brown sand lay the white, sterile sand of which the hill is composed.

Burials, either disturbed or *in situ*, were found in eleven of the test-trenches. Most of the trenches contained occasional fragments of human bone, often within the topsoil, which had been transported from elsewhere. All undisturbed burials, with the exception of that found in Trench 10, were orientated precisely or closely east to west, indicating that the cemetery belongs to the Christian era. The burial found in Trench 10 was orientated more closely north to south. The uncovering of parts of a skeleton where the bones were clearly arranged in the correct anatomical position was taken as adequate evidence of the existence of a burial in that location, and there was no deliberate policy of removing the human remains.

A ditch feature was discovered that appears to run north to south across the centre of the plateau. The occurrence of undisturbed burials close to the eastern side of this feature and the absence of any evidence of burial on its western side strongly suggest that this feature delineates the western boundary of the cemetery. The apparent discontinuation of bone in the section of the quarry face beyond a point 20m west of the ESB pylon corresponds with this evidence. Burials were also found right up to the edge of the plateau on all sides to the east of this ditch, and the section of the quarry face suggests that burial continued for some metres down the slope of the hill beyond the eastern edge of the plateau.

No specific attempt was made to determine the extent of stratified burial as to do so would have involved the opening of a larger area and the removal of some burials. The varying depths at which burials were found suggests that there had been occasional superimposition of interments, while the section face also gave some indication of stratified burial. However, the manner in which many of the exposed skeletons appeared to lie upon the sterile, white sand indicates that stratified burial was not the norm.

It is probable that the natural plateau on the summit of the hill acted as the focus of this burial-ground. While it is clear that an unknown portion of this burial-ground has been destroyed by quarrying on the south of the area tested, it appears that some of the western boundary of the cemetery, as defined by the ditch, is intact. It also appears likely that the topography to the north and east of the plateau has not been greatly altered, and thus the original boundary, as indicated approximately by the edge of the plateau, may be preserved on these sides.

Clare Mullins, 39 Kerdiff Park, Monread, Naas, Co. Kildare.

551. FRANKFORT
Shrunken settlement
SMR 45:22
20627 18482
98E0061
Trial-trenching on a site for a new house, just east of the Church of Ireland church in Dunkerrin village, revealed no features of archaeological significance. An old north–south field boundary was noted and dated to the 18th century or later.
Brian Hodkinson, Annaholty, Birdhill, Co. Tipperary.

552. FRANKFORT
Shrunken settlement
SMR 45:22
20627 18482
98E0095
Monitoring of groundworks for a small funeral home besides the Catholic church in Dunkerrin village and opposite where No. 551 (above) took place, revealed no features of deposits of archaeological significance.
Brian Hodkinson, Annaholty, Birdhill, Co. Tipperary.

553. LEMANAGHAN
Trackway
216641 228101 to 216582 227607
98E0464
An excavation was carried out as part of an assessment and mitigation project in Bord na Móna's Lemanaghan Bog, Boora Works, Co. Offaly. The work was carried out between 13 October and 5 November 1998 and concentrated on a single-plank walkway and three lesser structures.

The plank walkway was first identified in 1993 during field survey carried out by the Irish Archaeological Wetland Unit, when it was traced for 454m. During the 1998 assessment the site was traced further and was finally identified as surviving intermittently over a length of 870m. The site runs in a north–south direction, and at its northern end is a zone of 25 other smaller sites to the east and west. The excavations were concentrated along a 360m length at the southernmost end of the site.

The assessment recorded visible traces of the site at fourteen locations, and nine cuttings were established. On excavation the wood in the three most southerly cuttings (Nos 1–3) proved to have been redeposited by heavy machinery. This wood was roughly aligned on the projected line of the site and represented its former presence in the general area. Cuttings 4 and 5 each produced a single *in situ* peg indicating the line of the site, as well as fragments of disturbed and redeposited wood. Cuttings 6–8 produced the best surviving evidence of the structure of the sites.

In each cutting the site had been truncated by Bord na Móna drains and severely damaged and partly removed by surface milling. The general pattern of construction revealed in these cuttings showed an upper surface of single longitudinal planks laid end to end supported two layers of substructure. None of the upper planks survived intact, but the excavated evidence indicates that they ranged from *c.* 4m to 6m long, with mortises cut through the ends, through which pegs were driven. Supporting each end of the planks was an upper substructure of single transverse roundwoods or split timbers *c.* 1.1m long. The lower substructure consisted of pairs of longitudinally laid timbers *c.* 1.5m long set *c.* 0.5m apart, supporting each of the upper substructural timbers. The end of each of the superstructure planks was therefore supported by three timbers and additional lesser timbers as well as supporting pegs.

Cutting 9 produced no surviving horizontally laid timbers; however, a number of pegs survived indicating a continuation of the pattern of construction identified in other cuttings.

This form of trackway construction has not been excavated before and samples submitted for dendrochronological dating provided a date of after AD 590.
Conor McDermott, Irish Archaeological Wetland Unit, Department of Archaeology, University College Dublin, Belfield, Dublin 4.

554. TUMBEAGH BOG, TUMBEAGH
Bog body
215622 229398
98E0452
In mid-September the Irish Archaeological Wetland Unit was carrying out pre-mitigation surveys for Bord na Móna in the Lemanaghan group of bogs between Clara and Ferbane in County Offaly. During a resurvey of Tumbeagh Bog a member of the field crew, Cathy Moore, discovered what were soon to be confirmed as human remains. The remains lay on the milled surface of the bog and were visible as a small flap of damaged skin with crumbs of body fat. Initial inspection showed that skeletal material was present, and a disturbed tarsal bone was recovered from the field surface.

Consultation between *Dúchas*, the National Monuments Service, the National Museum of Ireland, Bord na Móna and the Irish Archaeological Wetland Unit culminated in an excavation designed to recover the *in situ* remains; to search for *ex situ* human remains and artefacts; to recover any associated archaeological objects and identify any associated features; to undertake a sampling project for palaeoenvironmental purposes, which included samples for beetle, pollen and ash content analysis as well as a peat stratigraphic survey. In addition a metal-detection survey was carried out, as well as film documentation of the excavation process. The excavation was carried out in close cooperation with Dr Máire Delaney of Trinity College Dublin.

The excavation involved trowelling *c.* 25m of the field surface on which the remains were found; shovelling and raking of the heavy, loose peat cover of the field immediately to the west of the find field; searching by hand a nearby stockpile for redeposited material; and defining the extent of *in situ* human remains by the digging of regularly placed hand-dug test-pits, followed by isolation of the human remains in a block of peat around which the excavation proceeded.

The raking of the peat on the adjacent western field produced a single, decalcified rib. The stockpile investigation resulted in the discovery of fragments of human skin as well as a lumbar vertebra, a left patella and the unfused proximal epiphyses of the left and right tibiae. The retrieval of these stray bones indicated that the body had already been extensively destroyed and served to verify that it had once been complete. Hand-dug tests-pits, excavated at half-metre intervals over an area of 3m x 3.5m, resulted in the definition of the extent of the *in situ* remains. These consist of either a left leg, tightly flexed, or the lower parts of a right and left leg. Skin and the proximal left tibia were visible once all disturbed peat had been removed from over the remains.

Immediately adjacent to the *in situ* remains a number of artefacts were recovered, which include a horizontal worked roundwood running in a northerly direction away from the area of the knee, three to four short lengths of worked brushwood, and a wooden withy as well as a stake that appeared to have been driven into the peat adjacent to the knee. In addition the metal-detection survey resulted in the recovery of four tiny strips of non-ferrous metal. Three were found within 1m of the *in situ* remains, and the fourth *c.* 5m distant. All were retrieved from disturbed, loose peat. The metal-detection survey also included the adjacent fields and stockpile, but no further finds were recovered.

Once the site was cleared of artefacts a 2m-wide and 1m-deep moat was excavated around a 1m x 1m peat block in which the remains had been isolated. The moat facilitated the lifting of the remains and allowed a pollen monolith to be taken and a peat stratigraphic study of the peat deposits in which the remains lay to be carried out, as well as fulfilling the archaeological requirement of determining the presence or absence of associated archaeological features (absence in this case).

On completion of the moat excavation the 1m x 1m x 1m peat block was reduced in size to facilitate lifting. The reduced-size block, 1.2m x 0.6m x 0.5m, was secured within a wooden frame filled by expanding polyurethane foam, which hardened to form a shell around the block. The secured block was removed to the National Museum and stored in a fridge. The peat block is to be excavated later in the Museum.

Nóra Bermingham, Irish Archaeological Wetland Unit, Department of Archaeology, University College Dublin, Belfield, Dublin 4.

ROSCOMMON

555. AUGHAMORE VILLAGE, BALLYKILCLINE
19th-century tenant village
M990860
98E0297

Excavations were conducted at the 19th-century village of Aughamore, Ballykilcline townland, Co. Roscommon, from 29 June and to 31 July 1998.

The townland of Ballykilcline, which contains the village, was a Crown estate. The Mahons, who lived in Strokestown Park House, around seven miles away, leased the land from the 1790s to 1834. From 1834 to 1847, however, the townland's tenants owed their rents directly to the English Crown. Before their wholesale eviction in 1847 the tenants refused to pay and were involved in a protracted and violent rent strike. Actions such as this made it possible for early 19th-century observers like John O'Donovan—lexicographer for the Ordnance Survey—to observe that 'the Parish of Kilglass...is proverbial...for its wickedness'. Bailiffs and cartographers were frequently afraid to travel into the townland without an armed escort.

Before excavation Kevin Barton, of the Applied Geophysics Unit of the National University of Ireland, Galway, made a detailed topographical map of the site and conducted a series of sub-surface geophysical surveys of the site area. The placement of cuttings was based on these tests as well as on information appearing on the Ordnance Survey map. Thirty-five 1m x 2m excavation units were examined.

A total of 1134 artefacts was collected. With the exception of eight isolated stone flakes, all of the artefacts date to the 1800–47 period. The artefact distribution breaks down as follows: ceramics (fine earthenware, coarse earthenware, porcelain and stoneware), 626 sherds (55.2% of total sample); glass (curved and flat), 402 sherds (35.4%); metal (iron, brass, lead and gilding), 62 (5.5%); and other (bone, charcoal sample, slate, animal tooth, whitewash), 44 (3.9%). From a purely historical standpoint perhaps the most interesting artefact was a partial bowl from a white clay smoking pipe discretely stamped '...PEAL', undoubtedly for 'REPEAL'.

Thirty-two contexts were identified. Two of these were narrow, stone alignments that probably constitute the remains of house walls. Another context was a cobbled yard area, just north of one of the stone walls. The stone walls will be excavated in 1999.

The soil stratigraphy at the site consisted of five layers: sod, topsoil, two horizons of dark yellowish/brown, loamy soil and a deeper, dark yellowish/brown, culturally sterile clay. Most of the artefacts and man-made features were found in the topsoil or just below, in the two layers of loam. Little if any mixing could be observed in these soil layers.

This excavation was conducted as part of a larger archaeological effort to examine the material basis of rural life on the eve of the Great Hunger. Although it is the third site tested as part of this research project, it is clearly the most interesting. The interpretations of Gorttoose (*Excavations 1996*, 95) and Mulliviltrin (*Excavations 1997*, 152–3) were confused by the substantial degree of post-abandonment disturbance that had taken place. A large amount of data was gathered from both sites on the material culture of the period. Much of this information can be used in the interpretation of the most recent excavation, but neither site permits the level of analysis that will be possible with the Aughamore material. Of the artefacts collected, the ceramic sample will prove especially important. The large amount of imported, English, fine earthenware in the sample is interesting because it implies that instead of paying their annual rents to the Crown the tenants used their meagre funds to improve their material conditions. In addition the collection of locally made coarse earthenware further argues for the importance of this industry to the men and women of the countryside.

The Aughamore site is important from both historical and archaeological standpoints, and it is expected that further excavations will broaden our understanding of early 19th-century rural life in this part of the country.

Charles E. Orser Jr., Illinois State University, Normal, IL 61790-4640, USA.

556. BALLYPHESAN
No archaeological significance
98E0438
Pre-development testing in the form of trial-trenches was carried out in the north-west portion of a proposed development at Ballyphesan, Co. Roscommon. Two trenches measuring 30m x 2m were mechanically excavated, with nothing of archaeological significance encountered.

Martin Fitzpatrick, Archaeological Consultancy, Ballydavid South, Athenry, Co. Galway.

557. DEMESNE
Possible tree ring?
98E0515
Trial-trenching was carried out at Demesne town-land, Castlerea, Co. Roscommon, for five days from 28 October 1998. The proposed development involved the construction of twelve houses. In the course of the planning process a hitherto unrecorded and unclassified earthen feature, a possible tree ring, was noted within the area of the development, and it was recommended that this feature be examined by an archaeologist under licence before the commencement of the development.

The site is of irregular shape, slightly more angular than circular, with several ill-defined, poorly preserved banks and ditches broadly enclosing a roughly square area. The apparent lack of accomplishment in the execution of these enclosing elements, coupled with the lack of clarity in deciphering them, makes a confident classification of the site as a tree ring impossible. Trees occupy just half of the site, and they were not planted on a continuous bank. Several gaps appear in the banks, and neither the line of the trees nor of the unplanted banks follows a well-executed shape.

The excavation of a single trial-trench through the feature did not produce conclusive evidence that this site was archaeologically significant. It did reveal evidence of human activity, and the indications are that the feature was man-made, as a deliberate cut and redeposited bank material were noted, but the remains do not satisfactorily fit the accepted classification criteria of a tree ring.

The exact function of the site could not be ascertained from the finds, which were almost exclusively of modern to 18th-century date and were highly mixed in two of the eight excavated contexts. A possible piece of worked flint was discovered in the topsoil side by side with modern glass and clay pipe fragments.

Anne Connolly, Archaeological Services Unit Ltd, Purcell House, Oranmore, Co. Galway.

558. DRUMSILLAGH
No archaeological significance
SMR 7:74
98E0589
Pre-development testing was undertaken on the site of a proposed development in Drumsillagh, Boyle, Co. Roscommon, in December 1998. The proposed development site lies within the designated archaeological area of SMR 7:74.

Four test-trenches were excavated by machine. No archaeological features or small finds were recovered from any of the trenches.

Gerry Walsh, Rathbawn Road, Castlebar, Co. Mayo.

559. GLEBE
Adjacent to castle
SMR 8:13
98E0325
Five test-trenches were dug in advance of house construction in the townland of Glebe, Castlemore, Ballaghaderreen, Co. Rosmommon. (The castle and surrounding area were formerly in County Mayo.) The nearest trench came within 30m of the castle remains and bawn wall.

Material from the trenches showed the area to be one of eskerine gravel, covered by basically similar, loamy topsoil, 0.35–0.65m deep. The ground appears not to have been interfered with or disturbed. No artefacts were found.

Leo Morahan, James Street, Kiltimagh, Co. Mayo.

560. GRALLAGH
Archaeological complex
SMR 22:56
98E0523
Pre-development testing was carried out on 31 October 1998 in advance of house construction. The area is one of great archaeological wealth, with a large area denoted as an archaeological complex. There are no surface traces of any archaeological features at or close to the development site; the nearest known monument is a rath 200m to the south-south-east.

Seven trenches were excavated, but the soil quality in all was more or less the same and nothing of archaeological significance was encountered. Boulder clay was encountered no more than 0.6m beneath ground level.

Leo Morahan, James Street, Kiltimagh, Co. Mayo.

561. KILTULLAGH HILL, KILTULLAGH

Inhumations

M530740

96E0179 ext.

Excavations on Kiltullagh Hill took place in 1994 and 1996 (F. McCormick, *Excavations 1994*, 76, 94E030; D.G. Coombs and K. Maude, *Excavations 1996*, 95, 96E0179) and over a three-week period in 1998. The hill is a small but distinctive eminence of carboniferous limestone that straddles the border of counties Roscommon and Mayo. The surrounding landscape is a subdued complex of esker and bog with slow and chaotic drainage.

Interest in the hill stems from the accidental find in 1991 of fragmentary human remains in a small quarry on the Mayo side of the border. Radiocarbon dates from these remains placed them in the late Iron Age. Subsequent excavation has concentrated on the Roscommon side of the border.

In previous seasons, excavation focused on the site of a standing stone (1994) where a single extended adult inhumation was recovered, and a small ring-barrow (1996) that produced the disturbed remains of two adult inhumations. On both occasions small, unprotected, cremation pits were also found. The excavation of the barrow also produced a single, small, blue glass bead. Radiocarbon dating of the inhumation remains at both sites suggested the possibility of Early Christian burials, while the standing stone, ring-barrow and cremation pits point to an earlier, pagan site. The excavation in 1998 was designed to allow positive identification of an Early Christian cemetery and to clarify other phases of site use.

A series of three complete inhumations was recovered. Two of these were adults, probably one male and one female, and one was a child. All three had been buried according to Christian tradition with their heads to the west and their feet to the east, in inhumation pits that were defined by discontinuous large stones and backfilled with a stony, calcareous loam. No grave-goods accompanied any of the burials. In addition to these complete inhumations excavation recovered the isolated skull of a child and part of the cranial vault of an adult, together with a single vertebra and some loose teeth. At the time of

writing no dates are available, but there seems to be good reason to suspect that the intact burials are Early Christian and that the summit of Kiltullagh Hill was a Christian cemetery.

A probable earlier phase of site use was also confirmed. Excavation recovered the inhumation of an incomplete pig, which was found on a large stone slab covering a charcoal-rich cremation pit. No grave-goods or ceramics accompanied the cremation. It seems possible, however, that the cremation was sealed by the stone slab and celebrated by the ritual slaughter of a pig. An Iron Age date is anticipated for these activities.

M.E. Robinson and D.G. Coombs, Department of Geography and Department of Art History and Archaeology, University of Manchester, Manchester M13 9PL, England.

562. ROCKINGHAM–CORTOBER ROAD PROJECT

Monitoring

Archaeological monitoring took place along the course of the Rockingham–Cortober road (N4), Co. Roscommon, in the townlands of Usna, Hughestown, Drumharlow, Woodbrook, Cloongownagh, Cuilty-coneen, Meera, Cloonmaan, Clonskeeveen and Cortober, during road widening. The excavation of soil-investigation trenches was monitored on behalf of Roscommon County Council; 82 trenches were excavated at 50m intervals.

A single feature found at Trench 27 consisted of a spread of burnt stones and charcoal, 0.05m thick, and may represent a destroyed *fulacht fiadh*. One piece of worked wood with toolmarks was recovered from Usna townland, from boggy ground. The remains of a ringfort, 63.4m in diameter north–south x 57m, and not previously recorded, were found in Cloongownagh townland. This site will undergo further investigation.

Deirdre Murphy, Archaeological Consultancy Services Ltd, 15 Trinity Street, Drogheda, Co. Louth.

563. VESNOY

No archaeological significance

SMR 23:171

98E0453

Pre-development testing was undertaken on the site of a proposed development in Vesnoy, Strokestown Co. Roscommon, in October 1998. The proposed development site lies within the designated archaeological area of a ringfort.

Five test-trenches were excavated by machine. Trench 1 was dug along the western boundary of the proposed development site adjacent to the ringfort. It ran in a north–south direction and measured 25m x 2m. The sod/topsoil layer directly overlay the boulder clay. Stratigraphy was similar in all the other trenches

No archaeological features or small finds were recovered from any of the trenches.

Gerry Walsh, Rathbawn Road, Castlebar, Co. Mayo.

SLIGO

564. AGHANAGH

No archaeological significance

SMR 40:171

98E0588

Planning permission was sought for an extension to

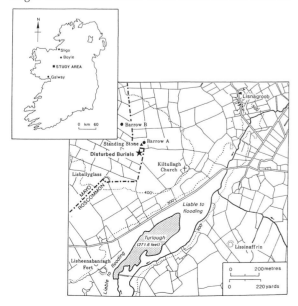

Location of site at Kiltullagh Hill.

an existing dwelling-house at Aghanagh, Ballinafad, Co. Sligo. Pre-construction testing was undertaken, as the development occurred within the constraint area of ecclesiastical remains.

Trenches were opened along the foundation lines, extending 8m east–west by 5m. They were excavated to a depth of *c.* 1.7m, into natural, orange gravel. No evidence of archaeology was uncovered.
Anne Marie Lennon, 9 Buenos Aires Court, Strandhill, Co. Sligo.

565. BALLINCAR
No archaeological significance
1676 3389
98E0390
Monitoring of topsoil-stripping along a 420m-long stretch of roadway, part of the realignment of the R291, the Sligo–Rosses Point road, was carried out on 2–4 September 1998, as a result of recommendations by the NMHPS following an Environmental Impact Survey prepared by Archaeological Services Unit Ltd in May 1998.

This section of the roadway lay *c.* 3 miles east of Rosses Point, in the townland of Ballincar. The topsoil-stripping was confined to the southern side of the existing roadway. The area excavated for the proposed realignment was 3–8.6m wide.

The stratigraphy encountered consisted of topsoil underlain by natural subsoil, redeposited subsoil, boulder clay and bedrock.

The only artefacts recovered, from the topsoil, were a number of pottery sherds of modern date and two modern glass bottles. The remains of a field drain, 0.3–0.4m wide and 0.2–0.3m deep, were also uncovered.

Nothing of archaeological significance was in evidence. The first 120m of proposed roadway at its western end had been disturbed in the recent past, having been acquired a number of years earlier by Sligo County Council and landscaped. Domestic water connections, Telecom cables and chambers were also laid within the road-take, adding to the disturbance.
Richard Crumlish, Archaeological Services Unit Ltd, Purcell House, Oranmore, Co. Galway.

566. CARROWHUBBUCK SOUTH
Adjacent to possible passage tombs
SMR 16:15 and 16:16
98E0342
The proposed construction of two private dwelling-houses on a small site at Carrowhubbuck South, Inishcrone, Co. Sligo, a short distance north-west of possible passage tombs, required pre-development testing. Machine-cut trenches revealed no archaeological material.
Suzanne Zajac, 1 Chapel Lane, Killala, Co. Mayo.

567. CARROWMORE
Megalithic tombs
Background
The Swedish archaeological excavations at Carrowmore, 1977–1982, revealed a series of data that made alternative explanations of the appearance of the megalithic tradition in Ireland and Europe possible, as well as of the underlying settlement-subsistence systems. The importance of the rich marine resources to the megalith-building popu-

lation in the Knocknarea area was strongly emphasised. The investigation highlighted the complicated, and artificial, boundary between the Mesolithic and the Neolithic periods, suggesting a slow, local, successive transformation rather than a migration of farmers. The archaeological results were strongly supported by the palaeoecological studies in the area. The remarkably early dates from the three tombs that produced datable material, Tomb Nos 4, 7 and 27, placed Carrowmore among the earliest megalithic cemeteries in Europe, and thereby in the world, and stressed the necessity of a rethinking of the Irish megalithic tradition.

The results from the Carrowmore excavations have since gained strong support from excavations in other areas in Europe, notably Brittany in France, where a series of dates now shows that the megalithic tradition in western France had commenced before 5000 BC, and that the underlying economy was heavily oriented towards marine resources.

An overall pattern concerning the Mesolithic–Neolithic transition and the appearance of megalithic traditions along the Atlantic coasts of Europe is emerging from recent excavations, and a series of new questions has arisen. The Carrowmore megalithic cemetery forms a central part in this important process.

Primary aims of the 1994–2000 excavation campaign
Since the first campaign of the Swedish archaeological excavations at Carrowmore was published a series of new interdisciplinary methods has developed. Several of them added considerable data to the interpretation of both internal and external chronology of the cemetery, as well as kinship analysis and sex determination of the cremated individuals buried in the tombs. Furthermore, these data will, used in a wider perspective, add considerable knowledge to the development of the Irish megalithic traditions as a whole, for example questions concerning internal chronological and ethnic relationship, or the arrival of possible migrants versus native developments.

Three of the four tombs excavated at Carrowmore in the 1970s provided samples from construction layers for radiocarbon dating. With traditional radiocarbon dating techniques the lack of rich deposits of charcoal limited the dates to five samples. Although all five did belong to the earliest in the Irish megalithic period, the inner time-span is still considerable, and little was known of the inner chronology of the Carrowmore cemetery. Were most tombs built around the earliest dates, or are these unique, leaving most of the tombs to have been built at the end of the local tradition? These are also essential questions in the relationship to other megalithic areas and tomb types in Ireland and to the megalithic traditions in Western Europe as a whole.

Radiocarbon dating advanced greatly when the accelerator mass spectrometric (AMS) method was introduced, in terms of both exactness and applicability. With the rarity of charcoal in the Carrowmore tombs, this new dating technique gives us the possibility to obtain a long series of additional, statistically valid dates for the construction of the tombs and use of the cemetery.

The ability to do kinship analyses and sex determinations based on ancient DNA has been known for some time. Recently a method to determine this from burnt bones has been developed, and analyses on ancient DNA applied to the Carrowmore material could give valuable results. DNA from burnt bones could complement the osteological analysis and might also be used for a kinship analysis within the megalithic cemetery, as well as within the megalithic traditions in Ireland and Western Europe as a whole. Also, in a longer perspective, the kinship relations between Mesolithic and Neolithic populations, as revealed from other excavations in Ireland, would provide data of immense importance to our understanding of the relations between the Stone Age populations of Ireland.

Details on the 1994–2000 excavation campaign
Tomb No. 4, 94E0032
Only one date from construction layers was obtained during the 1977–1982 campaign. As this date (*c.* 4800 BC) was the earliest then obtained from the Carrowmore cemetery, it was of great importance that additional data from the AMS dating technique would be available for the interpretation. In 1979 half of the monument was left unexcavated. One additional quadrant was excavated in 1994. A series of charcoal samples was taken for dating, and an even earlier date of *c.* 5400 BC has been processed from the cist.

Tombs Nos 1 (95E0022), 13 (see below), 52A (see below), 55 (see below) and 56 (94E0032)
Tombs Nos 7 and 27 revealed important information on some of the larger monument types at Carrowmore, a dolmen and a cruciform chamber. The dates and function of a series of smaller dolmens, as well as cist-like tombs, were unknown, and Nos 1, 13, 52A, 55 and 56 are tombs that could provide vital knowledge on the chronological position of these types. The fact that these tombs are situated in close vicinity to the Visitor Centre, as are Nos 4 and 51, means that these excavations provide public access possibilities during the tourist season. The excavation of Tomb No. 56 started in 1994 and was completed in 1995. The excavation of Tomb No. 1 was started in 1995 and completed in 1996.

Tomb No. 13, 98E0168
The rescue excavation of Tomb No. 13 took place during 1998. The monument, situated directly beside the Sligo road, was in danger of total collapse after a car accident some years ago, and there was also a risk that the roof-slab would slide off the supporting orthostats. Seven orthostats remained in the chamber, six standing and three supporting the roof-slab, while one had been knocked down by the car. All stones in the boulder circle are missing.

Before excavation the roof-slab was lifted off for safety. The central chamber and the surrounding area were completely excavated, 18m² altogether. No intact layers were found. The socket of another orthostat, a stone visible on a drawing by George Petrie from 1837 but long since removed, was found in the north-west part of the chamber. The reconstruction of Tomb No. 13 followed photographs taken during the 1977–1982 campaign, as they show the status of the monument before the accident. During the restoration work the fallen stone was re-erected and all orthostats were safely secured in concrete sockets. The roof-slab has been placed in its original position, gravel and topsoil have been put back, and grass seeds have been sown on the surface.

Tomb No. 51, 96E0020
In the archaeological survey of Carrowmore, Tomb No. 51, *Listoghil*, holds a central position for several reasons. The monument differs considerably from other tombs within the cemetery in both size and construction. Its location in the middle of the oval cluster of the other tombs makes it crucial to our understanding of the function and symbolism of the ritual landscape of the whole cemetery, and its chronological position is important in this context. It is the only monument in the cemetery from which can be seen both Ballisadare Bay, to the south, and Sligo Bay, to the north, as well as most of the other Carrowmore tombs.

The chamber, the area around the chamber and a large segment of the mound were excavated in order to fulfil three main aims: to provide valid dates for the construction and use of the monument; to provide a clear picture of the construction of chamber and mound that can be used for a reconstruction of the destroyed, once gigantic mound; and to provide evidence of the rituals and ceremonies of this monument. For the same reasons the burial traditions in this tomb have to be compared with those performed at the other tombs. Megalithic art has been discovered on the front of the roof-slab of the central chamber and also inside the chamber itself. The almost intact boulder circle, consisting of about one hundred large stones, has been completely exposed and thereby allows an exact calculation of the monument's original diameter and size. After the 1999 excavation season Tomb No. 51 will be completely reconstructed. A concrete vault and passage will be built, permitting public access to the central chamber, and the cairn will be restored to its original size.

There is no doubt that the actual position of Tomb No. 51 must have been of major interest in the original layout of the cemetery. This does not mean that the dominant chamber with its cairn is the first structure to have been built on this focal spot, as the ongoing excavation also has shown. Radiocarbon dates from the central chamber have shown that this was built in around 3600 BC. On the east side of the central chamber, below the intact cairn, three large gneiss boulders were found. The boulders form no part of the chamber. They seem to have been pushed aside during the chamber construction and may well be the remains of an earlier megalithic structure that pre-dates the preserved one.

The remains of burials in Tomb No. 51 are unburned human bones. A piece of skull, showing clear cut-marks probably resulting from defleshing, has been dated to the tomb's original period of use. As the common burial practice at Carrowmore is cremation, this highlights the fact that inhumation and cremation were practised at the same time within the Carrowmore tradition. From a social, ritual and maybe ethnic point of view this is an important contextual fact.

The excavation of Tomb No. 51 started in 1996

and was completed during 1998. The excavation of the main trench, including the central chamber area, was completed, as were two test-trenches towards the west and the east. A human cremation was found inside and in direct contact with a gneiss boulder in the boulder circle in the western test-trench. Inside the boulder circle an area of 250m² has been completely excavated. Thus, the planned reconstruction work at Tomb No. 51 can now proceed according to the time schedule suggested in 1997. A large series of radiocarbon samples allows for good possibilities to date both primary construction and successive stages of use of the monument. Deep test-trenches have been dug into the glacial deposits underneath the monument along the sections in order to control possible pre-site activity.

Outside and inside the boulder circle, on the south side of the monument, an area of 10m² around a limestone slab in the circle was excavated in 1998. An intact human cremation was found close to and behind the north corner of the limestone slab. Outside the slab a massive stone packing was unearthed, possibly the remains of a satellite tomb.

Tomb No. 55, 98E0169

Tomb No. 55 at Carrowmore, according to Wood-Martin's *Rude stone monuments of Ireland*, was, in the 19th century, completely covered with field stones. 'This circle, with its cromleac, which Petrie states was, in 1837, tolerably perfect, is now so covered with stones—the clearing of fields—which had been thrown on it, that a description is impossible' (Wood-Martin 1888, 52). In order to determine whether a megalithic tomb was hidden under the heap of stones, removal of the covering material with the help of light machinery took place during the 1998 season.

It was found that the covering material consisted of field stones, thrown up in recent times. Modern glass, fragments of clay pipes and porcelain were found down to the very bottom level of the cairn. On ground level three gneiss boulders were found, placed close together in a slightly rounded shape, but there were no visible remains of any chamber. To determine whether the boulders were also thrown into the heap from the surrounding fields or were the remains of a boulder circle of a destroyed megalithic tomb a 6m-long test-trench was laid out from the boulders towards the north. In the first layer more modern material was found, but in the second layer large amounts of cremated human bones were found, together with fragments of mushroom-headed antler pins and bone and stone beads. Radiocarbon samples were taken from among the cremations. One dated sample reveals that the tomb was in use in around 3800 BC. An area of 8m² was opened, and a full excavation is planned for the 1999 season.

The clearing of field walls at Carrowmore and the exposed Tomb No. 52A
In 1997 the OPW in Sligo decided that the recent field walls, cutting up the area of the Carrowmore megalithic cemetery, should be removed. At the same time the stones could be used in the ongoing reconstruction work of the cairn at Tomb No. 51, the site from where the stones most probably originally came. During surveillance the walls were removed

by machinery in November 1997. In one area, close to Tomb Nos 52 and 53, several gneiss boulders were visible in the field wall. They had not been mentioned by Petrie or Wood-Martin in the 19th century. In the Archaeological Survey the site is marked as a 'megalithic structure, possible'. This particular area was left to be hand-cleaned of bushes and field-wall stones during the 1998 season.

Modern material, glass and porcelain were found all through the wall. On reaching the level of the large boulders it could be determined that they were all, with the exception of the roof-slab, standing in their original position. All but one orthostat in a polygonal chamber are preserved, as are the stones along the entrance in the east. The roof-slab was found placed in the bottom of the field wall a few metres east of the chamber. Modern material has been found on the level exposed, and no excavation has taken place. A large stone slab is covering the inner area of the chamber. An excavation of the chamber is planned for the 1999 season.

The total station-based survey and mapping of Carrowmore
A detailed, total station-based mapping and landscape reconstruction work of the central area of the Carrowmore megalithic cemetery started in 1996 and was completed during the 1998 season. As well as for the scientific aims of this digital survey, the mapping can, together with aerial photography of the area, be used for reconstruction work, scale models and/or digital presentations in the planned new Visitors' Centre Exhibition.

The geophysical prospecting at Carrowmore
The geophysical prospecting of the Carrowmore megalithic cemetery started in 1997 and continued during the 1998 season. The aim is to determine the exact position of destroyed monuments that were recorded as megalithic tombs in the 19th century. Indications of possible destroyed megalithic structures have been found. The geophysical prospecting will continue during the 1999 excavation season.

The Primrose Grange hut site, field systems and megalithic tombs, 95E0021
Detailed survey of this vast archaeological landscape, 3km south-west of Carrowmore, started in 1995. It included total station mapping, human geographical analysis, phosphate survey and interpretation of aerial, infrared photography. The hut site is very similar to the Neolithic hut sites at Lough Gur in terms of both size and visible construction, and it is also possible that the Primrose Grange hut site is of Neolithic date and therefore extremely important in the cultural–historical context of Carrowmore. Furthermore, the existence of megalithic tombs, one of which has been recorded as a court tomb, in close proximity to the hut site and the field systems, may provide vital information about the cultural and chronological relationship between the two megalithic traditions in question: the passage tombs and the court tombs. Also, the excavation of this complex of sites would again add vital information to the important question of the economic background to the different stages of the megalithic traditions on the Knocknarea peninsula and in Ireland as a whole. Rich

deposits of unburned human bones, as well as artefacts made of flint, chert and bone, were found in PrimTomb 1. Several chert arrowheads of outstanding quality belong to the find material.

Morphologically, Primrose Grange Tomb 1 lacks all features that characterise the Carrowmore tombs, yet the ongoing excavation has shown that the tomb was in use at the same time as the Carrowmore cemetery. An intact deposition layer inside the chamber, excavated during 1997, has produced a date of around 4000 BC; the date of the tomb construction can be expected to pre-date that sample. All the burials found in PrimTomb 1 are inhumations.

The excavation of Primrose Grange Tomb 1 started in 1996 and was completed during 1998. An area of $52m^2$ has been excavated, and the tomb has produced large quantities of unburned human bones, as well as stone and bone artefacts. A large series of radiocarbon samples will provide good possibilities to date both primary construction and successive stages of use of the monument. A charcoal sample from the 1998 excavation season, from the foundation to one of the stones in the chamber, has given a date of around 6000 BC. Future control areas have been left unexcavated after the documentation of the first layer of stone packing. The site has been refilled with stones, clay and topsoil and returfed into its original status.

The artefacts associated with the burials from the Carrowmore tombs and the Primrose Grange tomb differ. The typical Carrowmore grave assemblage consists of mushroom-headed antler pins and stone/clay balls, artefacts that have not yet been found in the Primrose Grange context. Instead extraordinary pieces of chert artefacts are found in PrimTomb 1, mainly leaf-shaped or pointed arrow-heads.

Questions concerning the relation between the Carrowmore and Primrose Grange tombs are of utmost importance to our understanding of the demographic, social, ethnic and ritual situation in the Irish megalithic.

The complete 1998 excavation report (text) is available on the Internet on the Carrowmore home-page: www.hgo.se/carrowmore
Göran Burenhult, Department of Archaeology, Stockhlom University, S-106 91 Stockhlom, Sweden.

568. CALTRAGH, CUMEEN
Enclosure
G66353625
SMR 14:52
98E0545

The large and probably prehistoric enclosure of *Caltragh* lies in the townland of Cumeen, Co. Sligo. It surrounds a low, flat-topped hillock, in unimproved ground, overlooking Sligo Harbour to the north. It is defined by a low spread bank, which in places apparently turns into a low scarp, enclosing a roughly circular area some 130m in diameter. No internal features were visible above ground. On foot of an application to extend an existing planning permission westwards, closer to the enclosure, existing APs were examined. These suggested the presence of a possible second enclosing ditch. As a first step in investigating this feature a geophysical survey of the area through

which such a ditch was thought to run was commissioned. However, this proved inconclusive. Consequently, a second phase of investigation, involving more direct methods, was proposed.

The assessment took the form of a series of machine-dug trenches in the proposed extension area. Two trenches, excavated to the east of the enclosure, were designed to determine the presence or absence of a second, contemporary enclosing ditch.

Two further trenches were opened to the north-east of the enclosure to investigate the nature of the geophysical anomalies noted in this area.

The results from the trenches to the east of the enclosure were inconclusive. A number of linear features were uncovered, but it was possible that they were of relatively recent origin, at least in the case of the feature found closest to the enclosure. Examination of the fills of the 'ditch' uncovered the pipe of a live sewer. However, a smaller ditch or gully, uncovered some 50m from the enclosure, may be significant and requires further examination. The second trench, to the north, revealed nothing of significance.

The pair of trenches to the north-east of the enclosure uncovered only one feature of potential significance. This was a small ditch or gully, visible on the surface, curving around apparently concentric to the main enclosure. Its form, once exposed, was similar to the smaller ditch uncovered in the first trench to the east of the enclosure, and it is possible that they mark the continuous line of an outer, albeit badly truncated, enclosure.
Eoin Halpin, Archaeological Development Services Ltd, Unit 48, Westlink Enterprise Centre, 30–50 Distillery Street, Belfast BT12 5BJ.

569. CURLEW MOUNTAINS PROJECT
Fulachta fiadh
17620 31342
98E0202

All of the cluster of sites described below were revealed through the monitoring of the existing N4 from Hollybrook Estate to Castlebaldwin, Co. Sligo, a distance of 2km, when it was realigned and widened during the summer of 1998. The route lies at the base of the Curlew and Bricklieve Mountains and is only 1.2km from the megalithic cemetery at Carrowkeel.

At the northern end of the proposed routeway, and in close proximity to SMR 40:31, a holy well, and SMR 40:30, a flat-topped mound with an enclosure, six *fulachta fiadh* were discovered set within what is now a very boggy landscape, bordered to the west by a small stream known as the Brickeen Stream.

As all of the *fulachta fiadh* lay to the immediate west of the N4 routeway and in an area to be used as a tip for unwanted soil, it was not necessary to excavate them. They were left undisturbed by the removal of soil for the actual roadway, having being fully recorded and protected by the redeposition of peat. In many cases only the dimensions and height of the sites were noted, in other cases, where part of a *fulacht fiadh* was exposed in section, it was possible to gain further information on its make-up and stratigraphy.

All of the sites lay under a layer of topsoil and peat *c.* 0.1–0.5m deep. The smallest site measured 3m x 3m, and the largest 6m x 10m. Most of the mounds were low, with an average height of 0.5m, although there is some evidence that one or two of the mounds had been truncated at some time in the past, thereby severely reducing their profile. Owing to the high vegetation and growth of peat over the mounds, none of the sites was visible in the landscape before the monitoring of the realignment of the routeway. The make-up of the mounds, where revealed, was of the classic burnt mound type, with the presence of charcoal and fire-reddened soil with shattered and heat-cracked stones.

As none of the sites was excavated it is not possible to give an accurate date. However, it is possible to speculate that they were connected to the possible Bronze Age enclosure, SMR 40:30 that overlooked all six *fulachta fiadh* and that may indicate that the mounds were the result of domestic activity in the valley during that period.

Sylvia Desmond, 25 Rowan Hall, Millbrook Court, Milltown, Dublin 6.

570. GRANGE
Adjacent to castle
SMR 5:35
98E0513
Pre-development testing was undertaken on the site of a proposed development in Grange, Co. Sligo, in October 1998. The proposed development site lies within the designated area of a castle.

Three test-trenches were excavated by machine within the proposed development site. No archaeological features or small finds were recovered from any of these.

Gerry Walsh, Rathbawn Road, Castlebar, Co. Mayo.

571. GRANGE EAST
Pit
G640341
98E0215
This proposed development site of a single-storey house and garage lies some 5km south-west of Sligo town. Carrowmore and its associated megalithic cemetery complex lie to the east, and Knocknarea, surmounted by Maeve's Cairn, is to the west. The archaeological richness of the area can be readily seen from the amount of sites listed for the immediate vicinity in the Sites and Monuments Record. It was owing to this richness and associated high archaeological potential that an archaeological assessment of the site was recommended. This was carried out on 21 May 1998.

The house plan proposed for this site was tested by the machine-excavation of two trenches, with a further trench each for the garage and percolation area.

The trenches revealed that no recent ploughing had taken place as evidenced by the poorly defined plough horizon. There appeared to be little differentiation between the top and bottom of the horizon, with the entire 0.5m consisting of a fairly uniform, compacted, yellow/brown, stony loam.

Over much of the site this horizon rested directly on natural, which varied from a stony, light yellow/brown clay gravel to a light yellow/brown, gravelly clay. Some of the stones within the natural had rotted to a dark grey silt clay, which on first sight appeared to be archaeological in nature, suggestive of either organic material or, where the soil was particularly dark, patches of charcoal. However,

close examination in each case proved the soil to be a natural phenomenon.

The exception to this was at the western end of the test-trench positioned along the foundation line of the south wall of the house. Here a substantially broad but relatively shallow pit was uncovered. It appeared to consist of a light grey, very compacted, silty loam. Its light grey appearance is likely to have been caused by leaching. This interpretation is supported by the discovery, in section, of a well-formed iron pan along the sides of the pit. Though by no means a precise method, in the absence of any other dating evidence the presence of an iron pan suggests that the pit feature may be very old, possibly even prehistoric.

Overall, the proposed development area appears to be largely devoid of archaeology, with the exception of the large pit. The remainder of the areas tested produced nothing of archaeological significance.

Eoin Halpin, Archaeological Development Services Ltd, Unit 48, Westlink Enterprise Centre, 30–50 Distillery Street, Belfast BT12 5BJ.

572. GRANGE WEST
No archaeological significance
G627332
SMR 14:152 (adjacent to)
98E0381
There was no known archaeological potential within or near the area to be disturbed; SMR 14:152, a settlement platform site and midden site, is 50m uphill from it. Goran Burenhult carried out a minor excavation within this platform in 1981. A radiocarbon determination of 1160±50 BP (ad 790/ AD 900) suggests a phase of use in the Early Christian period for that monument.

The test excavation took place on 2 September 1998. Strip A was 1.5m x 16.6m; Strip B was 3.1m north–south by 6.3m; Strip C was 1.5m by 14.3m; and Strip D was 1.5m by 13.2m. In all areas the sod was 0.1–0.15m thick. This overlay 0.15–0.2m of thick, brown soil over reddish-brown soil, which in turn overlay the limestone bedrock.

The area tested was archaeologically sterile.

Martin A. Timoney, Bóthar an Corran, Keash, Co. Sligo.

573. KILLASPUGBRONE
Shell midden
98E0374
This project consisted of the improvement of the existing roadway, provision of a new road, foul and water drainage and general landscaping at Enterprise Park, Sligo Regional Airport, Strandhill, Co. Sligo.

During the course of monitoring of ground disturbance a shell midden was revealed in one of the trenches in the east of the site. It was uncovered at a depth of 1m below ground level and was 2.2m long, 1.7m wide and 0.25m deep. It consisted of a black, gritty sand layer with inclusions of cockle and oyster shell, as well as occasional charcoal inclusions. This layer came down onto a burnt, red, sandy layer, 0.1m deep. Underlying this layer was a grey, natural sand. It should be noted that the shell midden was only uncovered for a length of 2.2m but extends further north beyond the limit of the trench.

Fiona Rooney, Archaeological Consultancy, Ballydavid South, Athenry, Co. Galway.

Sligo

574. SHROOVE (LOUGH GARA)
Stone platform
SMR 46:29
97E0209

The excavations in Shroove townland at the shore of Lough Gara, Co. Sligo, continued this year. The main focus was an oval rise occupying a position in front of the causeway leading out to the artificial island investigated last year. The low rise stretched *c.* 17m from the north-east to the south-west and was more or less kidney shaped, with a small dip in the area nearest to the causeway resembling a burnt mound. It was found that the mound consisted of sand and the dip was the location of a small, cobbled stone floor, forming a forecourt area to the causeway.

The excavation of the small artificial island (*Excavations 1997*, 156) also continued this year. A brushwood floor circled by post-holes was found, covered by a small floor of flat stones.

Among the finds were what seem to be two ringed pins of iron (only X-ray will confirm this) and a fragment of a lignite bracelet.

The Crannog Research Programme thanks *Dúchas* The Heritage Service and the National Committee for Archaeology at the Royal Irish Academy for finances and support.
Christina Fredengren, Department of Archaeology, Stockholm University, S-106 91 Stockholm, Sweden.

575. SLIGO AND ENVIRONS WATER SUPPLY SCHEME
Urban
98E0395

The upper weir
The upper weir (1697 3359) on the Garvoge River in Rathquarter and Abbeyquarter North in Sligo town, built sometime between 1808 and 1815, may have been a successor to the weirs of Sligo's Dominican Abbey, *c.* 250m downriver. Newspaper references to clearing the bed of the river in the 1840s, upriver of the Upper Weir, may indicate the presence of earlier weirs and that the early 19th-century one was built with the protection of those earlier structures.

A bund was built in late 1997 around the old Upper Weir, and the worst section was broken through under archaeological observation. Nothing of an earlier structure was encountered, and so the old weir structure was progressively demolished. The structure was one of large blocks of limestone, presumably quarried from the bed of the river, used to form the sides and top of the weir, with smaller stones, down to the size of gravel, used to fill the core.

A damaged quernstone was discovered in the make-up of the weir near its north end in Rathquarter.

More interesting was the discovery of a layer of dense, sticky, blue clay, partially under but also upriver of the weir. It may be that the weir was built on this layer but, owing to the pressure of the water and damage to the weir, moved downriver by about a metre. No other archaeology was recovered. The new weir was completed in autumn 1998. It holds the water at what was the winter level on Lough Gill.

Rising main
Work on a new pumping station and initial work for a new rising main in Carns townland began in January 1998. There was archaeological involvement, though not from the outset. The greater part of the length of the strip for the pipeline proved to be archaeologically sterile.

At the north end of the pipeline the cut crossed (1703 3343) an old lane leading from a limestone quarry and a limekiln on the east side of Carns Hill towards Sligo town. A single layer of stones, generally no more than 0.15m in diameter, was used in the make-up of this road. Adjacent to the lane, but untouched by the development, are the foundations of a house (1704 3342) that may have been contemporary with the lane and the quarrying.

Midway along the pipeline and just downhill of the current road, which was constructed after 1837, are the probable foundations of another house of unknown antiquity (1711 3342), built on a platform cut into the slope between the current road and the pipeline. The development avoided this platform by less than 2m.

On the slopes downhill from the former Belvoir House and Belvoir Wood, in a stretch where the soil had considerable amounts of broken crockery, four concentrations of burnt stone and soil were encountered. The first three (1712 3340; 1713 3339; 1713 3338) were at the west edge of the cut and were not disturbed. Insufficient was exposed to establish the intensity or extents of use of these *fulachta fiadh* deposits. Their positions were marked by steel rods, and they were covered over with clay.

The fourth (1713 3337), the throw-out material from a *fulacht fiadha,* was more disturbed by the cut for the pipeline. The location had been soil-stripped, and the ground had been levelled by cutting into the hill to make a working platform for pipe-laying. This was done without the presence of an archaeologist until mid-January 1998. At the time of walking the line in early February 1998 there was no indication of any archaeological feature here or anywhere else on the line. When the pipe was being laid in July considerable deposits of burnt stone, black soil and sizeable pieces of charcoal were disturbed in an area 8m x 1.5m, within the area prepared by mid-January and then apparently devoid of any archaeological potential. This area was covered over with soil in September. There was no indication of a trough, a hearth or a cairn, and no objects were seen.

Water treatment plant field at the Fox's Den in Carns (Duke)
The water treatment plant field at the Fox's Den in Carns (Duke) lies between, but at a lower level than, the passage tomb cairns on Cairns Hill West (SMR 14:231) and Cairns Hill East (SMR 14:232). The cairns are at distances of 150m and 250m respectively. A geophysics survey of this field was carried out by GeoArc, and all the anomalies found had a geological explanation. Two hearths and the burning pit and burnt stones of a *fulacht fiadh* were encountered and recorded during the soil-stripping of this field. No indications of these were given until the topsoil had been completely removed and the B horizon material was being layered off. There were no finds, and the research is still incomplete.

Nothing else of an archaeological nature was encountered.

Further monitoring took place in several phases during the autumn in Carns (Carbury Barony) and

Carns (Duke) townlands. The third area covered by this licence, that for the break pressure tanks in Tonaphubble, will be excavated when weather conditions allow for transporting the soil through the suburban area of Tonaphubble.

Carns (Carbury Barony)
No archaeological significance
1713 3339
Monitoring of the laying of land drainage pipes down from the rising main between the new pumphouse in Carns and the new water treatment plant in Carns (Duke) took place in September 1998, in four separate but adjacent areas.

The first was in an area where the Garvoge River narrows as it leaves Lough Gill. A promontory fort, SMR 15:91, is on a dry hill at the edge of the river, just downriver of this first area. The very wet ground consisted of silts deposited in times of high water-levels. Approximately 220m of plastic drainage piping was laid in seven trenches 0.5–0.8m wide and averaging 0.6m deep. There was evidence of at least two earlier efforts to drain this area. Nothing of an archaeological nature was encountered.

The second area was a single conduit scour pipe to take the water accumulating along the rising main down to the Garvoge. The cut was 77m long and narrowed from 2m wide at the rising-main end to 0.5m wide at the river edge. At the rising-main end the cut was 2m deep and V-shaped, and thereafter it reduced to 0.6m deep.

Nothing of an archaeological nature was encountered, although a small area (1713 3338) of burnt stone and sooty soil had earlier been encountered but not disturbed 5m north-west of the rising-main end of this drainage pipe during the laying of the rising main itself.

The third area, just east of Belvoir Wood, was 40m x 30m, showed evidence of several springs and was very soft. Approximately 160m of land drainage piping was laid down in several sections. Nothing of an archaeological nature was encountered.

The fourth area was a single scour conduit pipe to take the water accumulating along the rising main down to the Garvoge. The cut was 65m long and narrowed from 3m wide at the top to 0.5m wide at the river edge, where it was through river silts. At the rising-main end the cut was 4m deep, and thereafter it reduced to 0.6m deep.

Nothing of an archaeological nature was encountered, although an area (1713 3337) of burnt stone, black soil and sizeable pieces of charcoal had earlier been encountered just north of the high end of this drainage pipe during the laying of the rising main.

Carns (Duke) and Carns (Carbury Barony)
No archaeological significance
1706 3340
There was no known archaeology within the length of 380m to be disturbed for the inter-connector pipeline between the old water treatment plant on the Green Road in Carns (Carbury Barony) and the new one in Carns (Duke). Monitoring took place from 26 August 1998. The cut for the pipe was 1.5m wide and varied in depth, depending on the topography, from 0.8m at the south end to 2.7m at the north end. A working strip 9m wide had to be

desodded to allow machinery and materials access. At one stage towards the south end the alignment of the cut had to be adjusted, and so the strip was almost double width for a length of *c.* 50m. Soil-stripping of the space, 20m x 20m, for a cattle crush (1705 3335) south of this strip and south-east of the old water treatment plant was also monitored. The limestone bedrock was immediately under the 50mm-thick sod. Nothing of an archaeological nature was encountered.
Martin A. Timoney, Bóthar an Corran, Keash, Co. Sligo.

576. SLIGO ENVIRONS WATER SCHEME
Fulacht fiadh
98E0533
Monitoring of all open trenching and pipe-laying is taking place. The project is divided into three phases: (1) Ballygawley/Ballintogher pipeline, 10.1km; (2) Strandhill village pipeline, 3km; (3) Rosses Point Peninsula pipeline, 6.2km.

The project has been ongoing since November 1998, and the first phase of the Ballygawley/Ballintogher line is nearing completion. To date, the open trenching has cut through one area of archaeological interest, the remains of a possible *fulacht fiadh*. All trenching in this section of the project has been undertaken along roadways.
Anne Marie Lennon, 9 Buenos Aires Court, Strandhill, Co. Sligo.

577. ABBEY STREET, SLIGO
Urban medieval/post-medieval
G69403585
97E0181
As a result of an archaeological impact assessment carried out by Eoin Halpin in 1997 (*Excavations 1997*, 156, 97E0181) an excavation was carried out at a site on the southern side of Abbey Street, Sligo, between 4 March and 17 April 1998. The site lies directly across the road from the 13th-century Holy Cross Dominican Abbey. The excavation took place in advance of a proposed retail and apartment development and was part of the planning condition.

The first area to be excavated, along the Abbey Street frontage, uncovered significant archaeological remains in the form of at least four phases of medieval activity on site. The first and earliest of these was a large ditch, aligned north–south, possibly connected with the boundary of the Abbey. The second phase consisted of another ditch, parallel to but slightly east of the first. This ditch contained the remains of a well-faced wall. The third phase took the form of east/west-oriented drainage ditches that cut both the Phase 1 and 2 ditch features. The final phase of medieval activity involved the construction of a building, probably a tower-house, over the infilled drainage ditch. This may be part of the structure known as O'Crean's Castle, one of the fortified residences known to have been built in this part of the town. Above these earlier phases of activity were successive layers of post-medieval occupation. Large quantities of disarticulated skeletal remains were retrieved from the excavation, but no evidence of a cemetery or grave cuts was uncovered.

The second area of the site to be excavated, along the eastern side, uncovered no evidence of any

medieval activity. Post-medieval activity took the form of pits cut into redeposited subsoil and the remains of 19th/20th-century houses. Again disarticulated skeletal remains were retrieved from all of these features.
Ruairí Ó Baoill, Archaeological Development Services Ltd, Unit 48, Westlink Enterprise Centre, 30–50 Distillery Street, Belfast BT12 5BJ.

578. ABBEY STREET LOWER, SLIGO
Urban
G695358
98E0216
An archaeological assessment was carried out on the site of a proposed apartment building in accordance with planning conditions. The site lies close to the remains of Holy Cross Priory. Excavation was by mechanical digger using a toothless bucket.

Owing to upstanding buildings on part of the site, only four of the proposed five trenches could be excavated. Archaeological material of possible medieval date was encountered in the trench closest to the abbey grounds. This consisted of a stony surface, possibly a metalled surface, and a small pit or post-hole, neither of which were excavated.

Large quarry pits were encountered in the most northerly trench. These contained large amounts of artefacts of post-medieval to modern date. Nothing of archaeological significance was recovered from either of the other two trenches.
Audrey Gahan, Archaeological Development Services Ltd, Unit 48, Westlink Enterprise Centre, 30–50 Distillery Street, Belfast BT12 5BJ.

579. ABBEY STREET LOWER, SLIGO
Urban post-medieval
G695358
As a result of the recommendations of an archaeological assessment carried out by Audrey Gahan during May 1998 (No. 578 above) this writer was requested to monitor the digging of foundation trenches and associated services for a proposed apartment development at a site at Abbey Street Lower, Sligo, close to the medieval Holy Cross Abbey. This work was carried out on 10 June 1998.

On arrival at site it was observed that the greater part of it had already had foundations excavated and filled with concrete. This appeared to have happened subsequent to the archaeological assessment. Of the portion of the site where ground disturbance had not taken place, no significant archaeological deposits were observed during the monitoring. Stratigraphy consisted of post-medieval build-up layers and house remains.
Ruairí Ó Baoill, Archaeological Development Services Ltd, Unit 48, Westlink Enterprise Centre, 30–50 Distillery Street, Belfast BT12 5BJ.

580. 8–9 LOWER ABBEY STREET, SLIGO
Medieval limekiln and post-medieval burials, adjacent to Dominican Priory (Sligo 'Abbey')
G695359
98E0216 ext.
Pre-development assessment, carried out by Audrey Gahan in May 1998, revealed the presence of human bones and a stone deposit, possibly of early date, at the south-west corner of the site.

Monitoring by this writer of the mechanical removal of the overburden from this corner of the site in November 1998 revealed the survival of a large, potentially medieval limekiln and several post-medieval human burials. The limited area where these features survived was excavated over a one-week period.

A large limekiln was the earliest feature revealed. Its northern side was truncated by modern building activity. The kiln had a large, round bowl and originally had two flues set at right angles to each other. The north-eastern of the two was entirely removed by modern disturbance. The south-eastern flue ended in a large, stone-lined pit that extended outside the area of the site. It was not a slaking-pit as no lime occurred on its sides; it probably served to hold the hot ashes raked out of the kiln.

The kiln could date either to *c.* 1253, when the nearby abbey was built, or to *c.* 1416, when it was rebuilt after a disastrous fire. ^{14}C dating of the timber fuel that survived in the base of the kiln will hopefully allow it to be dated with some accuracy.

Spreads of partly burnt stone occurred around the kiln; this was the deposit noted during the assessment.

After the kiln had been infilled the area appears to have been used for casual human burial. Three poorly preserved human inhumations were uncovered. The pottery associated with them suggests that they date to the 17th century. They were superseded by some slight evidence of 18th-century activity and finally by 19th- and 20th-century buildings.
Alan Hayden, Archaeological Projects Ltd, 25A Eaton Square, Terenure, Dublin 6W.

581. 14 STEPHEN STREET, SLIGO
Urban
98E0012
Two long trenches and a test-pit were machine-excavated as part of the assessment of this site. The northern trench and test-pit were investigated within the upstanding remains, owing to structural problems that may have arisen had the buildings been demolished before testing. The southern trench was excavated in the yard to the rear.

Results showed that the floors and associated hard-core of the buildings rested, at the northern end, directly on grey, natural till. About two-thirds of the way back the level at which the till appeared dropped and was overlain by a dark grey/brown, organic soil. This deposit was noted as a continuous feature to the southern end of the development area. It contained glass, fragments of clay pipe, red brick and pot, all of which suggested a post-medieval date, probably in the late 18th or early 19th century. This soil appears to be the remains of gardens that once existed to the rear of Stephen Street. Nothing else of archaeological significance was uncovered during the testing.
Eoin Halpin, Archaeological Development Services Ltd, Unit 48, Westlink Enterprise Centre, 30–50 Distillery Street, Belfast BT12 5BJ.

582. WATER LANE, SLIGO
Urban post-medieval
G69153590
Planning conditions for construction work on a site on Water Lane, between Grattan Street and Rockwood Parade, Sligo town, stipulated that as the site lay with-

in the zone of archaeological potential archaeological monitoring of the digging of foundation pads should take place. This work was carried out on 9 July 1998.

The site had undergone a pre-development site assessment by Eoin Halpin in July 1997 (*Excavations 1997*, 158, 97E0277). This showed that stratigraphy consisted of a substantial depth of post-medieval dump material raising the ground level significantly, presumably in an effort to reclaim land that lay within the River Garvoge tidal area.

Nothing of archaeological significance was found during the monitoring of the foundation pads. Stratigraphy appeared to consist of made ground and reflects the 18th-century expansion of Sligo on both sides of the river, as found elsewhere in the town during recent archaeological investigations.

Ruairí Ó Baoill, Archaeological Development Services Ltd, Unit 48, Westlink Enterprise Centre, 30–50 Distillery Street, Belfast BT12 5BJ.

TIPPERARY

583. BALLINA
Urban
SMR 25:9 (noon)
R706732

Part demolition of an existing warehouse and digging of the foundations on this site were monitored in compliance with a planning condition. The area had been cleared and reduced to the level of natural clay/rock sometime previously and used as a yard. Nothing of archaeological interest was noted.

Celie O Rahilly, Limerick Corporation, City Hall, Limerick.

584. BALLINTOTTY
Medieval hall-house
R910784
97E0328

Excavations were undertaken in advance of a major road construction scheme. The site took the form of a U-shaped river promontory, defended by a ditch and bank on the landward side. It measured 65m x 50m and was split into two parts by the erection of a second bank within the site itself. The ditch was 5–6m wide and up to 1.5m deep. The bank had maximum dimensions of 8m wide and 2m high.

A causewayed entrance lay in the south-west of the site. It was c. 3m wide and was defended by a possibly stone-fronted gate-tower. A metalled and roughly paved roadway led through the outer enclosure to a gateway in the second bank leading to the inner part of the enclosure.

The outer enclosure contained the ruin of a hall-house measuring 13.5m x 10m externally and 10m x 6.5m internally. Only the ground floor survived, to a maximum height of 1.8m from foundation level, with a cross-wall creating two rooms. The partial remains of a staircase were found within a projection in the north wall.

Adjacent to this and adjoining the western wall was the base of a small latrine tower. The entrance was on the ground floor but accessible only along a narrow path between the hall-house and the second bank.

The inner part of the enclosure revealed possible evidence of two smaller buildings constructed on

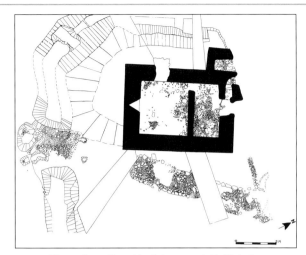

Plan of medieval hall-house at Ballintotty, Co. Tipperary.

timber sill-beams. The enclosure and all buildings were contemporary and were dated on the grounds of direct association with glazed 13th–14th-century pottery (including sherds of English and French ware) and Henry III coins.

Paul Logue, Archaeological Development Services Ltd, Unit 48, Westlink Enterprise Centre, 30–50 Distillery Street, Belfast BT12 5BJ.

585. BALLINTOTTY
Fulacht fiadh
R911785
98E0476

The site, investigated as part of the Nenagh Bypass, lay in Ballintotty townland, c. 4 miles east of Nenagh town, Co. Tipperary. AR 30 (an Anglo-Norman hall-house, *Excavations 1997*, 159) is situated to the west; Ballintotty Castle is to the south; and the Ballintotty River runs to the south and south-east of the site. The site consisted of a roughly circular/ovoid burnt stone mound, with adjacent spreads of burnt stone. The main mound measured c. 18m x 13m, and was c. 0.3–0.5m high.

Approximately 5m east of the main mound a marl embankment measured 31m x 17m. Peat and burnt stones were observed under portions of this marl bank. The embankment was orientated roughly south-south-east/west-north-west and may have been a natural build-up. Immediately south of this embankment more burnt stones were evident extending for c. 40–50m east–west by 14m. This area was extensively covered with peat sod, small bushes and reeds.

Approximately 10m north of the main mound was a burnt stone spread, which was excavated on 2–3 September 1998. This spread measured 12m x 8m and was 0.2m high. There were two fills: a 0.04–0.1m layer of peat overlain by a 0.04–0.1m layer of burnt stones. The site had been truncated by a number of narrow, modern field drains. There were no finds from this site, and no features were uncovered beneath the peat.

Neither the main burnt mound nor the mound material south of the marl embankment could be excavated further owing to safety concerns about serious flooding from the Ballintotty River.

Richard N. O'Brien, Archaeological Development Services Ltd, Windsor House, 11 Fairview Strand, Fairview, Dublin 3.

586. BALLYBRADO HOUSE
Mesolithic artefacts
S996200
98E0369

Trial excavations in the walled garden at Ballybrado House, Co. Tipperary, were initiated after a number of lithic artefacts were found by John Gardner while gardening. These were donated to the Tipperary SR Museum, where they were brought to the attention of Professor Peter Woodman, who instigated an excavation.

The assemblage of 45 pieces contained a couple of blades that suggested possible Early Mesolithic activity. Discussion with the finder suggested that *in situ* deposits may have been present. Unfortunately test excavations and test-pitting failed to reveal any buried soil horizon or to recover any diagnostic Mesolithic artefacts. A small lithic assemblage with later prehistoric affinities was recovered from garden soil, along with an assemblage of glazed pottery, clay pipe fragments and other 19th–20th-century domestic debris. Earlier garden features including a cobbled path and bedding trenches were also uncovered.

The fieldwork was funded by the Society of Antiquaries, London, and the Bob Smith Award from the Prehistoric Society.
Nyree Finlay and Peter Woodman, Department of Archaeology, University College Cork.

587. BALLYMACKEOGH–MULKEAR
CERTIFIED DRAINAGE SCHEME—see No. 385 above

588. BENEDIN
Bronze age
R866774
98E0444

This site was uncovered during the monitoring of topsoil-stripping to the immediate north of the Nenagh Bypass, in an area of higher ground that was to be used as fill elsewhere along the road. An area of just under 38000m² was monitored. The site is bounded along the north, east and west by pastureland and to the south by the N7 Bypass. Several pits had already been excavated along the road corridor in the immediate area (see No. 589 below), and it is likely that these also form part of the Bronze Age activity uncovered here.

Along the western half of the site twelve pits were excavated cutting into the natural subsoil and bedrock. These pits were mostly positioned some distance away from each other, although one cut through an earlier pit and several had small post-holes/stake-holes cutting through their base. They varied in size from 0.42m x 0.3m x 0.15m to 1m x 1.4m x 0.6m. They were generally filled with black, greasy clay and burnt, red clay—in some cases the surrounding subsoil had also been fired. Charred timber, a few pieces of burnt bone, hazelnut shells and some metal slag were recovered from some of the pits. Although nothing datable was recovered, it is likely that the finds form an integral part of the Bronze Age activity to the east of the site.

Along the eastern and higher end of the site an area of 16m x 7m was uncovered, containing numerous post-holes, pits and stake-holes. Upon excavation one circular setting of post-holes, with an internal diameter of 3.8m, was identified, probably forming a hut circle. A floor area of beaten clay lay within these post-holes. Numerous stake-holes and small pits, some of which were filled with charcoal-rich soil and burnt, red clay, were revealed both in and around the possible hut structure. Only a few finds were recovered: pottery, chert scrapers, burnt bone and slag, and these indicate a Bronze Age date for the site.
Cia McConway, Archaeological Development Services Ltd, Windsor House, 11 Fairview Strand, Fairview, Dublin 3.

589. BENEDIN
Possible Bronze Age
R826769–R923788
98E0430

This was a joint licence with Paul Logue, to facilitate the monitoring of topsoil-stripping along the full length of the Nenagh Bypass, from Carrigatogher to Clashnevin. Richard O'Brien also carried out some excavation under this licence.

In Benedin townland several pits were found and excavated. They varied in size from 0.2m diameter to 0.8m x 0.5m and had a maximum depth of 0.4m. They were filled with a mix of charcoal-rich soil and burnt, red clay, and almost all produced metal slag. Their proximity to No. 588 (above), in the same townland, and their similarity to the features excavated there suggest a possible Bronze Age date for these features.
Cia McConway, Archaeological Development Services Ltd, Windsor House, 11 Fairview Strand, Fairview, Dublin 3.

590. ABBEY STREET LOWER, CAHIR
Urban
98E0508

Pre-development testing was undertaken over two days in late October 1998. The site lay within the archaeological sensitive zone in Cahir town. The developer proposed to build five single-storey dwellings.

A series of trenches was opened along the foundation lines of the buildings. In the eastern area of the site bedrock occurred directly under the topsoil. The bedrock sloped downwards to the west of the site, where natural, compacted gravel overlay the rock. Modern infill of brick, mortar, stone etc. had been used to level this site in the last fifty years. No evidence of archaeology was uncovered during the testing.
Anne Marie Lennon, 9 Buenos Aires Court, Strandhill, Co. Sligo.

591. CAHIR ABBEY LOWER, CAHIR
Urban
20497 12493
SMR 75:48
98E0246

Testing was carried out in advance of the proposed construction of an oil distribution depot on a site on the opposite side of a narrow by-road to Cahir Abbey, now in ruins. A substantial, L-shaped, 19th-century mill formerly occupied the site.

Three test-trenches were opened on the site. They extended to a depth of 0.9m and had average dimensions of 3.9m x 1.4m. The trenches were excavated on the site of the proposed concrete base that will be laid to support the two storage tanks. The required depth for the base was 0.45m.

The findings from the trenches consisted of accumulated rubble fill intermixed with a mid-brown, coarse-grained, loose sand. The rubble fill had a very high stone content and contained timber planks, modern scraps of metal, lumps of concrete and mortar. This rubble fill was the residue from the demolition of the mill that formerly stood on the site. Towards the base of Trenches 1 and 2, at a depth of *c.* 0.6m, was a pocket of burnt material dumped with the building debris. It contained fragmented red brick, partly burnt wood, slate, ash, charcoal, coal and cinders.

Testing works ceased at a depth of 0.9m below modern ground level and did not extend into subsoils or archaeological remains that may have survived beneath the modern accumulated rubble fill.

Mary Henry, 1 Jervis Place, Clonmel, Co. Tipperary.

592. CARRICK-ON-SUIR
Urban
S215400
SMR 85:4
98E0259

The Carrick-on-Suir Main Drainage Scheme, Phase I, started in August 1998 and is currently ongoing. The scheme will see the laying of new storm and foul sewers in much of the town, including parts of the medieval town, and in its suburb of Carrickbeg on the south bank of the river. Pre-construction testing and monitoring of pipeline excavations are taking place. Initial work has been centred on the north-east of the town, in the area where the largest of the detention tanks is being built. Just west of this lies the Ormond Castle and Manor House. Archaeological work to date has revealed modern dump deposits in the immediate vicinity of the Castle and 18th/19th-century dump deposits in the area just east of Castle Lane.

During the course of the monitoring a mass burial comprising four human skeletons was found in Castle Park. They were buried in what would have originally been parkland, *c.* 200m in front of the castle. The remains were aligned north–south. Only one of the skeletons was neatly laid out, the remainder being roughly placed on top of each other. Three of the skeletons lay with their heads to the south, the other had its head to the north. Part of the latest burial had been removed by a later disturbance. These remains are tentatively dated to the early 19th century and may be associated with one of the outbreaks of cholera that affected Carrick-on-Suir in the 1830s. The original Fever Hospital is nearby.

Work on the project is continuing, with areas of the medieval town yet to be examined.

Florence M. Hurley, 8 Marina Park, Victoria Road, Cork.

593. CARRIGATOGHER/TULLAHEDY
Post-medieval
R826769–R835770
98E0160

A corridor 600m x 20m was monitored along the western limit of the N7, Nenagh Bypass, from Tullahedy (SMR 20:79) in the east, linking up with the N7 in the west. Concerns had been raised because of its proximity to the extensive Neolithic site at Tullahedy

excavated by Paul Logue (*Excavations 1997*, 180–1, 97E0472) and because the townland name, Carrigatogher, suggests the presence of a trackway.

During monitoring, large subrectangular pits, *c.* 2m x 1m, were uncovered, all lying within a 150m-long corridor. Upon excavation these pits were generally 0.5m deep, cut into the natural (a white lime marl) and were filled with a mixture of peat, clay and sand. Although nothing datable was recovered from the fills, it is likely that these pits form part of the extensive post-medieval/industrial archaeological landscape identified by Logue at Tullahedy, to the immediate north of these pits. The pits appear to have been dug for the purpose of excavating the lime marl, to be used as a fertilizer in the reclaiming of the surrounding bogland. Such activity was common during the 19th century.

Cia McConway, Archaeological Development Services Ltd, Windsor House, 11 Fairview Strand, Fairview, Dublin 3.

594. ST PATRICKSROCK/LADYSWELL/MOOR/ ST DOMINICKS ABBEY/CASHEL/LOUHGNAFINA/ GREEN/WAILER'S LOT/ASHWELLS LOT/HORE ABBEY AND COUNTRY TOWLANDS, CASHEL
Medieval and post-medieval town and vicinity of a Cistercian Abbey
20758 14070; 20689 14079; 20600 14112; 20776 13996 and 20780 14008
SMR 61:25, 61:23, 61:71, 61:24 and 61:135
98E0189

From April 1998 to January 1999 a new storm and foul network of pipes was laid in and around parts of the town of Cashel. A licence was held to monitor all ground disturbance works in association with this scheme. In addition to monitoring site works, extensive pre-construction testing was carried out in the following areas: The Green, The Upper Green, McCann Street, The Old Road (*Rian Bó Phádraig*), William Street, Colliers Lane, Circular Road, Camus Road, Mountjudkin Road, Hore Abbey and a narrow lane to the west of Camus Road.

The scheme provided an opportunity to look at the subsurface archaeological remains in diverse and well-dispersed areas in and around the town. There was pipe-laying inside the medieval walled town (William Street), immediately outside the walled town but close to the Dominican Abbey (Colliers Lane), to the rear of the Rock of Cashel (Circular Road, a road that sweeps around the back of 'The Rock'), possible medieval and/or post-medieval suburban areas (The Green and Upper Green, Camus Road, the lane off Camus Road and McCann Street) and along part of the ancient road known as *Rian Bó Pádraig* (The Old Road). The scheme was not just concentrated in the town of Cashel. Approximately 3km of pipeline was laid in the town's rural hinterland, extending in a westerly direction from the Treatment Fiant off the Cashel–Tipperary road to the River Suir. It was part of the original design in the scheme to lay new storm and sewer pipes near Hore Abbey, a National Monument. Hore Abbey is in a rural setting, *c.* 0.8km to the north-west of the town.

The scheme started in April 1998 in areas peripheral to the modern town centre and well outside the walled medieval town. These areas were, however, by and large inside the zone of archaeological potential as defined by the *Urban archaeological survey* (Office of Public Works, 1993) and may have been the focus of extra-mural suburban activity, of either medieval or post-medieval date. They included the streets The Green, Upper Green, McCann Street and Camus Road. Regarding The Green and Upper Green, an area of the town that is *c.* 40m to the south of the medieval walled town, there was no evidence to suggest the presence of extra-mural activity of medieval date.

The findings from pre-construction testing and monitoring uncovered evidence of earlier streets. In one substantial test-trench was evidence of two post-medieval metalled surfaces. Following the demise of the lower and earlier surface, there had been infilling with dumped material to raise the street level, and a new, more recent metalled surface was laid, of probable 18th/19th-century date. Other than the post-medieval streets, there was nothing found of archaeological or historical significance. Equally there was no evidence uncovered in McCann Street, a street *c.* 80m to the east of the walled town, to suggest that there ever was significant medieval or post-medieval activity in this part of the town. This part of the pipeline route proved to be very sterile. There were no traces of earlier street patterns, strata or structures of any significant archaeological date, other than services, found on McCann Street. It could be concluded that there was little or no tendency for the town of Cashel to expand in any large scale in an easterly or southerly direction beyond the walled town during the medieval period and in particular in the earlier part of the post-medieval period.

Another area looked at outside the walled town was Camus Road, 90m to the west of the west circuit of the walled town. Limited evidence was found of archaeological activity. A possible medieval cobbled surface was uncovered during pre-construction testing. The surface was sealed with a rich, black, organic dumped material.

The findings from Camus Road, though limited, tied into those found on the lane off Camus Road. This lane extended in a westerly direction away from the walled town and at right angles to the west of Camus Road. There was a dense network of cobbled surfaces, one superseding the other. In most instances the surfaces were separated by medieval, dumped, organic material. In addition to the medieval deposits and cobbled surfaces a substantial wall was uncovered in section. It was 7m long and had an average height of 0.5m. Though of medieval date, the wall was pre-dated by organic deposits and surfaces. It was not possible to determine the function of the wall. However, the findings from the excavation along the lane confirmed that there was extra-mural activity during the medieval and post-medieval period in this part of the town. Evidence of early streets was uncovered: their demise, the build-up of organic material, the laying of new cobbled surfaces and a substantial medieval wall, a possible wall of a large extra-mural building.

Two other areas investigated, peripheral to the town of Cashel, were the Old Road and Circular Road; both had great archaeological potential. However, bedrock was the predominant characteristic of both. The Old Road is sited to the south of the town and extends into its rural hinterland in a southerly direc-tion. It supposedly coincides with an ancient road known as *Rian Bó Pádraig* (an SMR site). There was no archaeological evidence found along the pipeline route to suggest that *Rian Bó Pádraig* ever extended along the part of the Old Road looked at during the scheme. However, a caveat should be noted: the Old Road is either built off or cuts through bedrock. It is possible that any evidence of the ancient road was obliterated during road construction or upgrading.

Circular Road is also outside the medieval town. It sweeps around the rear of the Rock of Cashel. The road itself post-dates 1840. However, its close proximity to 'The Rock' gave this area an added significance. It was borne in mind during the works that this road may have followed the line of an enclosing embankment or ditch that may have enclosed the late 4th/5th-century fortress site, now the Rock of Cashel, that accommodated successive Munster kings. In common with the Old Road there was no archaeological evidence found along the pipeline route that could be associated in any manner with the fortress that supposedly stood on 'The Rock' or, alternatively, with the medieval ecclesiastical centre there. It was quite possible that the activities on 'The Rock', during the first and part of the second millennium AD, were very much contained within this geographically strategic site. Similarly to the Old Road, bedrock was very pervasive throughout the entire pipeline route and in places occurred very close to the modern road surface.

Colliers Lane and William Street in the centre of the town were looked at. Both areas would have been at the heart of or close to commercial activity in the medieval market town. Colliers Lane, though just outside the walled town, would have been close to the activities in the medieval town, and the lane is very near the Dominican Abbey. Perhaps the most noteworthy feature of Colliers Lane was the very high level of disturbance and truncation of deposits by stone-lined culverts and dormant and live services. Any archaeology that may have survived from the medieval and/or post-medieval period would have been destroyed by the extensive ground disturbances along this lane during the late 19th and 20th century.

William Street provided the only opportunity to see what was going on inside the medieval walled town. It was strategically placed between two important medieval streets, John Street and Main Street, and would have extended alongside the backs of properties that fronted onto those streets and burgage plots. Although the trench for the new pipes was quite narrow, archaeological remains of a medieval date were identified during the monitoring of construction works. A post-medieval street surface was picked up. It overlay two earlier surfaces, again both of post-medieval date. The surfaces sealed dumped occupational debris of medieval date. The deposit was typical dumped domestic waste that is very common to medieval towns. No structures of medieval date were uncovered along the pipeline route. The deposits reflect typical medieval activity, the dumping and accumulation of the residue from everyday activities inside a medieval town.

Opportunities were provided on the scheme to look at rural areas near the town. Perhaps the most significant was the area around Hore Abbey. The findings from the test-trenches can be broadly summarised as representing aspects of medieval farming patterns. Agricultural furrows occurred at regular intervals in the test-trenches, a spread of lime, probably used for fertilization, was found in one of the trenches. Several post-holes were dispersed throughout the trenches, which perhaps represented temporary fencing. One sherd of medieval pottery was found in an excavated post-hole-like feature. Most of the post-holes and the agricultural furrows were not excavated. In some places it was only possible to remove the sod as archaeological remains were being encountered. Non-definable stone features and walls occurred immediately beneath the sod in one of the test-trenches. The stone wall in the sixth trench, with its extent still remaining undetermined, may have radiated from the north end of the abbey and extended across the width of the way-leave in a north-west/south-east orientation. The surfaces of both walls were only partly exposed. An extensive array of agricultural furrows and several post-holes were encountered in the trenches. A possible drainage ditch was found, extending across much of the width of the fifth test-trench. The ditch extended in a south-west/north-east direction across much of the trench and headed towards the nearby stream. The presence of drains in the trenches is of no surprise as the soil on the alluvial plain tends to become waterlogged. A drainage network would have been required by the Cistercians to carry out satisfactory cultivation in the fields around the abbey.

The findings from the test-trenches confirmed the presence of walls, which may possibly be associated with the Cistercian Abbey and its ancillary outbuildings or, alternatively, may have been used to demarcate field boundaries. The presence of an extensive network of furrows confirmed that arable farming was carried out. The presence of drains indicated that attempts were made to relieve drainage problems. The existence of post-holes may represent the use of temporary demarcating boundaries in the fields, although their close proximity to the furrows suggests that they may be associated with the cultivation activities in the fields. A significant spread of lime was uncovered in one of the test-trenches. It probably was used for fertilizing the soil. An embankment extends along the northern edge of the field and runs for several hundred metres. Its purpose remains unknown. It may have been a demarcation around the immediate property surrounding Hore Abbey. It should be remarked that there was a distinct difference in the soil make-up on either side of the embankment.

Following the results of pre-construction testing it was decided to reroute the pipeline away from the abbey. The findings from the testing clearly confirmed that the area around Hore Abbey is of great archaeological potential and should be viewed as an archaeological complex. The findings gave a keyhole glimpse into an intensively used medieval landscape and one that was shaped by the progressive Cistercians, the occupiers of the abbey.

Mary Henry, 1 Jervis Place, Clonmel, Co. Tipperary.

595. AGAR'S LANE, CASHEL
Urban
S077407
98E0217
Archaeological testing on the site of a two-storey

dwelling at Agar's Lane, Cashel, was carried out on 11 May 1998, in response to a condition of planning. Three 1m-wide test-trenches were mechanically excavated in the grounds of the old Community Hall.

Nothing of archaeological significance was revealed in any of the test-trenches. A cut feature found in Trench 1 may have been a plough furrow. A single sherd of post-medieval pottery from the fill suggested a late date.

The remains of a wall noted in Trench 2 may have dated to the building of the hall in 1842–3. The wall ran north–south for *c.* 4m, being 0.5m wide and terminating near the hall. Its fabric consisted of large, mortared stones with traces of red brick and roof slates. It may have been part of a previously unknown shed or outbuilding of the hall.

Richard N. O'Brien, Archaeological Development Services Ltd, Windsor House, 11 Fairview Strand, Fairview, Dublin 3.

596. COUNTY HOSPITAL, CASHEL
Urban medieval
S2075814070
SMR 61:25
98E0302
Test-trenches were excavated in advance of a proposed extension to the north of Our Lady's Hospital, Cashel, Co. Tipperary, by The South-Eastern Health Board. Thirteen test-pits excavated to examine the subsurface deposits in advance of building construction within the area enclosed by the medieval walled town were also monitored. The existing hospital lies to the south of the medieval walled town of Cashel.

The medieval town
The town was given its first charter defining it as a borough by Archbishop Donat O'Lonargan in 1212 (Finn, 1930) and probably developed into a medieval town in the period 1250–1350 (Thomas 1992, Vol. 1, 153). The enclosing town wall in Cashel appears to be a later development than the town itself in that the wall construction was begun in 1303 with the assistance of a murage grant (Thomas 1992, Vol. 2, 47). The whole town appears to have been enclosed by a wall by 1320 (Gleeson 1927, 234), and this wall would have been repaired up to the 18th century.

The wall enclosed an area of 14ha and was originally 1550m long. The wall circuit was punctuated by five gates, and these controlled access into the town. The site of archaeological investigation was on the southern section of the walled town, and the wall here is aligned roughly south-west/north-east. The wall is constructed from roughly coursed limestone blocks with a rubble core and has an average height of *c.* 3m. It is in relatively good condition, but sections of the inner (north) face have collapsed and are unstable. A sally-port was recorded along this stretch of wall by Wyse Jackson (1949, 24), although its precise location is unclear. The wall has been breached within the area under investigation and was recently filled in with modern concrete blocks. This breach is almost opposite the narrow William Street, which is at a right angle to the main street and turns again at a right angle towards the east, to link into John's Street. William Street may be an original medieval laneway, and its southernmost side is *c.* 50m from the inner face of the town wall.

Extracts from the Corporation Books (Thomas, 1992) indicate that the area of proposed development was a garden area and may never have been built upon. According to the Corporation Books, trees were planted in 1702 'in the most convenient part of the Green, adjacent to the town wall', and this was presumably in the field within the town wall where the new hospital extension is to be built. In 1704 permission was granted to Alderman Thomas Chardwick 'to make a door through the town wall' into the garden, and this new entrance into the medieval town may lie where the wall has recently been rebuilt as there is no other apparent break along the wall in the area of the Green. The door was supposedly 8ft (*c.* 2.4m) wide (O'Keeffe 1995, 164). The creation of a new 'door' through the wall also suggests that the walls were redundant in terms of defence. The area between the walls and the ends of the burgage plots appears not to have been developed until recent times.

The excavation

Archaeological input into the proposed development consisted of two main elements: monitoring of engineering test-pits, excavated to determine the suitability of the subsurface layers in order to access the site for building purposes, and excavation of test-trenches to determine whether archaeological horizons exist.

Thirteen test-pits were monitored within the walled town area of the proposed development. All but one were mainly sterile. The upper levels showed that there was a substantial overburden up to 1.2m thick in places and thicker on the eastern end of the site. This overburden lay on top of the sterile boulder clay levels. This soil was of a rich, organic composition and probably derived from the use of the site as a garden area over a considerable period of time.

A north/south-aligned section of a wall footing was exposed in one test-pit. This footing is *c.* 2.5m north of the medieval town wall and *c.* 6m east of the blocked-up breach in the town wall. The soil over the footing included red brick fragments, a wig curler, 19th-century clay pipe fragments and pottery. These may indicate an 18th/19th-century period for the accumulation/deposition of this soil. The wall was mortar-bonded and did not appear to be substantial.

Fourteen test-trenches were excavated on the south side of the town wall in the grounds of the hospital. Nothing of archaeological significance was recorded in them.

Four test-trenches were excavated to the north of the medieval town wall in the proposed development area. Three were excavated in areas where new buildings were proposed, but no archaeological features or stratigraphy were recorded in them. A fourth trench was excavated to examine the wall footing where a modern blocking of the medieval town wall was visible, to establish whether an ancient gateway existed at this location. The footing was exposed in the trench and appeared continuous across the area of excavation. The wall was constructed of roughly coursed, unmortared limestone flags. Five large limestone stones appeared to be displaced. This displacement may have occurred when a gateway was constructed at this location either in the 18th century (Alderman Chardwick's gateway of 1704?) or more recently, when the opening was created by wall collapse. The stones beneath those displaced were smaller than those in the eastern section of the wall exposed in the trench but were on the same line and may be part of the original wall construction.

The excavation did not uncover any real evidence of a sally-port at this location, such as original door jambs, road surface or any architectural feature dating to the medieval period. It appears from the excavated section that the medieval town wall remained virtually intact on the eastern side of the trench until the wall collapsed in the recent past.

References

Finn, A. 1930 *Cashel and its ancient corporation.* Dublin.

Gleeson, J. 1927 *Cashel of the kings.* Dublin.

Wyse Jackson, Rev. 1949 The walls of Cashel. *North Munster Antiquarian Journal* **6**, 24–5.

O'Keeffe, T. 1995 Cashel. In A. Simms and J.H. Andrews (eds), *More Irish country towns,* 157–167. Dublin.

Thomas, A. 1992 *The walled towns of Ireland.* 2 vols. Dublin.

Rose M. Cleary, Department of Archaeology, University College Cork.

597. FRIAR STREET, CASHEL

Urban medieval, post-medieval
S076402
95E0286

An excavation was carried out on the eastern side of Friar Street within the medieval town of Cashel, from 16 January to 26 February 1998. Friar Street led from Main Street through the Friars Gate to Clonmel and Fethard. A Franciscan friary (founded in 1265) stood adjacent to and outside the Friars Gate.

Cutting 1, the principal area excavated, measured 11.5m north–south by 8.5m. It was adjacent to the street front in the north-western corner of the site, between two large, concrete building foundations, 1m wide, that removed any archaeological deposits along the eastern and western baulk. Cuttings 2–4 were to the east and south of Cutting 1 and were opened to assess the survival of archaeological deposits across the remainder of the site.

The excavation identified two main phases of archaeological activity. The first dated to the medieval period and was subdivided into four separate sub-phases, where evidence of the layout of Friar Street, house construction, domestic occupation and property plot realignment was revealed. The second phase of activity dated to the post-medieval period; this again was subdivided into four separate sub-phases of occupation.

A range of stratified archaeological artefacts and ecofacts was recovered during the excavation, including medieval pottery, a bone gaming piece, a lead spindle whorl, faunal remains, macro fossil plant remains, seeds, pulses and coleoptera.

Edmond O'Donovan, Margaret Gowen & Co. Ltd, 2 Killiney View, Albert Road Lower, Glenageary, Co. Dublin.

598. OLD ROAD, CASHEL

Enclosure
20750 13850
SMR 61:135
97E0041 ext.

The site of a housing development to the south of a possible enclosure at Old Road, Cashel, had been tested for archaeological material on 28 February 1997 (*Excavations 1997*, 160). This was followed by monitoring of topsoil-stripping and the cutting of foundation trenches. No evidence of past settlement was found.

In January 1998 an archaeological investigation of the enclosure bank was carried out as it was believed that landscaping posed a threat to it. A trench 3m wide was initially opened before being narrowed to 1.6m.

Three generations of bank and ditch were identified. The earliest bank and ditch are likely to have formed part of a ringfort. Bone and charcoal in the primary fill of the ditch suggest occupation close by (unlike the clean fills of the two later ditches). Post-holes identified on top of the bank suggest a palisade or fence. No datable finds were recovered from the earliest two banks and ditches. The latest, stone-revetted bank and ditch were associated with post-medieval finds.

Jo Moran, 33 Woodlawn, Cashel, Co. Tipperary.

599. HUGHES MILL, LITTLE ISLAND, CLONMEL

No archaeological significance
S203222
98E0470

The second phase of archaeological monitoring took place in October 1998 on a development site at the 18th- and 19th-century Hughes Mill, on a natural rock outcrop island within the River Suir, immediately south of the medieval town of Clonmel. The development involved the demolition of the existing mill and the construction of nine townhouses and three apartment blocks.

Monitoring was concentrated on the installation and enabling works associated with the pile-driven foundations for the development. No archaeological soils or features were encountered.

Paul Stevens for Margaret Gowen & Co. Ltd, 2 Killiney View, Albert Road Lower, Glenageary, Co. Dublin.

600. COOLBAUN

Possible early fields
22138 14109
SMR 62:50
98E0008

Cropmarks recorded by the Geological Survey in a field at Coolbaun, Cooleagh, were checked in advance of proposed development of the land. It was clear from three long test-trenches (3m x *c.* 80m) that the cropmarks represented periglacial features and natural drainage. There was no indication that the land had been cultivated before the early 19th century. Part of a *fulacht fiadh* was intercepted, and two further trenches were cut into neighbouring hillocks in the hope of uncovering *fulachta fiadh* mounds intact. Both hillocks were part of the natural topography.

Dave Pollock, 33 Woodlawn, Cashel, Co. Tipperary.

601. DONOHILL LANDS, DONOHILL

Linear feature
98E0520

Pre-construction testing took place in advance of an extension to an existing landfill site to assess the nature of a linear feature identified during field inspection but not recorded on the Sites and Monuments Record. Three test-trenches were opened along and across the feature to determine whether it was an archaeological site.

There was no evidence found in the trenches to indicate that the linear feature was of archaeological origin. It was, in fact, a natural anomaly on the landscape.

Mary Henry, 1 Jervis Place, Clonmel, Co. Tipperary.

602. MAIN STREET, GOLDEN

Urban medieval and post-medieval
20155 13825
96E0353 ext.

The site was tested for archaeological material in April 1997 (*Excavations 1997*, 162). An 18th- or possibly late 17th-century building, believed to be a 'clubhouse', was identified on the street front at the west end of the site.

Monitoring of service trenches in 1998 established that the remains of the 'clubhouse' survived in fairly good condition, buried below flood silts and deliberate infill on the edge of the flood-plain; however, the plan and function of the building are still unclear. Sherds of 17th-century pottery sealed below the building suggest a late 17th/early 18th-century construction date.

Cobbled surfaces leading to the adjacent bridge over the River Suir underlie the 'clubhouse' walls.

Two clay-bonded, stone walls were uncovered towards the rear of the site, and two furnaces filled with charcoal and slag were uncovered close to the street front. Charcoal spreading out from the hearths contained several hearth bottoms and a quantity of iron waste. The ironworking and walls may pre-date the bridge. They may be associated with the tower-house on the island in the river, but pottery recovered overlying the walls and hearths (three sherds) is of 13th-century date.

Jo Moran, 33 Woodlawn, Cashel, Co. Tipperary.

603. *RIAN BÓ PHÁDRAIG*, KILDANOGE

Linear earthwork
20722 10814
SMR 91:00102
97E0482 ext.

The upgrading of a forestry road as part of the development of the Ardfinnan Regional Water Supply Scheme affected a section of the linear earthwork known as the *Rian Bó Phádraig*, situated in Kildanoge Td, on the slopes of the Knockmealdown Mountains in County Tipperary. The trackway lay on the east side of the Glengalla River, close to a fording point. It was proposed to build a bridge across the river at that point to provide vehicular access to the west side. The section of the trackway affected by the development was excavated in 1997 before the start of the project (*Excavations 1997*, 162).

Work on the embankment for the bridge began in January 1998, and the area on either side of the river was trenched. The trenches were cut through what

appeared to be natural gravel deposits, and no archaeological features were noted during the work on the bridge.
Mary G. O'Donnell, Archaeological Services Unit, University College Cork.

604. KILTINAN CASTLE, KILTINAN
Medieval and post-medieval castle
2233 1320
97E0062

Monitoring drain trenches at Kiltinan Castle led to a short excavation in the outer bawn. Cobbled surfaces and mortared stonework were unexpectedly well preserved, sealed under rubble interpreted as debris from Cromwell's bombardment of 1650.

The mortared stonework was the fabric of a bridge crossing a ditch and entering the inner bawn through a gateway. The bridge and gate were probably built together in the 16th century; the wall (lower part) and ditch are considerably older. A cobbled road crossed the bridge, and a cobbled path ran south between the end of the bridge and a wooden building. The wooden building was later dismantled, and the path was widened to a cobbled road. (One gateway can be seen in the outer bawn wall; remains of a second gate can probably be found a short distance beyond the excavation, on the line of the path.)

Before the construction of the bridge in the 16th century access to the castle yard (the present inner bawn) must have been from the south, where the main house stands today.
Dave Pollock, 33 Woodlawn, Cashel, Co. Tipperary.

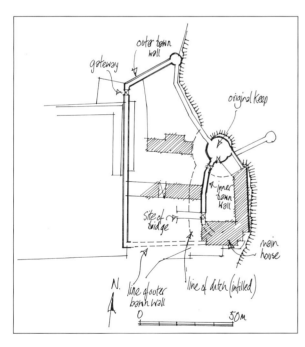

General plan of Kiltinan Castle.

605. KNOCKALTON LOWER
Prehistoric ditches
R902777
98E0471

The site, in Knockalton Lower townland, *c.* 3 miles east of Nenagh town, Co. Tipperary, and *c.* 1 mile south of the N7, consisted of two roughly linear ditches running approximately north-east/south-west. The southern end of Ditch No. 1 extended

beyond the CPO line of the Bypass. The ditches were separated from each other by a 2m gap—no features were noted in this immediate area.

Ditch No. 1 was 17.5m long, 0.8m wide and *c.* 0.3–0.4m deep, terminating at the southern end of Ditch No. 2. Ditch No. 2 was 28m long, 0.6m wide and 0.45–0.5m deep. Both drains were roughly U-shaped in section and contained similar fills of charcoal-flecked clays. A number of possible posts/ pits and a fire spot were noted adjacent to the northern end of Ditch No. 2, possibly representing the remains of a temporary structure.

Finds included slag, charcoal, struck chert flakes, a rough-out for a stone axe, disarticulated animal bones, antler and the skeleton of a dog(?). The finds all came from the fills of both drains, and the slag may suggest a date in the Bronze Age.

The southern end of Ditch No. 1 continued into the adjoining field, where a roughly circular depression was noted. As this area was outside the CPO line no investigation could take place, but its close proximity to the ditches may suggest an association.
Richard N. O'Brien, Archaeological Development Services Ltd, Windsor House, 11 Fairview Strand, Fairview, Dublin 3.

606. KNOCKALTON UPPER (SITE A)
Unknown
R893775
97E0320 ext.

This was an extension to the original licence issued to Paul Logue in 1997 for pre-development testing on the Nenagh Bypass (*Excavations 1997*, 177). Site A lay off the Knockalton Road and *c.* 70m north-east of a ringfort, AR27. It did not lie on the bypass road itself but on a new side road.

The site consisted of an irregular linear ditch, running north–south across the road-take for 20.8m and roughly U-shaped in section. At its south end it was 0.22m deep, and at its north end 0.32m deep. It had two clearly defined fills. The primary fill was a grey/brown, silty, sterile clay, which was not continuous within the whole ditch. The secondary fill was a moderately compact, dark brown, silty clay, with occasional charcoal-flecking, occurring over the entire length of the ditch. Neither ditch fill produced finds.

Approximately 3–5m south-west of the southern end of the ditch a number of small, hollow pits were found that may be associated with it. There were no finds or dating evidence from these pits.

In appearance and form the ditch resembled the two ditches found in Knockalton Lower (No. 605 above), the townland to the immediate east.

Although the site produced no finds and there was no dating evidence, its close resemblance in form to the ditches found at Knockalton Lower suggests that it is prehistoric in date. It may be possible to get enough of a charcoal sample from the fills to date the site.
Richard N. O'Brien, Archaeological Development Services Ltd, Windsor House, 11 Fairview Strand, Fairview, Dublin 3.

607. KNOCKALTON UPPER (SITE B)
Prehistoric structure?
R893776
97E0320 ext.

Site B lay to the south-east of AR27, and close to the

Knockalton Road, on the Nenagh Bypass. The site area was *c.* 10.5m north–south x 12m and consisted of a series of post- and stake-holes with a number of associated pits. The post-holes did not form a clearly identifiable structure. The largest pit lay immediately north of the series of post-holes. This pit measured 1.5m x 2m and was 0.45m deep, consisting of a charcoal- and burnt clay-flecked soil. The northern edge of the pit had been disturbed by a plough furrow. The western portion of the site area was disturbed by a modern test-pit.

Finds consisted of sherds of prehistoric pottery, charcoal and chert flakes, all from the surface of the site.

Richard N. O'Brien, Archaeological Development Services Ltd, Windsor House, 11 Fairview Strand, Fairview, Dublin 3.

608. KNOCKAUNKENNEDY
Fulacht fiadh
R903777
98E0472

The site was in Knockaunkennedy townland, *c.* 3 miles east of Nenagh town, Co. Tipperary, *c.* 1 mile south of the N7. A large trivallate ringfort in Curraheen townland lies *c.* 170m north of the site, the prehistoric ditches in Knockalton Lower townland (No. 605 above) lay *c.* 150m west of it. The site consisted of a low, burnt stone mound (Site A), with an adjacent spread of burnt stone material (Site B). The sites lay on marshland prone to flooding from a nearby stream.

Site A measured *c.* 16m x 9m with a *c.* 0.3–0.4m depth of burnt and heat-shattered stones. A 2m-wide machine-dug section was put through the burnt mound material. Further hand-excavation revealed an unlined rectangular trough filled with burnt stones, cut into natural. This trough measured 2.4m x 1.2m and was 0.32m deep. A post-hole was found at each internal corner of the trough edges. A possible pot boiler feature was 'attached' to the north-west edge of the trough, and beside this was a shallow linear cut—the remains of a windbreak. A number of additional pits and/or smaller troughs were cut into natural at the north-east and east edges of the mound; these features generally contained a basal fill of peat covered by burnt stones.

Site B lay *c.* 10m east-south-east of Site A and consisted of a roughly oval spread of burnt stones. It measured *c.* 11m x 9m with a *c.* 0.2m depth of burnt stones and peat. The centre of Site B was truncated by a number of modern field drains. The owner of the land knew of the existence of these burnt areas, saying that there was 'a nest of them here'. His family had carried out irrigation work in the area and had previously levelled some of the burnt stone material. This may account for the absence of a higher burnt mound on Site B.

A number of pits/small troughs filled with peat were found beneath the burnt stone material on Site B. There was further evidence of clusters of stake-holes around these pits/troughs. Although the central trough on the site had been truncated by a field drain, a number of deep post-holes within the trough edges were found. This closely resembled the main trough found on Site A.

The area between both sites consisted of a sterile, grey/white marl clay. There was further evidence of pits/troughs and series of stake-hole clusters cut into the marl clay. The northern area between both sites had a metalled stone surface surrounding some of the pits, perhaps indicative of connecting pathways. Finds from both sites consisted of small quantities of animal bone and teeth, some chert flakes, unworked wood and charcoal.

Richard N. O'Brien, Archaeological Development Services Ltd, Windsor House, 11 Fairview Strand, Fairview, Dublin 3.

609. LAHESSERAGH (SITE A)
Prehistoric settlement
R848769
98E0473

The site was *c.* 2 miles west of Nenagh, Co. Tipperary, and just off the Ballycahill Road. It lay on a natural incline that the road crosses, allowing commanding views of the landscape to the east and south.

The site area measured *c.* 40m x 30m. Within this area up to 50–60 randomly placed posts/pits, a short linear feature (*c.* 10m long and 0.4m wide) and two hearths/fire spots were found. It was apparent that around ten to twelve of the post-holes formed a subrectangular structure. Most of the site had outcrops of bedrock over the surface.

Finds consisted of worked flint and chert, a possible fragment of a chert arrowhead, an ovoid rubbing stone and charcoal. The ovoid rubbing stone was found on the surface of one of the hearths.

Richard N. O'Brien, Archaeological Development Services Ltd, Windsor House, 11 Fairview Strand, Fairview, Dublin 3.

610. LAHESSERAGH (SITE C)
Prehistoric house
R845769
98E0474

The site lay in Lahesseragh townland, at the base of the incline that is crossed by the Ballycahill Road. It measured *c.* 17m x 24m. There were a number of bedrock outcrops, and portions of the site area were truncated by modern field drains.

A small, circular hut structure, consisting of a foundation trench 3.3m x 3.7m in diameter and 0.05–0.2m deep, was found at the north-east area of the site. This structure appeared to have an internal habitation layer 0.01–0.07m deep, consisting of a light brown, silty clay with charcoal flecking. Beneath this layer was a linear arrangement of three post-holes, with two smaller supporting post-holes situated off-centre. At the north-east corner of the structure a possible entranceway was revealed, where a 1.4m gap in the foundation trench had been left. To one side of this entrance was a single post-hole; the opposite side was disturbed by later activity.

To the south-west of this structure was a series of random pits and post-holes. The fill of one post-hole contained a stone spindle whorl of the disc-shaped type, with centrally bored perforation. Also in this area were two large rubbish pits. The larger example measured 2.3m x 1.9m in diameter, containing a 1m depth of clay and large stones. A rubbing stone, burnt bone, wood fragments and a saddle quern came from it. The smaller rubbish pit measured 2m x 1.5m in diameter, with a 0.6m depth of clay and large stones. A grinding stone, burnt bone and another saddle quern came from this pit. Further finds consisted of charcoal, animal teeth and chert flakes.

Two small areas to the immediate south of Site C were investigated in Tullahedy townland under the same licence. Tullahedy Site E turned out to be a portion of a field drain of possible Famine date. Tullahedy Site F consisted of five small, charcoal-filled pits within a 10m x 11m area. One of the pit fills contained much charcoal and burnt nut kernels. There were no datable finds from the pits.

Richard N. O'Brien, Archaeological Development Services Ltd, Windsor House, 11 Fairview Strand, Fairview, Dublin 3.

611. LAHESSERAGH (SITE D)
Fulacht fiadh
R854771
98E0475

The site lay in Lahesseragh townland, *c.* 2 miles south of Nenagh, Co. Tipperary, beside the Newport Road and adjacent to the newly constructed Newport Bridge.

The site consisted of an extensive burnt mound, *c.* 22m x 28m in diameter and a maximum of 0.9m deep, situated on low-lying ground. Two hand-excavated test-trenches were placed across the mound material. Portions of the site had been severely disturbed by modern activity, in the form of two concrete pump stations built on the mound, covering *c.* 6m east–west x 12m north–south. A number of field drains traversed the mound in places, and deep root disturbance was evident from a number of felled trees.

All burnt stone material was removed by machine using a grading bucket. Owing to the high level of disturbance from the pump stations, and from a safety point of view, most of the centre of the mound was not excavated. A number of isolated large stones were found at the mound edges at the north-west, north and north-east corners. These may have been placed deliberately to delimit the mound in the landscape. A fire spot/hearth was revealed at the south-east extremity of the mound spread, sealed by the burnt stones. This produced charcoal remains that may be able to date the site. There were no finds from the hearth or from the rest of the site.

Richard N. O'Brien, Archaeological Development Services Ltd, Windsor House, 11 Fairview Strand, Fairview, Dublin 3.

612. LISHEEN MINE COMPLEX, BARNALISHEEN/COOLEENEY/ DERRYFADDA/KILLORAN
Archaeological complex
S193676–S212669
97E0372 ext.

Following the completion of assessment and wetland excavation in Derryville Bog (*Excavations 1995*, 93; *Excavations 1996*, 102–5; *Excavations 1997*, 163–77), the interdisciplinary archaeological study the Lisheen Archaeological Project continued with the archaeological monitoring and mitigation of all dry-land operations for the construction of the Lisheen Mine. This covered an area of 250ha across four townlands affected by the development. The Lisheen Arhaeological Project is funded in full by the developer, the Lisheen Mine Partnership Ltd,

and managed by Margaret Gowen & Co. Ltd Monitoring commenced in September 1997 and finished in August 1998.

Construction operations comprised large-scale topsoil removal for quarry sites; linear topsoil-stripping for access roads, peat excavation and stockpiling; trench cutting for drainage/ducting pipes; and keyhole excavations for service poles, stations and test-holes. Thirty-two archaeological sites were uncovered during monitoring and were spread broadly across the development area; a further two sites were revealed in adjacent areas through a campaign of field-walking. *Dúchas/* the National Museum of Ireland issued separate licence numbers in retrospect to this writer (*Excavations 1997*, 173, 174–5, Kil:03, 97E0036, Kil:04, 97E0051 and Kil:10, 97E0168) for discrete sites designated by them, whilst large sites required a separate licence holder: John Ó Néill (*Excavations 1997*, 173–4, Kil:08, 97E439) and Cara Murray (No. 614 below).

Archaeological monitoring and excavation continued from January to August 1998 following works carried out in 1997. A further two sites were revealed in field-walking in and around the development area. These were both burnt mounds from Cooleeney and Killoran townlands.

Barnalisheen 1
Burnt mound
S193676

This site was a burnt mound running into the baulk and was 3m+ x 1m in exposed length and width and 0.3m deep. The mound consisted of charcoal-rich, peaty soil with fire-cracked stone, heavily truncated.

Barnalisheen 2
Burnt pits
S193676

This site consisted of two small pits containing burnt mound material of fire-cracked stone and charcoal-rich silt.

Barnalisheen 3
Burnt pits
S193675

This site consisted of three small, oval pits containing burnt mound material of fire-cracked stone and charcoal-rich silt.

Killoran 12
Destroyed burnt mound
S202668

Revealed during tree clearance and trench cutting for the installation of an ESB pylon, the site had been destroyed by the field bank and ditch before development. It comprised a spoilheap of fire-cracked stone within a black, charcoal-rich, sandy silt matrix.

Killoran 13
Burnt mound
S201669

This site was revealed during trench cutting for a road drainage scheme. A large trench was excavated by machine. The site was a burnt mound revealed in section as a thick band of small fire-cracked stone (80% sandstone, 20% limestone), 0.54–1.26m thick.

Killoran 14
Fulacht fiadh
S200669

The site was a *fulacht fiadh* with a shallow, circular trough, 3.9m in diameter and 0.33m deep. The cut was filled by burnt mound material. The truncated burnt mound measured 14.8m east–west x 5.7m+ and was 0.24m deep and roughly horseshoe shaped. It consisted of small, fire-cracked stone (80% sandstone, 20% limestone).

Killoran 15
Burnt pit
S211666

The site consisted of a large, possibly medieval, burnt pit and a smaller pit. The burnt pit was oval and measured 2.46m east–west by 1.5m and was 0.4m deep. The pit sides were substantially reddened, and it was filled by several layers of clayey silt with intermittent layers of charcoal. A similar pit at Killoran 3 was dated to the 11th century AD (*Excavations 1997*, 173, 97E0036).

Killoran 17
Early Bronze Age *fulacht fiadh*
S212669

The site consisted of a *fulacht fiadh* with several intercutting troughs. The first subcircular trough measured *c.* 2.3m x 1.8m x 0.45m deep, and contained fills of grey clay and fire-cracked stone, charcoal and silty clay. Charcoal identified as *Evonymus*, *Quercus*, *Corylus*, *Pyrus/Malus*, *Ulmus* and *Fraxinus* (I.L. Stuijts, pers. comm.) produced a radiocarbon date for the site of 2585–2195 BC (Beat-117547).

A second oval trough partially cutting the northern edge of the first measured 2.1m x 1.8m x 0.47m deep. This contained a stake-hole cut into the base of the trough. The partially ploughed-out burnt mound of small, fire-cracked stone (80% sandstone, 20% limestone) was roughly circular and measured 10.8m east–west by 8m and 0.15m deep.

Killoran 19
Fulacht fiadh
S216663

The site was a *fulacht fiadh* with complex intercutting troughs. The earliest subrectangular trough measured *c.* 1.6m x 1.55m x 0.47m deep. In the base of the trough was a large, circular depression that served as a well or sump. The fill was fire-cracked stone in charcoal-rich peat, with large flags, possibly a disturbed stone lining. Two associated internal stake-holes were cut into the base of the trough.

The second trough complex was, in effect, several attempts at a successful trough. It consisted of the original pit cut and recut by shallow, oval or rectangular pits, to form a large irregular trough with flat base and oblong depression, representing a widened spring, with posts, and filled by burnt mound material and peat. The partially truncated burnt mound was roughly circular and measured 15m east–west by 5m+ and 0.17m in truncated depth.

Killoran 21
Fulacht fiadh
S205668

This *fulacht fiadh* contained a subcircular trough measuring 1.94m x 1.76m x 0.5m deep, with thirteen fills. The ploughed-out burnt mound covered an area of over 9.5m x 8m x 0.13m and consisted of small, fire-cracked stone (80% sandstone, 20% limestone).

Killoran 22: Structure 1
Fulacht fiadh
S211669

This heavily ploughed-out *fulacht fiadh* contained two troughs: one trough appeared to cut a second and was 1.4m in diameter and 0.58m deep, filled by sandy clay silt with burnt sandstone. The second subcircular trough was 1.25m in diameter and 0.25m deep and contained three fills of sand, silt and charcoal and burnt mound material. This trough showed signs of a burnt lining of light brushwood. Two teeth (*Ovis*—sheep/goat) were recovered from the upper fill. A possible hearth site in a rectangular feature measured 1.07m+ x 0.76m and was 0.24m deep. The ploughed-out burnt mound covered an area of 4.53m x 8m+ x 0.18m.

Killoran 22: Structure 2
Fulacht fiadh
S211669

This ploughed-out *fulacht fiadh* contained a shallow, subcircular trough, measuring 1.7m x 1.44m x 0.12m, filled by burnt mound material. A shallow, circular stake-hole was cut into the corner of the trough. A truncated hearth lay in an irregular depression measuring over 1.4m x 2.45m x 0.21m deep. The ploughed-out burnt mound was almost totally removed; it covered an approximate area of 4.53m+ x 7.5m+ x 0.18m and consisted of small, fire-cracked stone (80% sandstone, 20% limestone).

Killoran 23
Medieval boiling pit
S202671

The site consisted of a subcircular pit 1.8m in diameter and 0.55m deep. It had steep, straight or convex sides and was filled with several layers of charcoal-rich silt and fire-cracked stone. Charcoal from this sample was identified as *Quercus*, *Fraxinus*, *Betula* and *Pyrus/Malus* (I.L. Stuijts, pers. comm.) and produced a date of AD 660–880 (Beta-117550).

Killoran 24
Isolated flat cremations
S212669

The site consisted of two isolated cremations. The first was a steep-sided pit, measuring 0.34m x 0.24m x 0.18m deep, containing an abundance of cremated bone within a particularly charcoal-rich fill capped by redeposited, light grey clay subsoil and stone. The second cremation was a shallow, concave pit, 0.42m in diameter and 0.16m deep, which contained less charcoal, a few tiny fragments of burnt bone and some large fragments of fired clay.

Killoran 25
Burnt mound
S211669

The site was a partially ploughed-out burnt mound covering an area of over 30m x 23m x 0.8m. It was preserved to its full thickness under a field bank roughly central to the site, sealed by upcast subsoil from the associated field ditch. The burnt mound sealed peat and consisted of two layers of burnt material. The upper layer was 0.3m deep and composed of small, fire-cracked limestone. The lower layer was 0.37m deep and consisted of fire-cracked stone (95% sandstone, 5% limestone).

Killoran 26
Late Bronze Age *fulacht fiadh*
S216664

The site was a *fulacht fiadh* consisting of a subrectangular trough measuring 2.36m x 2m x 0.46m deep filled by a silt layer under an almost uniform layer of charcoal and charred wood, representing a burnt plank or roundwood lining, sealed by a hard packing of redeposited clay subsoil up against the sides, probably representing a relining of the trough for a second use. Charcoal from Dep. 4, identified as *Pyrus/Malus*, *Quercusg*, *Corylus* and *Fraxinus* (I.L. Stuijts, pers. comm.) produced a radiocarbon date of 1145–795 BC (Beta-117549).

A recut of the trough followed the burning of the initial lining and collapse of the side lining and was represented within the smaller area delimited by the redeposited clay packing. An associated stake-hole cut the edge of the trough. The ploughed-out spread of burnt mound material covered part of the trough and stake-hole and had been largely removed by machine during stripping. It appeared to cover an area 13m x 7m x 0.01m (80% sandstone, 20% limestone).

Killoran 27
Late Bronze Age *fulacht fiadh*
S205665

This site was a ploughed-out *fulacht fiadh* consisting of a large, sub-oval trough measuring 3.45m x 2.72m x 1.22m deep. It contained fills of silts, redeposited clay/sand subsoil and fire-cracked stone. A recut trough consisted of a subrectangular pit measuring 1.64m x 1.24m x 0.37m. The trough was filled by a thick layer of slumped, organic, silty clay containing wood fragments and also sheep/goat (*Ovis*) bone and teeth and occasional fire-cracked stone, sealed by sand. The upper level of the trough was delimited by an oak timber step, which produced a dendrochronological date of 932 BC (Q9698). The spread of burnt mound material had been largely removed by machine during stripping but appeared to cover an area of 10.7m x 6m x 0.2m.

Killoran 29
Fulacht fiadh
S211668

This site was a heavily ploughed-out *fulacht fiadh* with a sub-oval trough, partly sealed by thin patches of a heavily ploughed-out spread of burnt sandstone, silt and charcoal and peat, and an irregular feature, possibly a hearth. The sub-oval trough measured 1.91m x 1.78m x 0.23m and contained a basal fill of burnt mound material sealed by a layer of charcoal-flecked clay and peat. The ploughed-out burnt mound was almost entirely removed during mechanical stripping over an area of 12m+ north–south by 11m to a depth of 0.1m. A possible hearth measured 1.04m x 0.8mm x 0.1m.

Killoran 30
Fulacht fiadh
S211668

This site was a heavily ploughed-out *fulacht fiadh* with oblong trough, measuring 1.76m x 1.04m x 0.37m deep, containing several fills of inwashed silt and burnt mound material. The ploughed-out burnt mound was almost entirely non-existent and covered an area of 7.6m+ x 6.7m to a maximum depth of 0.01m.
Paul Stevens for Margaret Gowen & Co. Ltd, 2 Killiney View, 2 Albert Road Lower, Glenageary, Co. Dublin.

613. KILLORAN 10
Bronze Age flat cremation cemetery
S217662
97E0168 ext.

A second season of excavation was undertaken at this large, flat cremation cemetery site in August 1998 to determine its full extent. Features were revealed, recorded and then covered with thick gauge plastic and backfilled and the area fenced off, for preservation and protection.

The excavation consisted of two linear trenches opened on either side of the area previously excavated in 1997 (*Excavations 1997*, 174–5). The trenches measured 9.2m east–west, 2m wide, extending east, and 18.6m east–west, 2m wide, extending west. Excavation revealed twelve further small, circular pits in the eastern extension trench, six containing a charcoal-rich fill capped with clay and a further six containing charcoal-rich fills.

The entire site was therefore revealed to consist of 67 pits, containing at least 30 individual burials, within an area 11m long and 9m wide, orientated east–west. No visible trace of an enclosing ditch or boundary was noted to the north or south. The pits were clustered with no apparent regularity within a loose east–west alignment, with three lying outside the cluster to the north and several intercutting.

A charcoal sample from one, identified as *Alnus* (I.L. Stuijts, pers. comm.), produced a radiocarbon date of 1410–1285 BC (Beta-117546).
Paul Stevens for Margaret Gowen & Co. Ltd, 2 Killiney View, 2 Albert Road Lower, Glenageary, Co. Dublin.

614. KILLORAN 16
Iron Age house and Early Christian pit
222350 166900
98E0066

This excavation formed part of a large project for Lisheen Mines Development. The site was uncovered during the pre-development monitoring carried out by Paul Stevens (see No. 612 above, 98E0372). Killoran 16 lay on the eastern edge of a small ridge, north of Killoran House, with a series of glacial knolls to the east and more gentle, undulating landscape to the west. The ridge on which the site lay was composed of sand, gravel and mixed clays, forming a well-drained foundation in the immediate environs of the site, which was covered with a 0.3–0.4m deposit of topsoil. This topsoil had been ploughed, and the underlying archaeological deposits were truncated.

The house site comprised a series of posts forming a roughly circular structure 14.88m in diameter, with a central post. No pattern of specific structural posts was apparent. Instead it appears that the posts were inserted where possible to an appropriate depth. The main structural support appears to have come from the central post, and the posts of the outer doorway were load bearing. This doorway, which was facing south-east, was formed by four post-holes, with the partial remains of two shallow wall slots that formed a curved extension onto the front of the house. The doorway was a minimum of 1.05–1.09m wide and was 1.42–2m long across the porch.

Within the interior the partial remains of a series of smaller post- and stake-holes lay in the eastern area of the structure, west and south-west of the doorway. A ^{14}C date, produced from the fill of one of the door-posts, returned a date of 180 BC–AD 425 (Beta-117551). No finds were associated with any of the features apart from a small fragment of burnt bone in the fill of the central post-hole. This was the primary phase of activity at the site.

The second phase of activity related to a large pit 2.85m to the north, which was 3m in diameter and 1.08m deep. It had been backfilled with redeposited boulder clay, and a small piece of worked brushwood was found at the base. This sample produced a carbon date of AD 890–1040. Despite analysis of the fill no indication was found of the use of this pit. In the environs of the site were the partial remains of four areas of burning, which may have been associated with either phase of activity.

The final phase of activity, which had been truncated, related to the subsequent agricultural activity on the site.

Cara Murray, 10 Martello Avenue, Dun Laoghaire, Co. Dublin, for Margaret Gowen & Co. Ltd.

615. KILLORAN 31
Early Christian settlement
S210661
SMR 36:20
98E0269

An archaeological excavation was undertaken in advance of the installation of an ESB pole unit on the site of an Early Christian ecclesiastical enclosure. The site lies in Killoran townland, Moyne parish. The results form part of the Lisheen Archaeological Project, an integrated research project. Development was halted as part of the archaeological monitoring for the Lisheen mine and was allowed to proceed by *Dúchas*, provided archaeological excavation was undertaken for the footprint of the poles. This excavation was done in July 1998.

The site is a large, circular enclosure visible as a low, curving, scarped platform, continued in the line of the modern field boundary but with no visible trace to the north. The enclosure is 155m in diameter, surviving to a height of *c.* 0.5m. The site was naturally defensive, at the southern end of a glacial ridge, enclosed on three sides by bog (now reclaimed) and to the east by the Moyne Stream, 50–70m east of the monument.

Excavation consisted of a single cutting along the footprint of the development, measuring 6m north–south by 5m. Excavation revealed a cluster of oval burnt pits and post-holes used for ironworking, rich in ironworking waste, with one containing a broken furnace bowl. Samples of charcoal taken from these pits were identified by I.L. Stuijts (pers. comm.) as

Quercus and *Taxus* branches, and radiocarbon-dated to AD 450–690 (Beta-120521). The cutting was bisected by two overlapping parallel linear gullies associated with a cluster of roughly aligned post- and stake-holes post-dating the ironworking activity. A third linear gully was at right angles to the line of slots and stopped short of them. The three features delineated most of the features on the site, and represent slot-trenches for an internal wattle partition within the large enclosure.

A number of other associated or unassociated features of apparent antiquity were found within the trench. There were also several outlying features, mainly shallow post-holes. One cluster of post-holes around the north-western terminus did not appear to form an alignment. The enclosure was bisected by a recent field bank and ditch, running east–west.

The date of the site is within the lifetime of the Saint Odran, and it was probably founded by him, before AD 563 or 548. It may have continued to function as a monastery for some years.

Paul Stevens for Margaret Gowen & Co. Ltd, 2 Killiney View, 2 Albert Road Lower, Glenageary, Co. Dublin.

616. LISTUNNY
Bronze Age house site
R885776
98E0477

The site lay in Lissatunny townland, *c.* 1 mile south-east of Nenagh town, Co. Tipperary, and east of the Ballynaclogh Road, and was on the Nenagh Bypass. The site consisted of a roughly circular arrangement of six to eight charcoal-rich posts/pits, with a number of associated fire spots. The approximate dimensions of this circular area was 6m x 7m.

Approximately 24m east of this area a short, linear feature was also uncovered. This feature consisted of a charcoal and burnt clay spread, *c.* 6m long and 0.2m wide. A cursory examination of the surface of this feature revealed sherds of burnt, prehistoric pottery and a small fragment of curved, sheet bronze.

This site was severely damaged by construction work before the excavation commenced.

Richard N. O'Brien, Archaeological Development Services Ltd, Windsor House, 11 Fairview Strand, Fairview, Dublin 3.

617. LOUHGNAFINA
Enclosure
98E0414

During monitoring works on the Cashel Sewerage Scheme a new site was uncovered. It was noticed during the topsoil-stripping stage and lies about half a mile outside the town of Cashel.

The site was partly excavated. A trench 2.5m wide and 100m long was opened through its centre. Accordingly, it was only possible to get a limited look at the site. Restrictions on the width of the dig (2.5m wide) and its defined location limited the excavation, and a large percentage of the site remained unexcavated. Also, heavy truncation, particularly at the west end of the site, resulted in part of it being destroyed.

Approximately midway along the length of the trench a mound was uncovered. It was relatively close to the surface, 300mm below the present ground level. On the part of the mound excavated no archaeological evidence was found to indicate what function it served. The mound had been greatly truncated at its western side by a large number of interconnecting and overlying pits and cuts. Some of these were filled with gravel and stone. Within a pocket of gravel a very well-preserved zoomorphic penannular brooch was uncovered. Though out of context, the find was noteworthy for its excellent condition and the fact that such brooches have rarely been found in County Tipperary.

To the eastern edge of the mound was a well-preserved metalled surface. This may have extended around the entire mound, but, owing to the limited width of the excavation, it was not possible to establish its extent. It displayed all of the characteristics of having been used and frequently walked on. The surface appeared to have been contemporary with the mound. It extended and sloped downwards for a length of 15m away from the mound and suddenly stopped. At its lowest point it was *c.* 2m below ground level.

The surface had been truncated by a wide, deep ditch that was not related to the mound or enclosure and had been cut out later. It was *c.* 4m wide and had a maximum depth of 2.5m. It had been filled with several deposits and contained a reasonable amount of animal bone and pottery dating to the 13th and 14th century. In addition to the ditch being filled with deposits containing finds of medieval date, the metalled surface was covered and backfilled with a substantial number of deposits containing frequent amounts of animal bone and pottery from the 13th and 14th century. These deposits appear to have been brought to the site to backfill it and bring it up to the level of the surface of the mound, which was relatively close to modern ground level. There was no trace of an enclosing embankment or ditch. The wider and later ditch may have truncated the original bank and ditch on the east side of the mound, whereas on the west side of the mound there had been great disturbance by the opening of later cuts and pits that were subsequently filled with gravels, stone and mixtures of soil, stone and gravel. The mound itself had been greatly damaged, and there was no possibility of any enclosing ditch or embankment surviving.

No date was obtained for the mound or metalled surface. The mound was constructed with redeposited builder clay and was built off the natural subsoils. The metalled surface was laid on the natural subsoils. No finds were recovered to give dating clues for either. Regarding the wide ditch, it was dug out after the construction of the mound and the surface. However, it was possible to establish, from datable finds, that it was backfilled sometime before the mid-18th century.
Mary Henry, 1 Jervis Place, Clonmel, Co. Tipperary.

618. NENAGH BYPASS ROAD SCHEME
Various
98E0471–98E0477, 98E0540, 97E0320 ext.
Beginning in August 1998, monitoring work was carried out on the route of the Nenagh Bypass, Co. Tipperary, initially by Cia McConway and Paul Logue and from 30 August by this writer. Large-scale monitoring of the route was completed by the start of October 1998, although monitoring of a number of peripheral roads was undertaken again in December

1998 and March 1999. Excavations continued in tandem with the monitoring work and are ongoing at the time of writing. Ciara McManus was the assistant director at Lahesseragh Sites A and C (Nos 609 and 611 above), Knockalton Lower (No. 605 above) and Tullahedy Sites E and F.

Further possible archaeological features found during monitoring were investigated in the townlands of Ballintotty, Benedine, Clashnevin, Knockalton Lower, Lahesseragh and Tyone. These features generally consisted of single, isolated pits/fire spots of indeterminate date and function.
Richard N. O'Brien, Archaeological Development Services Ltd, Windsor House, 11 Fairview Strand, Fairview, Dublin 3.

619. 54 PEARSE STREET, NENAGH
Urban
SMR 20:37
98E0535
In the course of monitoring of manual excavations at the site of a proposed development at 54 Pearse Street, Nenagh, no finds or features of archaeological interest were encountered.

The entire site was covered by concrete, and the underlying stratigraphy comprised mainly redeposited materials that appeared to date to the 19th century. Natural, undisturbed subsoil was reached at a depth of 0.45–0.5m below ground level.
Anne Connolly, Archaeological Services Unit Ltd, Purcell House, Oranmore, Co. Galway.

620. CUCKOO HILL, NICHOLASTOWN
Adjacent to enclosure
SMR 82:39
21135 12242
98E0340
Pre-construction testing took place in advance of the construction of a farm effluent tank at Cuckoo Hill, Ballindoney East, Nicholastown, Cahir. The site of the proposed development lies *c.* 30m to the south-west of an enclosure. An area measuring 12.5m x 12m and 2.1m deep will be covered by the proposed development. Three test-trenches were opened on the site.

There were no archaeological remains found during testing works that could be associated with the enclosure site. The soil profile in all the test-trenches consisted of a mid-brown topsoil with pebbles, small stones and root tendrils. The underlying subsoils consisted of a sterile, yellowish-brown, sandy clay and an olive, yellowish-brown, boulder clay.
Mary Henry, 1 Jervis Place, Clonmel, Co. Tipperary.

621. ROSCREA SEWERAGE SCHEME, ROSCREA
No archaeological significance
22266 16613
97E0361 ext.
Monitoring of pipe-laying for the Roscrea Sewerage Scheme took place in the grounds of St Crónan's Catholic church and along the Bunnow River towards the Burgoo Bridge. The 15th-century friary lay across the river at one location where works were to take place, and the 'Roscrea pillar' lay in the grounds of St Crónan's, on the same bank on which the pipes were laid (although it is believed to have been moved there from Monaincha). Limited testing of the riverbank, in advance of construction, showed

that it had been regraded fairly recently.

No archaeological deposits were disturbed during pipe-laying, as both the riverbed and northern bank had been disturbed earlier this century during previous works.

John Ó Néill for Margaret Gowen & Co. Ltd, 2 Killiney View, Albert Road Lower, Glenageary, Co. Dublin.

622. KING JOHN'S TOWER, ROSCREA CASTLE, ROSCREA

Medieval castle, curtain tower
S134892
98E044

Excavations were undertaken over an eight-week period behind and inside one of the curtain towers, known as King John's Tower, in Roscrea Castle, in advance of its conservation.

The visible mural tower is D-shaped in plan and is probably of later 13th-century date. In the interior of the basement of the tower an earlier round tower was revealed. It is likely to have been of early 13th-century date, although no contemporary finds were recovered.

An intra-mural passageway, leading down a flight of steps to a well, was discovered and excavated in the north wall of the later curtain tower. It was infilled in the later 17th century, when its entrance was blocked.

The chute of the garderobe on the first floor of the tower was also excavated. It proved to be c. 7.15m deep and was also infilled in the later 17th century.

The area immediately behind the tower was also excavated to varying degrees, and a small part of a heavily truncated and possible early earthen bank was the only medieval feature uncovered. The work was funded by *Dúchas* The Heritage Service.

Alan Hayden, Archaeological Projects Ltd, 25A Eaton Square, Terenure, Dublin 6W.

623. RIVERRUN HOUSE, CORNAMULT, TERRYGLASS

Ditch features of unknown age
SMR 6:3
98E0421

It was proposed to develop three self-catering/ residential units, at Riverrun House, which lies inside the zone of archaeological potential for Terryglass, Nenagh, Co. Tipperary. In compliance with the planning conditions soil-stripping from the site was monitored on 16 September 1998.

Monitoring revealed two substantial cut features crossing the site. One of these (Feature 1), tested in two areas, was shown to be a large, curved ditch leading from the north-eastern end of the site, curving to the west, towards the river. The lower ditch fill consisted of sterile sands and gravel. The upper fill consisted of a thin band of dark grey, sandy silt, with frequent flecks of charcoal, followed by an orange/brown clay, with frequent large stones. The general uniformity of the lower backfill (from both test areas) may suggest a natural fill process.

The test-trenches produced two fragments of animal bone but no artefacts. There was no evidence of an earthen bank on either side of the ditch. The position and shape of the ditch suggested that it would terminate at the river, to the west. To the north-east the arc of the ditch appeared to be heading towards the present road junction. It was initially thought that

Feature 1 may have been a field drain; however, its shape, position and fill do not seem to support this theory. It seems to have been associated with the river, perhaps as a flood-relief mechanism or as a means of drawing water off the river, perhaps for a watermill.

A second substantial ditch feature was identified running south from the main ditch. The upper fill of the second ditch was similar to Feature 1; however, this was not tested. Some other pit and linear features were also identified but not tested.

Kenneth Hanley, 44 Eaton Heights, Cobh, Co. Cork.

624. RIVERRUN HOUSE, CORNAMULT, TERRYGLASS

Ringditch
M865004
98E0421 ext.

Monitoring took place in November 1998 of construction works for a small residential development, following an assessment by Ken Hanley in September 1998 (No. 623 above), which identified a large curvilinear ditch feature and several other features within the footprint of development. Following consultation with *Dúchas*, the foundations were raised and a pad-and-beam structure was employed to span the ditch, with remaining features protected with a geotextile mesh.

Archaeological investigation revealed the ditch to be 2.8m wide and 0.75m deep, with a primary gravel fill, suggesting that it was designed to fill with water. Later sand fills show that the ditch continued to hold water until it was deliberately backfilled with a stony clay fill. A lower charcoal layer with token crushed cremated bone above the primary gravel fill suggested that the structure was built as a prehistoric funerary monument—a ring-ditch or barrow. If circular, the structure would measure c. 40m in diameter and occupy part of the eastern flood-plain of the river.

No further archaeological mitigation is considered necessary for this development. However, any proposed further ground disturbance or development on the site should be subject to archaeological appraisal as it is likely that further archaeological issues will arise.

Paul Stevens for Margaret Gowen & Co. Ltd, 2 Killiney View, Albert Road Lower, Glenageary, Co. Dublin.

625. THE MUNSTER HOTEL, CATHEDRAL STREET, THURLES

Urban medieval
S130586
SMR 41:42
98E0598

An archaeological assessment took place in December 1998 in advance of redevelopment of a site on the east bank of the River Suir, opposite the site of the Camelite Friary (c. 1291–1300) and within the eastern medieval suburb of Thurles. The original Hotel Munster (two neighbouring properties and No. 22 Cathedral Street) was demolished following approval by *Dúchas*.

The assessment consisted of eleven test-trenches across the development area of 7100m² and revealed a substantial concentration of archaeological features cut into subsoil across the site. They include a cluster of pits, linear slots and post-holes parallel to the street frontage, representing medieval and post-medieval structures, with ancillary structures and features to the rear. A series of furrows revealed to the rear probably represents medieval or post-medieval ploughing, within burgage plots. Further work was recommended.

Paul Stevens for Margaret Gowen & Co. Ltd, 2 Killiney View, Albert Road Lower, Glenageary, Co. Dublin.

626. BOHERCROW ROAD, MURGASTY, TIPPERARY

Burial-ground/kiln/hut site
R365892
97E0026

An excavation was carried out in a green-field site (80m east–west x 35m), adjacent to a 19th-century church (St Mary's Church of Ireland), in advance of construction of a government office building. St Mary's is marked on the OS map (1st edition) as the site of an earlier church. Five skeletons were excavated here during test-trenching by Brian Hodkinson in 1997 (*Excavations 1997*, 180).

In 1998 an area measuring 15m (east–west) by 30m was opened around the location of those skeletons, and the topsoil in the remainder of the field was removed by machine, under supervision. A kiln and a hut site were uncovered. Post-medieval cultivation had caused disturbance of the archaeological remains throughout the field.

Sixteen burials were recorded during the 1998 excavations, three of which were very partial skeletal remains. They were orientated in a west–east direction, heads to the west, but a number were aligned slightly along a south-west/north-east axis. All were in simple graves with no traces of any coffins or grave-markers. They appeared to represent eleven adults, one juvenile and one neonate. When the burials excavated in 1997 are included, the burials in the field represent eleven adults, five juveniles and two neonates. Associated pottery suggested a post-medieval date for the burials.

An east–west-orientated kiln structure was cut into the sand subsoil to the north of the burials. This consisted of a linear flue leading to an elliptical bowl at the east end. It was 8.5m long, 3.48m wide and 1.2m deep and was keyhole-shaped in plan. The sides were stone-lined, and a single lintel stone was found over the flue. The kiln was filled with collapsed sand from the sides of the structure. There was a basal, charcoal-rich deposit under the stone lining, which may contain evidence of charred cereal grains, indicative of a corn-drying function. There were also small fragments of oxidised limestone in some of the overlying fills, which may suggest a limekiln function.

A circular hut site, 4m in diameter, was excavated in the north-east corner of the field, and no enclosing bank or ditch was uncovered. The upper level of the hut had been disturbed by cultivation activity, and there was a high amount of hollows in the interior caused by root/burrowing activity. A sherd of post-medieval pottery was found in a context severely disturbed by root/burrowing activity. The hut was surrounded by a narrow gully, 0.2–0.5m wide and 0.2m deep, containing no evident post-holes or stake-holes. It may have functioned as a bedding trench. The entrance in the north was indicated by a backfill of moderately compacted sand within the gully, and a hearth lay close to the centre of the hut. The interior of the hut was occupied by overlapping sand layers containing a number of small post-holes and stake-holes. They did not indicate any identifiable structures, apart from a possible spit over the hearth. There were two shallow pits in the north-east corner, and one of these contained a fragment of a jet/lignite bracelet.

Tony Cummins for Archaeological Services Unit, University College Cork.

627. TULLAHEDY

Neolithic landscape
R834772
SMR 102:79
97E0472

The site lies *c.* 3.3km to the west of Nenagh, Co. Tipperary, along the western limit of the N7 Bypass. The site consists primarily of a gravel and sand mound 110m x 125m, to the immediate north of the road-take, within a low-lying boggy landscape. It had been intended to quarry the mound for fill, but when the depth and complexity of the surviving archaeological deposits became apparent it was agreed to allow the lower slopes of the mound to remain intact. They have since been covered with terram and topsoil.

As excavated, the mound was almost entirely enclosed by a linear, ditch-type feature, scarping into the natural face of the mound, creating a very steep inner face and petering out as it ran into the surrounding bog. The ditch had a maximum depth of 1.86m, was 8m wide and was filled with a basal, charcoal-rich, black, peaty clay, overlain with a series of lightly charcoal-flecked, compact, stony, orange/grey clays. Polished stone axes, chert arrowheads, struck chert, stone beads and pendants were all recovered from the ditch fills. Along the inner edge of the ditch was evidence of a palisade that cut through both the undisturbed subsoil and the upper ditch fill.

Owing to the realignment of an open drain, the ditch and associated features are no longer within the catchment area for the road and have also been preserved.

Numerous pits, post-holes and stake-holes were excavated along the slopes of the mound, particularly in two areas. Along the southern slope a large pit was visible in the quarry face and, as survived, measured 8.8m x 6m x 2m. It had been entirely lined with wooden planks that were burnt *in situ*. A few pieces of Neolithic pottery, chert scrapers, chert arrowheads and bone were recovered from the fill. On removal of a plank along the eastern side of the pit a large, polished, shale axe almost 0.4m long was recovered. It is unlikely that an axe of such size was have been misplaced, and therefore it can be concluded that it was deliberately deposited during construction of the pit.

The eastern slope of the mound had been heavily landscaped and transformed in the prehistoric period. A large hollow 16m wide and, as excavated, 12m long had been quarried into the side of the mound to produce a large level platform through which numerous post-holes, pits and stake-holes were excavated. The area was extremely charcoal-rich, with extensive areas of burnt red clay, indicating that the hollowed-out area had been fired, possibly as part of the activity occurring here. After the activity had ceased in the hollowed-out area soil was tipped back into the depression, reinstating the natural slope of the mound. Numerous polished stone axes, chert arrowheads, rock crystal, Neolithic pottery and struck chert were recovered from these soils. Surrounding this large hollowed-out area were several much smaller hollowed-out platforms, each one also infilled after use to reinstate the natural slope of the mound. The large hollowed-out area and all to the east of it have been preserved under terram and topsoil.

Evidence suggests that Tullahedy had been the focus of extensive ritual activity on a scale and of a nature unique in the current Irish archaeological record.

Cia McConway, Archaeological Development Services Ltd, Windsor House, 11 Fairview Strand, Fairview, Dublin 3.

628. TULLAHEDY

Prehistoric/Early Medieval *fulachta fiadh*
R842771
98E0540

Three burnt mounds were found together in Tullahedy townland near the Nenagh–Limerick railway line, south-west of Nenagh town. Site A is *c.* 35m south of sites B and C, and the sites were originally separated by boggy marshland; now the Nenagh Bypass road runs between them. At the time of writing all three sites were still being excavated. Sites A and B were producing evidence of metalworking, perhaps from bog ore extraction/ processing.

Site A

The southern portion of Site A was destroyed when the railway line, to which it is adjacent, was built. The site now measures *c.* 18m east–west x 20m, and the burnt stone mound is *c.* 0.5–1m high and roughly circular in shape. Two hand-excavated test-trenches were placed across the mound material and bottomed down to natural. The test-trenches revealed homogeneous burnt stone material and peat accumulation at the north and north-west end of the site.

A number of clay-lined troughs, at least one hearth, areas of stone cobbling and clusters of stake-holes were found under the burnt stones. One of the troughs had a stone surround, and there was evidence of a possible spit in the clay lining in the form of three stake-holes. The troughs naturally filled with water and had been positioned nearest the boggy ground at the northern end of the site.

The south-east area of the site appears to have been used for smelting activity, where large quantities of waste slag, ash spreads and ore were found. A possible furnace pit with multiple stake-holes at one edge was found. Near this area was an animal cremation deposit within the burnt stone material. Mixed with the bones were over twenty finely crafted iron nails/fragments, much charcoal, burnt hazelnuts and apple seeds. At the time of writing, this area had still to be excavated fully, as had the entire south-west portion of the mound.

Finds included slag, burnt and unburned animal bones and teeth, two stone weights and flint, all from within the burnt stones. A stone bead, burnt flint and chert flakes were found in the old ground surface, sealed by the burnt stones. The stone bead closely resembled examples found on the late Neolithic ritual site of Tullahedy (*Excavations 1997*, 181; No. 627 above), half a mile to the west.

Site B

Site B lies *c.* 35m north of Site A. A portion of the north-west extremity was removed before excavation owing to drainage works, but the full extent of the site was accurately established. The site measures *c.* 22m north–south by *c.* 26m and is 1–1.5m high, giving a roughly circular shape. It was originally covered with dense briars and bushes, and a field boundary ran to the north. This had concealed the site before topsoil-stripping.

Sites B and C both lie on the edge of the 200ft contour, which traverses the field here. Thus the sites would originally have lain on the edge of the bog that extended westward as far as Carraigtogher townland. The upper burnt stone material at the south-west corner of the site was removed by machine using a grading bucket. A number of large field drains were found at the south-west extremity of the site.

Two hand-excavated test-trenches were put through the mound. Two clear phases of *fulacht* activity have been identified, separated by a distinct, grey silt layer. A number of clay-lined pits with associated cobbled areas were found cut into natural, beneath the primary *fulacht* material. A series of four post-holes, cut into the natural and up to 0.4m deep, was found near the mound centre.

A shallow ditch-like feature was found at the north-east edge of the mound running north–south; it in turn was dissected by a smaller ditch running north-east/south-west. These ditch features all respect the main field boundary at the north of the site. As yet there are no datable finds from the ditches, the primary *fulacht* phase or the grey layer. This grey layer appears to follow the contour of the land, oriented north-west/south-east, and is deepest at the southern end of the mound. The northern and southern ends of the mound have peat accumulation, and a cream-coloured shell layer was found at the northern end, sealed by the peat and burnt stones

Associated with the secondary *fulacht* phase is a distinct portion of the site centre where the stone material is reddish, from possible ore deposits/ waste. Elsewhere the mound material is more heavily charcoal-flecked and blacker. The secondary phase covers the entire site area and was more extensive than the primary phase. There are occasional large stones sealed by the burnt stone material that may form hearths/ovens.

One distinct arrangement of large stones within this *fulacht* phase may form part of a stone structure. The stones together measure *c.* 2m long, and *c.* 0.58m deep; the largest stone is 0.67m long and 0.21m deep. As yet these stones are only partially exposed in section. Much burnt and unburned bone has been found in this secondary *fulacht* phase, as well as rubbing stones, hone stones, a worked bone fragment, slag and the upper portion of a rotary quern.

An arrangement of sandstones that surrounds the mound edges appears to be the final phase of use on the site. These stones may have been placed to delimit the mound in the landscape or as storage for later submersion in the troughs. The stones lie at the south, south-east and east edges of the mound, and finds associated with this final phase are large quantities of burnt bones, charcoal, large quantities of metal waste/fragments, nails and a ring-headed bronze pin (ring missing).

At the time of writing, a 7m north–south x 26m strip of the southern end of the mound is being fully excavated, as this portion will be buried by the road embankment. A 5.2m north–south portion of the northern end of the mound was completely excavated to allow a road drain to be inserted here. This leaves *c.* 10m north–south by *c.* 26m by 1–1.5m deep of the mound surviving *in situ* outside the line of the road.

Approximately 9.5m to the north-west of Site B a ditch feature has been found in the section face of the road drain. The ditch is *c.* 4.6m wide, 1m deep and roughly U-shaped in section. It continues southward from the CPO line for *c.* 10.2m. The fill appears to consist of a charcoal-flecked clay with animal bones. This ditch cuts a sand bank running east–west and is exposed in the drain face. This sand bank is *c.* 14.2m long and 1.1m deep. Both the ditch and the sand bank follow the contour of the land and continue northward outside the CPO line of the bypass. This ditch is outside the road embankment and will thus survive *in situ*.

Site C
Site B, the larger burnt mound, was connected via a cobbled stone surface, 3m long, to an adjoining, smaller burnt mound, Site C, to the east. As at Site B, two phases of *fulacht* use have been identified at this site, separated by the grey silt layer.

The primary phase appears to consist of a general cobbled stone spread extending 18m east–west x 20m. The site terminated at the main field boundary to the north. At the southern end the cobbling was more rough and scattered. There was peat encroachment in this area from the adjoining bog. The same peat encroachment occurred on Site A. The peat was subsequently covered by a distinct sand bank running approximately north-west/south-east. The rest of the site was covered by the grey silt layer identical to that on Site B.

Near the centre of this stone spread is a raised platform of ground where more compacted layers of cobbles were laid. Here was a rectangular arrangement of four deep post-holes (1.2m x 2m), with supporting smaller stake-holes. Adjoining this structure at the south-east corner was a circular arrangement of shallow, thin stake-holes, with a number of internal stakes inside. Two possible troughs/pits lay to the south-east and east of this structure, with associated cobble paths. A further trough lay at the juncture of Sites B and C; this trough had evidence of much reuse, and a polished tusk came from the primary peat fill. All the troughs filled naturally with water as there are springs everywhere.

The rectangular structure was subsequently covered with stones and clay, and quantities of charcoal at the inner edges may suggest that it was wood-lined. Most of the rectangular structure and portions of the cobbles were subsequently covered by the secondary *fulacht* phase, which measured 12m x 12.5m and 0.3m deep. This was a homogeneous black burnt stone spread, roughly horseshoe-shaped. Finds from this final phase included burnt bones and some slag.

A small portion of the northern extremity of the site will survive outside the road embankment.
Richard N. O'Brien, Archaeological Development Services Ltd, Windsor House, 11 Fairview Strand, Fairview, Dublin 3.

TYRONE

629. COPNEY
Stone circle complex
H65747368
SMR 37:21
A tract of land in this site, which is in state care, was being made available to a farmer to allow access for animals. Before this happened the area was archaeologically examined.

Two previously unknown circles, K and L, were discovered, as were other stone settings and laid surfaces. Circle K was very disturbed, with three stones comprising its remains within the excavated area; further potential elements of the setting, however, could be detected within the bog, suggesting a diameter of *c.* 9m. Circle L was virtually intact, although some of its stones had toppled, and its dimensions were 10.5m north–south x 9m. The circles had been erected upon prepared surfaces of clay and small stones, and very compact banks of clay and stones were uncovered within them.
Norman Crothers, Archaeological Excavation Unit, Built Heritage, EHS, 5–33 Hill Street, Belfast.

630. LISDIVIN
Megalith
C38800485
SMR 2:12
The removal of the western element of a pair of standing stones, on either side of a bank that marked the townland boundary, prompted a brief investigation.

A trench, 4m x 2m, was opened up to the west of the bank. The stone socket and a shallow ditch flanking the bank were uncovered, as was a pit, 1.6m in diameter and 0.5m deep, filled with sandy loam and stones. An extension of the trench 1m to the west revealed another similar pit, 1.6m in diameter and 0.6m deep, again containing a sandy loam fill and stones. These pits could represent stone sockets, indicating that the remaining stones were the remnants of a more extensive megalith.
Declan P. Hurl, Built Heritage, EHS, 5–33 Hill Street, Belfast.

631. TREMOGE
Stone circle complex
H599782
SMR 27:33
The owner of the land on which these small, low-lying stone circles stood had ploughed over the site. The area was examined to determine the level of disturbance caused and to establish the extent of the features.

Eight trenches were opened: through the western circle and alignment; across a pair of linked circles in the east; and further upslope (north) to investigate the potential for other settings. The known settings were found to be intact, with the possible remains of a cairn uncovered within the western circle and the possible remains of a further three cairns found within the linked circles in the east. The exploratory trenches showed no indications of additional features, but the area had been deep-ploughed. Signs of further features were identified downslope from (south of) the circles but were not explored.

Norman Crothers, Archaeological Excavation Unit, Built Heritage, EHS, 5–33 Hill Street, Belfast.

WATERFORD

632. BALLYDUFF
No archaeological significance
2217 9416
SMR 30:28
98E0569
The development of a site at Ballyduff, Dungarvan, Co. Waterford, required an archaeological assessment. The site is adjacent to a univallate ringfort. Nine trenches were dug. Only one cut feature was found. This produced a modern piece of metal. No archaeological deposits or features were present.

Florence M. Hurley, 8 Marina Park, Victoria Road, Cork.

633. LISNAKILL, BUTLERSTOWN
Adjacent to church
SMR 17:23
98E0048
Despite the proximity of a 16th-century church in ruins in an adjacent field no archaeological features were disturbed by the digging here of foundations for a dwelling-house.

O. Scully, 7, Bayview, Tramore, Co. Waterford.

634. CHURCH STREET/EMMET STREET, DUNGARVAN
Late medieval/post-medieval urban
2262 0967
97E0325
The site for a residential development in the junction of Church Street and Emmett Street, Dungarvan, was tested for archaeological survival in 1997 (*Excavations 1997*, 182). The site is within the

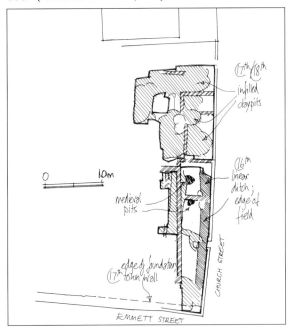

Plan of site at Church Street/Emmet Street, Dungarvan.

17th-century town wall, beside the main street from the castle to the medieval church (Church Street). In 1998 a large part of the roadside was investigated.

Two small pits and a few scraps of pebble surface are the only indications of medieval buildings close to the road. No post-holes, slots or hearths were found. Buildings were probably few and only standing for a short time. There were no suggestions of burgage divisions on site. By the 16th century a field occupied half of the roadside; a second field may have occupied the other half. With the 17th-century construction of a town wall (foundations were uncovered) on the line of Emmett Street, soil was stripped from the fields and houses were built beside Church Street. The buildings probably had clay-bonded stone walls, but virtually all traces of walls were removed by later buildings and clay pits.

Clay pits from the 17th and 18th century covered a good deal of the site. Clay extraction started before the construction of the town wall and continued in a belt behind the roadside houses, occasionally cutting away a roadside site. Ground level dropped beside the road and under it. The survival of pre-19th-century surfaces was poor.

Dave Pollock, 33 Woodlawn, Cashel, Co. Tipperary.

635. DUNGARVAN CASTLE, DUNGARVAN
Medieval and post-medieval castle
2262 0927
95E0080
During May and June 1998, in the fourth season of excavations ahead of consolidation, funded by the National Monuments Service, a piece of ground between the shell keep and the north curtain wall was taken down to the 16th/17th-century ground level to investigate the site of two possible towers. The sally-port or watergate in the wall of the shell keep was also investigated.

A ditch between the keep and the curtain wall was largely infilled by the 16th century; in the 16th or 17th century the remaining hollow immediately outside the main entrance to the keep was further infilled and the fill revetted with a clay-bonded wall. Beyond the revetment wall the battered base of the keep was blanketed with a layer of rubble and clay, a deliberate artillery protection matched by a similar rampart on the inside (uncovered in 1997). Traces of buildings were found in the disturbed ground inside the north curtain wall. A door in the curtain was inserted or rebuilt, probably in the 1640s, and provided with a flanking tower. The curtain wall was mined from the inside and exploded at the end of the 17th century. Shortly after barracks were built the curtain was reconstructed (as a thin wall) and the ground level was raised considerably.

The high tower shown on a late 17th-century watercolour of Dungarvan was never built against the keep. It may have been freestanding, but this is unlikely. It is matched exactly by a tower attached to the keep at Cardiff Castle; its presence on the Dungarvan picture is a mystery.

The presence of a second tower, a suspected medieval terminal on the north curtain wall, could not be ascertained. Medieval stonework did not survive at 16th-century ground level, owing to 17th-century rebuilding and late 17th-century demolition.

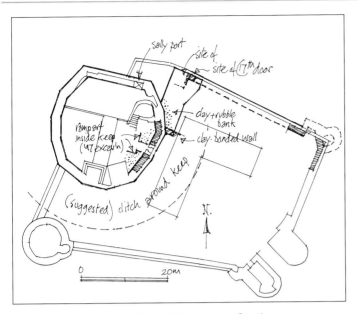

Plan of Dungarvan Castle.

Furthermore, in the crucial area, damage from 18th-and 19th-century drains threatened the stability of the thin 18th-century curtain wall standing above. For safety reasons excavation was not taken further.
Dave Pollock, 33 Woodlawn, Cashel, Co. Tipperary.

636. 44 MAIN STREET, DUNGARVAN
Late medieval/post-medieval urban
2262 0967
98E0600
During the refurbishment of a property on Main Street, within the 17th-century walled town, a trench was cut in the floor, ahead of a proposed drain. The ground had been truncated (to extract clay) shortly before the present building was erected in the 18th century. No earlier surface survived.
Dave Pollock, 33 Woodlawn, Cashel, Co. Tipperary.

637. KILMOVEE
Kilns, medieval?
24362 11114
SMR 8:30
98E0558
During the construction of a house close to a possible church site at Kilmovee, Portlaw, the remains of three small kilns/furnaces were investigated. The features were associated with iron waste, potentially part of a smithing rather than smelting operation. No domestic midden, datable finds or indications of buildings were found.
Dave Pollock, 33 Woodlawn, Cashel, Co. Tipperary.

638. 9 ARUNDEL SQUARE, WATERFORD
Urban medieval
98E0091
Excavation work at this site was monitored in spring 1998 following an archaeological assessment by Sarah McCutcheon (*Excavations 1997*, 184–5, 97E137). Construction work had already been amended to avoid the line of the city wall. Unforeseen work underpinning the wall of an adjacent property, however, necessitated further testing on the line of the wall. Its remains were uncovered running north-east/south-west along the eastern boundary of the site.

It was possible to avoid underpinning on the line of the wall. All archaeological features encountered during the monitoring were excavated by hand and archaeologically recorded.

At the eastern end of the site the remains of a sill-beam house fronting onto Arundel Square were uncovered. It was at least 7.3m long east–west, but only 1m of its north–south extent was exposed. The pottery found may indicate a late 12th-century date for this structure, but this occurred in such small amounts across the site that any dating can only be tentative (Clare McCutcheon, pers. comm.) To the rear of the building a backyard extended west for at least 10m, and there was evidence of some small structures within the yard.

At some stage in the later 12th or early 13th century a defensive clay bank was erected above the backyard. This extended roughly north–south across the western end of the site close to the line of the later city wall. It was constructed of a mix of clays, silts and deposits of occupation debris. It had a maximum excavated width of 7.64m but was probably at least 1–2m wider. It survived to a maximum estimated height of 1.4m above the occupation debris and sloped downwards from west to east. Three sherds of Ham Green cooking ware (early 12th/mid-13th century) were recovered from a clay layer that may have formed part of this bank.

The bank gradually went out of use and was partly covered by backyard occupation debris and cut by small pits. These apparently belonged to a second level of house building fronting onto Arundel Square. Small amounts of pottery associated with these layers again suggest a date in the late 12th or early 13th century.

Around this time a defensive stone wall was built into the bank clays 17.5m west of the modern street frontage on Arundel Square. An Inquisition of 1224 mentions an Arundel Gate on the city defences sited on Arundel Lane north of the site (Nicholls 1972, 109).

The wall extended north–south for 2.8m, where a post-medieval trench cut through it. It was constructed of rough-coursed limestone blocks measuring between 0.2m and 0.6m wide. These were bonded with yellow clay and decayed mortar.

The wall was 0.8m wide but was cut to the east by a post-medieval cellar. Its basal levels could not be excavated owing to water seepage, but it was exposed to a height of five courses (0.8m), where it was truncated by later cellars.

A stone-lined cesspit was also set into the remains of the bank. This pit went out of use and was backfilled some time in the mid-13th to early 14th century. Later a stone wall was erected along its eastern edge.

Reference
Nicholls, K. 1972 *Gaelic and Gaelicised Ireland in the Middle Ages*. Dublin.

Joanna Wren, The Mile Post, Waterford.

639. DEANERY GARDEN, WATERFORD
Medieval undercroft
S61051237
98E0447
To the rear of City Hall, at the east side of Cathedral

Square, what was originally a semi-underground building of 13th-century date had been buried to the level of the undercroft roof. Two trenches were excavated along the length of the rectangular building. The floor of the interior was also excavated. The front (west-facing) wall of the undercroft was exposed for a length of 14.2m to an average depth of 2.2m, and in one section the trench was dug to the off-set of the footing, a maximum depth of 3.45m. Three window opes/arrowloops were exposed, the fourth lies under an annexe to the Deanery (the present-day Finance Office of the Corporation). The rear wall of the building was also exposed, the construction trench for which was identified and voided, and the earlier medieval and possibly Viking layers cut by the construction trench were removed to the level of the old ground surface. Post-excavation work is now in progress.

Orla Scully, 7, Bayview, Tramore, Co. Waterford.

640. 92 THE QUAY, WATERFORD
No archaeological significance
S608125
98E0509

The proposed development consisted of an extension (8.8m x 6m) to the rear of the existing shop premises at No. 92 The Quay, Waterford. The site for proposed redevelopment lay within the zone of archaeological potential for the city of Waterford. Consequently archaeological monitoring of all construction works was requested as a planning condition.

Onsite works involved the excavation of foundation trenches, 0.6m deep and 0.5m wide, and ground clearance within the central area. At the depth of 0.6m there were no indications of archaeological material.

Cathy Sheehan, Hillview, Aglish, Carrigeen, South Kilkenny.

641. WATERSIDE MOTORS LTD, WATERSIDE, WATERFORD
City wall
60835 12060
98U2

Monitoring of the mechanical excavation of the foundation trenches of the three walls of the northward extension to the existing workshop took place on 2 and 3 November 1998. The trenches were dug to a maximum depth of *c.* 0.8m below existing ground level. The stratigraphy consisted of a series of loosely compacted deposits, predominantly of ashy or sandy material, with inclusions of red brick and crushed mortar laid down as recently as 1984. Beneath these deposits was, on the evidence of its appearance in all three trenches, an extensive cobbled pavement that is provisionally dated to the 19th/early 20th century. This feature, found at a depth of *c.* 0.75m below modern ground level, may be of interest to archaeologists in the future, so the few exposed areas of cobbles were sealed with polythene sheeting before the pouring of concrete.

The city wall along the western boundary of the premises was photographed in a series of overlapping shots taken at a constant distance of 12.5m from the base of the wall. The photographs were marked to indicate which parts of the fabric are original and which are of later addition. From these photographs

and the plan an elevation drawing accurate to a given scale can be prepared with the use of computer rectification technology available to *Dúchas*.

The wall forms the western boundary along the entire length of the premises; it is well preserved, and the original stonework survives to a height of 3m above present ground level. The outer opes of two archery loops are visible in the stretch of the wall that was surveyed at the rear of the premises. The sill of the northern loop lies barely above modern ground level, while that of the southern one is buried. These facts suggest that the ground level here has been elevated significantly since the medieval wall was built and that at the time that the wall was constructed the ground level declined from north to south, towards John's River. A further loop was noted at the front of the premises (not surveyed), and there may be others in areas currently obscured from view.

Andrew Gittins, 22 Lower Grange, Waterford.

WESTMEATH

642. BASTION STREET, ATHLONE
Urban post-medieval
2030 2410

Archaeological monitoring took place in October 1998 at a housing redevelopment at No. 16 Bastion Street, Athlone. The site lies on the northern side of Bastion Street, south of the 17th-century bastion wall, which runs parallel to the street and at right angles to the medieval town wall. The development area measures 19m north–south by 8m.

Development was in progress when archaeological monitoring was requested; no demolition or alteration to existing walls was planned; however, subsurface works were undertaken close to the wall, and these were all subject to an archaeological monitoring clause. In fact, only one trench was available to archaeologically monitor; however, all standing walls were visible.

The trench was opened for a foul water main supply and lay in the centre of the building on the site. The trench was 6m long, 1m wide and 0.4–1m deep and revealed two linear features of 17th/18th-century date below the existing property. These were revealed at a depth of 0.3–0.4m below ground level.

The line of the bastion wall appeared to be substantially altered and contained several phases of masonry and brick. No intact portion of the original bastion wall was noted during the assessment. Analysis of the other face of the wall revealed that the bastion wall had been rebuilt from a point east of the property, where it was listing and buttressed. It is therefore likely that the wall fell and was rebuilt using existing stone and brick additions.

Paul Stevens for Margaret Gowen & Co. Ltd, 2 Killiney View, Albert Road Lower, Glenageary, Co. Dublin.

643. NORTHGATE STREET, ATHLONE
Urban medieval
203790 241445
98E0210

Trial-trenching was undertaken at the site of a proposed hotel, leisure centre and apartment development on 27–9 April 1998. The work was undertaken in compliance with a condition of the grant of planning in respect of the development. Subsurface ground disturbance works had commenced on the site before the involvement of an archaeologist. However, following a report of such to the Garda by Athlone UDC, all works were halted until an archaeologist was present.

The site lies on the east bank of the River Shannon, north of the bridge, and is bounded on the east by Northgate Street. Before development the site consisted of a number of houses fronting onto the street, with the remainder of the site consisting, for the most part, of a disused factory unit. The upstanding remains of the Athlone gasworks building are also within the development site. Demolition of the houses and part of the factory had been completed; the levels had been reduced into the subsoil in much of the south-western quadrant of the site.

The site lies within the walled town of Athlone, and cartographic sources indicate the line of the medieval town wall running west towards the river, in the central part of the site. Furthermore, this wall was reinforced during the 17th century, and a demi-bastion was constructed at the river end. In addition a plan of Athlone dating to 1691 indicates that a number of trenches were dug along the waterfront, within the site, most probably by the Williamites following their breaching of the north bastion.

Trial-trenching indicated that the levels across the southern half of the site had been reduced, probably during the construction of the former factory premises, and that any features of archaeological interest had been removed.

However, investigations along the presumed line of the town wall uncovered the foundation remains of the wall. The nature of the foundations indicated that they are probably medieval in origin, although there were indications that portions were rebuilt, probably in the 17th century. The wall lay up to 4m below the present ground surface and stood to a maximum height of 1.65m. It was up to 1.83m wide and had a slight batter on the internal face.

No further features or finds of archaeological interest were revealed during the course of the evaluation.

The existence of undemolished sections of the former factory building and other extant buildings militated against further archaeological investigations of the site, particularly in the area of the mural defences. Therefore it was decided to cease the evaluation until the remaining demolition works were complete. However, the development ran into financial difficulties, and no further work has been undertaken.

A further planning application in relation to the site has been made, to replace the proposed hotel and leisure centre with apartments. It is intended that demolition works will commence in spring 1999, following which, further archaeological investigations, including the survey of the existing gasworks, will be undertaken.

Martin E. Byrne, 39 Kerdiff Park, Monread, Naas, Co. Kildare.

644. RETREAT PARK, ATHLONE
Enclosure
20550 24161
SMR 29:22
98E0308

Test excavation was undertaken from 6 to 10 July 1998. The site of the proposed development lies *c.* 500m east of the medieval walled town on the east bank of the River Shannon and contains an enclosure. The enclosure is probably the 'pond' site referred to in *The Sieges of Athlone 1690 and 1691* (H. Murtagh 1973, 3). Murtagh states that on 17 July 1690 the Williamite army arrived at Athlone and encamped about a quarter of a mile from the town. According to the footnotes, 'Strong local tradition says the encampment was in the townland of Retreat at a pond called the "Doctor's Pool". Here the troops washed their clothes, tended their wounds, and in the immediate area buried their dead. Local farmers have discovered skeletons when digging drains etc. It is possible the locality was similarly utilised at the second siege in 1691'. The pond is shown in open countryside in the estate grounds of Retreat House on the 1st edition of the OS 6-inch map (1841). The area now forms part of the suburbs of the modern town.

The site comprises a subrectangular green-field area measuring *c.* 170m north–south by 85m. A shallow depression near the centre of the park was pinpointed as representing the site of the pond. Test excavation comprised the mechanical excavation of two trial-trenches in this area. A mid-brown, loose, silty clay topsoil (0.2m thick) overlay a compacted, redeposited, yellowish-brown, silty clay and grey, silty, sand subsoil (0.3m). The redeposited subsoil overlay natural stratified layers of orange, silty clay and grey silty sand subsoil. The topsoil and redeposited subsoil contained occasional modern pottery sherds and glass fragments. It appears that the pond was drained and backfilled when the surrounding lands were developed in recent times.

No archaeological deposits or features were encountered. A couple of post-medieval pottery sherds were recovered during subsequent monitoring of topsoil removal in advance of development.
Dominic Delany, 31 Ashbrook, Oranmore, Co. Galway.

645. SEÁN COSTELLO STREET WEST (IRISHTOWN UPPER), ATHLONE
17th-century suburb
204372 241234
98E0383

Trial-trenching was undertaken at the site in compliance with a condition of planning and a request from the NMHPS, *Dúchas*. The proposed development comprised an extension to the rear of the existing Dunnes Stores premises, as well as

Town wall at Northgate Street, Athlone.

additional carparking. The work was carried out on 20 and 21 September 1998.

The site lies to the rear of Seán Costello Street West, which until quite recently was named Irishtown Upper. This street, stretching eastwards from the walled town, formed a linear suburb to Athlone that dates to at least the second half of the 17th century, being marked on Philips's map of 1683. (During the 17th century the entire town west of the Shannon was known as Irishtown. Later this term was used for the east town suburb adjacent to the Dublin road.)

The site lies to the rear property boundaries of premises fronting onto the street and was, for the most part, 'greenfield', except for an existing carpark. Furthermore, a small portion of the southern end of the site lay within the boundaries of a previous land-fill area, upon which the Golden Island shopping centre now stands.

Twelve trial-trenches, of varying lengths, were excavated by machine across the site. However, no features or deposits of archaeological interest were revealed. Indeed, it appeared that much of the area had been raised at some time in the past. One sherd of green glazed medieval pottery was recovered from the topsoil.

It can be inferred from the results of the trial-trenching that any settlement during the medieval and post-medieval periods was confined to along the street front or to an area between the northern limit of the testing and the street front.

It was recommended that no further archaeological involvement was required at the site.
Martin E. Byrne, 39 Kerdiff Park, Monread, Naas, Co. Kildare.

646. WATER STREET, CASTLEPOLLARD
Adjacent to church and graveyard
246415 270355
SMR 3:96
98E0347

An archaeological evaluation was undertaken at a proposed development site at Water Street, Castlepollard, on 5 August 1998. The work was carried out in compliance with two grants of planning in respect of two individual plots that make up the site of a housing development.

Six trenches were mechanically excavated in order to determine the nature and extent of any subsurface archaeological features that may exist within the external area adjacent to the boundary wall with Killefree graveyard. The area of testing was defined by the NMHPS, *Dúchas*.

No finds, features or structures of archaeological significance were uncovered during the course of the work, and it was recommended that no further archaeological involvement was required at the site.
Martin E. Byrne, 39 Kerdiff Park, Monread, Naas, Co. Kildare.

647. FORE
No archaeological significance
98E0253

Pre-development testing was carried out on 28 May 1998 at the site of a proposed development at Fore, Co. Westmeath, on behalf of Valerie J. Keeley Ltd. The proposed development lay within the area of archaeological potential in Fore as identified in the

Urban Survey of County Westmeath. The development involved the conversion of an existing, derelict building, which stood at the north end of the village abutting the public road, into a tourist office and coffee shop and the provision of toilet facilities and a carpark at the rear of the site.

In the course of the archaeological work no archaeological material was uncovered. Both areas examined, Area 1, to the east of the existing building, and Area 2, in a waterlogged, boggy area to the north, were completely sterile.
Anne Connolly, Archaeological Services Unit Ltd, Purcell House, Oranmore, Co. Galway.

648. KERINSTOWN AND BALROWAN
Vicinity of castle site
N547513
98E0267

Three test-trenches and three test-pits were excavated to test an area east of a possible roadway that appears to run southwards from the corner of the remains of a castle. The landowner intended to build a dwelling-house in the south-east corner of the field. The area tested was 30–40m east of the roadway. Nothing of archaeological interest was observed.
Rosanne Meenan, Roestown, Drumree, Co. Meath.

649. AUSTIN FRIARS STREET/McCURTAIN STREET, MULLINGAR
Urban post-medieval
244092 253082
98E0039

Archaeological testing was carried out in advance of a proposed commercial development at Austin Friars Street/McCurtain Street, Mullingar, Co. Westmeath. The site lies near the eastern boundary of the medieval town and close to the site of the former medieval Augustinian friary. Burials related to this institution had been discovered just west of the site.

Three trenches were excavated, two on Austin Friars Street and one on McCurtain Street. Trench 1 was 18m long, 1.4m wide and 1.6m deep. A layer of brown clay loam lay under the topsoil and extended to 1.1–1.5m deep. It contained white delft pottery and was probably of 18th-century date. This layer overlay boulder clay.

Trench 2 was 17m long, 1.3m wide and 1.5m deep and was parallel to Trench 1. Under topsoil a layer identical to that in Trench 1 extended to 0.5–1.5m deep and overlay boulder clay. It contained black-glazed earthenware and a clay pipe of probable 18th-century date.

Trench 3 was 8m long, 1.3m wide and 1.4m deep. Topsoil was 0.3m deep and overlay natural gravel.
Deirdre Murphy, Archaeological Consultancy Services Ltd, 15 Trinity Street, Drogheda, Co. Louth.

650. AUSTIN FRIARS STREET/ McCURTAIN STREET, MULLINGAR
Urban medieval
244605 253391
98E0156

Archaeological assessment took place at Austin Friars Street and McCurtain Street in advance of proposed commercial developments. A single trench oriented east–west was excavated at the site on

Austin Friars Street and was 12.5m long, 1.2m wide and 1.3m deep. Rubble and red brick extended to a depth of 0.2m, below which was a layer of brown clay loam containing red brick and modern pottery. At 1.3m the natural boulder clay was encountered.

Three trenches were excavated on McCurtain Street. Trench 2 was 12m long, 1.2m wide and 1.7m deep. Footpath foundation of 0.2m overlay a sandy, yellow gravel that extended for 0.8m and in turn overlay the natural, grey gravel. Trench 3 was 13m long, 1.2m wide and 1.7m deep and was excavated parallel to Trench 2. A yellow, sandy layer extended to 0.4m and contained fragments of industrial piping. It overlay natural, grey, stony gravel. Trench 4 was 14.5m long, 1.2m wide and 1.7m deep and was parallel to Trench 3. Black, silty topsoil 0.25m thick was removed onto a band of mortar. Underlying this was a brown, sandy clay loam containing 19th-century material. At a depth of 1–1.2m natural gravel was exposed.

Deirdre Murphy, Archaeological Consultancy Services Ltd, 15 Trinity Street, Drogheda, Co. Louth.

651. BARRACK STREET/FRIAR'S MILL ROAD, MULLINGAR

Site of post-medieval friary?
N450600
97E0091 ext.

The initial assessment of the site was undertaken in 1997 and revealed nothing of archaeological significance (*Excavations 1997*, 191). An additional block of apartments was to be built at the north-west corner of the site. This area was assessed in May 1998.

Five trenches were opened with a mechanical excavator. These revealed the demolished remains of a 19th-century water-powered cornmill, which is shown on the 1st edition of the OS map of the area. No evidence of any activity of an earlier date was uncovered.

Alan Hayden, Archaeological Projects Ltd, 25A Eaton Square, Terenure, Dublin 6W.

652. BLACKHALL STREET, MULLINGAR

Urban medieval
243619 252888
98E0138

Test-trenching was carried out on various dates in March and April 1998 at the site of the existing Employment Exchange at Blackhall Street, Mullingar. The work was carried out in compliance with a condition within the grant of planning for an extension to the existing building. The extension was to involve the construction of a building in the area of the courtyard at the front of the existing building and the construction of a boiler house and fire escape to the rear of the building.

Testing of the courtyard was by necessity limited to a trench inserted along its east side. A second test-trench was inserted along the open area at the rear of the building. Test-Trench 1 was positioned directly adjacent to the existing eastern site boundary wall. During the excavation of this trench what appeared to be a wall face became visible within the western side of the trench. The top of this wall was revealed at a depth of 1.1m below the surface, while the remaining depth of the visible wall face was *c*. 0.3m. A considerable amount of disturbance was noticed within the fill surrounding the wall, and the formation

level of the wall appeared to rest upon a brown, humic material containing flecks of charcoal, which may represent the original soil cover and which, in turn, rested upon a yellow/beige natural. However, no evidence of the date of the wall was uncovered.

Test-trench 2 was excavated to the rear of the existing building. It was aligned east–west and was 10m long. The stratigraphy in this trench consisted of rubble to a depth of 1.6m over the original topsoil, which had a depth of 0.9m. It appeared in places that the yellow natural was just beginning to appear at the base of the topsoil.

Monitoring was carried out of foundation trenches associated with the extension to the existing Employment Exchange, from 9 to 18 September 1998.

Three main foundation trenches were dug in the courtyard to the front of the existing building. In addition three box trenches were inserted along the east wall of the front part of the building, and some further box trenches were dug on the internal side of its northern wall. Trenches were dug to a depth of 2–2.5m.

Monitoring confirmed the existence of an old soil layer on the site, which consisted of a silty clay. It was organic in texture and contained occasional inclusions of minute fragments of wood, occasional fragments of charcoal and frequent inclusions of animal bone. The absence of modern inclusions within this material was striking, for it was overlain directly by modern rubble. The foundations of the existing building lay upon this layer and had not truncated it. This soil layer extended over the entire area of the courtyard to the front of the existing building and was generally *c*. 1m deep. It was particularly deep and undisturbed at the southern end and was also found to extend inside the building.

A number of stone walls were encountered in the trench sections. The existence of at least one wall was already indicated during the initial testing of the site. Excavation of a trench along the street front indicated that this wall had not run precisely parallel to the existing site boundary but diverged westwards slightly.

Another wall (No. 2) was encountered in Trench 2. The upper surface of this wall was at a depth of 1m, directly beneath the rubble. This wall ran east–west across the site and could be seen to continue beneath the front part of the existing building. It was also visible in section in Trench 1, and it is probable, on this evidence, that it was functionally related to the wall that ran roughly parallel to the present site boundary. Wall No. 2 was composed of roughly cut and squared blocks of limestone and was 0.9m thick. On its southern side a foundation cut could be seen, indicating that the wall, as observed, represented the foundation courses. These walls may represent relatively late structural walls; several structures are shown on the site on the 1st edition OS map.

At certain places within the trenches layers of a coloured, ashy substance were noticed, varying from light yellow to red. This material appeared to be in some way related to the old soil layer in that it always occurred directly beneath, within or over the soil layer. It was particularly extensive along the street front, where it occurred as a deep layer along the northern face of Trench 3, directly on top of the soil layer. Its presence within and above the old soil layer suggests a domestic origin, and it may represent spreads of ash from domestic fires.

A foundation trench and foundation base were excavated for the structures to the rear of the existing building. Monitoring of these proved that the layer of modern topsoil identified during testing extended to the depth of the natural at 2.5m beneath the existing ground level. There were no intervening layers.

Further monitoring of groundworks associated with this development is to take place in 1999.
Clare Mullins, 39 Kerdiff Park, Monread, Naas, Co. Kildare.

653. CHURCH AVENUE/PEARSE STREET, MULLINGAR
Post-medieval
98E0209
Archaeological work took place in Mullingar at two elongated sites running back from Pearse Street, formerly Main Street, and originally the main spinal road of the town. One (Site A) was a former supermarket that, before demolition, had a 19th-century facade and fabric and stood on the corner with Church Avenue. The second part of the site (Site B) had a 19th-century shop-cum-dwelling-house and early to mid-19th-century features. It also had some fine early 19th century panelling and wainscoting.

Eight areas were excavated in Site A, and a further nine in Site B. Excavation was initially carried out using a mechanical digger, and then areas were hand-dug and cleaned. The main archaeological features found were a series of pits and a spread of dark, organic soils that was generally found between 19th-century and modern builders' rubble and natural undisturbed deposits. The pits and spread contained 17th-century clay pipes, post-medieval bottles and ceramics, along with organic deposits containing large quantities of wood (branches, cut and shaped pieces, some sawn-off cuts and a deposit of twigs and reeds). In 1826 the OS 1:2500 map shows a saw-pit on the opposite site of the road in Church Avenue. The organic deposits excavated are clearly earlier than this, but one wonders if there was a saw-pit there previously, in the 17th century. Generally, however, saw-pits did not come into use until the 18th century in most places.

The ceramics included portion of a Westerwald chamber-pot, post-medieval smoothware, Buckley-type ware and plain, white, tin-glazed wares. These were found along with heavy, bulbous, thick-based glass bottles.

The most likely interpretation of the organic deposits in waterlogged contexts is that they represent domestic deposits made during the occupation of the site. That some of the deposits include a large amount of hazel and birch may suggest a link with some industrial activities. There were several tan-houses indicated in the Groove's survey of 1641.

By 1691 a rampart, as shown on the Richard's Map of the Williamite fortifications, seems to have been built diagonally across the site, and some of the bottles and pottery found may be as late as this period, although others are clearly some decades earlier.

Some time after the site was cleared of the fortifications the plots of lands involved seem to have been restored to their elongated 'burage plot-type' lengths.

Subsequent to the main monitoring work a cutting was made in Pearse Street for service trenches. No archaeological material survived in the trench.
Jim Higgins, 'St Gerards', 18 College Road, Galway.

654. DOMINIC STREET, MULLINGAR
Organic deposit
24300 25200
98E0037
Monitoring was carried out when a trench was dug along the pavement on the north side of Dominic Street. For most of its length the ground had been extensively disturbed by pipes and cables running out from the houses.

At the eastern end of the trench, near the junction with Mary Street, the trench ran southwards to meet an existing trench further out in the road. About 1.5m out from the kerb an organic deposit was found at a depth of 1m. No artefacts were found in this layer, but the presence of certain seed and nut remains, including cultivated flax seeds and bolls, suggested that it was composed of occupation debris. The date of this deposit is not known.
Thaddeus C. Breen, 13 Wainsfort Crescent, Dublin 6W, for Valerie J. Keeley Ltd.

655. 28 DOMINICK STREET, MULLINGAR
Urban medieval
N434532
98E0146
Three trenches tested this long, narrow site, at the west end of the medieval town. Trench 1, at the Dominick Street end, produced evidence of a pit or ditch terminal, 4m wide on its north–south axis and 1m deep. There were two layers of fill; the upper was a clay fill that produced two sherds of late 18th-century pottery, and the lower comprised silt with a high content of twigs and vegetable matter but no finds. While the date of this feature was not clear, a late 18th- or 19th-century date was suggested.

A survey of the standing building was also carried out before demolition and reconstruction behind the original facade. There was no evidence to suggest that the building was earlier than 19th century in date.
Rosanne Meenan, Roestown, Drumree, Co. Meath.

656. FRIARS HILL ROAD, MULLINGAR
Urban
98E0153
The site is well outside the medieval town walls of Mullingar. No buildings were present along much of the length of the road apart from two rectangular buildings adjoining the pound, which feature on a map of the area from 1858. The vast majority of the buildings that now flank the street are clearly of late 19th-century date.

Archaeological monitoring was carried out over seven days. An east-west-running trench was machine-dug for pipe-laying to an average depth of 0.72m and width of 0.7m. The total length of the trench was 210m. The trench was found to contain no intact archaeological deposits. The area had been dug previously and was riddled with sewage and water pipes, electricity wires etc. The fill of the trench consisted of gravel and stone beneath the modern surface. The only finds were 19th- and 20th-century fragments of glazed pottery, two pieces of late clay pipes and bottle glass.

Jim Higgins, 'St Geralds', 18 College Road, Galway.

657. LYNNBURY TERRACE, MULLINGAR
Urban medieval
369200 184032
98E0275

Archaeological assessment took place at a proposed school development at Lynnbury Terrace, Mullingar, Co. Westmeath. The site lies within the area of the medieval town. Three trenches were excavated across the site and revealed sod, ploughsoil and a sandy, grey, natural clay with frequent stones. No archaeological features or objects were recovered.

Donald Murphy, Archaeological Consultancy Services Ltd, 15 Trinity Street, Drogheda, Co. Louth.

658. McCURTAIN STREET, MULLINGAR
Urban medieval
244071 253093
98E0084

Archaeological assessment took place at McCurtain Street, Mullingar, Co. Westmeath, in advance of the instalment of a new foul sewer pipe. One trench was excavated, and natural gravel was exposed at 0.5m below the surface. The existence of burials at 0.7m below gravel on the north of the street may suggest that some of this was redeposited. It was excavated to 1m without evidence of human remains, and the sewer trench was restricted to 0.6m deep.

Deirdre Murphy, Archaeological Consultancy Services Ltd, 15 Trinity Street, Drogheda, Co. Louth.

659. 11–13 OLIVER PLUNKETT STREET, MULLINGAR
Urban medieval
N437530
98E0521

Supervision of the excavation of seven pads was required by planning permission; this was for an extension to the back of the AIB premises on Oliver Plunkett Street. The stratigraphy was constant throughout the site. It had been disturbed at the east where a previous extension was constructed on a raft and a deposit of sand and hard-core had been laid down as a base.

The stratigraphy comprised _c._ 7m of building and demolition rubble, brick, slate etc. in a matrix of loose, black clay. Underlying that was a loose, grey garden clay deposit, _c._ 1m deep. This layer did not produce finds, but there was no evidence to indicate that it had archaeological significance. The grey, garden clay layer bottomed on to yellow, natural boulder clay. No material of archaeological significance was observed.

Rosanne Meenan, Roestown, Drumree, Co. Meath.

WEXFORD

660. ADAMSTOWN
Adjacent to ecclesiastical site
SMR 31:23
98E0384

The property lay in close proximity to recorded ecclesiastical remains. Assessment in the form of test-trenches was requested as a planning condition for a dwelling-house and garage. Test-trenches to assess the presence of archaeological material were commensurate with the locations of the foundations of both the house and garage. Additional trenches were dug within the area of the proposed well bore, on the line of the driveway and also for the sewer line. Seventeen trenches were opened. There were no indications of archaeological material within the designated areas.

Cathy Sheehan, Hillview, Aglish, Carrigeen, South Kilkenny.

661. BALLYANNE
Medieval settlement
27460 13120
98E0137

Monitoring of groundworks for a bungalow was carried out at Ballyanne in response to a planning condition on 6 April 1998. The site lies _c._ 5 km north of New Ross, directly across the road from Ballyanne parish church and graveyard (SMR 29:2) and falls within the zone of archaeological potential for that site.

In situ burning and a few structural features, associated with 12th–14th-century pottery, were uncovered during monitoring, and groundworks were stopped.

Whilst the archaeological preservation was generally disappointing, a 3m-wide band of archaeological material survived running east–west across the site of the proposed house, between areas of cultivation.

A possible drip-gully, post-holes, flooring and associated pottery suggested that a medieval house once stood on the site, before being largely removed by agricultural activity. The drip-gully is likely to have followed the line of a house wall, but the post-holes did not appear to have supported the same structure.

A test-pit in the area of a proposed sump to the north-west of the house identified a layer of redeposited clay (possible flooring) overlying an early soil. Preservation appears to be better north-west of the house site and in the adjoining two properties.

Jo Moran and assistants, 33 Woodlawn, Cashel, Co. Tipperary.

662. COURTOWN
No archaeological significance
T195545
98E0341

The inspection of engineering test-trenches and pits along the proposed route of the Courtown Drainage Scheme was carried out under archaeological supervision. The monitoring of the site investigations forms part of the mitigation arising from the Environmental Impact Survey prepared by Markus Casey.

Courtown is a former medieval borough occupied during the 13th and 14th centuries and apparently deserted thereafter; its precise location is unknown. A motte and bailey (SMR 12:10) and graveyard (SMR 12:9) lie in the townland of Middletown. It is likely that these surviving monuments represent the site of the medieval borough. Before the Anglo-Norman invasion Courtown was known as 'Killellin', suggesting that it was the location of a pre-Norman ecclesiastical establishment, the site of which is likely to correspond to the graveyard (SMR 12:9). The only SMR site recorded close to the route is a cross-slab (SMR 12:6). References to Courtown as 'Killellin' in medieval documents indicate that a pre-Norman ecclesiastical site was replaced by a manor to which the name 'court' was applied.

The topography is a low-lying, undulating alluvial drift including some shell, sands and gravels. The area is now drained by the Aughboy River to the south, the Owenavaragh River to the north and other small streams. Rock is commonly found at depths of 5–6m or more below present ground level.

Fourteen geotechnical test-pits were inspected at the request of the local authority and design team. No archaeological inclusions were noted. The topsoil excavated was typically 25mm–300mm deep, and beneath this was a virtually stone-free silt with occasional lenses of sandy gravel. In general the water table lay *c*. 3m below present ground level. Many of the pits, excavated to depth of up to 3.8–4m, did not reach the water table.

Five trenches, measuring 5m x 1.2m, were opened, removing topsoil, ostensibly for archaeological purposes (as advised in the Environmental Impact Survey). The topsoil depth was similar to that noted in the geotechnical test-pits, and the silty soil beneath it displayed no archaeological indicators whatsoever. The discovery of a glacial relict deposit of gravel with a high, well-preserved wood content during the geotechnical investigation (to the south of our nominated study area) is of considerable interest from a palaeoenvironmental point of view.

The lack of archaeological material in the pits inspected in no way precludes the possibility that features will be revealed during construction after topsoil removal. An opportunity to take samples of the buried organic gravel deposit for dating and palaeoenvironmental study may be sought in the event that excavation during construction reveals the deposit again. Archaeological monitoring will remain a requirement.

Edmond O'Donovan, Margaret Gowen & Co. Ltd, 2 Killiney View, Albert Road Lower, Gleanageary, Co. Dublin.

663. MURPHY-FLOOD'S HOTEL, IRISH STREET, ENNISCORTHY

Urban medieval
2973 1398
98E0120

The proposed redevelopment was subject to an archaeological condition in the planning permission. Archaeological testing was required before site preparation works. This was carried out on 13 March 1998. The property lies in the medieval town of Enniscorthy *c*. 150m to the north-west of the castle. The development consisted of a two-storey building with a reduced yard surface, an extension of an existing basement and the insertion of a stairwell.

Two trenches were excavated on the footprint of the development. In Trench 1 boulder clay was recorded at 12.781m OD. A north–south retaining wall was exposed at the eastern end of the excavation. The foundation trench was cut through boulder clay. A second east–west wall was exposed, which corresponded to a demolished storehouse. A layer up to 0.5m deep of fine-grained, brown silt containing red brick, mortar, sherds of glass, glazed red earthenware and a clay pipe stem overlay boulder clay.

In Trench 2 boulder clay occurred at *c*. 13.949m OD. Internal layers associated with the storehouse were exposed; beyond the storehouse wall the strata were the same as in Trench 1. No layers of archaeological significance were exposed during the investigation. The drop in the level in the boulder clay across the site is consistent with the natural fall of ground.

Sarah McCutcheon, Brook Lodge, Bandon, Co. Cork.

664. PARNELL (LEMINGTON) ROAD, ENNISCORTHY

No archaeological significance
SMR 20:31
98E0264

Test excavation took place at a site on the western end of Parnell Road (also known as Lemington Road), Enniscorthy (at the rear of 20 Weafer Street), on 15 June 1998. The site lies just outside of and to the west of the zone of archaeological potential for Enniscorthy town.

The site is in an elevated position on a fairly steeply sloping hill (downhill to north) and would command a good view in most directions but for surrounding buildings. It had been part of a farm complex in the relatively recent past, and a number of sheds stood on it until recently. It could be seen that the site had been levelled out to do this, as a cutaway section was evident on the southern (uphill) side. Nothing of interest was noted in the section, where the topsoil layer was *c*. 0.3m deep.

Three test-trenches were opened; a long one (Trench A) running east–west and two shorter (Trenches B and C) running north–south, B being 8.8m from the western boundary of the site, and C being 10.8m from the eastern. Each trench was *c*. 1.06m wide.

At the western side of the site, where outbuildings formerly stood, once their concrete floors and sub-floors were removed the yellow subsoil was immediately apparent. Elsewhere in this area only 0.15m of demolition rubble/topsoil covered the natural. Further eastward the subsoil was found at a greater depth, maximum 0.5m.

The only features encountered were two stone-filled land drains. One, *c*. 12m from the western end of the site, ran north–south and was found at a depth of 0.46m below present ground level. As the foundations of the proposed development will not exceed 0.33m it will not be disturbed in the construction. The second was found in Trench C, 1.8m from the southern boundary of the site, at a depth of 0.7m below present ground level. It ran east–west and again will not be disturbed by the development. A dump of small stones was encountered inside the gate at the eastern end of the site. These were probably put down to provide a solid base for machinery entering the yard.

Nothing of archaeological significance was found on this excavation.

Isabel Bennett, Glen Fahan, Ventry, Tralee, Co. Kerry.

665. FERNS/FERNS DEMESNE/FERNS UPPER/ FERNS LOWER

Medieval and post-medieval town and vicinity of abbey

30210 14973 and 30261 14913
SMR 15:3 and 15:4
98E0132

During late March and April 1998 a licence was held to undertake pre-construction testing in advance of pipe-laying on the Ferns Sewerage Scheme. Pipe-laying works commenced in February 1999. The purpose of the site testing was to determine the presence or absence of archaeological remains and to establish how the proposed construction works could affect any archaeological remains that might be uncovered.

Several areas were looked at in and around the village of Ferns. No testing was carried out in the centre of the village as the scheme will not go through there. The first area tested was *c.* 2 miles to the south-east of the village, in a rural setting. Trenches were opened in this area owing to the possible presence of a large, oval enclosure and possible field system (SMR 15:4) that had been identified by aerial photography. The possible enclosure measured *c.* 100m x 60m. It was identified in the centre of the field. The proposed route for the pipeline was some distance away from the possible site. However, nine test-trenches were opened to establish whether the proposed works could in any way impinge on the site. There was nothing of any archaeological significance found in the test-trenches.

The second area looked at was closer to Ferns, along an approach road into the village and inside the zone of archaeological potential for the village. This part of the pipeline route will sweep around the outside of the perimeter walls of St Aedan's graveyard. It is possible that stray architectural fragments and memorials associated with the graveyard will be encountered along this part of the pipeline route. In addition to St Aedan's graveyard, the Augustinian Abbey is sited *c.* 80m to the north of the pipeline route. Given the close proximity of this part of the route to the Abbey and to St Aedan's graveyard, it was decided to open sixteen test-trenches. All of the test-trenches were sited on the road. All were opened in sterile ground, and nothing of archaeological significance found in any of them.

A third part of the proposed pipeline route was tested. This area lay about half a mile to the north-east of the village. Though within a rural setting, it was partly within the zone of archaeological potential for the village of Ferns. Six test-trenches were opened in this area. However, testing was abandoned following the uncovering of archaeology. A recommendation was made to reroute the pipeline away from this area.

In one test-trench a relatively modern field drain was uncovered. In another no archaeology was uncovered. In the other four test-trenches archaeological remains were uncovered. They consisted of a series of linear cuts, possible post-holes and burnt spreads. A small amount of Bronze Age pottery was uncovered from the fills within the cuts. The archaeology was not excavated, and testing ceased. It was decided to reroute the pipeline away from this area.

Mary Henry, 1 Jervis Place, Clonmel, Co. Tipperary.

666. MAIN STREET, FERNS

Adjacent to castle

3021 1497
SMR 15:3
98E0273

Archaeological assessment of a site in Main Street (Castleland), Ferns, was carried out over two days in June 1998. The site lies immediately north of Ferns Castle and extends right up to the north-east tower. The proposed development would have been built virtually up against the ruined tower. Previous excavations by Sweetman (*PRIA* **79**C, 1979) had revealed a large fosse, mostly rock-cut, on the southern and eastern sides of the castle. Testing found that construction of the previous buildings on the site had removed all of the soils down to bedrock, a distance of 10m back from the street front. The bedrock drops sharply downwards here. This may be partly due to a sewer pipe running across the site along this area.

The other half of the site showed areas of disturbance, with much modern rubble present. The area closest to the north-east tower had been completely disturbed by the insertion of an engine pit from the mechanic's workshop that formerly stood there. This disturbance extended down to the bedrock, 1.43m below present ground level. This pit is built right up to where the edge of the north-east tower should be; however, no trace of this was found.

The south-western corner of the site produced the clearest evidence of archaeological activity. Here the bedrock dropped away quite sharply to a depth of almost 1.5m below ground level. Given that bedrock is *c.* 1m above ground level in the base of the north-east tower, this is a considerable drop in height and, taken with the position of the bedrock in the centre of the site, suggests that the fosse, already found on two sides of the castle, is present here also. There was 1m of fill in the fosse comprising varying brown, sandy and silty clays. All of these were sterile with the exception of the uppermost one, which produced two sherds of blackware. Sweetman found the fosse around the castle to be at its widest (6m) on its eastern side. No sign of a southern edge of the fosse was uncovered during the testing. The break in the bedrock where the sewer pipe crosses the site may be associated with a possible northern edge. If so, then the fosse would be at least 9m wide. It would also be shallower than that found on the eastern side of the castle. There it was at least 5m deep, here it is only 2–3m deep.

The layout of the development was altered as a result of the testing, with further monitoring of construction taking place.

Florence M. Hurley, 8 Marina Park, Victoria Road, Cork.

667. FETHARD-ON-SEA

No archaeological significance

27937 10502
98E0393

An assessment was carried out at the football field in Fethard before the grant of planning permission for the erection of a residential dormer bungalow. Fethard-on-sea is on the eastern side of the

Shelbourne Peninsula at the entrance to Bannow Bay, some 4km south of Duncannon. The placename is derived from *Fiodh Ard*, 'the high wood'. The Down Survey refers to the existence of two castles at Fethard, one of which can be identified as the existing structure, the other presumably being the episcopal castle first mentioned in a charter of *c.* 1200. An account of 1684 describes the town as having 'two or three small castles, a stone house, and also a brick house' (Hore, P.H. [1900–11] *History of the town and county of Wexford*, Vol. IV, 314).

Three trenches were opened by mechanical digger. All were identical in stratigraphy, consisting of topsoil over a light brown stony clay becoming more compact and stonier at a depth of 2.2m. There was no evidence of features/artefacts of an archaeological nature.

Helen Kehoe, 11 Norseman Place, Stoneybatter, Dublin 7.

668. TOWN CENTRE, GOREY
Urban post-medieval
T155598
SMR 77:33
98E0134

Archaeological monitoring of site investigation works, which preceded the Gorey Regional Water Supply Scheme, was carried out in Gorey town centre between 18 March and 8 April 1998. Fifty-eight narrow slit-trenches were excavated through the town centre and its environs, 28 of these were excavated within the zone of archaeological potential as identified in the Urban Survey, and sixteen of these were monitored.

Only two features of archaeological interest were revealed in the course the monitoring. The first occurred in Trench 9 along The Avenue and appeared to be the remains of a robbed-out wall associated with 18th-century pottery. The second feature occurred in Trench 13 along McDermot Street and consisted of the remains of a north-east/south-west-orientated drain, constructed of hand-made red bricks. The remainder of the stratigraphy in the trenches consisted of the tarmacadam road surface overlying hard-core and natural geology.

Rob Lynch, for Margaret Gowen & Co. Ltd, 2, Killiney View, Albert Road Lower, Gleanageary, Co. Dublin.

669. HAGGARDSTOWN
Zone of archaeological potential
SMR 47:15
98E0531

Owing to the close proximity of the development area to the site of a church and graveyard, *Dúchas* The Heritage Service recommended that archaeological testing be a condition of any planning permission granted.

Test-trenching was carried out on 11 and 12 November 1998. Ten mechanically excavated test-trenches were opened but failed to reveal any archaeological remains, either in the form of subsoil features or portable finds.

Dermot Nelis, Irish Archaeological Consultancy Ltd, 8 Dungar Terrace, Dun Laoghaire, Co. Dublin, for Archaeological Development Services Ltd.

670. KILLURIN
Possible enclosure site
SMR 32:25
98E0469

Archaeological test excavation of a proposed development site in Killurin Td, Enniscorthy, Co. Wexford, took place on 27 October 1998. The field, in the eastern half of which two houses have already been constructed, may be the location of an enclosure, picked up through aerial photography. This, however, was discounted when the site was inspected during fieldwork for the *Archaeological inventory of Co. Wexford*, and it is not included in that publication. It was proposed to put two further houses in the western half of the field (that portion tested under the current licence), and planning permission for the same had been granted to the landowner.

There was no visible sign on the ground of the presence of an enclosure. Two long trenches were opened by machine in the western portion of the field, one running north–south, the other east–west, extending the full length of the site. Nothing of archaeological interest, apart from some ploughmarks, was noted.

The only small finds were a sherd of modern china and another of the neck of a black glass bottle.

Isabel Bennett, Clen Fahan, Ventry, Tralee, Co. Kerry, for Mary Henry and Associates.

671. KILLURIN
Medieval graveyard
SMR 37:2
98E0422

Testing took place on the site of the proposed extension to the north of Killurin graveyard, Co. Wexford. The standing church at Killurin was built in *c.* 1800 (O'Flanagan 1933, vol. 1, 360) on the site of an earlier medieval parish church and graveyard.

Five test-trenches were opened in the area of the extension. Identical stratigraphy was uncovered in all the trenches. There was an initial deposit of dark topsoil with plant roots 0.1m thick. At 128.09m above sea level this gave way to a sandy, yellow/brown clay with some flecks of charcoal. This deposit was 0.8–1.2m thick and gave way between 127.29m and 126.89m above sea level to yellow boulder clay and shale bedrock.

Reference

O'Flanagan, M. 1933 *Letters containing information relative to the antiquities of the county of Wexford collected during the progress of the ordinance survey in 1840.* 2 vols. Bray.

Joanna Wren, The Mile Post, Waterford for Archaeological Development Services Ltd.

672. BALL ALLEY LANE, NEW ROSS
Medieval
2720 1275
98E0324

Six trenches were dug on the proposed site of two local authority houses. All but one were archaeologically sterile; the exception contained a lens of mid-brown soil within the shale, which yielded a single sherd of early medieval pottery.

Orla Scully, 7, Bayview, Tramore, Co. Waterford.

673. BISHOPSLAND, NEW ROSS
No archaeological significance
7230 2725
98E0140
Nothing of archaeological significance was found during testing at this site.
Orla Scully, 7, Bayview, Tramore, Co. Waterford.

674. PRIORY STREET, NEW ROSS
Urban medieval
271563 127129
SMR 29:13
98E0271
Test-trenching was carried out at the site of a proposed development in Priory Street, New Ross, on 9 June 1998, in response to a request for further information pending a formal decision on the planning application. The development site lies off Priory Street, within a large green-field area just inside the walled town, and is surrounded on the north, south and west by buildings. That part of the site fronting onto Priory Street is quite level for several metres in from the street, but beyond this point the ground slopes steeply uphill in conformity with the land on either side. It is possible that some levelling of the land along Priory Street took place in the 18th century, when most of the houses in the area appear to have been built.

Three test-trenches were dug by machine in the areas of greatest impact from the development. The results appear to confirm that some reduction of ground levels had already taken place in the area closest to the street. There was a considerable increase in the depth of topsoil towards the rear and on the western side of the site, and the occurrence of animal bone and medieval pottery within the deeper horizons of this topsoil, together with the apparent absence of post-medieval contamination within it, suggests that this area had undergone minimal disturbance. This may indicate that, while no structural remains were uncovered during the course of the archaeological evaluation, medieval or earlier soil horizons that preserve information of archaeological significance may remain undisturbed in parts of the site.

Archaeological monitoring of groundworks associated with the development was recommended.
Clare Mullins, 39 Kerdiff Park, Monread, Naas, Co. Kildare.

675. MAYGLASS, POLLWITCH
18th-century earthen farmhouse
T019110
98E0587
The Heritage Council has recently approved an extensive conservation programme for an earthen farmhouse in Mayglass. Before the commencement of the project it was necessary to erect a temporary protective structure over the body of the main building. This consisted of a standard, open-sided, six-pillar barn. In order to ensure the stability of the structure the pillars were set into concrete foundation blocks to the front and rear of the dwelling-house. In order to accommodate the concrete blocks three pits were excavated to the rear of the house.

Within two of these garden soil was found to overlie boulder clay. The third pit revealed a previous ground surface level (possibly relating to the alterations to the eastern portion of the house) that underlay a band of redeposited boulder clay. This redeposited layer was in turn covered by topsoil. To the front of the house the foundation blocks were placed on the existing ground surface with a minimum removal of topsoil. To the north-east of the house, after the removal of c. 0.11m of topsoil, a linear arrangement of undressed stones representing the basal level of a drain or gully was exposed. This feature post-dates the alterations to the eastern section of the house.
Cathy Sheehan, Hillview, Aglish, Carrigeen, South Kilkenny.

676. SALVILLE
Adjacent to motte and boulder burial
98E0326
A development site for which first outline and then full planning permission was granted had a detailed condition relating to the potential archaeology of the site, in view of its position between two known monuments, SMR 26:14, a boulder burial, and 26:15, a motte. Although archaeological testing was a requirement of the permission, the development went ahead without any testing or monitoring taking place until this test excavation was carried out on 29 July 1998.

The site slopes very steeply to south, above a small stream that flows into the Slaney, only a short distance to the west. It has been substantially altered to provide a level platform on which the house was constructed, at the northern end of the site, and a smooth slope to the south, rather than the stepped one there previously. Inspection of the boundary along the western edge of the site also indicated that the ground level had been reduced in that immediate area to below subsoil level.

Neither the motte nor the boulder burial is visible from the site, although if the motte were less overgrown it might be possible to make it out.

At the extreme northern end of the site the original ground level was lowered by between 1.3m (at the eastern end) and 1.7m (at the western end) to provide a level platform for the house. But in front of it the ground was built up.

Given the severely altered nature of the ground it was difficult to find any original ground level left undisturbed, especially as the site was now covered with drawn-in topsoil and a lawn planted. Two trenches were dug, but nothing was found that was consistent with an original ground level, with only stony, redeposited topsoil encountered until the subsoil was reached, at an average depth of 0.4m or less.

Nothing of an archaeological nature was found.
Isabel Bennett, Glen Fahan, Ventry, Tralee, Co. Kerry, for Mary Henry and Associates.

677. MAIN STREET, TAGHMON
Vicinity of Early Christian and medieval sites
291857 119649
98E0483
An archaeological evaluation was carried out at a site at Main Street, Taghmon, Co. Wexford, on 15 and 16 October 1998. An archaeological assessment report had already been carried out on the site in

response to a request for further information from the Planning Authority. Some existing modern buildings were to be retained as store houses during construction, and therefore a two-phase plan for testing the site was agreed. Four SMR sites lie a short distance outside the eastern boundary of the site. These range in date from the Early Christian period to the Anglo-Norman. The site is bordered to the north and west by the gardens of street-frontage properties and to the the south by pastureland. The site was in recent years used as a cattle mart and was a traditional market site before that. The placename is derived from the Irish *Teach Munnu*, 'the house (church) of Munnu', the eponym in the name referring to St Fintan Munna, who founded a church in Taghmon and died in AD 636.

Eight test-trenches were inserted along four trench lines. Three of these were positioned along the lines of the proposed houses, while one was placed across an earthen bank at the southern end of the site. The topsoil had been stripped from much of the site in living memory, and this was apparent in the absence of a topsoil horizon across the northern and north-western areas of the site. A deep layer of gritty gravel (hard-core), which lay directly beneath the sod, was observed where topsoil was absent and represented an imported material that had been spread over the site as part of its preparation for use as a mart.

The test-trenches were generally dug to a depth of 0.8–1m. Over most of the site the natural was quite close to the surface, occurring at a depth of about 0.5m below the present ground surface.

Nine features of archaeological significance were identified. These occurred over the general area defined by the test-trenches but most were concentrated in the northern and north-western parts of the site. They consisted of localised cuts into the natural that contained charcoal-rich fills, as well as a number of possible ditch features that were filled with materials of a highly organic composition. In one case an additional test-trench, which had not formed part of the original testing strategy, was inserted to test the assumption that one of these features represented a ditch. The occurrence of a feature of similar proportions and composition a few metres to the north-east was taken as an indication that a linear feature was represented.

In view of the fact that the site had been heavily disturbed during the construction of the cattle mart and that this event resulted in the truncation of the archaeological features, a programme of monitoring of all groundworks associated with the development was recommended.

Monitoring of foundation trenches along the northern end of the site proceeded in December 1998. The results indicated the presence of at least two separate ditch features that run roughly north-west to south-east through the northern end of the site. These ditches appear to be parallel and possibly follow a concentric curve, with the westernmost ditch being the more substantial of the two. The fills of these ditches are complexly layered and organic matter, e.g. timber fragments, hazelnut shells and leaves, occurs as a frequent inclusion within the fill of the westernmost ditch; this ditch also contained timber planks within its basal layer. The remains of two substantial timber posts were also found near these ditches. The excavation and removal of these posts necessitated the extension of the foundation trenches. Some discrete charcoal-rich features were also found during this monitoring phase both in between and beyond the ditch features referred to above.

Further monitoring of groundworks, together with some open-plan excavation, is to take place in 1999.
Clare Mullins, 39 Kerdiff Park, Monread, Naas, Co. Kildare.

678. 13 THE FAYTHE, WEXFORD
No archaeological significance
SMR 37:32
96E0013
This development was a continuation of site works that commenced in January 1996. As The Faythe lies within the zone of archaeological importance for the town of Wexford the site was tested in accordance with the planning directive. In 1996 sixteen pits were opened. There were no indications of archaeological material.

The street frontage was unavailable for testing owing to the presence of standing buildings, consequently in January 1998 an extension to the licence was obtained to monitor the insertion of service trenches. Two distinct horizons were present. A rubble and silt fill overlay a basal layer of naturally deposited sand. The fill had been introduced in order to level the site, the original contours of which sloped downwards from east to west.
Cathy Sheehan for Archaeological Development Services Ltd, Windsor House, 11 Fairview Strand, Fairview, Dublin 3.

679. GEORGE'S STREET UPPER, WEXFORD
No archaeological significance
T045218
98E0329
Before redevelopment the site, which fronts onto George's Street Upper, was archaeologically tested in accordance with the planning directive. The property lies 110m west of the medieval town walls and is also adjacent to the priory precinct of St Selskar's and the site of St John's church and graveyard.

Test-trenching revealed 20th-century infill overlying boulder clay and gravel. There were no indications of stratigraphy or material of an archaeological nature.
Cathy Sheehan, Archaeological Development Services Ltd, Windsor House, 11 Fairview Strand, Fairview, Dublin 3.

680. KING STREET UPPER, WEXFORD
Viking Age (?)/urban medieval
301621 121368
98E0419
Trial-trenching was undertaken at a proposed development site adjacent to Nos 20–22 King Street Upper, Wexford, on 24 September 1998. The work was undertaken in compliance with a request from The National Monuments Service and commissioned by the developers.

The site lies in the south-western area of Wexford, outside but close to the line of the Scandinavian and later Anglo-Norman defences of the town. The site of the late 12th-century Norman castle, itself possibly constructed on the site of a Scandinavian fortress, is nearby. Furthermore, the development site lies between the churches of St Brigid and St Michael, around which, it is believed, were suburban settlements in Anglo-Norman and possibly Scandinavian times.

Three trenches were excavated by machine in order to determine the nature and extent of any features or deposits of archaeological interest that might exist within the boundaries of the site. In general, it appears that the ground level was raised at some time in the past because of flooding, an occurrence still prevalent in the area. The basal layer of silt was probably laid down as a result of such flooding episodes in the past. However, investigation of this material did not reveal any items that would aid in dating the layer, and it is unclear whether it is of archaeological interest. Indeed, the sterile nature of the material indicates that it is not.

Given that no features, structures or finds of archaeological interest were uncovered during the course of the evaluation it was recommended that no further archaeological involvement at the site was required.

Martin E. Byrne, 39 Kerdiff Park, Monread, Naas, Co. Kildare.

681. ROWE STREET, WEXFORD
Urban medieval
98E0350

The site lies within St Iberius Parish, Wexford town, just outside the western line of the existing town wall. East of the site, on Main Street, is the possible site of an intra-mural gate, just north of St Iberius Church (Hore 1910–11, 284). Mary Street to the south was probably the site of 'Fryers Gate' mentioned in 1663 (*ibid.*, 350). Outside this gate, south-west of the site, is the Franciscan Friary that was built on the site of a Templar's graveyard in 1230 (*ibid.*, 82). The church was set on fire in 1532, and much of the present church was built in 1689, but the modern building includes parts of the medieval friary.

The proposed development was for offices for *The People* newspapers. Eight trenches were opened revealing a deposit of dump material and garden soil, 1.3–2.2m thick, dating from the 19th and 20th centuries, which seemed to cover most of the site. In all the trenches opened this material was directly above the natural subsoil. It is possible that much of the 19th-century material was deposited when Rowe Street church was built. The later material seems to have accumulated when the site was left open over time. Repeated levelling of mounds of dump material has taken place within the site over the last thirty years. One trench opened at the foot of the town wall showed that the wall continued below the modern ground surface for 1.3m, where it appeared to rest directly on the boulder clay. It was constructed of rough-coursed limestone and red sandstone boulders, mortar bonded.

Reference
Hore, P.H. (ed.) 1900–11 *History of the town and county of Wexford*, vol. IV.

Joanna Wren, The Mile Post, Waterford for Archaeological Development Services Ltd.

682. WEXFORD MAIN DRAINAGE
Urban
95E0254

Archaeological monitoring of the Wexford Main Drainage Scheme continued into early 1998.

Skeffington Street
There were no indications of archaeological material within the trench limits. The stratigraphic profile revealed estuarine deposits underlying post-medieval and early modern infill.

North Main Street
During street landscaping works (pavement setting, insertion of lamp-posts etc.) a large pit was excavated immediately to the north of No. 54 North Main Street (adjacent to the property boundary with No. 58). This lay 0.57m from the shop frontage and extended into the street for a distance of 0.84m. Archaeological stratigraphy was recorded at *c.* 1.26m below the path surface. This consisted of an organic silt layer underlying a mixed deposit of gravel, shell and sand. The profile is consistent with previous results for this street, which indicate that during the medieval period the area was sea front and subject to tidal inundation.

The Bullring
Alterations to the square at The Bullring (insertion of paving, benches etc.) and remedial work on the existing sewer line revealed no archaeological material.

Cathy Sheehan, Archaeological Development Services, Windsor House, 11 Fairview Strand, Fairview, Dublin 3.

WICKLOW

683. ARKLOW BYPASS
Various
97E0083

Archaeological monitoring of topsoil-stripping on the route of the Arklow Bypass in former tillage fields north of Arklow resulted in the discovery of three sites.

Site 1, N176223
A small area of dark, charcoal-like material that lay 0.23m below the original surface of the ground in sandy, red-brown soil. No other material was associated with this deposit.

Site 2, N176155
This consisted of a deposit of charcoal associated with a scatter of cremated bone. It was in a layer of sandy, brown and reddish brown soil and appeared to have been partially protected by three relatively small field stones. The main deposit measures 0.5m north–south by 0.44m and is a maximum of 0.2m deep. It was apparent that this material, which originally lay *c.* 0.3m below the original ground surface, has suffered interference as a result of soil-stripping machines moving over the site as some of the charcoal and cremated bone had been spread northwards over a distance of some 4.5m.

Site 3, N176075
This was initially identified as an area of light grey

soil within which were sherds of decorated pottery. Cleaning showed that there were three separate pits present, as well as a larger, linear spread.

Pit A (diameter 0.9m, maximum depth 0.3m) contained a circular deposit of black clay and numerous sherds of pottery, charcoal and a fragment of bone. Six large stones were set around the north-eastern edge of the pit.

Pit B (0.9m north–south by 1m, depth 0.35m) contained numerous sherds of pottery, charcoal and some flints.

Pit C (diameter 0.7m, depth 0.4m) contained sherds of pottery, charcoal and flint, as well as fragments of burnt bone in the upper levels. At a lower level sherds of pottery and charcoal were found but no flint fragments. Five large stones were set around the edge of this feature.

Pit D (diameter 0.48m, depth 0.2m) had a matrix of mid-brown/yellow, redeposited sand containing two fragments of flint and occasional fragments of charcoal. A suggestion has been made that this may have been dug to hold a form of marker by which to position the other three pits.

In excess of fifty sherds of pottery and over thirty flakes of flint, half of which were worked, were found in Pits A–C. Examination of the deposits in the pits suggests that there were two separate deposits in each pit. It was clear from the position of the pottery fragments that the vessels had been broken in antiquity; the potsherds are identifiable as being of Beaker and food vessel type. As there was no evidence to suggest the former presence of an associated earthwork the site may be regarded as a flat cemetery.

Breandán Ó Riordáin, Burgage More, Blessington, Co. Wicklow, for Valerie J Keeley Ltd.

684. SOUTH QUAY, ARKLOW
Urban medieval
325858 173440
98E0187

Archaeological assessment took place at a proposed residential development at South Quay, Arklow, Co. Wicklow. Two trenches were dug. Trench 1 was 88m long, 1m wide and 2m deep. At the south end of the trench was a black, organic layer, 0.3m thick, containing 19th-century pottery. It sat on natural estuarine gravels. At the north end a layer of red brick rubble overlay the natural gravel.

Donald Murphy, Archaeological Consultancy Services Ltd, 15 Trinity Street, Drogheda, Co. Louth.

685. BALLINABARNEY
Monastic site
31408 18878
SMR 29:4
98E0448

Archaeological monitoring was carried out on this site, in advance of the construction of a private dwelling, on 1–3 October 1998. The proposed dwelling was situated adjacent to the possible site of a monastery, known as Disirkeyvyn, founded by St Kevin of Glendalough. No features of archaeological significance were identified in the course of monitoring.

Rob Lynch, Irish Archaeological Consultancy Ltd, 8 Dungar Terrace, Dun Laoghaire, Co. Dublin.

686. BALLYNATTIN
Prehistoric enclosure
32332 17114
98E0257

The site was discovered during archaeological monitoring, by Sarah McCutcheon, of topsoil removal from a 14m-wide corridor designed to provide access and services for a new industrial park development by the IDA, close to the new Arklow Bypass. It appeared under the topsoil as a band (c. 0.4m wide) of charcoal and burnt clay enclosing a rectangular area.

Excavation revealed the enclosing element to be a trench ranging from 0.34m to 0.44m wide and from 0.04m to 0.2m deep, enclosing a rectangular area measuring c. 14m east–west x 8m. The trench was U-shaped in profile with near-vertical sides. The enclosure had rounded corners, and, although little survives of the east side owing to disturbance by a modern field fence, this side appears to have been curved rather than straight. The entrance to the enclosure was in the south side and was 1.35m wide. A circular cut (diameter 0.27m, depth 0.09m) on the east side of the entrance is likely to be the base of a post-hole.

The fill of the trench consisted of a soft, light brown soil with charcoal concentrations of varying densities and numerous patches of burnt, ashy material. Numerous fragments of burnt wood of small diameter were found, suggesting the presence of twigs, such as might have been used in a post-and-wattle fence. Charcoal concentrations were most dense at the east end of the south side and midway along the north side, where the trench was at its deepest. In these areas the charcoal layer was c. 0.05m thick and was underlain by a 0.1m-thick layer of greyish, silty soil.

The amount of charcoal and burning present suggests that the trench held a wooden palisade that burnt down. The presence of only one post-hole, that at the east side of the entrance, suggests that the trench may have contained a sill-beam in which posts were set that have now decayed without trace.

One sherd of pottery and numerous pieces of flint were recovered, and, while none of these was definitively diagnostic, they suggest a late prehistoric date, possibly Bronze Age.

Eamonn Cotter, Ballynanelagh, Rathcormac, Co. Cork.

687. PRESENTATION COLLEGE, NEWCOURT, BRAY
Unknown
O270176
98E0022

A feature of possible archaeological interest was observed in a field that was the site of a proposed housing development. It consisted of a flat area enclosed by what appeared to be a circular ditch, c. 12m in diameter. A single hand-dug trench was cut through the feature, revealing that the ground level had been raised by the introduction of modern fill, and the ditch may instead have been a short surviving section of the ditch of a long-demolished field fence.

Rosanne Meenan, Roestown, Drumree, Co. Meath.

688. CARRICKMINES–BRAY GAS PIPELINE, FASSAROE/ KILBRIDE/ KILCRONEY/ WINGFIELD/HOLLYBROOK/BALLYWALTRIN
Wedge tomb, *fulachta fiadh*

98E0445
Please see report No. 125.
John Ó Néill, for Margaret Gowen & Co. Ltd, 2 Killiney View, Albert Road Lower, Glenageary, Co. Dublin.

689. MARKET SQUARE, DUNLAVIN
Urban medieval
SMR 15:16
287138 201662
98E0547
An archaeological evaluation was carried out at a site in Dunlavin, Co. Wicklow, on 21 November 1998. Planning permission had been granted for the construction of two small blocks of apartments to the rear of the gardens associated with the buildings that front onto Market Square. An archaeological condition within the grant of planning had requested archaeological testing of the site following demolition and in advance of construction works.

It was clear from the general appearance of the development site that it had long been in use for yards and outbuildings. Several old stone outbuildings are still extant in the general area, and the lower courses of the walls of other buildings, which have been demolished, exist in the immediate vicinity of the development site.

Two test-trenches were inserted, one each across the approximate central longitudinal axis of each of the proposed apartment blocks.

A number of features were identified during the course of test-trenching. A stone-and-mortar wall, which crossed the line of Trench 1 at a right angle, was 0.3–0.4m wide. It could be seen to rest directly upon the natural and survived to a height of only 0.2m. The other stone wall appeared to be more substantial but had been obscured by what was probably a modern stone sump to its immediate south-west. While a number of dilapidated stone walls and extant stone buildings exist in the immediate area of the development site, neither of these stone walls appeared to be associated with any of the existing walls. Another feature identified during testing may represent a medieval drain that led from the street front *c.* 70m to the south-east. The general impression from this feature was of a U-shaped linear cut. It had a minimum depth of 0.5m beneath the surface of the natural. Its fill produced animal bone, red brick, timber fragments and charcoal. These inclusions would most likely date the obsolescence of the feature.

Archaeological monitoring was recommended for the groundworks stage of the development.
Clare Mullins, 39 Kerdiff Park, Monread, Naas, Co. Kildare.

690. MARKET SQUARE, DUNLAVIN
Urban medieval
SMR 15:16
287138 201662
98E0547 ext.
Monitoring of foundation works associated with the construction of a block of holiday homes was undertaken on 23 December 1998. The work was carried out in compliance with a request from NMHPS, *Dúchas* The Heritage Service, following the submission of an archaeological evaluation report, prepared by Clare Mullins, in respect of the

development (No. 689 above).

Four features were uncovered during the course of the work, an earth-cut drain, a wall foundation and a soakage pit with an associated stone-lined drain. All but the latter feature had previously been identified during the course of the initial trial-trenching. No material was recovered that might aid in the dating of these features, and they may be post-medieval in origin.

One sherd of medieval pottery was recovered from the soakage pit but its association with relatively later material indicated that it was probably a stray find.

Further monitoring will take place during January 1999.
Martin E. Byrne, 39 Kerdiff Park, Monread, Naas, Co. Kildare.

691. REDFORD PARK, RATHDOWN, GREYSTONES
Medieval
97E0075 ext.
Archaeological monitoring of the placement of two ESB poles and associated stay-wires was carried out in October 1998, adjacent to St Crispen's Cell (SMR 8:12). Nothing of archaeological significance was identified during the monitoring.
Una Cosgrave, Archaeological Development Services Ltd, Windsor House, 11 Fairview Strand, Fairview, Dublin 3.

692. LOTT LANE, KILCOOLE
Late medieval ironworking
98E0244
Archaeological monitoring was undertaken during the excavation of the foundations of a dwelling-house near a medieval church and graveyard (SMR 13:29). During monitoring an old field drain and archaeological remains, in the form of two isolated 'bowl' (or smelting) furnaces, were discovered at the east and north-west sides of the site respectively. The discovery of the furnaces was reported to *Dúchas*, and rescue excavation was decided upon. Two cuttings were opened and excavated.

The first furnace was tadpole-shaped in plan and was 2.3m long, 0.48m wide and 0.4m at its maximum depth. The second furnace was pear-shaped in plan and was 1.52m long, 0.56m wide and 0.26m at its maximum depth. In both cases the bowl and flue were filled with a charcoal-rich, dark grey clay loam. In the case of the first furnace the bowl was also backfilled with a number of burnt stones. At the base of both the bowls were thin lenses of crushed charcoal, on average 20mm thick, but no evidence of the intensive firing or baking of the clay, thus suggesting that the features were not reused over any great period of time.

The finds recovered from the fill included a number of small pieces of iron slag, a piece of burnt, glazed, medieval pottery, an animal tooth, a flint flake and a struck flint pebble. When taken in conjunction with the *terminus post quem* provided by the burnt sherd of pottery the simple form of the furnaces suggests a date somewhere between the 13th and 15th centuries.

In addition a small number of prehistoric flints were recovered from the cultivation soil. Including the flake and struck pebble from the furnace fill, ten

pieces altogether were found.
Emmet Byrnes for Archaeological Development Services Ltd, Windsor House, 11 Fairview Strand, Fairview, Dublin 3.

693. KILQUADE
Adjacent to church
32815 20850
98E0143
Testing was carried out in advance of a residential development immediately south and south-west of a recorded monument (SMR 13:21), classified as a church (possible site), from which the townland name, Kilquade (*Cill (mh)ic Uaid*, 'MacQuaid's church'), presumably derives. Alternatively, the element 'quade' may derive from *coimhéad*, a 'look-out or watching place'. The present church at Kilquade, St Patrick's RC church, is a modern building. There is no conclusive evidence of an early church here, although a chapel is shown on Nevill's map of the site of 1760. The Chancery Inquisition records a grant of a rent of Killecovat to the Earl of Kildare in 1523, and this appears to be the earliest historical mention of the name Kilquade. The only archaeological evidence of a pre-modern church in Kilquade is provided by a late medieval granite font with a five-sided recess into which a circular bowl is cut, at present standing outside the main door of the church. There are no pre-19th-century grave-slabs in the graveyard.

The area of the proposed development consisted of a roughly L-shaped plot of grazing land on a gentle, west-facing slope of a drumlin ridge and a poorly drained hollow extending north–south across the west edge of the site, which separates this ridge and an adjacent one to the west. Archaeological testing of the area was based on the assessment of six machine-dug trenches (each 10m long and 1m wide and on average 1m deep) excavated in April 1998. Three of the trenches (two east–west and one north–south) were excavated across the south of the site. Three further trenches (two east–west and one north–south) were excavated across the north of the site. Analysis of the six trenches indicated (by the occurrence of china sherds) that the topsoil had been disturbed by ploughing in the 19th century. The underlying subsoils had not been disturbed and consisted of a variety of glacially deposited clays and gravels.

No archaeological features or finds were found in any of the trenches. Therefore, if the current 19-century church at Kilquade is constructed on the site of a late medieval or perhaps an even earlier church it appears that activity associated with such a church did not extend beyond the present southern or south-western limits of the graveyard surrounding the modern church.
Christiaan Corlett, 88 Heathervue, Greystones, Co. Wicklow.

694. RATH EAST
Adjacent to hillfort
29055 17318
98E0495
Pre-development archaeological testing was carried out on this site, which is adjacent to Rathgall Hillfort (SMR 37:16) and is within 15m of a known hut site, Knockeen Enclosure (SMR 37:19). Potentially archaeologically significant deposits were identified

in three of the eleven trenches. These deposits took the form of infrequent charcoal flecking at the base of F2, a mid-brown, sandy loam. No datable material was recovered from this deposit. The deposit rested on natural subsoils.

The pre-development surface-stripping was subsequently monitored, and nothing of archaeological significance was identified.
Una Cosgrave, Archaeological Development Services Ltd, Windsor House, 11 Fairview Strand, Fairview, Dublin 3.

695. 1 MILTON VILLAS, CHURCH HILL, WICKLOW
No archaeological significance
T316940
98E0298
This archaeological testing took place on 8 July 1998. Three trenches were machine-excavated to undisturbed natural without encountering anything of archaeological significance.

The results suggest that the construction of the old house in 1896 removed any significant archaeology from the area. The ground to the north-east, currently grass covered, was once the site of an orchard. Severe tree-root disturbance exists in the area of the proposed development. Nonetheless, no significant archaeological deposits were noted. Modern layers lie on either till or sand.

Nothing of archaeological significance was uncovered during the assessment.
Eoin Halpin, Archaeological Development Services Ltd, Unit 48, Westlink Enterprise Centre, 30–50 Distillery Street, Belfast BT12 5BJ.

696. CHURCH HILL STREET, WICKLOW
Urban
331344 194029
98E0555
Excavation for the purpose of relaying a sewer pipe along the southern side of Church Hill Street, Wicklow, involved ground disturbance to a depth of *c.* 1m and width of 0.5m. As the development was within the area of archaeological potential for the town archaeological monitoring was carried.

Monitoring of *c.* 180m north-west/south-east revealed a made-ground layer associated with the road construction, sealing a mid-orange, silty, clay natural. A *c.* 0.5m-wide stone drain of probable post-medieval date was the only feature recorded, while finds from the made-ground layer include modern pottery.
Dermot Nelis, Irish Archaeological Consultancy Ltd, 8 Dungar Terrace, Dun Laoghaire, Co. Dublin.

697. 2 CHURCH STREET, WICKLOW
Urban
T31349402
98E0128
Archaeological monitoring of the excavation of strip foundations for a small extension to an existing office building at 2 Church Street, Wicklow, did not reveal any archaeological structures, features or deposits.

No further archaeological work is required in advance of this development.
James Eogan, Archaeological Development Services Ltd, Windsor House, 11 Fairview Strand, Fairview, Dublin 3.

698. CHURCH STREET/WENTWORTH PLACE, WICKLOW

Urban
29055 17318
98E0431

Pre-development archaeological testing was carried out on this site in September 1998. A potentially archaeologically significant deposit was identified. The deposit was light brown, fine, sandy clay with occasional charcoal flecking, which rested on natural and underlay post-medieval and modern disturbance. Further excavations would have to be carried out to ascertain the true nature of this deposit.
Una Cosgrave, Archaeological Development Services Ltd, Windsor House, 11 Fairview Strand, Fairview, Dublin 3.

699. CHURCH STREET/WENTWORTH PLACE, WICKLOW

Urban
98E0431

The development site lies at the corner of Church Street and Wentworth Place, Wicklow, and is within the zone of archaeological potential for the town. Recent excavations by James Eogan in an adjoining property (*Excavations 1997*, 202, 97E0118) identified a series of medieval pits and two shallow ditches.

Test-trenching was carried out by Una Cosgrave and involved the mechanical excavation of two trenches (No. 698 above). Limited archaeological deposits consisting of a light brown, fine, sandy clay with occasional charcoal flecking were recorded in both trenches. No datable material was recovered from this layer.

Given the identification of potentially significant deposits revealed during the test-trenching programme, *Dúchas* The Heritage Service recommended the archaeological monitoring of all further subsurface works.

Monitoring took place over two days and revealed the same formation processes of modern rubble and gravels sealing rubble layers containing red brick as identified in the test-trenching programme. The potentially archaeologically significant clay with occasional charcoal flecking was revealed in the north-eastern corner of the site. However, as excavation for foundation trenches only proceeded to a depth of *c.* 0.65m in this area, only the top 50mm of this layer was exposed. As this layer was only revealed in a 1m-long east–west foundation trench, it was not possible to define fully its extent, character and condition. There would be no further disturbance caused to this layer by the development. No datable material was recovered, and no further archaeological features or finds were revealed.
Dermot Nelis, Irish Archaeological Consultancy Ltd, 8 Dungar Terrace, Dun Laoghaire, Co. Dublin, for Archaeological Development Services Ltd.

DUBLIN

AD1. ORCHARD LANE/THE NINTH LOCK ROAD, CLONDALKIN

Post-medieval
O070315
97E0331

Test excavation was carried out at a proposed development site to the north-west of the early ecclesiastic monastery of Clondalkin. The Cammock River forms the boundary on the southern side of the site. The site was formerly part of Clondalkin Paper Mills and was extensively developed with the construction of large industrial buildings in the latter half of the 20th century.

Clondalkin was the site of an Early Christian monastery founded in the 7th century by St Mochua. The monastery was plundered in 833 and burned in 1071 by the Vikings. Following the Anglo-Norman conquest Clondalkin was annexed to the deanery of St Patrick's Cathedral, Dublin. The round tower is still standing in the village centre, and two granite crosses and a granite basin survive in the Protestant church and graveyard across the road. The 16th-century remains of Tully Castle are present at the eastern end of the village. The present streetscape reflects the presence of the monastic enclosure at Clondalkin. The site lies outside and beyond the monastic enclosure.

Two large test-trenches were excavated along the length of the proposed new buildings. The trenches were up to 38.5m long. No archaeological features or deposits were identified. Three sherds of post-medieval pottery were retrieved from the riverbank at the southern end of the site. All are from the same vessel. The vessel appears to be a Westerwald stoneware jug. The fragments date to the 17th or 18th century. The pottery was discovered in loose surface material lying along the side of a large 19th-century mill-race channel feeding into the original river channel.
Edmond O'Donovan, Margaret Gowen & Co. Ltd, 2 Killiney View, Albert Road Lower, Glenageary, Co. Dublin.

AD2. 43/44 CLARENDON STREET, DUBLIN

Pre-Georgian wall containing fireplace; Georgian cellars
31582 23378
98E0311

Licensed monitoring of intermittent subsurface groundworks for a mixed-use development was carried out between August and December 1998 in compliance with a condition of planning permission issued by Dublin Corporation.

Two red brick, barrel-vaulted Georgian cellars were encountered under an open area behind the retained building at the front of plot No. 43. These cellars were poured with concrete to stabilise them and were also retained.

Excavation for the underpinning of the south-south-west wall of the Carmelite building at the front of plot No. 45 showed that this wall had been constructed on the remains of a stretch of earlier, pre-Georgian walling. The latter incorporates the springing for a stone-arched vault with a stone-built fireplace underneath and relates to the basement of a building that originally occupied the front of plot No. 44. The position of the fireplace suggests that the east-south-east wall of the pre-Georgian building lay under the present footpath or street. This building continued in use into Georgian times, as the fireplace was later narrowed using yellow, Georgian brick.

However, no evidence of a cellar existed underneath the building on plot No. 44, which was demolished at the start of the present development. The wall and fireplace were constructed on natural boulder till, and no archaeological strata relating to this earlier phase of activity were encountered in the course of the groundworks. The pre-Georgian stretch of walling was underpinned with concrete and retained *in situ*. It was further stabilised through the pouring of concrete into the fireplace opening.

Deposits removed in the course of the development consisted entirely of post-Georgian build-up and rubble infill resting on natural boulder till. Artefacts recovered were generally quite modern but included two sherds of medieval pottery and several sherds of gravel-tempered ware.

Noel Dunne, Arch-Tech Ltd, 32 Fitzwilliam Place, Dublin 2.

AD3. DUNDRUM CASTLE HOUSE, DUNDRUM
Medieval
0174279
97E0438 ext.
Monitoring took place near Dundrum Castle between 6 and 11 August 1998. The work was carried out as an extension to a licence held by James Eogan (*Excavations 1997*, 56) for test-trenching at Dundrum Castle House.

The area around the southern and eastern exterior of the castle was reduced to facilitate the construction of an access roadway. A stone drain of post-medieval date was uncovered at the southern side of the Castle during the mechanical excavation of the area. In addition a post-medieval stone wall was uncovered on the eastern side of the castle at a depth of 0.15m below the modern ground level

No medieval material was unearthed during the monitoring.

E. Eoin Sullivan, 39, Trees Road, Mount Merrion, Co. Dublin.

AD4. PATRICKSWELL LANE, FINGLAS
Probable 17th-century earthen rampart
312757 238705
SMR 14:06608
98E0180
This small, triangular development site for fifteen houses lies a short distance to the west-south-west of Finglas village. Immediately to the north-east of the site is an earthen bank known as King William's Rampart. A previous archaeological assessment by Eoin Halpin (*Excavations 1995*, 25, 95E215) showed evidence of a continuation of the rampart along the northern boundary of the development area. In order to investigate this feature further a condition of

planning permission issued by Dublin Corporation required the hand-excavation of two 5m x 5m squares immediately inside the northern perimeter. This excavation was undertaken between 6 and 24 April 1998.

Excavation revealed evidence of a mortared stone wall, buttressed on its south side, that extended parallel to the northern boundary, a distance of 2m–3.5m from it. The remainder of this feature was exposed mechanically, between 22 and 26 May 1998, under archaeological supervision.

The wall was mostly evident as a robbed-out foundation trench or with only the bottom course or courses surviving immediately under the sod. However, at the north-east side of the site it had a surviving height of up to 1.7m, where it acted as revetting for higher ground to the north. At the north-east perimeter the feature emerges on the surface and is visible in places as revetting extending along the southern slope of the rampart. No evidence was uncovered to show that the wall is contemporary with the earthen bank, and it is more likely to be a later 18th- or 19th-century property boundary that included the line of the rampart.

The wall acted as revetting for higher ground to the north. No evidence was uncovered to show that the rampart continued along the northern edge of the site or that this higher ground is the remains of the base of an earthen bank. On the contrary, soils to the north of the wall appear to be the result of cultivation over a quite long period of time.

Most of the artefacts uncovered are modern and include glass, delftware and metal objects. Early brick, bellarmine and gravel-tempered sherds and an early clay pipe bowl indicate activity on the site during the 17th century. These finds, however, cannot date the features precisely, as none is from a totally sealed context.

Noel Dunne, Arch-Tech Ltd, 32 Fitzwilliam Place, Dublin 2.

KILDARE

AD5. PUNCHESTOWN LITTLE
No archaeological significance
291712 215943
98E0502
A programme of archaeological testing was undertaken at Punchestown Racecourse on 29–30 October and 2–3 December 1998, before the development of a new stabling block. The racecourse lies in an archaeologically sensitive landscape containing standing stones, cists and a ring-barrow. The work was carried out in compliance with a condition of planning permission issued by Kildare County Council.

Four trenches with a total length of 190m were excavated mechanically. Three of these lay within the area of an existing carpark and showed that the soil stratigraphy here had been reduced to natural before the spreading of the hard-core parking surface. The fourth trench was excavated immediately to the north-west of the carpark and contained deep brown earths resting on natural sand deposits. No archaeological evidence was noted in any of the trenches.

Noel Dunne, Arch-Tech Ltd. 32 Fitzwilliam Place, Dublin 2.

AD6. THOLSEL STREET, CARLINGFORD
Urban medieval/post-medieval
31888 31159
97E0141

Testing was carried out on 14 January 1998 on a site in Tholsel Street, Carlingford, where planning permission had been granted for a commercial and residential development. The site lies on the west side of Tholsel Street between The Tholsel, a medieval gatehouse, and The Mint, a medieval stone house that is a National Monument in state care. The site has a street frontage of 27m and extends westwards for 21m, cutting back into a natural gravel ridge.

In a series of test-trenches modern and post-medieval rubble was excavated by machine to expose the surface of archaeological deposits. Thereafter excavation of a very limited nature was carried out by hand to assess the nature of the deposits and to retrieve evidence of date. The archaeological deposits consisted of stone walls and house floors ranging in date from the medieval period to the early 19th century. The deposits were uncovered at a depth of 0.5m below present street level and extended up to 4m from the street front. Natural gravel was exposed at ground level over the western part of the site.

Pottery of post-medieval date and iron slag was recovered from the upper floor levels. At the northern end of the site an oxidised clay floor appeared to be of early 18th-century date. A black, greasy soil containing charcoal, ash and frequent oyster and limpet shells overlay the floor. These deposits resemble those recorded by Gleeson and Moore in excavations on the opposite side of the street (*CLAJ* 1992). Four sherds of 13th–14th-century local ware were recovered from a floor deposit exposed at a depth of 0.5m towards the south end of the site.

Examined in a 0.3m x 0.4m test-pit midway along the front of the site, the deposits were shown to have an overall thickness of 0.45m. In the test-pit three deposits of shell- and charcoal-flecked soil were interleaved with 50mm-thick layers of clean gravel. No dating evidence was recovered from these earliest levels.

As a result of the archaeological investigations the foundations in the area of the archaeological deposits were redesigned as a raft construction.
Kieran Campbell, 6 St Ultans, Laytown, Drogheda, Co. Louth.

WEXFORD

AD7. IRISHTOWN, NEW ROSS
Urban medieval
98E0565

Monitoring of three phases of a housing development is ongoing. At present two phases are complete. The work involves the monitoring of access roadways, services and topsoil removal and the excavation of the foundations for the houses.

Two burnt pits below the level of the topsoil have been identified. No artefactual material has been uncovered, nor have any archaeological strata been encountered.
E. Eoin Sullivan, 39, Trees Road, Mount Merrion, Co. Dublin.

AD8. ASHTON, BLESSINGTON
18th/19th/20th-century tillage features
29740 21450
98E0425

An archaeological assessment and impact study were undertaken before a major residential development to the north-west of Blessington village. A programme of test excavation was subsequently agreed with the NMHPS, and this work was carried out between 14 and 21 September 1998.

The remains of a late 17th-century house, Downshire House (SMR 5:18), lie to the north-east of the development area, and the assessment showed some of the field boundaries on the site to be contemporary with the occupation of the house. The house was burnt and abandoned in 1798.

The development area extended over five fields. Four trenches, each 30m long, were mechanically excavated in each of the fields—an overall total of 600m of trenching. The excavations showed that sandy, brown earths rested on natural gravel deposits over the entire area. Tillage features, including furrows, drills and ridges, were encountered in some of the trenches along the interface between the clay and the gravel. These varied considerably in dimension and form and may range in date from the 18th to the 20th century. No other archaeological features were evident.

The artefacts recovered are relatively modern and include sherds of delftware, crockery, china and glass; fragments of clay pipe and red brick; and some iron objects. The pottery includes two sherds of gravel-tempered ware.
Noel Dunne, Arch-Tech Ltd. 32 Fitzwilliam Place, Dublin 2.

IRISH ARCHAEOLOGICAL WETLAND UNIT (IAWU) FIELDWORK 1998—COUNTIES OFFALY AND MAYO

During the summer of 1998 the Irish Archaeological Wetland Unit (IAWU) spent eight weeks completing the survey of the Boora group of bogs in County Offaly. Boora Works comprises a series of bogs north and south of the road between Tullamore and Cloghan in County Offaly. The survey of the Boora Works began in 1997, when over 31 sites had been recorded. The 1998 survey concentrated on ten Bord na Móna bogs in the Boora region (over 6849ha in area). Clowngawney More, Drinagh West, Drinagh East, Tumduff, Boora East, Boora West, Derrybrat and Monettia are bogs that produce milled peat. Derrinboy and Killaun bogs had only recently been ditched, and there had been no milling in these bogs. One of the main objectives of this survey was to complete all the bogs west of Tullamore in County Offaly so that all the sites could be included in the Sites and Monuments Record. This work led to the completion of the Boora Group of bogs in West Offaly. In addition to these projects a week was spent reinstating a crannog in Frenchgrove, Co. Mayo (No. 488 above), and a preliminary field survey was undertaken in Oweninny, Co. Mayo.

In working in these bogs a standard IAWU survey strategy was used. This involved walking every second of the parallel drainage ditches, which gives an interval of *c.* 30m. On the first walk sites are identified, and then these are revisited and recorded on a standard IAWU record sheet. Sixty-one sites were recorded in six of the Bord na Móna-owned bogs, and seventeen other sites were recorded in a privately owned bog near Drinagh. Although no sites were recorded in four of the bogs, this does not preclude the finding of sites in the future as peat extraction continues. This brings the total of archaeological sites surveyed and recorded by the IAWU in Boora to over 92. The locations of all the archaeological sites were recorded and transferred onto appropriate maps. A record was also compiled of the threats facing each bog surveyed by the IAWU in 1998. The locational information of each site, the accompanying maps and the bog threats have been submitted to the NMHPS for inclusion in its Sites and Monuments Record.

Clowngawney More

This is the most westerly of the bogs in the Boora area. It lies west of the road from Birr to Cloghan, and its total area is 1018ha. Much of the central axis of the bog has been planted in coniferous forestry. Ten archaeological sites were identified. They lie to the south of Madden's Derry bog island, on the eastern side of Clowngawney bog. Most of the sites are brushwood toghers situated close to the surface of the bog.

Drinagh West

Drinagh bog lies east of the road from Birr to Cloghan and has been divided into east and west for production purposes. The total area of the two bogs is 1568ha. The survey of Drinagh West revealed nineteen sites in the spur off the south-eastern side of the bog. Sites included a large, single-plank walkway, roundwood and brushwood toghers, worked wood *in situ* and some puddle toghers. A single-piece vessel and a woven basket with associated leather were also recorded. A further seventeen sites were recorded in an area of private peat cutting to the east of the main concentration of archaeology.

Drinagh East

There were no archaeological sites recorded during the 1998 IAWU survey in this bog.

Derrybrat

Derrybrat is a small bog that lies west of the road running from Ferbane power station to Kilcormac. There were no archaeological sites recorded in this bog during the 1998 survey. Four sites were excavated by Etienne Rynne in the early 1960s, but there was no trace of these sites in 1998 as the area is now covered in forest.

Boora West

Boora bog is at the centre of the complex and lies just south of the Cloghan to Blueball road. Boora bog is divided into east and west for production purposes. The total area of Boora West is 774ha. Although no archaeological sites were found during the 1998 survey, its proximity to the excavated Lough Boora Mesolithic site may result in sites being uncovered in the future.

Boora East

This is the largest of the bogs surveyed in 1998. The total area of Boora East is 2044ha. Most of this area is cut over and is now used for forestry. The only area currently under production and suitable for survey is in the south-eastern corner of the bog. One site was found in this area, very close to the road. It is a brushwood site with deep stratigraphy.

Tumduff

Tumduff is a large expanse of bog beside Boora East. One archaeological site was identified during the course of the survey. It lay in the area to the extreme south-western corner of the bog and consisted of a number of roundwoods with some possible stone toolmarks.

Derrinboy

This bog is removed from the main concentration of Boora bogs and lies to the south of Kilcormac. It is 334ha in total area. No sites were found in this bog. The drains in this bog had just been ditched, and this made the recognition of archaeological sites difficult.

Killaun

Killaun bog is also removed from the main concentration of Boora bogs and lies to the south of Kilcormac. It is 395ha in total area. In the north-eastern spur of the bog thirty archaeological sites were identified. The sites were constructed of brushwood and roundwood, and three of them ran across the width of the bog.

Monettia

This bog lies south of Tullamore, and half of it lies in County Laois. Its total area is 716ha. Owing to time constraints only half of this bog was surveyed in 1998. Three sites were found, consisting of scattered brushwood and roundwood. The hardness of the wood suggests that these sites may be quite late in date.

Frenchgrove, Co. Mayo
A week (20–4 April 1998) was spent on the reinstatement of a crannog in Frenchgrove, Co. Mayo (see No. 488 above). The site was found during land reclamation while a mechanical excavator was being used (*Excavations 1997*, 208). An amount of damage was caused to the site by the machine.

The work involved sieving the upcast material, backfilling the excavated hole using the sieved spoil, reburying the displaced timbers, recording the artefacts recovered and arranging conservation where necessary. Samples were also selected and processed for dating.

Oweninny, Co. Mayo
In May 1998 a one-week field survey was undertaken in the Bord na Móna bogs in the Oweninny Works, Bellacorrick, Co. Mayo. The object of this survey was to investigate the archaeological potential of the lowland blanket bog. The IAWU did not uncover any sites exposed in the peat face or on the surface of the bog during this survey.
Conor McDermott, Nóra Bermingham, Ellen O'Carroll and Jane Whitaker, Irish Archaeological Wetland Unit, Department of Archaeology, University College Dublin, Dublin 4.

APPENDIX II

A FIELD-WALKING SURVEY OF THE KNOCKNAREA MOUNTAIN AREA, CO. SLIGO
16283 33469
E998
A field-walking survey is being undertaken in the townlands of Knocknarea North, Knocknarea South, Grange North, Rathcarrick and Drinaghan, all in the Knocknarea Mountain area of County Sligo. The work commenced in December 1998 and will continue during 1999. It forms part of a research project called 'The Sacred Mountain. The identity of a landscape', which focuses on the role of the Knocknarea Mountain within the symbolic and physical world of the Neolithic *Cúil Irra* region. One of the main aims of the survey is to record the occurrence and extent of Neolithic activity within this prominent mountain.

The survey falls spatially into two different areas: the lower, eastern ridge covered by forestry; and the higher, grazed mountain to the west with the well-known group of passage tombs on the flat top. The survey within the forestry is almost complete and has shown that a large number of worked chert and chert implements are to be found within this ridge. Unfortunately, certain parts of the forestry are extremely densely planted, which has made sur-veying impossible.

A preliminary interpretation of the results so far is that the lower ridge of Knocknarea Mountain, which overlooks the Carrowmore cemetery, was an area with extensive activity during the Neolithic.
Stefan Bergh, Department of Archaeology, University of Stockholm, Sweden.

APPENDIX III

CORRECTION TO REPORT ON TEMPLERAINY, CO. WICKLOW, PUBLISHED IN *EXCAVATIONS 1997*
Prehistoric potsherds recovered from Site 3 at Templerainy and described as being of Beaker and food vessel type (*Excavations 1997*, 201) have since been examined in detail by Helen Roche and identified as being solely of Beaker ware.
Breandán Ó Ríordáin, Burage More, Blessington, Co. Wicklow, for Valerie J. Keeley Ltd.

Index of Excavations 1969–97 by year and number

Year	No.	County	Location 1	Location 2	Type	Excavator	Grid ref.
1969	1	Tyrone	Clogher	Clogher Demesne	Hillfort	Warner, R.B.	H538-513
1969	2	Fermanagh	Kiltierney	Archdall Deerpark	Cairn	Flanagan, L.N.W.	H218-627
1969	3	Antrim	Doonbought		Medieval defence work	McNeill, T.E.	J333-845
1969	4	Antrim	Carnmoney		Ringfort	Avery, M.	
1969	5	Antrim	Mad Man's Window		Neolithic chipping floor	Woodman, P.C.	
1969	6	Armagh	Emain Macha	Navan Fort	Multi-period site	Waterman, D.M.	H847-452
1969	7	Down	Scrabo		Hut circles	Owens, M.	J470-720
1969	8	Donegal	Shawly		Court cairn	Flanagan, L.N.W.	G649-748
1969	9	Donegal	Croaghbeg		Court cairn	Flanagan, L.N.W.	G649-748
1969	10	Tyrone	Ballynagilly	The Corbie	Neolithic settlement	ApSimon, A.M.	H743-827
1969	11	Meath	Newgrange		Passage grave	O'Kelly, M.J.	O007-727
1969	12	Meath	Knowth		Passage grave	Eogan, G.	N999-738
1969	13	Kildare	Dún Áillinne	Knockaulin	Hillfort	Wailes, B.	N820-078
1969	14	Wicklow	Rathgall	Rath East	Hillfort	Raftery, B.	S902-731
1969	15	Longford	Ardagh		Ringfort & early church site	de Paor, L.	
1969	16	Dublin	Dublin City	Winetavern Street	Hiberno-Norse town	Ó Ríordáin, A.B.	O151-338
1969	17	Dublin	Dublin City	High Street	Hiberno-Norse town	Ó Ríordáin, A.B.	O151-338
1969	18	Mayo	Behy		Court cairn	de Valera, R.	G050-400
1969	19	Mayo	Behy and Carrownaglogh		Field walls (pre-bog)	Herity, M. and Caulfield, S.	G050-400
1969	20	Kerry	Coomatloukane		Wedge tomb	Herity, M.	
1969	21	Cork	Dunboy		Castle	Fahy, E.M.	V670-440
1969	22	Tipperary	Leigh	Liathmore–Mochoemog	Medieval settlement	Glasscock, R.	S225-577
1969	23	Galway	Ardrahan	Grannagh	Early Iron Age mound	Rynne, E.	M511-100
1969	24	Galway	Lydacan		Enclosure	Rynne, E.	
1969	25	Mayo	Castlebar	Carrowbrack	Middle Bronze Age mound	Rynne, E.	
1969	26	Galway	Renmore	Lisbeg	Enclosure	Rynne, E.	M315-252
1969	27	Mayo	Ballyglass		Court cairn	Ó Nualláin, S.	G097-381
1970	1	Antrim	Carnmoney		Ringfort	Avery, M.	J333-845
1970	2	Antrim	Newferry	Ballyscullion	Neolithic occupation site	Woodman, P.C.	H990-980
1970	3	Antrim	Tully		Ringfort	Harper, A.	J163-807
1970	4	Armagh	Armagh City		Franciscan friary church	Lynn, C.J.	H879-448
1970	5	Armagh	Emain Macha	Navan Fort	Multi-period site	Waterman, D.M.	H847-452
1970	6	Clare	Inis Cealtra	Holy Island	Monastic settlement	de Paor, L.	R698-850
1970	7	Cork	Dunboy		Tower-house & military fort	Fahy, E.M.	V670-440
1970	8	Derry	Ballybriest	Carnanbane	Court cairn (dual)	ApSimon, A.M.	H762-886
1970	9	Derry	Ballybriest	Carnanbane	Wedge tomb	ApSimon, A.M.	H762-885
1970	10	Derry	Magheramore	Bannagher Old Church	Early Christian church	Lynn, C.J.	C675-065
1970	11	Derry	Dungiven		Augustinian priory	Harper, A.	C692-083
1970	12	Donegal	Croaghbeg		Court cairn	Flanagan, L.N.W.	G649-748
1970	13	Down	Ballylessan	Farrell's Fort	Ringfort	Collins, A.E.P.	J335-661
1970	14	Down	Gortgrib		Later Iron Age site	Warner, R.B. and Delaney, T.G.	J400-730
1970	15	Down	Greencastle		Castle	Lynn, C.J.	J247-118
1970	16	Down	Scrabo		Early Iron Age hut circle	Owens, M.	J470-720
1970	17	Dublin	Dublin City	High Street/ Winetavern Street	Viking/ medieval town	Ó Ríordáin, A.B.	O151-338
1970	18	Galway	Oran Beg		Ring-barrow	Rynne, E.	M420-255
1970	19	Kerry	Gallarus		Early Christian church site	Fanning, T.	Q355-049
1970	20	Kildare	Dún Áillinne	Knockaulin	Early Iron Age ritual site	Wailes, B.	N820-078

1970	21	Kilkenny	Kilkenny City	St Francis's Abbey	Franciscan friary church	Sweetman, P.D.	S506-562
1970	22	Mayo	Ballyglass		Court cairn	Ó Nualláin, S.	G097-381
1970	23	Mayo	Carrownaglogh	Glenurla	Prehistoric enclosure	Herity, M.	G360-190
1970	24	Mayo	Behy/Glenurla	Céide Fields	Prehistoric enclosure	Caulfield, S.	G050-400
1970	25	Meath	Knowth		Passage grave complex & Later Iron Age settlement	Eogan, G.	N999-738
1970	26	Meath	Monknewtown		Early Bronze Age circular enclosure	Sweetman, P.D.	O000-760
1970	27	Meath	Newgrange		Passage grave & Neolithic occupation site	O'Kelly, M.J.	O007-727
1970	28	Tipperary	Bowling Green		Ringfort	Fanning, T.	S137-592
1970	29	Tipperary	Holycross		Cistercian abbey	Ó hEochaidhe, M.	S090-540
1970	30	Tipperary	Leigh	Liathmore—Mochoemog	Monastic site/post-medieval settlement	Glasscock, R.	S225-577
1970	31	Tyrone	Carnkenny		Ring-cairn	Lynn, C.J.	H354-867
1970	32	Tyrone	Ballynagilly	The Corbie	Neolithic/Bronze Age settlements	ApSimon, A.M.	H743-827
1970	33	Tyrone	Feegarran		Stone causeway in bog	Williams, B.B.	H770-820
1970	34	Tyrone	Urney		Ringfort	Scott, B.	H301-905
1970	35	Wicklow	Rathgall	Rath East	Hillfort	Raftery, B.	S902-731
1971	1	Antrim	Ballymacrea		Neolithic settlement site	Collins, A.E.P.	C884-406
1971	2	Antrim	Antrim Town	Ballygortgarve	Ringfort	Lynn, C.J.	J146-760
1971	3	Antrim	Cloughorr		Souterrain	Harper, A.	C875-397
1971	4	Antrim	Glynn		Mesolithic/Neolithic raised beach	Woodman, P.C.	D408-001
1971	5	Antrim	Newferry	Ballyscullion	Mesolithic/Neolithic occupation site	Woodman, P.C.	H991-981
1971	6	Antrim	Poleglass		Ringfort	Harper, A.	J278-695
1971	7	Antrim	Seacash		Ringfort	Lynn, C.J.	J154-797
1971	8	Armagh	Lisdrumchor Upper		Ringfort	Collins, A.E.P.	H997-335
1971	9	Armagh	Tullyallen		Ringfort	Collins, A.E.P.	H985-347
1971	10	Clare	Inis Cealtra	Holy Island	Monastic settlement	de Paor, L.	R698-850
1971	11	Donegal	Croaghbeg		Court cairn	Flanagan, L.N.W.	G649-748
1971	12	Down	Crossnacreevy		Ringfort	Harper, A.	J396-702
1971	13	Down	Greencastle		Castle	Lynn, C.J.	J247-118
1971	14	Down	Scrabo		Early Iron Age hut circle	Owens, M.	J470-720
1971	15	Dublin	Swords	Swords Castle	Castle	Fanning, T.	O184-470
1971	16	Dublin	Dublin City	Winetavern Street	Viking/medieval settlement	Ó Ríordáin, A.B.	O151-338
1971	17	Galway	Abbeypark	Clontuskert Priory	Medieval priory—Augustinian	Fanning, T.	M856-206
1971	18	Galway	Ardrahan	Grannagh	Inauguration/assembly site?	Rynne, E.	M511-100
1971	19	Kildare	Dún Áillinne	Knockaulin	Hillfort	Wailes, B.	N820-078
1971	20	Kildare	Narraghmore		Ringfort	Fanning, T.	N788-001
1971	21	Kildare	Pollardstown		Ringfort	Fanning, T.	N775-151
1971	22	Kilkenny	Ballyoskill		Multiple cist cairn	Prendergast, E. and Ryan, M.F.	S474-765
1971	23	Kilkenny	Jerpoint West		Neolithic burial	Ryan, M.F.	S572-414
1971	24	Mayo	Ballyglass		Court cairn & Neolithic house site	Ó Nualláin, S.	G097-381
1971	25	Mayo	Behy/Glenurla	Céide Fields	Pre-bog enclosures & field systems	Caulfield, S.	G050-400
1971	26	Mayo	Belderg Beg		Pre-bog field system	Caulfield, S.	F982-410
1971	27	Mayo	Carrownaglogh	Glenurla	Pre-bog field system	Herity, M.	G360-190
1971	28	Meath	Knowth		Passage grave complex & medieval occupation	Eogan, G.	N999-738
1971	29	Meath	Monknewtown		Late Neolithic/Early Bronze Age	Sweetman, P.D.	O000-760

1971	30	Meath	Newgrange		Neolithic settlement	O'Kelly, M.J.	O007-727
1971	31	Meath	Trim	Trim Castle	Medieval castle	Sweetman, P.D.	N802-564
1971	32	Tyrone	Clogher	Clogher Demesne	Iron Age hillfort/ royal site	Warner, R.B.	H538-513
1971	33	Tyrone	Tullywiggan		Neolithic/Early Bronze Age occupation	Bamford, H.M.	H816-756
1971	34	Tyrone	Urney		Ringfort	Scott, B.	H301-905
1971	35	Wexford	Tomona		Circular enclosure	Fanning, T.	S867-460
1971	36	Wicklow	Rathgall	Rath East	Hillfort	Raftery, B.	S902-731
1972	1	Antrim	Ballyhenry	Ballyhenry I	Ringfort	Lynn, C.J.	J312-853
1972	2	Antrim	Ballyhenry	Ballyhenry II	Ringfort	Lynn, C.J.	J314-847
1972	3	Antrim	Carrickfergus		Medieval town	Delaney, T.G.	J413-874
1972	4	Antrim	Shane's Castle		Ringfort	Lynn, C.J.	J122-887
1972	5	Antrim	Baunogenasraid		Burial mound	Raftery, B.	S793-741
1972	6	Clare	Inis Cealtra	Holy Island	Monastic site	de Paor, L.	R698-850
1972	7	Cork	Castlemagner		Souterrain	Twohig, D.C.	R441-027
1972	8	Cork	Dunboy		Castle	Fahy, E.M.	V665-440
1972	9	Cork	Lisduggan North		Ringforts	Twohig, D.C. and O'Kelly, M.J.	R433-039
1972	10	Cork	Turkhead		Hut site	Danaher, P.	W024-282
1972	11	Donegal	Croaghbeg		Court cairn	Flanagan, L.N.W.	G649-748
1972	12	Down	Gransha		Early Christian settlement	Lynn, C.J.	J531-769
1972	13	Down	Greencastle		Castle	Lynn, C.J.	J247-118
1972	14	Dublin	Dublin City	High Street/ Winetavern Street	Viking/medieval town	Ó Ríordáin, A.B.	O151-338
1972	15	Galway	Athenry	Athenry Castle	Medieval castle	Foley, C.	M512-288
1972	16	Galway	Lisconly		Earthwork	Champion, S. and Champion, T.	M437-590
1972	17	Galway	Abbeypark	Clontuskert Priory	Medieval priory— Augustinian	Fanning, T.	M856-206
1972	18	Kerry	Reask		Monastic enclosure	Fanning, T.	Q365-043
1972	19	Kildare	Dún Áillinne	Knockaulin	Hillfort	Wailes, B.	N820-078
1972	20	Kilkenny	Dunbell		Ringfort	Foley, C.	S561-528
1972	21	Kilkenny	Kells	Rathduff— Kells Priory	Augustinian priory	Fanning, T.	S499-434
1972	22	Leitrim	Kilmore	Parke's Castle	Tower-house	Foley, C.	G782-352
1972	23	Mayo	Ballyglass		Neolithic settlement	Ó Nualláin, S.	G098-379
1972	24	Mayo	Belderg Beg		Neolithic settlement	Caulfield, S.	F985-406
1972	25	Mayo	Carrownaglogh	Glenurla	Field system	Herity, M.	G360-190
1972	26	Meath	Knowth		Early Christian settlement	Eogan, G.	N999-738
1972	27	Meath	Newgrange		Passage grave	O'Kelly, M.J.	O007-727
1972	28	Meath	Trim	Trim Castle	Medieval castle	Sweetman, P.D.	N802-564
1972	29	Tipperary	Cahir		Castle	Reynolds, J.F.	S050-246
1972	30	Tipperary	Poulnacapple		Ringfort	Reynolds, J.F.	S370-390
1972	31	Tyrone	Clogher	Clogher Demesne	Hillfort	Warner, R.B.	H538-513
1972	32	Wexford	Ferns	Castleland	Castle	Sweetman, P.D.	T002-500
1972	33	Wicklow	Brockagh	St Kevin's Road	Pilgrims' road	Ryan, M.F and Wallace, P.	O075-205
1972	34	Wicklow	Rathgall	Rath East	Hillfort	Raftery, B.	S902-731
1973	1	Antrim	Ballynoe		Enclosure	Lynn, C.J.	J187-906
1973	2	Antrim	Carrickfergus		Medieval urban	Delaney, T.G.	J413-874
1973	3	Antrim	Finkiltagh		Ringfort	Williams, B.B.	C991-072
1973	4	Antrim	Antrim Town	Massereene Park	Friary	Lynn, C.J.	J147-866
1973	5	Antrim	Muckamore		Priory site	Lynn, C.J.	J167-855
1973	6	Clare	Inis Cealtra	Holy Island	Monastic site	de Paor, L.	R698-850
1973	7	Cork	Coolowen		Ringfort	Twohig, D.C.	W623-789
1973	8	Cork	Dunboy		Tower-house	Fahy, E.M.	V670-440
1973	9	Cork	Lisduggan North	Lisduggan No. 3	Ringfort	Twohig, D.C. and O'Kelly, M.J.	R428-038
1973	10	Derry	Ballymacpeake Upr	Souterrain		Warner, R.B.	C928-010
1973	11	Derry	Lismurphy		Ringfort	Lynn, C.J.	C837-307
1973	12	Derry	Mount Sandel		Mesolithic settlement	Woodman, P.C.	C853-307
1973	13	Donegal	Croaghbeg		Court cairn	Flanagan, L.N.W.	G649-748

1973	15	Down	Bishopscourt	Bonfire Hill	Souterrain	Lynn, C.J.	J588-413
1973	16	Down	Cloughskelt		Bronze Age cemetery	Flanagan, L.N.W.	J231-415
1973	17	Dublin	Dublin City	Christchurch Place	Viking/medieval urban	Ó Ríordáin, A.B.	O151-338
1973	19	Kerry	Dromkeen East		*Fulacht fiadh*	Twohig, D.C.	Q833-308
1973	20	Kerry	Reask		Monastic enclosure	Fanning, T.	Q365-043
1973	21	Kildare	Dún Áillinne	Knockaulin	Hillfort	Wailes, B.	N820-078
1973	22	Kilkenny	Jerpoint Church		Medieval rural settlement	Foley, C.	S561-409
1973	23	Kilkenny	Kells	Rathduff— Kells Priory	Augustinian priory	Fanning, T.	S499-434
1973	24	Leitrim	Kilmore	Parke's Castle	Tower-house	Foley, C.	G782-352
1973	25	Limerick	Sluggary		Ringfort	Shee, E.	R558-535
1973	26	Mayo	Belderg Beg		Prehistoric settlement/field systems	Caulfield, S.	F982-410
1973	27	Mayo	Carrownaglogh	Glenurla	Pre-bog field system	Herity, M.	G360-190
1973	28	Meath	Knowth		Passage grave cemetery	Eogan, G.	N999-738
1973	29	Meath	Newgrange		Passage grave cemetery	O'Kelly, M.J.	O007-727
1973	30	Meath	Trim	Trim Castle	Medieval castle	Sweetman, P.D.	N802-564
1973	31	Sligo	Lough Gara	Shroove	Cisted cairn	Wallace, P.	G689-002
1973	32	Tipperary	Longstone		Earthwork	Danaher, P.	R797-392
1973	33	Tyrone	Clogher	Clogher Demesne	Hillfort	Warner, R.B.	H538-513
1973	34	Tyrone	Erlagh	Lough Dolough	Crannog	Williams, B.B.	
1973	35	Tyrone	Kinkit		Cist grave	Flanagan, L.N.W.	H314-886
1973	36	Westmeath	Killucan/ Corbetstown	Kilpatrick	Ecclesiastical enclosure	Swan, D.L.	N575-558
1973	37	Westmeath	Rathnarrow	Barrow 3	Barrow group	McCabe, J.	N546-525
1973	38	Wexford	Ferns	Castleland	Castle	Sweetman, P.D.	T002-500
1973	39	Wexford	Wexford Town	St Selskar's Abbey	Church	Fanning, T.	T047-221
1973	40	Wicklow	Rathgall	Rath East	Hillfort	Raftery, B.	S902-731
1973	41	Sligo	Breeoge		Wedge tomb	Rynne, E. and Timoney, M.	G649-319
1974	1	Antrim	Ballycastle U.D.		Glassworks	Bowie, G.	D120-410
1974	2	Antrim	Ballywee		Ringfort	Lynn, C.J.	J218-898
1974	3	Antrim	Carrickfergus	Joymount/ High Street	Medieval & later urban	Delaney, T.G.	J413-874
1974	4	Antrim	Dunsilly		Motte & ringfort	McNeill, T.E.	J141-889
1974	5	Antrim	Antrim Town	Massereene Park	Friary	Lynn, C.J.	J147-866
1974	6	Antrim	Muckamore		Priory	Lynn, C.J.	J167-855
1974	7	Carlow	Sliguff		Cist burial	Ryan, M.F.	S695-578
1974	8	Cavan	Killycluggin		Decorated stone	Raftery, B.	H239-160
1974	9	Clare	Inis Cealtra	Holy Island	Monastic settlement	de Paor, L.	R698-850
1974	10	Cork	Cork City	North Main Street	Medieval & later	Twohig, D.C.	W670-719
1974	11	Derry	Mount Sandel		Mesolithic settlement	Woodman, P.C.	C853-307
1974	12	Donegal	Kinnagoe Bay	*La Trinidad Valencera*	Armada wreck	Martin, C.	C630-460
1974	13	Down	Downpatrick	Downpatrick Cathedral	Cathedral church	Delaney, T.G.	J483-445
1974	14	Dublin	Dublin City	Christchurch Place	11th- & 12th-century urban	Ó Ríordáin, A.B.	O151-339
1974	15	Dublin	Dublin City	Wood Quay	Medieval & later urban	Wallace, P.	O151-342
1974	17	Kerry	Rathmore		*Fulachta fiadh*	Ryan, M.F.	W152-928
1974	18	Kerry	Reask		Monastic site	Fanning, T.	Q365-043
1974	19	Kildare	Dún Áillinne	Knockaulin	Hillfort	Wailes, B.	N820-078
1974	20	Kilkenny	Castletobin		Medieval earthwork	Sutton, D.	S432-452
1974	21	Kilkenny	Catstown		*Fulacht fiadh*	Ryan, M.F.	S480-380
1974	22	Kilkenny	Catstown		*Fulacht fiadh*	Ryan, M.F.	S480-380
1974	23	Kilkenny	Kells	Rathduff— Kells Priory	Augustinian priory	Fanning, T.	S499-434
1974	24	Leitrim	Kilmore	Parke's Castle	Tower-house	Foley, C.	G782-352
1974	25	Limerick	Aughinish Island	Aughinish Island Site 1	Stone fort	Kelly, E.P.	R285-535

1974	26	Limerick	Aughinish Island	Aughinish Island Site 2	Stone fort	Kelly, E.P.	R285-535
1974	27	Limerick	Aughinish Island	Aughinish Island Site 5	Enclosure	Hickey, H.	R283-530
1974	28	Limerick	Aughinish Island	Aughinish Island Site 7	Tower-house bawn	Lynch, A.	R285-531
1974	29	Limerick	Sluggary		Ringfort	Shee, E.	R560-663
1974	30	Limerick	Croom East		Ringfort	Shee, E.	R505-590
1974	31	Mayo	Belderg Beg		Prehistoric settlement/field system	Caulfield, S.	F982-410
1974	32	Meath	Knowth		Passage grave cemetery	Eogan, G.	N999-738
1974	33	Meath	Newgrange		Passage grave cemetery	O'Kelly, M.J.	O007-727
1974	34	Meath	Trim	Trim Castle	Medieval castle	Sweetman, P.D.	N802-564
1974	36	Tyrone	Clogher	Clogher Demesne	Early Christian	Warner, R.B.	H538-506
1974	37	Tyrone	Clogher	Clogher Demesne	Hillfort/ringfort	Warner, R.B.	H538-506
1974	38	Waterford	Killeenagh Mountain		Urn burial	Ryan, M.F.	X038-890
1974	39	Wexford	Ballintubrid		Urn burial	Ryan, M.F.	T150-370
1974	40	Wexford	Ferns	Ferns Castle	Castle	Sweetman, P.D.	T002-500
1974	41	Wexford	Wexford Town	Oyster Lane	Medieval urban	Wallace, P.	T150-220
1974	42	Wicklow	Rathgall	Rath East	Late Bronze Age burial	Raftery, B.	S902-731

Excavations 1975–6 in one volume

1975	1	Antrim	Ballymackaldrack		Court cairn	Collins, A.E.P.	D021-830
1975	2	Antrim	Carrickfergus	Joymount/High Street	Medieval & later urban	Delaney, T.G.	J413-874
1975	3	Antrim	Carrickfergus	Joymount/High Street	Medieval & later urban	Delaney, T.G.	J413-874
1975	4	Antrim	Deerfin Lower		Ringfort	Bratt, A.D.	D156-023
1975	5	Antrim	Dunsilly		Motte & ringfort	McNeill, T.E.	J141-889
1975	6	Armagh	Armagh City	Market Street	Medieval urban	Lynn, C.J.	H876-452
1975	7	Armagh	Tray	Rath East	Artificial pond	Lynn, C.J.	H838-455
1975	8	Armagh	Mullynure	Bishop's Court	Episcopal manor	Lynn, C.J.	H881-471
1975	9	Clare	Inis Cealtra	Holy Island	Monastic settlement	de Paor, L.	R698-850
1975	10	Cork	Cork City	South Main Street	Medieval & later urban	Twohig, D.C.	W670-716
1975	11	Derry	Dungiven		Early Christian church/Augustinian priory	Bratt, A.D.	C692-083
1975	12	Derry	Dungiven		Early Christian church/Augustinian priory	Bratt, A.D.	C694-085
1975	13	Derry	Mount Sandel		Motte	Collins, A.E.P.	C853-307
1975	14	Donegal	Kinnagoe Bay	*La Trinidad Valencera*	Armada wreck	Martin, C.	C630-460
1975	15	Dublin	Dublin City	Christchurch Place	Viking/medieval urban	Ó Ríordáin, A.B.	O150-340
1975	18	Fermanagh	Kiltierney	Archdall Deerpark	Ringfort	Williams, B.B.	H215-624
1975	19	Fermanagh	Kiltierney	Archdall Deerpark	Linear earthwork	Williams, B.B.	H218-627
1975	20	Fermanagh	Kiltierney	Archdall Deerpark	Stone circle	Williams, B.B.	H219-626
1975	21	Kerry	Reask		Monastic enclosure	Fanning, T.	Q365-043
1975	23	Kilkenny	Gallows Hill		Mound	Ryan, M.F.	S600-550
1975	24	Kilkenny	Kells	Rathduff—Kells Priory	Augustinian priory	Fanning, T.	S499-434
1975	25	Kilkenny	Kilkenny City	Kilkenny Castle	Castle	Sweetman, P.D.	S512-556
1975	26	Limerick	Adare	Desmond's Castle	Castle	Sweetman, P.D.	R473-468
1975	27	Limerick	Limerick City	St Saviour's Priory	Dominican friary	Shee, E.	R580-578
1975	28	Mayo	Belderg Beg		Prehistoric settlement/field system	Caulfield, S.	F982-410
1975	29	Mayo	Carrownaglogh	Glenurla	Pre-bog field system	Herity, M.	G360-190

1975	30	Meath	Knowth		Passage grave cemetery	Eogan, G.	N999-738
1975	31	Meath	Newgrange		Passage grave cemetery	O'Kelly, M.J.	O007-727
1975	32	Meath	Randalstown		Church & well	Kelly, E.P.	N839-712
1975	33	Meath	Randalstown	Simonstown	Ringfort	Kelly, E.P.	N857-705
1975	35	Tyrone	Clogher	Clogher Demesne	Hillfort/ringfort	Warner, R.B.	H538-506
1975	36	Westmeath	Killucan/ Corbetstown	Kilpatrick	Religious enclosure	Swan, D.L.	N575-558
1975	37	Wexford	Carnsore	St Vogue's Church	Church, enclosure, well	Lynch, A. and Cahill, M.	T120-040
1976	1	Antrim	Carrickfergus	Joymount	Medieval urban	Delaney, T.G.	J413-874
1976	2	Antrim	Carrickfergus	High Street	Medieval urban	Delaney, T.G.	J413-874
1976	3	Antrim	Carrickfergus	Irish Quarter	Medieval urban	Delaney, T.G.	J413-874
1976	4	Antrim	Carrickfergus	Sailors' Row	Medieval urban	Delaney, T.G.	J413-874
1976	5	Antrim	Carrickfergus	Castle Green	Medieval urban	Delaney, T.G.	J413-874
1976	6	Armagh	Armagh City	Scotch Street	Early Christian/ medieval urban	Lynn, C.J.	H875-544
1976	7	Armagh	Armagh City	Scotch Street	Early Christian/ medieval urban	Lynn, C.J.	H875-544
1976	8	Armagh	Armagh City	Castle Street/ Thomas Street	Early Christian/ medieval urban	Lynn, C.J.	H875-544
1976	9	Armagh	Armagh City	Abbey Street	Early Christian/ medieval urban	Lynn, C.J.	H875-544
1976	11	Cork	Cork City	South Main Street	Medieval & later urban	Twohig, D.C.	W670-716
1976	12	Derry	Big Glebe		Mound	Bratt, A.D. and Lynn, C.J.	C740-332
1976	13	Derry	Castle Roe		Mesolithic settlement	Sweetman, P.D.	C859-299
1976	14	Derry	Derry City		Post-medieval urban	Lacy, B.	C435-157
1976	15	Derry	Mount Sandel		Mesolithic settlement	Woodman, P.C.	C853-307
1976	16	Donegal	Carrickballydooey		Cist burial	Ryan, M.F.	C258-101
1976	17	Donegal	Keeldrum Lower		Circular stone-built enclosure	Kilbride-Jones, H.E.	B907-296
1976	18	Down	Ballinran	Killowen	Court cairn	Collins, A.E.P.	J194-154
1976	19	Dublin	Dublin City	Fishamble Street	Viking/medieval urban	Ó Ríordáin, A.B.	O150-340
1976	20	Dublin	Dublin City	Wood Quay	Medieval urban waterfront	Wallace, P.	O150-340
1976	21	Dublin	Kilmainham	Royal Hospital	Royal Hospital	Sweetman, P.D.	O132-340
1976	22	Fermanagh	Tully	Abbey Point	Court cairn	Waterman, D.M.	H124-561
1976	23	Limerick	Limerick City	King John's Castle	Medieval castle	Sweetman, P.D.	R582-576
1976	24	Louth	Drogheda	John Street	Medieval urban	Ó Floinn, R.	O078-750
1976	25	Mayo	Belderg Beg		Prehistoric settlement/field system	Caulfield, S.	F982-410
1976	26	Mayo	Carrownaglogh	Glenurla	Pre-bog field system	Herity, M.	G360-190
1976	27	Meath	Clonard		Medieval earthworks	Sweetman, P.D.	N660-448
1976	28	Meath	Ferganstown	Ballymacann	Cist burial	Kelly, E.P.	N888-689
1976	29	Meath	Knowth		Passage grave cemetery & later	Eogan, G.	N999-738
1976	30	Meath	Randalstown		Church & well	Kelly, E.P.	N839-712
1976	31	Westmeath	Keoltown		Cist burial	Kelly, E.P.	N401-469
1976	32	Westmeath	Knockmant		Souterrain	Kelly, E.P.	N538-510
1976	33	Wexford	Wexford Town		Town wall	Cahill, M. and Ryan, M.F.	T050-220

Break in publication between 1975/6 and 1985. *JIA* IV (1987/8) covered Excavations 1977–9

1977	1	Antrim	Ballyboley		Souterrain & settlement	Lynn, C.J.	D382-032
1977	2	Antrim	Ballykennedy		Ringfort	Brannon, N.F.	J207-767
1977	3	Antrim	Ballymurphy		Ringfort	Lynn, C.J.	J299-742
1977	4	Antrim	Bay	Carnlough	Mesolithic/Late Bronze Age habitation	Woodman, P.C.	D290-160

1977	5	Antrim	Carrickfergus		Medieval & later urban	Delaney, T.G. and Simpson, M.L	J413-874
1977	6	Antrim	Greencastle		Earthwork	Brannon, N.F.	J342-793
1977	7	Antrim	Antrim Town	Massereene Park	Friary	Lynn, C.J.	J147-866
1977	8	Antrim	Turraloskin	Kilcrue	Cross-carved pillar stone	Brannon, N.F.	D086-382
1977	9	Armagh	Armagh City	Abbey Street Old Meeting House	Early Christian/ medieval occupation	Lynn, C.J.	H875-544
1977	10	Armagh	Armagh City	Scotch Street	Early Christian/ medieval ecclesiastical	Lynn, C.J.	H878-544
1977	11	Armagh	Armagh City	Scotch Street	Neolithic/ Early Christian	Lynn, C.J.	H877-451
1977	12	Armagh	Dorsey		Earthworks	Lynn, C.J.	J950-196
1977	13	Armagh	Shewis		Ringfort	Brannon, N.F.	H928-463
1977	14	Cork	Rigsdale		Moated site	Sweetman, P.D.	W602-610
1977	15	Cork	Maughanasilly		Stone alignment	Lynch, A.	W105-058
1977	16	Derry	Ballygroll		Field wall etc.	Williams, B.B.	C532-640
1977	17	Derry	Ballykelly	Walworth House	Plantation bawn	Lacy, B.	C624-227
1977	18	Derry	Coleraine	Bishopsgate	Medieval & post-medieval urban	Brannon, N.F.	C847-323
1977	19	Derry	Killeague		Urn burial	Collins, A.E.P.	C835-245
1977	20	Derry	Derry City		Post-medieval urban	Lacy, B.	C435-157
1977	21	Derry	Mount Sandel		Mesolithic settlement	Woodman, P.C.	C853-307
1977	22	Derry	Movanagher		Post-medieval settlement	Blades, B.S.	C920-159
1977	23	Derry	Mullaboy		Field wall	Williams, B.B.	C532-640
1977	24	Derry	Oughtymore		Early Christian occupation	Woodman, P.C.	C360-660
1977	25	Donegal	Ardaravan		Cist	Kelly, E.P.	C350-318
1977	26	Donegal	Tievebane		Cist	Kelly, E.P.	C364-240
1977	27	Down	Carnalbanagh East		Ringfort	Brannon, N.F.	J152-604
1977	28	Down	Church Quarter		Motte	Brannon, N.F.	J418-739
1977	29	Down	Drumbroneth	Dromore	Ringforts	Brannon, N.F.	J198-526
1977	30	Down	Dundrum Sandhills		Urn burial	Collins, A.E.P.	J405-345
1977	31	Down	Glendhu		Bronze Age habitation	Woodman, P.C.	J383-763
1977	32	Down	Greencastle		Castle	Lynn, C.J.	J247-119
1977	33	Down	Nendrum		Cashel & ecclesiastical site	Brannon, N.F.	J524-636
1977	34	Down	Rathmullan Lower		Ringfort & motte	Lynn, C.J.	J477-374
1977	35	Down	St John's Point		Church	Brannon, N.F.	J527-338
1977	36	Dublin	Ballyman	Glenmunire	Habitation site	O'Brien, E.	O238-186
1977	37	Dublin	Dublin City	Fishamble Street/ John's Lane	Medieval urban	Wallace, P.	O150-340
1977	38	Dublin	Glassamucky		Cist & pit burial	Kelly, E.P.	O101-234
1977	39	Fermanagh	Carn		Cashel	Brannon, N.F.	H231-654
1977	40	Fermanagh	Kilsmullan		Bronze axe findspot	Williams, B.B.	H248-654
1977	41	Fermanagh	Lisdoo	Castle Balfour Demesne	Ringfort	Brannon, N.F.	H363-332
1977	42	Kerry	Ardamore		Cross-slab	Manning, C.	V520-998
1977	43	Kerry	Fahan	Dunbeg	Promontory fort	Barry, T.B.	V342-974
1977	44	Kerry	Gallarus		Souterrain	Kelly, E.P.	Q396-044
1977	45	Kildare	Kilteel	Kilteel Upper	Church	Manning, C.	N985-212
1977	46	Kildare	Naas	Blackcastle	Medieval urban	Campbell, K.	N883-195
1977	47	Kilkenny	Graiguenamanagh	Duiske Abbey	Cistercian abbey	Bradley, J. and Manning, C.	S710-438
1977	48	Kilkenny	Kilkenny City	Black Abbey	Dominican friary	Ó Floinn, R.	S503-561
1977	49	Limerick	Ballyduff		Earthwork	Cleary, R.M. and Hurley, V.	R210-795
1977	50	Limerick	Lough Gur	Ballynagallagh	Cist grave & primary cremation	Cleary, R.M. and Jones, C.	R392-643
1977	51	Limerick	Lough Gur	Knockadoon Hill	Multi-period site	Cleary, R.M.	R644-408
1977	52	Louth	Dundalk	Ballybarrack	Souterrains & enclosure	Kelly, E.P.	J035-054

1977	53	Louth	Port		Prehistoric pit	Kelly, E.P.	O149-893
1977	54	Mayo	Carrownaglogh	Glenurla	Cultivation—early	Herity, M.	G360-190
1977	55	Meath	Balronny		Souterrain	Eogan, G.	N983-769
1977	56	Meath	Betaghstown		Cist	Kelly, E.P.	O159-730
1977	57	Meath	Betaghstown		Iron Age cemetery	Kelly, E.P.	O159-730
1977	58	Meath	Knowth		Multi-period site	Eogan, G.	N999-738
1977	59	Meath	Nevinstown		Various	Cahill, M.	N690-850
1977	60	Meath	Ninch		Prehistoric burial mound	Sweetman, P.D.	O157-710
1977	61	Meath	Sarsfieldstown		Souterrain	Kelly, E.P.	O149-682
1977	62	Meath	Trim	Trim Castle	Medieval castle	Sweetman, P.D.	N802-564
1977	62	Offaly	Boora		Mesolithic site	Ryan, M.F.	N150-180
1977	63	Offaly	Clonmacnoise		Monastic site	Manning, C.	N009-304
1977	64	Offaly	Lehinch		Prehistoric cemetery	Ó Floinn, R.	N263-330
1977	65	Sligo	Carrowmore	Knocknarea North	Megalithic tombs	Burenhult, G.	G660-330
1977	66	Sligo	Knocknashammer		Tumulus	Timoney, M.A.	G672-331
1977	67	Tipperary	Ardcroney		Late Neolithic burial cairn	Wallace, P.	R880-873
1977	68	Tipperary	Lackenavorna	Killederdadrum	Early Christian enclosure	Manning, C.	R950-721
1977	69	Tyrone	Ballybriest	Altanagh	Prehistoric burial site	Williams, B.B.	H762-261
1977	70	Tyrone	Beaghmore		Cairn	Brannon, N.F.	H684-841
1977	71	Tyrone	Clogher	Clogher Demesne	Multi-period settlement	Warner, R.B.	H538-506
1977	72	Tyrone	Creggandevesky		Court cairn	Foley, C.	H643-750
1977	73	Tyrone	Radergan		Megalith	Brannon, N.F.	H555-644
1977	74	Waterford	Kilnagrange		Cooking place	Cahill, M.	S397-077
1977	75	Wicklow	Glendalough	Brockagh	Monastic site environs	Manning, C.	T125-967
1977	76	Wicklow	Carrignamuck		Hut sites	Brindley, A.M.	T040-339
1977	77	Wicklow	Rathgall	Rath East	Hillfort	Raftery, B.	S902-731

JIA V (1989/90) covered Excavations 1980–4

1980	2	Antrim	Ballyutoag		Early Christian upland settlement	Williams, B.B.	J273-795
1980	3	Antrim	Ballyutoag		Prehistoric enclosure	Yates, M.J.	J288-795
1980	4	Antrim	Ballyvollen		Early Christian ironworking site	Williams, B.B.	J130-729
1980	5	Antrim	Ballywee		Early Christian settlement	Lynn, C.J.	J219-899
1980	6	Antrim	Bay	Bay Farm	Neolithic & Bronze Age settlements	Mallory, J.P.	D290-165
1980	7	Antrim	Belfast	Castle Street	17th-century urban site	Brannon, N.F.	J336-743
1980	8	Antrim	Belfast	High Street	17th-century urban site	Brannon, N.F.	J341-744
1980	10	Antrim	Carnaghliss		Rectangular earthwork	Williams, B.B.	
1980	12	Antrim	Carnlough North	Windy Ridge	Neolithic site	Woodman, P.C. and Doggart, R.	D283-189
1980	13	Antrim	Carnlough North	Windy Ridge	Early Christian or medieval enclosure	Hamond, F.W.	D283-189
1980	14	Antrim	Carrickfergus	Antrim Street	Medieval urban	Brannon, N.F.	J414-875
1980	15	Antrim	Carrickfergus	Joymount	Town walls	Brannon, N.F.	J415-875
1980	16	Antrim	Deer Park Farms		Raised rath	Lynn, C.J.	D287-088
1980	18	Antrim	Donegore Hill	Freemanstown/ Tobergill	Neolithic site	Mallory, J.P.	J214-892
1980	19	Antrim	Drumnakeel		Urn burials	Williams, B.B.	D163-398
1980	21	Antrim	Glenmakeeran		Cist grave & settlement sites	Williams, B.B. and Robinson, P.S.	D165-374
1980	22	Antrim	Greenisland	Castle Lug	Post-medieval castle	Brannon, N.F.	J374-844
1980	23	Antrim	Killylane		Rectangular enclosure	Williams, B.B.	J277-990
1980	24	Antrim	Lambeg	Richmond Court	Coin hoard site	Brannon, N.F.	J283-667
1980	25	Antrim	Lemnalary Mountain	Lough-na-Trosk Cave	Prehistoric industrial site	Woodman, P.C.	D273-199

1980	26	Antrim	Lemnalary Mountain	Lough-na-Trosk Cave	Occupation site	Woodman, P.C.	D270-200
1980	27	Antrim	Lissanduff	Pool	Earthworks	Warner, R.B.	C930-422
1980	28	Antrim	Rathlin Island	Church Bay	Cist graves	Wiggins, K.	D150-508
1980	30	Antrim	Slievenacloy		18th-century earthwork	Williams, B.B.	J245-708
1980	31	Antrim	Tievebulliagh	Cloghs	Neolithic industrial site	Mallory, J.P.	D193-266
1980	32	Antrim	Tildarg		Rectangular earthwork	Brannon, N.F.	J240-966
1980	34	Armagh	Armagh City	Scotch Street	Early Christian cemetery	Lynn, C.J. and McDowell, J.A.	H877-450
1980	35	Armagh	Armagh City	Scotch Street	Ecclesiastical enclosure	McDowell, J.A.	H877-450
1980	38	Armagh	Castleraw		17th-century house	Brannon, N.F.	H927-529
1980	40	Armagh	Legarhill		Ecclesiastical enclosure	Lynn, C.J.	H863-452
1980	41	Carlow	Killinane		Cist	Moore, M.	S691-632
1980	45	Cork	Ballyrobert		Trivallate ringfort	Power, D.	W870-920
1980	47	Cork	Cappeen West	Cahervagliair	Ringfort	Manning, C.	W313-605
1980	48	Cork	Castlecooke		Tower-house environs	Cleary, R.M.	R877-035
1980	49	Cork	Castleredmond		*Fulacht fiadh*	Doody, M.G.	W893-720
1980	51	Cork	Cork City	Grattan Street	Medieval city wall	Power, D.	W670-710
1980	52	Cork	Cork City	St Peter's Market	Medieval urban	Hurley, M.F.	W676-718
1980	53	Cork	Cork City	Tobin Street	Medieval urban	Papazian, C.	W671-710
1980	54	Cork	Cork City	Tuckey Street	Medieval city wall	Power, D.	W670-710
1980	55	Cork	Dromnea		*Fulacht fiadh*	Cleary, R.M.	
1980	57	Cork	Glanworth	Boherash	Castle	Manning, C.	R757-041
1980	58	Cork	Kilcor South		*Fulacht fiadh*	Hurley, M.F.	W864-888
1980	59	Cork	Cork City	Leitrim Street	Tower-house environs	Walsh, G.	W670-711
1980	60	Cork	Liscahane		Ringfort	Ó Donnabháin, B.	W283-893
1980	61	Cork	Lisleagh		Ringfort	Monk, M.A.	R786-065
1980	62	Cork	Mount Gabriel		Bronze Age copper mines	O'Brien, B.	V939-348
1980	63	Derry	Ballymulholland		Iron Age settlement	Mallory, J.P.	C659-350
1980	64	Derry	Brackfield		Bawn	Brannon, N.F.	C511-096
1980	65	Derry	Coleraine	New Row	17th-century house site	Brannon, N.F.	C849-323
1980	66	Derry	Coleraine	St Mary's Dominican Priory	17th-century urban site	Brannon, N.F.	C849-323
1980	68	Derry	Derry City	Derry Walls	Water bastion	Brannon, N.F.	C435-167
1980	69	Derry	Dungiven		Post-medieval manor house	Brannon, N.F.	C692-091
1980	70	Derry	Knockoneill		Court cairn	Flanagan, L.N.W.	C820-087
1980	71	Derry	Macosquin		Ecclesiastical site	Brannon, N.F.	C826-287
1980	72	Derry	Mount Sandel		Mesolithic settlement	Woodman, P.C.	C853-307
1980	73	Derry	Tamnyrankin		Court cairn	Flanagan, L.N.W.	C834-103
1980	74	Donegal	Lisnamulligan		Cist burial	Ó Floinn, R.	H244-924
1980	75	Donegal	Tonbane Glebe		Medieval sandhills occupation	Lacy, B.	C167-446
1980	76	Down	Ballybeen		Standing stone	Mallory, J.P.	J426-731
1980	77	Down	Ballyginny		Souterrain	Brannon, N.F.	J370-347
1980	78	Down	Castlereagh		16th-century castle site	McNeill, T.E.	J374-710
1980	79	Down	Downpatrick	Demesne of Down	Medieval occupation site	Brannon, N.F.	J483-444
1980	81	Down	Gransha		Ringfort/mound	Lynn, C.J.	J531-769
1980	82	Down	Greencastle		Earthwork & castle	Lynn, C.J.	J247-118
1980	83	Down	Inch	Inch Abbey	Cistercian ecclesiastical site	Brannon, N.F.	J477-455
1980	84	Down	Inch	Inch Abbey	Cistercian ecclesiastical site	Meek, M.	J477-455
1980	85	Down	Kirkistown		17th-century tower-house	Brannon, N.F.	J646-580
1980	86	Down	Maghera	Carnacavill	Ecclesiastical site	Lynn, C.J.	J372-341

1980	87	Down	Movilla		Ecclesiastical site	Yates, M.J. and Ivens, R.J.	H842-460
1980	89	Down	Newtownards	Castle Street	17th-century house	Brannon, N.F.	J492-739
1980	91	Down	Tullylish		Ecclesiastical enclosure	Ivens, R.J.	J223-486
1980	92	Dublin	Artaine South	Artane	Church	McMahon, M.	O189-382
1980	93	Dublin	Auburn		Landscape feature	Keeling, D.	O207-445
1980	94	Dublin	Ballyman	Glenmunire	Multi-period site	O'Brien, E.	O238-186
1980	95	Dublin	Ballymount Great		Medieval/ post-medieval site	Stout, G.	O090-304
1980	97	Dublin	Dublin City	Bridge Street	Medieval urban	O Rahilly, C.	O144-340
1980	99	Dublin	Dublin City	Ship Street/ St Michael le Pole	Church	Campbell, K. and Gowen, M.	O153-337
1980	101	Dublin	Laughanstown	Tully	Grave-slab—early	Healy, P.	O234-235
1980	103	Dublin	Robswalls	Paddy's Hill	Flint scatter	Keeling, D.	O240-446
1980	104	Dublin	Taylor's Grange	The Brehon's Chair	Portal tomb	Keeley, V.J.	O130-265
1980	105	Fermanagh	Cloghcor		Stone circle	Williams, B.B.	H295-405
1980	106	Fermanagh	Coolcran		Ringfort	Williams, B.B.	H365-500
1980	107	Fermanagh	Glengesh		Megalith site	Williams, B.B.	H391-537
1980	108	Fermanagh	Killygreagh		Ringfort	Lynn, C.J.	H286-273
1980	109	Fermanagh	Kilsmullan		Early Iron Age stone structure	Williams, B.B.	H248-654
1980	110	Fermanagh	Kiltierney	Archdall Deerpark	Passage grave & Iron Age cemetery	Foley, C. Williams, B.B.	H218-627 H337-446
1980	111	Fermanagh	Shanco		Cist burial		
1980	112	Galway	Abbeyknockmoy	Abbert Demesne	Cistercian abbey	Sweetman, P.D.	M508-565
1980	113	Galway	Annaghkeen		Clot burial	Ó Floinn, R.	M010 101
1980	117	Kildare	Naas	Blackcastle	Medieval settlement	Sleeman, M.J.	S728-838
1980	118	Kildare	Cupidstown	The Pale Ditch	Linear earthwork	O'Donnell, M.	
1980	119	Kildare	Forenaghts Great		Burial mound	Grogan, E.	N928-207
1980	120	Kildare	Haynestown		Cist burial environs	Manning, C.	N943-195
1980	121	Kildare	Killeen Cormac	Colbinstown	Church site	O'Donnell, M.	
1980	122	Kildare	Punchestown Great		Cist burial	Kelly, E.P.	N928-151
1980	123	Kildare	Timolin		Cist burial	Ó Floinn, R.	S797-937
1980	124	Kildare	Timolin		Cist burial	O'Connor, N.	S797-940
1980	125	Kilkenny	Clohogue		*Fulacht fiadh*	O'Flaherty, B.	
1980	126	Kilkenny	Kells	Rathduff— Kells Priory	Augustinian priory	Fanning, T.	S499-434
1980	127	Kilkenny	Kilferagh		Medieval habitation site	Hurley, M.F.	S550-525
1980	128	Kilkenny	Rathcash West		Deserted village? site	Lehane, D.	
1980	129	Kilkenny	Kilferagh/ Sheastown	St Fiachra's Well	Holy well	Cotter, C.	S550-525
1980	130	Kilkenny	Shankill		Linear earthwork	O'Flaherty, B.	
1980	132	Limerick	Limerick City	Charlotte's Quay	Medieval town defences	Lynch, A.	R577-575
1980	134	Louth	Drogheda	James' Street	Medieval & post-medieval urban	Campbell, K.	O095-750
1980	135	Louth	Drogheda	Shop Street	Medieval quayside	Sweetman, P.D.	O090-751
1980	136	Louth	Dundalk	Market Square	Post-medieval urban	Campbell, K.	J048-073
1980	137	Louth	Dundalk	Marshes Upper	Early Christian settlement	Gosling, P.	J066-049
1980	138	Louth	Dundalk	Marshes Upper	Early Christian settlement	Gosling, P.	J060-048
1980	141	Louth	Millockstown		Iron Age/Early Christian settlement	Manning, C.	N977-875
1980	142	Louth	Newtownbalregan		Cist burial	Manning, C.	J018-077
1980	145	Mayo	Greenwood		Wedge tomb	Sheehan, J.	M442-803
1980	146	Mayo	Shrule	Moyne	Early ecclesiastical enclosure	Manning, C.	M255-500
1980	147	Meath	Boolies Lower		Souterrain & lintel graves	Sweetman, P.D.	O041-655
1980	148	Meath	Duleek	Commons	Motte site	Campbell, K.	O049-686

1980	149	Meath	Fourknocks		Early Bronze Age habitation/ burial site	King, H.A.	O113-621
1980	151	Meath	Moynagh Lough	Brittas	Crannog	Bradley, J.	N818-860
1980	152	Meath	Newgrange		Pit circle	Sweetman, P.D.	O007-727
1980	153	Meath	Newgrange		Late Neolithic/ Early Bronze Age habitation	Sweetman, P.D.	O006-727
1980	154	Meath	Newtown Trim	St John's	Priory of Fratres Cruciferi	Sweetman, P.D.	N817-568
1980	156	Monaghan	Aghareagh	Black Pig's Dyke	Linear earthwork	Walsh, A.	H510-170
1980	157	Offaly	Cloncraff/ Bloomhill	The Giant's Road	Bog road	Breen, T.C.	N070-337
1980	158	Roscommon	Boyle	Knocknashee	Cistercian abbey	Lynch, A.	G802-032
1980	159	Roscommon	Cloonelt		Standing stone?	Gosling, P.	M604-818
1980	160	Roscommon	Glenballythomas	Dathi's Mound	Ring-barrow	Waddell, J.	M800-830
1980	162	Sligo	Ballymote		Castle	Sweetman, P.D.	G661-155
1980	163	Sligo	Carrowmore	Knocknarea North	Megalithic tombs	Burenhult, G.	G660-330
1980	165	Sligo	Carrowmore	Knocknarea North	Hut site	Burenhult, G.	G660-330
1980	166	Tipperary	Ashley Park		Neolithic burial mound	Manning, C.	R874-869
1980	167	Tipperary	Ballycullin		Ringfort environs	Doody, M.G.	S315-371
1980	168	Tipperary	Ballyveelish		Multi-period site	Doody, M.G.	S180-270
1980	169	Tipperary	Cashel	St Patrick's Rock	Cross	Lynch, A.	S075-407
1980	170	Tipperary	Curraghatoor		Late Bronze Age habitation	Doody, M.G.	S010-178
1980	171	Tipperary	Curraghtarsna		*Fulacht fiadh*	Buckley, V.M.	S104-410
1980	172	Tipperary	Derrynaflan	Lurgoe	Monastic site	Cahill, M.	S108-495
1980	173	Tipperary	Drumlummin		17th-century house	Cleary, R.M.	R988-165
1980	174	Tipperary	Garryntemple		Souterrain	Hurley, M.F.	S130-222
1980	175	Tipperary	Kilcash		Church	Sweetman, P.D.	S323-272
1980	176	Tipperary	Moorabbey		Franciscan friary	Lynch, A.	R801-208
1980	177	Tipperary	Rochestown		Tower-house & church environs	Hurley, M.F.	
1980	178	Tipperary	Roscrea	Townsparks	Castle	Stout, G.	S136-892
1980	179	Tyrone	Altanagh		Cairn & ringfort	Williams, B.B.	H623-693
1980	181	Tyrone	Castletown	Mellon House	17th-century house	Brannon, N.F.	H434-769
1980	183	Tyrone	Creggandevesky		Court cairn	Foley, C.	H646-750
1980	184	Tyrone	Derryloran		Ecclesiastical site	Brannon, N.F.	H805-768
1980	185	Tyrone	Doras		Ecclesiastical enclosure	McDowell, J.A.	H815-678
1980	186	Tyrone	Dunmisk	Dunmisk Fort	Early Christian ecclesiastical enclosure	Ivens, R.J.	H628-706
1980	188	Tyrone	Farrest		Earthwork enclosure	Lynn, C.J.	H443-792
1980	190	Tyrone	Ballybriest	Killyliss	Ringfort	Ivens, R.J.	H757-605
1980	191	Tyrone	Tamlaght		Ringfort	Foley, C.	
1980	192	Tyrone	The Bonn		Bawn	Brannon, N.F.	H714-710
1980	193	Tyrone	Tremoge		Cist burial	Foley, C.	H667-733
1980	194	Tyrone	Tully		Mound	Ivens, R.J.	H417-766
1980	195	Tyrone	Tullylinton		Standing stone	Yates, M.J.	H610-586
1980	196	Waterford	Waterford City	Lady Lane	Medieval urban	Moore, M.	S607-118
1980	197	Westmeath	Ballaghkeeran		Viking longfort?	Fanning, T.	N073-445
1980	198	Westmeath	Clonickilvant		Cist burial	Cahill, M.	N528-524
1980	199	Westmeath	Killucan/ Corbetstown	Kilpatrick	Early ecclesiastical site	Swan, D.L.	N575-558
1980	200	Westmeath	Killarecastle	Uisneach	Cist burial	Sheehan, J.	
1980	201	Westmeath	Newtownlow		Crannog	Bourke, C.	N379-369
1980	202	Wexford	Ferrycarrig	Newtown	Ringwork	Bennett, I.	T013-230
1980	203	Wexford	Tintern		Cistercian abbey	Lynch, A.	S795-100
1980	204	Wexford	Wexford Town	Bride Street	Town wall	Meenan, R.	T049-213
1980	205	Wexford	Wexford Town	Custom House Quay	Medieval urban?	Keeling, D.	T049-218
1980	206	Wicklow	Ballyremon Commons		*Fulacht fiadh*	Buckley, V.M.	O219-122
1980	207	Wicklow	Britonstown		Long cist graves	Clinton, M.	N946-082
1980	209	Wicklow	Glassnamullen	The Moat	Pit graves	Ó Floinn, R.	O220-102

Excavations resumes publication

1985	1	Antrim	Ballycraigy		Ring-ditch & stone circle	Brannon, N.F.	D384-039
1985	2	Antrim	Ballyhill Lower		Ringfort	Williams, B.B.	J223-870
1985	3	Antrim	Craigs		Passage grave	Williams, B.B.	C974-172
1985	4	Antrim	Craigs		Settlement site	Williams, B.B.	C977-176
1985	5	Antrim	Deer Park Farms		Raised rath	Lynn, C.J.	D288-088
1985	6	Antrim	Donegore Hill	Six-Mile Water	Neolithic ditched enclosure	Mallory, J.P.	J214-892
1985	7	Antrim	Carrickfergus	Woodburn Abbey	Abbey	Brannon, N.F.	J403-870
1985	8	Armagh	Armagh City	Scotch Street	Early Christian cemetery & medieval/ post-medieval settlement	McDowell, J.A.	H875-544
1985	9	Clare	Ballyconry		Enclosure	Blair Gibson, D.	M280-990
1985	10	Cork	Cork City	Grand Parade	Medieval urban	Hurley, M.F.	W672-716
1985	11	Cork	Clashroe		*Fulacht fiadh*	Hurley, M.F.	R305-135
1985	12	Cork	Mount Gabriel		Mines—primitive	O'Brien, B.	V938-348
1985	13	Cork	Timoleague		Medieval friary	Manning, C.	W473-437
1985	14	Derry	Maghera	Craigadick	Early Christian/ medieval settlement	Brannon, N.F.	C855-002
1985	15	Derry	Cuilbane		Stone circle	Yates, M.J.	C830-122
1985	16	Derry	Straid		Cist burials	Brannon, N.F.	C596-058
1985	17	Derry	Tullynure		Ecclesiastical enclosure boundary	Brannon, N.F.	H806-828
1985	18	Donegal	Dohallion Upper		Cist	Cahill, M.	C818-107
1985	19	Donegal	Carrickfin		Coastal midden	Raftery, B.	B780-225
1985	20	Down	Downpatrick	Demesne of Down	Standing stone	Brannon, N.F.	J485-434
1985	21	Down	Newtownards		Medieval urban	Brannon, N.F.	J493-739
1985	22	Dublin	Ballyman	Glenmunire	Early Christian/ medieval church site	O'Brien, E.	O238-186
1985	23	Dublin	Broomfield		Circular ditched enclosure	O'Brien, E.	O163-546
1985	24	Dublin	Dublin City	Dublin Castle	Pre-Norman to 18th-century	Lynch, A.	O154-340
1985	25	Dublin	Dublin City	Inns Quay Ward	Medieval & post-medieval	McMahon, M.	O149-342
1985	26	Dublin	Scholarstown	Fairy Fort	Ringfort	Keeley, V.J.	O115-260
1985	27	Dublin	Taylor's Grange	The Brehon's Chair	Portal tomb	Keeley, V.J.	O130-265
1985	28	Galway	Athenry		Town wall fosse	Rynne, E.	M505-278
1985	29	Galway	Athenry	Ballydavid South	Mound	Rynne, E.	M503-285
1985	30	Galway	Killeaney	Temple Benan/ Tighlagheany	Churches	Manning, C.	L893-068
1985	31	Kerry	Ferriter's Cove	Ballyoughteragh South	Mesolithic/Neolithic settlement	Woodman, P.C.	Q321-055
1985	32	Kerry	Derrynane More	Abbey Island	Monastic site	Power, C.	V516-584
1985	33	Kerry	Dromkeen East		Lintel graves	Bennett, I.	Q829-308
1985	34	Kerry	Loher		Cashel	O'Flaherty, B.	V560-615
1985	35	Kilkenny	Castletown	Kilkieran	Early Christian monastic settlement	Hurley, M.F.	S421-274
1985	36	Limerick	Lough Gur	Knockadoon Hill	Neolithic? habitation site	Cleary, R.M.	R644-408
1985	37	Longford	Corlea	Cloonbreany, Derryoughil	Bog road	Raftery, B.	N095-628
1985	38	Longford	Melkagh	Dermot & Grania's Bed	Portal tomb	Cooney, G.	N161-879
1985	39	Louth	Drogheda	James' Street	Medieval urban	Campbell, K.	O095-750
1985	40	Louth	Dundalk	Marshes Upper	Early Christian settlement	Buteaux, S.	J065-049
1985	41	Meath	Moynagh Lough	Brittas	Crannog	Bradley, J.	N818-860
1985	42	Meath	Crossakeel		Cist	Cahill, M.	N655-752
1985	43	Meath	Knowth		Passage grave & other activities	Eogan, G.	N999-738
1985	44	Meath	Randalstown		Early Christian souterrain	Campbell, K.	N842-715
1985	45	Offaly	Clonmacnoise		Monastic site	Manning, C.	N008-307

1985	46	Offaly	Durrow Demesne	Sheeon Hill	Cemetery	Ó Floinn, R.	N323-306
1985	47	Roscommon	Cartron		Castle site	Morahan, L.	M990-423
1985	48	Sligo	Drumcliffe South	St Columba's Church	Monastic site	Enright, J.	G681-420
1985	49	Sligo	Glen		Bank	Bergh, S.	G636-275
1985	50	Sligo	Glen		Passage grave	Bergh, S.	G636-275
1985	51	Sligo	Primrose Grange		Enclosure	Bergh, S.	G637-329
1985	52	Tipperary	Glenbane		Church & burial site	Power, C.	R797-364
1985	53	Tipperary	Derrynaflan	Lurgoe	Monastic settlement	Ó Floinn, R.	S108-490
1985	54	Tipperary	Cashel	St Patrick's Rock	Ecclesiastical site	Manning, C.	S075-407
1985	55	Waterford	Waterford City	High Street/ Exchange Street	Medieval & post-medieval urban	Stevens, S.	S607-122
1985	56	Waterford	Waterford City	Deanery Garden	Medieval & post-medieval urban	O Rahilly, C.	S607-121
1985	57	Waterford	Waterford City	Grady's Yard/ John Street	Medieval urban	Murtagh, B.	S607-119
1985	58	Westmeath	Newtownlow		Crannog	Bourke, C.	N379-369
1985	59	Wexford	MacMurroughs		Castle site & prehistoric? activity	Cotter, C.	S729-302
1985	60	Wicklow	Carrig		Cist cairn	Grogan, E.	N998-122
1986	1	Antrim	Ballyvaston		Prehistoric settlement	Williams, B.B.	J310-790
1986	2	Antrim	Connor	Rectory Field	Early Christian ecclesiastical site	Brannon, N.F.	J150-969
1986	3	Antrim	Deer Park Farms		Raised rath	Lynn, C.J.	D288-088
1986	4	Antrim	Galboly Lower	Garron	Prehistoric field wall	Hartwell, B.	D239-239
1986	5	Antrim	Glengormley		Ringfort	Brannon, N.F.	J314-815
1986	6	Antrim	Kilcoan More		Ecclesiastical site	Williams, B.B.	J460-985
1986	7	Antrim	Nappan		Neolithic site	Sheridan, A.	D289-236
1986	8	Antrim	Templemoyle	Kells Abbey	Augustinian church	Brannon, N.F.	J141-971
1986	9	Armagh	Armagh City	Scotch Street	Early Christian/ medieval	McDowell, J.A.	H875-544
1986	10	Carlow	Kilgraney		Cist grave	Cahill, M.	S556-708
1986	11	Clare	Poulnabrone		Portal tomb	Lynch, A.	M235-010
1986	12	Clare	Teaskagh		Unenclosed domestic habitation	Blair Gibson, D.	R282-963
1986	13	Cork	Ballynageeragh		Medieval? occupation features	Tarbett, C. *et al.*	R553-148
1986	14	Cork	Cloughlucas South		Round house & *fulacht fiadh*	Tarbett, C. and Crone, J.	R546-019
1986	15	Cork	Ballintra West	Guileen	Prehistoric site	Johnson, G.	W875-603
1986	16	Cork	Pepperhill		Neolithic habitation site	Tarbett, C. and Crone, J.	R525-081
1986	17	Cork	Poul Gorm	Glengarriff	Shell midden	McCarthy, A.	V930-562
1986	18	Donegal	Magheracar	Giant's Grave	Passage grave	Cody, E.	G795-588
1986	19	Down	Downpatrick	Demesne of Down	Early Christian/ medieval church site	Brannon, N.F.	J483-444
1986	20	Down	Downpatrick	Demesne of Down	Medieval urban	Brannon, N.F.	J486-446
1986	21	Dublin	Ballyman	Glenmunire	Early Christian/ medieval church site	O'Brien, E.	O238-186
1986	22	Dublin	Grange	Grange Abbey	Medieval church	Swan, D.L. and Ní Ghabhláin, S.	O224-403
1986	23	Dublin	Dublin City	Merchants' Quay	Early Christian/ medieval church environs	McMahon, M.	O153-341
1986	24	Dublin	Rathfarnham	Rathfarnham Castle	Castle	Carroll, J.	O144-268
1986	25	Dublin	Dublin City	Dublin Castle	Medieval/ post-medieval castle	Lynch, A.	O154-340
1986	26	Dublin	Taylor's Grange	The Brehon's Chair	Portal tomb	Keeley, V.J.	O130-265
1986	27	Galway	Ard	Lough Corrib	Long stone cist?	Casey, M.	M173-433
1986	28	Galway	Tuam	St Mary's Cathedral	Cathedral & graveyard	Clyne, M.	M443-518
1986	29	Kerry	Ballybunion		Shell middens	McCarthy, A.	Q865-412
1986	30	Kerry	Ferriter's Cove	Ballyoughteragh South	Mesolithic/ Neolithic	Woodman, P.C. Manning, C.	Q321-055 V447-805
1986	31	Kerry	Kimego West	Cahergal	Stone fort		
1986	32	Kerry	Sceilg Mhichíl (Great Skellig)		Early Christian monastic site	Lynch, A.	V248-609

1986	33	Kildare	Rathcoffey Demesne	Rathcoffey Castle	Castle	Byrne, G.	N890-320
1986	34	Kildare	Timahoe West		Trackway (togher)	Munro, M.	N747-325
1986	35	Laois	Aghaboe		Medieval monastic site	Candon, A.	S324-856
1986	36	Limerick	Adamstown		Bronze Age ditch & enclosed features	Grogan, E.	R674-313
1986	37	Limerick	Ballycahane Lower		*Fulacht fiadh*	Walsh, C.	R546-461
1986	38	Limerick	Ballycahane Upper		*Fulacht fiadh*	Walsh, C.	R551-448
1986	39	Limerick	Ballygrennan		Standing stone	Ó Donnabháin, B.	R623-345
1986	40	Limerick	Ballynatona		Bronze Age? pit	Walsh, C.	R776-269
1986	41	Limerick	Boherygeela		Ancient? road/ trackway	Gowen, M.	R589-390
1986	42	Limerick	Cloghnaclocka		*Fulacht fiadh*	Walsh, C.	R536-496
1986	43	Limerick	Doonmoon		Ring-barrow	Tarbett, C.	R696-306
1986	44	Limerick	Duntryleague		Group of pits	Walsh, C.	R762-277
1986	45	Limerick	Duntryleague		Bronze Age ring-ditch?	Grogan, E.	R761-277
1986	46	Limerick	Duntryleague		Bronze Age pits	Walsh, C.	R761-277
1986	47	Limerick	Duntryleague		Bronze Age features	Walsh, C. and Grogan, E.	R759-278
1986	48	Limerick	Duntryleague		Bronze Age? pit	Grogan, E.	R759-278
1986	49	Limerick	Elton		Bronze Age features	Gowen, M.	R686-309
1986	50	Limerick	Lough Gur	Knockadoon Hill	Prehistoric occupation site	Cleary, R.M.	R644-408
1986	51	Limerick	Mitchelstown East		Bronze Age pit	Walsh, C.	R742-287
1986	52	Limerick	Mitchelstown East		Cremation pits	Walsh, C.	R735-289
1986	53	Limerick	Mitchelstown North		Cremation pit cemetery	Grogan, E.	R717-295
1986	54	Limerick	Mitchelstown North		No archaeological significance	Gowen, M.	R735-289
1986	55	Limerick	Raheen		Ring-barrow	Walsh, C.	R747-286
1986	56	Limerick	Raheen		*Fulacht fiadh*	Grogan, E. and Walsh, C.	R748-285
1986	57	Limerick	Rathcahill West		Cist grave	Kelly, E.P.	R224-277
1986	58	Limerick	Shanaclogh		Ring-barrow	Gowen, M. *et al.*	R545-465
1986	59	Limerick	Spittle		Curvilinear ditch	Walsh, C.	R781-265
1986	60	Limerick	Spittle		Bronze Age pits	Grogan, E.	R772-265
1986	61	Limerick	Tankardstown		Neolithic house	Tarbett, C.	R584-282
1986	62	Longford	Corlea	Cloonbreany, Derryoughil	Bog road	Raftery, B.	N095-628
1986	63	Longford	Melkagh	Dermot & Grania's Bed	Portal tomb	Cooney, G.	N161-879
1986	64	Meath	Knowth		Passage grave	Eogan, G.	N995-735
1986	65	Meath	Randalstown		Souterrain & well	Campbell, K.	N850-713
1986	66	Offaly	Cloncraff/ Bloomhill	The Giant's Road	Medieval roadway	Breen, T.C.	N070-337
1986	66	Westmeath	Ballynahownwood	The Giant's Road	Medieval roadway	Breen, T.C.	N070-337
1986	67	Sligo	Carrickahorna East	Passage grave	Bergh, S.		G755-116
1986	68	Sligo	Drumcliffe South	St Columba's Church	Early Christian monastic site	Enright, J.	G681-420
1986	69	Tipperary	Ballynaraha		Corn-drying kiln	O'Donnell, M.	S311-247
1986	70	Tipperary	Derrynaflan	Lurgoe	Monastic settlement	Ó Floinn, R.	S108-490
1986	71	Tyrone	Doras		Ecclesiastical structure	McDowell, J.A.	H815-678
1986	72	Tyrone	Dunmisk	Dunmisk Fort	Ecclesiastical structure	Ivens, R.J.	H828-706
1986	73	Tyrone	Gortatray		Penannular enclosure	Laverty, D.	H860-705
1986	74	Waterford	Bally Lough	Fornaught Strand	Mesolithic/ Neolithic sites	Zvelebil, M., Moore, J.A., and Green S.W.	S707-036
1986	74	Waterford	Bally Lough	Monvoy	Mesolithic/ Neolithic sites	Zvelebil, M., Moore, J.A. and Green, S.W.	S570-030

1986	74	Waterford	Bally Lough	Knockavelish	Mesolithic/ Neolithic sites	Zvelebil, M., Moore, J.A. and Green, S.W.	S690-038
1986	74	Waterford	Bally Lough	Corbally More	Mesolithic/ Neolithic sites	Zvelebil, M., Moore, J.A. and Green, S.W.	S707-036
1986	75	Waterford	Waterford City	St Peter's Church	Medieval urban	Gittings, A.S.R.	S607-123
1986	76	Waterford	Waterford City	Grady's Yard/ John Street	Medieval/ post-medieval urban	Murtagh, B.	S607-119
1986	77	Waterford	Mayfield	Rockett's Castle	Lintel grave	O'Donnell, M.	S473-266
1986	78	Westmeath	Newtownlow		Crannog	Bourke, C.	N739-369
1986	79	Wexford	Ferrycarrig	Newtown	Ringwork	Cotter, C.	T013-230
1986	Apx1.1	Cork	Mallow	Goatisland	Gas pipeline	Gowen, M.	W193-358
1986	Apx1.3	Waterford	Ballyveelish		Gas pipeline	Gowen, M.	
1986	Apx1.2	Limerick	Barnakyle	Corracunna	Gas pipeline	Gowen, M.	R524-497
1986	Apx2	Cork/Kerry	Coastal sites		Hunter/gatherer sites	Woodman, P.C.	
1986	Apx3	Waterford	Bally Lough		Mesolithic/Neolithic colonisation	Green, S.W., Moore, J.A. and Zvelebil, M.	S707-036
1987	1	Antrim	Deer Park Farms		Raised rath	Lynn, C.J. and McDowell, J.A.	D288-088
1987	2	Antrim	Dunluce	Dunluce Castle	Post-medieval domestic	Brannon, N.F.	C904-413
1987	3	Antrim	Lyles Hill	Toberagnee	Neolithic enclosure	Simpson, D.D.A.	J248-929
1987	4	Antrim	The Dane's Cast	Killyfaddy	Linear earthwork	Lynn, C.J. *et al.*	H876-389
1987	5	Armagh	Tray	Haughey's Fort	Bronze Age/Iron Age hillfort/enclosure	Mallory, J.P.	H835-453
1987	6	Cavan	Clogh Oughter Castle	Lough Oughter	Castle	Manning, C.	H357-078
1987	7	Cork	Lisnagun	Darrara	Ringfort	O'Sullivan, J.	W413-415
1987	8	Cork	Sherkin Island	Farrancoush	Franciscan friary	Lynch, A.	W103-025
1987	9	Derry	Creggan Rath	Creggan	Ringfort	Hadfield, J.I.	C425-168
1987	10	Donegal	Magheracar	Giant's Grave	Passage grave	Cody, E.	G795-588
1987	11	Donegal	Rinnaraw		Cashel & house site	Fanning, T.	C038-368
1987	12	Down	Downpatrick	Demesne of Down	Medieval urban site	Brannon, N.F.	J483-444
1987	13	Down	Greengraves	The Kempe Stones	Portal tomb	Williams, B.B.	J445-736
1987	14	Down	Ryan		Cashel	Williams, B.B.	J142-283
1987	15	Dublin	Dundrum	Dundrum Castle	Castle	O'Brien, E.	O174-279
1987	16	Dublin	Taylor's Grange	The Brehon's Chair	Multi-period activity	Keeley, V.J.	O130-265
1987	17	Fermanagh	Enniskillen	Castle Barracks	Medieval/ post-medieval castle	Brannon, N.F.	H231-442
1987	18	Fermanagh	Killadeas Graveyard	Rockfield	Early Christian graveyard	Lanigan Wood, H.	H206-540
1987	19	Galway	Loughrea	Fairgreen	Town wall	Hayden, A.	M620-170
1987	20	Galway	Galway City	Merchants' Road	Late medieval town defences	Walsh, G.	M300-254
1987	21	Galway	Galway City	Middle Street	Post-medieval urban	Clyne, M.	M298-249
1987	22	Kerry	Ballybunion		Long stone cist	Ó Floinn, R.	Q866-405
1987	23	Kerry	Ferriter's Cove	Ballyoughteragh South	Mesolithic/ Neolithic	Woodman, P.C.	Q321-055
1987	24	Kerry	Killelton	Killelton Oratory	Church site	Manning, C.	Q719-101
1987	25	Kerry	Sceilg Mhichíl (Great Skellig)		Early Christian monastic site	Lynch, A.	V248-609
1987	26	Kildare	Crinstown		Medieval settlement site	Channing, J. and Keeley, V.J.	N919-365
1987	27	Kildare	Kilgowan		Burial-ground	Keeley, V.J.	
1987	28	Kildare	Moneycooly		Earthworks environs	Raftery, J. and Keeley, V.J.	N943-351
1987	29	Kildare	Walshetown		Mound	Byrne, G. and Keeley, V.J.	N804-128
1987	30	Limerick	Baggotstown		Cist grave in mound	Ó Floinn, R.	R657-355
1987	31	Limerick	Limerick City	Broad Street, Custom House	Medieval urban	Tarbett, C.	R581-573
1987	32	Limerick	Limerick City	John's Street, Custom House	Medieval urban	Hodkinson, B.J.	R581-573
1987	33	Limerick	Lough Gur	Knockadoon Hill	Soil-sampling near settlement	Almgren, E.	R642-406

1987	34	Limerick	Lough Gur	Knockadoon Hill	Prehistoric occupation site	Cleary, R.M.	R644-408
1987	35	Limerick	Tankardstown South		Neolithic house	Tarbett, C. and Gowen, M.	R585-281
1987	36	Longford	Corlea	Cloonbreany, Derryoughil	Bog road	Raftery, B.	N095-628
1987	37	Longford	Lough Kinale	Tonymore North	Crannog	Kelly, E.P., O'Connor, N. and Farrell, R.T.	N382-803
1987	38	Louth	Piperstown		Deserted village?	Barry, T.B.	O086-825
1987	39	Meath	Moynagh Lough	Brittas	Crannog	Bradley, J.	N818-860
1987	40	Meath	Knowth		Passage grave cemetery	Eogan, G.	N995-735
1987	41	Meath	Kells	Townparks	Monastic site environs	Byrne, G.	N739-760
1987	42	Meath	Trim	High Street	Medieval urban	Walsh, C.	N810-575
1987	43	Tipperary	Curraghatoor		Late Bronze Age habitation	Doody, M.G.	S001-108
1987	44	Tipperary	Derrynaflan	Lurgoe	Monastic settlement	Ó Floinn, R.	S108-490
1987	45	Tipperary	Derrynaflan	Lurgoe	Togher	Ó Floinn, R.	S108-490
1987	46	Tyrone	Lislear	Baronscourt	Ringfort	Simpson, D.D.A.	H364-837
1987	47	Tyrone	Crouck	Dun Ruadh	Cairn & henge	Simpson, D.D.A.	H624-845
1987	48	Tyrone	Dunmisk	Dunmisk Fort	Hillfort	Brennan, M.	H628-707
1987	49	Tyrone	Knockroe		Bronze Age cist	Williams, B.B.	H366-891
1987	50	Waterford	Coxtown East		Neolithic settlement	Zvelebil, M.	S689-019
1987	51	Waterford	Waterford City	High Street/ Peter Street	Medieval urban	Walsh, C.	S607-123
1987	52	Waterford	Waterford City	Bakehouse Lane, St Peter's Church	Medieval urban	Gittings, A.S.R.	S607-123
1987	53	Waterford	Waterford City	Lady Lane/ Bakehouse Lane	Medieval urban	Hayden, A.	S607-123
1987	54	Waterford	Waterford City	Peter Street II	Medieval urban	Hurley, M.F.	S607-123
1987	55	Waterford	Bally Lough	Knockavelish	Later Mesolithic sites	Green, S.W., Moore, J.A. and Zvelebil, M.	S690-038
1987	56	Wexford	Ferrycarrig	Newtown	Ringwork	Cotter, C.	T013-230
1987	57	Wexford	Portersgate	Brecaun Church	Medieval church	Breen, T.C.	S760-004
1987	58	Wicklow	Ballyla & Clonmannon	The *Aid*	Shipwreck	Gowen, M.	T311-991
1987	Apx1.1	Limerick	Limerick City		Inner city project	O Rahilly, C.	
1987	Apx1.2	Waterford	Waterford City		Medieval city	Hurley, M.F.	
1987	Apx2	Waterford	Bally Lough		Mesolithic/Neolithic colonisation	Green, S.W.	S707-036
1987	Apx3	Wicklow	Ballyla & Clonmannon	The *Aid*	Shipwreck	Gowen, M.	T311-991
1988	1	Antrim	Dooey		Settlement	Williams, B.B.	C940-425
1988	2	Antrim	Lyles Hill	Toberagnee	Neolithic enclosure	Gibson, A.M. and Simpson, D.D.A.	J248-929
1988	3	Clare	Ballykeel South		Lintel grave	Cahill, M.	M178-904
1988	4	Clare	Gragan West		Bronze Age/Early Christian settlement	Cotter, C.	M200-018
1988	5	Clare	Poulnabrone		Portal tomb	Lynch, A.	M235-010
1988	6	Cork	Carrigtwohill	Barryscourt Castle	Tower-house	Lennon, A.M.	W821-724
1988	7	Cork	Cork City	White Street (carpark)	Urban	Lennon, A.M.	W675-717
1988	8	Cork	Lisnagun	Darrara	Ringfort	O'Sullivan, J.	W413-415
1988	9	Cork	Cork City	Crosse's Green, Harte's Timber Yard	Urban	Lennon, A.M.	W668-717
1988	10	Donegal	Ramelton	Old Meetinghouse	Presbyterian meeting house	Carroll, J.	C235-208
1988	11	Donegal	Rinnaraw		Cashel & house site	Fanning, T.	C038-368
1988	12	Down	Downpatrick	Demesne of Down (Denvir's Hotel)	Medieval/ post-medieval urban	Brannon, N.F.	J486-446
1988	13	Dublin	Ballinascorney Upper		Burial cairn	Healy, P.	O070-235
1988	14	Dublin	Dalkey		Pale boundary	Gowen, M.	O262-270
1988	15	Dublin	Dundrum	Dundrum Castle	Castle	O'Brien, E.	O174-279

1988	16	Dublin	Gracedieu		Early Christian cemetery & enclosure	Gowen, M.	O170-526
1988	17	Dublin	Gracedieu		Medieval & post-medieval	Gowen, M.	O170-526
1988	18	Dublin	Kilshane		Christian cemetery	Gowen, M.	O106-431
1988	19	Dublin	Saucerstown		Medieval farmyard?	Halpin, E.	O152-491
1988	20	Dublin	Dublin City	Winetavern Street	Medieval urban	Gowen, M.	O152-341
1988	21	Dublin	Westereave	Skephubble	Christian cemetery	Gowen, M.	O143-472
1988	22	Dublin	Dublin City	Merchants' Quay	Medieval waterfront?	Meenan, R.	O150-342
1988	23	Fermanagh	Cornacully		Sweathouse	Williams, B.B.	H025-436
1988	24	Fermanagh	Slapragh		Lime kiln	Williams, B.B.	H034-446
1988	25	Galway	Garryduff	Annaghcorrib	Togher	Raftery, B.	M940-250
1988	26	Galway	Galway City	Spanish Arch	Medieval urban	Casey, M.	M297-249
1988	27	Kerry	Ballinskelligs	Ballinskelligs Castle	Tower-house	Sheehan, J.	V434-654
1988	28	Kerry	Coarhamore		*Fulacht fiadh*	Sheehan, J.	V378-736
1988	29	Kerry	Kill		Skeleton in souterrain	Cahill, M.	Q758-258
1988	30	Kerry	Killelton	Killelton Oratory	Church site	Manning, C.	Q719-101
1988	31	Kildare	Greenhills		Prehistoric burial-ground	Keeley, V.J.	N836-119
1988	32	Kildare	Greenhills		Tumulus	Keeley, V.J.	N835-116
1988	33	Kildare	Hillsborough		18th-century house	Keeley, V.J.	N832-131
1988	34	Kildare	Hillsborough	St Augustine's Well	Well	Keeley, V.J.	N818-128
1988	35	Kildare	Knockbounce		Ringfort	Keeley, V.J.	N834-046
1988	36	Kildare	Oldtown		No archaeological significance	Keeley, V.J.	N831-131
1988	37	Limerick	Limerick City	John's Street, Custom House	Medieval urban	Hodkinson, B.J.	R581-573
1988	38	Limerick	Limerick City	Irishtown/ The Linear Park	Medieval town wall	Hodkinson, B.J.	R581-573
1988	39	Limerick	Lough Gur	Knockadoon Hill	Prehistoric occupation site	Cleary, R.M.	R644-408
1988	40	Limerick	Tankardstown South		Neolithic/Bronze Age	Gowen, M.	R585-281
1988	41	Derry	Salterstown	Ballymultrea	English Plantation village	Miller, O.	H953-824
1988	42	Derry	Derry City	Bishop Street Within	Post-medieval urban	Brannon, N.F.	C434-165
1988	43	Derry	Shantallow		Cist burial	Brannon, N.F.	C432-207
1988	44	Longford	Corlea	Cloonbreany, Derryoughil	Togher	Raftery, B.	N095-628
1988	45	Louth	Dromiskin		Souterrains & later features	Halpin, E.	O060-979
1988	46	Louth	Drogheda	Lagavoreen/ Duleek Street	Medieval urban	Swan, D.L.	O075-746
1988	47	Mayo	Aghleam		Souterrain?	Conroy, G.	F627-209
1988	48	Mayo	Shrule	Moyne	Ecclesiastical enclosure/church	Higgins, J.	M255-500
1988	49	Meath	Blackfriary		Dominican friary	Meenan, R. and Kennedy, W.J.	N802-573
1988	50	Meath	Moynagh Lough	Brittas	Crannog	Bradley, J.	N818-860
1988	51	Meath	Colp West		Early Christian enclosure & cemetery	Gowen, M.	O122-746
1988	52	Meath	Drumbaragh		Lintel grave	Cahill, M.	N757-704
1988	53	Meath	Knowth		Passage grave cemetery & later activities	Eogan, G.	N995-735
1988	54	Meath	Newgrange		Passage grave	Lynch, A.	O006-735
1988	55	Meath	Smithstown		Early Christian settlement? & souterrains	Gowen, M.	O130-704
1988	56	Meath	Spiddal	Ballynee	Souterrains	Eogan, G.	N825-849
1988	57	Meath	Kells	Townparks	Monastic site environs	Byrne, G.	N739-760
1988	58	Tipperary	Caherabbey Lower	Sand Pit Grove	Cemetery	Cahill, M. and Holland, P.	S053-260
1988	59	Tipperary	Cashel	Main Street	Medieval urban	O'Donnell, M.	S073-404

1988	60	Tipperary	Curraghatoor		Late Bronze Age habitation	Doody, M.G.	S001-108
1988	61	Waterford	Waterford City	Peter Street/ Olaf Street	Viking/ medieval urban	Walsh, C.	S607-123
1988	62	Waterford	Waterford City	St Peter's Church	Medieval urban church & undercroft	Gittings, A.S.R.	S607-123
1988	63	Waterford	Waterford City	Lady Lane/ Bakehouse Lane	Viking/medieval urban	Hayden, A.	S607-123
1988	64	Westmeath	Burnellstown		Cist grave	Moore, F.	N457-499
1988	65	Westmeath	Fore	Donaghfeighin	Holy pool	Dillon, F.F.D.	N510-700
1988	66	Wexford	Coolnaboy		Pit burial	Cahill, M.	S307-321
1988	67	Wexford	Wexford Town	Bride Street/ South Main Street	Medieval urban	Bourke, E.C.	T049-213
1988	68	Wexford	Wexford Town	North Main Street	Urban	Roche, H.	T045-217
1988	69	Wexford	Wexford Town	Townparks	Urban	Bourke, E.C.	T046-219
1988	Apx1	Antrim	North Antrim		Field-walking	Marshall, J.D.C.	
1988	Apx2	Dublin/Louth	Dublin/Dundalk		North-Eastern Gas Pipeline	Gowen, M.	
1988	Apx3	Kildare	Kilcullen		Kilcullen Link Motorway excavation	Keeley, V.J.	
1988	Apx4	Waterford	Waterford City		Urban	Hurley, M.F.	
1989	1	Antrim	Ballygalley	Croft Manor	Neolithic settlement site	Simpson, D.D.A.	D374-075
1989	2	Antrim	Drumaheglish	Drumaheglish Marina	Multi-period	Marshall, J.D.C.	C910-230
1989	3	Armagh	Armagh City	English Street	Urban	Lynn, C.J.	H875-454
1989	4	Armagh	Dorsey		Earthworks	Lynn, C.J.	H947-194
1989	5	Armagh	Legarhill		Church site?	Neill, K.A. and Lynn, C.J.	H863-452
1989	6	Armagh	Tray	Haughey's Fort	Bronze Age hillfort	Mallory, J.P.	H835-453
1989	7	Clare	Bunratty East		Bridge	Gibbons, E.	R453-613
1989	8	Cork	Altar	The Altar	Wedge tomb	O'Brien, B.	V859-302
1989	9	Cork	Ballycommane		Boulder burial & stone row	O'Brien, B.	V976-436
1989	10	Cork	Cooradarrigan		Boulder burials	O'Brien, B.	V937-331
1989	11	Cork	Lisnagun	Darrara	Ringfort	O'Sullivan, J.	W413-415
1989	12	Cork	Dunboy	Dunboy Castle	Post-medieval fortification	Klingelhöfer, E.	V667-439
1989	13	Cork	Lisleagh	Lisleagh II	Ringfort	Monk, M.A.	R178-106
1989	14	Cork	Cork City	Barrack Street/ French's Quay	Medieval urban	O'Brien, M.A.	W670-711
1989	15	Derry	Bellaghy	Bellaghy Bawn	Plantation houses & bawn	Brannon, N.F.	H953-963
1989	16	Derry	Moneyconey	Ballinascreen Church	Church	Meek, M.	H730-907
1989	17	Derry	Moneymore	Conyngham Street	Post-medieval urban	Brannon, N.F.	H858-834
1989	18	Donegal	Lisnamulligan		Bronze Age cist	Ó Floinn, R.	H244-924
1989	19	Donegal	Rinnaraw		Cashel & house site	Fanning, T.	C038-368
1989	20	Down	Raholp	Raholp Old Church	Church	Neill, K.A.	J541-479
1989	21	Dublin	Balgriffin	St Doulough's	Church, baptistry & holy well	Swan, D.L.	O210-420
1989	22	Dublin	Coolmine		Enclosure?	Keeley, V.J.	O065-402
1989	23	Dublin	Dundrum	Dundrum Castle	Medieval castle	O'Brien, E.	O174-279
1989	24	Dublin	Glasnevin	Glasnevin Road	Early Christian monastic site?	McMahon, M.	O159-375
1989	25	Dublin	Inchicore North	Con Colbert Road	Medieval/ post-medieval	Healy, P.	O122-338
1989	26	Dublin	Islandbridge		Viking habitation?	O'Brien, E.	O122-333
1989	27	Dublin	Old Connaught	Toole's Moat	Burial site	Keeley, V.J.	O253-200
1989	28	Dublin	Shankill	Palermo Estate	Tree ring?	Keeley, V.J.	O254-193
1989	29	Dublin	Dublin City	Winetavern Street	Medieval town wall	McMahon, M.	O152-341
1989	30	Dublin	Dublin City	Bridge Street Lower	Medieval urban	Cotter, C.	O149-341
1989	31	Dublin	Dublin City	Bridge Street Lower	Medieval settlement	McMahon, M.	O148-341
1989	32	Dublin	Dublin City	Christchurch Place	Medieval town wall	Gowen, M.	O152-349
1989	33	Dublin	Dublin City	Christchurch Synod Hall	Urban	Cotter, C.	O151-339
1989	34	Dublin	Dublin City	High Street	Medieval urban	Murtagh, D.	O151-339

1989	35	Dublin	Dublin City	High Street	Medieval urban	Murtagh, D.	O151-339
1989	36	Dublin	Dublin City	High Street	Medieval urban	Murtagh, D.	O151-339
1989	37	Dublin	Dublin City	High Street	Medieval urban	Cotter, C.	O150-339
1989	38	Dublin	Dublin City	High Street—	Medieval parish St Audoen's Church	McMahon, M. church	O149-339
1989	39	Dublin	Dublin City	Merchants' Quay	Bore-holes	Meenan, R.	O105-342
1989	40	Dublin	Dublin City	Merchants' Quay	Medieval waterfront?	Meenan, R.	O150-342
1989	41	Galway	Abbeytown	Kilnamonagh	Early Christian & medieval ecclesiastical	Higgins, J.	M312-503
1989	42	Galway	Carrownamanagh	Killererin Church	Medieval church & graveyard	Lavelle, D.	M417-474
1989	43	Galway	Creevaghabaun	Creevaghabaun Church	Church ruin	Lavelle, D.	M493-494
1989	44	Galway	Kilcolgan		Post-medieval/ modern	Holland, M.	M414-181
1989	45	Galway	Killeely Beg		Earthworks	Zajac, S.	M429-187
1989	46	Galway	Galway City	Abbeygate Street Upper	Urban	Clyne, M.	M298-252
1989	47	Galway	Galway City	Barrack Lane	Post-medieval urban fortification	Clyne, M.	M230-253
1989	48	Galway	Galway City	Merchants' Road II	City wall & tower	Delaney, D.	M298-248
1989	50	Galway	Galway City	Whitehall Lane	Medieval urban	Zajac, S.	M299-253
1989	51	Kerry	Ardfert	St Brendan's Cathedral	Medieval cathedral	Moore, F.	Q786-214
1989	52	Kerry	Dromteewakeen		Stone row & boulder burial?	Sheehan, J.	V763-808
1989	53	Kerry	Glen Fahan	Clochán na mBó	Clochán	Bennett, I.	V327-969
1989	54	Kildare	Ballymany		Church site	Keeley, V.J.	N794-131
1989	55	Kildare	Greenhills		Prehistoric burial-ground	Keeley, V.J.	N836-119
1989	56	Kildare	Greenhills		Tumulus	Keeley, V.J.	N835-116
1989	57	Kildare	Kildare Town	Kildare Castle	Castle	O'Carroll, F.	N729-123
1989	58	Kildare	Naas	Poplar Square, Lawlor's Hotel	No archaeological significance	Murtagh, B.	N891-191
1989	59	Kildare	Roestown		No archaeological significance	Keeley, V.J.	N900-375
1989	60	Kildare	Treadstown		Land drains	Keeley, V.J.	N910-372
1989	61	Kilkenny	Dysart		Early Christian/ 13th-century	Murtagh, B. and Hall, M.E.	S597-393
1989	62	Kilkenny	Kilkenny City	James' Street	Medieval urban	Cotter, C.	S505-559
1989	63	Limerick	Limerick City	Broad Street/ Curry Lane	Medieval/ post-medieval urban	Wiggins, K.	R582-570
1989	64	Limerick	Limerick City	Curry Lane/ Grattan Street	Medieval/ post-medieval urban	Wiggins, K.	R582-570
1989	65	Limerick	Limerick City	Charlotte's Quay	Medieval/ post-medieval urban	Tarbett, C. and Wiggins, K.	R581-573
1989	66	Limerick	Adare	Desmond's Castle	No archaeological significance	O Rahilly, C.	R471-466
1989	67	Limerick	Limerick City	King's Island	Undercroft & castle	Hodkinson, B.J.	R583-577
1989	68	Limerick	Killacolla	Prospect Hill	Cist grave & field systems	Doody, M.G.	R164-477
1989	69	Limerick	Tankardstown South		Neolithic house	Tarbett, C. and Gowen, M.	R585-281
1989	70	Louth	Drogheda	St Mary d'Urso	Medieval priory & hospital	Halpin, E.	O086-755
1989	71	Mayo	Behy/Glenurla	Céide Fields	Neolithic field system	Byrne, G.	G051-408
1989	72	Meath	Moynagh Lough	Brittas	Crannog	Bradley, J.	N818-860
1989	73	Meath	Dowth		Passage grave	Lynch, A.	O024-740
1989	74	Meath	Knowth		Multi-period site	Eogan, G. and Roche, H.	N995-735
1989	75	Meath	Newgrange		Passage grave	Lynch, A.	O006-735
1989	76	Meath	Raffin	Raffin Fort	Ringfort?	Newman, C.	N820-828
1989	77	Meath	Trim		Garden feature	Dillon, F.F.D.	N805-567
1989	78	Offaly	Clonmacnoise		Early Christian monastic site	Manning, C.	N009-306
1989	79	Roscommon	Correenbeg	Correen Ford	Ford	Kelly, E.P.	M901-256

1989	80	Roscommon	Creggan		No archaeological significance	Kelly, E.P.	M934-253
1989	81	Roscommon	Erris	Templedriney Church	Church, burial-ground, habitation	Ó Ríordáin, A.B.	G822-027
1989	82	Roscommon	Erris		Ringfort & *fulacht fiadh*	Ó Ríordáin, A.B.	G821-033
1989	83	Roscommon	Boyle	Keeloges	Cairn mound	Ó Ríordáin, A.B.	G829-021
1989	84	Roscommon	Sheepwalk	Sheepwalk Rath	Multivallate fort	Killeen, J.J.	M715-925
1989	85	Sligo	Culleens		Cist	Cherry, S. and Ryan, M.F.	G349-313
1989	86	Sligo	Lecarrow		Ringfort with enclosure	Ó Ríordáin, A.B.	G799-090
1989	87	Tipperary	Curraghatoor		Late Bronze Age habitation	Doody, M.G.	S001-108
1989	88	Tipperary	Cashel	St Patrick's Rock	Ecclesiastical	Manning, C.	S075-409
1989	89	Tipperary	Roscrea	Roscrea Castle	Castle	Manning, C.	S134-892
1989	90	Waterford	Coxtown East		Neolithic site	Green, S.W., Judge, C. and Peterson, J.	S689-019
1989	91	Waterford	Waterford City	Peter Street	Medieval urban	Scully, O.M.B.	S607-123
1989	92	Waterford	Waterford City	St Peter's Church	Medieval urban church	Hurley, M.F. and Murtagh, B.	S607-123
1989	93	Waterford	Waterford City	Peter Street	Gateway in city wall	Murtagh, B. and Hurley, M.F.	S607-123
1989	94	Waterford	Waterford City	Peter Street	Medieval urban	Reid, M.	S607-123
1989	95	Waterford	Dungarvan	St Augustine Street	Town ditch & well	Power, C.	X226-930
1989	96	Waterford	Monvoy		Rhyolite quarry	Zvelebil, M., Moth, E. and Peterson, J.	S570-030
1989	97	Westmeath	Clonbrusk		River bed	Kelly, E.P.	N030-427
1989	98	Westmeath	Lough Ennel	Cro-Inis—Dysart	Crannog	Farrell, R.T.	N389-469
1989	99	Wexford	Gorey		Urn burial	Ó Floinn, R.	T152-591
1989	100	Wicklow	Ballyla & Clonmannon	The *Aid*	Shipwreck	Linnie, M.	T311-991
1989	101	Wicklow	Glendalough	St Kevin's Cross	High cross	Lynch, A.	T312-196
1989	Apx1	Louth	Mount Oriel		Field-walking project	Cooney, G.	N960-850
1989	Apx2	Waterford	Bally Lough		Mesolithic/Neolithic colonisation	Zvelebil, M.	S707-036
1989	Apx3	Westmeath	Lough Ennel	Cro-Inis—Dysart	Crannog project	Farrell, R.T.	N389-469
1989	Apx4	Wicklow	Ballyla & Clonmannon	The *Aid*	Shipwreck	Linnie, M.	T311-991
1990	1	Antrim	Ballygalley	Croft Manor	Neolithic settlement site	Simpson, D.D.A.	D374-075
1990	2	Antrim	Ballyshanaghill	Ballyshanaghill Rath	Ringfort	Halpin, E.	J148-758
1990	3	Antrim	Belfast	Donegall Street	Urban	Brannon, N.F.	J341-744
1990	4	Antrim	Belfast	Winetavern Street	Clay pipe factory	Brannon, N.F.	J336-747
1990	5	Antrim	Linford		Multi-phase upland	Williams, B.B.	D317-074
1990	6	Armagh	Armagh City	English Street	Urban	Lynn, C.J.	H875-454
1990	7	Armagh	Tray	Haughey's Fort	Bronze Age hillfort	Mallory, J.P.	H835-453
1990	8	Cavan	Drumlane		No archaeological significance	Halpin, E.	H342-122
1990	9	Clare	Ballinphunta		Wedge tomb	Hodkinson, B.J.	R515-938
1990	10	Clare	Bunratty West		Medieval borough	King, H.A.	R446-608
1990	11	Clare	Meelick	Clonrush Church	Church site	McCarthy, C.	R760-868
1990	12	Clare	Noughaval		House site	Ní Ghabhláin, S.	R121-197
1990	13	Clare	Tullaher	St Senan's Altar	Altar	Cotter, C.	Q928-618
1990	14	Cork	Sherkin Island	Farrancoush— Sherkin Island Friary	Franciscan friary	Lynch, A.	W103-025
1990	15	Cork	Garranes	Lisnacaheragh	Ringfort	O'Donnell, M.	W743-640
1990	16	Cork	Kilcummer Lower		Flint scatter	Anderson, E.	R696-006
1990	17	Cork	Leckaneen		Ring-barrow	O'Shaughnessy, J.	W432-768
1990	18	Cork	Lisleagh	Lisleagh II	Ringfort	Monk, M.A.	R178-106
1990	19	Cork	Mogeely	Mogeely Castle	Post-medieval settlement	Klingelhöfer, E.	W960-940
1990	20	Cork	Shanlaragh		Standing stones	O'Shaughnessy, J.	W257-593
1990	21	Cork	Skeam West		Church site—early	Cotter, C.	V990-288
1990	22	Cork	Cork City	Greenmount	Mass grave	Cherry, S.	W699-708

1990	23	Cork	Toormore		Wedge tomb	O'Brien, B.	V854-308
1990	24	Derry	Bellaghy	Bellaghy Bawn	Bawn, houses & ringfort	Brannon, N.F.	H953-963
1990	25	Donegal	Rinnaraw		Cashel & house site	Fanning, T.	C038-368
1990	26	Down	Ballynahatty	Ballynahatty 5	Palisaded enclosure	Hartwell, B.	J326-679
1990	27	Down	Newry	The Abbey	Urban	Brannon, N.F.	J087-265
1990	28	Down	Spittle Quarter		Souterrain	Brannon, N.F.	J530-404
1990	29	Dublin	Balally	Cross Church of Moreen	Church site & enclosure	Mount, C.	O179-260
1990	30	Dublin	Balally	St Olaf's Church	Church site	Cotter, C.	O178-260
1990	31	Dublin	Balgriffin	St Doulough's	Church, baptistry & holy well	Swan, D.L.	O210-420
1990	32	Dublin	Booterstown	St Helen's	Cropmark/tree ring	Halpin, A.	O199-300
1990	33	Dublin	Coolock	St John's Church	Early Christian & later site	Swan, D.L.	O198-382
1990	34	Dublin	Dundrum	Dundrum Castle	Castle	O'Brien, E.	O174-279
1990	35	Dublin	Garristown	Garristown Church	Medieval	McMahon, M.	O070-587
1990	36	Dublin	Glasnevin	Bons Secours Hospital	Early monastic site?	McMahon, M.	O158-375
1990	37	Dublin	Dublin City	Usher's Quay	Medieval urban	King, H.A.	O145-340
1990	38	Dublin	Oldcourt	Killininny	Castle/tower-house site	Swan, D.L.	O310-225
1990	39	Dublin	Porterstown		Bronze Age/ Early Christian?	Cotter, C.	O060-369
1990	40	Dublin	Dublin City	Arran Quay	Medieval river frontage	Hayden, A.	O145-344
1990	41	Dublin	Dublin City	Patrick Street	Medieval urban	Walsh, C.	O152-336
1990	42	Dublin	Tallaght	Main Street	Medieval boundaries	O'Brien, E.	O093-278
1990	43	Dublin	Tallaght	Old Bawn Road	Early Christian? ditch	O'Brien, E.	O093-278
1990	44	Dublin	Tallaght	Old Bawn Road	Medieval occupational remains	Gowen, M.	O093-278
1990	45	Dublin	Tallaght	St Maelruan's	Early Christian site	Newman, C.	O091-278
1990	46	Dublin	Dublin City	Essex Street West	Medieval street frontage	Hayden, A.	O156-342
1990	47	Dublin	Dublin City	Exchange Street Lower	Medieval urban	Gowen, M.	O154-342
1990	48	Dublin	Dublin City	High Street	Medieval urban	Gowen, M.	O151-339
1990	49	Dublin	Dublin City	Bridge Street	Waterfront?	Meenan, R.	O105-342
1990	50	Dublin	Dublin City	Merchants' Quay	Medieval urban	Murtagh, D.	O105-342
1990	51	Dublin	Dublin City	Merchants' Quay	Waterfront?	Meenan, R.	O105-342
1990	52	Fermanagh	Aghnagrane		No archaeological significance	Williams, B.B.	H363-454
1990	53	Fermanagh	Enniskillen	Castle Barracks	Bawn/castle	Halpin, E.	H231-442
1990	54	Galway	Athenry	Athenry Castle	Medieval castle	Papazian, C.	M512-288
1990	55	Galway	Omey Island	Goreen & Sturakeen	Burial & domestic site	O'Keeffe, T.	L562-566
1990	56	Galway	Graigue		Souterrain	Fitzpatrick, M.	M632-181
1990	57	Galway	Kilbeg Lower	Rosshill Abbey	Church & graveyard	Clyne, M.	M094-568
1990	58	Galway	Galway City	Abbeygate Street Lower	Urban	O'Regan, C.	M300-252
1990	59	Galway	Galway City	Abbeygate Street Lower	Modern urban	Connolly, A.	M299-352
1990	60	Galway	Galway City	Eglinton Street	Urban	Clyne, M.	M298-254
1990	61	Galway	Galway City	Merchants' Road III	Medieval urban	Delaney, D.	M298-248
1990	62	Galway	Galway City	Merchants' Road IV	Medieval urban	Delaney, D.	M298-248
1990	63	Galway	Galway City	Quay Street	Medieval/ post-medieval urban	Casey, M.	M295-250
1990	64	Galway	Galway City	St Augustine Street	Urban	O'Regan, C.	M297-247
1990	65	Galway	Galway City	St Augustine Street	Medieval town wall	Clyne, M.	M299-250
1990	66	Kerry	Ardfert	St Brendan's Cathedral	Medieval cathedral	Moore, F.	Q786-214
1990	67	Kerry	Kimego West	Cahergal	Stone fort	Manning, C.	V447-805
1990	68	Kildare	Castledermot	Main Street/ McEvoy's Well	Post-medieval urban	O'Brien, E.	S781-856
1990	69	Kildare	Leixlip	Main Street (The Factory)	No archaeological significance	Walsh, C.	O005-362

1990	70	Kildare	Naas	Abbey Road	Moat environs (Moatville)	O'Brien, E.	N289-219
1990	71	Kildare	Naas	St David's Church	Medieval church	Ó Ríordáin, A.B.	N891-191
1990	72	Kilkenny	Dunbell Big	Dunbell 5	Ringfort	Cassidy, B.	S557-521
1990	73	Kilkenny	Kilkenny City	Dean Street	Medieval urban	Cotter, C.	S505-561
1990	74	Kilkenny	Kilkenny City	Dean Street	Urban	Bourke, E.C.	S505-561
1990	75	Kilkenny	Graiguenamanagh	Duiske Abbey	Cistercian abbey	Hayden, A.	S710-439
1990	76	Kilkenny	Knockroe	The Caiseal	Passage grave	Bourke, E.C.	S408-312
1990	77	Kilkenny	Kilkenny City	Prior's Orchard	Post-medieval urban	King, H.A.	S508-561
1990	78	Kilkenny	Kilkenny City	Pennyfeather Lane	Medieval & post-medieval urban	King, H.A.	S503-558
1990	79	Kilkenny	Kilkenny City	Talbot Bastion	Medieval mural tower	Bourke, E.C.	S505-561
1990	80	Limerick	Limerick City	John's Street	Medieval urban	Hodkinson, B.J.	R581-572
1990	81	Limerick	Limerick City	King's Island	Medieval urban	Hodkinson, B.J.	R578-578
1990	82	Limerick	Limerick City	St Mary's Cathedral	Medieval urban	O Rahilly, C.	R578-575
1990	83	Limerick	Lough Gur	Knockadoon Hill	Prehistoric habitation site	Cleary, R.M.	R640-407
1990	84	Limerick	Limerick City	King John's Castle	Medieval castle	Wiggins, K.	R577-577
1990	85	Limerick	Stradbally North		Burial-ground	Hodkinson, B.J.	R661-624
1990	86	Louth	Dundalk	Clanbrassil Street	Urban	Halpin, E.	J047-076
1990	87	Mayo	Carrowsteelagh		Lintel graves	Cahill, M.	G202-383
1990	88	Mayo	Behy/Glenurla	Céide Fields	Neolithic field system	Byrne, G. and Dunne, N.	G050-400
1990	89	Mayo	Rathlackan		Court cairn & pre-bog settlement	Byrne, G.	G166-388
1990	90	Meath	Donaghmore	Blackcastle Demesne	Cist cemetery	Roche, H.	N875-685
1990	91	Meath	Bobsville	Clonabreany Churchyard	Graveyard	Meenan, R.	N615-743
1990	92	Meath	Donore	Donore Quarry	Monitoring	Gowen, M.	O045-735
1990	93	Meath	Knowth		Multi-period site	Roche, H. and Eogan, G.	N995-735
1990	94	Meath	Raffin	Raffin Fort	Iron Age enclosure?	Newman, C.	N820-828
1990	95	Offaly	Clonfinlough		Palisaded enclosure	Moloney, A.	N034-292
1990	96	Offaly	Clonmacnoise		Early Christian monastic site	Manning, C.	N009-306
1990	97	Offaly	Clonmacnoise	New Graveyard	Early Christian settlement & monastic site	King, H.A.	N011-308
1990	98	Offaly	Banagher/Kylebeg	Banagher Fort	Post-medieval military fort	Cassidy, B.	N003-155
1990	99	Roscommon	Lackagh and	Doon of Drumsna Drumcleavry	Linear earthwork	Buckley, V.M. and Condit, T.	M993-966
1990	100	Tipperary	Ballyvanran		Multivallate earthwork	O'Sullivan, M.	R905-742
1990	101	Tipperary	Clonmel	Emmet Street	Medieval urban	Zajac, S.	S203-225
1990	102	Tipperary	Cashel	Main Street	Urban	Stevens, S.	S075-409
1990	103	Tipperary	Cashel	Main Street	Medieval urban	Hayden, A.	S075-405
1990	104	Tipperary	Curraghatoor		Late Bronze Age settlement	Doody, M.G.	S001-108
1990	105	Tipperary	Littleton Bog	Longford Pass North	Togher	Cherry, S., Geraghty, S. and Ryan, M.F.	S234-592
1990	106	Tipperary	Cashel	St Patrick's Rock	Rock of Cashel environs	Hurley, M.F.	S075-407
1990	107	Tipperary	Roscrea	Roscrea Castle	Castle	Manning, C.	S134-892
1990	108	Waterford	Waterford City	Arundel Square	Medieval urban	Hurley, M.F. *et al.*	S608-124
1990	109	Waterford	Waterford City	Bakehouse Lane II	Pre-Norman city defences	Scully, O.M.B.	S607-123
1990	110	Waterford	Waterford City	Parnell Street (Waterford Arms)	Urban	Wren, J.	S609-122
1990	111	Waterford	Waterford City	Double Tower	Tower of city wall	Murtagh, B.	S606-199
1990	112	Waterford	Waterford City	Railway Square, Watch Tower	City wall & tower	Murtagh, B.	S607-199
1990	113	Westmeath	Marlinstown		Ringfort	Keeley, V.J.	N463-527
1990	114	Westmeath	Mullingar	McCurtain Street	Graveyard?	Meenan, R.	N440-530
1990	115	Westmeath	Petitswood		Ringfort	Keeley, V.J.	N458-537
1990	116	Westmeath	Portnashangan	Portnashangan I	Ringfort	Keeley, V.J.	N414-603

1990	117	Westmeath	Portnashangan	Portnashangan III	Ringfort	Keeley, V.J.	N415-600
1990	118	Westmeath	Rathconrath		Cist graves	Ó Floinn, R. and Cherry, S.	N315-530
1990	119	Westmeath	Robinstown		Stone platform	Brady, N.	N402-453
1990	120	Wexford	Ballinesker	Moudlinstown	Bronze Age hoard?	Cahill, M.	T117-288
1990	121	Wexford	Wexford Town	West Gate	Urban	Bourke, E.C.	T049-219
1990	122	Wicklow	Ballynerrin Lower		Burial site	Scally, G.	J313-942
1990	123	Wicklow	Glendalough	Lugduff	Early Christian site environs	Cotter, C.	T110-962
1991	1	Antrim	Antrim Town	Antrim Castle	Formal gardens	Reeves-Smyth, T.	J144-760
1991	2	Antrim	Ballygalley	Croft Manor	Neolithic settlement & industrial site	Simpson, D.D.A.	D374-075
1991	3	Antrim	Ballyshanaghill	Ballyshanaghill Rath	Ringfort	Halpin, E.	J148-758
1991	4	Antrim	Carrickfergus	Carrickfergus Castle	Medieval castle	Brannon, N.F.	J414-872
1991	5	Antrim	Carrickfergus		Medieval town	Ó Baoill, R.	J414-872
1991	6	Antrim	Dunloy	Giant's Grave	Megalith site	Williams, B.B.	D015-187
1991	7	Antrim	Linford		Multi-phase upland landscape	Williams, B.B.	D317-074
1991	8	Antrim	Minnis North		Shell midden	Simpson, D.D.A. and Conway, M.G	D339-131
1991	9	Antrim	Solar		Church site	Lynn, C.J.	D341-120
1991	10	Antrim	Toome	Toome Castle	Castle	Ó Baoill, R.	H990-901
1991	11	Antrim	Tunarobert		Souterrain	Williams, B.B.	D077-332
1991	12	Armagh	Armagh City	English Street	Urban	Crothers, N.	H875-454
1991	13	Armagh	Ballyrea	Navan Sanctuary	Multi-period site	Mallory, J.P.	H845-448
1991	14	Armagh	Breagh	Levaghery	River dredgings	Bourke, C.	
1991	15	Armagh	Clonmore		River dredgings	Bourke, C.	H880-610
1991	16	Armagh	Corr	Dunavally	River dredgings	Bourke, C.	H850-550
1991	17	Armagh	Corr	Dunavally	Underwater searching	Ramsey, G.	H850-550
1991	18	Armagh	Tray	Haughey's Fort	Late Bronze Age enclosure	Mallory, J.P.	H835-453
1991	19	Clare	Bunratty East		Medieval occupation	O Rahilly, C.	R453-613
1991	20	Clare	Ennis	Chapel Lane	Post-medieval urban	O Rahilly, C.	R339-777
1991	21	Clare	Ennis	Old Barracks Street	No archaeological significance	O Rahilly, C.	R337-774
1991	22	Cork	Garranes	Lisnacaheragh	Ringfort	O'Donnell, M.	W473-640
1991	23	Cork	Killavillig		Early ecclesiastical enclosure	O'Shaughnessy, J.	R408-101
1991	24	Cork	Knockawillin		*Fulacht fiadh*	O'Shaughnessy, J.	R364-120
1991	25	Cork	Cork City	Leitrim Street	Test-pits	Scully, O.M.B.	W670-711
1991	26	Cork	Lisleagh	Lisleagh II	Ringfort	Monk, M.A.	R178-106
1991	27	Cork	Mogeely	Mogeely Castle	Post-medieval settlement	Klingelhöfer, E.	W960-940
1991	28	Cork	Shandon		Urban	Lane, S.	W672-723
1991	29	Down	Ballynahatty	Ballynahatty 3	Cropmark	Hartwell, B.	J326-677
1991	30	Down	Newry	The Abbey	Urban ecclesiastical site	Crothers, N.	J087-265
1991	31	Dublin	Clonshaugh		Mound	Keeley, V.J.	O186-415
1991	32	Dublin	Dublin City	Bishop Street, old Jacob's factory	No archaeological significance	Gowen, M.	O154-335
1991	33	Dublin	Dublin City	Castle Street	Bore-holes	Murtagh, D.	O153-339
1991	34	Dublin	Dublin City	Castle Street	Urban	Hayden, A.	O155-340
1991	35	Dublin	Dublin City	Dublin Castle clock-tower	Medieval urban	Meenan, R.	O154-339
1991	36	Dublin	Dublin City	Francis Street	Medieval urban	Halpin, A.	O149-339
1991	37	Dublin	Dublin City	Nicholas Street	Town moat	Walsh, C.	O152-337
1991	38	Dublin	Dublin City	Nicholas Street	Town wall	Walsh, C.	O152-337
1991	39	Dublin	Dublin City	Patrick Street	Medieval urban	Hayden, A.	O153-342
1991	40	Dublin	Dublin City	Parliament Street	Medieval urban	Scally, G.	O158-341
1991	41	Dublin	Dublin City	Stephen Street Lower	Medieval hospital?	Meenan, R.	O157-338
1991	42	Dublin	Dublin City	Stephen Street Lower	Medieval church & graveyard	Hayden, A.	O157-338
1991	43	Dublin	Dublin City	Usher's Quay	Urban medieval waterfront	Swan, D.L.	O145-340
1991	44	Dublin	Dublin City	Westland Row	Urban	Meenan, R.	O167-340
1991	45	Dublin	Dundrum	Dundrum Castle	Castle	O'Brien, E.	O174-279

1991	46	Dublin	Dunsink		Mound	Keeley, V.J.	O096-388
1991	47	Dublin	Dunsink		Cropmark	Keeley, V.J.	O048-394
1991	48	Dublin	Finglas West	King William's Rampart	Medieval/ post-medieval rampart	Cotter, C.	O140-489
1991	49	Dublin	Lambay Island		Burial	Ó Floinn, R. and Cherry. S.	O307-508
1991	50	Dublin	Loughlinstown	Graves' Moat	Early medieval zcemetery	Ó Floinn, R.	O238-247
1991	51	Dublin	Lusk	Barrack Lane	Ecclesiastical enclosure	Stout, G.	O215-544
1991	52	Dublin	Margaretstown		Slab-lined grave	Stout, G.	O221-593
1991	53	Dublin	Tallaght	St Maelruan's	Medieval	Gowen, M.	O091-278
1991	54	Galway	Ballylee	Ballylee Mill	Mill	Delaney, D.	M481-063
1991	55	Galway	Ballynakill	Ballynakill	Medieval church & Graveyard	Henry, M.	M170-266 graveyard
1991	56	Galway	Iorras Beag Thiar	Port na Feadóige (Dogs' Bay)	Settlement site	Gibbons, E.	L692-380
1991	57	Galway	Beagh	Kilconly Graveyard	Graveyard	Clyne, M.	M351-586
1991	58	Galway	Galway City	Bollingbrook Fort	Cromwellian fort	Kiely, H.	M306-263
1991	59	Galway	Kellysgrove		River fords	Kelly, E.P.	M878-280
1991	60	Galway	Moycullen	Moycullen Graveyard	Church & graveyard	Clyne, M.	M231-331
1991	61	Galway	Oileán Ghorumna	Teampall Bhaile na Clé	Church & graveyard	Gibbons, E.	L865-220
1991	62	Kerry	Ardfert	St Brendan's Cathedral	Medieval cathedral	Moore, F.	Q786-214
1991	63	Kerry	Ballinrannig		Ogham stone, environs	Cotter, C	Q368-056
1991	64	Kerry	Ballinskelligs	Ballinskelligs Castle	Tower-house	Sheehan, J.	V434-654
1991	65	Kerry	Ballyegan		Cashel with souterrain	Byrne, M.E.	Q966-110
1991	66	Kerry	Ballyeigh		Enclosure site, environs	Bennett, I.	Q868-384
1991	67	Kerry	Brackloon		Lintel grave	Moore, F.	Q601-017
1991	68	Kerry	Ferritersquarter		No archaeological significance	Bennett, I.	Q313-011
1991	69	Kerry	Na Gorta Dubha	Dunurlin Church	Medieval church	Ó Coilleáin, M.	Q341-049
1991	70	Kerry	Kimego West	Cahergal	Stone fort	Manning, C.	V447-805
1991	71	Kerry	Sceilg Mhichíl (Great Skellig)		Early Christian monastery	Cotter, C.	V250-606
1991	72	Kildare	Castledermot	Carlow Street	Medieval	Scally, G.	S783-850
1991	73	Kildare	Kildare Town	White Abbey Road, Crosskeys	Urban potential	O'Carroll, F.	N723-213
1991	74	Kildare	Graigues	Mulhall's Fort	Ringfort	Scally, G.	N797-268
1991	75	Kildare	Grey Abbey		Medieval	Murtagh, B.	N727-109
1991	76	Kildare	Naas	Poplar Square, The Random Inn	Urban	Swan, D.L.	N897-195
1991	77	Kildare	Nicholastown	New Abbey Stud	No archaeological significance	Scally, G.	N847-093
1991	78	Kilkenny	Dysart		Early Christian/ medieval ecclesiastical & settlement site	Murtagh, B.	S597-393
1991	79	Kilkenny	Kilkenny City	College Park	Medieval urban	King, H.A.	S511-560
1991	80	Kilkenny	Kilkenny City	James' Street	Medieval urban	Channing, J.	S505-559
1991	81	Kilkenny	Kilkenny City	Kilkenny Castle	12th/19th-century castle	Murtagh, B.	S509-556
1991	82	Kilkenny	Kilkenny City	New Street	Post-medieval urban	Gittings, A.S.R.	S505-554
1991	83	Kilkenny	Kilkenny City	Parliament Street, Rothe House	Post-medieval	Halpin, A.	T251-157
1991	84	Kilkenny	Knockroe	The Caiseal	Passage grave	O'Sullivan, M.	S408-312
1991	85	Limerick	Adare		Medieval?	King, H.A.	R463-460
1991	86	Limerick	Ballybronoge South	Killasragh Children's Burial Ground	Trackway	Hanley, K.	R510-480
1991	87	Limerick	Castletroy		Post-medieval linear bank	Hanley, K.	R620-588
1991	88	Limerick	Killacolla	Glin Castle	Tower-house environs	O Rahilly, C.	R121-474

1991	89	Limerick	Lough Gur	Knockadoon Hill	Prehistoric habitation site	Cleary, R.M.	R640-407
1991	90	Limerick	Newcastle West	Maiden Street	Medieval urban	O Rahilly, C.	R279-337
1991	91	Longford	Aghadegnan	Templemichael—Aghadegnan Ringfort	Ringfort	Carroll, J.	N213-275
1991	92	Louth	Cappoge		No archaeological significance	Channing, J.	O048-899
1991	93	Louth	Carlingford	Carlingford Priory	Dominican priory	Cassidy, B.	J189-114
1991	94	Louth	Dundalk	Marshes Upper	Ringforts/souterrains?	Walsh, C.	J060-055
1991	95	Louth	Drogheda	Magdalene Street Upper	Dominican priory	Halpin, A.	O309-276
1991	96	Louth	Dundalk	Seatown	Graveyard	Halpin, E.	J051-075
1991	97	Mayo	Cross	Cross Abbey	Medieval abbey	Zajac, S.	F612-489
1991	98	Mayo	Behy/Glenurla	Céide Fields	Neolithic field system	Byrne, G. and Dunne, N.	G050-400
1991	99	Mayo	Achill	The Deserted Village, Slievemore (Toir)	Multi-phase landscape	Halpin, E. and McDonald, T.	F630-075
1991	100	Meath	Drumgill Lower		Enclosure (ploughed-out)	Walsh, C.	N859-925
1991	101	Meath	Dunshaughlin	St Secudinus' Church	Early ecclesiastical site	Meenan, R.	N969-525
1991	102	Meath	Ferganstown	Ballymacann	No archaeological significance	Swan, D.L.	N890-697
1991	103	Meath	Killbeg Upper		Anglo-Norman bailey	Meenan, R.	N778-818
1991	104	Meath	Knowth		Multi-period site	Roche, H. and Eogan, G.	N995-735
1991	105	Meath	Navan	Watergate Street	Medieval urban	Cotter, C.	N868-678
1991	106	Meath	Newtown		Neolithic house	Halpin, E. and Gowen, M.	N751-890
1991	107	Meath	Raffin	Raffin Fort	Ritual enclosure	Newman, C.	N820-828
1991	108	Meath	Ratoath		Medieval potential	Cotter, C.	O018-520
1991	109	Offaly	Birr	Bridge Street/Mill Lane	Post-medieval urban	King, H.A.	N057-045
1991	110	Offaly	Clonmacnoise	New Graveyard	Early Christian settlement & monastic site	King, H.A.	N011-308
1991	111	Offaly	Killeigh		Monastery environs	Kehoe, H.	N363-183
1991	112	Roscommon	Trinity Island	Holy Trinity Abbey	Abbey—Premonstratensian	Clyne, M.	G833-045
1991	113	Sligo	Lackan	The Fisherman's Grave	Lintel grave	Buckley, V.M.	G305-363
1991	114	Sligo	Sligo Town	Tullynagracken North	No archaeological significance	Brady, N.	G695-340
1991	115	Tipperary	Ballyvanran		Ringfort	O'Sullivan, M.	R905-742
1991	116	Tipperary	Clonmel	Kickham Street	Town wall	Channing, J.	S205-223
1991	117	Tipperary	Curraghatoor		Late Bronze Age settlement	Doody, M.G.	S001-108
1991	118	Tipperary	Fethard		Town walls	Scally, G.	S208-349
1991	119	Tyrone	Casslesessiagh	Castlederg Castle	Plantation castle	Newman, C.	H262-844
1991	120	Tyrone	Culrevog	Moy	River dredgings	Bourke, C.	H850-550
1991	121	Tyrone	Dromore	Dromore Old Church	Church	Halpin, E.	H349-627
1991	122	Waterford	Waterford City	Alexander Street	Test-pits	Scully, O.M.B.	S607-123
1991	123	Waterford	Waterford City	Manor Street	Medieval urban	Halpin, A.	S261-113
1991	124	Westmeath	Athlone	Athlone Castle	Medieval/post-medieval castle	Halpin, A.	N039-420
1991	125	Westmeath	Athlone	The Docks/Williams Yard	Urban	Halpin, A.	N039-420
1991	126	Westmeath	Marlinstown		Ringfort	Keeley, V.J.	N463-527
1991	127	Westmeath	Mullingar	Friars' Mill Road	Archaeological potential	Keeley, V.J.	N440-530
1991	128	Westmeath	Mullingar	Martin's Lane	Post-medieval urban	Meenan, R.	N440-530
1991	129	Westmeath	Robinstown		Stone platform	Brady, N.	N402-453
1991	130	Westmeath	Tyrellspass	Tyrellspass Castle	Tower-house	Meenan, R.	N411-374
1991	131	Wexford	Clonee Lower		Enclosure site	Bennett, I.	T048-538
1991	132	Wexford	Fethard	Grange	Test-pits	Scully, O.M.B.	S781-052

1991	133	Wexford	Wexford Town		Medieval urban	O'Rourke, D.	T064-219
1991	134	Wicklow	Delgany	Killincarrick	Bronze Age remains	Gowen, M.	O280-105
1991	135	Wicklow	Killegar	Killegar Quarry	No archaeological significance	Scally, G.	O215-186
1991	136	Wicklow	Kindlestown Upper		Medieval	Halpin, A.	O372-211
1991	137	Wicklow	Wicklow Town	Wicklow Friary	Medieval	Gowen, M.	T313-940
1992	1	Antrim	Ballygalley	Croft Manor	Neolithic settlement & industrial site	Simpson, D.D.A.	D374-075
1992	2	Antrim	Carrickfergus		Medieval town	Ó Baoill, R.	J414-875
1992	3	Armagh	Armagh City	English Street	Urban	Hurl, D.P.	H875-456
1992	4	Armagh	Ballyrea		Linear ditch	Crothers, N.	H844-446
1992	5	Armagh	Shanmullagh	Ballycullen	River dredgings	Bourke, C.	H842-533
1992	6	Cavan	Aughrim		Wedge tomb	Channing, J.	H274-211
1992	7	Cavan	Blackhills Lower		Early Christian occupation site	McConway, L. and Halpin, E.	N701-932
1992	8	Cavan	Cloughballybeg		*Fulacht fiadh*	Gowen, M.	N680-848
1992	9	Clare	Bunratty East		Medieval settlement?	O Rahilly, C.	R453-613
1992	10	Clare	Cappagh		Barracks	O Rahilly, C.	Q985-540
1992	11	Clare	Castlecrine	Moygalla	Ringfort/children's burial-ground environs	O Rahilly, C.	R490-675
1992	12	Clare	Ennis	Abbey Street	Abbey environs	O Rahilly, C.	R337-774
1992	13	Clare	Mooghaun South		Hillfort (trivallate)	Bennett, I. and Grogan, E.	R408-706
1992	14	Clare	Ruan		Medieval church environs	O Rahilly, C.	R331-870
1992	15	Cork	Ballintaggert		Ecclesiastical enclosure?	Gowen, M.	W771-644
1992	16	Cork	Carrigtwohill	Barryscourt Castle	Tower-house	Finch, O.	W821-724
1992	17	Cork	Blackpool	Curraglass	Post-medieval settlement	Myles, F. and Klingelhöfer, E.	W969-938
1992	18	Cork	Bridgetown	Bridgetown Priory	Augustinian priory	O'Keeffe, T.	R690-009
1992	19	Cork	Carrigeen East		Post-medieval settlement	Myles, F. and Klingelhöfer, E.	W950-942
1992	20	Cork	Carrigtwohill	Fota Island	Multi-period	O'Connell, P. and Rutter, A.E	W790-720
1992	21	Cork	Conva		Cropmark enclosures	Doody, M.G.	W720-998
1992	22	Cork	Cork City	Grand Parade	Medieval city wall	Wren, J.	W671-715
1992	23	Cork	Cork City	Kyrl's Quay	Medieval urban/ North Main Street	Hurley, M.F.	W671-721
1992	24	Cork	Cork City	Red Abbey Yards	Medieval	Sheehan, C.	W675-714
1992	25	Cork	Cork City	Shandon Street/ Brownes Hill	Urban	Stack, J.D.	W672-722
1992	26	Cork	Curraheen		Domestic pits & pit burial	Byrne, E.	R790-100
1992	27	Cork	Old Head of Kinsale	Downmacpatrick	Prehistoric/historic settlement site	Cleary, R.M.	W632-402
1992	28	Cork	Killanully		Ringfort, souterrain & rectangular enclosure	Mount, C.	W692-636
1992	29	Cork	Killavillig		Early ecclesiastical enclosure	O'Shaughnessy, J.	R414-101
1992	30	Cork	Lisleagh	Lisleagh II	Ringfort	Monk, M.A.	R178-106
1992	31	Cork	Youghal	Ashe Street/ Chapel Lane	Medieval urban	Power, C.	X105-780
1992	32	Donegal	Rinnaraw		Cashel & house site	Fanning, T.	C038-368
1992	33	Down	Ballynahatty	Ballynahatty 5 & 6	Crop-marked pit enclosure	Hartwell, B.	J326-677
1992	34	Down	Downpatrick	Cathedral Hill	Early Christian/ medieval	Ó Baoill, R.	J483-445
1992	35	Down	Inch	Inch Abbey, River Quoile	River bed	Foley, C. (with Ramsey, G.)	J480-450
1992	36	Down	Newtownards	Castle Gardens	Ecclesiastical	Hurl, D.P.	J493-738
1992	37	Down	Ringmackilroy		Ringfort	Crothers, N.	J141-94Z
1992	38	Dublin	Drimnagh	Drimnagh Castle	Castle	Mullins, C.	O109-318
1992	39	Dublin	Brownsbarn		Cropmarks	Tierney, M.	O047-276
1992	40	Dublin	Chapelizod	Kingshall	Medieval manor?	Hayden, A.	O096-350
1992	41	Dublin	Chapelizod	Main Street	Post-medieval	Reid, M.	O101-345

1992	42	Dublin	Chapelizod	Martin's Row	Medieval settlement & burial	King, H.A.	O101-345
1992	43	Dublin	Crumlin	Fortostman	Mound	Halpin, A.	O134-323
1992	44	Dublin	Dalkey	St Joseph's	Medieval town	Hayden, A.	O265-165
1992	45	Dublin	Dublin City	Aungier Street	Post-medieval	Rennie, G.	O156-335
1992	46	Dublin	Dublin City	Back Lane	Medieval urban	Walsh, C.	O150-338
1992	47	Dublin	Dublin City	Bow Lane West/ Kennedy's Villas	No archaeological significance	Halpin, A.	O136-338
1992	48	Dublin	Dublin City	Bride Street/ Golden Lane	Urban	Halpin, A.	O153-337
1992	49	Dublin	Dublin City	Bridge Street Upper	Medieval urban	Meenan, R.	O148-344
1992	50	Dublin	Dublin City	Bridge Street Upper	Medieval urban defences	Hayden, A.	O144-340
1992	51	Dublin	Dublin City	Castle Street/ Lord Edward Street	Medieval urban	Byrne, M.E.	O156-341
1992	52	Dublin	Dublin City	Christchurch Place, Jury's Inn	Medieval	Gowen, M.	O151-349
1992	53	Dublin	Dublin City	Christchurch Place, Jury's Inn	Medieval urban defences & settlement	Hayden, A.	O152-349
1992	54	Dublin	Dublin City	Cook Street	Medieval urban	Meenan, R.	O149-341
1992	55	Dublin	Dublin City	Cornmarket/ Francis Street	Medieval urban defences & extra-mural industrial	Hayden, A.	O149-338
1992	56	Dublin	Dublin City	Dean Street/ Patrick Street	Urban	Halpin, A.	O151-335
1992	57	Dublin	Dublin City	Digges' Lane, Mercer's Hospital	Medieval ecclesiastical foundation	Hayden, A.	O157-338
1992	58	Dublin	Dublin City	Digges' Lane, Mercer's Hospital	Medieval church & hospital	Halpin, E.	O157-338
1992	59	Dublin	Dublin City	Essex Street East (Poddle Culvert)	Post-medieval	Gowen, M.	O158-341
1992	60	Dublin	Dublin City	Essex Street West, SS Michael & John's	Medieval urban	O'Flanagan, N.	O156-342
1992	61	Dublin	Dublin City	Eustace Street	Medieval/ post-medieval	Gowen, M.	O158-341
1992	62	Dublin	Dublin City	Eustace Street	18th-century	Gowen, M.	O158-341
1992	63	Dublin	Dublin City	Fownes Street Lower	Post-medieval	Gowen, M.	O158-341
1992	64	Dublin	Dublin City	Fownes Street Upper	No archaeological significance	Gowen, M.	O158-341
1992	65	Dublin	Dublin City	Francis Street	Medieval	Gowen, M.	O151-336
1992	66	Dublin	Dublin City	Francis Street/ Hanover Lane	Medieval urban	Halpin, A.	O150-336
1992	67	Dublin	Dublin City	South Great Georges Street	Urban	Halpin, A.	O156-338
1992	68	Dublin	Dublin City	High Street— St Audoen's Church	Medieval church	McMahon, M.	O149-340
1992	69	Dublin	Dublin City	James' Street— St Patrick's Hospital	No archaeological significance	Hayden, A.	O136-338
1992	70	Dublin	Dublin City	Liffey Street/ Strand Street	Urban	Hurley, F.M.	O157-343
1992	71	Dublin	Dublin City	Meath Place	Post-medieval	Gowen, M.	O141-329
1992	72	Dublin	Dublin City	Parliament Street	Post-medieval	Scally, G. and Gowen, M.	O158-341
1992	73	Dublin	Dublin City	Patrick Street	Medieval urban	Hurley, F.M.	O153-340
1992	74	Dublin	Dublin City	Poolbeg Street	Post-medieval graveyard	Channing, J.	O162-343
1992	75	Dublin	Dublin City	Queen Street	No archaeological significance	Walsh, C.	O145-345
1992	76	Dublin	Dublin City	Ship Street Little	Medieval urban	Scally, G.	O147-337
1992	77	Dublin	Dublin City	Stephen Street Lower	Medieval urban	Meenan, R.	O158-336
1992	78	Dublin	Dublin City	Wellington Quay	Post-medieval	Gowen, M.	O158-341
1992	79	Dublin	Finglas	Cappagh Road/ Patrickswell Place	Urban	O'Flanagan, N.	O128-388

1992	80	Dublin	Finglas	Church Road	No archaeological significance	McMahon, M.	O129-389
1992	81	Dublin	Howth	Howth House	Medieval stone building	Hayden, A.	O286-393
1992	82	Dublin	Donabate	Turvey	Post-medieval	Rennie, G.	O212-509
1992	83	Galway	Annaghcorrib		Togher	Moloney, A. and Jennings, D.	M940-250
1992	84	Galway	Ardrahan South		Medieval borough	Breen, C.	M461-123
1992	85	Galway	Galway City	Flood Street/ New Dock Street	Medieval urban	Walsh, C.	M298-249
1992	86	Galway	Galway City	Kirwan's Lane/ Cross Street Upper	Late medieval houses	Walsh, G.	M300-250
1992	87	Galway	Galway City	Mary Street (Abbey Lane)	City wall	O'Brien, M.A.	M300-252
1992	88	Galway	Galway City	Merchants' Road/ Abbeygate Street Lower	Medieval urban	Delaney, D.	M299-248
1992	89	Galway	Galway City	Merchants' Road/ Flood Street	Urban	O'Flanagan, N.	M298-251
1992	90	Galway	Galway City	Quay Street	No archaeological significance	Stierle, K.	M300-254
1992	91	Galway	Galway City	Spanish Parade	Medieval urban	Delaney, D.	M297-247
1992	92	Galway	Omey Island	Goreen & Sturakeen	Monastic site	O'Keeffe, T.	L570-560
1992	93	Galway	Áran (Inis Mór)	Dún Aonghasa (Kilmurvey)	Cliff fort	Cotter, C.	L817-079
1992	94	Galway	Rinville West	Rathnapoura	Ringfort	Ó Faoláin, D.	M350-227
1992	95	Galway	Ballyconneely	Truska, Mallinmore, Mallinbeg	Coastal middens	McCormick, F.	L640-450
1992	96	Galway	Tuam	Townparks, The Clareen	Early Christian, medieval & post-medieval complex	Higgins, J.	M437-519
1992	97	Galway	Tuam	Townparks	Pottery kiln	Connolly, A.	M437-519
1992	98	Kerry	Ardfert	St Brendan's Cathedral	Medieval cathedral	Moore, F.	Q786-214
1992	99	Kerry	Ballybeg		Ringfort environs	Bennett, I.	Q457-016
1992	100	Kerry	Ferriter's Cove	Ballyoughteragh North	Mesolithic/Neolithic settlement	Woodman, P.C. and O'Brien, M.Q	330-052
1992	101	Kerry	Dingle	Goat Street (Upper Main Street)	Urban	Bennett, I.	Q446-012
1992	102	Kerry	Dingle	Green Street	Urban	Bennett, I.	Q443-010
1992	103	Kerry	Illaunloughan		Early Christian hermitage	Walsh, C.	V362-733
1992	104	Kerry	Kilmore	Ballyhoneen	Pre-bog wall	Ó Coilleáin, M.	Q530-085
1992	105	Kerry	Ross Island		Copper mine	O'Brien, W.	V944-880
1992	106	Kerry	Shanakeal	Lissaroe	Ringfort environs	Bennett, I.	Q762-032
1992	107	Kildare	Carragh	Carragh Graveyard	Ecclesiastical site	O'Flanagan, N.	N840-218
1992	108	Kildare	Curragh		Circular feature	Duffy, C. and Keeley, V.J.	N763-123
1992	109	Kildare	Kildare Town	Grey Abbey	Abbey environs	Duffy, C. and Keeley, V.J.	N727-109
1992	110	Kildare	Rathernan	Resurexit	Ecclesiastical site	O'Flanagan, N.	N788-235
1992	111	Kilkenny	Ardra		Cist grave	Ó Floinn, R.	N535-753
1992	112	Kilkenny	Kilkenny City	Chapel Lane	Urban	Opie, H.	S504-559
1992	113	Kilkenny	Kilkenny City	High Street, Langton House	Medieval building	Scully, O.M.B.	S510-560
1992	114	Kilkenny	Kilkenny City	James' Street, Presentation Convent & Old Brewery	Medieval	Channing, J.	S505-559
1992	115	Kilkenny	Kilkenny City	Kilkenny Castle	12th/19th-century castle	Murtagh, B.	S509-556
1992	116	Kilkenny	Kilkenny City	Ormonde Road— Cleere's Factory	Medieval urban	Channing, J.	S508-557
1992	117	Kilkenny	Kilkenny City	Parliament Street	Urban	Opie, H.	S510-560
1992	118	Kilkenny	Kilkenny City	Parliament Street, Rothe House	Post-medieval	O'Flanagan, N.	T551-157
1992	119	Laois	Meeleck		*Fulachta fiadh?*	Keeley, V.J.	S480-950

1992	120	Laois	Rathbrennan		Mounds	Keeley, V.J.	S512-992
1992	121	Limerick	Abington	Abbey Owney	16th-century house site near Cistercian abbey	O Rahilly, C.	R714-536
1992	122	Limerick	Adare	Desmond's Castle	Medieval castle	O Rahilly, C.	R469-463
1992	123	Limerick	Annagh		Neolithic cave burial	Ó Floinn, R.	R693-581
1992	124	Limerick	Lough Gur	Ballynagallagh	No archaeological significance	Cleary, R.M.	R635-395
1992	125	Limerick	Glennameade		No archaeological significance	O Rahilly, C.	
1992	126	Limerick	Limerick City	King's Island— St John's Hospital	Medieval urban	O Rahilly, C.	R583-570
1992	127	Limerick	Limerick City	St Mary's Cathedral	Medieval cathedral	Hodkinson, B.J.	R578-575
1992	128	Limerick	Lough Gur	Patrickswell	Major site environs	O Rahilly, C.	R642-410
1992	129	Limerick	Rathkeale	Abbeylands	Medieval abbey, burial-ground	O Rahilly, C.	R362-415
1992	130	Limerick	Rathkeale	Englishtenements	No archaeological significance	O Rahilly, C.	R362-415
1992	131	Limerick	Mitchelstown West		Ring-ditches/ ring-barrows	Daly, A. and Grogan, E.	R724-287
1992	132	Limerick	Skehacreggaun		Monastic settlement	O Rahilly, C.	R544-531
1992	133	Louth	Carlingford	Holy Trinity Church	Medieval/ post-medieval burials	Gleeson, G. and Moore, D.	J189-120
1992	134	Louth	Carlingford	Tholsel Street	Urban	Gleeson, G. and Moore, D.	J190-119
1992	135	Louth	Dawson's Demesne	Castle Guard	Motte environs	Keeley, V.J.	N971-905
1992	136	Louth	Dawson's Demesne		Mound	Keeley, V.J.	N972-904
1992	137	Louth	Drogheda	Old Abbey Lane, Narrow West Street	Abbey	Meenan, R.	O085-752
1992	138	Louth	Glebe		Mound	Keeley, V.J.	N800-853
1992	139	Louth	Dundalk	Haynestown	Souterrain	Keeley, V.J.	J040-036
1992	140	Louth	Riverstown	Liss	Motte?	Keeley, V.J.	N965-913
1992	141	Mayo	Boofeenaun		Crannog & *fulachta fiadh*	Moloney, A. and Keane, M.	G113-041
1992	142	Mayo	Carrowcanada		Ringfort	Walsh, G.	G374-981
1992	143	Mayo	Cloonlara		Ringfort	Walsh, G.	G398-004
1992	144	Mayo	Glenbaun		Enclosure	Grant, C. and Loughran, A.	L875-782
1992	145	Mayo	Behy/Glenurla	Céide Fields	Neolithic field system	Byrne, G.	G066-389
1992	146	Mayo	Lislackagh		Ringfort	Walsh, G.	M356-975
1992	147	Mayo	Rathlackan		Court cairn & pre-bog settlement	Byrne, G.	G166-388
1992	148	Mayo	Achill	The Deserted Village, Slievemore (Toir)	Multi-phase landscape	Halpin, E. and McDonald, T.	F632-071
1992	149	Meath	Tara	Castleboy (St Patrick's Church)	Ecclesiastical	Meenan, R.	N921-598
1992	150	Meath	Cormeen		Souterrain & ringfort	McConway, L. and Halpin, E.	N738-891
1992	151	Meath	Knowth		Multi-period site	Eogan, G. and . Roche, H	N995-735
1992	152	Meath	Macetown		Burial	O'Connor, N.	N998-599
1992	153	Meath	Raffin	Raffin Fort	Ritual enclosure	Newman, C.	N820-828
1992	154	Meath	Ratoath	Fairyhouse Road	No archaeological significance	Ryan, F.	O019-518
1992	155	Meath	Stalleen		River excavation	Gregory, N.	
1992	156	Offaly	Banagher	Harbour Street	Plantation town/ early monastic site	King, H.A.	N001-154
1992	157	Offaly	Clonmacnoise	New Graveyard	Early Christian settlement	King, H.A.	N011-308
1992	158	Offaly	Clonmacnoise	St Kieran's NS	Monastic site	Ó Floinn, R.	N008-305
1992	159	Offaly	Clorhane		Field system	King, H.A.	M996-280
1992	160	Offaly	Toberdaly		Folly	Connolly, A.	N252-125
1992	161	Roscommon	Trinity Island	Holy Trinity Abbey	Abbey— Premonstratensian	Clyne, M.	G833-045

1992	162	Sligo	Carrigeens		Early Bronze Age cist burial	Cahill, M.	G589-459
1992	163	Sligo	Deechomade		Enclosure	Keane, M. and Farrelly, J.	G636-130
1992	164	Tipperary	Cashel	St Patrick's Rock—Cormac's Chapel	Romanesque church	Hodkinson, B.J.	S075-410
1992	165	Tipperary	Chancellorsland		Barrow cemetery & earthworks	Doody, M.G.	R758-358
1992	166	Tipperary	Clonmel	Dowd's Lane	Medieval/post-medieval urban	Henry, M.	S203-225
1992	167	Tipperary	Clonmel	Dowd's Lane	Medieval urban	Opie, H.	S203-225
1992	168	Tipperary	Clonmel	Gladstone Street/O'Connell Street	Urban	Scully, O.M.B.	S200-220
1992	169	Tipperary	Clonmel	New Quay	Medieval urban	Scully, O.M.B.	S200-220
1992	170	Tipperary	Nenegh	Pearse Street	Urban	Hodkinson, B.J.	R870-790
1992	171	Tipperary	Roscrea	Roscrea Castle	Medieval gatehouse	Wren, J.	S134-892
1992	172	Tyrone	Casslesessiagh	Castlederg Castle	Plantation castle	Halpin, E.	H261-844
1992	173	Waterford	Waterford City	Barrowstrand Street	Urban	Sheehan, C.	S607-123
1992	174	Waterford	Waterford City	Keyser Street/High Street	Medieval urban	Scully, O.M.B.	S608-124
1992	175	Waterford	Waterford City	Peter Street	Medieval urban	Scully, O.M.B.	S608-123
1992	176	Westmeath	Ballynahownwood	The Giant's Road	Medieval roadway	Moloney, A. and McDermott, C.	N070-337
1992	177	Westmeath	Fore	Fore Abbey (the Gatehouse)	Medieval	Scally, G.	N510-700
1992	178	Westmeath	Kilbeggan	Main Street	No archaeological significance	Ryan, F.	N332-351
1992	179	Westmeath	Petitswood		Enclosure	Channing, J.	N458-537
1992	180	Westmeath	Robinstown		Stone platform	Brady, N.	N402-453
1992	181	Westmeath	Templemacateer		No archaeological significance	Scally, G.	N264-395
1992	182	Wexford	Wexford Town	West Gate (Halligan's)	Town wall	Meenan, R.	T044-022
1992	183	Wicklow	Wicklow Town		No archaeological significance	Gowen, M.	T315-939
1992	Apx1	Dublin	North Dublin		Ploughzone Archaeology Survey	Guinan, B.	
1992	Apx2	Mayo	Achill	The Deserted Village, Slievemore (Toir)	Village survey	Halpin, E. and McDonald, T.	F632-071
1992	Apx3	Sligo	Carrowtemple		Early Christian slabs replacement	Timoney, M.A.	G625-021
1992	Apx4	Sligo	Knocknarea	Misgaun Maedbh	Passage grave reconstruction	Timoney, M.A.	G625-345
1993	1	Antrim	Ballygalley	Croft Manor	Neolithic settlement & industrial site	Simpson, D.D.A., Moore, G.G. and Conway, M.G	D374-075
1993	2	Antrim	Ballywee		Early Christian settlement complex	Crothers, N.	J219-899
1993	3	Antrim	Carrickfergus		Medieval town	Ó Baoill, R.	J414-872
1993	4	Antrim	Carrickfergus	Carrickfergus Castle	Castle	Donnelly, C.J. and McCooey, P.	J415-873
1993	5	Antrim	Rathlin Island	Corvally	Standing stone	Hurl, D.P.	D131-347
1993	6	Antrim	Forthill	Templecorran	Ecclesiastical enclosure	Crothers, N.	J449-937
1993	7	Antrim	Solar		Ecclesiastical site	Hurl, D.P.	D344-122
1993	8	Armagh	Ballyrea		Ditch	Crothers, N.	H846-448
1993	9	Armagh	Shanmullagh	Ballycullen	River dredgings	Bourke, C.	H843-438
1993	10	Clare	Ennis	Old Barracks Street	Urban	O Rahilly, C.	R337-774
1993	11	Clare	Lifford		No archaeological significance	O Rahilly, C.	R343-782
1993	12	Clare	Mooghaun South		Hillfort (trivallate)	Grogan, E.	R408-706
1993	13	Clare	Newtown	Newtown Castle	Castle	Lavelle, D.	M217-065
1993	14	Cork	Aghacross	Templemolagga Church	Medieval church	Monk, M.A.	R173-111
1993	15	Cork	Allihies	Trá na Fearla (the *Pearl*)	Shipwreck	Breen, C.	V570-450

1993	16	Cork	Ballindeasig	Tabor Lodge Ringfort	Ringfort	Breen, C.	W736-535
1993	17	Cork	Ballynagrumoolia		Standing stone	Tierney, J.	W632-647
1993	18	Cork	Castleblagh	Claidh Dubh, Ballydague	Linear earthwork	Doody, M.G.	N702-974
1993	19	Cork	Castlefreke	Rathbarry Castle	Tower-house environs	Crumlish, R.	W340-352
1993	20	Cork	Coraliss		Ringfort environs	Cleary, R.M.	R550-215
1993	21	Cork	Cork City	Blackmore Lane/ Meade Street	No archaeological significance	Lane, S.	W673-714
1993	22	Cork	Cork City	Douglas Street	Urban	Cleary, R.M.	W681-714
1993	23	Cork	Cork City	Evergreen Road bacon factory	No archaeological significance	Cleary, R.M.	W678-708
1993	24	Cork	Cork City	Gould's Square	Urban	O'Shaughnessy, J.	W675-713
1993	25	Cork	Cork City	Grattan Street	Post-medieval urban	Stack, J.D.	W670-719
1993	26	Cork	Cork City	Hanover Street	No archaeological significance	Lane, S.	W673-724
1993	27	Cork	Cork City	Mary Street	Abbey environs	Cleary, R.M.	W672-716
1993	28	Cork	Cork City	Pope's Quay	No archaeological significance	Cleary, R.M.	W667-720
1993	29	Cork	Cork City	Pope's Quay	No archaeological significance	Lane, S.	W671-722
1993	30	Cork	Cork City	Gill Abbey (St Mary's of the Isle)	Dominican priory	Hurley, M.F.	W671-715
1993	31	Cork	Cork City	Washington Street	No archaeological significance	Lane, S.	W673-724
1993	32	Cork	Inchiquin		Unknown	Cotter, E.	X038-748
1993	33	Cork	Kinsale	Abbeylands	Priory environs & town wall site	Cleary, R.M.	W637-505
1993	34	Cork	Lisleagh	Lisleagh II	Ringfort	Monk, M.A.	R178-106
1993	35	Cork	Youghal	Ashe Street/ Chapel Lane	Urban	Wren, J.	X105-780
1993	36	Derry	Coleraine	Stone Row	Urban	Gahan, A.	C848-323
1993	37	Donegal	Lifford	Town Hall	Urban	O'Flanagan, N.	C330-985
1993	38	Donegal	Letterkenny	ESB line	No archaeological significance	Crumlish, R.	C250-100
1993	39	Down	Ballymacarret	Ravenhill Road Pottery	Industrial	Francis, P.	J340-720
1993	40	Down	Ballynahatty	Ballynahatty 5 & 6	Cropmarks	Hartwell, B.	J326-677
1993	41	Down	Inch	Inch Abbey	Cistercian abbey	Hurl, D.P.	J480-450
1993	42	Down	Newtownards	Court Square	Medieval urban	Halpin, E.	J492-738
1993	43	Down	Tullyboard		Windmill	Hurl, D.P.	J599-505
1993	44	Dublin	Cabinteely		Standing stone	Carroll, J.	O229-246
1993	45	Dublin	Chapelizod	Martin's Row	Post-medieval urban	Halpin, E.	O102-350
1993	46	Dublin	Chapelizod	Martin's Row	Medieval settlement & burial	King, H.A.	O101-345
1993	47	Dublin	Clondalkin	St Brigid's Well	Holy well	Channing, J.	O070-306
1993	48	Dublin	Drimnagh	Drimnagh Castle	Castle	Mullins, C.	O109-318
1993	49	Dublin	Drimnagh	Drimnagh Castle	Castle	Swan, R.	O109-318
1993	50	Dublin	Dublin City	Arran Quay	Medieval urban	Simpson, L.	O148-342
1993	51	Dublin	Dublin City	Aungier Street	Medieval urban	Meenan, R.	O156-333
1993	52	Dublin	Dublin City	Aungier Street	Urban	Swan, D.L.	O157-336
1993	53	Dublin	Dublin City	Aungier Street	Urban	McConway, L.	O157-336
1993	54	Dublin	Dublin City	Aungier Street	No archaeological significance	Cassidy, B.	O157-336
1993	55	Dublin	Dublin City	Bride Street	Medieval urban	McMahon, M.	O153-337
1993	56	Dublin	Dublin City	Bride Street	Urban	Carroll, J.	O152-337
1993	57	Dublin	Dublin City	Castle Street	Viking/medieval urban	Byrne, M.E.	O156-341
1993	58	Dublin	Dublin City	Christchurch Place	Medieval urban	Gowen, M.	O152-349
1993	59	Dublin	Dublin City	Christchurch Place	Medieval urban	Walsh, C. and Hayden, A.	O152-349
1993	60	Dublin	Dublin City	Christchurch Place, Geneval's Tower	Medieval urban	Gowen, M.	O151-348
1993	61	Dublin	Dublin City	Church Street/ Bow Street	Urban	Cassidy, B.	O149-343
1993	62	Dublin	Dublin City	Church Street	Urban	Hayden, A.	O149-343

1993	63	Dublin	Dublin City	Cook Street	Medieval urban riverfront	Meenan, R.	O149-341
1993	64	Dublin	Dublin City	Coombe Relief Road	Medieval suburban	Hayden, A.	O140-330
1993	65	Dublin	Dublin City	Dame Street	No archaeological significance	Gowen, M.	O157-341
1993	66	Dublin	Dublin City	Echlin Street	Urban	Carroll, J.	O141-338
1993	67	Dublin	Dublin City	Essex Street East/ Wellington Quay	Post-medieval	Gowen, M.	O156-342
1993	68	Dublin	Dublin City	Eustace Street/ Dame Street	Urban	Carroll, J.	O156-345
1993	69	Dublin	Dublin City	Eustace Street	No archaeological significance	Gowen, M.	O156-341
1993	70	Dublin	Dublin City	Exchange Street Lower—Isolde's Tower	Medieval urban	Simpson, L.	O153-341
1993	71	Dublin	Dublin City	South Circular Road—Greenville Avenue	No archaeological significance	Swan, D.L.	O145-327
1993	72	Dublin	Dublin City	High Street	Medieval urban	Hurley, F.M.	O150-339
1993	73	Dublin	Dublin City	Loftus Lane	Urban	Scally, G.	O152-349
1993	74	Dublin	Dublin City	Meath Street	Post-medieval urban	Hanley, K.	O141-329
1993	75	Dublin	Dublin City	Meeting House Square	Medieval occupation	Gowen, M.	O156-341
1993	76	Dublin	Dublin City	Meeting House Square	Medieval urban	Reid, M.	O158-341
1993	77	Dublin	Dublin City	Collins Barracks	No archaeological significance	Hayden, A.	O136-346
1993	78	Dublin	Dublin City	North King Street	Post-medieval urban	Hanley, K.	O150-348
1993	79	Dublin	Dublin City	North King Street	Urban	Ryan, F.	O153-345
1993	80	Dublin	Dublin City	Ormond Quay Lower	No archaeological significance	Hayden, A.	O156-343
1993	81	Dublin	Dublin City	Parliament Street	Medieval urban	Gowen, M.	O155-341
1993	82	Dublin	Dublin City	Parliament Street	Hiberno-Norse/ medieval	Scally, G.	O146-343
1993	83	Dublin	Dublin City	Patrick Street	Urban	Halpin, E.	O152-336
1993	84	Dublin	Dublin City	Ship Street Little	Medieval urban	Hayden, A.	O153-338
1993	85	Dublin	Dublin City	Ship Street	Medieval urban	Simpson, L.	O148-342
1993	86	Dublin	Dublin City	Smithfield	No archaeological significance	McMahon, M.	O146-385
1993	87	Dublin	Dublin City	Temple Bar, West End	Medieval urban	Gowen, M.	O156-342
1993	88	Dublin	Dublin City	Temple Bar	Post-medieval activity	Gowen, M.	O156-342
1993	89	Dublin	Dublin City	Temple Bar, Temple Bar Gallery	Post-medieval activity	Gowen, M.	O157-342
1993	90	Dublin	Dublin City	Temple Bar, Temple Bar Gallery	Post-medieval waterfront	Reid, M.	O158-341
1993	91	Dublin	Dublin City	Temple Lane, The Green Building	Medieval burials	Gowen, M.	O156-341
1993	92	Dublin	Dublin City	Temple Lane, The Green Building	Medieval urban	Reid, M.	O156-341
1993	93	Dublin	Dublin City	Ward's Hill	No archaeological significance	Swan, D.L.	O146-322
1993	94	Dublin	Dublin City	Winetavern Street	Medieval urban	Halpin, A.	O152-341
1993	95	Dublin	Finglas		No archaeological significance	Opie, H.	O128-389
1993	96	Dublin	Lambay Island		Stone axe production site?	Cooney, G.	O315-505
1993	97	Dublin	Loughshinny	Ballough, gas pipeline	Bronze Age & later features	Gowen, M.	O225-258
1993	98	Dublin	Oxmanstown	George's Hill (Presentation Convent)	Urban	Ryan, F.	O143-348
1993	99	Dublin	Lusk	Raheny	Multi-period site	Cassidy, B.	O224-252
1993	100	Dublin	Rathfarnham	Rathfarnham Castle	Castle	Carroll, J.	O145-289
1993	101	Dublin	Swords	Bridge Street, 'The Pound'	Castle environs	Swan, D.L.	O182-470
1993	102	Dublin	Tallaght	Old Blessington Road/Main Street	Ecclesiastical enclosure	Meenan, R.	O093-277

1993	103	Dublin	Donabate	Turvey House	Castle site	Murtagh, D.	O212-509
1993	104	Fermanagh	Derryharney		Burial mounds/linear barrow cemetery	Conway, M.G.	H298-365
1993	105	Fermanagh	Derryhowlaght East		Crannog	Williams, B.B.	H300-364
1993	106	Galway	Abbeypark	Clontuskert Priory	Medieval priory—Augustinian	King, H.A.	M856-206
1993	107	Galway	Ballinderry		Tower-house	Fitzpatrick, M.	M445-462
1993	108	Galway	Galway City	Gleninagh Heights (St James' Church)	Church & graveyard	Higgins, J.	M299-250
1993	109	Galway	Galway City	Kirwan's Lane	Urban	O'Flanagan, N.	M300-250
1993	110	Galway	Galway City	Merchants' Road	Urban	Mount, C.	M298-515
1993	111	Galway	Omey Island	Goreen & Sturakeen	Prehistoric midden & early medieval settlement	O'Keeffe, T.	L562-566
1993	112	Galway	Áran (Inis Mór)	Dún Aonghasa (Kilmurvey)	Cliff fort	Cotter, C.	L817-097
1993	113	Galway	Loughrea	The Square	Urban	Lavelle, D.	M619-165
1993	114	Galway	Rahoon		Enclosure	Fitzpatrick, M.	M270-250
1993	115	Galway	Williamstown	Croaghill	Ringfort	Delaney, D.	M594-713
1993	116	Kerry	Ferriter's Cove	Ballyoughteragh North	Mesolithic/Neolithic settlement	Woodman, P.C.	Q330-052
1993	117	Kerry	Valentia Island	Bray Head	Medieval corn-drying kiln	Hayden, A.	V344-737
1993	118	Kerry	Caherlehillan		Early ecclesiastical & *ceallúnach*	Sheehan, J.	V571-834
1993	119	Kerry	Clasheen		Ringfort	Connolly, M.	W006-898
1993	120	Kerry	Valentia Island	Coarha More	Bronze Age settlement	Hayden, A.	V378-736
1993	121	Kerry	Dingle		Anglo-Norman town	Crumlish, R.	Q447-013
1993	122	Kerry	Emlagh West		Souterrain	Connolly, M.	Q444-077
1993	123	Kerry	Glin North		Clocháns	Bennett, I.	Q445-071
1993	124	Kerry	Sceilg Mhichíl (Great Skellig)	Monks' Garden	Monastic site	Bourke, E.C.	V245-604
1993	125	Kerry	Illaunloughan		Early Christian hermitage	Walsh, C. and White-Marshall, J.	V362-733
1993	126	Kerry	Ross Island		Bronze Age copper mines	O'Brien, W.	V944-880
1993	127	Kildare	Brewel West	Brewel Hill	Barrows etc.	Keeley, V.J.	N836-011
1993	128	Kildare	Clongowes	Castlebrown	Pale boundary earthwork	Donaghy, C.	N878-298
1993	129	Kildare	Grey Abbey		No archaeological significance	Donaghy, C.	N735-109
1993	130	Kildare	Kildare Town	Church Lane	Enclosure environs	Meenan, R.	N725-126
1993	131	Kildare	Kildare Town	Monasterevin Road, Crosskeys	No archaeological significance	Meenan, R.	N720-129
1993	132	Kildare	Kildare Town	St Brigid Square, Áras Bhríde	No archaeological significance	Meenan, R.	N726-123
1993	133	Kildare	Kilkea	Kilkea Castle	Medieval	McMahon, M.	S749-886
1993	134	Kildare	Kill		Monastic enclosure?	Halpin, E.	N942-229
1993	135	Kildare	Rathmore		No archaeological significance	Halpin, E.	N966-195
1993	136	Kilkenny	Gorteens		Castle & post-medieval settlement	King, H.A.	S652-135
1993	137	Kilkenny	Kilkenny City	Parliament Street, Rothe House	Post-medieval	O'Flanagan, N.	S511-557
1993	138	Laois	Coolbanagher	Coolbanagher Church	Ecclesiastical	Delaney, D.	N514-032
1993	139	Laois	Garrans	Chapel Hill	Mass house?	Delaney, D.	S587-977
1993	140	Laois	Port Laoise	The Heath	Archaeological potential	Keeley, V.J.	N525-018
1993	141	Laois	Port Laoise	Main Street	Urban	Byrne, M.E.	S470-990
1993	142	Laois	Dunamase	The Rock of Dunamase	Castle	Hodkinson, B.J.	S530-981
1993	143	Leitrim	Creevelea		Abbey environs	Crumlish, R.	G798-314
1993	144	Limerick	Clondrinagh		Deserted settlement?	O Rahilly, C.	R534-584
1993	145	Limerick	Killuragh	Killuragh Cave	Cave burial	O'Shaughnessy, J.	R778-497

1993	146	Limerick	Limerick City	King John's Castle	Medieval castle	Wiggins, K.	R577-577
1993	147	Limerick	Limerick City	Milk Market	City wall	O Rahilly, C.	R579-570
1993	148	Longford	Aghadegnan		*Fulacht fiadh*	Channing, J.	N132-759
1993	149	Longford	Aghadegnan	Aghadegnan II	*Fulacht fiadh* site	Swan, D.L.	N134-768
1993	150	Longford	Lisnamuck	Lisnamuck III	No archaeological significance	Swan, D.L.	N149-755
1993	151	Longford	Lisnamuck	Lisnamuck V	No archaeological significance	Swan, D.L.	N148-752
1993	152	Longford	Aghadegnan	Templemichael—Aghadegnan Ringfort	Ringfort	Carroll, J.	N132-759
1993	153	Louth	Ardee	William Street	Medieval mill site?	Swan, D.L.	N962-901
1993	154	Louth	Carlingford	Carlingford Priory	Dominican priory	Channing, J.	J898-141
1993	155	Louth	Drogheda	Old Abbey Lane	Ecclesiastical	Meenan, R.	O085-752
1993	156	Louth	Drogheda	Duleek Gate,	Urban	Mount, C.	O075-746
				Priest's Lane			
1993	157	Louth	Drogheda	Priest's Lane/Duleek Street	Urban	Swan, D.L.	O075-746
1993	158	Louth	Drogheda	Shop Street	Medieval urban	Meenan, R.	O091-750
1993	159	Louth	Drogheda	Stockwell Lane	Medieval urban	Meenan, R.	O089-752
1993	160	Louth	Drogheda	Stockwell Lane	Urban	McConway, L.	O089-752
1993	161	Louth	Drogheda	West Street, Westcourt Hotel	Medieval urban	Meenan, R.	O089-751
1993	162	Louth	Dundalk	Bachelor's Walk	No archaeological significance	Meenan, R.	J045-075
1993	163	Louth	Dundalk	Clanbrassil Street	Medieval urban	McMahon, M.	J045-075
1993	164	Louth	Dundalk	The Long Walk	Urban	Halpin, E.	J045-076
1993	165	Louth	Dundalk	The Long Walk	No archaeological significance	Meenan, R.	J047-076
1993	166	Louth	Gibstown		Souterrain?	Breen, T.C.	J030-035
1993	167	Louth	Dundalk	Haynestown	Corn-drying kiln & ring-barrow etc.	O'Sullivan, M.	J040-036
1993	168	Louth	Dundalk	Navan	Bronze Age	Opie, H.	J061-105
1993	169	Louth	Oldbridge	Sheephouse	Monitoring	Cassidy, B.	O045-760
1993	170	Louth	Whiterath		Souterrain?	Channing, J.	O039-986
1993	171	Mayo	Ballintubber		Medieval abbey	Ryan, F.	M115-279
1993	172	Mayo	Boheh		Rock art	Walsh, G.	L975-786
1993	173	Mayo	Church Island		Medieval	Ryan, F.	M116-275
1993	174	Mayo	Ballinrobe	Friarsquarter West—Ballinrobe Abbey	Friary	Morahan, L.	M195-649
1993	175	Mayo	Glenbaun		Enclosure	Grant, C. and Loughran, A.	L875-782
1993	176	Mayo	Behy/Glenurla	Céide Fields	Neolithic field system	Byrne, G.	G050-400
1993	177	Mayo	Rathlackan		Court cairn & pre-bog settlement	Byrne, G.	G166-388
1993	178	Mayo	Achill	The Deserted Village, Slievemore (Toir)	Multi-phase landscape	McDonald, T. and Halpin, E.	F630-075
1993	179	Meath	Boherard	Killallon Churchyard	Graveyard	Meenan, R.	N621-704
1993	180	Meath	Duleek	Navan Road	Early Christian/medieval urban	Donaghy, C.	O027-208
1993	181	Meath	Glebestown		No archaeological significance	Meenan, R.	O022-531
1993	182	Meath	Knowth		Multi-period site	Eogan, G. and Roche, H.	N995-735
1993	183	Meath	Raffin	Raffin Fort	Ritual enclosure	Newman, C.	N820-828
1993	184	Meath	Skreen		Ecclesiastical?	Meenan, R.	N951-603
1993	185	Offaly	Clonlyon Glebe	Belmont	Earthwork & enclosure	King, H.A.	N075-270
1993	186	Offaly	Clonmacnoise		High crosses	King, H.A.	N011-308
1993	187	Offaly	Clonmacnoise	New Graveyard	Early Christian settlement	King, H.A.	N011-308
1993	188	Offaly	Clonmacnoise		Early Christian	King, H.A.	N011-308
1993	189	Offaly	Clonmacnoise		No archaeological significance	King, H.A.	N011-306
1993	190	Offaly	Frankfort	Dunkerrin	Deserted medieval borough	O Rahilly, C.	S069-842
1993	191	Offaly	Tullamore	Collins Lane	Earthwork enclosure	King, H.A.	N326-265

1993	192	Roscommon	Ardcarn	'Ardcarna'	Monastic enclosure environs	Halpin, E.	G868-021
1993	193	Roscommon	Dysert	Cummeen	Ecclesiastical	Higgins, J.	
1993	194	Roscommon	Erris		Adjacent to features	Channing, J.	G821-033
1993	195	Roscommon	Erris	Templedriney Church	Church & enclosure	Channing, J.	G822-027
1993	196	Roscommon	Boyle	Keeloges	Enclosure?	Channing, J.	G829-021
1993	197	Sligo	Agharrow	Staad Abbey	Midden	McCormick, F.	G629-493
1993	198	Sligo	Ardrea Lough		Lakeside settlement	Moloney, A.	G683-165
1993	199	Sligo	Carnaweeleen		Passage grave	Buckley, V.M.	G717-132
1993	200	Sligo	Deechomade		Enclosure	Keane, M. and Farrelly, J.	G636-130
1993	201	Sligo	Sligo Town	Fort Hill (the Green Fort)	Artillery fort	Halpin, E.	G695-361
1993	202	Sligo	Sligo Town	Rockwood Parade	Post-medieval urban	Halpin, E.	G690-360
1993	203	Tipperary	Cashel	St Patrick's Rock—Cormac's Chapel	Church & graveyard	Hodkinson, B.J.	S075-410
1993	204	Tipperary	Chancellorsland		Bronze Age settlement	Doody, M.G.	R766-357
1993	205	Tipperary	Clonmel	Joyce's Lane, Irishtown	Urban	Henry, M.	S202-223
1993	206	Tipperary	Clonmel	Market Street	Medieval urban	Cleary, R.M.	S205-227
1993	207	Tipperary	Clonmel	Mary Street	Urban	Pollock, D.	S202-224
1993	208	Tipperary	Clonmel	Mary Street	Urban	Wren, J.	S202-222
1993	209	Tipperary	Clonmel	New Quay	Medieval urban	Scully, O.M.B.	S200-220
1993	210	Tipperary	Clonmel	Old Quay	Medieval urban	Henry, M.	S202-223
1993	211	Tipperary	Clonmel	Parnell Street, Town Hall	Urban	Henry, M.	S202-223
1993	212	Tipperary	Clonmel	Sarsfield Street, Quays	Post-medieval urban	Henry, M.	S202-223
1993	213	Waterford	Waterford City	Beau Street	Urban	Sheehan, C.	S607-123
1993	214	Waterford	Waterford City	Coffee House Lane	Urban	Gittings, A.S.R.	S609-124
1993	215	Waterford	Waterford City	Coffee House Lane	Medieval/ post-medieval urban	Wren, J.	S609-124
1993	216	Waterford	Waterford City	High Street	Medieval urban	McCutcheon, S.	S609-123
1993	217	Waterford	Waterford City	High Street	Medieval urban	Reid, M.	S608-124
1993	218	Waterford	Waterford City	Lady Lane	Urban	Sheehan, C.	S608-123
1993	219	Waterford	Waterford City	Little Patrick Street	Medieval/ post-medieval urban	Wren, J.	S607-123
1993	220	Waterford	Williamstown		No archaeological significance	Scully, O.M.B.	S607-120
1993	221	Westmeath	Portnashangan		Ringforts	Opie, H.	N414-603
1993	222	Wexford	Duncannon	Duncannon Fort	Post-medieval fort	Reid, M.	S727-081
1993	223	Wexford	Enniscorthy	Abbey Square	Medieval urban	Scully, O.M.B.	S975-399
1993	224	Wexford	Ferns	Main Street, Celtic Arms	No archaeological significance	Meenan, R.	T013-499
1993	225	Wexford	Taghmon	Main Street	Early Christian/ medieval	Wren, J.	S918-200
1993	226	Wexford	Enniscorthy	Templeshannon, Vinegar Hill	Battlefield	Bennett, I.	S984-401
1993	227	Wexford	Tintern	Tintern Abbey	Abbey	O'Donnell, M.	S795-100
1993	228	Wexford	Wexford Town	North Main Street	Urban	Scully, O.M.B.	T044-220
1993	229	Wexford	Wexford Town	South Main Street	Urban	Meenan, R.	T049-213
1993	230	Wicklow	Kilnacarrig		*Fulacht fiadh* & Bronze Age cultivation	Hayden, A.	O280-105
1993	231	Wicklow	Rathdown Upper		Prehistoric activity	Mount, C.	O328-135
1993	ApxI	Sligo	Rathdooney Beg		Geophysical survey	Mount, C.	G661-184
1993	ApxII	Wexford	Fethard		Survey	Murtagh, B.	S793-052
1994	1	Antrim	Antrim Town	Antrim Castle	Formal gardens & woodland bosquet	Conway, M.G.	J144-670
1994	2	Antrim	Antrim Town	Market Square	Urban	Crothers, N.	J147-666
1994	3	Antrim	Ballyaghagan	Cave Hill	Late Bronze Age dress-fastener findspot	Warner, R.B.	J321-792
1994	4	Antrim	Ballygalley	Croft Manor	Neolithic/Bronze Age settlement/industrial site	Simpson, D.D.A., Conway, M.G. and Moore, D.G.	D374-075
1994	5	Antrim	Ballygalley	Croft Manor	Neolithic	Halpin, E.	D371-077

1994	6	Antrim	Ballywee		Early Christian settlement complex	Crothers, N.	J218-898
1994	7	Antrim	Forthill	Templecorran	Multi-period	Crothers, N.	J448-936
1994	8	Antrim	Rathlin Island	Knockans South, 'Shandragh'	Late Neolithic settlement & industrial site	Conway, M.G.	D130-515
1994	9	Antrim	Vow	Bann drainage dump	River dredgings	Bourke, C.	C915-167
1994	10	Armagh	Cavanpole	Kennedies	Stone setting	Hurl, D.P.	H833-436
1994	11	Armagh	Killuney		Church & graveyard	Halpin, E.	H892-458
1994	12	Cavan	Lismeen		Ringfort environs	Meenan, R.	N915-541
1994	13	Clare	Cappakea	Cromwell's Road	Road	O Rahilly, C.	R665-644
1994	14	Clare	Clenagh		Hilltop enclosure	Daly, A. and Grogan, E.	R360-647
1994	15	Clare	Ennis	Ennis Friary (the Cloister)	Friary	O'Flanagan, N.	R337-774
1994	16	Clare	Ennis	Parnell Street, Salt House Lane	Historic town	O Rahilly, C.	R337-774
1994	17	Clare	Gragan West	Gragan Castle	Tower-house & bawn	Lavelle, D.	M203-036
1994	18	Clare	Knocknalappa		Late Bronze Age lakeside platform	O'Sullivan, A.	R444-688
1994	19	Clare	Mooghaun South		Hillfort (trivallate)	Grogan, E.	R408-706
1994	20	Clare	Newtown	Newtown Castle	Tower-house	Lavelle, D.	M217-065
1994	21	Cork	Carrigeen East		Post-medieval settlement	Klingelhöfer, E. and Myles, F.	W950-942
1994	22	Cork	Cork City	Cove Street	Medieval graveyard	Cleary, R.M.	W670-717
1994	23	Cork	Cork City	Cove Street	Test-pits	Cleary, R.M.	W670-717
1994	24	Cork	Cork City	Hanover Street	Test-pits	Cleary, R.M.	W664-712
1994	25	Cork	Cork City	North Gate	Medieval urban	Hurley, M.F.	W670-720
1994	26	Cork	Cork City	Wandsfort Quay & Pope's Quay	Urban	Lane, S.	W673-724
1994	27	Cork	Crushyriree		Horizontal-wheeled watermill	Cotter, E.	W727-802
1994	28	Cork	Killanully		Medieval church environs	Cleary, R.M.	W698-645
1994	29	Cork	Kilcolman Middle	Kilcolman Castle	Medieval castle, post-medieval fortification	Klingelhöfer, E.	R581-113
1994	30	Cork	Kilquane		Medieval church	Cotter, E.	W547-885
1994	31	Cork	Kinsale	Main Street	Suburban	Cleary, R.M.	W638-505
1994	32	Cork	Kinsale	Rose Abbey	Urban	Cleary, R.M.	W637-504
1994	33	Cork	Shanagarry	Shanagarry Castle	Tower-house	Cotter, E.	W980-651
1994	34	Cork	Youghal	Chapel Lane	Urban	Cleary, R.M.	X104-782
1994	35	Cork	Youghal	North Main Street	Urban	Power, C.	X104-782
1994	36	Derry	Maghera	Church Street	Urban	Hurl, D.P.	C856-002
1994	37	Derry	Portstewart	Coleraine Road, Crossreagh West	Megalith (remains)	Hurl, D.P.	C821-365
1994	38	Derry	Portstewart	Coleraine Road, Glebe	Settlement?	Hurl, D.P.	C823-365
1994	39	Donegal	Dunfanaghy	Kill	No archaeological significance	Walsh, G.	C022-367
1994	40	Down	Downpatrick	Cathedral Hill	Medieval urban	Ó Baoill, R.	J482-445
1994	41	Down	Newtownards	Castle Gardens, Court Square	Ecclesiastical/bawn	Hurl, D.P.	J492-738
1994	42	Down	Shinn		Standing stone site	Halpin, E.	J132-315
1994	43	Dublin	Balrothery		Tower-house & church environs	Opie, H.	O190-622
1994	44	Dublin	Blanchardstown	Ballycoolin Industrial Park	Mound & moat?	Gowen, M.	O095-409
1994	45	Dublin	Chapelizod	Chapelizod Road	Post-medieval	Gowen, M.	O104-344
1994	46	Dublin	Chapelizod	Martin's Row	Medieval settlement & burial	King, H.A.	O101-345
1994	47	Dublin	Chapelizod		No archaeological significance	Carroll, J.	O102-345
1994	48	Dublin	Clontarf	St Gabriel's Road	No archaeological significance	McMahon, M.	O206-360

1994	49	Dublin	Coolock	Malahide Road, Cadbury Ireland	Mound environs	Gowen, M.	O201-394
1994	50	Dublin	Drimnagh	Drimnagh Castle	Castle	Swan, R.	O109-318
1994	51	Dublin	Dublin City	Augustine Street	Medieval town wall	Hayden, A.	O144-342
1994	52	Dublin	Dublin City	Aungier Street	Urban site?	Swan, D.L.	O157-336
1994	53	Dublin	Dublin City	Back Lane	Urban	Murtagh, D.	O150-338
1994	54	Dublin	Dublin City	Back Lane (St V. de P. Night Shelter)	Viking/medieval?	Byrne, M.E.	O151-233
1994	55	Dublin	Dublin City	Benburb Street, Collins Barracks	Urban	Swan, D.L.	O131-344
1994	56	Dublin	Dublin City	Beresfort Lane, Fyffe's Yard	Urban	O'Flanagan, N.	O150-340
1994	57	Dublin	Dublin City	Bow Lane West	No archaeological significance	Hayden, A.	O132-340
1994	58	Dublin	Dublin City	Capel Street	No archaeological significance	Hayden, A.	O157-344
1994	59	Dublin	Dublin City	Castle Street	Viking/medieval urban	Byrne, M.E.	O156-343
1994	60	Dublin	Dublin City	Digges' Lane, Mercer's Hospital	Medieval cultivation/ post-medieval dumping	Hayden, A.	O157-338
1994	61	Dublin	Dublin City	Dublin Castle	Post-medieval urban	Simpson, L.	O154-339
1994	62	Dublin	Dublin City	East Arran Street	Urban?	Swan, D.L.	O153-344
1994	63	Dublin	Dublin City	Essex Street West	Medieval urban	Simpson, L.	O153-341
1994	64	Dublin	Dublin City	Eustace Street	Urban	Murtagh, D.	O156-341
1994	65	Dublin	Dublin City	Fishamble Street (Kinlay House)	Medieval urban	Gowen, M.	O153-340
1994	66	Dublin	Dublin City	Fishamble Street	Urban	Murtagh, D.	O153-342
1994	67	Dublin	Dublin City	Francis Street	Medieval friary— Franciscan	Murtagh, D.	O150-336
1994	68	Dublin	Dublin City	Francis Street	Post-medieval burial	Hayden, A.	O148-337
1994	69	Dublin	Dublin City	Francis Street	No archaeological significance	Gowen, M.	O150-337
1994	70	Dublin	Dublin City	Francis Street	Urban	O'Flanagan, N.	O149-337
1994	71	Dublin	Dublin City	Grand Canal Street (Sir Patrick Dun's)	No archaeological significance	Hayden, A.	O170-336
1994	72	Dublin	Islandbridge	Salmon Pool	Urban	O'Flanagan, N.	O135-346
1994	73	Dublin	Dublin City	Jervis Street (Hospital Site)	Post-medieval urban	Simpson, L.	O154-345
1994	74	Dublin	Dublin City	Jervis Street/ Wolfe Tone Street/ Parnell Street	Urban	Halpin, A.	O154-346
1994	75	Dublin	Dublin City	Mount Brown Mills, Kilmainham	Mills site	Swan, D.L.	O132-336
1994	76	Dublin	Dublin City	Lord Edward Street	Medieval urban	Gowen, M.	O153-340
1994	77	Dublin	Dublin City	Lord Edward Street (Carnegie Trust)	Medieval urban	Byrne, M.E.	O158-343
1994	78	Dublin	Dublin City	Meath Street/ Earl Street South	Urban	Halpin, A.	O146-338
1994	79	Dublin	Dublin City	Brunswick Street North (Richmond Hospital)	Post-medieval	Simpson, L.	O148-348
1994	80	Dublin	Dublin City	Palace Street/ Exchange Court	Urban	Swan, D.L.	O154-333
1994	81	Dublin	Dublin City	Parliament Street	Viking & Hiberno-Norse	Scally, G.	O156-344
1994	82	Dublin	Dublin City	Queen Street/ Haymarket	Urban	Murphy, D.	O145-345
1994	83	Dublin	Dublin City	Schoolhouse Lane	Urban	Halpin, A.	O162-337
1994	84	Dublin	Dublin City	Stephen Street Lower	Medieval urban	Meenan, R.	O157-338
1994	85	Dublin	Dublin City	Thomas Street	Medieval urban	Hurley, F.M.	O143-338
1994	86	Dublin	Dublin City	Usher's Quay	Urban	Gowen, M.	O147-341
1994	87	Dublin	Dublin City	Werburgh Street	Hiberno-Viking urban settlement & defences	Hayden, A.	O155-339
1994	88	Dublin	Dublin City	Wexford Street	Urban?	Swan, D.L.	O154-331
1994	89	Dublin	Dublin City	Winetavern Street (Civic Offices)	Medieval urban	Halpin, A.	O152-341

1994	90	Dublin	Dunsink		Pits	Duffy, C.	O108-388
1994	91	Dublin	Dunsoughly	Dunsoughly Castle	Medieval tower-house	Murphy, D.	O154-410
1994	92	Dublin	Finglas	Finglas Bypass	Ecclesiastical enclosure?	Halpin, E.	O129-393
1994	93	Dublin	Finglas	Finglas Bypass	Ecclesiastical enclosure?	Halpin, E.	O129-393
1994	94	Dublin	Howth	Church Street	Medieval urban	Meenan, R.	O278-393
1994	95	Dublin	Lambay Island		Neolithic site/stone axe production site	Cooney, G.	O315-505
1994	96	Dublin	Lucan	Ballyowen Lane, Ballyowen Castle	No archaeological significance	Hayden, A.	O052-345
1994	97	Dublin	Raheny	Main Street	No archaeological significance	Carroll, J.	O215-382
1994	98	Dublin	Rathfarnham	Rathfarnham Castle Estate	Castle environs	Carroll, J.	O145-289
1994	99	Dublin	Swords	Main Street	No archaeological significance	O'Flanagan, N.	O182-470
1994	100	Dublin	Swords	Swords Castle	Castle environs	Channing, J.	O182-470
1994	101	Dublin	Tallaght	Belgard Road (Docfield)	Monastic enclosure environs	Meenan, R.	O093-277
1994	102	Dublin	Tallaght	St Maelruan's	Early Christian enclosure	McConway, C.	O091-278
1994	103	Dublin	Tyrellstown Big		*Fulacht fiadh*	Campbell, K.	O240-557
1994	104	Fermanagh	Derrybrusk		Burnt mound	Carroll, F.	H286-389
1994	105	Fermanagh	Derryvullen	Mound No. 1	Burnt mound	Carroll, F.	H268-406
1994	106	Fermanagh	Derryvullen	Mound No. 2	Burnt mound	Carroll, F.	H266-406
1994	107	Fermanagh	Doon	The Grey Stone	Prehistoric (Bronze Age?)	Halpin, E.	H347-473
1994	108	Fermanagh	Enniskillen	Enniskillen Castle	Castle	Crothers, N.	H315-422
1994	109	Fermanagh	Enniskillen		Burnt mound	Carroll, F.	H247-441
1994	110	Galway	Doughiska		Various	Crumlish, R.	M360-250
1994	111	Galway	Áran (Inis Mór)	Dún Aonghasa (Kilmurvey)	Cliff fort	Cotter, C.	L817-097
1994	112	Galway	Knocknacarragh Cross		Horizontal mill site	O'Brien, M.A.	M261-239
1994	113	Galway	Lettershea		Prehistoric	Gibbons, M.	L730-498
1994	114	Galway	Portumna	Portumna Castle	17th-century castle	King, H.A.	M855-014
1994	115	Galway	Truska	False Bay	Midden	McCormick, F.	L560-462
1994	116	Galway	Ballnavenooragh	Cathair Fionnúrach	Cashel	Gibbons, E.	Q429-107
1994	117	Kerry	Valentia Island	Bray Head—Crompeol	Early medieval farm to late medieval village	Hayden, A.	V342-736
1994	118	Kerry	Caherlehillan		Early ecclesiastical & *ceallúnach*	Sheehan, J.	V571-834
1994	119	Kerry	Valentia Island	Coarha Beg	Early Christian clochán	Hayden, A.	V349-758
1994	120	Kerry	Deer Park		Field system?	Bennett, I.	V971-919
1994	121	Kerry	Dingle	Green Street	Urban	Bennett, I.	Q447-013
1994	122	Kerry	Dingle		Monitoring in medieval town	Crumlish, R.	Q447-013
1994	123	Kerry	Sceilg Mhichíl (Great Skellig)	Monks' Garden	Monastic site	Bourke, E.C.	V245-604
1994	124	Kerry	Illaunloughan		Early Christian hermitage	Walsh, C. and White-Marshall, J.	V362-733
1994	125	Kerry	Killurly West		No archaeological significance	Walsh, C.	V413-684
1994	126	Kerry	Knockercreeveen		Enclosure?	O Rahilly, C.	Q856-315
1994	127	Kerry	Lahard		Ringfort	Connolly, M.	V866-930
1994	128	Kerry	Moybella North		Ringfort	Connolly, M.	Q909-387
1994	129	Kerry	Ross Island		Copper mine—early	O'Brien, W.	V944-880
1994	130	Kerry	Tralee	Mary Street	Urban	Bennett, I.	Q830-135
1994	131	Kildare	Athy		Town	Neary, P.	S690-935
1994	132	Kildare	Blackhall		Ring-barrows?	Channing, J.	
1994	133	Kildare	Brewel West	Brewel Hill	Ring-barrow site	Opie, H.	N836-011
1994	134	Kildare	Collinstown	Blakestown	No archaeological significance	Hurley, M.F.	N980-370
1994	135	Kildare	Naas	Millbrook	No archaeological significance	Byrne, M.E.	N109-899

1994	136	Kildare	Tipperkevin		No archaeological significance	Gowen, M.	N934-148
1994	137	Kilkenny	Gorteens	Gorteens II	No archaeological significance	Hurley, M.F.	S660-135
1994	138	Kilkenny	Kilkenny City	Greensbridge Street/ New Street	Graveyard environs	Gowen, M.	S510-560
1994	139	Kilkenny	Kilkenny City	John Street	Urban	Gowen, M.	S510-570
1994	140	Kilkenny	Knockroe	The Caiseal	Passage grave	O'Sullivan, M.	S408-312
1994	141	Laois	Aghaboe	Fairgreen, Aghaboe Abbey	Archaeological complex	Delaney, D.	S327-857
1994	142	Laois	Coolbanagher	Coolbanagher Church	Ecclesiastical remains	Delaney, D.	N514-032
1994	143	Laois	Maganey	Grange Castle	Castle	Delaney, D.	S712-831
1994	144	Laois	Dunamase	The Rock of Dunamase	Castle	Hodkinson, B.J.	S530-981
1994	145	Leitrim	Crickeen		*Fulacht fiadh?*	Channing, J.	
1994	146	Leitrim	Drumlease	Dromahaire Castle— the Lodge	Plantation castle environs	Halpin, E.	G800-315
1994	147	Leitrim	Drumsna		*Fulacht fiadh*	Opie, H.	N005-980
1994	148	Leitrim	Drumsna	Jamestown, Annaduff, Tully, Kildorragh	Various sites	Opie, H.	N001-970
1994	149	Leitrim	Kildorragh		*Fulacht fiadh* & round house	Opie, H.	M980-982
1994	150	Leitrim	Kiltycarney		*Fulacht fiadh*	Opie, H.	M980-990
1994	151	Leitrim	Lisseeghan		Ringfort	Opie, H.	M980-990
1994	152	Leitrim	Minkill		Burnt material spread	Opie, H.	M982-982
1994	153	Leitrim	Tully		*Fulacht fiadh*	Neary, P.	M982-982
1994	154	Limerick	Abington	Abbey Owney	Abbey environs	Byrne, M.E.	R714-536
1994	155	Limerick	Askeaton		Medieval urban	O Rahilly, C.	R341-503
1994	156	Limerick	Lough Gur	Ballynagallagh	Enclosure	Cleary, R.M.	R644-392
1994	157	Limerick	Coolalough		Prehistoric earthwork	Cross, S. and Grogan, E.	R718-353
1994	158	Limerick	Limerick City	St Saviour's Priory	Medieval priory— Dominican	Moran, J.	R580-578
1994	159	Limerick	Limerick City	Convent Street	Medieval urban	O Rahilly, C.	R578-575
1994	160	Limerick	Limerick City	King John's Castle	Medieval castle	Wiggins, K.	R577-577
1994	161	Limerick	Limerick City	Mungret Street	Medieval urban	O Rahilly, C.	R580-571
1994	162	Limerick	Limerick City	Nicholas Street	Medieval urban	O Rahilly, C.	R578-576
1994	163	Limerick	Limerick City	Nicholas Street	Medieval urban	O Rahilly, C.	R579-576
1994	164	Limerick	Newcastle West	Desmond	Historic town	O Rahilly, C.	R279-337
1994	165	Louth	Carlingford	Ghan House Banqueting Hall	Midden & watercourse	Gibbons, E.	J187-115
1994	166	Louth	Carlingford	Newry Street	Medieval urban	Murphy, D.	J188-119
1994	167	Louth	Carlingford	Tholsel Street	Medieval urban	Murphy, D.	J187-115
1994	168	Louth	Collon	Lower Street	Urban	Campbell, K.	N998-818
1994	169	Louth	Dundalk	Dowdallshill	Rectangular fosse	Channing, J.	J059-092
1994	170	Louth	Dundalk	Dowdallshill II	*Fulacht fiadh*	Breen, T.C.	J059-092
1994	171	Louth	Drogheda	Dominick Street/ Linenhall Street	Urban	Murphy, D.	O084-756
1994	172	Louth	Drogheda	Fair Street	Urban	Murphy, D.	O088-753
1994	173	Louth	Drogheda	Magdalene Tower	Dominican priory	Murphy, D.	O089-755
1994	174	Louth	Drogheda		Urban	Campbell, K.	O090-750
1994	175	Louth	Drogheda	West Street	Urban	McMahon, M.	O089-751
1994	176	Louth	Dundalk	Ballybarrack	Post-medieval farm buildings	Murphy, D.	J033-052
1994	177	Louth	Dundalk	The Long Walk	Medieval urban	Meenan, R.	J047-077
1994	178	Louth	Dundalk	Blackrock, Haggardstown	Medieval activity?	Murphy, D.	J062-032
1994	179	Louth	Dundalk	Seatown	Urban	Campbell, K.	J053-075
1994	180	Louth	Dundalk	Haggardstown	Ringfort	Campbell, K.	J067-026
1994	181	Louth	Ardee	Harristown	Early Christian ringfort?	Murphy, D.	N995-905
1994	182	Louth	Louth Village	Priorstate—Louth Monastery (St Mochta's)	Early monastic site	Murphy, D.	H956-014

1994	183	Louth	Termonfeckin	Duffsfarm	No archaeological significance	Murphy, D.	O150-810
1994	184	Mayo	Ballinrobe	Ballinrobe Sewage Scheme	Various sites	Walsh, G.	M191-643
1994	185	Mayo	Boleyboy		Burial mound	Ryan, F.	
1994	186	Mayo	Croagh Patrick	Glaspatrick	Oratory	Walsh, G.	L906-820
1994	187	Mayo	Westport	Westport Industrial Park	House	Ryan, F.	L998-840
1994	188	Mayo	Achill	The Deserted Village, Slievemore (Toir)	Multi-phase landscape	McDonald, T.	F630-075
1994	189	Meath	Donaghmore	Blackcastle Demesne	Bronze Age cist cemetery	Roche, H.	N875-685
1994	190	Meath	Moynagh Lough	Brittas	Crannog	Bradley, J.	N818-860
1994	191	Meath	Knowth		Multi-period site	Eogan, G. and Roche, H.	N995-735
1994	192	Meath	Navan	Abbey Road (Old Fire Station)	Medieval urban	Meenan, R.	N870-679
1994	193	Meath	Navan	Athlumney— Athlumney Castle	Tower-house/ 16th-century house	Meenan, R.	N876-674
1994	194	Meath	Sheephouse		*Fulachta fiadh*	Campbell, K.	O045-731
1994	195	Offaly	Banagher		Urban	King, H.A.	N001-154
1994	196	Offaly	Clonmacnoise		High crosses	King, H.A.	N011-308
1994	197	Offaly	Clonmacnoise	New Graveyard	Early Christian settlement	King, H.A.	N011-308
1994	198	Offaly	Clonmacnoise		Monastic site environs	King, H.A.	N011-308
1994	199	Offaly	Daingean	Killaderry	Enclosure?	King, H.A.	N465-285
1994	200	Roscommon	Carrowntemple	'The Nunnery'	Church, nunnery & cemetery	Higgins, J.	
1994	201	Roscommon	Kiltullagh		Standing stone	McCormick, F.	M530-740
1994	202	Roscommon	Loughlackagh	Moore Cemetery	Souterrain	Lavelle, D.	M938-219
1994	203	Sligo	Carrowmore		Megalithic cemetery environs	Mount, C.	G661-337
1994	204	Sligo	Collooney		Church site	Simpson, L.	G680-270
1994	205	Sligo	Killaraght		No archaeological significance	Mount, C.	G176-298
1994	206	Sligo	Knoxspark		Promontory fort & Iron Age/Early Christian cemetery	Mount, C.	G672-287
1994	207	Sligo	Rathdooney Beg		Barrow cemetery	Mount, C.	G661-184
1994	208	Sligo	Sligo Town	Rockwood Parade, Tobergal Lane	Post-medieval urban	Halpin, E.	G692-361
1994	209	Tipperary	Boytonrath		Medieval rural	Moran, J.	S204-135
1994	210	Tipperary	Cahir	Cahir Abbey Lower	Medieval priory	Pollock, D.	S049-249
1994	211	Tipperary	Chancellorsland		Bronze Age settlement	Doody, M.G.	R758-358
1994	212	Tipperary	Fethard		Medieval town wall	Moran, J.	S221-350
1994	213	Tyrone	Copney		Stone circles	MacDonough, M.	H599-780
1994	214	Tyrone	Goles		Stone alignment	Halpin, E.	H699-947
1994	215	Waterford	Waterford City	John Street/ Waterside	Medieval urban	McCutcheon, S.	S119-607
1994	216	Westmeath	Ballymore	Low Street	Urban	Campbell, K.	N225-490
1994	217	Westmeath	Kinnegad		Underbridge	Neary, P.	N600-450
1994	218	Westmeath	Mullingar	Austin Friar Street (A)	Medieval urban	Meenan, R.	N441-530
1994	219	Westmeath	Mullingar	Austin Friar Street (B)	Medieval urban	Meenan, R.	N440-530
1994	220	Westmeath	Mullingar	Austin Friar Street	Cemetery	Duffy, C.	N440-530
1994	221	Wexford	Enniscorthy	St John's	Ecclesiastical site?	Channing, J.	S970-380
1994	222	Wexford	New Ross	Mary Street	No archaeological significance	Scully, O.M.B.	S720-270
1994	223	Wexford	Wexford Town	The Faythe	No archaeological significance	Scully, O.M.B.	T052-211
1994	224	Wexford	Wexford Town	Faythe Lane, Mount Folly	Medieval urban	Meenan, R.	T052-211
1994	225	Wexford	Wexford Town	George's Street Upper	Medieval urban/rural	Pollock, D.	T046-220

1994	226	Wexford	Wexford Town	Kevin Barry Street (St Michael's Graveyard)	Burial site	Scally, G.	T050-201
1994	227	Wexford	Wexford Town	Rowe Street Lower	Post-medieval	Moran, J.	T048-219
1994	228	Wexford	Wexford Town	West Gate	Urban	O'Flanagan, N.	T052-211
1994	229	Wexford	Wexford Town		Urban	Wren, J.	T048-219
1994	230	Wicklow	Kilnacarrig		*Fulacht fiadh*	Hayden, A.	O280-105
1994	231	Wicklow	Irishtown		Post-medieval metalworking site	Simpson, L.	O269-163
1994	232	Wicklow	Rathdown Upper		Early Christian/ medieval	Halpin, E.	O285-138
1994	233	Wicklow	Rathdown Upper	Rathdown Castle	Castle & environs	Gowen, M.	O291-128
1994	ApxI	Cork	Carrigtwohill	Barryscourt Castle	Resistivity survey	Byrne, M.E.	W821-724
1994	ApxII	Limerick/Clare	Shannon Estuary & tributaries		Intertidal survey	O'Sullivan, A.	
1995	1	Antrim	Ballygalley	Croft Manor	Neolithic/Bronze Age	Moore, D.G.	D371-077
1995	2	Antrim	Carrickfergus		Urban	Ó Baoill, R.	J414-875
1995	3	Antrim	Cushendun	Castle Park, 'Castle Carra'	Tower-house, later killeen, over prehistoric site	Hurl, D.P.	D249-334
1995	4	Antrim	Grange of Mallusk		Souterrain	Crothers, N.	J286-833
1995	5	Antrim	Gortgole/ Ferrystown	River Bann	Dredgings	Bourke, C.	C960-980
1995	6	Antrim	Island Magee	Skernaghan Point	Mesolithic/Neolithic raised beach	James, H.F.	D430-002
1995	7	Antrim	Jordanstown	Meadowbank Rath	Raised rath	Halpin, E. and Crothers, N.	J361-850
1995	8	Antrim	Larne	Larne Harbour	Raised beach	Halpin, E.	D414-025
1995	9	Antrim	Antrim coast	*Taymouth Castle* wreck	Post-medieval shipwreck	Breen, C.	D260-435
1995	10	Armagh	Tray	Haughey's Fort	Bronze Age enclosure	Mallory, J.P.	H835-453
1995	11	Carlow	Carlow Town	Mill Lane	Medieval urban	Pollock, D.	S716-765
1995	12	Cavan	Belturbet	Willow Avenue	Post-medieval urban	Campbell, K.	H364-171
1995	13	Clare	Barntrick		Earthwork complex environs	O Rahilly, C.	
1995	14	Clare	Dromoland		Castle site?	O Rahilly, C.	R388-705
1995	15	Clare	Dysert	O'Dea's Castle	Castle	Blair Gibson, D.	R282-850
1995	16	Clare	Ennis	O'Connell Street	Historic town	O Rahilly, C.	R337-774
1995	17	Clare	Ennis	Parnell Street/ Carmody Street/ Summerhill	Historic town	O Rahilly, C.	R337-774
1995	18	Clare	Ennis	Parnell Street/ Curtain's Lane	Historic town	O Rahilly, C.	R337-774
1995	19	Clare	Mooghaun South		Hillfort (trivallate)	Grogan, E.	R408-706
1995	20	Clare	Parknabinnia		Habitation	Jones, C.	
1995	21	Clare	Tomgreany		Ecclesiastical enclosure?	O Rahilly, C.	R637-829
1995	22	Cork	Bere Island	Lonehort Harbour, Ardnaragh East	Viking harbour?	Breen, C. and Sheehan, J.	V753-438
1995	23	Cork	Ballynoe		Medieval parish church	Cotter, E.	W934-896
1995	24	Cork	Baneshane		Uncertain	Cotter, E.	W867-722
1995	25	Cork	Cork City	Gill Abbey, Craig More, Connaught Avenue	Medieval?	Lane, S.	W664-714
1995	26	Cork	Cork City	Griffith Lane/ Barrack Street	Urban	Hurley, M.F.	W670-710
1995	27	Cork	Cork City	North Mall	Medieval urban?	Lane, S.	W671-721
1995	28	Cork	Cork City	Old Friary Road	Medieval urban?	Cleary, R.M.	W680-730
1995	29	Cork	Cork City	Travers' Street	Medieval urban?	Lane, S.	W673-714
1995	30	Cork	Kilcolman Middle	Kilcolman Castle	Castle	Klingelhöfer, E.	R581-113
1995	31	Cork	Killanully		Medieval church environs	Cleary, R.M.	W698-645
1995	32	Cork	Kinsale	Blind Gate Street	Historic town	Cleary, R.M.	W637-502
1995	33	Cork	Kinsale	Carmel Avenue	Historic town	Cleary, R.M.	W641-502
1995	34	Cork	Kinsale	Newman's Mall/ Chimney Lane	Historic town	Cleary, R.M.	W641-502

1995	35	Cork	Labbamolaga Middle		Early Christian & medieval ecclesiastical site	Cleary, R.M.	R767-185
1995	36	Cork	Old Head of Kinsale	Downmacpatrick	Coastal promontory fort	Cleary, R.M.	W632-402
1995	37	Cork	Spital		Early Christian & medieval site environs	Cleary, R.M.	W678-918
1995	38	Cork	Youghal	Cross Lane	Urban	Power, C.	X102-782
1995	39	Cork	Youghal	Emmet Place, the College grounds	Medieval & post-medieval	Power, C.	X101-782
1995	40	Cork	Youghal	Seafield	Historic town environs	Cleary, R.M.	X096-768
1995	41	Derry	Beagh	Temporal	Natural mound	Halpin, E.	C859-071
1995	42	Derry	Bellaghy	Bellaghy Bawn— Old Town Deer Park	Plantation bawn/ ringfort	Hurl, D.P.	H953-963
1995	43	Donegal	Ballylosky		Early ecclesiastical site	Walsh, G.	C466-445
1995	44	Down	Strangford Lough	Ballyhenry Bay (the *Nimble*)	Post-medieval shipwreck	Breen, C.	J580-518
1995	45	Down	Ballynahatty	Giant's Ring	Late Neolithic ritual enclosure	Hartwell, B.	J326-677
1995	46	Dublin	Ballycoolin	Cappoge/Grange	No archaeological significance	Murphy, D.	O098-408
1995	47	Dublin	Bremore	Bremore Castle	Post-medieval castle	Swan, D.L.	O199-646
1995	48	Dublin	Chapelizod	Chapelizod Road (Esso petrol station)	Medieval urban	Gowen, M.	O108-343
1995	49	Dublin	Chapelizod	The Island	Medieval urban	Gowen, M.	O103-345
1995	50	Dublin	Chapelizod	Martin's Row School	Urban, possible burial-ground	Walsh, C.	O101-345
1995	51	Dublin	Clondalkin	Tower Road	No archaeological significance	Swan, R.	O303-308
1995	52	Dublin	Cooldrinagh		Ring-barrow	Mullins, C.	O007-356
1995	53	Dublin	Courtlough		Cropmark	Breen, T.C.	O186-586
1995	54	Dublin	Dalkey	Castle Street	Medieval urban	Simpson, L.	O264-261
1995	55	Dublin	Donnybrook	Brookvale Avenue (St Mary's)	Medieval	McConway, C.	O173-320
1995	56	Dublin	Donnybrook	Simmonscourt Road	Medieval	McConway, C.	O232-390
1995	57	Dublin	Ballsbridge	RDS, Anglesea Road	Urban	Swan, D.L.	O232-318
1995	58	Dublin	Dublin City	Arran Quay	Medieval urban	Simpson, L.	O147-342
1995	59	Dublin	Dublin City	Back Lane/ Lamb Alley	Medieval urban habitation & defences	Gowen, M.	O149-338
1995	60	Dublin	Ballsbridge	Johnson, Mooney & O'Brien site	Urban	Gowen, M.	O179-324
1995	61	Dublin	Dublin City	Bishop Street	Post-medieval urban?	Walsh, C.	O154-335
1995	62	Dublin	Dublin City	Bow Lane East	Medieval	McMahon, M.	O157-336
1995	63	Dublin	Dublin City	Capel Street	Medieval/ 17th-century house	McConway, C.	O152-346
1995	64	Dublin	Dublin City	Capel Street	Medieval/ 17th-century house	McConway, C.	O155-343
1995	65	Dublin	Dublin City	Capel Street	No archaeological significance	Gowen, M.	O154-346
1995	66	Dublin	Dublin City	Carmen's Hall	Medieval	Opie, H.	O147-337
1995	67	Dublin	Dublin City	Cecilia Street/ Fownes Street	Friary & environs?	Gowen, M.	O156-341
1995	68	Dublin	Dublin City	Dame Street	Medieval urban	Murphy, D.	O150-340
1995	69	Dublin	Dublin City	Earl Street South— St Thomas's Abbey	Medieval abbey precinct	Hayden, A.	O140-339
1995	70	Dublin	Dublin City	Earl Street South	Medieval urban	Walsh, C.	O141-338
1995	71	Dublin	Dublin City	Eastmoreland Place—Hibernian Hotel	Castle environs?	Carroll, J.	O178-329
1995	72	Dublin	Dublin City	Fishamble Street	Medieval urban environs	Gowen, M.	O153-342
1995	73	Dublin	Dublin City	Francis Street	No archaeological significance	Hayden, A.	O150-460
1995	74	Dublin	Dublin City	Francis Street	No archaeological significance	Walsh, C.	O150-464

1995	75	Dublin	Dublin City	Fyffe's Yard/ George's Hill	Medieval	McConway, C.	O150-345
1995	76	Dublin	Dublin City	Liffey Street— Arnott's	Medieval urban	Gowen, M.	O159-345
1995	77	Dublin	Dublin City	Green Street Little— Keeling's	Medieval urban	Gowen, M.	O152-347
1995	78	Dublin	Dublin City	Lurgan Street	Urban	Simpson, L.	O141-348
1995	79	Dublin	Dublin City	Montpelier Hill	No archaeological significance	Murphy, D.	O136-346
1995	80	Dublin	Dublin City	Ormond Quay Lower	No archaeological significance	Walsh, C.	O155-343
1995	81	Dublin	Dublin City	Parliament Street	Post-medieval urban	Simpson, L.	O154-341
1995	82	Dublin	Dublin City	Parnell Street	Medieval urban	Halpin, E.	O156-347
1995	84	Dublin	Dublin City	Parnell Street	Urban	Murphy, D.	O155-348
1995	85	Dublin	Dublin City	Parnell Street	No archaeological significance	Hayden, A.	O150-350
1995	86	Dublin	Rathfarnham	Rathfarnham Road	Ecclesiastical?	Swan, D.L.	O145-289
1995	87	Dublin	Dublin City	Stephen's Green Centre	Medieval urban	Gowen, M.	O158-335
1995	88	Dublin	Dublin City	Smithfield Distillery	Urban	Carroll, J.	O147-345
1995	89	Dublin	Dublin City	Thomas Street	Medieval urban	Gowen, M.	O147-343
1995	90	Dublin	Dublin City	Thomas Street	Medieval urban	Gowen, M.	O147-339
1995	91	Dublin	Dublin City	Thomas Street— NCAD	Medieval urban	Gowen, M.	O148-339
1995	92	Dublin	Dublin City	Thomas Street— Statoil filling station	Medieval urban	Gowen, M.	O143-339
1995	93	Dublin	Dublin City	Usher's Quay	Medieval urban	Walsh, C.	O314-234
1995	94	Dublin	Dublin City	Westland Row	Urban	Meenan, R.	O167-340
1995	95	Dublin	Dublin City	York Street—RCSI	Urban	Reid, M.	O157-335
1995	96	Dublin	Finglas	Ballygall Road West	Ecclesiastical urban?	Swan, D.L.	O133-238
1995	97	Dublin	Finglas	Cappagh Road (Holy Faith Convent)	Medieval urban	Halpin, E.	O129-388
1995	98	Dublin	Finglas	Patrickswell Place	Rampart	Halpin, E.	O128-388
1995	99	Dublin	Killiney	Marino Road— Abbeylands Cottage	Church site	Simpson, L.	O242-236
1995	100	Dublin	Lambay Island	The Point	Human burial site	Cooney, G.	O305-504
1995	101	Dublin	Lambay Island		Neolithic, including stone axe production site?	Cooney, G.	O315-505
1995	102	Dublin	Cherrywood	Leehaunstown Camp	18th-century military camp	Gowen, M.	O238-235
1995	103	Dublin	Cabinteely	Mount Offaly (Esso petrol station)	Medieval urban	Gowen, M.	O233-242
1995	104	Dublin	Lucan	Ballyowen Lane, Ballyowen Castle	15th–17th-century defended house	Simpson, L.	O052-345
1995	105	Dublin	Lucan	Main Street	Urban?	Swan, D.L.	O030-350
1995	106	Dublin	Palmerstown Upper		Earthwork	McCutcheon, S.	O073-350
1995	107	Dublin	Rathfarnham	Rathfarnham Castle Estate	Unknown	Carroll, J.	O145-289
1995	108	Dublin	Rathfarnham	Rathfarnham Castle Estate	18th/19th-century underground passage	Carroll, J.	O145-289
1995	109	Dublin	Swords	Bridge Street	Medieval urban	Gowen, M.	O190-470
1995	110	Dublin	Swords	New Road	Well environs	Swan, R.	O178-457
1995	111	Dublin	Tallaght	St Maelruan's	Medieval	McConway, C.	O091-278
1995	112	Galway	Bredagh		Burnt mound?	Fitzpatrick, M.	
1995	113	Galway	Caherwalter		Early ecclesiastical remains, environs	Connolly, A.	M626-168
1995	114	Galway	Knockacarrigeen	Carrowntemple	Hillfort	Connolly, A.	M378-488
1995	115	Galway	Claretuam	Claretuam Castle	Tower-house site	Crumlish, R.	M400-495
1995	116	Galway	Doughiska		Burnt mound	Fitzpatrick, M.	M360-250
1995	117	Galway	Áran (Inis Mór)	Dún Eoghanachta (Eoghanacht)	Stone fort	Cotter, C.	L811-097
1995	118	Galway	Iorras Beag Thiar	Port na Feadóige (Dogs' Bay)	Fire-pits	Kelly, E.P.	L692-382
1995	119	Galway	Galway City	Abbeygate Street Lower	Late medieval urban, domestic	Higgins, J.	M300-250

1995	120	Galway	Galway City	Eyre Street	Urban defences	Simpson, L.	M300-250
1995	121	Galway	Galway City	Kirwan's Lane	Medieval	Ryan, F.	M300-250
1995	122	Galway	Galway City	Mainguard Street	Post-medieval house	Stevens, P.	M298 252
1995	123	Galway	Galway City	Quay Street/ Kirwan's Lane	Urban	Stevens, P.	M298-252
1995	124	Galway	High Island		Early Christian oratory	Scally, G.	L501-572
1995	125	Galway	Áran (Inis Mór)	Dún Aonghasa (Kilmurvey)	Cliff fort	Cotter, C.	L817-097
1995	126	Galway	Portumna	Portumna Castle	17th-century castle	Murphy, D.	M040-843
1995	127	Galway	Tuam	Townparks	Enclosure site	Crumlish, R.	M430-526
1995	128	Galway	Tuam	Various	Pipeline corridor	Crumlish, R.	
1995	129	Kerry	Ardfert	St Brendan's Cathedral	Medieval cathedral	Reid, M.	Q786-214
1995	130	Kerry	Ferriter's Cove	Ballyoughteragh North	Late Mesolithic coastal settlement	Woodman, P.C.	Q328-054
1995	131	Kerry	Beaufort		Souterrain	Connolly, M.	V867-925
1995	132	Kerry	Valentia Island	Bray Head	Earthworks & hut	Walsh, C.	V242-738
1995	133	Kerry	Caherlehillan		Early ecclesiastical & *ceallúnach*	Sheehan, J.	V571-834
1995	134	Kerry	Dingle		Monitoring	Gracie, C.D.	Q446-012
1995	135	Kerry	Dingle		Medieval town	Cotter, E.	Q447-013
1995	136	Kerry	Sceilg Mhichíl (Great Skellig)	Monks' Garden	Monastic site	Bourke, E.C.	V245-604
1995	137	Kerry	Illaunloughan		Early Christian hermitage	Walsh, C. and White-Marshall, J.	V362-733
1995	138	Kerry	Leamnaguila		Ringfort	Bennett, I.	V948-995
1995	139	Kerry	Ross Island		Copper mine	O'Brien, W.	V944-880
1995	140	Kildare	Athy	Dominican Church Road	Town wall? environs	Byrne, M.E.	S681-938
1995	141	Kildare	Athy	Duke Street	Medieval? urban	Mullins, C.	S680-938
1995	142	Kildare	Athy	Meeting Lane	No archaeological significance	Gracie, C.D.	N685-938
1995	143	Kildare	Athy	St John's Lane, St John's House	Medieval urban	Byrne, M.E.	S682-973
1995	144	Kildare	Ballysaxhills		No archaeological significance	Gowen, M.	N819-084
1995	145	Kildare	Castledermot	Main Street	Medieval urban	O'Donovan, E.	S783-848
1995	146	Kildare	Castlefarm		Castle site?	Mullins, C.	N779-006
1995	147	Kildare	Celbridge		Urban	Gowen, M.	N974-330
1995	148	Kildare	Celbridge	Main Street	Urban	Swan, R.	O983-345
1995	149	Kildare	Cloncurry		Early Christian/ medieval	Murphy, D.	N805-410
1995	150	Kildare	Curryhills		Ringfort	Meenan, R.	N828-266
1995	151	Kildare	Kilkea	Kilkea Castle	Medieval	McMahon, M.	S749-886
1995	152	Kildare	Kilmeague		Church environs	Meenan, R.	N775-230
1995	153	Kildare	Leixlip	Parsonstown— Hewlett-Packard site	Cropmarks & mound	Breen, T.C.	N990-347
1995	154	Kildare	Leixlip	Parsonstown, Rinawade	No archaeological significance	Gracie, C.D.	N989-343
1995	155	Kildare	Leixlip	Silleachain Lane	No archaeological significance	Mullins, C.	O010-363
1995	156	Kildare	Maynooth		Urban	Gowen, M.	N938-382
1995	157	Kildare	Naas	Abbey Street	Medieval cemetery	Reid, M.	N109-899
1995	158	Kildare	Naas	Canal Street	Monitoring	Ó Ríordáin, A.B.	N109-899
1995	159	Kildare	Naas	Corban's Lane	Urban	Meenan, R.	N894-190
1995	160	Kildare	Naas	Dublin Road	Medieval burial-ground	Mullins, C.	N882-198
1995	161	Kildare	Naas	Main Street, Bank of Ireland	Early Christian, medieval	McConway, C.	N893-194
1995	162	Kildare	Naas	North Main Street (Naas Courthouse)	Medieval urban	Gowen, M.	N895-193
1995	163	Kildare	Naas	Town Centre (West)	Urban	Gowen, M.	N895-190
1995	164	Kildare	Straffan	Barberstown Castle	Tower-house	O'Carroll, F.	N931-312
1995	165	Kilkenny	Kells	Garrynamann Lower	Motte & bawn (nearby)	Pollock, D.	S493-435
1995	166	Kilkenny	Kilkenny City	Abbey Street	Medieval urban	Walsh, C.	S502-562

1995	167	Kilkenny	Kilkenny City	Abbey Street	Medieval urban	McCutcheon, S.	S508-556
1995	168	Kilkenny	Kilkenny City	Abbey Street	Urban	Meenan, R.	S502-560
1995	169	Kilkenny	Kilkenny City	John Street, Bridge House	Urban	Gowen, M.	S503-576
1995	170	Kilkenny	Kilkenny City	St Kieran's Street, Kytler's Inn	Medieval urban	Gowen, M.	S505-565
1995	171	Kilkenny	Kilkenny City	Pudding Lane	Medieval urban	Gowen, M.	S501-506
1995	172	Kilkenny	Knockroe	The Caiseal	Passage grave	O'Sullivan, M.	S408-312
1995	173	Laois	Ballydavis		Early Iron Age complex	Keeley, V.J.	N950-250
1995	174	Laois	Derry		*Fulacht fiadh*	Duffy, C.	
1995	175	Laois	Grantstown		Tower-house	Delaney, D.	S332-797
1995	176	Laois	Dunamase	The Rock of Dunamase	Castle on Early Christian defence works	Hodkinson, B.J.	S530-981
1995	177	Laois	Port Laoise	The Heath	Monitoring	Ó Ríordáin, A.B. . and Keeley, V.J	N523-019
1995	178	Limerick	Baunmore		Enclosure	O Rahilly, C.	R638-231
1995	179	Limerick	Caherguillamore		Area of many sites	Cleary, R.M.	R605-403
1995	180	Limerick	Limerick City	Castle Street	Medieval urban	O Rahilly, C.	R578-577
1995	181	Limerick	Limerick City	Island Road	City wall line	Hodkinson, B.J.	R578-579
1995	182	Limerick	Limerick City	King John's Castle	Medieval castle	Wiggins, K.	R577-577
1995	183	Limerick	Limerick City	Mary Street	Medieval urban	O Rahilly, C.	R579-575
1995	184	Limerick	Limerick City	Nicholas Street/ Peter Street	Medieval urban	O Rahilly, C.	R579-576
1995	185	Longford	Ballinalee	Bully's Acre	Burial site	Carroll, J.	N222-280
1995	186	Louth	Balgatheran		Barrow?	Coughlan, T.	O385-783
1995	187	Louth	Dundalk	Ballybarrack	Enclosure environs	Campbell, K.	J351-524
1995	188	Louth	Carlingford	Castle Hill	Urban	Campbell, K.	J872-203
1995	189	Louth	Carlingford	Dundalk Street	Urban	Murphy, D.	J189-115
1995	190	Louth	Carlingford	Newry Street	Medieval urban	Murphy, D.	J188-119
1995	191	Louth	Carlingford	Taaffe's Castle	Urban tower-house	Moore, D.G.	J188-117
1995	192	Louth	Collon	Drogheda Street	Medieval/ post-medieval urban	Campbell, K.	O000-819
1995	193	Louth	Commons		No archaeological significance	Gracie, C.D.	O045-999
1995	194	Louth	Drogheda	Bachelor's Lane (Calendar Building)	Medieval urban	Murphy, D.	O091-752
1995	195	Louth	Drogheda	Bachelor's Lane	Medieval/ post-medieval urban	Campbell, K.	O091-752
1995	196	Louth	Drogheda	Duleek Gate, Duleek Street	Medieval urban	Swan, D.L.	O750-746
1995	197	Louth	Drogheda	Dyer Street	Medieval/ post-medieval urban	Campbell, K.	O089-750
1995	198	Louth	Drogheda	Fair Street	Urban	Breen, T.C.	O086-753
1995	199	Louth	Drogheda	Millmount	Martello tower	Ó Ríordáin, A.B. and Keeley, V.J.	O084-753
1995	200	Louth	Drogheda	Peter Street	Medieval urban	Murphy, D.	O090-760
1995	201	Louth	Drogheda	St Mary d'Urso	Medieval priory & hospital	Murphy, D.	O085-752
1995	202	Louth	Termonfeckin	Duffsfarm	Early Christian	Murphy, D.	O143-804
1995	203	Louth	Dundalk	Castletown	Medieval settlement	Murphy, D.	J031-086
1995	204	Louth	Dundalk	Chapel Street	Medieval urban	Murphy, D.	J050-074
1995	205	Louth	Dundalk	Clanbrassil Street— Queen Medb Hotel	Medieval urban	Campbell, K.	J048-074
1995	206	Louth	Dundalk	Clanbrassil Street	Medieval	McConway, C.	J047-072
1995	207	Louth	Dundalk	Demesne	Post-medieval urban	Campbell, K.	J047-071
1995	208	Louth	Dundalk	Farrandreg	Medieval settlement?	Murphy, D.	J030-080
1995	209	Louth	Dundalk	Farrandreg	Medieval settlement?	Murphy, D.	J032-082
1995	210	Louth	Dundalk	Jocelyn Street	Medieval urban	Halpin, E.	J050-073
1995	211	Louth	Dundalk	John Street	Post-medieval urban	Campbell, K.	J047-079
1995	212	Louth	Dundalk	Mill Street	Medieval urban	Campbell, K.	J056-075
1995	213	Louth	Dundalk	Park Street	No archaeological significance	Gowen, M.	J050-075
1995	214	Louth	Dundalk	Park Street	Medieval urban	Murphy, D.	J048-071
1995	215	Louth	Dundalk	Roden Place	Urban	Murphy, D.	J050-075

1995	216	Louth	Dundalk	Seatown—Priory of St Leonard	Medieval priory	Campbell, K.	J050-074
1995	217	Louth	Dundalk	Seatown	Urban	Campbell, K.	J052-074
1995	218	Louth	Dunmahon		Souterrains?	Murphy, D.	J031-019
1995	219	Louth	Gallstown		Prehistoric landscape?	Murphy, D.	H077-842
1995	220	Louth	Haggardstown		Souterrain	McConway, C.	J068-030
1995	221	Louth	Louth Village	Mullavally	Early Christian	Murphy, D.	H956-014
1995	222	Louth	Louth Village	Priorstate—Louth Monastery (St Mochta's)	Early Christian	Murphy, D.	H956-014
1995	223	Mayo	Clooneen		Cist	Kelly, E.P.	M278-693
1995	224	Mayo	Croagh Patrick	Glaspatrick/Teevenacroagh	Hillfort	Walsh, G.	L906-820
1995	225	Mayo	Money		Souterrain	Walsh, G.	
1995	226	Mayo	Achill	The Deserted Village, Slievemore (Toir)	Multi-phase landscape	McDonald, T.	F630-075
1995	227	Mayo	Westport	Church Street, Pollnacappul	Ritual pool?	Walsh, G.	L998-840
1995	228	Meath	Moynagh Lough	Brittas	Crannog	Bradley, J.	N818-860
1995	229	Meath	Dowth	Glebe House	Passage grave environs	Murphy, D.	O023-736
1995	230	Meath	Dunshaughlin	St Secudinus' Church	Early ecclesiastical centre	Simpson, L.	N289-589
1995	231	Meath	Knowth		Multi-period site	Eogan, G.	N995-735
1995	232	Meath	Newtown Trim	St John's	Medieval bridge, priory & tower-house environs	Meenan, R.	N816-568
1995	233	Meath	Oldbridge		Skeletal remains—animal	Stout, G.	O038-760
1995	234	Meath	Randalstown	Simonstown	Sites?	Campbell, K.	N857-705
1995	235	Meath	Slane		Souterrain environs	Meenan, R.	N966-749
1995	236	Meath	Stamullin		Early Christian/medieval ecclesiastical	Swan, D.L.	O150-657
1995	237	Meath	Trim	Trim Castle	Medieval castle	Hayden, A.	N802-564
1995	238	Offaly	Ballykeane		Ecclesiastical remains	Delaney, D.	N489-194
1995	239	Offaly	Clonmacnoise		Bridge	Boland, D.	N011-308
1995	240	Offaly	Clonmacnoise	New Graveyard	Early Christian settlement	King, H.A.	N011-308
1995	241	Offaly	Killeigh	Killeigh 1	Archaeological complex	Delaney, D.	N365-183
1995	242	Offaly	Killeigh	Killeigh 2	Archaeological complex	Delaney, D.	N365-183
1995	243	Roscommon	Glebe		Graveyard environs	Connolly, A.	M827-577
1995	244	Sligo	Ballysadare		Burial-ground	Opie, H.	G673-290
1995	245	Sligo	Belladrihid		Mound	Opie, H.	G674-307
1995	246	Sligo	Carrowgobbadagh		Ringfort	Opie, H.	G681-319
1995	247	Sligo	Carrowgobbadagh	Fort William	Fort & settlement complex	Opie, H.	G677-311
1995	248	Sligo	Rathdooney Beg		Iron Age barrow cemetery	Mount, C.	G661-184
1995	249	Tipperary	Ballypatrick	Lisnatubbrid	Ringfort	Moran, J.	S252-278
1995	250	Tipperary	Cashel	William Street	Medieval urban	Pollock, D.	S074-402
1995	251	Tipperary	Chancellorsland		Bronze Age settlement	Doody, M.G.	R758-358
1995	252	Tipperary	Clonmel	Bridge Street/Grubb's Quay	Medieval urban	Henry, M.	S202-223
1995	253	Tipperary	Clonmel	Emmet Street, Richmond Mill	Medieval urban mill	Pollock, D.	S203-228
1995	254	Tipperary	Clonmel	Market Street	Historic town	Cleary, R.M.	S205-227
1995	255	Tipperary	Clonmel	Market Street	Medieval urban	Henry, M.	S202-223
1995	256	Tipperary	Clonmel	Morton Street	Medieval urban	Henry, M.	S202-223
1995	257	Tipperary	Clonmel	Main Guard	Medieval	Henry, M.	S202-223
1995	258	Tipperary	Fethard	Barrack Street & Burke Street	Medieval urban	Moran, J. and Pollock, D.	S215-348
1995	259	Tipperary	Knockgraffon		Deserted medieval town	Pollock, D.	R048-295

1995	260	Tipperary	Knockroe	Drangan	Churchyard	Pollock, D.	S284-140
1995	261	Tipperary	Thurles	Black Castle Theatre	Urban	Gowen, M.	S128-588
1995	262	Tyrone	Derryloughan		Trackway	McConway, C.	H906-645
1995	263	Tyrone	Doras		Ecclesiastical enclosure	Halpin, E.	H815-678
1995	264	Tyrone	Killymoon Demesne		Bronze Age industrial complex?	Hurl, D.P.	H827-771
1995	265	Waterford	Dungarvan	Dungarvan Castle	Medieval castle	Pollock, D.	X262-930
1995	266	Westmeath	Ardnagross		Early Christian inhumation cemetery	Eogan, J.	N445-777
1995	267	Westmeath	Ardnagross		Early Christian inhumation cemetery	Murray, C.	N445-777
1995	268	Westmeath	Mullingar	Bishopsgate Street	Urban	Meenan, R.	N435-533
1995	269	Westmeath	Mullingar	College Street	Urban	Meenan, R.	N434-532
1995	270	Westmeath	Mullingar	Austin Friar Street	No archaeological significance	Gracie, C.D.	N437-530
1995	271	Westmeath	Mullingar	Pearse Street	Medieval urban deposits (potential)	Breen, T.C.	N441-530
1995	272	Westmeath	Tyrellspass	Tyrellspass Castle	Tower-house	Meenan, R.	N411-374
1995	273	Wexford	Ferns	Castleland	Medieval urban	Gowen, M.	T023-498
1995	274	Wexford	Enniscorthy	Templeshannon	No archaeological significance	Bennett, I.	S980-403
1995	275	Wexford	Gorey	Church Street	Medieval urban	Gowen, M.	T155-598
1995	276	Wexford	Knockbrack		Cist burial	Cahill, M.	T090-662
1995	277	Wexford	New Ross		Medieval urban	McCutcheon, S.	S718-275
1995	278	Wexford	Wexford Town	Barrack Street	Post-medieval urban	Moran, J.	T048-215
1995	279	Wexford	Wexford Town	Crescent Quay	Medieval/ post-medieval urban	Pollock, D.	T052-215
1995	280	Wexford	Wexford Town	George's Street	Town wall	Moore, D.G.	T046-220
1995	281	Wexford	Wexford Town	George's Street	Town wall	Moran, J.	T046-223
1995	282	Wexford	Wexford Town	North Main Street (AIB)	Medieval urban	Moran, J.	T048-219
1995	283	Wexford	Wexford Town	Redmond Road	Ferry point?	McConway, C.	T048-220
1995	284	Wexford	Wexford Town	Trinity Street (Talbot Hotel)	Urban	Scally, G.	T057-212
1995	285	Wexford	Wexford Town	Trinity Street (Gasworks)	Medieval defences?	McConway, C.	T057-212
1995	286	Wexford	Wexford Town	West Gate	Medieval	McConway, C.	T046-220
1995	287	Wexford	Wexford Town	Wexford Main Drainage	Medieval/ post-medieval urban	Wren, J.	T049-218
1995	288	Wicklow	Ballinagore		Early Bronze Age cemetery	Ó Donnabháin, B.	T315-174
1995	289	Wicklow	Bray	Killarney	Wooden structure	McDermott, C.	O268-180
1995	290	Wicklow	Kilpeddar	Tinnapark Demesne	Medieval settlement	Gowen, M.	O326-209
1995	ApxI	Tipperary	Littleton Bog		Survey	Irish Archaeological Wetland Unit	S234-592
1995	ApxII	Limerick/Clare	Shannon Estuary		Intertidal survey	O'Sullivan, A.	
1996	1	Antrim	Ballycastle		Harbour	McCooey, P.	D121-413
1996	2	Antrim	Island Magee	Ballydown	Multi-period site	Crothers, N.	D431-009
1996	3	Antrim	Island Magee	Ballydown	Medieval ditch	Crothers, N.	D435-005
1996	4	Antrim	Ballygalley	Croft Manor	Tower-house & bawn	Hurl, D.P.	D372-078
1996	5	Antrim	Ballyharry		Neolithic house	Crothers, N.	J469-981
1996	6	Antrim	Ballyharry		Neolithic house	Crothers, N.	J470-978
1996	7	Antrim	Island Magee	Ballylumford, Ballycronan	Burnt mound & material?	Duffy, P.	D437-027
1996	8	Antrim	Ballyutoag		Booley-houses	McSparron, C.	J291-799
1996	9	Antrim	Craigarogan	Roughfort	Medieval church	Hurl, D.P.	J369-840
1996	10	Antrim	Kilcoan More		Burnt mound	Crothers, N.	J460-996
1996	11	Antrim	Middle Division		Burnt mound	Crothers, N.	J402-906
1996	12	Antrim	Muckamore		Augustinian priory	Halpin, E. and McDonagh, M.	J166-854
1996	13	Antrim	Templepatrick	Castle Upton	Neolithic/ Bronze Age	Gahan, A.	J225-859
1996	14	Antrim	Whitehouse		Fortified house	McSparron, C.	J350-808
1996	15	Armagh	Cavanpole		Early Christian	Crothers, N.	H782-435
1996	16	Armagh	Killygarn	River Bann	Dredgings	Bourke, C.	H992-988

1996	17	Armagh	Tray	Haughey's Fort	Bronze Age enclosure	Mallory, J.P.	H835-453
1996	18	Carlow	Carlow Town	Carlow Castle	Medieval castle	O'Connor, K.	S715-771
1996	19	Carlow	Carlow Town		Medieval/ post-medieval urban?	Halpin, E. *et al.*	S714-755
1996	20	Clare	Ballaghaline		Unknown	Lynch, A.	R056-969
1996	21	Clare	Ballyogan		No archaeological significance	O Rahilly, C.	R384-184
1996	22	Clare	Bunratty		No archaeological significance	Hodkinson, B.J.	R453-613
1996	23	Clare	Coad	Coad Road	Church environs	Hodkinson, B.J.	
1996	24	Clare	Dough		Ringfort	Murphy, D.	Q008-879
1996	25	Clare	Dysert	O'Dea's Castle	Castle bakery	Blair Gibson, D.	R282-850
1996	26	Clare	Ennis	Market Place	Urban	Hodkinson, B.J.	R337-774
1996	27	Clare	Ennis	O'Connell Street	Historic town	O Rahilly, C.	R337-774
1996	28	Clare	Ennis	Old Ground Hotel, O'Connell Street	Medieval/ post-medieval urban	Henry, M.	R337-774
1996	29	Clare	Killaloe		Urban	Delaney, D.	R701-172
1996	30	Clare	Knockanean		No archaeological significance	O Rahilly, C.	R365-790
1996	31	Clare	Knocknalappa		Bronze Age lake settlements	O'Sullivan, A.	R444-688
1996	32	Clare	Knockyclovaun		*Fulacht fiadh*	Gowen, M.	R701-729
1996	33	Clare	Latoon South		Post-medieval enclosure & field systems	Hanley, K.	R378-714
1996	34	Clare	Sixmilebridge	Owenogarney River	No archaeological significance	McConway, C.	Q148-162
1996	35	Clare	Smithstown	Smithstown or Ballynagowan Castle	Tower-house	Crumlish, R.	R147-941
1996	36	Cork	Ardcloyne		Horizontal watermill undercroft	Cleary, R.M.	W606-510
1996	37	Cork	Ballynoe		Medieval parish church	Cotter, E.	W934-896
1996	38	Cork	Barnahely		Assessment	O'Donovan, E.	W772-637
1996	39	Cork	Carrigtwohill	Barryscourt Castle	Late medieval castle	Pollock, D.	W821-724
1996	40	Cork	Cobh	Middleton Street	Graveyard?	Cleary, R.M.	W797-667
1996	41	Cork	Cork City	Grattan Street/ Adelaide Street	Medieval urban	Hurley, M.F.	W669-719,
1996	42	Cork	Cork City	Green Street	Urban	Lane, S.	W699-712
1996	43	Cork	Cork City	Hanover Street/ South Main Street	Medieval urban	Cleary, R.M.	W671-715
1996	44	Cork	Cork City	Liberty Street to Marina	Urban	Lane, S.	W671-718
1996	45	Cork	Cork City	North Main Street/ Castle Street	Medieval/ post-medieval urban	Power, C.	W670-720
1996	46	Cork	Cork City	Washington Street	Medieval urban	Cleary, R.M.	W681-702
1996	47	Cork	Old Head of Kinsale	Downmacpatrick	Tower-house environs, bawn wall & extra-mural ditch	Cleary, R.M.	W632-402
1996	48	Cork	Sherkin Island	Farrancoush	Late medieval Observantine friary	O'Sullivan, J.	W103-025
1996	49	Cork	Firville West		Mound	Cleary, R.M.	W103-997
1996	50	Cork	Glanbannoo Lower		Ringfort environs	Conway, M.G.	W005-408
1996	51	Cork	Kilcolman Middle	Kilcolman Castle	Late medieval tower-house, bawn, Plantation residence	Klingelhöfer, E.	R581-113
1996	52	Cork	Kinsale	Friary Lane	Medieval urban	Cleary, R.M.	W638-509
1996	53	Cork	Kinsale	The Glen	Medieval urban?	Cleary, R.M.	W640-505
1996	54	Cork	Leherfineen		Medieval urban	Cleary, R.M.	W552-568
1996	55	Cork	Monkstown	Monkstown Castle	Fortified house	Lane, S.	W765-662
1996	56	Cork	Youghal	Seafield	No archaeological significance	Power, C.	X096-768
1996	57	Cork	Youghal	Dolphin Square	No archaeological significance	Power, C.	X096-768
1996	58	Derry	Shantallow	Ballyarnet Lake	Neolithic trackway?	Hurl, D.P.	C447-215
1996	59	Donegal	Creevy	Park Fort	Enclosure environs	Crumlish, R.	J849-644

1996	60	Donegal	Greencastle		Medieval	Ó Baoill, R. and Halpin, E.	C653-403
1996	61	Down	Ballynahatty	Giant's Ring	Neolithic settlement	Hartwell, B.	J326-679
1996	62	Down	Ballyspurge	White House	Fortified house & bawn	Hurl, D.P.	J642-550
1996	63	Down	Downpatrick	Scotch Street/ Church Street	Medieval/ post-medieval	Gahan, A.	J487-488
1996	64	Dublin	Balally	Central Bank of Ireland Mint	Pale ditch/ church/tree ring?	Gracie, C.D.	O181-260
1996	65	Dublin	Stepaside	Ballyogan	House?	Breen, T.C.	O215-242
1996	66	Dublin	Carrickmines Great		Post-medieval	Connolly, A.	O218-246
1996	67	Dublin	Clondalkin	Brideswell Lane	Medieval	Desmond, S.	O073-301
1996	68	Dublin	Clondalkin	Kilmahuddrick— Grange/ Nangor Castle	Medieval	McConway, C.	O045-312
1996	69	Dublin	Clontarf	Clontarf Castle	Medieval urban	O'Donovan, E.	O194-364
1996	70	Dublin	Crumlin	St Agnes' Road	Urban	Scally, G.	O115-318
1996	71	Dublin	Dalkey	Castle Street	Urban	Murtagh, D.	O263-269
1996	72	Dublin	Dublin City	Back Lane/ Lamb Abbey	Medieval urban	Coughlan, T.	O149-338
1996	73	Dublin	Dublin City	Beresfort Street/ Cuckoo Lane	Medieval urban	O'Donovan, E.	O150-338
1996	74	Dublin	Dublin City	Brunswick Street	Urban	Scally, G.	O151-361
1996	75	Dublin	Dublin City	Brunswick Street/ Church Street	Medieval urban	Coughlan, T.	O149-348
1996	76	Dublin	Dublin City	Brunswick Street North/Red Cow Lane	Medieval urban	Coughlan, T.	O147-353
1996	77	Dublin	Dublin City	Camden Street/ Charlotte Street— The Bleeding Horse	Urban	Scally, G.	O144-332
1996	78	Dublin	Dublin City	Cecilia Street West	Medieval friary	Simpson, L.	O156-341
1996	79	Dublin	Dublin City	Church Street	Medieval urban	Delaney, D.	O150-344
1996	80	Dublin	Dublin City	Church Street	Urban	Murtagh, D.	O149-344
1996	81	Dublin	Dublin City	Crane Lane	Medieval urban	Kehoe, H.	O154-340
1996	82	Dublin	Dublin City	Dame Street	Medieval urban	Gowen, M.	O157-341
1996	83	Dublin	Dublin City	Dame Street	Urban	Carroll, J.	O155-340
1996	84	Dublin	Dublin City	Davis Place	Medieval urban	Conway, M.G.	O150-334
1996	85	Dublin	Dublin City	Digges' Lane	Medieval urban	McConway, C.	O160-334
1996	86	Dublin	Dublin City	Drury Street	Medieval urban	Murphy, D.	O157-333
1996	87	Dublin	Dublin City	Essex Gate/ Exchange Street Upper	Medieval urban	Scally, G.	O147-334
1996	88	Dublin	Dublin City	Fishamble Street	Medieval urban	O'Flanagan, N.	O153-342
1996	89	Dublin	Dublin City	Fishamble Street/ Essex Street West	Medieval urban	Kehoe, H.	O153-342
1996	90	Dublin	Dublin City	Fownes Street Upper/Temple Bar	Medieval urban	Gowen, M.	O158-339
1996	91	Dublin	Dublin City	Francis Street	Urban	McMahon, M.	O149-338
1996	92	Dublin	Dublin City	Francis Street	Medieval urban	Coughlan, T.	O149-338
1996	93	Dublin	Dublin City	Francis Street	Medieval urban	Kehoe, H.	O149-338
1996	94	Dublin	Dublin City	Gardiner Street/ Beresford Street	Urban— 17th/18th-century	Simpson, L.	O160-341
1996	95	Dublin	Dublin City	Golden Lane/ Ship Street	Urban	McMahon, M.	O154-331
1996	96	Dublin	Dublin City	Green Street	Urban	Murtagh, D.	O152-346
1996	97	Dublin	Dublin City	High Street— Tailors' Hall	Medieval urban	Kehoe, H.	O151-339
1996	98	Dublin	Dublin City	James' Street/ Bow Lane West	Urban	Delaney, D.	O138-388
1996	99	Dublin	Dublin City	Kevin Street Lower	Urban	Murtagh, D.	O155-334
1996	100	Dublin	Dublin City	Liffey Street— Arnott's	Medieval urban	Gowen, M.	O159-345
1996	101	Dublin	Dublin City	Lincoln Place— Dental Hospital	Post-medieval	Meenan, R.	O168-339
1996	102	Dublin	Dublin City	Mary's Lane— Fyffe's Yard	Medieval urban	O'Flanagan, N.	O152-347

1996	103	Dublin	Dublin City	May Lane/ Bow Street	Medieval urban/ post-medieval burials	McConway, C.	O149-344
1996	104	Dublin	Dublin City	Meath Street/ Hanbury Lane	Urban	Halpin, E.	O147-337
1996	105	Dublin	Dublin City	New Row South	Medieval urban	Scally, G.	O149-338
1996	106	Dublin	Dublin City	Ormond Quay	Medieval urban	Gowen, M.	O153-342
1996	107	Dublin	Dublin City	Parkgate Street (Aishling Hotel)	Urban	Hurley, M.F.	O138-344
1996	108	Dublin	Dublin City	Parnell Square	Urban	Swan, D.L.	O235-315
1996	109	Dublin	Dublin City	Queen Street	Urban	Murtagh, D.	O315-234
1996	110	Dublin	Dublin City	Ship Street	Medieval urban	Simpson, L.	O154-337
1996	111	Dublin	Dublin City	Sycamore Street	Medieval urban	Gowen, M.	O156-341
1996	112	Dublin	Dublin City	Tara Street— Fire Station	Urban	Hurley, M.F.	O163-343
1996	113	Dublin	Dublin City	Temple Lane/ Cecilia Street	Medieval urban	Gowen, M.	O156-341
1996	114	Dublin	Dublin City	Thomas Street	Medieval urban	O'Donovan, E.	O146-337
1996	115	Dublin	Dublin City	Thomas Street— Frawley's	Medieval urban	Gowen, M.	O148-340
1996	116	Dublin	Dublin City	Thomas Street— NCAD	Medieval urban	Simpson, L.	O146-339
1996	117	Dublin	Dublin City	Westland Row	Urban	Meenan, R.	O167-339
1996	118	Dublin	Dublin City	Whitefriar Street	Medieval urban	Gowen, M.	O155-336
1996	119	Dublin	Finglas	Cardiff's Castle	No archaeological significance	Scally, G.	O123-403
1996	120	Dublin	Finglas	Spanish Convent	Medieval/ post-medieval	Halpin, E.	O132-386
1996	121	Dublin	Finglas	Spanish Convent	Medieval/ post-medieval	McConway, C.	O132-386
1996	122	Dublin	Finglas East	Jamestown Road	Medieval urban	Coughlan, T.	O133-392
1996	123	Dublin	Glasnevin	Bons Secours Hospital	Ecclesiastical settlement	Carroll, J.	O152-376
1996	124	Dublin	Glasnevin	Glasnevin Hill	Mound & Early Christian church environs	Meenan, R.	O160-372
1996	125	Dublin	Islandbridge	Conyngham Road	No archaeological significance	Scally, G.	O130-343
1996	126	Dublin	Islandbridge	Hospital Lane	Medieval post-medieval	McConway, C.	O128-343
1996	127	Dublin	Islandbridge	South Circular Road	Urban	Delaney, D.	O127-349
1996	128	Dublin	Kilmainham	Bow Bridge/ Irwin Street	Urban	Murtagh, D.	O135-338
1996	129	Dublin	Lambay Island		Neolithic, including stone axe production site?	Cooney, G.	O317-508
1996	130	Dublin	Loughlinstown	Beechgrove	House	Breen, T.C.	O243-234
1996	131	Dublin	Lucan	Main Street	Medieval burgage plots?	Coughlan, T.	O030-235
1996	132	Dublin	Lucan	Main Street	Urban	Swan, D.L.	O030-350
1996	133	Dublin	Lucan	Main Street— St Andrew's Church	Urban	Swan, R.	O033-235
1996	134	Dublin	Lucan	Palmerstown Upper	Early modern	Scully, O.M.B.	O073-350
1996	135	Dublin	Lusk	Treen Hill	No archaeological significance	McMahon, M.	O210-550
1996	136	Dublin	Raheny	Cahill Motors	Ecclesiastical settlement	Carroll, J.	O215-383
1996	137	Dublin	Saggart		Ringfort & ecclesiastical site environs	Coughlan, T.	O037-266
1996	138	Dublin	Sutton	St Fintan's Church	Graveyard & church environs	Meenan, R.	O270-381
1996	139	Dublin	Swords	Bridge Street	Medieval urban	Gowen, M.	O190-470
1996	140	Dublin	Swords	North Street	Medieval urban	Gowen, M.	O182-460
1996	141	Dublin	Swords	The Old Vicarage	Medieval urban	Kehoe, H.	O157-452
1996	142	Dublin	Tallaght	St Maelruan's	Ecclesiastical environs	Meenan, R.	O091-278
1996	143	Dublin	Taylor's Grange	The Brehon's Chair	Portal tomb environs	Coughlan, T.	O130-265
1996	144	Dublin	Templeogue	Templeogue House	Castle site	Swan, D.L.	O128-288

1996	145	Dublin	Tobertown		Burnt material deposits	Lynch, P.	
1996	146	Fermanagh	Killynure		Bronze Age?	Ó Baoill, R.	H247-441
1996	147	Galway	Athenry	Swangate	Archaeological potential	Connolly, A.	M502-271
1996	148	Galway	Kilkreest	Cloughaun Castle	Tower-house	Connolly, A.	M537-108
1996	149	Galway	Curryoughter		No archaeological significance	Stevens, P.	M417-437
1996	150	Galway	Galway City	Barrack Lane (The Barracks)	Medieval urban	Simpson, L.	M340-148
1996	151	Galway	Galway City	Dominic Street Upper	Urban	Crumlish, R.	M295-247
1996	152	Galway	Galway City	Eyre Street	Medieval urban	Simpson, L.	M313-233
1996	153	Galway	Galway City	Kirwan's Lane	Medieval urban	O'Flanagan, N.	M300-250
1996	154	Galway	Galway City	Prospect Hill	Modern urban	Connolly, A.	M298-252
1996	155	Galway	Galway City	Quay Street/ Kirwan's Lane	Medieval urban	Connolly, A.	M298-252
1996	156	Galway	Galway City	Quay Street (Blake's Tower)	Tower-house—urban	Connolly, A.	M298-252
1996	157	Galway	High Island		Early Christian monastery	Scally, G.	L501-572
1996	158	Galway	Áran (Inis Mór)	Kilmurvey	Early Christian	King, H.A.	L820-100
1996	159	Galway	Knocknacarragh	Main Drainage Scheme	Monitoring	Connolly, A.	M261-239
1996	160	Galway	Lackan		Ringfort environs	Fitzpatrick, M.	M477-128
1996	161	Galway	Áran (Inis Mór)	Oighil— Mainistir Chiaráin	Early Christian monastery/ post-medieval house site & midden	Ní Ghabhláin, S. and Moran, J.	L810-120
1996	162	Galway	Oranmore		Sewage scheme	Walsh, G.	
1996	163	Galway	Portumna	Portumna Castle	17th-century castle	Murphy, D.	M040-843
1996	164	Kerry	Ballycarty		Hilltop enclosure & passage tomb	Connolly, M.	Q871-123
1996	165	Kerry	Caherlehillan		Early ecclesiastical enclosure & *ceallúnach*	Sheehan, J.	V571-834
1996	166	Kerry	Caherquin		Burials	Bennett, I.	Q360-057
1996	167	Kerry	Cordal West		Ringfort environs	Connolly, M.	R053-078
1996	168	Kerry	Sceilg Mhichíl (Great Skellig)	Monks' Garden	Monastic site	Bourke, E.C.	V245-604
1996	169	Kerry	Termons		Circular enclosure (levelled)	Lane, S.	V522-679
1996	170	Kerry	Tralee	Ashe Sreett— The Old Rectory	Medieval parish church environs	Byrne, M.E.	Q837-145
1996	171	Kerry	Tralee	Upper Castle Street	Medieval urban	Byrne, M.E.	Q838-143
1996	172	Kerry	Tralee	Mary Street	Dominican priory environs	Byrne, M.E.	Q834-142
1996	173	Kildare	Athy	Dominican Church Road	Medieval urban	Byrne, M.E.	S681-938
1996	174	Kildare	Athy	Kirwan's Lane	Medieval urban	Byrne, M.E.	S685-941
1996	175	Kildare	Ballysaxhills		No archaeological significance	Gowen, M.	N819-084
1996	176	Kildare	Castledermot	Main Street	Medieval urban	O'Donovan, E.	S780-856
1996	177	Kildare	Castledermot	Skenagun	Archaeological potential	Connolly, A.	S781-851
1996	178	Kildare	Celbridge	Main Street	Urban	Ó Ríordáin, A.B.	O898-345
1996	179	Kildare	Celbridge	Main Street	Medieval urban	Byrne, M.E.	O973-331
1996	180	Kildare	Celbridge	Oakley Park	Urban	Swan, R.	N969-328
1996	181	Kildare	Clane	Carrigeen	Motte environs	Ó Ríordáin, A.B.	N870-280
1996	182	Kildare	Collinstown		Habitation site	Delaney, D.	N724-345
1996	183	Kildare	Jigginstown	Jigginstown Castle	17th-century castle	Simpson, L.	N288-218
1996	184	Kildare	Kill		Ecclesiastical?	Halpin, E.	O942-228
1996	185	Kildare	Lackagh More	Cherryville	No archaeological significance	Gracie, C.D.	N680-118
1996	186	Kildare	Leixlip	Parsonstown— Hewlett-Packard site	*Fulacht fiadh*?	Gracie, C.D.	N989-343
1996	187	Kildare	Leixlip	Parsonstown— Hewlett-Packard site	No archaeological significance	Ó Ríordáin, A.B.	N989-343

1996	188	Kildare	Leixlip	Pound Street	No archaeological significance	Hayden, A.	O095-362
1996	189	Kildare	Maddenstown	The Curragh Gallop	Prehistoric (unprotected)	Conway, M.G.	N706-102
1996	190	Kildare	Maynooth	Maynooth Castle	Castle	Hayden, A.	N934-375
1996	191	Kildare	Maynooth	Old Carton	Castle site environs?	Byrne, M.E.	N938-396
1996	192	Kildare	Milltown		Watermill (disused), environs	Ó Ríordáin, A.B.	N760-170
1996	193	Kildare	Monasterevin	Moore Abbey	Cistercian Abbey complex, environs	Mullins, C.	N627-099
1996	194	Kildare	Naas	Abbey Street/ Basin Street	Augustinian cemetery?	Lynch, P.	N109-899
1996	195	Kildare	Naas	Abbey Road (Moatville)	Urban	Murtagh, D.	N289-219
1996	196	Kildare	Naas	Corban's Lane/ South Main Street	Town ditch	O'Carroll, F.	N890-190
1996	197	Kildare	Naas	St David's Church	Medieval church	Ó Ríordáin, A.B.	N891-191
1996	198	Kildare	Naas	Main Street	Medieval urban	Mullins, C.	N893-193
1996	199	Kildare	Naas	North Main Street (Naas Courthouse)	Medieval urban	Gowen, M.	N895-193
1996	200	Kildare	Celbridge	Parsonstown— The New Bridge	Bridge	Fitzpatrick, M.	N989-343
1996	201	Kildare	Timolin		Monastic complex environs	Mullins, C.	S799-931
1996	202	Kildare	Timolin	National School	Monastic complex environs	Byrne, M.E.	S800-932
1996	203	Kilkenny	Gowran	Main Street	Urban	Campbell, K.	S633-535
1996	204	Kilkenny	Kilkenny City	Abbey Street	Medieval urban	Reid, M.	S510-560
1996	205	Kilkenny	Kilkenny City	Collier's Lane	No archaeological significance	Conway, M.G.	S504-558
1996	206	Kilkenny	Kilkenny City	Evans' Lane	Medieval urban	O'Donovan, E.	S505-561
1996	207	Kilkenny	Kilkenny City	Greensbridge Street	Medieval urban	Coughlan, T.	S504-565
1996	208	Kilkenny	Kilkenny City	High Street	Urban	Swan, R.	S504-557
1996	209	Kilkenny	Kilkenny City	John Street, Smithwicks Brewery	Medieval urban	Gowen, M.	S503-470
1996	210	Kilkenny	Kilkenny City	John Street	Medieval urban	O'Donovan, E.	S509-560
1996	211	Kilkenny	Kilkenny City	New Building Lane—Abbey View	Medieval urban	Conway, M.G.	S503-560
1996	212	Kilkenny	Kilkenny City	New Building Lane	Medieval urban	McCutcheon, S.	S500-550
1996	213	Kilkenny	Kilkenny City	New Building Lane	Medieval urban	O'Donovan, E.	S500-560
1996	214	Kilkenny	Kilkenny City	Ormonde Road— Cleere's Factory	Medieval urban	O'Donovan, E.	S506-554
1996	215	Kilkenny	Kilkenny City	William Street	Medieval/ post-medieval urban	Moran, J.	S505-558
1996	216	Kilkenny	Outrath		Ringfort/cemetery environs	Reid, M.	
1996	217	Kilkenny	Kells	Rathduff— Kells Priory	Augustinian priory	Clyne, M.	S499-434
1996	218	Kilkenny	Thomastown	Chapel Lane	Archaeological potential	Gracie, C.D.	S586-418
1996	219	Kilkenny	Ullard		Early Christian	Kehoe, H.	S728-478
1996	220	Laois	Clonaddadoran		No archaeological significance	Crumlish, R.	S466-945
1996	221	Laois	Coolbanagher		Ringfort	Breen, T.C.	N517-024
1996	222	Laois	Coolbanagher	Coolbanagher church & castle	Church & castle	Breen, T.C.	N514-032
1996	223	Laois	Dunamase	The Rock of Dunamase	Castle	Hodkinson, B.J.	S530-981
1996	224	Laois	Port Laoise	Church St— Old Gaol	18th-century building adjoining old graveyard	Breen, T.C.	S470-984
1996	225	Laois	Port Laoise	Peppers Lane	Urban	Delaney, D.	S471-984
1996	226	Laois	Straboe	Straboe Church	Church	Breen, T.C.	S495-025
1996	227	Leitrim	Drumlease	Dromahaire Castle— the Lodge	Test-trenching	Halpin, E.	G800-315
1996	228	Leitrim	Jamestown		Archaeological potential	Walsh, G.	

1996	229	Limerick	Adare	Main Street	Medieval urban	Cosgrave, U.	R461-460
1996	230	Limerick	Askeaton		Historic town	O Rahilly, C.	R341-503
1996	231	Limerick	Askeaton		Medieval urban	Hodkinson, B.J.	R341-503
1996	232	Limerick	Aughinish Island	Aughinish West	Enclosure	Byrne, M.E.	R275-522
1996	233	Limerick	Ballybronoge South		No archaeological significance	Eogan, J.	R512-483
1996	234	Limerick	Ballycummin		Assessment	McConway, C.	R545-521
1996	235	Limerick	Ballycummin		19th-century houses	Eogan, J.	R561-505
1996	236	Limerick	Lough Gur	Ballynagallagh— Red Bog	Prehistoric enclosure	Cleary, R.M.	R644-392
1996	237	Limerick	Barnakyle		Enclosure	McConway, C.	R524-497
1996	238	Limerick	Caherguillamore		Prehistoric/historic settlement area	Cleary, R.M.	R605-403
1996	239	Limerick	Cloghnaclocka		Mound	Eogan, J.	R534-504
1996	240	Limerick	Derryknockane		No archaeological significance	Eogan, J.	R555-514
1996	241	Limerick	Dooradoyle		No archaeological significance	McConway, C.	R572-535
1996	242	Limerick	Killuragh	Killuragh Cave	Mesolithic— Bronze Age cave	Woodman, P.C.	R778-497
1996	243	Limerick	Limerick City	Courthouse Lane/ River Lane	Urban	O Rahilly, C.	R580-575
1996	244	Limerick	Limerick City	Exchange Street	Medieval urban	Henry, M.	R580-573
1996	245	Limerick	Limerick City	King John's Castle	Medieval castle	Wiggins, K.	R577-577
1996	246	Limerick	Limerick City	King's Island— St Francis' Abbey	Franciscan friary	Hurley, F.M.	R578-575
1996	247	Limerick	Limerick City	Little Gerard Griffin Street	Post-medieval urban	O Rahilly, C.	R584-570
1996	248	Limerick	Limerick City	Northern Relief Road, Phase I	Medieval urban	O Rahilly, C.	R577-578
1996	249	Limerick	Limerick City	Northern Relief Road, Phase II	Urban	O Rahilly, C.	R580-576
1996	250	Limerick	Limerick City	Pennywell— The Devil's Battery	Town wall	O Rahilly, C.	R584-570
1996	251	Limerick	Limerick City	St Mary's Cathedral	Medieval cathedral	Hodkinson, B.J.	R578-575
1996	252	Limerick	Newcastle West	Desmond Castle	Castle	Hanley, K.	R297-337
1996	253	Limerick	Raheenamadra		Barrow	Buckley, V.M.	R729-302
1996	254	Limerick	Singland	Cromwell's Fort	Star-shaped fort	Cleary, R.M.	R592-564
1996	255	Longford	Ballinalee	Bully's Acre	Ecclesiastical?	Carroll, J.	N222-280
1996	256	Louth	Ardee	Riverstown	No archaeological significance	Murphy, D.	N974-922
1996	257	Louth	Ardee	Tierney Street	Urban	Swan, D.L.	N961-290
1996	258	Louth	Ballymascanlan		Ringfort?	Campbell, K.	J071-105
1996	259	Louth	Ballymascanlan		Ringfort/souterrain environs	Meenan, R.	J072-107
1996	260	Louth	Carlingford	Back Lane	Medieval urban	Murphy, D.	J188-177
1996	261	Louth	Carlingford	Dundalk Street	Medieval urban	Murphy, D.	J189-117
1996	262	Louth	Carlingford	Dundalk Street/ Market Square	Medieval urban	Murphy, D.	J188-116
1996	263	Louth	Carlingford	Newry Street/ Market Square— Carlingford Arms	Medieval urban	Murphy, D.	J188-116
1996	264	Louth	Carlingford	Station Road	Urban	Campbell, K.	J189-116
1996	265	Louth	Commons		No archaeological significance	Lynch, P.	O045-999
1996	266	Louth	Drogheda	Bessexwell Lane	Urban	Campbell, K.	O090-750
1996	267	Louth	Drogheda	Dyer Street	Medieval urban	Murphy, D.	O088-749
1996	268	Louth	Drogheda	Fair Street	Post-medieval urban	Murphy, D.	O088-753
1996	269	Louth	Drogheda	Greenlanes	Medieval urban	Murphy, D.	O089-755
1996	270	Louth	Drogheda	Harpur's Lane— Baker Building	Medieval urban	Murphy, D.	O089-751
1996	271	Louth	Drogheda	John Street	Medieval urban	Murphy, D.	O088-748
1996	272	Louth	Drogheda	John Street	Medieval urban	Scally, G.	O083-745
1996	273	Louth	Drogheda	Moneymore	Medieval urban	Murphy, D.	O088-750
1996	274	Louth	Drogheda	North Strand	Medieval/ post-medieval urban	Murphy, D.	O092-754
1996	275	Louth	Drogheda	Patrickswell Lane	Medieval urban	Murphy, D.	O085-752

1996	276	Louth	Drogheda	St Laurence Street—Grammar School	Medieval urban	Murphy, D.	O091-752
1996	277	Louth	Drogheda	Shop Street	Medieval/post-medieval urban	Murphy, D.	O089-751
1996	278	Louth	Drogheda	Sunday's Gate	Post-medieval urban	Murphy, D.	O089-755
1996	279	Louth	Drogheda	West Street	Urban	O'Flanagan, N.	O085-753
1996	280	Louth	Dromiskin		*Fulacht fiadh?*	Campbell, K.	O053-979
1996	281	Louth	Dundalk	Carnbeg	Enclosure & henge?	Murphy, D.	J041-099
1996	282	Louth	Dundalk	Chapel St—Priory & Hospital of St Leonard	Medieval priory	Campbell, K.	J051-074
1996	283	Louth	Dundalk	Church Street	Urban	Campbell, K.	J047-078
1996	284	Louth	Dundalk	Church Street—Dundalk House	Medieval urban	O'Flanagan, N.	J047-072
1996	285	Louth	Dundalk	Mary Street North	Urban	McConway, C.	J053-170
1996	286	Louth	Dundalk	Mill Street	Medieval urban	Meenan, R.	J056-075
1996	287	Louth	Dundalk	Park Street	Medieval urban	Murphy, D.	J048-071
1996	288	Louth	Dundalk	Park Street	No archaeological significance	Murphy, D.	J048-071
1996	289	Louth	Dundalk	Rampart Road	Urban	Campbell, K.	J047-070
1996	290	Louth	Dundalk	Faughert Lower	Enclosures, environs	Campbell, K.	J053-118
1996	291	Louth	Galtrimsland		Enclosure environs	Campbell, K.	J196-070
1996	292	Louth	Knocklore	Cookstown	Oval platform & linear earthwork	Fitzpatrick, M.	N972-952
1996	293	Louth	Termonfeckin	Main Street	Early Christian monastic enclosure	Murphy, D.	O141-804
1996	294	Louth	Termonfeckin	Thunder Hill	Medieval tower-house & Early Christian enclosure	Murphy, D.	O143-803
1996	295	Mayo	Ardoley	St Columbkille's Well	Ecclesiastical complex	Walsh, G.	
1996	296	Mayo	Balla		Ecclesiastical site environs	Walsh, G.	M252-845
1996	297	Mayo	Ballykine Upper		Cist cairn—multiple	Buckley, V.M.	M116-560
1996	298	Mayo	Castleaffy		Tower-house environs	Walsh, G.	
1996	299	Mayo	Coolavally		*Fulacht fiadh*	Ryan, F.	M119-254
1996	300	Mayo	Gorteendrunagh		Mound	Walsh, G.	
1996	301	Mayo	Gweesadan	Kilbrenan Church	Ecclesiastical	Ryan, F.	M121-282
1996	302	Mayo	Knockbrack		Enclosure	Walsh, G.	
1996	303	Mayo	Achill	The Deserted Village, Slievemore (Toir)	Multi-phase landscape	McDonald, T.	F630-075
1996	304	Meath	Beauparc	Rossnaree	No archaeological significance	Murphy, D.	N997-718
1996	305	Meath	Dulane		Early Christian	Meenan, R.	N740-737
1996	306	Meath	Duleek	Main Street	Medieval urban/motte site?	Meenan, R.	O049-733
1996	307	Meath	Gormanstown		Burnt mound?	Ryan, F.	O161-345
1996	308	Meath	Kells	Maudlin Street	Medieval urban	O'Donovan, E.	N740-758
1996	309	Meath	Killeen		Tower-house	Meenan, R.	N932-548
1996	310	Meath	Knowth		Multi-period site	Eogan, G.	N995-735
1996	311	Meath	Knowth		No archaeological significance	Murphy, D.	N995-735
1996	312	Meath	Moynalty		Medieval church site?	Murphy, D.	N734-827
1996	313	Meath	Randalstown		Cropmark	Campbell, K.	N854-725
1996	314	Meath	Rath		Rectangular enclosure	Lynch, P.	H647-160
1996	315	Meath	Trim		Medieval urban	Meenan, R.	N810-575
1996	316	Meath	Trim	Trim Castle	Medieval castle	Hayden, A.	N802-564
1996	317	Monaghan	Monaghan Town	Dawson Street/Dublin Road	Urban	Swan, R.	H672-337
1996	318	Monaghan	Monaghan Town	Dublin Road (carpark)	Urban	Swan, D.L.	H672-336
1996	319	Monaghan	Monaghan Town	Dublin Street	Urban	Swan, R.	H672-339
1996	320	Monaghan	Monaghan Town	Glasslough Street	Urban	Swan, R.	H673-339
1996	321	Monaghan	Monaghan Town	Market Road/Dawson Street	Urban	Swan, R.	H673-336
1996	322	Monaghan	Monaghan Town	Market Road/Park Street	Urban	Swan, D.L.	H672-337

1996	323	Monaghan	Monaghan Town	New Road—Tirkeenan	Urban	Swan, D.L.	H672-332
1996	324	Offaly	Clonmacnoise	New Graveyard	Early Christian settlement	King, H.A.	N011-308
1996	325	Offaly	Kilcomin		No archaeological significance	Hodkinson, B.J.	
1996	326	Offaly	Leabeg/Castlearmstrong	Cornafurrish/Corrabeg	Pathway (single-plank)—togher	Bermingham, N.	N229-110
1996	327	Offaly	Lemanaghan		togher	O'Carroll, E.	N229-110
1996	328	Roscommon	Dunamon	Carrigan's Park	Archaeological complex, environs	Ryan, F.	M178-267
1996	329	Roscommon	Cloonshanville		Abbey environs	Walsh, G.	
1996	330	Roscommon	Erris		Burnt mound/trackways	Opie, H.	G821-033
1996	331	Roscommon	Glenballythomas		Rathcroghan archaeological complex	Connolly, A.	M804-830
1996	332	Roscommon	Gorttoose		Agricultural village/head tenant home site	Orser, C. E. Jr	M995-795
1996	333	Roscommon	Kiltullagh	Kiltullagh Hill	Ring-barrow	Coombs, D.G. and Maude, K.	M530-740
1996	334	Roscommon	Moneylea		Archaeological complex, environs	Ryan, F.	M178-285
1996	335	Roscommon	Rathcroghan		Ritual complex	Waddell, J. *et al.*	M798-830
1996	336	Roscommon	Tintagh		*Fulacht fiadh*	Opie, H.	
1996	337	Roscommon	Tully	Kilmore	Ringfort environs	Ryan, F.	M199-292
1996	338	Sligo	Ballysadare		Burial-ground	Opie, H.	G673-290
1996	339	Sligo	Cottlestown		Fortified house environs	Walsh, G.	
1996	340	Sligo	Farranyharpy		No archaeological significance	Timoney, M.A.	G519-326
1996	341	Sligo	Sligo Town	Abbey Street	Medieval urban	Halpin, E.	G695-358
1996	342	Sligo	Sligo Town	High Street/Market Yard	Medieval/post-medieval?	Halpin, E.	G692-356
1996	343	Sligo	Sligo Town	John F. Kennedy Parade	Medieval/post-medieval?	Halpin, E. and Murtagh, D.	G694-359
1996	344	Sligo	Sligo Town	Market Street	Urban	Halpin, E.	G692-358
1996	345	Sligo	Sligo Town	Quay Street (Murray's Yard)	Medieval/post-medieval?	Halpin, E.	G689-362
1996	346	Sligo	Sligo Town	Riverside	No archaeological significance	Halpin, E.	G696-359
1996	347	Sligo	Sligo Town	Stephen Street	Medieval?	Halpin, E.	G692-361
1996	348	Sligo	Sligo Town	Wine Street (carpark)	Medieval/post-medieval?	Halpin, E.	G689-359
1996	349	Sligo	Sligo Town	Wine Street	Urban	Scally, G.	G691-363
1996	350	Tipperary	Ballintotty		Defensive tower?	McConway, C.	R910-784
1996	351	Tipperary	Cahir		Monitoring of sewage system	Ryan, F.	S050-250
1996	352	Tipperary	Cahir	Abbey Mills	Urban	Pollock, D.	S048-253
1996	353	Tipperary	Carrigatogher		Post-medieval farm	McConway, C.	R828-771
1996	354	Tipperary	Cashel	Friar Street	Medieval/post-medieval urban	Henry, M.	S075-407
1996	355	Tipperary	Cashel	Friar Street	Medieval urban	O'Donovan, E.	S076-402
1996	356	Tipperary	Chancellorsland		Early historic site	Doody, M.G.	R758-358
1996	357	Tipperary	Clonmel	Denis Burke Park	Post-medieval harbour	Henry, M.	S220-225
1996	358	Tipperary	Clonmel	Upper Gladstone Street	Medieval/post-medieval urban	Henry, M.	S220-225
1996	359	Tipperary	Clonmel	Kickham Street—Richmond House	Medieval/post-medieval cultivation	Pollock, D.	S220-225
1996	360	Tipperary	Clonmel	New Quay/Nelson Street	Post-medieval urban	Henry, M.	S200-223
1996	361	Tipperary	Clonmel	O'Connell Street	Medieval urban	Henry, M.	S200-223
1996	362	Tipperary	Clonmel	O'Connell Street	Medieval/post-medieval urban	Henry, M.	S200-223
1996	363	Tipperary	Clonmel	Old St Mary's Church	Medieval church	Pollock, D.	S200-225

1996	364	Tipperary	Cooleeny/ Derryfadda	Derryville/ Templetouhy	Prehistoric archaeological complex	Conway, M.G.	S203-606
1996	365	Tipperary	Derryville/ Derryfadda	Killoran/Cooleeny	Prehistoric archaeological complex	Murray, C. *et al.*	S226-661
1996	366	Tipperary	Gurtnahoe	Clonamicklon Castle	Tower-house & bawn	Moran, J.	S280-555
1996	367	Tipperary	Knockalton Upper		Unknown	Eogan, J.	R896-776
1996	368	Tipperary	Lahesseragh		No archaeological significance	McConway, C.	R850-769
1996	369	Tipperary	Lisronagh		Medieval town	Henry, M.	S203-921
1996	370	Tipperary	Lissenhall		Marl pit?	McConway, C.	R828-771
1996	371	Tipperary	Lisvernane	Moneynaboola	Burial cist	Pollock, D.	R859-282
1996	372	Tipperary	Modreeny		Post-medieval quarry pits & cultivation	Pollock, D.	
1996	373	Tipperary	Nenagh	Abbey Street (The Friary)	Medieval urban	Desmond, S.	R866-790
1996	374	Tipperary	Nenagh	Church View	Urban	Hodkinson, B.J.	R865-790
1996	375	Tipperary	Nenagh	Nenagh Castle	Castle	Hodkinson, B.J.	R865-790
1996	376	Tipperary	Nenagh	Pearse Street/ Abbey Street	Urban	Delaney, D.	R866-790
1996	377	Tipperary	Thurles	Racecourse	Quarry	Moran, J.	S100-600
1996	378	Tipperary	Tipperary Town	Supervalu	Urban	Pollock, D.	R891-358
1996	379	Tipperary	Tullaheddy		No archaeological significance	Eogan, J.	R832-771
1996	380	Tipperary	Tullaheddy		No archaeological significance	Eogan, J.	R834-771
1996	381	Tipperary	Tullaheddy		Post-medieval house	Eogan, J.	R830-773
1996	382	Tipperary	Tullaheddy		Post-medieval field enclosure	Eogan, J.	R830-773
1996	383	Tipperary	Tullaheddy		Banks	McConway, C.	R830-773
1996	384	Tipperary	Tyone		No archaeological significance	Eogan, J.	R875-774
1996	385	Waterford	Ardmore	Ardocheasty	Round tower	Lynch, A.	X188-777
1996	386	Waterford	Dungarvan	Davitt's Quay	Post-medieval town wall	Pollock, D.	X262-927
1996	387	Waterford	Dungarvan	Dungarvan Castle	Castle	Pollock, D.	X262-930
1996	388	Waterford	Dungarvan	Tannery	Medieval town/post-medieval town wall	Pollock, D.	X227-092
1996	389	Waterford	Tramore	Moonvoy	Prehistoric	Scully, O.M.B.	S580-010
1996	390	Waterford	Waterford City	Jenkins Lane— Beach Tower	Medieval	Scully, O.M.B.	S603-118
1996	391	Waterford	Waterford City	John Street	Medieval urban?	Cleary, R.M.	S603-118
1996	392	Waterford	Waterford City	Palace Lane	Medieval	Scully, O.M.B.	S603-118
1996	393	Westmeath	Kilkenny West	Kilkenny Castle	Castle environs	Campbell, K.	N122-489
1996	394	Westmeath	Mullingar	Austin Friar Street/ Barrack Street	Medieval urban	Ó Ríordáin, A.B.	N440-530
1996	395	Westmeath	Mullingar	Dominick Place	Medieval urban?	Meenan, R.	N435-529
1996	396	Westmeath	Mullingar	Friars' Mill Road/ Bishop's Gate Street	No archaeological significance	Gracie, C.D.	N437-530
1996	397	Westmeath	Mullingar	Pearse Street	Medieval urban	Meenan, R.	N440-531
1996	398	Westmeath	Mullingar	Pearse Street	Medieval urban	O'Flanagan, N.	N441-530
1996	399	Wexford	Balwinstown	Balwinstown Castle	Medieval	Scully, O.M.B.	
1996	400	Wexford	Enniscorthy	Templeshannon	Urban	Bennett, I.	S980-403
1996	401	Wexford	Ferns Upper		Castle environs	McCutcheon, S.	T017-498
1996	402	Wexford	Fethard	Grange	Early Christian/ medieval	Scully, O.M.B.	S790-045
1996	403	Wexford	Gorey	Esmonde Street	Urban	Meenan, R.	T156-597
1996	404	Wexford	Wexford Town	Anne Street	Urban	Reid, M.	T052-215
1996	405	Wexford	Wexford Town	George's Street	Urban	McConway, C.	T045-218
1996	406	Wexford	Wexford Town	South Main Street	Medieval/ post-medieval urban	Moran, J.	T049-225
1996	407	Wexford	Wexford Town	Paul Quay— Stafford's Yard	Urban	Reid, M.	T052-215
1996	408	Wicklow	Blessington	Burgage More	Moat?	Duffy, C.	N973-132
1996	409	Wicklow	Blessington	Eagers Field	Barrow environs	Conway, M.G.	N982-144
1996	410	Wicklow	Blessington	Tinode	Earthwork?	Reid, M.	O001-190

1996	411	Wicklow	Glendalough	An Óige Hostel	Medieval urban	Gowen, M.	T123-968
1996	412	Wicklow	Johnstown South		Enclosure	Fitzpatrick, M.	T280-771
1996	413	Wicklow	Oldcourt	Oldcourt House	Tower-house	Simpson, L.	O022-147
1996	ApxI	Antrim	Muckamore		Geophysical survey	McCleary, A.	J167-854
1996	ApxII	Derry	Ballybriest		Stone circle complex survey	MacDonough, M.	H756-889
1996	ApxIII	Derry	Glebe		Geophysical survey	McCleary, A.	C822-367
1996	ApxIV	Down	Ballyspurge	White House	Geophysical survey	McCleary, A.	J643-551
1996	ApxV	Down	Ballyspurge		Intertidal survey	Gahan, A. and McCleary, A.	J643-550
1996	ApxVI	Down	Newtownards	Strangford Lough	Intertidal survey	Gahan, A. and Ó Baoill, R.	J499-723
1996	ApxVII	Down	Strangford Lough		Intertidal survey	O'Sullivan, A. *et al.*	J580-518
1996	ApxVIII	Fermanagh	Tully	Abbey Point	Geophysical survey	McCleary, A.	H123-568
1996	ApxIX	Limerick/Clare	Shannon Estuary		Intertidal survey & excavations	O'Sullivan, A.	
1996	ApxX	Offaly	Lemanaghan	Bellair Works	Surveys of mining site	Irish Archaeological Wetland Unit	N229-110
1996	ApxXI	Sligo	Knocknarea	Misgaun Maedbh	Passage grave reconstruction	Timoney, M.A.	G625-345
1997	1	Antrim	Island Magee	Ballycronan More	No archaeological significance	Neighbour, T.	D433-018
1997	2	Antrim	Antrim Town	Ballygortgarve	Ecclesiastical	Reilly, A.	J146-760
1997	3	Antrim	Antrim Town	Ballygortgarve	*Fulacht fiadh?*	O'Neill, J.	J146-762
1997	4	Antrim	Belfast	Donegall Quay (Telfords)	Urban	Francis, P.	J343-745
1997	5	Antrim	Glebe	St Patrick's Church	Ecclesiastical	Hurl, D.P.	D009-046
1997	6	Antrim	Templepatrick	Castle Upton	Landscape— prehistoric/ Early Christian	Gahan, A.	J225-859
1997	7	Armagh	Tray	Haughey's Fort	Bronze Age enclosure	Mallory, J.P.	H835-453
1997	8	Carlow	Ballymoon		Castle environs	Hurley, M.F.	S739-615
1997	9	Carlow	Strawhill	Graigue	No archaeological significance	Gilmore, S.	S720-748
1997	10	Carlow	Strawhill		River bank	Duffy, C.	S720-748
1997	11	Cavan	Cavan Bypass		Monitoring	Coughlan, T.	
1997	12	Cavan	Corgreagh	Belturbet–Aghalane	No archaeological significance	Conway, M.G.	
1997	13	Cavan	Cloughergoole		Fort? environs	Meenan, R.	H468-074
1997	14	Cavan	Shercock	Nolagh	No archaeological significance	Murphy, D.	H693-014
1997	15	Clare	Ballinphunta		Church environs	Hodkinson, B.J.	R515-938
1997	16	Clare	Ballyea		Ringfort environs	Hodkinson, B.J.	R304-721
1997	17	Clare	Ballyogan		Souterrain environs	Hodkinson, B.J.	R384-184
1997	18	Clare	Coolnatullagh		Prehistoric cairn & field system	Eogan, J.	M307-203
1997	19	Clare	Crag		Enclosure	Hodkinson, B.J.	R095-867
1997	20	Clare	Drumcullaun		Post row	O'Carroll, E.	R173-824
1997	21	Clare	Ennis	Cabey's Lane/ Curtin's Lane	Urban	Hodkinson, B.J.	R337-224
1997	22	Clare	Ennis	Cornmarket Street	Mill	Crumlish, R.	R337-774
1997	23	Clare	Ennis	Mill Road	Urban	Connolly, A.	R337-774
1997	24	Clare	Ennis	Parnell Street	Urban	Hodkinson, B.J.	R337-774
1997	25	Clare	Ennis	Parnell Street	Urban	Tierney, J.	R337-774
1997	26	Clare	Ennis	Parnell Street	Urban	Tierney, J.	R337-774
1997	27	Clare	Sixmilebridge		Post-medieval	Gilmore, S. and Dowd, M.	Q148-162
1997	28	Clare	Moys	Rowlagh	No archaeological significance	Gilmore, S.	R460-390
1997	29	Cork	Aghacross	Templemolagga Church	Medieval church	Dunne, L.	R173-111
1997	30	Cork	Ballynora		Ringfort environs	Cleary, R.M.	W612-678
1997	31	Cork	Bandon	South Main Street/ Markey Quay	Medieval urban	Lane, S.	W492-551
1997	32	Cork	Leap	Brade	Graveyard & church	McCarthy, M.	

1997	33	Cork	Buttevant	Kerry Lane (off)	Medieval urban	Lane, S.	R542-089
1997	34	Cork	Carrigtwohill	Barryscourt Castle	Late medieval castle	Pollock, D.	W821-724
1997	35	Cork	Codrum Rural		No archaeological significance	Tierney, J.	W314-733
1997	36	Cork	Cork City	Grattan Street	Medieval urban	Hurley, M.F.	W675-717
1997	37	Cork	Cork City	North Main Street	Medieval & post-medieval urban	Power, C.	W670-720
1997	38	Cork	Cork City	Philips Lane/ Grattan Street	Urban	O'Donnell, M.	W669-720
1997	39	Cork	Cork City	St Peter's Avenue	Medieval urban	Hurley, M.F.	W676-718
1997	40	Cork	Cork City	Skiddy's Lane	Urban	O'Donnell, M.	W670-721
1997	41	Cork	Cork City	Tuckey Street	Hiberno-Norse/ medieval urban	O'Donnell, M.	W675-718
1997	42	Cork	Kill-Saint-Ann South		Fortified house environs	Cotter, E.	W841-926
1997	43	Cork	Kilmore		Early ecclesiastical enclosure	O'Sullivan, J.	R159-671
1997	44	Cork	Knockacullen		Circular enclosure (levelled)	McCarthy, M.	
1997	45	Cork	Knockagarrane East		Ringfort environs	Tierney, J.	R302-468
1997	46	Cork	Loughane East		Ringfort environs	Cleary, R.M.	W577-788
1997	47	Cork	Mallow	Bridewell Lane	Monitoring	Kiely, J.	W565-985
1997	48	Cork	Mallow	Bridge Street	Urban	Lane, S.	W569-977
1997	49	Cork	Mallow	Davis Street (Central Cinema)	Medieval urban	Lane, S.	W568-797
1997	50	Cork	Mallow	St Joseph's Road	Medieval urban	Lane, S.	W569-778
1997	51	Cork	Mohera		No archaeological significance	Cleary, R.M.	W845-925
1997	52	Cork	Rafeen		Ringfort environs	Lane, S.	W740-658
1997	53	Cork	Rosscarbery	Church Road (Anglers' Rest)	Medieval urban	Hurley, M.F.	W288-365
1997	54	Cork	Youghal	Dolphin Square	Urban	Power, C.	X105-780
1997	55	Derry	Ballybriest	Carnanbane	Wedge tomb	Hurl, D.P.	H764-886
1997	56	Derry	Coleraine	Bishopsgate	Medieval & post-medieval urban	Gahan, A.	C847-323
1997	57	Derry	Derry City	Fahan Street	Urban	Carroll, J.	C435-157
1997	58	Derry	Magilligan Point	Lower Doaghs	Coastal defence systems—WWII	McErlean, T.	C660-387
1997	59	Donegal	Ballymacaward		Multi-period burial cairn	O'Brien, E.	G835-627
1997	60	Donegal	Ballyshannon	Castle Street	No archaeological significance	Corlett, C.	G879-615
1997	61	Donegal	Ballyshannon	Main Street	No archaeological significance	Corlett, C.	G877-614
1997	62	Donegal	Cark Mountain	Ballygallen/ Meenadaura	Monitoring	Dunne, L.	C084-045
1997	63	Donegal	Carrownamaddy		Early Christian/ medieval	Ó Baoill, R. and Logue, P.	H368-213
1997	64	Donegal	Conwal		Graveyard	Crumlish, R.	C213-410
1997	65	Donegal	Donegal Town		Various	King, P.	
1997	66	Donegal	Magheracar		No archaeological significance	Walsh, G.	G795-588
1997	67	Donegal	Tory Island	West Town	Prehistoric or Early Christian	Ó Baoill, R.	B855-465
1997	68	Down	Ballybarnes		Booley-house?	McSparron, C.	J468-759
1997	69	Down	Ballynahatty	Giant's Ring	Neolithic settlement	Hartwell, B.	J327-679
1997	70	Down	Downpatrick	Belfast Road (Marsh Lane)	Post-medieval/ industrial urban	McConway, C.	J438-420
1997	71	Down	Downpatrick	Cathedral Hill	Ecclesiastical	Brannon, N.F.	J483-444
1997	72	Down	Downpatrick	English Street (Denvir's Hotel)	Post-medieval building	Brannon, N.F.	J485-446
1997	73	Down	Drumbroneth		Ringfort	Halpin, E.	J199-527
1997	74	Down	Inch	Ballyrenan	Ringfort	Mac Manus, C.	J471-462
1997	75	Down	Killaghy		No archaeological significance	Hurl, D.P.	J565-757
1997	76	Down	Ringcreevy	Rough Island	Mound	McElrean, T.	J495-689

1997	77	Down	Round Island		Mound	Williams, B.B.	J577-566
1997	78	Dublin	Ballsbridge	RDS, Anglesea Road	No archaeological significance	Corlett, C.	O232-318
1997	79	Dublin	Ballymount Great		Ditched enclosure & 17th-century manorial complex	Conway, M.G.	O090-304
1997	80	Dublin	Stepaside	Ballyogan	Iron Age? & medieval	Reid, M.	O200-245
1997	81	Dublin	Balrothery	Main Street	Medieval?	Walsh, C.	O200-615
1997	82	Dublin	Balscaddin Newtown		Cinerary urn	Lynch, P.	H633-173
1997	83	Dublin	Beaumont		Unknown	Meenan, R.	O171-376
1997	84	Dublin	Carrickmines	Herenford Lane	Field system?	Sullivan, E.E.	O230-226
1997	85	Dublin	Loughlinstown	Leehaunstown/ Cherrywood	Neolithic/ post-medieval	O'Donovan, E.	O240-235
1997	86	Dublin	Clondalkin	Kilmahuddrick— Grange/Nangor Castle	Medieval?	McConway, C.	O045-312
1997	87	Dublin	Clondalkin	Kilmahuddrick— Grange/Nangor Castle	Medieval	O'Brien, R.N.	O045-312
1997	88	Dublin	Clondalkin	Áras Chrónáin	Urban	Walsh, C.	O650-317
1997	89	Dublin	Clontarf	Clontarf Castle	Castle environs	O'Donovan, E.	O193-364
1997	90	Dublin	Leixlip	Cooldrinagh— Leixlip Waterworks	Area of archaeological potential	Byrne, M.E.	O006-356
1997	91	Dublin	Leixlip	Cooldrinagh— Leixlip Waterworks	Area of archaeological potential	Mullins, C.	O006-356
1997	92	Dublin	Balbriggan	Balbriggan Bypass	Various	Lynch, P.	
1997	93	Dublin	Dalkey	Castle Street	Medieval urban	Murphy, D.	O259-273
1997	94	Dublin	Dalkey	Castle Street	Medieval urban	Conway, M.G.	O259-273
1997	95	Dublin	Dalkey	Castle Street	Medieval urban	McConway, C.	O263-269
1997	96	Dublin	Dalkey	Castle Street	Medieval urban	Swan, R.	O264-268
1997	97	Dublin	Dalkey	Castle Street	Medieval urban	Conway, M.G.	O264-268
1997	98	Dublin	Dalkey	Castle Street (Our Lady's Hall)	Medieval urban	O'Donovan, E.	O264-268
1997	99	Dublin	Drumcondra	All Hallows Lane	Post-medieval	Logue, P.	O164-371
1997	100	Dublin	Drummans		Pits	Lynch, P.	H650-158
1997	101	Dublin	Dublin City	Adelaide Road/ Hatch Street	19th-century church site	Coughlan, T.	O161-329
1997	102	Dublin	Dublin City	Anglesea Street (The Auld Dubliner)	Late medieval urban	Byrne, M.E.	O156-344
1997	103	Dublin	Dublin City	Augustine Street/ Oliver Bond Street	Medieval urban	Walsh, C.	O142-342
1997	104	Dublin	Dublin City	Augustine Street/ John Street West	Medieval urban	Cosgrave, U.	O148-340
1997	105	Dublin	Dublin City	Back Lane/ Lamb Alley	Urban	Coughlan, T.	O149-338
1997	106	Dublin	Dublin City	Blackhall Place/ Arbour Hill	Post-medieval urban	Eogan, J.	O144-347
1997	107	Dublin	Dublin City	Camden Street Upper	Medieval urban	Kehoe, H.	O144-332
1997	108	Dublin	Dublin City	Capel Street	Medieval Urban	Sullivan, E.E.	O153-342
1997	109	Dublin	Dublin City	Capel Street	Urban	Walsh, C.	O160-337
1997	110	Dublin	Dublin City	Carmen's Hall	Urban	Channing, J.	O147-337
1997	111	Dublin	Dublin City	Castle Street	Medieval urban	Hayden, A.	O155-340
1997	112	Dublin	Dublin City	Cecilia Street	Medieval urban	Conway, M.G.	O156-341
1997	113	Dublin	Dublin City	Christchurch Cathedral	Monitoring	Seaver, M.	O152-349
1997	114	Dublin	Dublin City	Church Street	Medieval urban	Meenan, R.	O149-344
1997	115	Dublin	Dublin City	Church Street Upper	Urban	O'Rourke, D.	O150-340
1997	116	Dublin	Dublin City	Clare Lane/ Clare Street	Urban	McMahon, M.	O162-338
1997	117	Dublin	Dublin City	College Street	Urban	Carroll, J.	O150-340
1997	118	Dublin	Dublin City	Cook Street	Medieval urban	Meenan, R.	O149-341
1997	119	Dublin	Dublin City	The Coombe (Holy Faith Convent)	Medieval urban	Conway, M.G.	O149-335
1997	120	Dublin	Dublin City	Crane Lane	Medieval urban	Kehoe, H.	O154-340
1997	121	Dublin	Dublin City	Davis Place	Medieval urban	Conway, M.G.	O150-334
1997	122	Dublin	Dublin City	Essex Street East	Medieval urban	Cosgrave, U.	O152-346
1997	123	Dublin	Dublin City	Essex Street East	Medieval urban	Gowen, M.	O156-342

1997	124	Dublin	Dublin City	Essex Street West	Medieval urban	Simpson, L.	O153-341
1997	125	Dublin	Dublin City	Eustace Street	Medieval urban	Simpson, L.	O156-341
1997	126	Dublin	Dublin City	Exchange Street Lower	Medieval and post-medieval urban	Scally, G.	O144-345
1997	127	Dublin	Dublin City	Exchange Street Upper	Viking, Hiberno-Norse & medieval urban	Scally, G.	O145-344
1997	128	Dublin	Dublin City	Fownes Street Upper	Medieval urban	Simpson, L.	O158-339
1997	129	Dublin	Dublin City	Francis Street (The Iveagh Markets)	Medieval urban	Kehoe, H.	O150-336
1997	130	Dublin	Dublin City	Francis Street	Medieval suburban & 17th–19th-century clay pipe manufacture	Hayden, A.	O150-460
1997	131	Dublin	Dublin City	Francis Street	Urban	Scally, G.	O144-345
1997	132	Dublin	Dublin City	Francis Street/ Swift's Alley	Medieval urban	Walsh, C.	O149-338
1997	133	Dublin	Dublin City	Green Street	Urban	Walsh, C.	O152-347
1997	134	Dublin	Dublin City	Hill Street	Medieval urban	Kehoe, H.	O150-350
1997	135	Dublin	Dublin City	James' Street/ Bow Lane West	Urban	Meenan, R.	O135-342
1997	136	Dublin	Dublin City	James' Street	Medieval urban	Sullivan, E.E.	O137-338
1997	137	Dublin	Dublin City	John Street West	Urban	McMahon, M.	O155-339
1997	138	Dublin	Dublin City	Kevin Street Lower	Medieval and post-medieval urban	McConway, C.	O155-334
1997	139	Dublin	Dublin City	North King Street/ Brunswick Street North	Urban	Walsh, C.	O145-347
1997	140	Dublin	Dublin City	Lincoln Place	Urban	Swan, R.	O165-338
1997	141	Dublin	Dublin City	Little Britain Street	Post-medieval urban	McConway, C.	O153-347
1997	142	Dublin	Dublin City	Little Mary Street	Urban	Murphy, D.	O160-349
1997	143	Dublin	Dublin City	Longford Street/ Steeven's Street	Urban	Reid, M.	O157-335
1997	144	Dublin	Dublin City	Clanbrassil Street Lower	Post-medieval urban	Eogan, J.	O149-330
1997	145	Dublin	Dublin City	Gardiner Street Lower	Urban	McMahon, M.	O160-348
1997	146	Dublin	Dublin City	Meath Street/ Hanbury Lane	Medieval urban	Halpin, E.	O148-338
1997	147	Dublin	Dublin City	Middle Abbey Street/The Lotts	Medieval urban	O'Donovan, E.	O158-334
1997	148	Dublin	Dublin City	Gardiner Street Middle	Medieval urban	Kehoe, H.	O158-346
1997	149	Dublin	Dublin City	Montpelier Hill	No archaeological significance	McMahon, M.	O139-345
1997	150	Dublin	Dublin City	Montpelier Hill	No archaeological significance	McMahon, M.	O133-346
1997	151	Dublin	Dublin City	Mountjoy Square	18th-century urban	McMahon, M.	O172-361
1997	152	Dublin	Dublin City	New Row South	Medieval urban	Scally, G.	O149-338
1997	153	Dublin	Dublin City	North King Street	Urban	Walsh, C.	O149-343
1997	154	Dublin	Dublin City	North King Street	No archaeological significance	Murphy, D.	O147-348
1997	155	Dublin	Dublin City	Ormond Quay	Urban	Kehoe, H.	O153-342
1997	156	Dublin	Dublin City	Ormond Quay Lower	Urban	Opie, H.	O155-343
1997	157	Dublin	Dublin City	Parkgate Street (Aishling Hotel)	Urban	Reid, M.	O138-344
1997	158	Dublin	Dublin City	Parkgate Street	No archaeological significance	Corlett, C.	O137-345
1997	159	Dublin	Dublin City	Parnell Street (Parnell Centre)	No archaeological significance	Conway, M.G.	O155-348
1997	160	Dublin	Dublin City	Phoenix Park (Ordnance Survey)	No archaeological significance	McMahon, M.	O101-360
1997	161	Dublin	Dublin City	Ship Street Great	Medieval urban	Kehoe, H.	O154-337
1997	162	Dublin	Dublin City	Ship Street Little (Osmond House)	Medieval urban	Gowen, M.	O148-342
1997	163	Dublin	Dublin City	Ship Street Little (Osmond House)	Medieval urban	O'Donovan, E. and Kehoe, H.	O148-342

1997	164	Dublin	Dublin City	Earl Street South	Urban	Swan, R.	O146-337
1997	165	Dublin	Dublin City	Earl Street South	Urban	Walsh, C.	O140-338
1997	166	Dublin	Dublin City	Earl Street South (Meath Market)	Medieval urban	Walsh, C.	O141-341
1997	167	Dublin	Dublin City	Suir Road	Medieval urban	Kehoe, H.	
1997	168	Dublin	Dublin City	Temple Bar	Urban	Swan, R.	O154-234
1997	169	Dublin	Dublin City	Townsend Street/ Luke Street	Post-medieval river frontage & dock	Hayden, A.	O163-343
1997	170	Dublin	Dublin City	Vicar Street/ Thomas Street	Medieval urban	Carroll, J.	O143-339
1997	171	Dublin	Dublin City	Wellington Place	Post-medieval quay front	Corlett, C.	O315-234
1997	172	Dublin	Dublin City	Whitefriars Place	Medieval urban	Kehoe, H.	O155-336
1997	173	Dublin	Dublin City	Wolfe Tone Street	Urban	McConway, C.	O154-346
1997	174	Dublin	Dundrum	Dundrum Castle	Castle environs	O'Donovan, E.	O174-278
1997	175	Dublin	Dundrum	Dundrum Castle House	Castle environs	Eogan, J.	O174-279
1997	176	Dublin	Finglas	Cappagh Road (Holy Faith Convent)	Medieval?	Halpin, E.	O129-388
1997	177	Dublin	Finglas	Cappagh Road (Holy Faith Convent)	Manor site	Cosgrave, U.	O128-388
1997	178	Dublin	Gallanstown	Park West Industrial Estate	No archaeological significance	Murphy, D.	O083-329
1997	179	Dublin	Kiltalown	Kiltalown House	Standing stone?	Swan, R.	O064-261
1997	180	Dublin	Lambay Island		Neolithic axe production site	Cooney, G.	O317-508
1997	181	Dublin	Lusk	Church Road	Early Christian foundation	Murphy, D.	O210-550
1997	182	Dublin	Lusk	The Green	Medieval friary	Murphy, D.	O208-554
1997	183	Dublin	Quarryvale		Post-medieval	Scully, O.M.B.	O073-350
1997	184	Dublin	Rathfarnham	Butterfield Avenue (Old Orchard Inn)	Medieval occupation & burials	Carroll, J.	O135-289
1997	185	Dublin	Ringsend	Irishtown Road— Seapoint Terrace	Post-medieval	Walsh, C.	O193-133
1997	186	Dublin	Swords	The Old Vicarage	Burials	Dunne, G.	O157-452
1997	187	Dublin	Tallaght	St Maelruan's	Early ecclesiastical	Walsh, C.	O091-275
1997	188	Dublin	Whitechurch	St Columba's College	No archaeological significance	Hayden, A.	O156-356
1997	189	Fermanagh	Belcoo	Mullycovet Mill	Corn mill & grain-drying kiln	Donnelly, C.J.	H121-393
1997	190	Fermanagh	Enniskillen	Portora Castle	Fortified house & bawn	Brannon, N.F. and McSparron, C.	H222-345
1997	191	Galway	Athenry		No archaeological significance	Walsh, G.	M505-278
1997	192	Galway	Athenry	Back Lane	Anglo-Norman town	Delaney, D.	M502-277
1997	193	Galway	Carrowkeel	Caheratoother	Stone fort environs	Walsh, G.	
1997	194	Galway	Castlegar	Castlegar Castle	Tower-house environs	Higgins, J.	
1997	195	Galway	Claregalway	Summerfield	No archaeological significance	Higgins, J.	M365-326
1997	196	Galway	Garryduff	Coolacarta East— Garryduff Bog	Red deer in pitfall trap?	Bermingham, N.	M949-228
1997	197	Galway	Doonloughan		Early Christian coastal habitation sites	McCormick, F. and Murray, E.	L640-450
1997	198	Galway	Galway City	Court House Lane (Custom House)	Medieval urban	Walsh, G.	M298-252
1997	199	Galway	Galway City	Court House Lane/ Flood Street	Medieval urban	Delaney, D.	M298-252
1997	200	Galway	Galway City	Cross Street	Urban	O'Flanagan, N.	M298-251
1997	201	Galway	Galway City	Francis Street (Franciscan priory)	Urban ecclesiastical	Higgins, J.	
1997	202	Galway	Galway City	Kirwan's Lane	Urban	O'Flanagan, N.	M300-250
1997	203	Galway	Galway City	New Dock Street	Urban	O'Flanagan, N.	M298-249
1997	204	Galway	Galway City	Prospect Hill	No archaeological significance	Crumlish, R.	M302-254

1997	205	Galway	Galway City	Prospect Hill	Urban	Crumlish, R.	M301-253
1997	206	Galway	Galway City	Prospect Hill (Hackett's Shop)	Urban	Higgins, J.	M298-252
1997	207	Galway	Galway City	Quay Street (Blake's Tower)	Medieval urban	Connolly, A.	M298-252
1997	208	Galway	Galway City	Spanish Arch	Urban	Connolly, A.	M298-250
1997	209	Galway	Gort	Bridge Street	Post-medieval urban	Ó Baoill, R. and Logue, P.	M451-020
1997	210	Galway	High Island		Early Christian monastery	Scally, G.	L501-572
1997	211	Galway	Kilcloony		No archaeological significance	Crumlish, R.	M423-608
1997	212	Galway	Kilcolgan		No archaeological significance	Crumlish, R.	M415-178
1997	213	Galway	Kilcolgan		No archaeological significance	Crumlish, R.	M412-177
1997	214	Galway	Áran (Inis Mór)	Kilmurvey	Early Christian	King, H.A.	L820-100
1997	215	Galway	Knocknacarragh/ Rahoon		No archaeological significance	Connolly, A.	M261-239
1997	216	Galway	Loughrea	Abbey Street	Urban	Crumlish, R.	M618-166
1997	217	Galway	Loughrea	Barracks Street	Urban	Higgins, J.	
1997	218	Galway	Loughrea	Bride Street	Urban	Crumlish, R.	M623-166
1997	219	Galway	Loughrea	Dunkellin Street	Urban	Rooney, F.	
1997	220	Galway	Marble Hill		Megaliths, environs	Fitzpatrick, M.	
1997	221	Galway	Áran (Inis Mór)	Oighil— Mainistir Chiaráin	Early Christian monastery/ post-medieval house site & midden	Ní Ghabhláin, S.	L810-120
1997	222	Galway	Portumna	Portumna Castle	17th-century castle	Murphy, D.	M855-014
1997	223	Galway	Rinville West		Souterrain? environs	Gowen, M.	M350-227
1997	224	Galway	Tuam	Bishop Street	Ecclesiastical	Walsh, G.	M443-518
1997	225	Galway	Tuam	Bishop Street (Super-Valu)	Urban	Walsh, G.	M443-518
1997	226	Kerry	Ardfert	Ardfert Community Centre	Monastic site environs	Bennett, I.	Q785-211
1997	227	Kerry	Ballingleanna		No archaeological significance	Bennett, I.	Q320-999
1997	228	Kerry	Cathair Fionnúrach	Cathair a' Bhogaisín	Cashel/stone fort	Gibbons, E.	Q429-107
1997	229	Kerry	Ballyvelly		Ogham stone	Tierney, J.	Q824-152
1997	230	Kerry	Valentia Island	Bray Head	Early medieval hut	Walsh, C.	V242-738
1997	231	Kerry	Valentia Island	Bray Head	Early medieval farm & village	Hayden, A.	V344-737
1997	232	Kerry	Caherlehillan		Early ecclesiastical enclosure	Sheehan, J.	V572-835
1997	233	Kerry	Caherquin		Inhumation	Bennett, I.	Q360-057
1997	234	Kerry	Castlegregory		Castle	Dunne, L.	Q621-133
1997	235	Kerry	Coomacullen		*Fulacht fiadh?*	Connolly, M.	V101-822
1997	236	Kerry	Corbally		Monitoring	Dunne, L.	V818-970
1997	237	Kerry	Curragraigue		Ring-barrow?	Bennett, I.	Q816-111
1997	238	Kerry	Dingle	John Street	Town wall site?	Bennett, I.	Q446-011
1997	239	Kerry	Dingle	Main Street	Post-medieval urban	Dunne, L.	Q447-014
1997	240	Kerry	Dingle	The Mall	No archaeological significance	Bennett, I.	Q446-011
1997	241	Kerry	Dingle	Main Street (Market House)	Castle?	Dunne, L.	Q447-014
1997	242	Kerry	Dromthacker		Ringfort, enclosure & *fulachta fiadh*	Cleary, R.M.	Q154-837
1997	243	Kerry	Emlagh West		Ringfort environs	Tierney, J.	Q447-100
1997	244	Kerry	Sceilg Mhichíl (Great Skellig)	Monks' Garden	Monastic site	Bourke, E.C.	V245-604
1997	245	Kerry	Reacashlagh		Monitoring	Bennett, I.	R135-152
1997	246	Kerry	Scrahane		Cropmark	O'Donnell, M.	V963-897
1997	247	Kerry	Scrahane		Bronze Age metalworking site	Breen, T.C.	V964-896
1997	248	Kerry	Tralee	Abbey Carpark	Dominican priory	Byrne, M.E.	Q833-114

1997	249	Kerry	Tralee	The Basin	No archaeological significance	Bennett, I.	Q829-139
1997	250	Kerry	Tralee	Carrigeendaniel (Mount Hawk)	Monitoring	Bennett, I.	Q823-115
1997	251	Kerry	Tralee	Mount Hawk 1	Late Bronze Age cemetery & settlement site?	Dunne, L.	Q822-164
1997	252	Kerry	Tralee	Mount Hawk 2	Monitoring	Dunne, L.	Q824-158
1997	253	Kerry	Tralee	Listowel Road (Meadowlands Hotel)	No archaeological significance	Bennett, I.	Q852-158
1997	254	Kerry	Tralee	Prince's Quay—Mount Brandon Hotel	Urban	Bennett, I.	Q833-142
1997	255	Kerry	Tralee	Prince's Quay	Urban	Bennett, I.	Q834-143
1997	256	Kildare	Athy	Duke Street	Medieval urban	Mullins, C.	S680-938
1997	257	Kildare	Athy	Kildare Road	Medieval urban	Mullins, C.	S687-942
1997	258	Kildare	Barnhall		Cropmark—enclosure?	Gowen, M.	N986-356
1997	259	Kildare	Tipperkevin	Bawnogue/Walshestown	Monitoring	Delaney, D.	N934-148
1997	260	Kildare	Tipperkevin	Bawnogue/Walshestown	Monitoring	Quinn, B.	N934-148
1997	261	Kildare	Bishopslane	Bishopslane (Site 2)	Medieval borough	Hayden, A.	N940-096
1997	262	Kildare	Bishopslane	Bishopslane (Sites 1, 3–6)	Medieval borough	Hayden, A.	N940-096
1997	263	Kildare	Brownstown	Corbally and Silliot Hill	Prehistoric	Purcell, A.	N127-850
1997	264	Kildare	Celbridge	Main Street	Urban	Delaney, D.	S973-330
1997	265	Kildare	Celbridge	Stacumny House	Medieval ecclesiastical	Cosgrave, U.	N999-326
1997	266	Kildare	Clane		Urban	Brady, N.	N875-277
1997	267	Kildare	Clane	Main Street	Medieval urban	Mullins, C.	N876-273
1997	268	Kildare	Curragh		Prehistoric & later	Ó Ríordáin, A.B.	N750-137
1997	269	Kildare	Curragh	Curragh Camp	Archaeological complex, environs	Byrne, M.E.	N764-183
1997	270	Kildare	Forenaghts Great	Furness	Rock art environs	O'Carroll, F.	N934-200
1997	271	Kildare	Kilkea	Kilkea Castle	Castle	McMahon, M.	S749-887
1997	272	Kildare	Killhill		Motte environs	Swan, R.	N944-226
1997	273	Kildare	Laraghbryan East		Church environs	Coughlan, T.	N923-378
1997	274	Kildare	Leixlip		Medieval? & 18th-century church	McMahon, M.	O004-350
1997	275	Kildare	Leixlip	Leixlip Demesne	Drainage scheme	Duffy, C.	
1997	276	Kildare	Leixlip	Main Street	Medieval urban	Hayden, A.	O008-360
1997	277	Kildare	Leixlip	St Catherine's Park	Walls & drain	Connolly, A.	O017-360
1997	278	Kildare	Maynooth		Urban	Brady, N.	N938-377
1997	279	Kildare	Milltown		No archaeological significance	Meenan, R.	N760-170
1997	280	Kildare	Monasterevin		Road Bypass	Duffy, C.	
1997	281	Kildare	Monasterevin	Moore Abbey	Cistercian abbey environs	Mullins, C.	N627-099
1997	282	Kildare	Mount Prospect		No archaeological significance	Meenan, R.	
1997	283	Kildare	Naas	Clongowes Wood College	Pre-development testing	Halpin, E.	N877-298
1997	284	Kildare	Naas	North Main Street	Medieval urban	Byrne, M.E.	N895-193
1997	285	Kildare	Naas	North & South Main Streets	Urban	Ó Ríordáin, A.B.	N895-193
1997	286	Kildare	Leixlip	Parsonstown—Hewlett-Packard site	Monitoring	Ó Ríordáin, A.B.	N989-343
1997	287	Kildare	Leixlip	Parsonstown—Hewlett-Packard site	No archaeological significance	Lynch, P.	N989-343
1997	288	Kildare	Sherlockstown		Medieval archaeological complex, environs	Byrne, M.E.	N902-245
1997	289	Kildare	Walterstown		Medieval archaeological complex, environs	Byrne, M.E.	N703-055

1997	290	Kilkenny	Kellsborough	Hutchinson's Mill	Post-medieval mill	Pollock, D.	
1997	291	Kilkenny	Kilkenny City	Kilkenny City Main Drainage	Medieval urban	Neary, P.	S505-560
1997	292	Kilkenny	Kilkenny City	Abbey Street	Medieval urban	King, P.	S505-560
1997	293	Kilkenny	Kilkenny City	Abbey Street (Freren Court)	Urban	Neary, P.	S505-560
1997	294	Kilkenny	Kilkenny City	Black Abbey	Urban	Fredengren, C.	S503-561
1997	295	Kilkenny	Kilkenny City	Collier's Lane	Urban	Reid, M.	S505-558
1997	296	Kilkenny	Kilkenny City	Friary Street/ Garden Row	Medieval urban	O'Donovan, E.	S505-557
1997	297	Kilkenny	Kilkenny City	Friary Street	Urban	Breen, T.C.	S505-557
1997	298	Kilkenny	Kilkenny City	Garden Row	Urban	Reid, M.	S505-550
1997	299	Kilkenny	Kilkenny City	High Street	Medieval urban	Reid, M.	S505-560
1997	300	Kilkenny	Kilkenny City	Lower New Street	Urban	Kiely, J.	S505-560
1997	301	Kilkenny	Kilkenny City	New Building Lane	Medieval urban	O'Donovan, E.	S503-560
1997	302	Kilkenny	Kilkenny City	New Building Lane	Medieval urban	Conway, M.G.	S503-560
1997	303	Kilkenny	Kilkenny City	New Building Lane—Abbey View	Urban	Breen, T.C.	S503-561
1997	304	Kilkenny	Kilkenny City	Kilkenny Castle (The Parade)	Castle— 12th–19th-century	Murtagh, B.	S508-557
1997	305	Kilkenny	Kilkenny City	Patrick Street	Urban	Carroll, J.	S503-558
1997	306	Kilkenny	Kilkenny City	Poyntz's Lane	Urban	Reid, M.	S505-558
1997	307	Kilkenny	Kilkenny City	St Canice's Place	Late medieval urban	O'Donovan, E.	S504-563
1997	308	Kilkenny	Kilkenny City	St Francis' Abbey (Smithwicks Brewery)	Medieval	O'Donovan, E.	S506-562
1997	309	Kilkenny	Kilkenny City	St Kieran's Street	Medieval urban	Ó Baoill, R.	S504-557
1997	310	Kilkenny	Kilkenny City	William Street	Urban	Reid, M.	S505-557
1997	311	Kilkenny	Kilkenny City	William Street	Medieval urban	Sullivan, E.E.	S505-557
1997	312	Kilkenny	Barrow River		EIS (part)	Brady, N.	
1997	313	Kilkenny	Thomastown	Chapel Lane	Urban	Murtagh, B.	S586-418
1997	314	Laois	Clonaddadoran		*Fulacht fiadh*	Crumlish, R.	N469-947
1997	315	Laois	Dunamase	The Rock of Dunamase	Castle	Hodkinson, B.J.	S530-981
1997	316	Laois	Graigue		No archaeological significance	Gilmore, S.	S720-784
1997	317	Leitrim	Carrick-on-Shannon	Main Street (Priest's Lane)	Urban	Timoney, M.A.	G939-997
1997	318	Leitrim	Drumlease	Dromahaire Castle—the Lodge	No archaeological significance	Halpin, E.	G805-311
1997	319	Leitrim	Jamestown		No archaeological significance	Ryan, F.	
1997	320	Limerick	Adare	Blackabbey (Dunraven Arms Hotel)	No archaeological significance	O Rahilly, C.	R461-460
1997	321	Limerick	Croom	Anhid East—Site 2	No archaeological significance	Breen, T.C.	R516-392
1997	322	Limerick	Croom	Anhid West—Site 4	No archaeological significance	Breen, T.C.	R514-395
1997	323	Limerick	Croom	Anhid West—Site 5	No archaeological significance	Breen, T.C.	R515-396
1997	324	Limerick	Ashfort		Ringfort	Gahan, A.	R550-512
1997	325	Limerick	Askeaton	Coláiste Mhuire	Urban	Hodkinson, B.J.	R341-503
1997	326	Limerick	Attyflin		*Fulacht fiadh*	McConway, C.	R516-490
1997	327	Limerick	Attyflin		Medieval (moated site?)	Eogan, J.	R511-478
1997	328	Limerick	Attyflin		*Fulacht fiadh*	Gahan, A.	R520-491
1997	329	Limerick	Attyflin		Garden feature?	Gahan, A.	R515-487
1997	330	Limerick	Attyflin		Medieval enclosure	Logue, P.	R511-477
1997	331	Limerick	Lough Gur	Ballynagallagh	Enclosure	Cleary, R.M.	R644-392
1997	332	Limerick	Barnakyle		No archaeological significance	Gahan, A.	R524-497
1997	333	Limerick	Barnakyle		Post-medieval	Logue, P.	R524-497
1997	334	Limerick	Connigar		Standing stone	Moran, J. and Pollock, D.	R522-551
1997	335	Limerick	Croom	Site 6	Circular enclosure	Breen, T.C.	R513-400
1997	336	Limerick	Croom	Site 7	Enclosure	Breen, T.C.	R512-402

1997	337	Limerick	Croom	Site 9	No archaeological significance	Breen, T.C.	R512-404
1997	338	Limerick	Dooradoyle		*Fulachta fiadh*	Gahan, A.	R572-535
1997	339	Limerick	Dooradoyle		*Fulacht fiadh*	McConway, C.	R573-536
1997	340	Limerick	Fanningstown		Earthwork enclosure	Gracie, C.D.	R505-446
1997	341	Limerick	Fanningstown		No archaeological significance	Gracie, C.D.	R505-444
1997	342	Limerick	Fanningstown		Cropmark	Gracie, C.D.	R505-440
1997	343	Limerick	Fanningstown		Cropmark	Gracie, C.D.	R506-433
1997	344	Limerick	Gorteen		Moated site?	Gahan, A.	R495-475
1997	345	Limerick	Kilmallock	Sheares Street	Urban	O Rahilly, C.	R610-278
1997	346	Limerick	Kilmallock		Medieval urban	O'Donovan, E.	R610-278
1997	347	Limerick	Kilmallock		Medieval urban	O'Donovan, E.	R610-278
1997	348	Limerick	Limerick City	Athlunkard Street—Sir Harry's Mall	Urban	O Rahilly, C.	R580-576
1997	349	Limerick	Limerick City	Church Street/Old Dominick Street	Urban	O Rahilly, C.	R577-578
1997	350	Limerick	Limerick City	Courthouse Lane	Urban	O Rahilly, C.	R581-575
1997	351	Limerick	Limerick City	Fish Lane/Sir Harry's Mall	Medieval urban	Hanley, K.	R580-576
1997	352	Limerick	Limerick City	James' Street	Urban	O Rahilly, C.	R581-569
1997	353	Limerick	Limerick City	King John's Castle	Medieval castle	Wiggins, K.	R577-578
1997	354	Limerick	Limerick City	Little Creagh Lane	Medieval urban	O Rahilly, C.	R579-574
1997	355	Limerick	Limerick City	Mary Street	Urban	O Rahilly, C.	R579-575
1997	356	Limerick	Limerick City	Mungret Street	Medieval urban	Byrne, M.E.	R577-569
1997	357	Limerick	Limerick City	Mungret Street	Urban	O Rahilly, C.	R583-570
1997	358	Limerick	Limerick City	St Mary's Cathedral	Medieval urban	Hodkinson, B.J.	R578-575
1997	359	Limerick	Newcastle West	Market Place	Urban	Bennett, I.	R279-337
1997	360	Limerick	Raheen		Burials adjacent to churchyard	Hodkinson, B.J.	R748-285
1997	361	Limerick	Rathbane South		Mound—ring-barrow?	Gahan, A.	R595-540
1997	362	Limerick	Rathbranagh		No archaeological significance	Gracie, C.D.	R505-437
1997	363	Limerick	Rossbrien		Not excavated	Gahan, A.	R580-543
1997	364	Louth	Agnaskeagh		Megalithic tombs	Murphy, D.	J076-137
1997	365	Louth	Ardee	Ardee Castle	Urban tower-house	Campbell, K.	N962-904
1997	366	Louth	Ardee	Tierney Street	Medieval urban	Murphy, D.	N962-905
1997	367	Louth	Ardee	William Street/College Lane	Mill site?	Swan, R.	N962-901
1997	368	Louth	Carlingford	Back Lane	Medieval urban	Murphy, D.	J188-118
1997	369	Louth	Carlingford	River Street	Medieval urban	Murphy, D.	J188-116
1997	370	Louth	Dundalk	Cleremont	No archaeological significance	Lynch, P.	
1997	371	Louth	Darver		Tower-house environs	Campbell, K.	O009-987
1997	372	Louth	Drogheda	Bachelor's Lane	Medieval urban	Murphy, D.	O091-755
1997	373	Louth	Drogheda	Bachelor's Lane	Medieval urban	Murphy, D.	O091-754
1997	374	Louth	Drogheda	Bessexwell Lane	Medieval urban	Meenan, R.	O091-753
1997	375	Louth	Drogheda	Constitution Hill/North Strand	Urban	Meenan, R.	O092-752
1997	376	Louth	Drogheda	Constitution Hill	Urban	Meenan, R.	O917-752
1997	377	Louth	Drogheda	Dyer Street	Medieval/post-medieval urban	Murphy, D.	O088-749
1997	378	Louth	Drogheda	Dyer Street	Medieval/post-medieval urban	Campbell, K.	O089-750
1997	379	Louth	Drogheda	George's Hill	Medieval urban	Murphy, D.	O083-758
1997	380	Louth	Drogheda	Laurence Street	Medieval urban	Murphy, D.	O091-752
1997	381	Louth	Drogheda	The Mall	Medieval urban	Murphy, D.	O091-753
1997	382	Louth	Drogheda	Moneymore	Medieval urban	Murphy, D.	O088-750
1997	383	Louth	Drogheda	North Quay/Bessexwell Lane	Medieval urban	Murphy, D.	O092-755
1997	384	Louth	Drogheda	Shop Street	Medieval urban	Murphy, D.	O090-750
1997	385	Louth	Drogheda	Trinity Street	Medieval urban	Murphy, D.	O081-757
1997	386	Louth	Drogheda	Wellington Quay	No archaeological significance	Corlett, C.	O090-756

1997	387	Louth	Drogheda	West Street	Medieval urban	Murphy, D.	O086-751
1997	388	Louth	Dundalk	Bridge Street	Medieval pottery kiln	Campbell, K.	J047-079
1997	389	Louth	Dundalk	Church Street (Carroll's Village)	Medieval urban	Murphy, D.	J047-076
1997	390	Louth	Dundalk	Church Street	Medieval/ post-medieval urban	Campbell, K.	J041-011
1997	391	Louth	Dundalk	Laurels Road	Medieval/ post-medieval urban	Campbell, K.	J046-011
1997	392	Louth	Dundalk	Park Street	Urban	Meenan, R.	J047-070
1997	393	Louth	Dundalk	Park Street	Post-medieval urban	Campbell, K.	J041-010
1997	394	Louth	Dundalk	Seatown (Sutton Court)	No archaeological significance	Murphy, D.	J056-074
1997	395	Louth	Dunleer		No archaeological significance	Murphy, D.	O057-881
1997	396	Louth	Monasterboice	Tower House	No archaeological significance	Murphy, D.	O042-810
1997	397	Louth	Termonfeckin	Yellow Gap	No archaeological significance	Murphy, D.	O143-803
1997	398	Mayo	Balla		No archaeological significance	Walsh, G.	M252-845
1997	399	Mayo	Balla		Ecclesiastical site environs	Walsh, G.	M252-845
1997	400	Mayo	Carrowbeg		No archaeological significance	Morahan, L.	M137-299
1997	401	Mayo	Carrownalurgan	Carrownalurgan Island	Enclosure	Byrne, M.E.	F981-283
1997	402	Mayo	Churchfield & Ardoley		Ecclesiastical remains	Byrne, M.E.	F971-284
1997	403	Mayo	Clonkeen	Islandeady	Enclosure environs	Walsh, G.	
1997	404	Mayo	Cloonlaur		No archaeological significance	Morahan, L.	L756-765
1997	405	Mayo	Erris	Regional water supply	No archaeological significance	Walsh, G.	
1997	406	Mayo	Kilbree Lower	Cloonkeen	Bullaun stone	Walsh, G.	
1997	407	Mayo	Kilkeeran	Ballyovey Church	Church & graveyard	Morahan, L.	
1997	408	Mayo	Kiltimagh		No archaeological significance	Walsh, G.	
1997	409	Mayo	Knappaghmore		No archaeological significance	Walsh, G.	
1997	410	Mayo	Murrisk Demesne		No archaeological significance	King, P.	
1997	411	Mayo	Achill	The Deserted Village, Slievemore (Toir)	Multi-phase landscape	McDonald, T.	F630-075
1997	412	Mayo	Strade	Strade Abbey	Medieval friary	Murphy, D.	M258-976
1997	413	Mayo	Westport–Belclare	Road realignment scheme	Various	Byrne, M.E.	F981-283
1997	414	Meath	Athboy	The Station House	Medieval/ post-medieval urban	Campbell, K.	N718-641
1997	415	Meath	Athboy	Townparks	Medieval urban	Murphy, D.	N718-645
1997	416	Meath	Various	Balbriggan Bypass	Various	Lynch, P.	
1997	417	Meath	Beamore		Medieval gatehouse	Murphy, D.	O095-725
1997	418	Meath	Moynagh Lough	Brittas	Crannog	Bradley, J.	N818-860
1997	419	Meath	Tara	Rath na Ríogh	Prehistoric enclosure	Roche, H.	N915-597
1997	420	Meath	Duleek	Abbeylands	Medieval settlement	McSparron, C.	O046-686
1997	421	Meath	Duleek	Main Street	No archaeological significance	Murphy, D.	O046-684
1997	422	Meath	Gormanstown		Burning	Lynch, P.	O161-345
1997	423	Meath	Kells	Market Cross	High cross	King, H.A.	N742-758
1997	424	Meath	Kilcairn	Athlumney House	Souterrain?	Sullivan, E.E.	N875-661
1997	425	Meath	Knockharley		No archaeological significance	Opie, H.	N950-680
1997	426	Meath	Knowth		Multi-period	Eogan, G.	N995-375
1997	427	Meath	Navan	Navan Moat	Motte	Breen, T.C.	N859-676
1997	428	Meath	Navan	Athlumney	Monitoring	Reid, M.	N876-674
1997	429	Meath	Navan	Metges Lane	Medieval urban	Meenan, R.	N870-679
1997	430	Meath	Teltown	The Knockans	Linear earthwork	Waddell, J. and O'Brien, M.	N809-743

1997	431	Meath	Peterstown		Early Christian/ medieval cemetery	Murphy, D.	N813-575
1997	432	Meath	Ratoath		Medieval urban	Murphy, D.	O020-519
1997	433	Meath	Ratoath	Curragha Road	Medieval borough	Meenan, R.	O322-523
1997	434	Meath	Sarsfieldstown		Bronze Age cremated burials?	Lynch, P.	O155-676
1997	435	Meath	Slane	Slane Castle Demesne/St Erc's Hermitage	Hermitage	Channing, J.	N966-749
1997	436	Meath	Tobertown & Rath		Pits & subrectangular feature	Lynch, P.	H643-163
1997	437	Meath	Trim	Castle Street (Trim Courthouse)	Urban	Delaney, D.	N801-569
1997	438	Meath	Woodpole		Cist burial	Cahill, M.	N671-782
1997	439	Monaghan	Monaghan Town	Mill Street	No archaeological significance	Swan, R.	H672-334
1997	440	Offaly	Ballicknahee		Burials	Murphy, D.	N280-338
1997	441	Offaly	Banagher		Monitoring	Kiely, J.	N001-154
1997	442	Offaly	Ballybritt	Kinnity Castle	Trial-trenching	Higgins, J.	N201-050
1997	443	Offaly	Ballyburley		Church & graveyard environs	Mullins, C.	N551-351
1997	444	Offaly	Banagher	Lower Main Street	Urban	Delaney, D.	N001-154
1997	445	Offaly	Birr	Main Street	Urban	Delaney, D.	N055-050
1997	446	Offaly	Carrowkeey & Clonfinlough	Esker Hill/ Fighting Hill	No archaeological significance	Gracie, C.D.	N070-300
1997	447	Offaly	Clonmacnoise		Early medieval bridge	O'Sullivan, A. and Boland, D.	N006-306
1997	448	Offaly	Clonmacnoise	New Graveyard	Early Christian settlement	King, H.A.	N011-308
1997	449	Offaly	Croghan Demesne		Burials	Delaney, D.	N483-333
1997	450	Offaly	Bannagher	Garrycastle	Archaeological complex	Delaney, D.	
1997	451	Offaly	Killeigh		Archaeological complex	Delaney, D.	N365-183
1997	452	Roscommon	Ardnafinnan		Linear earthworks environs	Timoney, M.A.	M198-296
1997	453	Roscommon	Cooltona		Medieval church site	Murphy, D.	M957-601
1997	454	Roscommon	Glebe		No archaeological significance	Dunne, L.	M827-577
1997	455	Roscommon	Moigh Lower		Burnt stone mound	Coombs, D.G. and Robinson, M.	M530-740
1997	456	Roscommon	Mulliviltrin		19th-century village	Orser, C.E. Jr	M809-650
1997	457	Roscommon	Rathkineely		No archaeological significance	Dunne, L.	M766-847
1997	458	Roscommon	Roscommon Town	Main Street (Roscommon Jail)	Urban	Higgins, J.	M872-641
1997	459	Roscommon	Tulsk		No archaeological significance	Walsh, G.	
1997	460	Sligo	Ballaghboy		*Fulacht fiadh?*	Channing, J.	G782-081
1997	461	Sligo	Ballinafad		*Fulacht fiadh*	Channing, J.	G779-085
1997	462	Sligo	Belladrihid		No archaeological significance	Channing, J.	G674-307
1997	463	Sligo	Bellaghy		No archaeological significance	Morahan, L.	G148-320
1997	464	Sligo	Carrowhubbuck South		No archaeological significance	Walsh, G.	
1997	465	Sligo	Doonaveeragh		No archaeological significance	Timoney, M.A.	G768-112
1997	466	Sligo	Farranyharpy		No archaeological significance	Timoney, M.A.	G519-326
1997	467	Sligo	Gortalough		Castle & road environs	Timoney, M.A.	G780-088
1997	468	Sligo	Inishmurray	Trahaun Ó Riain	Early medieval altar; cross-inscribed slab	O'Sullivan, J.	G566-533
1997	469	Sligo	Knoxspark		Burials, environs	Channing, J.	G288-672
1997	470	Sligo	Lough Gara	Shroove	Stone platform	Fredengren, C.	G689-002
1997	471	Sligo	Sligo Town	Abbey Street	Burials	Halpin, E.	G693-358

1997	472	Sligo	Sligo Town	Abbey Street Lower	Post-medieval urban	Ó Baoill, R.	G695-358
1997	473	Sligo	Sligo Town	John F. Kennedy Parade	Urban	Halpin, E.	G693-358
1997	474	Sligo	Sligo Town	John F. Kennedy Parade	Urban	Halpin, E.	G695-359
1997	475	Sligo	Sligo Town	Rockwood Parade	Urban	Halpin, E.	G692-359
1997	476	Sligo	Sligo Town	Stephen Street	Post-medieval urban	Ó Baoill, R.	G692-359
1997	477	Sligo	Sligo Town	Stephen Street	Post-medieval urban	Ó Baoill, R.	G692-359
1997	478	Sligo	Sligo Town	Stephen Street	Post-medieval urban	Ó Baoill, R.	G692-359
1997	479	Sligo	Sligo Town	Stephen Street (Stephen House)	Urban	Halpin, E.	G692-359
1997	480	Sligo	Sligo Town	Thomas Street	Urban	Halpin, E.	G693-358
1997	481	Sligo	Sligo Town	Watery Lane	Urban	Halpin, E.	G691-359
1997	482	Sligo	Sligo Town	Wine Street	Urban	Gowen, M.	G691-363
1997	483	Sligo	Tonefortes		Henge environs	Channing, J.	
1997	484	Tipperary	Ballintotty		Medieval strong house	McConway, C.	R910-785
1997	485	Tipperary	Cahir		Monitoring	Ryan, F.	S050-250
1997	486	Tipperary	Cahir	Mall Lane	Urban	Breen, T.C.	S050-248
1997	487	Tipperary	Cashel	Lower Gate Street	Medieval urban	Henry, M.	S075-407
1997	488	Tipperary	Cashel	Old Road	Enclosure environs	Moran, J.	S070-397
1997	489	Tipperary	Clonmel	Gladstone Street	Medieval/ post-medieval urban	Henry, M.	S202-223
1997	490	Tipperary	Clonmel	Grubb's Court	Medieval/ post-medieval urban	Henry, M.	S202-223
1997	491	Tipperary	Clonmel	Joyce's Lane	Medieval/ post-medieval urban	Henry, M.	S202-223
1997	492	Tipperary	Clonmel	Mary Street	Urban	Moran, J.	S202-222
1997	493	Tipperary	Coolaholloga		Post-medieval	Logue, P.	R851-801
1997	494	Tipperary	Drummin		No archaeological significance	Logue, P.	R862-806
1997	495	Tipperary	Fethard	Kiltinan Castle	Castle	Pollock, D.	S232-320
1997	496	Tipperary	Golden	Main Street	Urban	Moran, J.	S000-384
1997	497	Tipperary	Grallagh		Post-medieval	Logue, P.	R839-787
1997	498	Tipperary	Kildanoge	*Rian Bó Phádraig*	Linear earthwork	O'Donnell, M.	S072-081
1997	499	Tipperary	Lisheen Project		General introduction	Gowen, M. and Ó Néill, J.	S226-661
1997	500	Tipperary	Lisheen Project— DER240	Derryville Bog, Killoran	*Fulacht fiadh*	Ó Néill, J.	S226-661
1997	501	Tipperary	Lisheen Project— DER241, 243, 314, 316	Derryville Bog, Killoran	Trackways & burnt mound	Ó Néill, J.	S226-661
1997	502	Tipperary	Lisheen Project— DER235	Derryville Bog, Killoran	Trackway	Ó Néill, J.	S226-661
1997	503	Tipperary	Lisheen Project— DER265	Derryville Bog, Killoran	*Fulacht fiadh* with timber platform	Ó Néill, J.	S226-661
1997	504	Tipperary	Lisheen Project— DER253	Derryville Bog, Killoran	*Fulacht fiadh* with platform	Ó Néill, J.	S226-661
1997	505	Tipperary	Lisheen Project— DER304	Derryville Bog, Killoran	*Fulacht fiadh*	Stevens, P.	S221-662
1997	506	Tipperary	Lisheen Project— DER18 (DER302 & DER305)	Killoran	Stone causeway	Stevens, P.	S221-662
1997	507	Tipperary	Lisheen Project— DER302	Killoran	Wooden causeway	Stevens, P.	S221-662
1997	508	Tipperary	Lisheen Project— DER305	Killoran	Wooden trackway	Stevens, P.	S221-662
1997	509	Tipperary	Lisheen Project— DER69	Killoran	Wooden trackway	Stevens, P.	S221-662
1997	510	Tipperary	Lisheen Project— DER306 (DER300)	Killoran	Wooden trackway	Stevens, P.	S221-662
1997	511	Tipperary	Lisheen Project— DER246	Killoran	Wooden platform	Stevens, P.	S221-662
1997	512	Tipperary	Lisheen Project— DER226	Killoran	Wooden trackway	Stevens, P.	S221-662
1997	513	Tipperary	Lisheen Project— DER301	Killoran	Wooden trackway	Stevens, P.	S221-662

1997	514	Tipperary	Lisheen Project—DER248	Killoran	Wooden trackway	Stevens, P.	S221-662
1997	515	Tipperary	Lisheen Project	Killoran	No archaeological significance	Stevens, P.	S221-662
1997	516	Tipperary	Lisheen Project	Derryville Bog, Killoran	Introduction	Cross, S.	S222-666
1997	517	Tipperary	Lisheen Project—DER237	Killoran	Wooden platform	Cross, S.	S222-666
1997	518	Tipperary	Lisheen Project—DER229	Killoran	Roundwood scatter	Cross, S.	S222-666
1997	519	Tipperary	Lisheen Project—DER230	Killoran	Wooden trackway	Cross, S.	S222-666
1997	520	Tipperary	Lisheen Project—DER234	Killoran	Wooden trackway	Cross, S.	S222-666
1997	521	Tipperary	Lisheen Project—DER75	Killoran	Wooden trackway	Cross, S.	S222-666
1997	522	Tipperary	Lisheen Project—DER312	Killoran	Brushwood trackway	Cross, S.	S222-666
1997	523	Tipperary	Lisheen Project DER315	Killoran	Wooden trackway	Cross, S.	S222-666
1997	524	Tipperary	Lisheen Project—DER31	Cooleeny	Composite trackway	Cross, S.	S222-666
1997	525	Tipperary	Lisheen Project—DER325	Cooleeny	Brushwood scatter	Cross, S.	S222-657
1997	526	Tipperary	Lisheen Project	Lisheen Mine	Introduction	Stevens, P.	S193-665
1997	527	Tipperary	Lisheen Project—KIL:01	Killoran	*Fulacht fiadh* & parallel linear field ditches	Stevens, P	S206-668
1997	528	Tipperary	Lisheen Project—KIL:02	Killoran	Burnt spreads & linear field ditches	Stevens, P.	S220-664
1997	529	Tipperary	Lisheen Project—KIL:05	Killoran	*Fulacht fiadh*	Stevens, P.	S212-666
1997	530	Tipperary	Lisheen Project—KIL:06	Killoran	Isolated cremation	Stevens, P.	S213-665
1997	531	Tipperary	Lisheen Project—KIL:07	Killoran	Isolated cremation	Stevens, P.	S213-666
1997	532	Tipperary	Lisheen Project—KIL:09	Killoran	Post-medieval roadway	Stevens, P.	S220-664
1997	533	Tipperary	Lisheen Project—KIL:11	Killoran	Medieval/post-medieval features	Stevens, P.	S204-667
1997	534	Tipperary	Lisheen Project—KIL:03	Killoran	Neolithic activity?	Stevens, P. and Ó Néill, J.	S217-663
1997	535	Tipperary	Lisheen Project—KIL:04	Killoran	Prehistoric flat cremation cemetery	Stevens, P.	S213-666
1997	536	Tipperary	Lisheen Project—KIL:08	Killoran	Later prehistoric unenclosed settlement	Ó Néill, J.	S220-667
1997	537	Tipperary	Lisheen Project—KIL:10	Killoran	Flat cremation cemetery	Stevens, P.	S217-662
1997	538	Tipperary	Lisheen Project	Derryville Bog	Introduction	Murray, C.	S222-659
1997	539	Tipperary	Lisheen Project—DER218	Derryfadda	Degraded platform	Murray, C.	S226-659
1997	540	Tipperary	Lisheen Project—DER22	Cooleeny	Single-plank walkway	Murray, C.	S223-660
1997	541	Tipperary	Lisheen Project—DER57	Killoran	Roundwood path	Murray, C.	S225-659
1997	542	Tipperary	Lisheen Project—DER311	Derryfadda	Stone track	Murray, C.	S226-657
1997	543	Tipperary	Lisheen Project—DER17	Derryfadda	Stone track	Murray, C.	S227-669
1997	544	Tipperary	Lisheen Project—DER20	Killoran	Pool filler	Murray, C.	S226-663
1997	545	Tipperary	Lisheen Project—DER64	Cooleeny	Brushwood togher	Murray, C.	S222-660
1997	546	Tipperary	Lisheen Project—DER54 & DER56	Killoran	Complex stake row & brushwood structure	Murray, C.	S224-665

1997	547	Tipperary	Knockalton		Early Christian settlement?	Logue, P.	R891-775
1997	548	Tipperary	Nenagh	Abbey Lane	Urban	Hodkinson, B.J.	R866-790
1997	549	Tipperary	Nenagh	Abbey Street (The Friary)	Medieval urban	Desmond, S.	R866-790
1997	550	Tipperary	Nenagh	Ball Alley Lane	Urban	Hodkinson, B.J.	R866-790
1997	551	Tipperary	Nenagh	Connolly Street	Urban	Hodkinson, B.J.	R866-790
1997	552	Tipperary	Nenagh	Lower Sarsfield Street	Urban	Hodkinson, B.J.	R866-790
1997	553	Tipperary	Nenagh	Nenagh Castle	Castle	Hodkinson, B.J.	R866-790
1997	554	Tipperary	Roolagh		No archaeological significance	Gilmore, S.	R460-390
1997	555	Tipperary	Roscrea		12th-century cross	Manning, C.	S136-894
1997	556	Tipperary	Roscrea	Roscrea Sewage System	No archaeological significance	Conway, M.G.	S134-892
1997	557	Tipperary	Roscrea	Glebe View	Urban	Carroll, J.	S134-892
1997	558	Tipperary	Sharragh		Togher	Whitaker, J.	
1997	559	Tipperary	Terryglass		Castle bawn	Hodkinson, B.J.	M864-004
1997	560	Tipperary	Thurles	Bowling Green	Ringfort environs	Stevens, P.	S137-492
1997	561	Tipperary	Tipperary Town	Muragasty (Bohercrow Road)	Burials adjacent to church	Hodkinson, B.J.	R891-358
1997	562	Tipperary	Tullaheddy		Post-medieval	Logue, P.	R830-773
1997	563	Tipperary	Tullaheddy		Prehistoric landscape	McConway, C.	R834-773
1997	564	Tyrone	Copney		Stone circles	Gardiner, M.	H599-780
1997	565	Waterford	Ballynatray		Monitoring	Tierney, J.	X080-828
1997	566	Waterford	Dungarvan	Castle Street/ Quay Street	Medieval urban	Pollock, D.	X262-927
1997	567	Waterford	Dungarvan	Castle Street/ Emmet Street	Medieval urban	Pollock, D.	X262-927
1997	568	Waterford	Dungarvan	Davitt's Quay	Medieval urban	Pollock, D.	X262-927
1997	569	Waterford	Dungarvan	Davitt's Quay/ Thompson's Lane	Medieval urban	Pollock, D.	X262-927
1997	570	Waterford	Dungarvan	Dirty Lane	Medieval urban	Pollock, D.	X262-927
1997	571	Waterford	Dungarvan	Dungarvan Castle	Castle	Pollock, D.	X262-930
1997	572	Waterford	Dungarvan	Quay Street	Medieval urban	Pollock, D.	X262-927
1997	573	Waterford	Dungarvan	Quay Street	Medieval urban	Tierney, J.	X262-927
1997	574	Waterford	Faithlegg		Ecclesiastical remains environs	Scully, O.M.B.	
1997	575	Waterford	Waterford City	Arundel Square	Medieval urban	McCutcheon, S.	S605-122
1997	576	Waterford	Waterford City	Christchurch	Cathedral	O'Donovan, E.	S607-121
1997	577	Waterford	Waterford City	Conduit Lane/ Cathedral Lane	Medieval urban	Hurley, M.F.	S607-125
1997	578	Waterford	Waterford City	Grattan Quay	Urban	Breen, T.C.	S602-122
1997	579	Waterford	Waterford City	Meagher's Quay	Medieval urban	McCutcheon, S.	S606-125
1997	580	Waterford	Waterford City	Reginald's Tower	Medieval tower of city wall	Murtagh, B.	S607-123
1997	581	Westmeath	Athlone	Irishtown Lower	Post-medieval urban	Ó Baoill, R.	N039-415
1997	582	Westmeath	Athlone	Irishtown Upper	Medieval urban	O'Donovan, E.	N045-413
1997	583	Westmeath	Athlone	Pearse Street	Post-medieval urban	Conway, M.G.	N045-413
1997	584	Westmeath	Athlone	The Quay	Medieval urban	Sullivan, E.E.	N039-413
1997	585	Westmeath	Glebe		Early Christian/ medieval	O'Carroll, F.	N568-251
1997	586	Westmeath	Knockdomney		Monitoring	Murphy, D.	N163-394
1997	587	Westmeath	Mullingar	Barrack Street	No archaeological significance	Hayden, A.	N450-600
1997	588	Westmeath	Mullingar	Bishopsgate	Urban	Lynch, P.	N435-533
1997	589	Westmeath	Mullingar	Friars' Mill Road	Urban	Gracie, C.D.	N437-532
1997	590	Westmeath	Mullingar	Harbour Street	No archaeological significance	Gracie, C.D.	N441-533
1997	591	Westmeath	Mullingar	Pearse Street	Medieval urban	Byrne, M.E.	N438-530
1997	592	Westmeath	Mullingar	Pearse Street	Urban	Duffy, C.	N438-530
1997	593	Wexford	Courthoyle Old		Church (site of) and graveyard	Henry, M.	S818-254
1997	594	Wexford	Duncannon	Duncannon Fort	16th-century star-shaped fort	McCutcheon, S.	S727-081
1997	595	Wexford	Enniscorthy		No archaeological significance	Channing, J.	S975-399

1997	596	Wexford	Enniscorthy	Railway Square	Urban	McCutcheon, S.	S973-398
1997	597	Wexford	Enniscorthy	The Shannon	Urban	Bennett, I.	S973-398
1997	598	Wexford	Enniscorthy	Templeshannon	Urban	Bennett, I.	S975-398
1997	599	Wexford	Enniscorthy	Templeshannon	Medieval/ post-medieval urban	Henry, M.	S975-397
1997	600	Wexford	Enniscorthy	Templeshannon	Urban	Bennett, I.	S975-398
1997	601	Wexford	New Ross	Main Drainage	Medieval urban	McCutcheon, S.	S718-275
1997	602	Wexford	New Ross	Trinity Place, Priory Street	Medieval urban	Sullivan, E.E.	S718-272
1997	603	Wexford	St Helens	Ballyhire Castle	Castle environs	O'Donovan, E.	T141-105
1997	604	Wexford	Taghmon		Ecclesiastical enclosure environs	Hurley, M.F.	S918-200
1997	605	Wexford	Wexford Town	Anne Street	Urban	Reid, M.	T052-215
1997	606	Wexford	Wexford Town	Custom House Quay	Urban	McConway, C.	T049-218
1997	607	Wexford	Wexford Town	The Pillar	Medieval urban	Sullivan, E.E.	T049-212
1997	608	Wexford	Wexford Town	South & North Main Streets	Medieval urban	Sheehan, C.	T049-213
1997	609	Wicklow	Ballynattin		Burnt mound	Connolly, A.	T231-716
1997	610	Wicklow	Coolboy		Burnt mound	Gracie, C.D.	T324-175
1997	611	Wicklow	Donard	Donard Community Centre	No archaeological significance	Eogan, J.	T929-974
1997	612	Wicklow	Greystones	Rathdown Lower	Prehistoric & medieval	Eogan, J. and O'Brien, R.N.	O287-136
1997	613	Wicklow	Johnstown North		*Fulacht fiadh*	Lynch, P.	T265-775
1997	614	Wicklow	Johnstown North		Burnt mound	Gregory, N.	T265-774
1997	615	Wicklow	Johnstown North		Enclosure	Fitzpatrick, M.	T280-771
1997	616	Wicklow	Kilbride		Bronze Age settlement site	Breen, T.C.	T237-748
1997	617	Wicklow	Newcastle		Medieval?	Walsh, C.	O291-035
1997	618	Wicklow	Arklow	Templerainey	Prehistoric	Ó Ríordáin, A.B.	T269-768
1997	619	Wicklow	Wicklow Town	Church Street	Medieval urban	Eogan, J.	T313-940
1997	620	Wicklow	Wicklow Town	Church Street (Wentworth House)	Medieval urban with prehistoric?	McConway, C.	T313-940
1997	621	Wicklow	Wicklow Town	Church Street (Wentworth House)	Medieval urban	Eogan, J.	T313-940
1997	622	Wicklow	Wicklow Town	South Quay	Post-medieval urban	Eogan, J.	T313-940
1997	623	Wicklow	Wicklow Town	South Quay	Medieval urban	Gowen, M.	T313-940
1997	624	Wicklow	Wicklow Town	South Quay/ The Mall	Medieval urban	Gowen, M.	T313-940
1997	Ad1	Clare	Ballyconneely		Standing stone & field boundaries	Grant, C.	
1997	Ad2	Clare	Ennis	Parnell Street	Urban	Grant, C.	R337-774
1997	Ad3	Donegal	Doon Glebe		Standing stone	Grant, C.	
1997	Ad4	Galway	Galway City	Lower Fairhill	Urban	Grant, C.	
1997	Ad5	Limerick	Ballyouragan		No archaeological significance	Grant, C.	
1997	Ad6	Limerick	Croom		No archaeological significance	Grant, C.	R515-396
1997	Ad7	Limerick	Croom		No archaeological significance	Grant, C.	R515-396
1997	Ad8	Limerick	Croom		No archaeological significance	Grant, C.	R515-396
1997	Ad9	Limerick	Skagh		Cultivation ridges	Grant, C.	
1997	ApxI	Galway	Clonfert		Research survey (Clonfert Research Project Survey)	Higgins, J. and Cuniffe, C.	M967-211
1997	ApxII	Limerick	Killuragh	Killuragh Cave	Amendment to 1996	Woodman, P.C.	R778-497
1997	ApxIII	Offaly/ Westmeath/ Mayo		Bord na Móna Bogs	Research survey (IAWU)	McDermott, C. *et al.*	

Index of Excavations 1969–97 by location

Location	Volume/excavation no.
Abbey Street, Armagh City	1976/009
Abbey Street (Freren Court), Kilkenny City	1997/293
Abbey Street, Kilkenny City	1995/166, 1995/167, 1995/168, 1996/204, 1997/292
Abbey Street Old Meeting House, Armagh City	1977/009
Abbeygate Street Lower, Galway City	1990/058, 1990/059, 1995/119
Abbeygate Street Upper, Galway City	1989/046
Abbeyknockmoy, Co. Galway	1980/112
Abbeypark, Co. Galway	1971/017, 1972/017, 1993/106
Abbeytown, Co. Galway	1989/041
Abington, Co. Limerick	1992/121, 1994/154
Achill, Co. Mayo	1991/099, 1992/148, 1992/Apx 2, 1993/178, 1994/188, 1995/226, 1996/303, 1997/411
Adamstown, Co. Limerick	1986/036
Adare, Co. Limerick	1975/026, 1989/066, 1991/085, 1992/122, 1996/229, 1997/320
Adelaide Road/Hatch Street, Dublin City	1997/101
Aghaboe, Co. Laois	1986/035, 1994/141
Aghacross, Co. Cork	1993/014, 1997/029
Aghadegnan, Co. Longford	1991/091, 1993/148, 1993/149, 1993/152
Aghareagh, Co. Monaghan	1980/156
Agharrow, Co. Sligo	1993/197
Aghleam, Co. Mayo	1988/047
Aghnagrane, Co. Fermanagh	1990/052
Agnaskeagh, Co. Louth	1997/364
Alexander Street, Waterford City	1991/122
Allihies, Co. Cork	1993/015
Altanagh, Co. Tyrone	1980/179
Altar, Co. Cork	1989/008
Anglesea Street (The Auld Dubliner), Dublin City	1997/102
Annagh, Co. Limerick	1992/123
Annaghcorrib, Co. Galway	1992/083
Annaghkeen, Co. Galway	1980/113
Antrim coast, Co. Antrim	1995/009
Antrim Town, Co. Antrim	1971/002, 1973/004, 1974/005, 1977/007, 1991/001, 1994/001, 1994/002, 1997/002, 1997/003
Áran (Inis Mór), Co. Galway	1992/093, 1993/112, 1994/111, 1995/117, 1995/125, 1996/158, 1996/161, 1997/214, 1997/221
Ard, Co. Galway	1986/027
Ardagh, Co. Longford	1969/015
Ardamore, Co. Kerry	1977/042
Ardaravan, Co. Donegal	1977/025
Ardcarn, Co. Roscommon	1993/192
Ardcloyne, Co. Cork	1996/036
Ardcroney, Co. Tipperary	1977/067
Ardee, Co. Louth	1993/153, 1994/181, 1996/256, 1996/257, 1997/365, 1997/366, 1997/367
Ardfert, Co. Kerry	1989/051, 1990/066, 1991/062, 1992/098, 1995/129, 1997/226
Ardmore, Co. Waterford	1996/385
Ardnafinnan, Co. Roscommon	1997/452
Ardnagross, Co. Westmeath	1995/266, 1995/267
Ardoley, Co. Mayo	1996/295
Ardra, Co. Kilkenny	1992/111
Ardrahan, Co. Galway	1969/023, 1971/018
Ardrahan South, Co. Galway	1992/084
Ardrea Lough, Co. Sligo	1993/198
Arklow, Co. Wicklow	1997/618
Armagh City, Co. Armagh	1970/004
Arran Quay, Dublin City	1990/040, 1993/050, 1995/058
Artaine South, Co. Dublin	1980/092
Arundel Square, Waterford City	1990/108, 1997/575
Ashfort, Co. Limerick	1997/324
Ashley Park, Co. Tipperary	1980/166
Askeaton, Co. Limerick	1994/155, 1996/230, 1996/231, 1997/325
Athboy, Co. Meath	1997/414, 1997/415

Ballycastle, Co. Antrim	1996/001
Ballycommane, Co. Cork	1989/009
Ballyconneely, Co. Clare	1997/Ad1
Ballyconneely, Co. Galway	1992/095
Ballyconry, Co. Clare	1985/009
Ballycoolin, Co. Dublin	1995/046
Ballycraigy, Co. Antrim	1985/001
Ballycullin, Co. Tipperary	1980/167
Ballycummin, Co. Limerick	1996/234, 1996/235
Ballydavis, Co. Laois	1995/173
Ballyduff, Co. Limerick	1977/049
Ballyea, Co. Clare	1997/016
Ballyegan, Co. Kerry	1991/065
Ballyeigh, Co. Kerry	1991/066
Ballygalley, Co. Antrim	1989/001, 1990/001, 1991/002, 1992/001, 1993/001, 1994/004, 1994/005, 1995/001, 1996/004
Ballyginny, Co. Down	1980/077
Ballyglass, Co. Mayo	1969/027, 1970/022, 1971/024, 1972/023
Ballygrennan, Co. Limerick	1986/039
Ballygroll, Co. Derry	1977/016
Ballyharry, Co. Antrim	1996/005, 1996/006
Ballyhenry, Co. Antrim	1972/001, 1972/002
Ballyhill Lower, Co. Antrim	1985/002
Ballykeane, Co. Offaly	1995/238
Ballykeel South, Co. Clare	1988/003
Ballykelly, Co. Derry	1977/017
Ballykennedy, Co. Antrim	1977/002
Ballykine Upper, Co. Mayo	1996/297
Ballyla and Clonmannon, Co. Wicklow	1987/058, 1987/Apx 3, 1989/100, 1989/Apx 4
Ballylee, Co. Galway	1991/054
Ballylessan, Co. Down	1970/013
Ballylosky, Co. Donegal	1995/043
Ballymacarret, Co. Down	1993/039
Ballymacaward, Co. Donegal	1997/059
Ballymackaldrack, Co. Antrim	1975/001
Ballymacpeake Upper, Co. Derry	1973/010
Ballymacrea, Co. Antrim	1971/001
Ballyman, Co. Dublin	1977/036, 1980/094, 1985/022, 1986/021
Ballymany, Co. Kildare	1989/054
Ballymascanlan, Co. Louth	1996/258, 1996/259
Ballymoon, Co. Carlow	1997/008
Ballymore, Co. Westmeath	1994/216
Ballymote, Co. Sligo	1980/162
Ballymount Great, Co. Dublin	1980/095, 1997/079
Ballymulholland, Co. Derry	1980/063
Ballymurphy, Co. Antrim	1977/003
Ballynageeragh, Co. Cork	1986/013
Ballynagilly, Co. Tyrone	1969/010, 1970/032
Ballynagrumoolia, Co. Cork	1993/017
Ballynahatty, Co. Down	1990/026, 1991/029, 1992/033, 1993/040, 1995/045, 1996/061, 1997/069
Ballynahownwood, Co. Westmeath	1986/066, 1992/176
Ballynakill, Co. Galway	1991/055
Ballynaraha, Co. Tipperary	1986/069
Ballynatona, Co. Limerick	1986/040
Ballynatray, Co. Waterford	1997/565
Ballynattin, Co. Wicklow	1997/609
Ballynerrin Lower, Co. Wicklow	1990/122
Ballynoe, Co. Antrim	1973/001
Ballynoe, Co. Cork	1995/023, 1996/037
Ballynora, Co. Cork	1997/030
Ballyogan, Co. Clare	1996/021, 1997/017
Ballyoskill, Co. Kilkenny	1971/022
Ballyouragan, Co. Limerick	1997/Ad5
Ballypatrick, Co. Tipperary	1995/249
Ballyrea, Co. Armagh	1991/013, 1992/004, 1993/008
Ballyremon Commons, Co. Wicklow	1980/206

Ballyrobert, Co. Cork — 1980/045
Ballysadare, Co. Sligo — 1995/244, 1996/338
Ballysaxhills, Co. Kildare — 1995/144, 1996/175
Ballyshanaghill, Co. Antrim — 1990/002, 1991/003
Ballyshannon, Co. Donegal — 1997/060, 1997/061
Ballyspurge, Co. Down — 1996/062, 1996/Apx IV, 1996/Apx V
Ballyutoag, Co. Antrim — 1980/002, 1980/003, 1996/008
Ballyvanran, Co. Tipperary — 1990/100, 1991/115
Ballyvaston, Co. Antrim — 1986/001
Ballyveelish, Co. Tipperary — 1980/168
Ballyveelish, Co. Waterford — 1986/Apx 1.3
Ballyvelly, Co. Kerry — 1997/229
Ballyvollen, Co. Antrim — 1980/004
Ballywee, Co. Antrim — 1974/002, 1980/005, 1993/002, 1994/006
Balrenny, Co. Meath — 1977/055
Balrothery, Co. Dublin — 1994/043, 1997/081
Balscaddin Newtown, Co. Dublin — 1997/082
Balwinstown, Co. Wexford — 1996/399
Banagher, Co. Offaly — 1992/156, 1994/195, 1997/441, 1997/444
Banagher/Kylebeg, Co. Offaly — 1990/098
Bandon, Co. Cork — 1997/031
Baneshane, Co. Cork — 1995/024
Bannagher, Co. Offaly — 1997/450
Barnahely, Co. Cork — 1996/038
Barnakyle, Co. Limerick — 1986/Apx 1.2, 1996/237, 1997/332, 1997/333
Barnhall, Co. Kildare — 1997/258
Barntrick, Co. Clare — 1995/013
Barrack Lane (The Barracks), Galway City — 1996/150
Barrack Lane, Galway City — 1989/047
Barrack Street/French's Quay, Cork City — 1989/014
Barrow River, Co. Kilkenny — 1997/312
Barrowstrand Street, Waterford City — 1992/173
Baunmore, Co. Limerick — 1995/178
Baunogenasraid, Co. Antrim — 1972/005
Bay, Co. Antrim — 1977/004, 1980/006
Beagh, Co. Derry — 1995/041
Beagh, Co. Galway — 1991/057
Beaghmore, Co. Tyrone — 1977/070
Beamore, Co. Meath — 1997/417
Beau Street, Waterford City — 1993/213
Beaufort, Co. Kerry — 1995/131
Beaumont, Co. Dublin — 1997/083
Beauparc, Co. Meath — 1996/304
Behy and Carronaglogh, Co. Mayo — 1969/019
Behy, Co. Mayo — 1969/018
Behy/Glenurla, Co. Mayo — 1970/024, 1971/025, 1989/071, 1990/088, 1991/098, 1992/145, 1993/176

Belcoo, Co. Fermanagh — 1997/189
Belderg Beg, Co. Mayo — 1971/026, 1972/024, 1973/026, 1974/031, 1975/028, 1976/025
Belfast, Co. Antrim — 1980/007, 1980/008, 1990/003, 1990/004, 1997/004
Belladrihid, Co. Sligo — 1995/245, 1997/462
Bellaghy, Co. Derry — 1989/015, 1990/024, 1995/042
Bellaghy, Co. Sligo — 1997/463
Belturbet, Co. Cavan — 1995/012
Benburb Street, Collins Barracks, Dublin City — 1994/055
Bere Island, Co. Cork — 1995/022
Beresfort Lane, Fyffe's Yard, Dublin City — 1994/056
Beresfort Street/Cuckoo Lane, Dublin City — 1996/073
Betaghstown, Co. Meath — 1977/056, 1977/057
Big Glebe, Co. Derry — 1976/012
Birr, Co. Offaly — 1991/109, 1997/445
Bishop Street Within, Derry City — 1988/042
Bishop Street, Dublin City — 1995/061
Bishop Street, Old Jacob's Factory, Dublin City — 1991/032
Bishopscourt, Co. Down — 1973/015
Bishopslane, Co. Kildare — 1997/261, 1997/262
Black Abbey, Kilkenny City — 1977/048, 1997/294

Blackfriary, Co. Meath	1988/049
Blackhall Place/Arbour Hill, Dublin City	1997/106
Blackhall, Co. Kildare	1994/132
Blackhills Lower, Co. Cavan	1992/007
Blackmore Lane/Meade Street, Cork City	1993/021
Blackpool, Co. Cork	1992/017
Blanchardstown, Co. Dublin	1994/044
Blessington, Co. Wicklow	1996/408, 1996/409, 1996/410
Bobsville, Co. Meath	1990/091
Boheh, Co. Mayo	1993/172
Boherard, Co. Meath	1993/179
Boherygeela, Co. Limerick	1986/041
Bohullion Upper, Co. Donegal	1985/018
Boleyboy, Co. Mayo	1994/185
Bollingbrook Fort, Galway City	1991/058
Boofeenaun, Co. Mayo	1992/141
Boolies Lower, Co. Meath	1980/147
Boora, Co. Offaly	1977/062
Booterstown, Co. Dublin	1990/032
Bord na Móna bogs, cos Offaly/Westmeath/Mayo	1997/Apx III
Bow Lane East, Dublin City	1995/062
Bow Lane West, Dublin City	1994/057
Bow Lane West/Kennedy's Villas, Dublin City	1992/047
Bowling Green, Co. Tipperary	1970/028
Boyle, Co. Roscommon	1980/158, 1989/083, 1993/196
Boytonrath, Co. Tipperary	1994/209
Brackfield, Co. Derry	1980/064
Brackloon, Co. Kerry	1991/067
Bray, Co. Wicklow	1995/289
Breagh, Co. Armagh	1991/014
Bredagh, Co. Galway	1995/112
Breeoge, Co. Sligo	1973/041
Bremore, Co. Dublin	1995/047
Brewel West, Co. Kildare	1993/127, 1994/133
Bride Street, Dublin City	1993/055, 1993/056
Bride Street/Golden Lane, Dublin City	1992/048
Bridge Street, Dublin City	1980/097, 1990/049
Bridge Street Lower, Dublin City	1989/030, 1989/031
Bridge Street Upper, Dublin City	1992/049, 1992/050
Bridgetown, Co. Cork	1992/018
Britonstown, Co. Wicklow	1980/207
Broad Street, Custom House, Limerick City	1987/031
Broad Street/Curry Lane, Limerick City	1989/063
Brockagh, Co. Wicklow	1972/033
Broomfield, Co. Dublin	1985/023
Brownsbarn, Co. Dublin	1992/039
Brownstown, Co. Kildare	1997/263
Brunswick Street, Dublin City	1996/074
Brunswick Street/Church Street, Dublin City	1996/075
Brunswick Street North (Richmond Hospital), Dublin City	1994/079
Brunswick Street North/Red Cow Lane, Dublin City	1996/076
Bunratty, Co. Clare	1996/022
Bunratty East, Co. Clare	1989/007, 1991/019, 1992/009
Bunratty West, Co. Clare	1990/010
Burnellstown, Co. Westmeath	1988/064
Buttevant, Co. Cork	1997/033
Cabinteely, Co. Dublin	1993/044, 1995/103
Caherabbey Lower, Co. Tipperary	1988/058
Caherguillamore, Co. Limerick	1995/179, 1996/238
Caherlehillan, Co. Kerry	1993/118, 1994/118, 1995/133, 1996/165, 1997/232
Caherquin, Co. Kerry	1996/166, 1997/233
Caherwalter, Co. Galway	1995/113
Cahir, Co. Tipperary	1972/029, 1994/210, 1996/351, 1996/352, 1997/485, 1997/486
Camden Street/Charlotte Street— The Bleeding Horse, Dublin City	1996/077
Camden Street Upper, Dublin City	1997/107

Clonickilvant, Co. Westmeath	1980/198
Clonkeen, Co. Mayo	1997/403
Clonlyon Glebe, Co. Offaly	1993/185
Clonmacnoise, Co. Offaly	1977/063, 1985/045, 1989/078, 1990/096, 1990/097, 1991/110, 1992/157, 1992/158, 1993/186, 1993/187, 1993/188, 1993/189, 1994/196, 1994/197, 1994/198, 1995/239, 1995/240, 1996/324, 1997/447, 1997/448
Clonmel, Co. Tipperary	1990/101, 1991/116, 1992/166, 1992/167, 1992/168, 1992/169, 1993/205, 1993/206, 1993/207, 1993/208, 1993/209, 1993/210, 1993/211, 1993/212, 1995/252, 1995/253, 1995/254, 1995/255, 1995/256, 1995/257, 1996/357, 1996/358, 1996/359, 1996/360, 1996/361, 1996/362, 1996/363, 1997/489, 1997/490, 1997/491, 1997/492
Clonmore, Co. Armagh	1991/015
Clonshaugh, Co. Dublin	1991/031
Clontarf, Co. Dublin	1994/048, 1996/069, 1997/089
Clooneen, Co. Mayo	1995/223
Cloonelt, Co. Roscommon	1980/159
Cloonlara, Co. Mayo	1992/143
Cloonlaur, Co. Mayo	1997/404
Cloonshanville, Co. Roscommon	1996/329
Clorhane, Co. Offaly	1992/159
Cloughballybeg, Co. Cavan	1992/008
Cloughergoole, Co. Cavan	1997/013
Cloughlucas South, Co. Cork	1986/014
Cloughorr, Co. Antrim	1971/003
Cloughskelt, Co. Down	1973/016
Coad, Co. Clare	1996/023
Coarhamore, Co. Kerry	1988/028
Coastal sites, cos Cork/Kerry	1986/Apx 2
Cobh, Co. Cork	1996/040
Codrum Rural, Co. Cork	1997/035
Coffee House Lane, Waterford City	1993/214, 1993/215
Coleraine, Co. Derry	1977/018, 1980/065, 1980/066, 1993/036, 1997/056
College Park, Kilkenny City	1991/079
College Street, Dublin City	1997/117
Collier's Lane, Kilkenny City	1996/205, 1997/295
Collins Barracks, Dublin City	1993/077
Collinstown, Co. Kildare	1994/134, 1996/182
Collon, Co. Louth	1994/168, 1995/192
Collooney, Co. Sligo	1994/204
Colp West, Co. Meath	1988/051
Commons, Co. Louth	1995/193, 1996/265
Conduit Lane/Cathedral Lane, Waterford City	1997/577
Connigar, Co. Limerick	1997/334
Connor, Co. Antrim	1986/002
Conva, Co. Cork	1992/021
Convent Street, Limerick City	1994/159
Conwal, Co. Donegal	1997/064
Cook Street, Dublin City	1992/054, 1993/063, 1997/118
Coolaholloga, Co. Tipperary	1997/493
Coolalough, Co. Limerick	1994/157
Coolavally, Co. Mayo	1996/299
Coolbanagher, Co. Laois	1993/138, 1994/142, 1996/221, 1996/222
Coolboy, Co. Wicklow	1997/610
Coolcran, Co. Fermanagh	1980/106
Cooldrinagh, Co. Dublin	1995/052
Cooleeney/Derryfadda, Co. Tipperary	1996/364
Coolmine, Co. Dublin	1989/022
Coolnaboy, Co. Wexford	1988/066
Coolnatullagh, Co. Clare	1997/018
Coolock, Co. Dublin	1990/033, 1994/049
Coolowen, Co. Cork	1973/007
Cooltona, Co. Roscommon	1997/453
Coomacullen, Co. Kerry	1997/235
Coomatloukane, Co. Kerry	1969/020
Coombe Relief Road, Dublin City	1993/064

Dawson's Demesne, Co. Louth	1992/135, 1992/136
Dean Street, Kilkenny City	1990/073, 1990/074
Dean Street/Patrick Street, Dublin City	1992/056
Deanery Garden, Waterford City	1985/056
Deechomade, Co. Sligo	1992/163, 1993/200
Deer Park Farms, Co. Antrim	1980/016, 1985/005, 1986/003, 1987/001
Deer Park, Co. Kerry	1994/120
Deerfin Lower, Co. Antrim	1975/004
Delgany, Co. Wicklow	1991/134
Derry City, Co. Derry	1976/014, 1977/020
Derry Walls, Derry City	1980/068
Derry, Co. Laois	1995/174
Derrybrusk, Co. Fermanagh	1994/104
Derryharney, Co. Fermanagh	1993/104
Derryhowlaght East, Co. Fermanagh	1993/105
Derryknockane, Co. Limerick	1996/240
Derryloran, Co. Tyrone	1980/184
Derryloughan, Co. Tyrone	1995/262
Derrynaflan, Co. Tipperary	1980/172, 1985/053, 1986/070, 1987/044, 1987/045
Derrynane More, Co. Kerry	1985/032
Derryville/Derryfadda, Co. Tipperary	1996/365
Derryvullen, Co. Fermanagh	1994/105, 1994/106
Digges' Lane, Dublin City	1996/085
Digges' Lane, Mercer's Hospital, Dublin City	1992/057, 1992/058, 1994/060
Dingle, Co. Kerry	1992/101, 1992/102, 1993/121, 1994/121, 1994/122, 1995/134, 1995/135, 1997/238, 1997/239, 1997/240, 1997/241
Dominic Street Upper, Galway City	1996/151
Donabate, Co. Dublin	1992/082, 1993/103
Donaghmore, Co. Meath	1990/090, 1994/189
Donard, Co. Wicklow	1997/611
Donegal Town, Co. Donegal	1997/065
Donegore Hill, Co. Antrim	1980/018, 1985/006
Donnybrook, Co. Dublin	1995/055, 1995/056
Donore, Co. Meath	1990/092
Dooey, Co. Antrim	1988/001
Doon, Co. Fermanagh	1994/107
Doon Glebe, Co. Donegal	1997/Ad3
Doonaveeragh, Co. Sligo	1997/465
Doonbought, Co. Antrim	1969/003
Doonlaughan, Co. Galway	1997/197
Doonmoon, Co. Limerick	1986/043
Dooradoyle, Co. Limerick	1996/241, 1997/338, 1997/339
Doras, Co. Tyrone	1980/185, 1986/071, 1995/263
Dorsey, Co. Armagh	1977/012, 1989/004
Double Tower, Waterford City	1990/111
Dough, Co. Clare	1996/024
Doughiska, Co. Galway	1994/110, 1995/116
Douglas Street, Cork City	1993/022
Downpatrick, Co. Down	1974/013, 1980/079, 1985/020, 1986/019, 1986/020, 1987/012, 1988/012, 1992/034, 1994/040, 1996/063, 1997/070, 1997/071, 1997/072
Dowth, Co. Meath	1989/073, 1995/229
Drimnagh, Co. Dublin	1992/038, 1993/048, 1993/049, 1994/050
Drogheda, Co. Louth	1976/024, 1980/134, 1980/135, 1985/039, 1988/046, 1989/070, 1991/095, 1992/137, 1993/155, 1993/156, 1993/157, 1993/158, 1993/159, 1993/160, 1993/161, 1994/171, 1994/172, 1994/173, 1994/174, 1994/175, 1995/194, 1995/195, 1995/196, 1995/197, 1995/198, 1995/199, 1995/200, 1995/201, 1996/266, 1996/267, 1996/268, 1996/269, 1996/270, 1996/271, 1996/272, 1996/273, 1996/274, 1996/275, 1996/276, 1996/277, 1996/278, 1996/279, 1997/372, 1997/373, 1997/374, 1997/375, 1997/376, 1997/377, 1997/378, 1997/379, 1997/380, 1997/381, 1997/382, 1997/383, 1997/384, 1997/385, 1997/386, 1997/387
Dromiskin, Co. Louth	1988/045, 1996/280
Dromkeen East, Co. Kerry	1973/019, 1985/033
Dromnea, Co. Cork	1980/055
Dromoland, Co. Clare	1995/014

Dromore, Co. Tyrone	1991/121
Dromteewakeen, Co. Kerry	1989/052
Dromthacker, Co. Kerry	1997/242
Drumaheglish, Co. Antrim	1989/002
Drumbaragh, Co. Meath	1988/052
Drumbroneth, Co. Down	1977/029, 1997/073
Drumcliffe South, Co. Sligo	1985/048, 1986/068
Drumcondra, Co. Dublin	1997/099
Drumcullaun, Co. Clare	1997/020
Drumgill Lower, Co. Meath	1991/100
Drumlane, Co. Cavan	1990/008
Drumlease, Co. Leitrim	1994/146, 1996/227, 1997/318
Drumlummin, Co. Tipperary	1980/173
Drummans, Co. Dublin	1997/100
Drummin, Co. Tipperary	1997/494
Drumnakeel, Co. Antrim	1980/019
Drumsna, Co. Leitrim	1994/147, 1994/148
Drury Street, Dublin City	1996/086
Dublin Castle Clock Tower, Dublin City	1991/035
Dublin Castle, Dublin City	1985/024
Dublin Castle, Dublin City	1986/025
Dublin Castle, Dublin City	1994/061
Dublin/Dundalk, Cos Dublin/Louth	1988/902
Dulane, Co. Meath	1996/305
Duleek, Co. Meath	1980/148, 1993/180, 1996/306 1997/420, 1997/421
Dún Áillinne, Co. Kildare	1969/013, 1970/020, 1971/019, 1972/019, 1973/021, 1974/019
Dunamase, Co. Laois	1993/142, 1994/144, 1995/176, 1996/223, 1997/315
Dunamon, Co. Roscommon	1996/328
Dunbell Big, Co. Kilkenny	1990/072
Dunbell, Co. Kilkenny	1972/020
Dunboy, Co. Cork	1969/021, 1970/007, 1972/008, 1973/008, 1989/012
Duncannon, Co. Wexford	1993/222, 1997/594
Dundalk, Co. Louth	1977/052, 1980/136, 1980/137, 1980/138, 1985/040, 1990/086, 1991/094, 1991/096, 1992/139, 1993/162, 1993/163, 1993/164, 1993/165, 1993/167, 1993/168, 1994/169, 1994/170, 1994/176, 1994/177, 1994/178, 1994/179, 1994/180, 1995/187, 1995/203, 1995/204, 1995/205, 1995/206, 1995/207, 1995/208, 1995/209, 1995/210, 1995/211, 1995/212, 1995/213, 1995/214, 1995/215, 1995/216, 1995/217, 1996/281, 1996/282, 1996/283, 1996/284, 1996/285, 1996/286, 1996/287, 1996/288, 1996/289, 1996/290, 1997/370, 1997/388, 1997/389, 1997/390, 1997/391, 1997/392, 1997/393, 1997/394
Dundrum Sandhills, Co. Down	1977/030
Dundrum, Co. Dublin	1987/015, 1988/015, 1989/023, 1990/034, 1991/045, 1997/174, 1997/175
Dunfanaghy, Co. Donegal	1994/039
Dungarvan, Co. Waterford	1989/095, 1995/265, 1996/386, 1996/387, 1996/388, 1997/566, 1997/567, 1997/568, 1997/569, 1997/570, 1997/571, 1997/572, 1997/573
Dungiven, Co. Derry	1970/011, 1975/011, 1975/012, 1980/069
Dunleer, Co. Louth	1997/395
Dunloy, Co. Antrim	1991/006
Dunluce, Co. Antrim	1987/002
Dunmahon, Co. Louth	1995/218
Dunmisk, Co. Tyrone	1980/186, 1986/072, 1987/048
Dunshaughlin, Co. Meath	1991/101, 1995/230
Dunsilly, Co. Antrim	1974/004, 1975/005
Dunsink, Co. Dublin	1991/046, 1991/047, 1994/090
Dunsoughly, Co. Dublin	1994/091
Duntryleague, Co. Limerick	1986/044, 1986/045, 1986/046, 1986/047, 1986/048
Durrow Demesne, Co. Offaly	1985/046
Dysart, Co. Kilkenny	1989/061, 1991/078
Dysert, Co. Clare	1995/015, 1996/025
Dysert, Co. Roscommon	1993/193
Earl Street South, Dublin City	1995/070, 1997/164, 1997/165
Earl Street South (Meath Market), Dublin City	1997/166

Earl Street South—St Thomas' Abbey, Dublin City	1995/069
East Arran Street, Dublin City	1994/062
Eastmoreland Place—Hibernian Hotel, Dublin City	1995/071
Echlin Street, Dublin City	1993/066
Eglinton Street, Galway City	1990/060
Elton, Co. Limerick	1986/049
Emain Macha, Co. Armagh	1969/006, 1970/005
Emlagh West, Co. Kerry	1993/122, 1997/243
English Street, Armagh City	1989/003, 1990/006, 1991/012, 1992/003
Ennis, Co. Clare	1991/020, 1991/021, 1992/012, 1993/010, 1994/015, 1994/016, 1995/016, 1995/017, 1995/018, 1996/026, 1996/027, 1996/028, 1997/021, 1997/022, 1997/023, 1997/024, 1997/025, 1997/026, 1997/Ad2
Enniscorthy, Co. Wexford	1993/223, 1993/226, 1994/221, 1995/274, 1996/400, 1997/595, 1997/596, 1997/597, 1997/598, 1997/599, 1997/600
Enniskillen, Co. Fermanagh	1987/017, 1990/053, 1994/108, 1994/109, 1997/190
Erris, Co. Mayo	1997/405
Erris, Co. Roscommon	1989/081, 1989/082, 1993/194, 1993/195, 1996/330
Eskragh, Co. Tyrone	1973/034
Essex Gate/Exchange Street Upper, Dublin City	1996/087
Essex Street East, Dublin City	1997/122, 1997/123
Essex Street East (Poddle Culvert), Dublin City	1992/059
Essex Street East/Wellington Quay, Dublin City	1993/067
Essex Street West, Dublin City	1990/046, 1994/063, 1997/124
Essex Street West, SS Michael and John's, Dublin City	1992/060
Eustace Street, Dublin City	1992/061, 1992/062, 1993/069, 1994/064, 1997/125
Eustace Street/Dame Street, Dublin City	1993/068
Evans' Lane, Kilkenny City	1996/206
Evergreen Road Bacon Factory, Cork City	1993/023
Exchange Street Lower, Dublin City	1990/047, 1997/126
Exchange Street Lower—Isolde's Tower, Dublin City	1993/070
Exchange Street Upper, Dublin City	1997/127
Exchange Street, Limerick City	1996/244
Eyre Street, Galway City	1995/120, 1996/152
Fahan, Co. Kerry	1977/043
Fahan Street, Derry City	1997/057
Faithlegg, Co. Waterford	1997/574
Fanningstown, Co. Limerick	1997/340, 1997/341, 1997/342, 1997/343
Farranyharpy, Co. Sligo	1996/340, 1997/466
Farrest, Co. Tyrone	1980/188
Feegarran, Co. Tyrone	1970/033
Ferganstown, Co. Meath	1976/028, 1991/102
Ferns, Co. Wexford	1972/032, 1973/038, 1974/040, 1993/224, 1995/273
Ferns Upper, Co. Wexford	1996/401
Ferriter's Cove, Co. Kerry	1985/031, 1986/030, 1987/023, 1992/100, 1993/116, 1995/130
Ferritersquarter, Co. Kerry	1991/068
Ferrycarrig, Co. Wexford	1980/202, 1986/079, 1987/056
Fethard, Co. Tipperary	1991/118, 1994/212, 1995/258, 1997/495
Fethard, Co. Wexford	1991/132, 1993/Apx II, 1996/402
Finglas, Co. Dublin	1992/079, 1992/080, 1993/095, 1994/092, 1994/093, 1995/096, 1995/097, 1995/098, 1996/119, 1996/120, 1996/121, 1997/176, 1997/177
Finglas East, Co. Dublin	1996/122
Finglas West, Co. Dublin	1991/48
Finkiltagh, Co. Antrim	1973/003
Firville West, Co. Cork	1996/049
Fish Lane/Sir Harry's Mall, Limerick City	1997/351
Fishamble Street, Dublin City	1976/019, 1994/066, 1995/072, 1996/088
Fishamble Street (Kinlay House), Dublin City	1994/065
Fishamble Street/Essex Street West, Dublin City	1996/089
Fishamble Street/John's Lane, Dublin City	1977/037
Flood Street/New Dock Street, Galway City	1992/085
Fore, Co. Westmeath	1988/065, 1992/177
Forenaghts Great, Co. Kildare	1980/119, 1997/270
Forthill, Co. Antrim	1993/006, 1994/007
Fourknocks, Co. Meath	1980/149

Fownes Street Lower, Dublin City	1992/063
Fownes Street Upper, Dublin City	1992/064, 1997/128
Fownes Street Upper/Temple Bar, Dublin City	1996/090
Francis Street (Franciscan Priory), Galway City	1997/201
Francis Street, Dublin City	1991/036, 1992/065, 1994/067, 1994/068, 1994/069, 1994/070, 1995/073, 1995/074, 1996/091, 1996/092, 1996/093, 1997/130, 1997/131
Francis Street (the Iveagh Markets), Dublin City	1997/129
Francis Street/Hanover Lane, Dublin City	1992/066
Francis Street/Swift's Alley, Dublin City	1997/132
Frankfort, Co. Offaly	1993/190
Friary Street, Kilkenny City	1997/297
Friary Street/Garden Row, Kilkenny City	1997/296
Fyffe's Yard/Georges Hill, Dublin City	1995/075
Galboly Lower, Co. Antrim	1986/004
Gallanstown, Co. Dublin	1997/178
Gallarus, Co. Kerry	1970/019, 1977/044
Gallows Hill, Co. Kilkenny	1975/023
Gallstown, Co. Louth	1995/219
Galtrimsland, Co. Louth	1996/291
Garden Row, Kilkenny City	1997/298
Gardiner Street/Beresford Street, Dublin City	1996/094
Gardiner Street Middle, Dublin City	1997/148
Gardiner Street Lower, Dublin City	1997/145
Garranes, Co. Cork	1990/015, 1991/022
Garrans, Co. Laois	1993/139
Garristown, Co. Dublin	1990/035
Garryduff, Co. Galway	1997/196, 1988/025
Garryntemple, Co. Tipperary	1980/174
Gibstown, Co. Louth	1993/166
Gill Abbey (St Mary's of the Isle), Cork City	1993/030
Gill Abbey, Craig More, Connaught Avenue, Cork City	1995/025
Glanbannoo Lower, Co. Cork	1996/050
Glanworth, Co. Cork	1980/057
Glasnevin, Co. Dublin	1989/024, 1990/036, 1996/123, 1996/124
Glassamucky, Co. Dublin	1977/038
Glassnamullen, Co. Wicklow	1980/209
Glebe, Co. Antrim	1997/005
Glebe, Co. Derry	1996/Apx III
Glebe, Co. Louth	1992/138
Glebe, Co. Roscommon	1995/243, 1997/454
Glebe, Co. Westmeath	1997/585
Glebestown, Co. Meath	1993/181
Glen, Co. Sligo	1985/049, 1985/050
Glen Fahan, Co. Kerry	1989/053
Glenballythomas, Co. Roscommon	1980/160, 1996/331
Glenbane, Co. Tipperary	1985/052
Glenbaun, Co. Mayo	1992/144, 1993/175
Glendalough, Co. Wicklow	1977/075, 1989/101, 1990/123, 1996/411
Glendhu, Co. Down	1977/031
Glengesh, Co. Fermanagh	1980/107
Glengormley, Co. Antrim	1986/005
Gleninagh Heights (St James' Church), Galway City	1993/108
Glenmakeeran, Co. Antrim	1980/021
Glennameade, Co. Limerick	1992/125
Glin North, Co. Kerry	1993/123
Glynn, Co. Antrim	1971/004
Golden, Co. Tipperary	1997/496
Golden Lane/Ship Street, Dublin City	1996/095
Goles, Co. Tyrone	1994/214
Gorey, Co. Wexford	1989/099, 1995/275, 1996/403
Gormanstown, Co. Meath	1996/307, 1997/422
Gort, Co. Galway	1997/209
Gortalough, Co. Sligo	1997/467
Gortatray, Co. Tyrone	1986/073
Gorteen, Co. Limerick	1997/344

Inis Cealtra, Co. Clare	1970/006, 1971/010, 1972/006, 1973/006, 1974/009, 1975/009
Inishmurray, Co. Sligo	1997/468
Inns Quay Ward, Dublin City	1985/025
Iorras Beag Thiar, Co. Galway	1991/056, 1995/118
Irishtown, Co. Wicklow	1994/231
Irishtown/The Linear Park, Limerick City	1988/038
Island Magee, Co. Antrim	1995/006, 1996/002, 1996/003, 1996/007, 1997/001
Island Road, Limerick City	1995/181
Islandbridge, Co. Dublin	1989/026, 1994/072, 1996/125, 1996/126, 1996/127
James' Street—St Patrick's Hospital, Dublin City	1992/069
James' Street, Presentation Convent and Old Brewery, Kilkenny City	1992/114
James' Street, Dublin City	1997/136
James' Street/Bow Lane West, Dublin City	1996/098, 1997/135
James' Street, Kilkenny City	1989/062, 1991/080
James' Street, Limerick City	1997/352
Jamestown, Co. Leitrim	1996/228, 1997/319
Jenkins Lane—Beach Tower, Waterford City	1996/390
Jerpoint Church, Co. Kilkenny	1973/022
Jerpoint West, Co. Kilkenny	1971/023
Jervis Street/Wolfe Tone Street/Parnell Street, Dublin City	1994/074
Jervis Street (Hospital Site), Dublin City	1994/073
Jigginstown, Co. Kildare	1996/183
John Street, Kilkenny City	1994/139, 1996/210
John Street, Bridge House, Kilkenny City	1995/169
John Street, Smithwicks Brewery, Kilkenny City	1996/209
John Street, Waterford City	1996/391
John Street/Waterside, Waterford City	1994/215
John Street West, Dublin City	1997/137
John's Street, Limerick City	1990/080
John's Street, Custom House, Limerick City	1987/032, 1988/037
Johnstown North, Co. Wicklow	1997/613, 1997/614, 1997/615
Johnstown South, Co. Wicklow	1996/412
Jordanstown, Co. Antrim	1995/007
Keeldrum Lower, Co. Donegal	1976/017
Kells, Co. Kilkenny	1972/021, 1973/023, 1974/023, 1975/024, 1980/126, 1995/165, 1996/217
Kells, Co. Meath	1987/041, 1988/057, 1996/308, 1997/423
Kellsborough, Co. Kilkenny	1997/290
Kellysgrove, Co. Galway	1991/059
Keoltown, Co. Westmeath	1976/031
Kevin Street Lower, Dublin City	1996/099, 1997/138
Keyser Street/High Street, Waterford City	1992/174
Kilbeg Lower, Co. Galway	1990/057
Kilbeggan, Co. Westmeath	1992/178
Kilbree Lower, Co. Mayo	1997/406
Kilbride, Co. Wicklow	1997/616
Kilcairn, Co. Meath	1997/424
Kilcash, Co. Tipperary	1980/175
Kilcloony, Co. Galway	1997/211
Kilcoan More, Co. Antrim	1986/006, 1996/010
Kilcolgan, Co. Galway	1989/044, 1997/212, 1997/213
Kilcolman Middle, Co. Cork	1994/029, 1995/030, 1996/051
Kilcomin, Co. Offaly	1996/325
Kilcor South, Co. Cork	1980/058
Kilcullen, Co. Kildare	1988/Apx 3
Kilcummer Lower, Co. Cork	1990/016
Kildanoge, Co. Tipperary	1997/498
Kildare Town, Co. Kildare	1989/057, 1991/073, 1992/109, 1993/130, 1993/131, 1993/132
Kildorragh, Co. Leitrim	1994/149
Kilferagh, Co. Kilkenny	1980/127
Kilferagh/Sheastown, Co. Kilkenny	1980/129
Kilgowan, Co. Kildare	1987/027
Kilgraney, Co. Carlow	1986/010
Kilkea, Co. Kildare	1993/133, 1995/151, 1997/271

Kilkeeran, Co. Mayo	1997/407
Kilkenny Castle, Kilkenny City	1975/025, 1991/081, 1992/115
Kilkenny Castle (The Parade), Kilkenny City	1997/304
Kilkenny City Main Drainage, Kilkenny City	1997/291
Kilkenny West, Co. Westmeath	1996/393
Kilkreest, Co. Galway	1996/148
Kill, Co. Kerry	1988/029
Kill, Co. Kildare	1993/134, 1996/184
Killacolla, Co. Limerick	1989/068, 1991/088
Killadeas Graveyard, Co. Fermanagh	1987/018
Killaghy, Co. Down	1997/075
Killaloe, Co. Clare	1996/029
Killanully, Co. Cork	1992/028, 1994/028, 1995/031
Killaraght, Co. Sligo	1994/205
Killarecastle, Co. Westmeath	1980/200
Killavillig, Co. Cork	1991/023, 1992/029
Killbeg Upper, Co. Meath	1991/103
Killeague, Co. Derry	1977/019
Killeaney, Co. Galway	1985/030
Killeely Beg, Co. Galway	1989/045
Killeen, Co. Meath	1996/309
Killeen Cormac, Co. Kildare	1980/121
Killeenagh Mountain, Co. Waterford	1974/038
Killegar, Co. Wicklow	1991/135
Killeigh, Co. Offaly	1991/111, 1995/241, 1995/242, 1997/451
Killelton, Co. Kerry	1987/024, 1988/030
Killhill, Co. Kildare	1997/272
Killinane, Co. Carlow	1980/041
Killiney, Co. Dublin	1995/099
Kill-Saint-Ann South, Co. Cork	1997/042
Killucan/Corbetstown, Co. Westmeath	1973/036, 1975/036, 1980/199
Killuney, Co. Armagh	1994/011
Killuragh, Co. Limerick	1993/145, 1996/242, 1997/Apx II
Killurly West, Co. Kerry	1994/125
Killycluggin, Co. Cavan	1974/008
Killygarn, Co. Armagh	1996/016
Killygreagh, Co. Fermanagh	1980/108
Killylane, Co. Antrim	1980/023
Killymoon Demesne, Co. Tyrone	1995/264
Killynure, Co. Fermanagh	1996/146
Kilmainham, Co. Dublin	1976/021, 1996/128
Kilmallock, Co. Limerick	1997/345, 1997/346, 1997/347
Kilmeague, Co. Kildare	1995/152
Kilmore, Co. Cork	1997/043
Kilmore, Co. Kerry	1992/104
Kilmore, Co. Leitrim	1972/022, 1973/024, 1974/024
Kilnacarrig, Co. Wicklow	1993/230, 1994/230
Kilnagrange, Co. Waterford	1977/074
Kilpeddar, Co. Wicklow	1995/290
Kilquane, Co. Cork	1994/030
Kilshane, Co. Dublin	1988/018
Kilsmullan, Co. Fermanagh	1977/040, 1980/109
Kiltalown, Co. Dublin	1997/179
Kilteel, Co. Kildare	1977/045
Kiltierney, Co. Fermanagh	1969/002, 1975/018, 1975/019, 1975/020, 1980/110
Kiltimagh, Co. Mayo	1997/408
Kiltullagh, Co. Roscommon	1994/201, 1996/333
Kiltycarney, Co. Leitrim	1994/150
Kimego West, Co. Kerry	1986/031, 1990/067, 1991/70
Kindlestown Upper, Co. Wicklow	1991/136
King John's Castle, Limerick City	1976/023, 1990/084, 1993/146, 1994/160, 1995/182, 1996/245,
King's Island, Limerick City	1989/067, 1990/081
King's Island—St Francis' Abbey, Limerick City	1996/246
King's Island—St John's Hospital, Limerick City	1992/126
Kinkit, Co. Tyrone	1973/035
Kinnagoe Bay, Co. Donegal	1974/012, 1975/014
Kinnegad, Co. Westmeath	1994/217

Kinsale, Co. Cork	1993/033, 1994/031, 1994/032, 1995/032, 1995/033, 1995/034, 1996/052, 1996/053
Kirkistown, Co. Down	1980/085
Kirwan's Lane, Galway City	1993/109, 1995/121, 1996/153, 1997/202
Kirwan's Lane/Cross Street Upper, Galway City	1992/086
Knappaghmore, Co. Mayo	1997/409
Knockacarrigeen, Co. Galway	1995/114
Knockacullen, Co. Cork	1997/044
Knockagarrane East, Co. Cork	1997/045
Knockalton, Co. Tipperary	1997/547
Knockalton Upper, Co. Tipperary	1996/367
Knockanean, Co. Clare	1996/030
Knockawillin, Co. Cork	1991/024
Knockbounce, Co. Kildare	1988/035
Knockbrack, Co. Mayo	1996/302
Knockbrack, Co. Wexford	1995/276
Knockdomney, Co. Westmeath	1997/586
Knockercreeveen, Co. Kerry	1994/126
Knockgraffon, Co. Tipperary	1995/259
Knockharley, Co. Meath	1997/425
Knocklore, Co. Louth	1996/292
Knockmant, Co. Westmeath	1976/032
Knocknacarragh, Co. Galway	1996/159
Knocknacarragh Cross, Co. Galway	1994/112
Knocknacarragh/Rahoon, Co. Galway	1997/215
Knocknalappa, Co. Clare	1994/018, 1996/031
Knocknarea, Co. Sligo	1992/Apx 4, 1996/Apx XII
Knocknashammer, Co. Sligo	1977/066
Knockoneill, Co. Derry	1980/070
Knockroe, Co. Kilkenny	1990/076, 1991/084, 1994/140, 1995/172
Knockroe, Co. Tipperary	1995/260
Knockroe, Co. Tyrone	1987/049
Knockyclovaun, Co. Clare	1996/032
Knowth, Co. Meath	1969/012, 1970/025, 1971/028, 1972/026, 1973/028, 1974/032, 1975/030, 1976/029, 1977/058, 1985/043, 1986/064, 1987/040, 1988/053, 1989/074, 1990/093, 1991/104, 1992/151, 1993/182, 1994/191, 1995/231, 1996/310, 1996/311, 1997/426
Knoxspark, Co. Sligo	1994/206, 1997/469
Kyrl's Quay/North Main Street, Cork City	1992/023
Labbamolaga Middle, Co. Cork	1995/035
Lackagh and Drumcleavry, Co. Roscommon	1990/099
Lackagh More, Co. Kildare	1996/185
Lackan, Co. Galway	1996/160
Lackan, Co. Sligo	1991/113
Lackenavorna, Co. Tipperary	1977/068
Lady Lane, Waterford City	1980/196, 1993/218
Lady Lane/Bakehouse Lane, Waterford City	1987/053, 1988/063
Lahard, Co. Kerry	1994/127
Lahesseragh, Co. Tipperary	1996/368
Lambay Island, Co. Dublin	1991/049, 1993/096, 1994/095, 1995/100, 1995/101, 1996/129, 1997/180
Lambeg, Co. Antrim	1980/024
Laraghbryan East, Co. Kildare	1997/273
Larne, Co. Antrim	1995/008
Latoon South, Co. Clare	1996/033
Laughanstown, Co. Dublin	1980/101
Leabeg/Castlearmstrong, Co. Offaly	1996/326
Leamnaguila, Co. Kerry	1995/138
Leap, Co. Cork	1997/032
Lecarrow, Co. Sligo	1989/086
Leckaneen, Co. Cork	1990/017
Legarhill, Co. Armagh	1980/040, 1989/005
Leherfineen, Co. Cork	1996/054
Lehinch, Co. Offaly	1977/064
Leigh, Co. Tipperary	1969/022, 1970/030
Leitrim Street, Cork City	1980/059

Lisheen Project—KIL:11, Co. Tipperary	1997/533
Lislackagh, Co. Mayo	1992/146
Lisleagh, Co. Cork	1980/061, 1989/013, 1990/018, 1991/026, 1992/030, 1993/034
Lislear, Co. Tyrone	1987/046
Lismeen, Co. Cavan	1994/012
Lismurphy, Co. Derry	1973/011
Lisnagun, Co. Cork	1987/007, 1988/008, 1989/011
Lisnamuck, Co. Longford	1993/150, 1993/151
Lisnamulligan, Co. Donegal	1980/074, 1989/018
Lisronagh, Co. Tipperary	1996/369
Lissanduff, Co. Antrim	1980/027
Lisseeghan, Co. Leitrim	1994/151
Lissenhall, Co. Tipperary	1996/370
Lisvernane, Co. Tipperary	1996/371
Little Britain Street, Dublin City	1997/141
Little Creagh Lane, Limerick City	1997/354
Little Gerard Griffin Street, Limerick City	1996/247
Little Mary Street, Dublin City	1997/142
Little Patrick Street, Waterford City	1993/219
Littleton Bog, Co. Tipperary	1990/105, 1995/Apx I
Loftus Lane, Dublin City	1993/073
Loher, Co. Kerry	1985/034
Longford Street/Steeven's Street, Dublin City	1997/143
Longstone, Co. Tipperary	1973/032
Lord Edward Street, Dublin City	1994/076
Lord Edward Street (Carnegie Trust), Dublin City	1994/077
Lough Ennel, Co. Westmeath	1989/098, 1989/Apx 3
Lough Gara, Co. Sligo	1973/031, 1997/470
Lough Gur, Co. Limerick	1977/050, 1977/051, 1985/036, 1986/050, 1987/033, 1987/034, 1988/039, 1990/083, 1991/089, 1992/124, 1992/128, 1994/156, 1996/236, 1997/331
Lough Kinale, Co. Longford	1987/037
Loughane East, Co. Cork	1997/046
Loughlackagh, Co. Roscommon	1994/202
Loughlinstown, Co. Dublin	1991/050, 1996/130, 1997/085
Loughrea, Co. Galway	1987/019, 1993/113, 1997/216, 1997/217, 1997/218, 1997/219
Loughshinny, Co. Dublin	1993/097
Louth Village, Co. Louth	1994/182, 1995/221, 1995/222
Lower Fairhill, Galway City	1997/Ad4
Lower New Street, Kilkenny City	1997/300
Lucan, Co. Dublin	1994/096, 1995/104, 1995/105, 1996/131, 1996/132, 1996/133, 1996/134
Lurgan Street, Dublin City	1995/078
Lusk, Co. Dublin	1991/051, 1993/099, 1996/135, 1997/181, 1997/182
Lydacan, Co. Galway	1969/024
Lyles Hill, Co. Antrim	1987/003, 1988/002
Macetown, Co. Meath	1992/152
MacMurroughs, Co. Wexford	1985/059
Macosquin, Co. Derry	1980/071
Mad Man's Window, Co. Antrim	1969/005
Maddenstown, Co. Kildare	1996/189
Maganey, Co. Laois	1994/143
Maghera, Co. Derry	1985/014, 1994/036
Maghera, Co. Down	1980/086
Magheracar, Co. Donegal	1986/018, 1987/010, 1997/066
Magheramore, Co. Derry	1970/010
Magilligan Point, Co. Derry	1997/058
Mainguard Street, Galway City	1995/122
Mallow, Co. Cork	1986/Apx 1.1, 1997/047, 1997/048, 1997/049, 1997/050
Manor Street, Waterford City	1991/123
Marble Hill, Co. Galway	1997/220
Margaretstown, Co. Dublin	1991/052
Market Street, Armagh City	1975/006
Marlinstown, Co. Westmeath	1990/113, 1991/126
Mary Street, Cork City	1993/027
Mary Street, Limerick City	1995/183, 1997/355

Mullaboy, Co. Derry	1977/023
Mullingar, Co. Westmeath	1990/114, 1991/127, 1991/128, 1994/218, 1994/219, 1994/220, 1995/268, 1995/269, 1995/270, 1995/271, 1996/394, 1996/395, 1996/396, 1996/397, 1996/398, 1997/587, 1997/588, 1997/589, 1997/590, 1997/591, 1997/592
Mulliviltrin, Co. Roscommon	1997/456
Mullynure, Co. Armagh	1975/008
Mungret Street, Limerick City	1994/161, 1997/356, 1997/357
Murrisk Demesne, Co. Mayo	1997/410
Na Gorta Dubha, Co. Kerry	1991/069
Naas, Co. Kildare	1977/046, 1980/117, 1989/058, 1990/070, 1990/071, 1991/076, 1994/135, 1995/157, 1995/158, 1995/159, 1995/160, 1995/161, 1995/162, 1995/163, 1996/194, 1996/195, 1996/196, 1996/197, 1996/198, 1996/199, 1997/283, 1997/284, 1997/285
Nappan, Co. Antrim	1986/007
Narraghmore, Co. Kildare	1971/020
Navan, Co. Meath	1991/105, 1994/192, 1994/193, 1997/427, 1997/428, 1997/429
Nenagh, Co. Tipperary	1992/170, 1996/373, 1996/374, 1996/375, 1996/376, 1997/548, 1997/549, 1997/550, 1997/551, 1997/552, 1997/553
Nendrum, Co. Down	1977/033
Nevinstown, Co. Meath	1977/059
New Building Lane, Kilkenny City	1996/212, 1996/213, 1997/301, 1997/302
New Building Lane—Abbey View, Kilkenny City	1996/211, 1997/303
New Dock Street, Galway City	1997/203
New Ross, Co. Wexford	1994/222, 1995/277, 1997/601, 1997/602
New Row South, Dublin City	1996/105, 1997/152
New Street, Kilkenny City	1991/082
Newcastle, Co. Wicklow	1997/617
Newcastle West, Co. Limerick	1991/090, 1994/164, 1996/252, 1997/359
Newferry, Co. Antrim	1970/002, 1971/005
Newgrange, Co. Meath	1969/011, 1970/027, 1971/030, 1972/027, 1973/029, 1974/033, 1975/031, 1980/152, 1980/153, 1988/054, 1989/075
Newry, Co. Down	1990/027, 1991/030
Newtown, Co. Clare	1993/013, 1994/020
Newtown, Co. Meath	1991/106
Newtown Trim, Co. Meath	1980/154, 1995/232
Newtownards, Co. Down	1980/089, 1985/021, 1992/036, 1993/042, 1994/041, 1996/Apx VI
Newtownbalregan, Co. Louth	1980/142
Newtownlow, Co. Westmeath	1980/201, 1985/058, 1986/078
Nicholas Street, Dublin City	1991/037, 1991/038
Nicholas Street, Limerick City	1994/162, 1994/163
Nicholas Street/Peter Street, Limerick City	1995/184
Nicholastown, Co. Kildare	1991/077
Ninch, Co. Meath	1977/060
North Antrim, Co. Antrim	1988/Apx 1
North Dublin, Co. Dublin	1992/Apx 1
North Gate, Cork City	1994/025
North King Street, Dublin City	1993/078, 1993/079, 1997/153, 1997/154
North King Street/Brunswick Street North, Dublin City	1997/139
North Main Street, Cork City	1974/010, 1997/037
North Main Street/Castle Street, Cork City	1996/045
North Mall, Cork City	1995/027
Northern Relief Road, Phase I, Limerick City	1996/248
Northern Relief Road, Phase II, Limerick City	1996/249
Noughaval, Co. Clare	1990/012
Oileán Ghorumna, Co. Galway	1991/061
Old Connaught, Co. Dublin	1989/027
Old Friary Road, Cork City	1995/028
Old Head of Kinsale, Co. Cork	1992/027, 1995/036, 1996/047
Oldbridge, Co. Louth	1993/169
Oldbridge, Co. Meath	1995/233
Oldcourt, Co. Dublin	1990/038
Oldcourt, Co. Wicklow	1996/413
Oldtown, Co. Kildare	1988/036
Omey Island, Co. Galway	1990/055, 1992/092, 1993/111

Scholarstown, Co. Dublin	1985/026
Schoolhouse Lane, Dublin City	1994/083
Scotch Street, Armagh City	1976/006, 1976/007, 1977/010, 1977/011, 1980/034, 1980/035, 1985/008, 1986/009
Scrabo, Co. Down	1969/007, 1970/016, 1971/014
Scrahane, Co. Kerry	1997/246, 1997/247
Seacash, Co. Antrim	1971/007
Shanaclogh, Co. Limerick	1986/058
Shanagarry, Co. Cork	1994/033
Shanakeal, Co. Kerry	1992/106
Shanco, Co. Fermanagh	1980/111
Shandon Street/Brownes Hill, Cork City	1992/025
Shandon, Co. Cork	1991/028
Shane's Castle, Co. Antrim	1972/004
Shankill, Co. Dublin	1989/028
Shankill, Co. Kilkenny	1980/130
Shanlaragh, Co. Cork	1990/020
Shanmullagh, Co. Armagh	1992/005, 1993/009
Shannon Estuary and tributaries, Cos Limerick/Clare	1994/Apx II
Shannon Estuary, Cos Limerick/Clare	1995/Apx II, 1996/Apx IX
Shantallow, Co. Derry	1988/043, 1996/058
Sharragh, Co. Tipperary	1997/558
Shawly, Co. Donegal	1969/008
Sheephouse, Co. Meath	1994/194
Sheepwalk, Co. Roscommon	1989/084
Shercock, Co. Cavan	1997/014
Sherkin Island, Co. Cork	1987/008, 1990/014, 1996/048
Sherlockstown, Co. Kildare	1997/288
Shewis, Co. Armagh	1977/013
Shinn, Co. Down	1994/042
Ship Street, Dublin City	1993/085,1996/110
Ship Street/St Michael le Pole, Dublin City	1980/099
Ship Street Great, Dublin City	1997/161
Ship Street Little, Dublin City	1992/076, 1993/084
Ship Street Little (Osmond House), Dublin City	1997/162, 1997/163
Shrule, Co. Mayo	1980/146, 1988/048
Singland, Co. Limerick	1996/254
Sixmilebridge, Co. Clare	1996/034, 1997/027
Skagh, Co. Limerick	1997/Ad9
Skeam West, Co. Cork	1990/021
Skehacreggaun, Co. Limerick	1992/132
Skiddy's Lane, Cork City	1997/040
Skreen, Co. Meath	1993/184
Slane, Co. Meath	1995/235, 1997/435
Slapragh, Co. Fermanagh	1988/024
Slievenacloy, Co. Antrim	1980/030
Sligo Town, Co. Sligo	1991/114, 1993/201, 1993/202, 1994/208, 1996/341, 1996/342, 1996/343, 1996/344, 1996/345, 1996/346, 1996/347, 1996/348, 1996/349, 1997/471, 1997/472, 1997/473, 1997/474, 1997/475, 1997/476, 1997/477, 1997/478, 1997/479, 1997/480, 1997/481, 1997/482
Sliguff, Co. Carlow	1974/007
Sluggary, Co. Limerick	1973/025, 1974/029
Smithfield, Dublin City	1993/086
Smithfield Distillery, Dublin City	1995/088
Smithstown, Co. Clare	1996/035
Smithstown, Co. Meath	1988/055
Solar, Co. Antrim	1991/009, 1993/007
South Circular Road—Greenville Avenue, Dublin City	1993/071
South Great Georges Street, Dublin City	1992/067
South Main Street, Cork City	1975/010, 1976/011
Spanish Arch, Galway City	1988/026, 1997/208
Spanish Parade, Galway City	1992/091
Spiddal, Co. Meath	1988/056
Spital, Co. Cork	1995/037
Spittle, Co. Limerick	1986/059, 1986/060
Spittle Quarter, Co. Down	1990/028

St Augustine Street, Galway City	1990/064, 1990/065
St Canice's Place, Kilkenny City	1997/307
St Francis' Abbey, Kilkenny City	1970/021
St Francis' Abbey (Smithwick's Brewery), Kilkenny City	1997/308
St Helens, Co. Wexford	1997/603
St John's Point, Co. Down	1977/035
St Kieran's Street, Kilkenny City	1997/309
St Kieran's Street, Kytler's Inn, Kilkenny City	1995/170
St Mary's Cathedral, Limerick City	1990/082, 1992/127, 1996/251, 1997/358
St Peter's Avenue, Cork City	1997/039
St Peter's Church, Waterford City	1986/075, 1988/062, 1989/092
St Peter's Market, Cork City	1980/052
St Saviour's Priory, Limerick City	1975/027, 1994/158
Stalleen, Co. Meath	1992/155
Stamullin, Co. Meath	1995/236
Stepaside, Co. Dublin	1996/065, 1997/080
Stephen Street Lower, Dublin City	1991/041, 1991/042, 1992/077, 1994/084
Stephen's Green Centre, Dublin City	1995/087
Straboe, Co. Laois	1996/226
Stradbally North, Co. Limerick	1990/085
Strade, Co. Mayo	1997/412
Straffan, Co. Kildare	1995/164
Straid, Co. Derry	1985/016
Strangford Lough, Co. Down	1995/044, 1996/Apx VII
Strawhill, Co. Carlow	1997/009, 1997/010
Suir Road, Dublin City	1997/167
Sutton, Co. Dublin	1996/138
Swords, Co. Dublin	1971/015, 1993/101, 1994/099, 1994/100, 1995/109, 1995/110, 1996/139, 1996/140, 1996/141, 1997/186
Sycamore Street, Dublin City	1996/111
Taghmon, Co. Wexford	1993/225, 1997/604
Talbot Bastion, Kilkenny City	1990/079
Tallaght, Co. Dublin	1990/042, 1990/043, 1990/044, 1990/045, 1991/053, 1993/102, 1994/101, 1994/102, 1995/111, 1996/142, 1997/187
Tamlaght, Co. Tyrone	1980/191
Tamnyrankin, Co. Derry	1980/073
Tankardstown, Co. Limerick	1986/061
Tankardstown South, Co. Limerick	1987/035, 1988/040, 1989/069
Tara, Co. Meath	1992/149, 1997/419
Tara Street—Fire Station, Dublin City	1996/112
Taylor's Grange, Co. Dublin	1980/104, 1985/027, 1986/026, 1987/016, 1996/143
Teaskagh, Co. Clare	1986/012
Teltown, Co. Meath	1997/430
Temple Bar, Dublin City	1993/088, 1997/168
Temple Bar, Temple Bar Gallery, Dublin City	1993/089, 1993/090
Temple Bar, West End, Dublin City	1993/087
Temple Lane, The Green Building, Dublin City	1993/091, 1993/092
Temple Lane/Cecilia Street, Dublin City	1996/113
Templemacateer, Co. Westmeath	1992/181
Templemoyle, Co. Antrim	1986/008
Templeogue, Co. Dublin	1996/144
Templepatrick, Co. Antrim	1996/013, 1997/006
Termonfeckin, Co. Louth	1994/183, 1995/202, 1996/293, 1996/294, 1997/397
Termons, Co. Kerry	1996/169
Terryglass, Co. Tipperary	1997/559
The Bonn, Co. Tyrone	1980/192
The Coombe (Holy Faith Convent), Dublin City	1997/119
The Dane's Cast, Co. Antrim	1987/004
Thomas Street, Dublin City	1994/085, 1995/089, 1995/090, 1996/114
Thomas Street—Frawley's, Dublin City	1996/115
Thomas Street—NCAD, Dublin City	1995/091, 1996/116
Thomas Street—Statoil Filling Station, Dublin City	1995/092
Thomastown, Co. Kilkenny	1996/218, 1997/313
Thurles, Co. Tipperary	1995/261, 1996/377, 1997/560
Tievebane, Co. Donegal	1977/026
Tievebulliagh, Co. Antrim	1980/031

Tildarg, Co. Antrim — 1980/032
Timahoe West, Co. Kildare — 1986/034
Timoleague, Co. Cork — 1985/013
Timolin, Co. Kildare — 1980/123, 1980/124, 1996/201, 1996/202
Tintagh, Co. Roscommon — 1996/336
Tintern, Co. Wexford — 1980/203, 1993/227
Tipperary Town, Co. Tipperary — 1996/378, 1997/561
Tipperkevin, Co. Kildare — 1994/136, 1997/259, 1997/260
Toberdaly, Co. Offaly — 1992/160
Tobertown, Co. Dublin — 1996/145
Tobertown and Rath, Co. Meath — 1997/436
Tobin Street, Cork City — 1980/053
Tomgreany, Co. Clare — 1995/021
Tomona, Co. Wexford — 1971/035
Tonbane Glebe, Co. Donegal — 1980/075
Tonefortes, Co. Sligo — 1997/483
Toome, Co. Antrim — 1991/010
Toormore, Co. Cork — 1990/023
Tory Island, Co. Donegal — 1997/067
Townsend Street/Luke Street, Dublin City — 1997/169
Tralee, Co. Kerry — 1994/130, 1996/170, 1996/171, 1996/172, 1997/248, 1997/249, 1997/250, 1997/251, 1997/252, 1997/253, 1997/254, 1997/255
Tramore, Co. Waterford — 1996/389
Travers' Street, Cork City — 1995/029
Tray, Co. Armagh — 1975/007, 1987/005, 1989/006, 1990/007, 1991/018, 1995/010, 1996/017, 1997/007
Treadstown, Co. Kildare — 1989/060
Tremoge, Co. Tyrone — 1980/193
Trim, Co. Meath — 1971/031, 1972/028, 1973/030, 1974/034, 1977/062, 1987/042, 1989/077, 1995/237, 1996/315, 1996/316, 1997/437
Trinity Island, Co. Roscommon — 1991/112, 1992/161
Truska, Co. Galway — 1994/115
Tuam, Co. Galway — 1986/028, 1992/096, 1992/097, 1995/127, 1995/128, 1997/224, 1997/225
Tuckey Street, Cork City — 1980/054, 1997/041
Tullaheddy, Co. Tipperary — 1996/379, 1996/380, 1996/381, 1996/382, 1996/383, 1997/562, 1997/563
Tullaher, Co. Clare — 1990/013
Tullamore, Co. Offaly — 1993/191
Tully, Co. Antrim — 1970/003
Tully, Co. Fermanagh — 1976/022, 1996/Apx VIII
Tully, Co. Leitrim — 1994/153
Tully, Co. Roscommon — 1996/337
Tully, Co. Tyrone — 1980/194
Tullyallen, Co. Armagh — 1971/009
Tullyboard, Co. Down — 1993/043
Tullylinton, Co. Tyrone — 1980/195
Tullylish, Co. Down — 1980/091
Tullynure, Co. Derry — 1985/017
Tullywiggan, Co. Tyrone — 1971/033
Tulsk, Co. Roscommon — 1997/459
Tunarobert, Co. Antrim — 1991/011
Turkhead, Co. Cork — 1972/010
Turraloskin, Co. Antrim — 1977/008
Tyone, Co. Tipperary — 1996/384
Tyrellspass, Co. Westmeath — 1991/130, 1995/272
Tyrellstown Big, Co. Dublin — 1994/103

Ullard, Co. Kilkenny — 1996/219
Urney, Co. Tyrone — 1970/034, 1971/034
Usher's Quay, Dublin City — 1990/037, 1991/043, 1994/086, 1995/093

Valentia Island, Co. Kerry — 1993/117, 1993/120, 1994/117, 1994/119, 1995/132, 1997/230, 1997/231
Vicar Street/Thomas Street, Dublin City — 1997/170
Vow, Co. Antrim — 1994/009

Walshetown, Co. Kildare	1987/029
Walterstown, Co. Kildare	1997/289
Wandsfort Quay and Pope's Quay, Cork City	1994/026
Ward's Hill, Dublin City	1993/093
Washington Street, Cork City	1993/031, 1996/046
Waterford City, Co. Waterford	1987/Apx 1.2, 1988/Apx 4
Wellington Place, Dublin City	1997/171
Wellington Quay, Dublin City	1992/078
Werburgh Street, Dublin City	1994/087
Westereave, Co. Dublin	1988/021
Westland Row, Dublin City	1991/044, 1995/094, 1996/117
Westport, Co. Mayo	1994/187, 1995/227
Westport–Belclare, Co. Mayo	1997/413
Wexford Street, Dublin City	1994/088
Wexford Town, Co. Wexford	1973/039, 1974/041, 1976/033, 1980/204, 1980/205, 1988/067, 1988/068, 1988/069, 1990/121, 1991/133, 1992/182, 1993/228, 1993/229, 1994/223, 1994/224, 1994/225, 1994/226, 1994/227, 1994/228, 1994/229, 1995/278, 1995/279, 1995/280, 1995/281, 1995/282, 1995/283, 1995/284, 1995/285, 1995/286, 1995/287, 1996/404, 1996/405, 1996/406, 1996/407, 1997/605, 1997/606, 1997/607, 1997/608
White Street (carpark), Cork City	1988/007
Whitechurch, Dublin	1997/188
Whitefriars Place, Dublin City	1997/172
Whitefriars Street, Dublin City	1996/118
Whitehall Lane, Galway City	1989/050
Whitehouse, Co. Antrim	1996/014
Whiterath, Co. Louth	1993/170
Wicklow Town, Co. Wicklow	1991/137, 1992/183, 1997/619, 1997/620, 1997/621, 1997/622, 1997/623, 1997/624
William Street, Kilkenny City	1996/215, 1997/310, 1997/311
Williamstown, Co. Galway	1993/115
Williamstown, Co. Waterford	1993/220
Winetavern Street, Dublin City	1969/016, 1971/016, 1988/020, 1989/029, 1993/094
Winetavern Street (Civic Offices), Dublin City	1994/089
Wolfe Tone Street, Dublin City	1997/173
Wood Quay, Dublin City	1974/015, 1976/020
Woodpole, Co. Meath	1997/438
York Street—RCSI, Dublin City	1995/095
Youghal, Co. Cork	1992/031, 1993/035, 1994/034, 1994/035, 1995/038, 1995/039, 1995/040, 1996/056, 1996/057, 1997/054

Index of Excavations 1969–97 by type

Excavation type	Volume/excavation no.
11th- and 12th-century urban	1974/014
12th-century cross	1997/555
12th/19th-century castle	1991/081, 1992/115
15th–17th-century defended house	1995/104
16th-century castle site	1980/078
16th-century house site near Cistercian abbey	1992/121
16th-century star-shaped fort	1997/594
17th-century castle	1994/114, 1995/126, 1996/163, 1996/183, 1997/222
17th-century house	1980/038, 1980/089, 1980/173, 1980/181
17th-century house site	1980/065
17th-century tower-house	1980/085
17th-century urban site	1980/007, 1980/008, 1980/066
18th-century	1992/062
18th-century building adjoining old graveyard	1996/224
18th-century earthwork	1980/030
18th-century house	1988/033
18th-century military camp	1995/102
18th-century urban	1997/151
18th/19th-century underground passage	1995/108
19th-century church site	1997/101
19th-century houses	1996/235
19th-century village	1997/456
Abbey	1985/007, 1992/137, 1993/227
Abbey environs	1992/012, 1992/109, 1993/027, 1993/143, 1994/154, 1996/329
Abbey—Premonstratensian	1991/112, 1992/161
Adjacent to features	1993/194
Agricultural village/head tenant home site	1996/332
Altar	1990/013
Ancient? road/trackway	1986/041
Anglo-Norman bailey	1991/103
Anglo-Norman town	1993/121, 1997/192
Archaeological complex	1994/141, 1995/241, 1995/242, 1997/450, 1997/451
Archaeological complex, environs	1996/328, 1996/334, 1997/269
Archaeological potential	1991/127, 1993/140, 1996/147, 1996/177, 1996/218, 1996/228
Area of archaeological potential	1997/090, 1997/091
Area of many sites	1995/179
Armada wreck	1974/012, 1975/014
Artificial pond	1975/007
Artillery fort	1993/201
Assessment	1996/038, 1996/234
Augustinian cemetery?	1996/194
Augustinian church	1986/008
Augustinian priory	1970/011, 1972/021, 1973/023, 1974/023, 1975/024, 1980/126, 1992/018, 1996/012, 1996/217
Bank	1985/049
Banks	1996/383
Barracks	1992/010
Barrow	1996/253
Barrow?	1995/186
Barrow cemetery	1994/207
Barrow cemetery and earthworks	1992/165
Barrow environs	1996/409
Barrow group	1973/037
Barrows etc.	1993/127
Battlefield	1993/226
Bawn	1980/064, 1980/192
Bawn/castle	1990/053
Bawn, houses and ringfort	1990/024
Bog road	1980/157, 1985/037, 1986/062, 1987/036
Booley-house?	1997/068
Booley-houses	1996/008

Bore-holes | 1989/039, 1991/033
Boulder burial and stone row | 1989/009
Boulder burials | 1989/010
Bridge | 1989/007, 1995/239, 1996/200
Bronze Age | 1993/097
Bronze Age? | 1993/168
Bronze Age and later features | 1996/146
Bronze Age cemetery | 1973/016
Bronze Age cist | 1987/049, 1989/018
Bronze Age cist cemetery | 1994/189
Bronze Age copper mines | 1980/062, 1993/126
Bronze Age cremated burials? | 1997/434
Bronze Age ditch and enclosed features | 1986/036
Bronze Age/Early Christian? | 1990/039
Bronze Age/Early Christian settlement | 1988/004
Bronze Age enclosure | 1995/010, 1996/017, 1997/007
Bronze Age features | 1986/047, 1986/049
Bronze Age habitation | 1977/031
Bronze Age hillfort | 1989/006, 1990/007
Bronze Age hoard? | 1990/120
Bronze Age industrial complex? | 1995/264
Bronze Age/Iron Age hillfort/enclosure | 1987/005
Bronze Age lake settlements | 1996/031
Bronze Age metalworking site | 1997/247
Bronze Age pit | 1986/051
Bronze Age? pit | 1988/018, 1988/048
Bronze Age pits | 1986/046, 1986/060
Bronze Age remains | 1991/134
Bronze Age ring-ditch? | 1986/045
Bronze Age settlement | 1993/120, 1993/204, 1994/211, 1995/251
Bronze Age settlement site | 1997/616
Bronze axe findspot | 1977/040
Brushwood scatter | 1997/525
Brushwood togher | 1997/545
Brushwood trackway | 1997/522
Bullaun stone | 1997/406
Burial | 1991/049, 1992/152
Burial and domestic site | 1990/055
Burial cairn | 1988/013
Burial cist | 1996/371
Burial-ground | 1987/027, 1990/085, 1995/244, 1996/338
Burial mound | 1972/005, 1980/119, 1994/185
Burial mounds/linear barrow cemetery | 1993/104
Burial site | 1989/027, 1990/122, 1994/226, 1995/185
Burials | 1996/166, 1997/186, 1997/440, 1997/449, 1997/471
Burials adjacent to church | 1997/561
Burials adjacent to churchyard | 1997/360
Burials, environs | 1997/469
Burning | 1997/422
Burnt material deposits | 1996/145
Burnt material spread | 1994/152
Burnt mound | 1994/104, 1994/105, 1994/106, 1994/109, 1995/116, 1996/010, 1996/011, 1997/609, 1997/610, 1997/614
Burnt mound? | 1995/112, 1996/307
Burnt mound and material? | 1996/007
Burnt mound/trackways | 1996/330
Burnt spreads and linear field ditches | 1997/528
Burnt stone mound | 1997/455

Cairn | 1969/002, 1977/070
Cairn and henge | 1987/047
Cairn and ringfort | 1980/179
Cairn mound | 1989/083
Cashel | 1977/039, 1985/034, 1987/014, 1994/116
Cashel and ecclesiastical site | 1977/033
Cashel and house site | 1987/011, 1988/011, 1989/019, 1990/025, 1992/032
Cashel with souterrain | 1991/065

Cashel/stone fort	1997/228
Castle	1969/021, 1970/015, 1971/013, 1971/015, 1972/008, 1972/013, 1972/029, 1972/032, 1973/038, 1974/040, 1975/025, 1975/026, 1977/032, 1980/057, 1980/162, 1980/178, 1986/024, 1986/033, 1987/006, 1987/015, 1988/015, 1989/057, 1989/089, 1990/034, 1990/107, 1991/010, 1991/045, 1992/038, 1993/004, 1993/013, 1993/048, 1993/049, 1993/100, 1993/142, 1994/050, 1994/108, 1994/143, 1994/144, 1995/015, 1995/030, 1996/190, 1996/223, 1996/252, 1996/375, 1996/387, 1997/234, 1997/271, 1997/315, 1997/495, 1997/553, 1997/571
Castle?	1997/241
Castle—12th–19th-century	1997/304
Castle and environs	1994/233
Castle and post-medieval settlement	1993/136
Castle and road environs	1997/467
Castle bakery	1996/025
Castle bawn	1997/559
Castle environs	1993/101, 1994/098, 1994/100, 1996/393, 1996/401, 1997/008, 1997/089, 1997/174, 1997/175, 1997/603
Castle environs?	1995/071
Castle site	1985/047, 1993/103, 1996/144
Castle site?	1995/014, 1995/146
Castle site and prehistoric? activity	1985/059
Castle site environs?	1996/191
Castle on Early Christian defence works	1995/176
Castle/tower-house site	1990/038
Cathedral	1997/576
Cathedral and graveyard	1986/028
Cathedral church	1974/013
Cave burial	1993/145
Cemetery	1985/046, 1988/058, 1994/220
Christian cemetery	1988/018, 1988/021
Church	1973/039, 1977/035, 1977/045, 1980/092, 1980/099, 1980/175, 1989/016, 1989/020, 1991/121, 1996/226
Church and burial site	1985/052
Church and castle	1996/222
Church and enclosure	1993/195
Church and graveyard	1990/057, 1991/060, 1991/061, 1993/108, 1993/203, 1994/011, 1997/407
Church and graveyard environs	1997/443
Church and well	1975/032, 1976/030
Church, baptistry and holy well	1989/021, 1990/031
Church, burial-ground, habitation	1989/081
Church, enclosure, well	1975/037
Church environs	1995/152, 1996/023, 1997/015, 1997/273
Church, nunnery and cemetery	1994/200
Church ruin	1989/043
Church site	1987/024, 1988/030, 1989/054, 1990/011, 1990/030, 1991/009, 1994/204, 1995/099
Church site?	1989/005
Church site and enclosure	1990/029
Church site—early	1990/021
Church site environs	1980/121
Church (site of) and graveyard	1997/593
Churches	1985/030
Churchyard	1995/260
Cinerary urn	1997/082
Circular ditched enclosure	1985/023
Circular enclosure	1971/035, 1997/335
Circular enclosure (levelled)	1996/169, 1997/044
Circular feature	1992/108
Circular stone-built enclosure	1976/017
Cist	1977/025, 1977/026, 1977/056, 1980/041, 1985/018, 1985/042, 1989/085, 1995/223
Cist and pit burial	1977/038
Cist burial	1974/007, 1976/016, 1976/028, 1976/031, 1980/074, 1980/111, 1980/113, 1980/120, 1980/122, 1980/123, 1980/124, 1980/142,

Decorated stone	1974/008
Defensive tower?	1996/350
Degraded platform	1997/539
Deserted medieval borough	1993/190
Deserted medieval town	1995/259
Deserted settlement?	1993/144
Deserted village?	1987/038
Deserted village? site	1980/128
Ditch	1993/008
Ditched enclosure and 17th-century manorial complex	1997/079
Domestic pits and pit burial	1992/026
Dominican friary	1975/027, 1977/048, 1988/049
Dominican priory	1991/093, 1991/095, 1993/030, 1993/154, 1994/173, 1997/248
Dominican priory environs	1996/172
Drainage scheme	1997/275
Dredgings	1995/005, 1996/016
Early Bronze Age cemetery	1995/288
Early Bronze Age circular enclosure	1970/026
Early Bronze Age cist burial	1992/162
Early Bronze Age habitation/burial site	1980/149
Early Christian	1993/188, 1995/202, 1995/221, 1995/222, 1996/015, 1996/158, 1996/219, 1996/305, 1997/214
Early Christian?	1974/036
Early Christian/13th-century	1989/061
Early Christian and later site	1990/033
Early Christian and medieval ecclesiastical	1989/041
Early Christian and medieval ecclesiastical site	1995/035
Early Christian and medieval site environs	1995/037
Early Christian cemetery	1980/034
Early Christian cemetery and enclosure	1988/016
Early Christian cemetery and medieval/ post-medieval settlement	1985/008
Early Christian church	1970/010
Early Christian church/Augustinian priory	1975/011, 1975/012
Early Christian church site	1970/019
Early Christian clochán	1994/119
Early Christian coastal habitation sites	1997/197
Early Christian? ditch	1990/043
Early Christian ecclesiastical enclosure	1980/186
Early Christian ecclesiastical site	1986/002
Early Christian enclosure	1977/068, 1994/102
Early Christian enclosure and cemetery	1988/051
Early Christian foundation	1997/181
Early Christian graveyard	1987/018
Early Christian hermitage	1992/103, 1993/125, 1994/124, 1995/137
Early Christian inhumation cemetery	1995/266, 1995/267
Early Christian ironworking site	1980/004
Early Christian, medieval	1995/161
Early Christian/medieval	1986/009, 1992/034, 1993/225, 1994/232, 1995/149, 1996/402, 1997/063, 1997/585
Early Christian, medieval and post-medieval complex	1992/096
Early Christian/medieval cemetery	1997/431
Early Christian/medieval church environs	1986/023
Early Christian/medieval church site	1985/022, 1986/019, 1986/021
Early Christian/medieval ecclesiastical	1977/010, 1995/236
Early Christian/medieval ecclesiastical and settlement site	1991/078
Early Christian/medieval occupation	1977/009
Early Christian/medieval settlement	1985/014
Early Christian/medieval urban	1976/006, 1976/007, 1976/008, 1976/009, 1993/180
Early Christian monastery	1991/071, 1996/157, 1997/210
Early Christian monastery/ post-medieval house site and midden	1996/161, 1997/221
Early Christian monastic enclosure	1996/293
Early Christian monastic settlement	1985/035

Early Christian monastic site	1986/032, 1986/068, 1987/025, 1989/078, 1990/096
Early Christian monastic site?	1989/024
Early Christian occupation	1977/024
Early Christian occupation site	1992/007
Early Christian or medieval enclosure	1980/013
Early Christian oratory	1995/124
Early Christian ringfort?	1994/181
Early Christian settlement	1972/012, 1972/026, 1980/005, 1980/137, 1980/138, 1985/040,
	1992/157, 1993/187, 1994/197, 1995/240, 1996/324, 1997/448
Early Christian settlement?	1997/547
Early Christian settlement and monastic site	1990/097, 1991/110
Early Christian settlement? and souterrains	1988/055
Early Christian settlement complex	1993/002, 1994/006
Early Christian site	1990/045
Early Christian site environs	1990/123
Early Christian slabs replacement	1992/Apx 3
Early Christian souterrain	1985/044
Early Christian upland settlement	1980/002
Early ecclesiastical	1997/187
Early ecclesiastical and *ceallúnach*	1993/118, 1994/118, 1995/133
Early ecclesiastical centre	1995/230
Early ecclesiastical enclosure	1980/146, 1991/023, 1992/029, 1997/043, 1997/232
Early ecclesiastical enclosure and *ceallúnach*	1996/165
Early ecclesiastical remains, environs	1995/113
Early ecclesiastical site	1980/199, 1991/101, 1995/043
Early historic site	1996/356
Early Iron Age complex	1995/173
Early Iron Age hut circle	1970/016, 1971/014
Early Iron Age mound	1969/023
Early Iron Age ritual site	1970/020
Early Iron Age stone structure	1980/109
Early medieval altar; cross-inscribed slab	1997/468
Early medieval bridge	1997/447
Early medieval cemetery	1991/050
Early medieval farm and village	1997/231
Early medieval farm to late medieval village	1994/117
Early medieval hut	1997/230
Early modern	1996/134
Early monastic site	1994/182
Early monastic site?	1990/036
Earthwork	1972/016, 1973/032, 1977/006, 1977/049, 1995/106
Earthwork?	1996/410
Earthwork and castle	1980/082
Earthwork and enclosure	1993/185
Earthwork complex, environs	1995/013
Earthwork enclosure	1980/188, 1993/191, 1997/340
Earthworks	1977/012, 1980/027, 1989/004, 1989/045
Earthworks and hut	1995/132
Earthworks, environs	1987/028
Ecclesiastical	1989/088, 1992/036, 1992/149, 1993/138, 1993/155, 1993/193,
	1996/301, 1997/002, 1997/005, 1997/071, 1997/224
Ecclesiastical?	1993/184 1995/086 1996/184 1996/255
Ecclesiastical/bawn	1994/041
Ecclesiastical complex	1996/295
Ecclesiastical enclosure	1973/036 1980/035 1980/040 1980/091 1980/185 1991/051
	1993/006 1993/102 1995/263 1996/142
Ecclesiastical enclosure?	1992/015, 1994/092, 1994/093, 1995/021
Ecclesiastical enclosure boundary	1985/017
Ecclesiastical enclosure/church	1988/048
Ecclesiastical enclosure environs	1997/604
Ecclesiastical remains	1994/142, 1995/238, 1997/402
Ecclesiastical remains, environs	1997/574
Ecclesiastical settlement	1996/123, 1996/136
Ecclesiastical site	1980/071, 1980/086, 1980/087, 1980/184, 1985/054, 1986/006,
	1992/107, 1992/110, 1993/007
Ecclesiastical site?	1994/221
Ecclesiastical site, environs	1996/296, 1997/399

Ecclesiastical structure	1986/071, 1986/072
Ecclesiastical urban?	1995/096
EIS (part)	1997/312
Enclosure	1969/024, 1969/026, 1973/001, 1974/027, 1985/009, 1985/051, 1992/144, 1992/163, 1992/179, 1993/114, 1993/175, 1993/200, 1994/156, 1995/178, 1996/232, 1996/237, 1996/302, 1996/412, 1997/019, 1997/331, 1997/336, 1997/401, 1997/615
Enclosure?	1989/022, 1993/196, 1994/126, 1994/199
Enclosure and henge?	1996/281
Enclosure, environs	1993/130, 1995/187, 1996/059, 1996/291, 1997/403, 1997/488
Enclosure (ploughed-out)	1991/100
Enclosure site	1991/131, 1995/127
Enclosure site, environs	1991/066
Enclosures, environs	1996/290
English Plantation village	1988/041
Episcopal manor	1975/008
Ferry point?	1995/283
Field system	1972/025, 1992/159
Field system?	1994/120, 1997/084
Field-walking	1988/Apx 1
Field-walking project	1989/Apx 1
Field wall	1977/023
Field wall etc.	1977/016
Field walls (pre-bog)	1969/019
Fire-pits	1995/118
Flat cremation cemetery	1997/537
Flint scatter	1980/103, 1990/016
Folly	1992/160
Ford	1989/079
Formal gardens	1991/001
Formal gardens and woodland bosquet	1994/001
Fort and settlement complex	1995/247
Fort? environs	1997/013
Fortified house	1996/014, 1996/055
Fortified house and bawn	1996/062, 1997/190
Fortified house environs	1996/339, 1997/042
Franciscan friary	1980/176, 1987/008, 1990/014, 1996/246
Franciscan friary church	1970/004, 1970/021
Friary	1973/004, 1974/005, 1977/007, 1993/174, 1994/015
Friary and environs?	1995/067
Fulacht fiadh	1973/019, 1974/021, 1974/022, 1980/049, 1980/055, 1980/058, 1980/125, 1980/171, 1980/206, 1985/011, 1986/037, 1986/038, 1986/042, 1986/056, 1988/028, 1991/024, 1992/008, 1993/148, 1994/103, 1994/147, 1994/150, 1994/153, 1994/170, 1994/230, 1995/174, 1996/032, 1996/299, 1996/336, 1997/314, 1997/326, 1997/328, 1997/339, 1997/461, 1997/500, 1997/505, 1997/529, 1997/613
Fulacht fiadh?	1994/145, 1996/186, 1996/280, 1997/003, 1997/235, 1997/460
Fulacht fiadh and Bronze Age cultivation	1993/230
Fulacht fiadh and parallel linear field ditches	1997/527
Fulacht fiadh and round house	1994/149
Fulacht fiadh site	1993/149
Fulacht fiadh with platform	1997/504
Fulacht fiadh with timber platform	1997/503
Fulachta fiadh	1974/017, 1994/194, 1997/338
Fulachta fiadh?	1992/119
Garden feature	1989/077
Garden feature?	1997/329
Gas pipeline	1986/Apx 1.1, 1986/Apx 1.2, 1986/Apx 1.3
Gateway in city wall	1989/093
Geophysical survey	1993/Apx I, 1996/Apx I, 1996/Apx III, 1996/Apx IV, 1996/Apx VIII
Glassworks	1974/001
Grave-slab—early	1980/101
Graveyard	1990/091, 1991/057, 1991/096, 1993/179, 1997/064
Graveyard?	1990/114, 1996/040

Late Bronze Age settlement	1990/104, 1991/117
Late medieval castle	1996/039, 1997/034
Late medieval houses	1992/086
Late medieval Observantine friary	1996/048
Late medieval tower-house, bawn, Plantation residence	1996/051
Late medieval town defences	1987/020
Late medieval urban	1997/102, 1997/307
Late medieval urban, domestic	1995/119
Late Mesolithic coastal settlement	1995/130
Late Neolithic burial cairn	1977/067
Late Neolithic/Early Bronze Age	1971/029
Late Neolithic/Early Bronze Age habitation	1980/153
Late Neolithic ritual enclosure	1995/045
Late Neolithic settlement and industrial site	1994/008
Later Iron Age site	1970/014
Later Mesolithic sites	1987/055
Later prehistoric unenclosed settlement	1997/536
Limekiln	1988/024
Linear ditch	1992/004
Linear earthwork	1975/019, 1980/118, 1980/130, 1980/156, 1987/004, 1990/099, 1993/018, 1997/430, 1997/498
Linear earthworks, environs	1997/452
Lintel grave	1986/077, 1988/003, 1988/052, 1991/067, 1991/113
Lintel graves	1985/033, 1990/087
Long cist graves	1980/207
Long stone cist	1987/022
Long stone cist?	1986/027
Major site environs	1992/128
Manor site	1997/177
Marl pit?	1996/370
Martello tower	1995/199
Mass grave	1990/022
Mass house?	1993/139
Medieval	1990/035, 1991/053, 1991/072, 1991/075, 1991/136, 1991/137, 1992/024, 1992/052, 1992/065, 1992/114, 1992/177, 1993/133, 1993/173, 1995/055, 1995/056, 1995/062, 1995/066, 1995/075, 1995/111, 1995/121, 1995/151, 1995/206, 1995/257, 1995/286, 1996/060, 1996/067, 1996/068, 1996/390, 1996/392, 1996/399, 1997/087, 1997/308
Medieval?	1991/085, 1995/025, 1996/347, 1997/081, 1997/086, 1997/176, 1997/617
Medieval/17th-century house	1995/063, 1995/064
Medieval abbey	1991/097, 1993/171
Medieval abbey, burial-ground	1992/129
Medieval abbey precinct	1995/069
Medieval activity?	1994/178
Medieval? and 18th-century church	1997/274
Medieval and later	1974/010
Medieval and later urban	1974/003, 1974/015, 1975/002, 1975/003, 1975/010, 1976/011, 1977/005
Medieval and post-medieval	1985/025, 1988/017, 1995/039
Medieval and post-medieval urban	1977/018, 1980/134, 1985/055, 1985/056, 1990/078, 1997/037, 1997/056, 1997/126, 1997/138
Medieval archaeological complex, environs	1997/288, 1997/289
Medieval borough	1990/010, 1992/084, 1997/261, 1997/262, 1997/433
Medieval boundaries	1990/042
Medieval bridge, priory and tower-house, environs	1995/232
Medieval building	1992/113
Medieval burgage plots?	1996/131
Medieval burial-ground	1995/160
Medieval burials	1993/091
Medieval castle	1971/031, 1972/015, 1972/028, 1973/030, 1974/034, 1976/023, 1977/062, 1989/023, 1990/054, 1990/084, 1991/004, 1992/122, 1993/146, 1994/160, 1995/182, 1995/237, 1995/265, 1996/018, 1996/245, 1996/316, 1997/353
Medieval castle, post-medieval fortification	1994/029

Medieval cathedral	1989/051, 1990/066, 1991/062, 1992/098, 1992/127, 1995/129, 1996/251
Medieval cemetery	1995/157
Medieval church	1986/022, 1987/057, 1990/071, 1991/069, 1992/068, 1993/014, 1994/030, 1996/009, 1996/197, 1996/363, 1997/029
Medieval church and graveyard	1989/042, 1991/042, 1991/055
Medieval church and hospital	1992/058
Medieval church environs	1992/014, 1994/028, 1995/031
Medieval church site	1997/453
Medieval church site?	1996/312
Medieval city	1987/Apx 1.2
Medieval city wall	1980/051, 1980/054, 1992/022
Medieval corn-drying kiln	1993/117
Medieval cultivation/post-medieval dumping	1994/060
Medieval defence work	1969/003
Medieval defences?	1995/285
Medieval ditch	1996/003
Medieval earthwork	1974/020
Medieval earthworks	1976/027
Medieval ecclesiastical	1997/265
Medieval ecclesiastical foundation	1992/057
Medieval enclosure	1997/330
Medieval farmyard?	1988/019
Medieval friary	1985/013, 1996/078, 1997/182, 1997/412
Medieval friary—Franciscan	1994/067
Medieval gatehouse	1992/171, 1997/417
Medieval graveyard	1994/022
Medieval habitation site	1980/127
Medieval hospital?	1991/041
Medieval manor?	1992/040
Medieval mill site?	1993/153
Medieval (moated site?)	1997/327
Medieval monastic site	1986/035
Medieval mural tower	1990/079
Medieval occupation	1991/019, 1993/075
Medieval occupation and burials	1997/184
Medieval? occupation features	1986/013
Medieval occupation site	1980/079
Medieval occupational remains	1990/044
Medieval parish church	1989/038, 1995/023, 1996/037
Medieval parish church, environs	1996/170
Medieval/post-medieval	1989/025, 1992/061, 1996/063, 1996/120, 1996/121, 1996/126
Medieval/post-medieval?	1996/342, 1996/343, 1996/345, 1996/348
Medieval/post-medieval burials	1992/133
Medieval/post-medieval castle	1986/025, 1987/017, 1991/124
Medieval/post-medieval cultivation	1996/359
Medieval/post-medieval features	1997/533
Medieval/post-medieval rampart	1991/048
Medieval/post-medieval site	1980/095
Medieval/post-medieval urban	1986/076, 1988/012, 1989/063, 1989/064, 1989/065, 1990/063, 1992/166, 1993/215, 1993/219, 1995/192, 1995/195, 1995/197, 1995/279, 1995/287, 1996/028, 1996/045, 1996/215, 1996/274, 1996/277, 1996/354, 1996/358, 1996/362, 1996/406, 1997/377, 1997/378, 1997/390, 1997/391, 1997/414, 1997/489, 1997/490, 1997/491, 1997/599
Medieval/post-medieval urban?	1996/019
Medieval potential	1991/108
Medieval pottery kiln	1997/388
Medieval priory	1994/210, 1995/216, 1996/282
Medieval priory and hospital	1989/070, 1995/201
Medieval priory—Augustinian	1971/017, 1972/017, 1993/106
Excavation priory—Dominican	1994/158
Medieval quayside	1980/135
Medieval river frontage	1990/040
Medieval roadway	1986/066, 1986/066, 1992/176
Medieval rural	1994/209
Medieval rural settlement	1973/022

	1997/108, 1997/111, 1997/112, 1997/114, 1997/118, 1997/119, 1997/120, 1997/121, 1997/122, 1997/123, 1997/124, 1997/125, 1997/128, 1997/129, 1997/132, 1997/134, 1997/136, 1997/146, 1997/147, 1997/148, 1997/152, 1997/161, 1997/162, 1997/163, 1997/166, 1997/167, 1997/170, 1997/172, 1997/198, 1997/199, 1997/207, 1997/256, 1997/257, 1997/267, 1997/276, 1997/284, 1997/291, 1997/292, 1997/296, 1997/299, 1997/301, 1997/302, 1997/309, 1997/311, 1997/346, 1997/347, 1997/351, 1997/354, 1997/356, 1997/358, 1997/366, 1997/368, 1997/369, 1997/372, 1997/373, 1997/374, 1997/379, 1997/380, 1997/381, 1997/382, 1997/383, 1997/384, 1997/385, 1997/387, 1997/389, 1997/415, 1997/429, 1997/432, 1997/487, 1997/549, 1997/566, 1997/567, 1997/568, 1997/569, 1997/570, 1997/572, 1997/573, 1997/575, 1997/577, 1997/579, 1997/582, 1997/584, 1997/591, 1997/601, 1997/602, 1997/607, 1997/608, 1997/619, 1997/621, 1997/623, 1997/624
Medieval? urban	1995/141
Medieval urban?	1980/205, 1995/027, 1995/028, 1995/029, 1996/053, 1996/391, 1996/395
Medieval urban church	1989/092
Medieval urban church and undercroft	1988/062
Medieval urban defences	1992/050
Medieval urban defences and extra-mural industrial	1992/055
Medieval urban defences and settlement	1992/053
Medieval urban deposits (potential)	1995/271
Medieval urban environs	1995/072
Medieval urban habitation and defences	1995/059
Medieval urban mill	1995/253
Medieval urban/motte site?	1996/306
Medieval urban/post-medieval burials	1996/103
Medieval urban river front	1993/063
Medieval urban/rural	1994/225
Medieval urban site	1987/012
Medieval urban waterfront	1976/020
Medieval urban with prehistoric?	1997/620
Medieval waterfront?	1988/022, 1989/040
Megalith	1977/073
Megalith (remains)	1994/037
Megalith site	1980/107, 1991/006
Megalithic cemetery, environs	1994/203
Megalithic tombs	1977/065, 1980/163, 1997/364
Megaliths, environs	1997/220
Mesolithic–Bronze Age cave	1996/242
Mesolithic/Late Bronze Age habitation	1977/004
Mesolithic/Neolithic	1986/030, 1987/023
Mesolithic/Neolithic colonisation	1986/Apx 3, 1987/Apx 2, 1989/Apx 2
Mesolithic/Neolithic occupation site	1971/005
Mesolithic/Neolithic raised beach	1971/004, 1995/006
Mesolithic/Neolithic settlement	1985/031, 1992/100, 1993/116
Mesolithic/Neolithic sites	1986/074, 1986/074, 1986/074, 1986/074
Mesolithic settlement	1973/012, 1974/011, 1976/013, 1976/015, 1977/021, 1980/072
Mesolithic site	1977/062
Midden	1993/197, 1994/115
Midden and watercourse	1994/165
Middle Bronze Age mound	1969/025
Mill	1991/054, 1997/022
Mill site?	1997/367
Mills site	1994/075
Mines—primitive	1985/012
Moat?	1996/408
Moat environs	1990/070
Moated site	1977/014
Moated site?	1997/344
Modern urban	1990/059, 1996/154
Monastery environs	1991/111
Monastic complex, environs	1996/201, 1996/202

Monastic enclosure	1972/018, 1973/020, 1975/021
Monastic enclosure?	1993/134
Monastic enclosure, environs	1993/192, 1994/101
Monastic settlement	1970/006, 1971/010, 1974/009, 1975/009, 1985/053, 1986/070, 1987/044, 1992/132
Monastic site	1972/006, 1973/006, 1974/018, 1977/063, 1980/172, 1985/032, 1985/045, 1985/048, 1992/092, 1992/158, 1993/124, 1994/123, 1995/136, 1996/168, 1997/244
Monastic site, environs	1977/075, 1987/041, 1988/057, 1994/198, 1997/226
Monastic site/post-medieval settlement	1970/030
Monitoring	1990/092, 1993/169, 1995/134, 1995/158, 1995/177, 1996/159, 1997/011, 1997/047, 1997/062, 1997/113, 1997/236, 1997/245, 1997/250, 1997/252, 1997/259, 1997/260, 1997/286, 1997/428, 1997/441, 1997/485, 1997/565, 1997/586
Monitoring in medieval town	1994/122
Monitoring of sewage system	1996/351
Motte	1975/013, 1977/028, 1997/427
Motte?	1992/140
Motte and bawn (nearby)	1995/165
Motte and ringfort	1974/004, 1975/005
Motte environs	1992/135, 1996/181, 1997/272
Motte site	1980/148
Mound	1975/023, 1976/012, 1980/194, 1985/029, 1987/029, 1991/031, 1991/046, 1992/043, 1992/136, 1992/138, 1995/245, 1996/049, 1996/239, 1996/300, 1997/076, 1997/077
Mound and Early Christian church, environs	1996/124
Mound and moat?	1994/044
Mound environs	1994/049
Mound—ring-barrow?	1997/361
Mounds	1992/120
Multi-period	1989/002, 1992/020, 1994/007, 1997/426
Multi-period activity	1987/016
Multi-period burial cairn	1997/059
Multi-period settlement	1977/071
Multi-period site	1969/006, 1970/005, 1977/051, 1977/058, 1980/094, 1980/168, 1989/074, 1990/093, 1991/013, 1991/104, 1992/151, 1993/099, 1993/182, 1994/191, 1995/231, 1996/002, 1996/310
Multi-phase landscape	1991/099, 1992/148, 1993/178, 1994/188, 1995/226, 1996/303, 1997/411
Multi-phase upland	1990/005
Multi-phase upland landscape	1991/007
Multiple cist cairn	1971/022
Multivallate earthwork	1990/100
Multivallate fort	1989/084
Natural mound	1995/041
Neolithic	1994/005
Neolithic activity?	1997/534
Neolithic and Bronze Age settlements	1980/006
Neolithic axe production site	1997/180
Neolithic/Bronze Age	1988/040, 1995/001, 1996/013
Neolithic/Bronze Age settlement/industrial site	1994/004
Neolithic/Bronze Age settlements	1970/032
Neolithic burial	1971/023
Neolithic burial mound	1980/166
Neolithic cave burial	1992/123
Neolithic chipping floor	1969/005
Neolithic ditched enclosure	1985/006
Neolithic/Early Bronze Age occupation	1971/033
Neolithic/Early Christian	1977/011
Neolithic enclosure	1987/003, 1988/002
Neolithic field system	1989/071, 1990/088, 1991/098, 1992/145, 1993/176
Neolithic habitation site	1986/016
Neolithic? habitation site	1985/036
Neolithic house	1986/061, 1987/035, 1989/069, 1991/106, 1996/005, 1996/006
Neolithic, including stone axe production site?	1995/101, 1996/129
Neolithic industrial site	1980/031

Neolithic occupation site	1970/002
Neolithic/post-medieval	1997/085
Neolithic settlement	1969/010, 1971/030, 1972/023, 1972/024, 1987/050, 1996/061, 1997/069
Neolithic settlement and industrial site	1991/002, 1992/001, 1993/001
Neolithic settlement site	1971/001, 1989/001, 1990/001
Neolithic site	1980/012, 1980/018, 1986/007, 1989/090
Neolithic site/stone axe production site	1994/095
Neolithic trackway?	1996/058
No archaeological significance	1986/054, 1988/036, 1989/058, 1989/059, 1989/066, 1989/080, 1990/008, 1990/052, 1990/069, 1991/021, 1991/032, 1991/068, 1991/077, 1991/092, 1991/102, 1991/114, 1991/135, 1992/047, 1992/064, 1992/069, 1992/075, 1992/080, 1992/090, 1992/124, 1992/125, 1992/130, 1992/154, 1992/178, 1992/181, 1992/183, 1993/011, 1993/021, 1993/023, 1993/026, 1993/028, 1993/029, 1993/031, 1993/038, 1993/054, 1993/065, 1993/069, 1993/071, 1993/077, 1993/080, 1993/086, 1993/093, 1993/095, 1993/129, 1993/131, 1993/132, 1993/135, 1993/150, 1993/151, 1993/162, 1993/165, 1993/181, 1993/189, 1993/220, 1993/224, 1994/039, 1994/047, 1994/048, 1994/057, 1994/058, 1994/069, 1994/071, 1994/096, 1994/097, 1994/099, 1994/125, 1994/134, 1994/135, 1994/136, 1994/137, 1994/183, 1994/205, 1994/222, 1994/223, 1995/046, 1995/051, 1995/065, 1995/073, 1995/074, 1995/079, 1995/080, 1995/085, 1995/142, 1995/144, 1995/154, 1995/155, 1995/193, 1995/213, 1995/270, 1995/274, 1996/021, 1996/022, 1996/030, 1996/034, 1996/056, 1996/057, 1996/119, 1996/125, 1996/135, 1996/149, 1996/175, 1996/185, 1996/187, 1996/188, 1996/205, 1996/220, 1996/233, 1996/240, 1996/241, 1996/256, 1996/265, 1996/288, 1996/304, 1996/311, 1996/325, 1996/340, 1996/346, 1996/368, 1996/379, 1996/380, 1996/384, 1996/396, 1997/001, 1997/009, 1997/012, 1997/014, 1997/028, 1997/035, 1997/051, 1997/060, 1997/061, 1997/066, 1997/075, 19970/78, 1997/149, 1997/150, 1997/154, 1997/158, 1997/159, 1997/160, 1997/178, 1997/188, 1997/191, 1997/195, 1997/204, 1997/211, 1997/212, 1997/213, 1997/215, 1997/227, 1997/240, 1997/249, 1997/253, 1997/279, 1997/282, 1997/287, 1997/316, 1997/318, 1997/319, 1997/320, 1997/321, 1997/322, 1997/323, 1997/332, 1997/337, 1997/341, 1997/362, 1997/370, 1997/386, 1997/394, 1997/395, 1997/396, 1997/397, 1997/398, 1997/400, 1997/404, 1997/405, 1997/408, 1997/409, 1997/410, 1997/421, 1997/425, 1997/439, 1997/446, 1997/454, 1997/457, 1997/459, 1997/462, 1997/463, 1997/464, 1997/465, 1997/466, 1997/494, 1997/515, 1997/554, 1997/556, 1997/587, 1997/590, 1997/595, 1997/611
North-Eastern Gas Pipeline	1988/Apx 2
Not excavated	1997/363
Occupation site	1980/026
Ogham stone	1997/229
Ogham stones, environs	1991/063
Oratory	1994/186
Oval platform and linear earthwork	1996/292
Pale boundary	1988/014
Pale boundary earthwork	1993/128
Pale ditch/church/tree ring?	1996/064
Palisaded enclosure	1990/026, 1990/095
Passage grave	1969/011, 1969/012, 1972/027, 1985/003, 1985/050, 1986/018, 1986/064, 1986/067, 1987/010, 1988/054, 1989/073, 1989/075, 1990/076, 1991/084, 1993/199, 1994/140, 1995/172
Passage grave and Iron Age cemetery	1980/110
Passage grave and Neolithic occupation site	1970/027
Passage grave and other activities	1985/043
Passage grave cemetery	1973/028, 1973/029, 1974/032, 1974/033, 1975/030, 1975/031, 1987/040
Passage grave cemetery and later	1976/029
Passage grave cemetery and later activities	1988/053
Passage grave complex and later Iron Age settlement	1970/025

Passage grave complex and medieval occupation	1971/028
Passage grave environs	1995/229
Passage grave reconstruction	1992/Apx 4, 1996/Apx XI
Pathway (single-plank)—togher	1996/326
Penannular enclosure	1986/073
Pilgrims' road	1972/033
Pipeline corridor	1995/128
Pit burial	1988/066
Pit circle	1980/152
Pit graves	1980/209
Pits	1994/090, 1997/100
Pits and subrectangular feature	1997/436
Plantation bawn	1977/017
Plantation bawn/ringfort	1995/042
Plantation castle	1991/119, 1992/172
Plantation castle environs	1994/146
Plantation houses and bawn	1989/015
Plantation town/early monastic site	1992/156
Ploughzone Archaeology Survey	1992/Apx 1
Pool filler	1997/544
Portal tomb	1980/104, 1985/027, 1985/038, 1986/011, 1986/026, 1986/063, 1987/013, 1988/005
Portal tomb environs	1996/143
Post row	1997/020
Post-medieval	1991/083, 1992/041, 1992/045, 1992/059, 1992/063, 1992/071, 1992/072, 1992/078, 1992/082, 1992/118, 1993/067, 1993/137, 1994/045, 1994/079, 1994/227, 1996/066, 1996/101, 1997/027, 1997/099, 1997/183, 1997/185, 1997/333, 1997/493, 1997/497, 1997/562
Post-medieval activity	1993/088, 1993/089
Post-medieval building	1997/072
Post-medieval burial	1994/068
Post-medieval castle	1980/022, 1995/047
Post-medieval domestic	1987/002
Post-medieval enclosure and field systems	1996/033
Post-medieval farm	1996/353
Post-medieval farm buildings	1994/176
Post-medieval field enclosure	1996/382
Post-medieval fort	1993/222
Post-medieval fortification	1989/012
Post-medieval graveyard	1992/074
Post-medieval harbour	1996/357
Post-medieval house	1995/122, 1996/381
Post-medieval/industrial urban	1997/070
Post-medieval linear bank	1991/087
Post-medieval manor house	1980/069
Post-medieval metalworking site	1994/231
Post-medieval military fort	1990/098
Post-medieval mill	1997/290
Post-medieval/modern	1989/044
Post-medieval quarry pits and cultivation	1996/372
Post-medieval quay front	1997/171
Post-medieval river frontage and dock	1997/169
Post-medieval roadway	1997/532
Post-medieval settlement	1977/022, 1990/019, 1991/027, 1992/017, 1992/019, 1994/021
Post-medieval shipwreck	1995/009, 1995/044
Post-medieval town wall	1996/386
Post-medieval urban	1976/014, 1977/020, 1980/136, 1987/021, 1988/042, 1989/017, 1990/068, 1990/077, 1991/020, 1991/082, 1991/109, 1991/128, 1993/025, 1993/045, 1993/074, 1993/078, 1993/202, 1993/212, 1994/061, 1994/073, 1994/208, 1995/012, 1995/081, 1995/207, 1995/211, 1995/278, 1996/247, 1996/268, 1996/278, 1996/360, 1997/106, 1997/141, 1997/144, 1997/209, 1997/239, 1997/393, 1997/472, 1997/476, 1997/477, 1997/478, 1997/581, 1997/583, 1997/622
Post-medieval urban?	1995/061
Post-medieval urban fortification	1989/047

Post-medieval waterfront	1993/090
Pottery kiln	1992/097
Pre-bog enclosures and field systems	1971/025
Pre-bog field system	1971/026, 1971/027, 1973/027, 1975/029, 1976/026
Pre-bog wall	1992/104
Pre-development testing	1997/283
Prehistoric	1994/113, 1996/389, 1997/263, 1997/618
Prehistoric activity	1993/231
Prehistoric and later	1997/268
Prehistoric and medieval	1997/612
Prehistoric archaeological complex	1996/364, 1996/365
Prehistoric (Bronze Age?)	1994/107
Prehistoric burial-ground	1988/031, 1989/055
Prehistoric burial mound	1977/060
Prehistoric burial site	1977/069
Prehistoric cairn and field system	1997/018
Prehistoric cemetery	1977/064
Prehistoric earthwork	1994/157
Prehistoric enclosure	1970/023, 1970/024, 1980/003, 1996/236, 1997/419
Prehistoric field wall	1986/004
Prehistoric flat cremation cemetery	1997/535
Prehistoric habitation site	1990/083, 1991/089
Prehistoric/historic settlement area	1996/238
Prehistoric/historic settlement site	1992/027
Prehistoric industrial site	1980/025
Prehistoric landscape	1997/563
Prehistoric landscape?	1995/219
Prehistoric midden and early medieval settlement	1993/111
Prehistoric occupation site	1986/050, 1987/034, 1988/039
Prehistoric or Early Christian	1997/067
Prehistoric pit	1977/053
Prehistoric settlement	1986/001
Prehistoric settlement/field system	1974/031, 1975/028, 1976/025
Prehistoric settlement/field systems	1973/026
Prehistoric site	1986/015
Prehistoric (unprotected)	1996/189
Pre-Norman city defences	
Pre-Norman to 18th-century	1990/109
1985/024	
Presbyterian meeting house	1988/010
Priory	1974/006
Priory environs and town wall site	1993/033
Priory of Fratres Cruciferi	1980/154
Priory site	1973/005
Promontory fort	1977/043
Promontory fort and Iron Age/Early Christian cemetery	1994/206
Quarry	1996/377
Raised beach	1995/008
Raised rath	1980/016, 1985/005, 1986/003, 1987/001, 1995/007
Rampart	1995/098
Rathcroghan archaeological complex	1996/331
Rectangular earthwork	1980/010, 1980/032
Rectangular enclosure	1980/023, 1996/314
Rectangular fosse	1994/169
Red deer in pitfall trap?	1997/196
Religious enclosure	1975/036
Research survey (Clonfert Research Project Survey)	1997/Apx I
Research survey (IAWU)	1997/Apx III
Resistivity survey	1994/Apx I
Rhyolite quarry	1989/096
Ring-barrow	1970/018, 1980/160, 1986/043, 1986/055, 1986/058, 1990/017, 1995/052, 1996/333
Ring-barrow?	1997/237
Ring-barrow site	1994/133
Ring-barrows?	1994/132

Ring-cairn	1970/031
Ring-ditch and stone circle	1985/001
Ring-ditches/ring-barrows	1992/131
Ringfort	1969/004, 1970/001, 1970/003, 1970/013, 1970/028, 1970/034, 1971/002, 1971/006, 1971/007, 1971/008, 1971/009, 1971/012, 1971/020, 1971/021, 1971/034, 1972/001, 1972/002, 1972/004, 1972/020, 1972/030, 1973/003, 1973/007, 1973/009, 1973/011, 1973/025, 1974/002, 1974/029, 1974/030, 1975/004, 1975/018, 1975/033, 1977/002, 1977/003, 1977/013, 1977/027, 1977/041, 1980/047, 1980/060, 1980/061, 1980/106, 1980/108, 1980/190, 1980/191, 1985/002, 1985/026, 1986/005, 1987/007, 1987/009, 1987/046, 1988/008, 1988/035, 1989/011, 1989/013, 1990/002, 1990/015, 1990/018, 1990/072, 1990/113, 1990/115, 1990/116, 1990/117, 1991/003, 1991/022, 1991/026, 1991/074, 1991/091, 1991/115, 1991/126, 1992/030, 1992/037, 1992/094, 1992/142, 1992/143, 1992/146, 1993/016, 1993/034, 1993/115, 1993/119, 1993/152, 1994/127, 1994/128, 1994/151, 1994/180, 1995/138, 1995/150, 1995/246, 1995/249, 1996/024, 1996/221, 1997/073, 1997/074, 1997/324
Ringfort?	1989/076, 1996/258
Ringfort and early church site	1969/015
Ringfort and ecclesiastical site environs	1996/137
Ringfort and *fulacht fiadh*	1989/082
Ringfort and motte	1977/034
Ringfort/promontory environs	1996/216
Ringfort/children's burial-ground, environs	1992/011
Ringfort, enclosure and *fulachta fiadh*	1997/242
Ringfort environs	1980/167, 1992/099, 1992/106, 1993/020, 1994/012, 1996/050, 1996/160, 1996/167, 1996/337, 1997/016, 1997/030, 1997/045, 1997/046, 1997/052, 1997/243, 1997/560
Ringfort/mound	1980/081
Ringfort, souterrain and rectangular enclosure	1992/028
Ringfort/souterrain, environs	1996/259
Ringfort with enclosure	1989/086
Ringforts	1972/009, 1977/029, 1993/221
Ringforts/souterrains?	1991/094
Ringwork	1980/202, 1986/079, 1987/056
Ritual complex	1996/335
Ritual enclosure	1991/107, 1992/153, 1993/183
Ritual pool?	1995/227
River bank	1997/010
River bed	1989/097, 1992/035
River dredgings	1991/014, 1991/015, 1991/016, 1991/120, 1992/005, 1993/009, 1994/009
River excavation	1992/155
River fords	1991/059
Road	1994/013
Road bypass	1997/280
Rock art	1993/172
Rock art environs	1997/270
Rock of Cashel environs	1990/106
Romanesque church	1992/164
Round house and *fulacht fiadh*	1986/014
Round tower	1996/385
Roundwood path	1997/541
Roundwood scatter	1997/518
Royal Hospital	1976/021
Settlement	1988/001
Settlement?	1994/038
Settlement site	1985/004, 1991/056
Sewage scheme	1996/162
Shell midden	1986/017, 1991/008
Shell middens	1986/029
Shipwreck	1987/058, 1987/Apx 3, 1989/100, 1989/Apx 4, 1993/015
Single-plank walkway	1997/540
Sites?	1995/234

Skeletal remains—animal	1995/233
Skeleton in souterrain	1988/029
Slab-lined grave	1991/052
Soil-sampling near settlement	1987/033
Souterrain	1971/003, 1972/007, 1973/010, 1973/015, 1976/032, 1977/044, 1977/055, 1977/061, 1980/077, 1980/174, 1990/028, 1990/056, 1991/011, 1992/139, 1993/122, 1994/202, 1995/004, 1995/131, 1995/220, 1995/225
Souterrain?	1988/047, 1993/166, 1993/170, 1997/4241988/047, 1993/166, 1993/170, 1997/424
Souterrain and lintel graves	1980/147
Souterrain and ringfort	1992/150
Souterrain and settlement	1977/001
Souterrain and well	1986/065
Souterrain environs	1995/235, 1997/017
Souterrain? environs	1997/223
Souterrains	1988/056
Souterrains?	1995/218
Souterrains and enclosure	1977/052
Souterrains and later features	1988/045
Standing stone	1980/076, 1980/195, 1985/020, 1986/039, 1993/005, 1993/017, 1993/044,1994/201,1997/334, 1997/Ad3
Standing stone?	1980/159, 1997/179
Standing stone and field boundaries	1997/ 1
Standing stone site	1994/042
Standing stones	1990/020
Star-shaped fort	1996/254
Stone alignment	1977/015, 1994/214
Stone axe production site?	1993/096
Stone causeway	1997/506
Stone causeway in bog	1970/033
Stone circle	1975/020, 1980/105, 1985/015
Stone circle complex survey	1996/Apx II
Stone circles	1994/213, 1997/564
Stone fort	1974/025, 1974/026, 1986/031, 1990/067, 1991/070, 1995/117
Stone fort environs	1997/193
Stone platform	1990/119, 1991/129, 1992/180, 1997/470
Stone row and boulder burial?	1989/052
Stone setting	1994/010
Stone track	1997/542, 1997/543
Sub-urban	1994/031
Survey	1993/Apx II, 1995/Apx I
Surveys of mining site	1996/Apx X
Sweathouse	1988/023
Test-pits	1991/025, 1991/122, 1991/132, 1994/023, 1994/024
Test-trenching	1996/227
Togher	1987/045, 1988/025, 1988/044, 1990/105, 1992/083, 1996/327, 1997/558
Tower-house	1972/022, 1973/008, 1973/024, 1974/024, 1988/006, 1988/027, 1991/064, 1991/130, 1992/016, 1993/107, 1994/020, 1994/033, 1995/164, 1995/175, 1995/272, 1996/035, 1996/148, 1996/309, 1996/413
Tower-house/16th-century house	1994/193
Tower-house and bawn	1994/017, 1996/004, 1996/366
Tower-house and church environs	1980/177, 1994/043
Tower-house and military fort	1970/007
Tower-house bawn	1974/028
Tower-house environs	1980/048, 1980/059, 1991/088, 1993/019, 1996/298, 1997/194, 1997/371
Tower-house environs, bawn wall and extra-mural ditch	1996/047
Tower-house, later killeen, over prehistoric site	1995/003
Tower-house site	1995/115
Tower-house—urban	1996/156
Tower of city wall	1990/111
Town	1994/131
Town ditch	1996/196

	1997/437, 1997/444, 1997/445, 1997/458, 1997/473, 1997/474,
	1997/475, 1997/479, 1997/480, 1997/481, 1997/482, 1997/486,
	1997/492, 1997/496, 1997/548, 1997/550, 1997/551, 1997/552,
	1997/557, 1997/578, 1997/588, 1997/589, 1997/592, 1997/596,
	1997/597, 1997/598, 1997/600, 1997/605, 1997/606, 1997/Ad2,
	1997/Ad4
Urban?	1994/062, 1994/088, 1995/105
Urban—17th/18th-century	1996/094
Urban defences	1995/120
Urban ecclesiastical	1997/201
Urban ecclesiastical site	1991/030
Urban medieval waterfront	1991/043
Urban, possible burial-ground	1995/050
Urban potential	1991/073
Urban site?	1994/052
Urban tower-house	1995/191, 1997/365
Urn burial	1974/038, 1974/039, 1977/019, 1977/030, 1989/099
Urn burials	1980/019
Various	1977/059, 1994/110, 1997/065, 1997/092, 1997/413, 1997/416
Various sites	1994/148, 1994/184
Viking and Hiberno-Norse	1994/081
Viking habitation?	1989/026
Viking harbour?	1995/022
Viking, Hiberno-Norse and medieval urban	1997/127
Viking longfort?	1980/197
Viking/medieval?	1994/054
Viking/medieval settlement	1971/016
Viking/medieval town	1970/017, 1972/014
Viking/medieval urban	1973/017, 1975/015, 1976/019, 1988/061, 1988/063, 1993/057,
	1994/059
Village survey	1992/Apx 2
Walls and drain	1997/277
Water bastion	1980/068
Waterfront?	1990/049, 1990/051
Watermill (disused), environs	1996/192
Wedge tomb	1969/020, 1970/009, 1973/041, 1980/145, 1989/008, 1990/009,
	1990/023, 1992/006, 1997/055
Well	1988/034
Well environs	1995/110
Windmill	1993/043
Wooden causeway	1997/507
Wooden platform	1997/511, 1997/517
Wooden structure	1995/289
Wooden trackway	1997/508, 1997/509, 1997/510, 1997/512, 1997/513, 1997/514,
	1997/519, 1997/520, 1997/521, 1997/523